THE VISUAL GUIDE TO
ISLAM

THE VISUAL GUIDE TO
ISLAM

HISTORY • PHILOSOPHY • TRADITIONS • TEACHINGS • ART & ARCHITECTURE

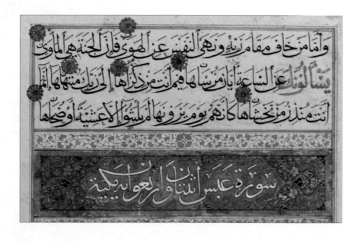

RAANA BOKHARI & DR MOHAMMAD SEDDON

CONSULTANTS: DR RIAD NOURALLAH & MOYA CAREY

WITH CONTRIBUTIONS BY
CAROLINE CHAPMAN • MELANIE GIBSON • GEORGE MANGINIS •
ANNA McSWEENEY • CHARLES PHILLIPS • IAIN ZACZEK

HERMES
HOUSE

CONTENTS

*Above A candlestick from
the 13th century, decorated
with scenes from daily life.*

*Above An interior view
of the dome in the Great
Mosque of Córdoba, Spain.*

Above The mihrab *(arched
niche) of the Tanjal Mosque,
Tripoli, Lebanon.*

*Above Detail from a Persian
carpet of a warrior surrounded
by flowers and animals.*

Above A 16th-century manuscript painting in the Mughal style.

Above 'No Conqueror But God', an inscription from the Alhambra Palace, Spain.

Above The minarets of the Sultan Hassan Mosque, Cairo, Egypt.

Above Suleyman the Magnificent, Venetian woodcut, 1540–50.

Above Dome of the Rock, a Muslim shrine built in Jerusalem 691.

Above Brickwork from the 9th-century Mausoleum of Ismail Samani in Bukhara.

Above Muqarnas and tiles in the Seljuks' 11th-century Friday Mosque in Isfahan.

Above The early 12th-century Bahram Shah minaret, in Ghazni.

Above Detail of tiles from the Gur-e Amir Mausoleum, in Samarkand.

Above Alhambra, residence of Muslim rulers in Granada, built in the 14th century.

Above Detail from a mid-16th-century illustration, produced in Mughal India.

Above Sultan Qaboos Mosque, built in Oman between 1995 and 2001.

INTRODUCTION

Islam is believed to be the world's second largest religion, second to Christianity. It has more than 1.3 billion followers making up about a fifth of the global population. The meaning and message of Islam is one of peaceful submission to the will of one God, who is referred to in Arabic as 'Allah'.

Arabic is the language in which the Quran – according to Islam, a divine revelation – was disclosed to Muhammad, the 'Prophet of Islam', in 610 in Makkah. Muslims believe that what followed over the next 23 years was a series of revelations to guide and instruct people to lead deeply spiritual, moral and upright lives, with God at the centre as sacred creator, and men and women seeking to live in peace through worship.

Above *Verses from the Quran, believed by Muslims to be divine revelation, the very words of God given to Muhammad.*

Below *The* maghrib *(sunset) prayer offered at the Prophet's Mosque in Madinah, Saudi Arabia.*

Within 100 years of Muhammad's death, the faith that had transformed Arabian society had extended as far as what is now Spain in the West and China in the East. The spread of Islam heralded a great time in Muslim civilization, marked by many mosques, forts and gardens that still stand today in Andalusian Spain, Moghul India and Abbasid Baghdad.

THE PROPHET OF ISLAM

Muslims consider the Quran to be the direct word of God and so do not challenge its authenticity, but a critical science of interpretation developed around the text over the centuries. Islam teaches that people cannot lead Godly lives through personal search and obedience to rules alone, but that they must depend on guidance from their

creator. This guidance, Muslims believe, came through prophets who were selected by God and sent to every nation: Adam is considered the first of these prophets and Muhammad the last.

Muhammad is central to Islam, which holds that there can be no belief in God without belief in Muhammad as his messenger. Known by Muslims as the Prophet, Muhammad is viewed not as the founder of a new religion, but rather as the restorer of monotheistic belief as practised by Ibrahim (Abraham), Moses, Jesus and others. Islam claims to be the culmination of Judaeo-Christian monotheism. The Prophet's life, as narrated in hadith (collections of the Prophet's sayings) and biographies, is the exemplary model that all Muslims aspire to follow.

ISLAM AS A WAY OF LIFE

The prescriptive and binding nature of Islam touches every aspect of life. Therefore, a Muslim's life is regulated by discipline. The five pillars of faith – declaring belief, prayers, giving alms, fasting and pilgrimage – give a ritualistic form to worship, but many Muslims believe that such observances should be imbued with inner spirituality.

Great scholarly activity after the death of Muhammad saw works in theology, philosophy, spirituality and law, as well as in the arts, sciences and medicine, being produced by independent scholars to ensure that people knew how to apply Islamic teachings to their lives.

HOW THE BOOK IS SET OUT

Because the Prophet and his teachings are so central to Islam, Part One of the book begins with the story of the life of Muhammad, and the importance of the revelations he received, his teachings (hadith) and his life example (sunnah) to Muslim belief. It includes chapters concerning the

history and development of Islam, theological beliefs and ritual worship practices within Muslim life, and issues of morality, including controversial topics such as medical bioethics and 'just war'.

Part One concludes with a review of the unity and division among the Muslim community worldwide, for while all Muslims claim to be part of the global *ummah* (community), there are many points of difference, notably between Sunni and Shiah. Most of this book represents the majority of Sunni views.

A variety of pictures have been used to illustrate the beauty and breadth of Muslim life. Islam forbids the depiction of Muhammad in art, but Islamic history is full of vivid depictions of places and people. As it is a sensitive issue regarding the Prophet, he is generally portrayed either without facial features, veiled or surrounded by divine light.

Part Two of the book turns to the art and architecture of Islam. There are chapters on arts such as calligraphy, painting, manuscript illumination and bookbinding, as well as furnishings, ceramics, luxury

items made from precious metals and alloys, ivory, rock crystal, gemstones, glass and wood, and also textiles and carpets. The architectural wonders of Islam are represented by glorious buildings, from palaces to whole cities, and from mosques to bazaars. A section at the back of the book lists the best places to see Islamic art.

A NOTE ON ARABIC TERMS

As Arabic is the literary language of Islam, Arabic terms have been used and explained throughout the book, and a glossary of the major words appears at the back of the book. Spellings considered to be correct by the wider Muslim academic community have been adopted: for example 'Makkah' and 'Muslims' rather than 'Mecca' and 'Moslems'. It is customary for peace and salutations to follow the names both of Islamic prophets and of Muhammad's companions, but these have been omitted in this book.

Below Pilgrims circumambulate the Kaabah *in the Sacred Mosque in Makkah, the holiest site in Islam.*

PART ONE

THE HISTORY, PHILOSOPHY, TRADITIONS AND TEACHINGS OF ISLAM

Left Muslims pray in Malaysia during the Friday prayer. Offering collective worship in mosques is an important part of Muslim community life.

THE GLOBAL ISLAMIC COMMUNITY

SINCE THE EARLIEST PERIOD OF ISLAMIC HISTORY, MUSLIMS HAVE MIGRATED AND TRAVELLED TO NEW AREAS, AND COMMUNITIES OF MUSLIMS NOW LIVE ON EVERY CONTINENT IN THE WORLD.

The phenomenon of migration is perhaps at the heart of understanding the establishment of the *ummah*, or universal Muslim community. Muhammad's migration (*hijrah*) from his home city of Makkah to Madinah in 622 was the turning point for his message in the creation of an Islamic citadel and the first Muslim community. The Muslims of Madinah were ethnically different from the first Muslims and religiously pluralistic.

DIVERSITY AND UNITY

Today, Muslims are truly global and extremely diverse – ethnically, culturally, theologically, socially, geographically, economically and politically. Across the Muslim world, Islam is reflected in the geo-cultural expressions of its varied adherents, the most noticeable differences being in the way people dress, speak and eat, and the ways in which they celebrate their rites of passage. There is, therefore, no single way that one can think of a Muslim.

Muslim diversity is seen as a cause for celebration in the Quran, which states 'O Mankind! Verily We have created you from a single male and female and made you into tribes and nations so that you may know each other. Indeed, the best of you with God are those who attain piety. Surely God is all-knowing, best-aware' (49:13).

Above Two Muslim men talk outside the gates of a madrasa in Fez, Morocco. Islam encourages fraternity, teaching that all Muslims are brothers in faith.

Below This demographic map illustrates the percentage of the Islamic population around the world. Muslims total more than one-fifth of the world's population.

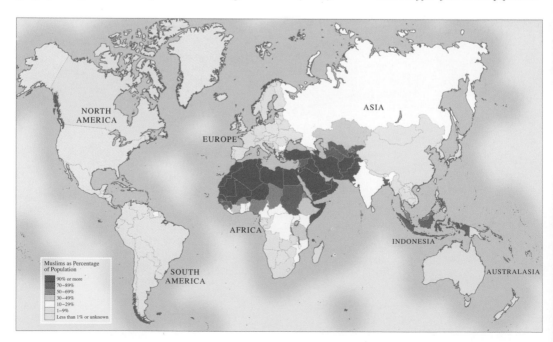

Muslims as Percentage of Population
- 90% or more
- 70–89%
- 50–69%
- 30–49%
- 10–29%
- 1–9%
- Less than 1% or unknown

NORTH AMERICA

EUROPE

ASIA

AFRICA

INDONESIA

SOUTH AMERICA

AUSTRALASIA

Left The Quran is preserved and recited in its original Arabic by Muslims throughout the world and is believed by all Muslims to be the sacred word of God as revealed to Muhammad.

The global Muslim community can be understood best through its beliefs and practices. Much of the Western scholarship on Islam has represented the faith as harsh and indignant, but for the majority of Muslims worldwide, the overarching characteristics of God are his endless mercy and immeasurable compassion. Their attitude to him is, therefore, one of grateful worship rather than fearful obedience.

Yet, despite their incredible diversity, Muslims are unified by their core Islamic beliefs and practices. For example, believers in every mosque from Beijing to Boston and Moscow to Makkah worship the same God, offer the same congregational prayers, read from the same Quran and loyally follow the teachings of the same prophet, Muhammad. Muhammad once declared that 'the Muslim *ummah* is like one body. If the eye is in pain then the whole body is in pain and if the head is in pain then the whole body is in pain.'

CHANGE AND CONSTANCY

Muslim contributions to human civilization and scholarship in the fields of science and technology have all been inspired by the religion of Islam. Although Muslim societies are constantly evolving – as are all human societies – the fundamental beliefs of Islam have remained constant since the time of the Prophet Muhammad, more than 1,500 years ago.

Right Muslims offering Friday prayers in Kuwait. Community life in Islam is centred around the mosque as a place of ritual prayer and social interaction.

CHAPTER 1

MUHAMMAD: MAN AND PROPHET

To make sense of the religion of Islam, it is essential to gain an understanding of Muhammad's life and the early medieval Arabian society in which he lived. Before Muhammad's prophethood and the advent of Islam, Arabia was divided into hostile tribes who worshipped many gods. Their religious effigies were housed in and around the *Kaabah*, an ancient temple attributed to the prophet Ibrahim (Abraham) in Makkah, the city where Muhammad was born.

During Muhammad's early life, Makkah was established as the site of religious pilgrimage for the polytheist Arabian tribes. Muhammad the man became God's prophet, and the divine revelations he received, known as al-Quran, 'The Recitation', proclaimed him the 'Seal of the Prophets' (33:40). Within a generation, he united his tribal society and established a belief system based on absolute monotheism that eventually gave rise to one of the world's most influential religious civilizations.

Opposite The Prophet Muhammad's mosque at Madinah. The green dome is situated directly above the original site of Muhammad's house, in which he is buried.

Above The 'Mountain of Light' outside Makkah houses the cave where Muhammad is said to have received the first revelations of the Quran from Archangel Jibril (Gabriel).

ARABIA BEFORE ISLAM

UNTIL THE ADVENT OF ISLAM, ARAB CIVILIZATION HAD LITTLE IMPACT ON NEIGHBOURING ROMAN AND PERSIAN EMPIRES. THE PRE-ISLAMIC ERA WAS MARKED BY POLYTHEISM AND TYRANNY.

The city and desert dwellers of Arabia were traditionally two distinct peoples, who were shaped and conditioned by their different surroundings. Historically, the Arab Bedouins roamed the desert plains, living in territorial regions that were loosely held together by tribal codes and agreed treaties (*assabiyah*). Sedentary Arabs were originally grouped together in tribes, but in the urban setting, tribal divisions were generally social rather than geographical.

In pre-Islamic Arabia, the life of the Bedouins was romanticized by urbanized Arabs as pure, chivalrous and unrestricted. The desert Arabs were considered to embody all the noble characteristics of the Arab peoples. As a result, city children were often temporarily fostered with nomads to learn aspects of traditional Arab culture, such as the pure Arabic language, desert living, camel rearing and goat herding.

THE CITY OF MAKKAH

While the deserts of 6th-century Arabia and their inhabitants were largely overlooked by the powerful neighbouring empires of Abyssinia, Byzantium and Persia, the oasis city of Makkah was already an important Arab metropolis. It had long been established as a trading nexus between Arabia and Africa to the west, Yemen and India to the south and Egypt and Syria to the north. Trade brought wealth and status to Makkah's ruling tribes, increasing their power and influence way beyond the city.

The leading Makkan tribe of the Quraysh, the bloodline descendants of the prophet Ibrahim (Abraham),

Above The arid deserts of the Arabian Peninsula provided a breathtaking backdrop for the desert's unique people and their journey to Islam.

were the religious custodians of the ancient temple, the *Kaabah*. This square stone structure was originally built by Ibrahim, and the Quran asserts that the *Kaabah* was the first place of worship dedicated to Allah (God) (2:15–127). Elements of religious monotheism still existed in the minority communities of Jews in Yathrib (Madinah) and among

Below For thousands of years, caravans wound their way along the ancient trade routes, cutting through the oasis towns.

ORAL TRADITION

From as early as the 5th century BCE, the Arabs, originally a largely illiterate people who were proud of their tribal genealogies and histories, developed an incredibly descriptive and rhythmic language. This was achieved mostly through the custom of memorizing oral narratives from generation to generation. As the ancient nomadic cultural traditions were lost as a result of urban settlement, they were recaptured in the collective consciousness through the art of poetry and story-telling. These unique tribal narratives included genealogies of their ancestors and the extensive pedigrees of their prized camels and thoroughbred horses.

Left Bedouin Arabs socialize as they drink coffee. This is the time when they can enjoy their ancient customs of story-telling and poetry recital.

individual Arab Christians living in Makkah. However, the religion taught and practised by Ibrahim had long since been replaced by polytheism, and by the time Muhammad and his followers eventually conquered the city in 630CE, it was filled with no less than 360 statues and other images of devotion.

Below Antar, the 6th-century Arabian poet and warrior, epitomized the noble qualities of pre-Islamic desert Arabs.

BELIEFS AND SUPERSTITIONS

Polytheism prevailed in the pre-Islamic era – a period referred to in Islam as *jahiliyyah*, or 'the days of ignorance' – and every pagan Arab tribe possessed its own idol housed in the *Kaabah*. People believed that these devotional images would act as intercessors between humans and Allah (literally 'the one God'), and that by offering sacrifices and making pilgrimages to the idols they would ultimately earn God's grace and favour.

A few of the rites from the time of Ibrahim had been preserved – circumambulation, pilgrimage and animal sacrifice, for example – but they existed alongside superstitious beliefs and the worship of images. Omens, amulets, astrology and divination (by the casting of arrows) were important practices in deciding serious matters, such as when to travel, marry or go to war.

TRIBALISM AND SOCIETY

Social and tribal hierarchies also meant that the pre-Islamic period was marked by oppression, tyranny and racism. The conflicts between dissenting tribes led to continuous hostilities and strife. Slavery was a common practice, as was female infanticide, and while ownership of slaves was perceived as a sign of great wealth and power, daughters were often seen as an expensive liability. Women, whether married or not, as well as slaves were treated as personal property that could be sold or exchanged, and polygamy (the practice of marrying more than one woman) was common in pre-Islamic Arabia.

But Muhammad's prophetic call to Islam would soon transform Arabian society into a new civilization based on absolute monotheism, social egalitarianism and a fraternity of faith.

MUHAMMAD'S CHILDHOOD

WHILE MUHAMMAD WAS STILL A CHILD, AND INDEED EVEN BEFORE HE WAS BORN, THERE WERE INDICATIONS THAT THIS BOY WOULD TRANSFORM THE ARABIAN SOCIETY IN WHICH HE LIVED.

Muhammad is said to have been born in 570CE, a year that became known as the Year of the Elephant. According to a chapter of the Quran entitled 'The Elephant', Abyssinian Christians, led by army commander Abraha al-Ashram, invaded Makkah in an attempt to eradicate polytheism and destroy the ancient temple, the *Kaabah*.

Terrified, the inhabitants fled the city. But before leaving, the formal tribal shaykh (trible elder leader) Abd al-Muttalib (who was later to become Muhammad's grandfather), dared to ask the Abyssinian general to return 200 camels that had been taken from him. When Abraha expressed surprise that Abd al-Muttalib was more concerned with the camels than the religion and its shrine that he had come to destroy, Abd al-Muttalib replied, 'I am the

lord of the camels, and the temple likewise has a lord who will defend it!' According to the Quran, the Abyssinians were miraculously bombarded by huge flocks of birds, forcing them to retreat before they could even approach the *Kaabah*.

The retreat was seen as a miracle by the Arab tribesmen, who believed they had witnessed Allah's divine intervention to protect the *Kaabah* after their abandonment of it. The Quraysh, the ancient custodians of the *Kaabah*, interpreted the attack as an omen, a precursor to a possible future event connected to the temple that had been built by Ibrahim to honour the one God.

MIRACULOUS CHILDHOOD

Later that year, Muhammad ibn Abdullah, grandson to the former tribal *shaykh* (teacher) of the

Above Abraha's elephants attacking the Kaabah. This event reputedly occurred in the year of Muhammad's birth.

Quraysh, Abd al-Muttalib, was born. Muhammad's father, Abdullah ibn Abd al-Muttalib, had unfortunately died some months earlier.

In his infancy, Muhammad was given to the care of a nursemaid, Halimah. He was fostered with her, staying with her tribe, Banu Sa'd, intermittently for the first five years of his life. The custom of foster-mothering their newborn with the Bedouins was common among the Quraysh, who wanted to imbue their children with the traditional Arab customs and pure language of the nomad Arabs.

According to a Sunni Hadith narration of Muhammad, it was during Muhammad's stay in the desert as a child that Archangel Jibril (Gabriel) came to him while he was playing with other boys. The angel allegedly held him down and split open his chest. Taking out his heart and removing a clump, he said 'this was Satan's portion of you'. He then washed Muhammad in a basin

Left During the 5th and 6th centuries, Abyssinian Christianity and civilization ruled over most of the south of the Arabian Peninsula.

Right Muhammad, cradled in his veiled mother's arms, is presented to his grandfather, Abd al-Muttalib, while the inhabitants of Makkah look on.

of gold, with water from the sacred Well of Zamzam in the *Kaabah's* precinct, before sealing his chest. The boys then ran to Halimah, shouting, 'Muhammad has been killed'. When they approached the boy, they found him pale and in a state of shock.

BAHIRA THE MONK

Muhammad's mother died when he was only six years old. The boy's paternal grandfather, Abd al-Muttalib, took charge of him, but unfortunately, he, too, died only two years later. Thereafter, Muhammad was raised by his father's younger brother, Abu Talib, a merchant and a leader of the Quraysh tribe. Muhammad benefited from the love and kindness that his uncle bestowed upon him and he would occasionally accompany him on his caravan trading trips.

When he was about 12 years old, Muhammad travelled with his uncle to Syria. Reaching the town of Busra, they met with a Christian monk called Bahira, who, unusually and for no apparent reason, insisted that they dine with him. The young Muhammad did not at first join the guests, remaining behind with the caravan's camels, perhaps to keep watch over valuable merchandise. But when Bahira saw that the boy was absent from the invited party, he asked Abu Talib to fetch him.

When Muhammad arrived, the priest immediately began to ask him a series of questions. As a result of the answers that Bahira received, he asked for permission to inspect a birthmark between Muhammad's shoulder blades. He then advised Abu Talib to take good care of his nephew, who, he declared earnestly, would become a great leader of men. Upon receiving this counsel, Muhammad's uncle concluded his business and immediately returned with his nephew to Makkah.

Although Abu Talib intuitively knew that Muhammad was special, as the Christian monk had confirmed, he could not have realized that Muhammad was, in fact, destined to become a fulfilment of Ibrahim's prophetic promise to the people of Makkah and beyond. As later asserted in the revelations of the Quran: 'and remember when Ibrahim raised the foundations of the House (*Kaabah*) with Ismail, supplicating, "Our Lord! Accept (this service) from us: for you are the All-Hearing, the All-Knowing... Our Lord send amongst them (Ismail's progeny) a messenger of their own, who will rehearse Your signs to them and and instruct them in wisdom and purify them; for You are the Exalted in Might, the Wise." ' (2:127–129)

MUHAMMAD'S IMPACT ON SOCIETY

MUHAMMAD'S EXEMPLARY CHARACTER, CARING NATURE AND WISDOM WERE RENOWNED IN THE CITY OF MAKKAH, AND HE WAS OFTEN CALLED UPON TO RESOLVE DISPUTES.

Muhammad was born into a family of noble lineage that belonged to the tribe of Banu Hashim of the Quraysh, who claimed descent from Ibrahim's son Ismail (Ismael). Pre-Islamic Arab society was based on tribal hierarchy, in which a tribe could be led to extinction in defence of its honour and that of anyone under its agreed protection.

Muhammad's family had been the ruling tribal family of Makkah at the time of his grandfather, Abd al-Muttalib. Muhammad's father, Abdullah, was the youngest and most loved son of Abd al-Muttalib but soon after marrying Aminah bint Wahb, Abdullah left with a trading caravan to Syria and never returned. The caravan came back with news of his sickness on the return journey through Yathrib (Madinah), where he eventually died. His son was born a short time later and was named 'Muhammad', meaning 'Praiseworthy', by his grieving grandfather. As Abd al-Muttalib later explained, 'I wanted Allah to praise him in heaven and mankind to praise him on earth.'

THE 'ALLIANCE OF VIRTUE'

As Muhammad reached maturity under the gentle care of his loving uncle, Abu Talib, his virtuousness earned him the title of al-Amin, 'the Trustworthy', among the inhabitants of Makkah. As a result, people would often entrust their valuables to him for safekeeping, and consult him to resolve their

Above Two Bedouin women playfully carry their children, a scene that has changed very little since the Prophet Muhammad's era.

problems and disagreements. Even as a young man, Muhammad showed commitment to issues of social justice, regardless of tribe.

A religious practice adhered to faithfully by the pagan Makkan tribes was observance of the sanctity of the month of pilgrimage, *Dhul-Hijjah*, which included a complete prohibition of hostilities. When Muhammad was 15, however, war broke out between the Quraysh and the tribe of Hawazin, which involved four years of protracted violence and bloody revenge.

The senseless bloodshed caused great loss and hardship to many people from both tribes, but as a result of their common suffering, a spirit of goodwill slowly began to prevail. Finally, another of Muhammad's uncles, al-Zubayr, took the initiative to find a

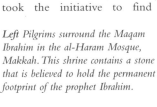

Left Pilgrims surround the Maqam Ibrahim in the al-Haram Mosque, Makkah. This shrine contains a stone that is believed to hold the permanent footprint of the prophet Ibrahim.

Above The shahadah – *'There is no God but God and Muhammad is His Messenger' – adorns the Topkapi Palace in Istanbul, Turkey.*

resolution to the conflict. He called for a meeting of representatives from both tribes, in which a charitable foundation, *Hilf ul-Fudul* ('Alliance of Virtue') was established to address the needs of the needy, poor and oppressed.

Muhammad was present, and joined the foundation, stating years later, 'I witnessed an alliance with my uncles at the house of Abdullah ibn Jadan and I would not wish to exchange it for the choicest luxuries. If I were called in Islam to participate in it I would respond.'

THE BLACK STONE

On another occasion, after a flood destroyed the *Kaabah* and repairs had been completed, tribal elders were having difficulty in deciding which nobleman should replace the decorative corner piece, *al-Hajar al-Aswad*, or the 'Black Stone'. (According to tradition, this ancient relic was sent from the heavens to adorn the *Kaabah*.) As the task was one of great honour, there was much dissent. Finally, exhausted

from arguing, the elders agreed that the first person to enter the *Kaabah*'s precinct would decide. When Muhammad entered, the elders were delighted, as he was renowned for his fairness and honesty. He advised them to place the stone on to a cloth to be held at each corner by a tribal elder, and he himself then placed the stone into position. Muhammad's wise and peaceful resolution to the problem averted bloodshed and united the various tribes of Makkah.

There was little doubt that Muhammad was not only a noble tribesman of great intelligence and integrity, but also that he was very generous and kind-hearted. In addition, his honesty was without question, and his ability to resolve serious problems and feuds was widely accepted. However, his rejection of the beliefs of his tribal peers, as well as his sudden claim to be an appointed prophet of God, was soon to test both the trust and the loyalties of the people of Makkah.

Right After the Kaabah was rebuilt, arguments arose about who should have the honour of replacing the Black Stone. Muhammad's diplomacy averted tribal bloodshed.

MUHAMMAD AND ORPHANS

Muhammad received much love and attention from his uncle Abu Talib after he was orphaned when only six years old, but he realized that the plight of most orphans did not reflect his own stable and protected upbringing and that many suffered from neglect and abuse.

Islam reflects Muhammad's concerns regarding orphans, and the Quran enshrines rights and protective measures: 'Give unto orphans their wealth. Exchange not the good for the bad (in your management thereof) nor absorb their wealth into your wealth' (4:2). And 'Come not near the property of orphans except to improve it, until he attains the age of strength (adulthood), and fulfil every agreed promise for every promise will be enquired into' (17:34).

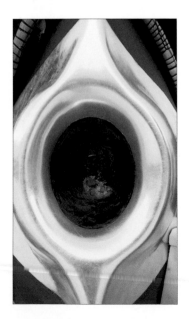

MARRIAGE TO KHADIJAH

MUHAMMAD'S WIFE, KHADIJAH, WAS A CAPTIVATING WOMAN AND 15 YEARS HIS SENIOR. SHE ENCOURAGED HER HUSBAND'S CONTEMPLATIVE LIFE AND ACCEPTED HIS MISSION AS A PROPHET.

The Quraysh tribesmen were accomplished merchants, and Muhammad's uncle Abu Talib was a wealthy businessman who encouraged his adopted nephew to become a trader. Muhammad's good character and reputation for honesty made him an ideal partner.

At the age of 25, Muhammad was employed by Khadijah bint Khuwaylid to trade for her in Syria. Khadijah was a highly successful businesswoman who employed men to work for her for an agreed percentage of the profits. After hearing of Muhammad's great honesty, she offered him a higher percentage than others in order to secure his employment. She also sent her trusted servant, Maysarah, to assist him on the long caravan.

MARRIAGE PROPOSAL

Muhammad's trading in Syria was extremely profitable, and Khadijah was pleased with both his business acumen and his outstanding moral behaviour, as observed by her servant on the trip. After discussing the matter with her close friend, Nafisah bint Munabbah, Khadijah expressed her wish to marry Muhammad, and Nafisah was asked to approach him with a proposal of marriage on her friend's behalf.

Khadijah was known for her beauty and intelligence. Many prominent men had asked for her hand in marriage, but she had consistently refused their proposals. She had been widowed and then later divorced for a number of years from her second husband, Abu Halah, and at the time of her proposal to Muhammad, she was 40 years old, some 15 years his senior.

Khadijah was a respected and wealthy woman, admired for her integrity and independence, and, like Muhammad, she was from the ruling Quraysh tribe. Muhammad willingly accepted her offer of marriage and asked his uncles, Abu Talib and Hamza, to make all the necessary wedding arrangements. As a part of the marriage dowry, Muhammad presented Khadijah with 20 pedigree camels. A modest wedding ceremony was conducted by Abu Talib at the bride's home.

MUHAMMAD'S CHILDREN

The couple lived happily until Khadijah's death at 65. His wife was a source of great comfort to Muhammad and they were blessed with two boys, al-Qasim and

Above A 14th-century manuscript painting depicts Muhammad with his wife Khadijah behind him. The third figure, on the left, is Muhammad's young cousin Ali ibn Abu Talib.

Abdullah, and according to Sunnis, with four girls, Zaynab, Ruqqaya, Umm Kulthum and Fatimah. Sadly, all Muhammad's sons died in their infancy, including Ibrahim, born to a later wife, Maria, a Coptic Christian from Egypt who later converted to Islam. Even after the death of his first-born son, al-Qasim, Muhammad was known by his *kunya* (a respectful but intimate Arab way of describing someone as 'the father of ...') Abul Qasim.

In a society that prized sons and denigrated daughters, Muhammad's loss of his male progeny became a point of ridicule among the Arabs. They mocked his prophetic mission by proclaiming, 'what we are involved in [polytheism] is more lasting than what the amputated *sunburn* [a date palm whose roots are broken] is involved in', meaning that Muhammad had no heirs to continue the propagation of Islam.

Left Ruins of the 14th-century Mosque of Fatimah, Busra, Syria. It was named for Muhammad's daughter Fatimah.

THE *HUNAFA*

Throughout his union with Khadijah, Muhammad continued the life of contemplation and seclusion that he had chosen before his marriage. He kept away from the adultery, drinking, gambling, and rivalries of pre-Islamic Makkan life and shunned the polytheism of his people. At the same time he successfully conducted his business activities and cared for the less privileged from his society.

Ibrahimic monotheism had not been completely abandoned in Arabia, and there existed a small group of people there who, like Muhammad, rejected the pervading polytheism of their tribal peers. These individuals were referred to collectively as *hunafa* (singular *hanif*), meaning 'one who follows the primordial belief in a single deity'. One such *hanif* was Zayd ibn Amr ibn Nufayl, who was known to proclaim, 'O Quraysh! By God none of you is following the religion of Ibrahim but me.'

THE REVELATION

Like Zayd, Muhammad was a *hanif*, and he would regularly visit a remote mountain cave outside Makkah to retreat in prayer and contemplation. Khadijah accepted and encouraged these retreats as a devotion that her husband had observed before their marriage.

It was during one such retreat in the month of Ramadan in 610 that Muhammad is believed to have received a visit from the Archangel Jibril, who revealed to him the first few verses of the Quran (81:22–3, 96:1–5). He returned home shaken, where he was comforted by Khadijah, who thereafter accepted her husband as a prophet. This event signalled the beginning of Muhammad's prophetic mission, the religion of Islam.

Below The 'Mountain of Light' is found on the outskirts of Makkah. Muhammad frequently made spiritual retreats on the mountain and it was here he received the first Quranic revelations.

Above Archangel Jibril is depicted in a handwritten Persian text dated to around the 14th century. According to Islamic tradition, Jibril often appeared to Muhammad in human form.

THE SIGNIFICANCE OF MAKKAH

MAKKAH IS HISTORICALLY IMPORTANT AS AN OASIS ON THE CARAVAN TRADING ROUTES ACROSS ARABIA, AS THE SITE OF THE ANCIENT TEMPLE, THE *KAABAH*, AND AS THE BIRTHPLACE OF MUHAMMAD.

Makkah is located in the Hijaz (literally 'barrier') region in the modern-day Kingdom of Saudi Arabia, a narrow tract of land punctuated by the Tropic of Cancer that runs some 1,400km (875 miles) north to south on the eastern side of the Red Sea and the chain of Sarat mountains. Between the volcanic peaks of the Sarat and the busy entrepot coast, there are sweltering barren deserts and desolate sandy passes. The landscape is both breathtakingly expansive and fiercely uninhabitable except by the hardiest of nomadic Arabs.

As the desert plains slowly rise toward the mountains, they give way to a series of arid, sun-baked rocky valleys. In one such valley is located the ancient city of Makkah with its temple and Well of Zamzam, which Muslims believe appeared miraculously in the desert. Makkah is also known to the Arabs as Wadi Ibrahim ('the valley of Ibrahim').

EARLY FOUNDATIONS

The moon-like terrain of this region is linked to a number of ancient Biblical characters. In a long prophetic hadith, Adam and Eve are said to have reunited on the plains of Arafah, just outside Makkah, after having been separated on their descent from heaven. The hadith recounts that Adam placed the foundation for Ibrahim's later temple, and states that Adam was buried near Makkah and Eve in nearby Jeddah. Muslims also believe that Noah's son Seth lived in the Hijaz and that Noah's Ark was constructed at Mount Budh, India, and was carried northward across the flooded plains to its resting place at Mount Judi (11:25–49).

THE WELL OF ZAMZAM

The story of the ancient Well of Zamzam that gave importance to Makkah as an ancient oasis and trading centre is associated with the patriarch Ibrahim, his wife Hajar and their baby, Ismail.

According to a hadith, Ibrahim brought his family from Egypt to the desert plains of Arabia before resting under a thorn tree in the valley of Makkah. The place was isolated and totally uninhabited. Leaving Hajar and Ismail with only a bag of dates and a leather water carrier, Ibrahim marched onward alone. Hajar cried after him,

Above The harsh rocky landscape surrounding Makkah, with its mountain peaks overshadowing narrow valleys passes, has changed little since the time of the Prophet Muhammad.

'Ibrahim, where are you going leaving us in this desert where there is no one and nothing? Is it by God's command?' When Ibrahim confirmed it was, the desperate Hajar replied, 'Then he will not let us go to waste.'

After the dates and water were finished and Hajar's breast milk was exhausted, both mother and child became thirsty. Hajar fretted as Ismail lay crying and writhing. In desperation, she ran to the top of a nearby hillock (Safa) and looked down over the valley for help. Seeing no one, she ran across the short plain to another hill (Marwa), again searching for assistance. Seven times she ran between the two hills beseeching God's mercy. Then an angel appeared, striking the ground with his wing at the midway point between the hills, at which a spring gushed forth. The infant cried 'Zamzam' (which is said to mean 'abundance'), and the well was established with this name.

Right Muhammad's grandfather, Abd al-Muttalib, and al-Harith, rediscovered the sacred Well of Zamzam in the precinct of Ibrahim's ancient temple, the Kaabah, in Makkah.

IBRAHIM'S *KAABAH*

A prophetic hadith recounts that when Ibrahim and Ismail were beginning the construction of their temple, a wind entered the Makkan valley, swirling violently around a particular site. They dug deep into the ground to reveal Adam's foundations, then began to collect huge stones, assembling them into a cube shape. When the walls reached the height of a man, Ismail brought a stone block for his father to work from. A stone, complete with Ibrahim's footprint, remains a holy relic in the *haram* ('sacred') precinct. At the corner of the building, an ornate stone, *al-Hajar al-Aswad* (the 'Black Stone') was inset to mark where circumambulatory rites begin.

Ibrahim's humble edifice – the only 'house of God' in its time – was eventually surrounded by colossal pyramids and monumental towers

Above This 16th-century painting depicts Ibrahim about to sacrifice his son Ismail as an angel brings a substitute lamb. The Makkan tribes claimed descent from Ismail.

constructed to celebrate pervading polytheistic beliefs, yet it was Ibrahim's simple 'cube' that was to permanently change the course of religion in the region.

THE CITY TODAY

Makkah is Islam's primary religious centre, the spiritual heartland to 1.3 billion Muslims around the world, who all face in the direction of the *Kaabah* as a part of their five daily prayers. More than two million Muslims make the annual pilgrimage (*Hajj*) to Makkah. Yet this barren and remote desert valley city would not even exist but for the story of Ibrahim.

Below Muslims congregate from around the world to make pilgrimage and to offer ritual circumambulations around the Kaabah *in Makkah, just as they believe Ibrahim did in ancient times.*

CALLED AS A PROPHET

THE QURAN RELATES THAT, FROM THE AGE OF 40, MUHAMMAD RECEIVED MANY ANGELIC VISITATIONS. THE QURAN WAS DICTATED TO HIM AND HE WAS COMMANDED TO CALL PEOPLE TO ISLAM.

Before Muhammad's call to Islam, the dominant religious beliefs and practices in Arabia were polytheistic, but there were also a number of minority groups from different monotheistic traditions.

THE MONOTHEISTS

As the religious centre of pre-Islamic Arabia, Makkah was a focus for polytheism and the *Kaabah* housed many statues and devotional images within its precincts. In contrast to the regions of Yathrib and Najran, communities of Christians and Jews were largely absent from Makkah. In this almost universally polytheistic society, they were generally prohibited from the *Kaabah* and were permitted to live – as slaves or servants – only on the outskirts of the city.

As a *hanif* (one who followed the original teachings of Ibrahim), Muhammad would have been one of the few religious monotheists living in Makkah itself. Another such man was Waraqa ibn Nawfal, a devout Christian and Khadijah's elderly cousin.

MUHAMMAD'S RETREATS

Muhammad is thought to have regularly observed spiritual retreats in a cave in the mountains on the outskirts of Makkah. Here he would spend weeks at a time in fasting, prayer and contemplation, grieving over what he saw as the erroneous religious practices and excessive lifestyles of his people. He also lamented the grave social injustices of the society in which he lived, which were often based on racial and tribal hierarchies: infant daughters were buried alive, women were traded and bartered like chattel, and slaves were treated no better than livestock.

RECEIVING REVELATIONS

According to prophetic hadith, Muhammad's many prayers and devotions to God were rewarded at the age of 40 by an unexpected angelic visitation. The story tells that Archangel Jibril appeared before Muhammad in every direction in which he gazed and that he was surrounded by a blinding light.

Above Jibril, accompanied by a group of angels, visits Muhammad. The artist has obscured Muhammad's face as a sign of respect for the Prophet.

Then, gripping Muhammad so tightly that he could barely breathe, the angel ordered him to 'Read!' Muhammad replied, 'I cannot read!' Jibril repeated the command, and on receiving the same reply, directed Muhammad to 'Read in the name of thy Lord who created, Created man from a clot, Read: and thy Lord is the Bounteous, Who teaches man with the pen, Teaches man that which he knows not' (96:1–5).

Ibn Ishaq's 8th-century biography of Muhammad, *Sirat Rasulillah*, relates that after his traumatic experience, Muhammad quickly returned home, frightened and confused. Khadijah hurriedly called for Waraqa, her Christian cousin, who, upon hearing Muhammad's encounter, concluded, 'This is the

Left Pilgrims visit the Hira cave on the 'Mountain of Light' overlooking Makkah. It was here that Muhammad is said to have received the revelations of the Quran from Archangel Jibril.

angel that God sent to Moses. I wish I were younger to witness your people exile you!' Muhammad cried 'Will they drive me out?', to which Waraqa replied, 'Anyone previously who came with something similar to what you have brought was treated with hostility: if I were to live until that day of rejection, I would strongly support you.'

THE PUBLIC CALL TO ISLAM

A lengthy period of time passed before Muhammad received further revelations, but eventually he was instructed to call his people to submit to God's will.

He began by inviting those nearest to him, starting with family and friends. After Khadijah, the first to become a declared Muslim was Ali ibn Abu Talib, the Prophet's young cousin, followed by Zayd ibn Harithah, a freed slave whom Muhammad had adopted as his son, followed by his friend Abu Bakr.

In the beginning, Muhammad's public call to Islam was merely scorned by his tribesmen, who claimed his new religion appealed only to the young, elderly and slaves. However, as the popularity of Islam spread and conversions increased, his enemies began to apply brute force and torture against its adherents.

MIGRATION TO ABYSSINIA

To relieve the oppression faced by many of his followers, Muhammad permitted a small band of Muslims to migrate to the Christian kingdom of Abyssinia. They received welcome and support from the Abyssinian King (Negus) and his subjects, despite pressure from the pagans to return them to Makkah.

They remained under the protection of the Christian king for almost two decades, living as loyal Muslim citizens, before returning to Arabia to join the burgeoning Islamic community at Madinah.

Below Muhammad's claims to have received angelic visitations and his call to the religion of Islam provoked much discussion among the tribal leaders of the Quraysh of Makkah.

Above The Prophet Muhammad and his trusted friend Abu Bakr are depicted taking refuge from the pursuing pagans in a cave during the migration (hijrah) to Madinah.

EXILE FROM MAKKAH

FEARING THAT THEIR PAGAN BELIEFS AND SOCIAL HIERARCHIES WERE
UNDER THREAT FROM ISLAM, TRIBAL ELDERS BEGAN TO PERSECUTE
AND TORTURE MUSLIMS AND TO PLOT MUHAMMAD'S ASSASSINATION.

The first exile of Muslims from the mounting hostilities of the Makkan pagans occurred around 615, when Muhammad sanctioned the migration of around 80 Muslims to Abyssinia. His public call to Islam was beginning to compromise the very fragile tribal allegiances and protection extended to him and his increasing number of followers. Muhammad's message of absolute monotheism (*tawhid*) and social equality was an anathema to the Makkan establishment.

PERSECUTION OF MUSLIMS

At the beginning of the fourth year of Muhammad's prophetic mission, the polytheists carefully aimed their persecution of Muslims at those unprotected by any tribal bonds. This meant that those already most vulnerable were targeted. When it was found that this strategy was having little impact on stemming conversions to Islam, leaders began pressuring anyone from their tribe found to be Muslim.

One of Muhammad's fiercest enemies was his uncle Abdul Uzza ibn Abd al-Muttalib, known as Abu Lahab ('the father of the flame'). Abu Jahl worked relentlessly to undermine Islam, persecuting and torturing many Muslims. A few were even killed for their beliefs.

DELEGATIONS TO ABU TALIB

In an effort to prevent conversions to Islam, a delegation of Quraysh leaders visited Muhammad's uncle Abu Talib. They complained that Muhammad was mocking their religion, cursing their gods and finding fault with their way of life. However, although Abu Talib managed to pacify the angry tribesmen, Muhammad continued to proselytize. According to Ibn Ishaq's biography of Muhammad, he told his uncle, 'if they put the sun on one hand and the moon in the other [as a reward for abandoning his mission], I would not leave it until Allah has made me victorious or I perish.'

Above A Muslim cavalryman with lance and shield rides his camel into battle, much as the Muslims would have done against the Makkan Arab pagans.

Realizing that Muhammad would not end his preaching and that Abu Talib would not forsake his nephew, Muhammad's enemies increased their oppression and torture, even plotting to kill him. On one occasion, a group led by Abu Jahl set about Muhammad while he was praying at the *Kaabah*.

When the news of Muhammad's persecution reached another of his uncles, Hamzah, an accomplished huntsman and warrior, he was so outraged that he immediately approached Abu Jahl and his accomplices. Ibn Ishaq records that, striking Abu Jahl violently across his back with his bow, he declared 'Ah! You have been abusing Muhammad: I too follow his religion and profess whatever he teaches!' The surprise conversion of Hamzah was a real blow to Muhammad's enemies.

THE YEAR OF GRIEF

A protracted series of negotiations, boycotts and plots followed in the next few years, until, in 619, Abu Talib died. Then, within a few

Left Abu Jahl, Muhammad's arch-enemy, is depicted attacking the Prophet as he offers his prayers at the Kaabah.

months, Muhammad's beloved wife Khadijah passed away. These two painful events added to his trials: he had lost not only his protector but also his greatest love and spiritual companion. The pagans took advantage of this misfortune and increased their hostilities.

Muhammad is said to have suffered even greater humiliations when he visited nearby Taif to invite its people to Islam. There, the citizens set their children on him, chasing him from the city and pelting him with stones.

THE TREATY OF AQABAH

During the pilgrimage season in 621, Muhammad approached a group of pilgrims from the Khazraj tribe of Yathrib (Madinah). They were aware of the Judaeo-Christian

Below This building outside Makkah marks the site where pilgrims from Yathrib (Madinah) accepted Islam.

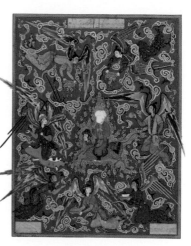

Right According to Islamic tradition, Muhammad was taken on a night journey to heaven on a winged horse, al-Buraq, a year before the migration (hijrah) to Madinah.

claims of a 'promised prophet' and had heard of Muhammad back in Yathrib. Muhammad explained the teachings of Islam and recited parts of the Quran to them, with the result that they were persuaded to convert to Islam.

A year later, these pilgrims returned to Makkah, along with a delegation of Muslim converts from Yathrib, and invited Muhammad and his followers to settle in their city. Muhammad ordered his followers to emigrate in small groups to avoid detection by the Quraysh, before leaving himself.

This migration, known as the *hijrah*, became a turning point for Islam. Muhammad went on to establish an Islamic community in the city, where he initiated a series of important treaties with some neighbouring tribes of both Arabs and Jews, and entered into a number of marriages with women from noble families and important tribes. The *hijrah* now marks the beginning of the Islamic calendar.

THE MADINAN COMMUNITY

THE MIGRATION (*HIJRAH*) OF MUHAMMAD AND HIS FOLLOWERS TO YATHRIB (MADINAH) TO ESCAPE PERSECUTION WAS TO BECOME PIVOTAL FOR ISLAM AND ITS SPREAD IN THE ARABIAN PENINSULA.

The persecution of Muslims in Makkah had intensified almost to the state of civil war. The two pledges that had been agreed at Aqabah between Muhammad and the Yathribite pilgrims, who had converted to Islam after their first meeting with him, became a lifeline for his prophetic mission.

Muhammad's enemies from the Quraysh were plotting a cunning assassination that would include a youth from each of the four major clans, thus avoiding any subsequent tribal bloodletting and feuding. However, when the youths attacked Muhammad's home intent on murdering him, their plot was frustrated. They found only his cousin Ali present; Muhammad had already departed from Makkah a few days earlier, and was heading for Yathrib, along with his trusted friend Abu Bakr.

Above A late 16th-century Ottoman manuscript painting shows early Muslims building the Prophet's Mosque in Madinah in 622.

ARRIVAL AT YATHRIB

After the first agreement at Aqabah, Muhammad had sent his envoy Musab ibn Umayr with the Yathribites to teach them the doctrines of their new faith and to help them propagate Islam among their fellow citizens. Musab was so successful in this mission that by the time the Yathribites returned to Makkah the following year, there was hardly a house in Yathrib without a Muslim.

The migration of many Muslims from Makkah came at considerable personal cost. Not only were most of them forsaken by their families and tribe, but their hasty exile meant that they left with virtually nothing. However, the Yathribites were generous, sharing their homes, businesses and belongings with the Muslim migrants.

Left A plan of the Prophet's Mosque in Madinah showing his pulpit, date orchard and house. It was both a religious building and political institution.

Eventually, Muhammad arrived in the city, after an eventful and dangerous journey in which he was forced to hide in a cave from the persuing Makkans. The Yathribites had been awaiting his arrival with great anticipation, and many broke out in song when they saw him on the distant horizon.

After Muhammad's migration to Yathrib, the city was renamed Madinat un-Nabi, 'City of the Prophet', in his honour.

THE ISLAMIC CITADEL

The Quranic revelations that Muhammad is believed to have received at Madinah are markedly different from those said to have been revealed to him in Makkah. While the Makkan verses concentrate on the main Quranic themes of divine unity, the coming resurrection and judgement and righteous conduct, the Madinan ones are concerned with social and political issues. These range from social relations between Muslims and others to verses communicating Shariah (divine law). Treaties and agreements between Muslims and confederate pagan-Arab and Jewish tribes are also mentioned.

These 'Madinan revelations' formed the basis of all social and political interactions and the regulating of Muslim society, state formation and Islamic dominance in the region. Muhammad was firmly established as Prophet-ruler of a virtual Islamic state within the heartlands of pagan Arabia.

Muhammad encouraged a spirit of brotherhood between the Madinite Muslims, known as al-ansar ('the helpers'), and the Makkan migrants, or al-muhajiroun, and developed a multicultural and religiously plural city-state. This was achieved by a pledge between the Christian and Jewish communities, who wished to retain their faith but pledged allegiance to Muhammad.

Right Muhammad's followers suffered a demoralizing defeat at the Battle of Uhud in 625. The prophet planned and organized his military campaigns from Madinah.

DECISIVE BATTLES

As the *ummah* began to establish itself under Muhammad's guidance at Madinah, his Makkan enemies continued in their determination to destroy Islam. This led to a number of decisive battles, some of which were won and some lost by the Muslims.

In 624, at wells of Badr near Madinah, the Muslims gained a notable victory, despite being heavily outnumbered by their opponents. However, their resilience was severly tested at Uhud, a mountain at the city boundary. In the battle here, Muslims broke their ranks, which led to a serious defeat.

Madinah was in danger of capture by 10,000 Makkans in 627 when they laid siege to the city for more than two weeks. However, the construction of a series of defensive ditches (*khandaq*) around Madinah kept the invaders at bay, eventually forcing a retreat.

BLOODLESS VICTORY

Two years after the Hudaybiyah treaty with the Makkans, which granted the Muslims permission to make pilgrimage, Muhammad marched upon Makkah with 10,000 followers. However, he did not take the city by force: instead, he granted a general amnesty. This peaceful gesture resulted in reciprocal goodwill and a mass conversion to Islam, and thus helped establish the city as the religion's spiritual centre.

Left Muhammad is flanked by angels on his triumphant return to Makkah, some eight years after the migration (hijrah) to Madinah.

ISLAM IN THE PENINSULA

BY FORGING USEFUL LINKS WITH NEIGHBOURING KINGDOMS AND
TRIBES, MUHAMMAD TRANSFORMED THE ARABIAN PENINSULA WITH
HIS PROPHETIC MESSAGE AND ISLAM SOON DOMINATED THE REGION.

Having established what was effectively an Islamic state at Madinah, Muhammad was able to send emissaries to surrounding tribal leaders and sovereigns. In the process he gained some important adherents, whose influence was essential to the successful long-term Islamization of the region.

TREATIES AND ALLEGIANCES

The early covenant between the Makkan Muslims and the Yathribite pilgrims at Aqabah provided an opportunity for Muhammad's message to flourish in the peninsula through the agreed migration (*hijrah*) to their city. The Yathribite tribes of Aws and Khazraj were neither Jews nor Christians, and the treaty was a useful experience for the Muslims in building alliances and propagating the doctrines of Islam to less hostile tribes in Arabia.

Once he had established Muslim ascendancy in Madinah, Muhammad quickly forged strong links with neighbouring communities. In

order to accomplish his mission to promulgate Islam, it was necessary to create the right conditions for religious dialogue. To this end, Muhammad's envoys travelled to the nearby rulers of Abyssinia, Egypt, Persia, Syria and Yemen.

THE NAJRAN CHRISTIANS

Around 630, Muhammad received a delegation of some 60 Christian clergy and leaders from Najran in Yemen. They were orthodox Trinitarians who were under the protection of the Byzantium empire, and Muhammad allowed them to use the mosques to offer their Christian worship. He also took the opportunity of their visit to invite the Jews of Madinah to a tripartite religious dialogue.

During the congress, Muhammad criticized both faiths, accusing them of compromising their monotheism and tampering with their divine scriptures, thus perverting the teachings of the prophets from whom they were originally received.

Above A letter sent by the Prophet Muhammad to Chosroes II, King of Persia, inviting him to accept Islam after his defeat by the Byzantines in 629.

The Najranis acknowledged Muhammad's legitimacy as a prophet but most declined his call to Islam at that time. However, they allowed one of his companions, Abu Ubaydah ibn al-Jarrah, to accompany them to Yemen as a missionary envoy for Islam. Within a few years, the majority of Yemen, including the Christians of Najran, had converted to Islam.

THE ABYSSINIAN PRIESTS

The Christian kingdom of Abyssinia had provided asylum for a number of early Muslims, whose emigration is referred to as 'the first migration in Islam'. Relations between the Negus of Abyssinia and Muhammad were extremely cordial, to the extent that the king sent a delegation of seven priests and five monks to Madinah. They were instructed to observe Muhammad and study his revelations.

Left A Byzantine mosaic from the Umayyad Mosque, Damascus. The city came under Muslim rule in 635.

Right A mountain village mosque near Taizz. Christianity dominated Yemen until the Byzantine bishops from Najran pledged allegiance with Muhammad.

The Abyssinian clergy were visibly moved by the verses they heard and the incident was later referred to in the Quran: 'And thou wilt find the nearest in affection, to those who believe, those who say, Lo! We are Christians. That is because from amongst them are priests and monks and they are not given to arrogance.' (5:82)

In response, Muhammad sent a letter inviting the king to accept Islam. It is unclear if the Negus actually became a Muslim, but when he passed away, Muhammad announced his death and offered the congregational funeral prayer in absentia. After the 'first migration', Islam continued to flourish throughout Abyssinia.

THE JEWS OF MADINAH

Relations between the Muslims and the Jews of Madinah were at times fraught, though a large number converted to Islam. In an effort to secure peace in the city, a treaty with the remaining Jews and Christians was signed. However, although they were subject to their own religious scriptures and exempted from many duties incumbent upon Muslims, some Jews broke their agreement. They were given two options: defend against the pagan Makkans, with whom they had allied against the Muslims, or face exile. After initially refusing to do either, they left for a region called Khaybar and launched offensives against the Muslims. The consequences of this revolt were concluded at the Battle of Ahzab ('confederates') and the later Muslim offensive at Khaybar, in which the Jewish tribes and their allies were defeated.

Once the Makkans and their allies had been defeated, Muhammad turned his attention to the establishment of peace treaties with surrounding Bedouin tribes in an effort to facilitate the spread of Islam throughout the peninsula and beyond.

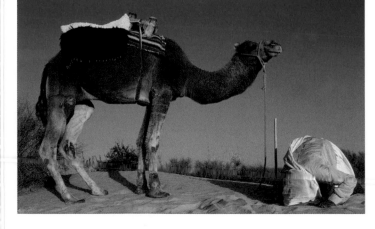

Left A Bedouin Muslim prays in the Sahara. Muslims used their knowledge of ancient trading caravan routes to spread Islam throughout the peninsula and into Byzantium, Persia and Africa.

ISLAMIC CALLIGRAPHY

THE OUTSTANDING WORK PRODUCED BY MUSLIM CALLIGRAPHERS
IS ONE OF THE CROWNING ACHIEVEMENTS OF ISLAMIC CULTURE. AS
A SPECIALIST SKILL, CALLIGRAPHY WAS HELD IN VERY HIGH REGARD.

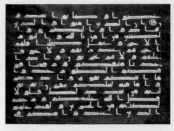

*Above A classic example of early kufic
script, from a 10th-century Quran
produced in North Africa. The long,
horizontal strokes of some characters
were a feature of the Western kufic style.*

Throughout the Islamic world,
calligraphers enjoyed a more
exalted status than artists until the
latter part of the Middle Ages. This
is reflected in a tale from the *Arabian
Nights*, 'The Second Dervish', in
which an unfortunate prince is
transformed into an ape. Undaunted,
he demonstrates his regal nature by
writing out a succession of verses,
using six different types of script.
His knowledge of calligraphy proved
that he was not only a human, but
also a highly cultivated one.

The development of elaborate
calligraphy owed much to religion.
In early societies, where literacy was
scarce, the written word assumed a
mysterious, almost magical aura.
Calligraphers exploited this, using
ever more elaborate forms of script
to beautify the sacred word. This is
evident in both Christian and
Muslim manuscripts, but the full
potential of calligraphy was explored
far more thoroughly by Islamic
artists, because of their restrictions
on other forms of decoration.

EARLY SCRIPTS

In the earliest phase of their history,
Muslims preferred to transmit their
learning orally. However, the need
to circulate a standardized version
of the Quran created a shift in
attitudes. In the 7th century, Caliph
Uthman ibn-Affan sent master texts
to leading Islamic centres, where
they were copied by local scribes.
These early manuscripts were chiefly
written in *kufic*, a blocklike, angular
script that took its name from the
Iraqi stronghold of Kufa.

Kufic had several regional
variations, but it remained the
preferred style of writing until
around the 10th century, when it
was gradually superseded by a
number of more rounded, cursive
scripts. These were more fluid in

appearance, as calligraphers in this
field were trained to focus on
whole words, rather than individual
letters. *Nashki* became the most
popular of these, though it did not
prevail everywhere. In the Islamic
West, for example, in Spain and
North Africa, calligraphers preferred
to use the Maghribi script, a cursive
form that managed to retain the
grandeur of *kufic* lettering.

DEVELOPING SCRIPTS

Islamic calligraphy underwent a
profound transformation in the
10th century following the reforms
of Ibn Muqla (886–940). He
rationalized the system, ensuring
that each character in the *nashki*
alphabet was written out in a
consistent, well-proportioned way.
He also promoted a number of
other scripts, such as *muhaqqaq*,
rayhani and *thuluth*. Each of these
served a different function, although
they could often appear in the same
manuscript. It was not unusual, for
example, to find the text of a Quran
copied out in *nashki*, but with the
headings in *kufic*.

*Left Calligraphers liked to combine
different scripts on the same page. In
this 16th-century Persian manuscript,
the main text is written in* nashki,
while the headings are in thuluth.

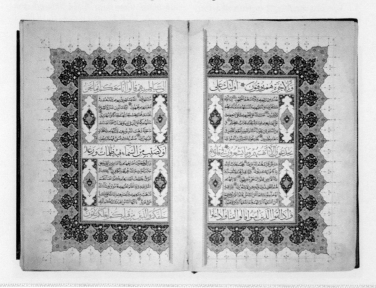

EPIGRAPHS

None of the Arabic scripts were confined solely to manuscripts. The chief reason why Islamic calligraphy is so rich and varied is because there was considerable interaction between the different media in which it was employed.

Architectural inscriptions, known as epigraphs, date back to the 7th century, featuring on the Dome of the Rock in Jerusalem. From the outset, their content was very varied. Sometimes, they simply referred to the foundation date and the patron of a building, but more often the inscriptions consisted of blessings or verses from the Quran.

Kufic was the most widely used script, but its form was modified far more drastically than it was in manuscripts. In many cases, the shafts of the letters were interlaced – a decorative ploy that was borrowed from early coinage. Alternatively, they were enveloped in leafy scrolls and floral motifs. Occasionally, the letters themselves sprouted buds or leaves.

Legibility was not always a high priority. Often the calligraphy was set in vertical panels, even though Arabic is read horizontally, from right to left. In other instances, it was enclosed in rigid, geometric patterns, with the letters distorted, in order to fit into the design. As a result, the maze-like inscriptions became virtually indecipherable.

CALLIGRAPHY AND CRAFTS

Calligraphy was employed in virtually every art form, featuring in the designs of a diverse range of objects, from carpets and tiles to metalwork and ivory. Here, the effect could sometimes be more playful. Inscriptions on a series of medieval metal vessels, for instance, featured ribbon-like *nashki* script, topped with comical human heads or imaginary animals.

Above A seal inscribed with a Quranic verse on the Prophet's form: 'And we have not sent you [Muhammad] except as a mercy for all creation...'

Below Decorative bands of calligraphy, citing verses from the Quran, encircle the red sandstone shaft of the Qutb Minar in Delhi. The lettering itself is combined with intricate floral motifs.

SEEKING KNOWLEDGE

'READ IN THE NAME OF THY LORD': THE FIRST WORDS BELIEVED TO HAVE BEEN REVEALED TO MUHAMMAD CHARACTERIZED HIS PROPHETIC MISSION TO EDUCATE AND CIVILIZE HIS SOCIETY.

Islam transformed a predominantly illiterate society into a leading civilization virtually within a single generation. The Quran provided a means of uniting diverse peoples into a single faith community, while developing their intellectual capacity through rulings that encouraged objective scientific and philosophical inquiry in the pursuit of a better understanding of Allah as al-Alim, 'the Source of all Knowledge'.

Muhammad was quite typical of his people in being an *ummi* (illiterate). The first revealed verses of the Quran are emphatic in their instruction to read and write – and thereby to seek knowledge: 'Read in the name of thy Lord who created, Created man from a clot! Read and your Lord is most Generous, Who teaches man by means of the pen, teaches Man what he does not know' (96:1–5).

SCIENCE AND LEARNING

Upon receiving this revelation, Muhammad immediately set about educating his followers to read and write. After the Battle of Badr, he decreed that any literate pagan captive who taught ten Muslims to read and write would gain freedom.

The Arabs had always used the stars to navigate their way across the deserts nocturnally. After their Islamization, they developed their knowledge of astronomy to map out the direction and times of prayers, and measure distances for travel, inventing instruments such as astrolabes, celestial globes, quadrants and sextants.

In order to obey the Quranic command to travel and experience the world that God had created, Muslims developed specific sciences that would aid exploration, and measure, analyze and quantify data and specimens. This led them to excel in the fields of science and technology.

CIVILIZATION AND CULTURE

Across the expanding Muslim world of the medieval era, from Delhi to Timbuktu and from Baghdad to Granada, Islamic culture and

Left This 14th-century astrolabe helped Muslims to explore the universe in pursuit of knowledge of the natural world, as inspired by the Quran.

Above Medieval Muslim astronomers, geographers and cartographers map out the heavens and earth, guided by the teachings of the Quran regarding natural phenomena.

learning began to advance. In Spain, the paved public footpaths of Córdoba and Seville were illuminated by street lamps. The cities incorporated public baths for the first time, and, even as early as the 9th century, underground sewers and city dumps were built to the benefit of all.

Baghdad and Cairo became the intellectual and academic centres of the Muslim world with the creation of the first universities and scientific centres, which specialized in astronomy and chemistry, philosophy and the arts.

The thirst for knowledge and the advancement in sciences and technology was not a result of market economy materialism, but rather was a living testament to the Quran's rhetorical question, 'Are those who have knowledge equal to those who do not have knowledge' (39:9)? It was also an obedient response to the Prophet

Muhammad's declaration that 'the seeking of knowledge is an obligation on every Muslim.'

Throughout the ages, Muslims have always understood the pursuit of knowledge and learning to be an act of worship that fulfils divine instructions and benefits human civilization and culture through scientific inquiry and critical thought. In no way do Muslims consider that learning results in a loss of faith or an alienation from the Islamic view of the universe.

Right The Great Mosque at Córdoba, Spain. By the 10th century, the Islamic world had become a bastion of civilization and scientific learning that stretched from Iraq right across to Spain.

PHILOSOPHY AND ART

As Muslims applied themselves to some of the more spiritual and philosophical aspects of the Quran, a number of theological disciplines emerged, including Sufism, which is often understood as Islamic mysticism. Sufism focuses on the esoteric meanings of the Quran and developed into a sophisticated branch of Islamic learning and practice. Another discipline to appear at this time was *kalam*, which is concerned with understanding the Quran through discussion of the attributes of God and theological posits on issues such as free will, sin and the nature of the Quran.

In art, the Arabesque developed an abstract and symmetrical form based on the circle and the dot, which represents God at the centre of creation. The circle and its intersecting geometric lines denote God's infinite creation as the patterns are repeated endlessly.

Left Religious devotion, geometry, acoustic sciences and skilled craftsmanship combine to produce a glorious mosque and centre of learning at the Masjid-e-Shah in Isfahan, Iran.

THE WAY OF THE PROPHET

THE QURAN TEACHES THAT THE PROPHET MUHAMMAD WAS SENT BY GOD FOR THE BENEFIT OF HUMANKIND. MUSLIMS THEREFORE BELIEVE THAT HIS LIFE EXAMPLE IS THE BEST MODEL TO EMULATE.

Above Reciting the Quran during Ramadhan is considered an emulation of Muhammad's ritual practice.

The Islamic declaration of faith, the *shahadah* – 'There is no God but God and Muhammad is His Messenger' – is a covenant comprised of two distinct parts. The first, 'There is no God but God', is seen by Muslims as both a negation of all false gods and an affirmation of the one true God. The second part, 'Muhammad is the messenger of God', states the Islamic belief that Muhammad is God's Prophet and that, as such, he must be obeyed and followed. Muslims believe that to obey the Prophet is to obey God, and loyalty to Muhammad's teachings and practices is therefore considered as a manifestation of belief in God.

HADITH AND SUNNAH

Islam teaches that the Prophet Muhammad is the gateway to God and that the pathway is formed of his hadith and sunnah. 'Hadith' literally means 'speech', or 'saying', and refers to anything that Muhammad is thought to have said, that is the thousands of transmitted and recorded sayings of the Prophet as remembered and passed down by his early followers.

The Arabs' oral tradition and custom of memorizing genealogies, stories and poems proved invaluable in the preservation of Muhammad's hadith. A couple of generations after his death, the prophetic sayings were compiled into various hadith collections by a small number of important Islamic scholars, who also included the chain of transmitters. A transmitter is an individual who faithfully memorized a particular hadith and its chain of narrators leading to the Prophet. In Islam, the hadith collections are second only to the Quran in importance.

The word 'sunnah' refers to the life example of the Prophet. Sunnah includes Muhammad's hadith and the particular way in which he lived – the way he ate, dressed, interacted with people and performed his religious duties. Islam teaches that

Left The mihrab of the Prophet's mosque in Madinah, from where he led his congregation in prayer.

Right A pilgrim has a moment of reflection at the shrine of Ali ibn Abu Talib in Mazar-e Sharif, Afghanistan.

the sunnah represents the perfect life example for Muslims to follow. The accounts of Muhammad's sunnah can be found in hadith but are more commonly recorded in the biographical accounts of his life known as the *Sirah*.

EMULATING THE PROPHET

Muslims believe that Muhammad's character provides the perfect example for them to emulate in their everyday lives. The imitation of the Prophet's practices is seen as an effective way of correcting personal character traits, and in doing so, Muslims believe that they will attain God's reward.

Following the sunnah is also seen as a measure of an individual's love of the Prophet, and Muslims are particular in their appearance and conduct in an effort to faithfully imitate him. The sunnah provides a means of developing a deep spiritual bond with the Prophet.

Without Muhammad the religion of Islam could not have been realized, and Muslims believe that it is only by following his example – one seen as demonstrating love and mercy – that they are able

to practise all aspects of their religious teachings. For many Muslims, love of the Prophet surpasses the love of all other humans to the point that they may

become emotional at the mention of his name, to which they will often supplicate *'sallallahu alayhi wa sallam'*, meaning 'the prayers and peace of God be upon him'.

THE HADITH OF MUHAMMAD'S LAST SERMON

One of the most famous prophetic hadiths is that said to relate Muhammad's final sermon at the plains of Arafah, which he gave to his followers after his farewell pilgrimage in 632. According to this hadith, Muhammad informed his followers, 'O people listen to what I say to you for I do not know whether I will meet with you after this year in this place again…' He reminded the congregation of their duties, urging them to treat each other with kindness, then concluded by announcing to his followers, '…I have left with you that which if you hold fast to will save you from all error, a clear indication, the Book of God and the word of his prophet. O people hear my words and understand.'

Left Muhammad delivers a sermon from his Minbar, or pulpit, at the Madinah mosque in this 17th-century manuscript painting.

PRESERVING THE PROPHET'S SAYINGS

IN ISLAM, THE PROPHET'S SAYINGS ARE A SOURCE OF AUTHORITY SECOND ONLY TO THE QURAN. AUTHENTICATING WHAT MUHAMMAD ACTUALLY SAID WAS THEREFORE A PRIORITY FOR EARLY MUSLIMS.

When Muslims began to commit their religious teachings to the written word, safeguarding the authenticity and integrity of the original narrations was paramount to preserving their religion. In the process of its written compilation, the Quran was subjected to continuous scrutiny by successive caliphs and their councils. Similarly, the narrations of Muhammad needed to be collated and verified for their authenticity. Prophetic sayings are important to understanding the Quran, religious practices and legal injunctions. Preserving the correct accounts was therefore important for the development of Islamic scholarship.

BIOGRAPHIES OF THE PROPHET

The early biographies of the Prophet Muhammad are documents that capture both the critical events and developments of his mission. The works are known collectively as the *Sirah*, and the earliest is that of Muhammad ibn Ishaq ibn Yasr (d.767), who produced the book *Siratu Rasulillah (Life of the Messenger of Allah)*. These first accounts also reflect the collective memory of the Muslim community relating to the spread of Islam during Muhammad's lifetime.

Through their particular literary style, these accounts also document the love and veneration that

Muhammad's first community had for him. According to ibn Ishaq, Abu Bakr's comment upon the Prophet's death was designed to affirm Muhammad's human status as compared with the eternal nature of God, who had revealed his guidance to humankind through his messenger. Abu Bakr reminded his fellow believers of God's word: 'Muhammad is but a messenger; messengers have passed away before him, will it be that when he dies or is killed, you will turn back on your heels?' (3:144) Thus Muhammad's companions were careful to avoid him becoming an object of worship in his death by focusing on the continuation of his divine mission.

However, the biography written by ibn Ishaq, while it provides details of the major events of Muhammad's life, is not more than

Above A 13th-century copy of the Quran preserves in handwritten Arabic script the original oral revelations that Muhammad is believed to have received some 600 years earlier.

a general portrait of him sketched from the shared memory of his contemporaries. Collecting the Prophet's actual hadith necessitated a more rigorous approach.

Right A trainee Muslim scholar learns hadith in the traditional way, at the feet of his shaykh, or teacher, in the Islamic madrasa in Shiraz, Iran.

RECORDING HADITH

Two specific terms became associated with the process of writing down the Prophet's hadith: *matn*, which refers to the actual content of a hadith, and isnad, which relates to the chain of transmitters linking the Prophet to a particular hadith.

The collection of hadith gathered great momentum in the first two centuries of Islam. This was largely because the memorized accounts had been either lost with the deaths of previous generations or taken from the community at Madinah by migrating Muslims. Frequently, a hadith would find its way back to Madinah, carried by Muslims settling there who had learnt it at their place of origin from an early emigrant.

Often, early compilers would travel huge distances in order to record a single narration. For example, one scholar set out from

Below Islamic scholars in Qom, Iran, discuss religion and memorize the Quran in the precincts of the Grand Mosque, a tradition that has endured for over a millenium.

Madinah to Damascus to seek out Abu al-Darda, a companion of Muhammad who was a transmitter of a particular hadith. The journey took a month, and necessitated some degree of discomfort, which demonstrates the extraordinary dedication of these scholars to the pursuit of religious knowledge.

THE SCIENCE OF HADITH

The collected hadiths were selected for their considered authenticity after a critical analysis of the chronological accuracy, linguistic content, geographical parameters and the character of individual transmitters connected to them.

Scrutinizing each of the links in the chain of a hadith became a biographical science called *ilm ar-rijal* (literally 'knowledge of men'). Scholars researched the reliability of character of the transmitters and also tried to establish whether linked individuals had met or if they had any political or sectarian motives. Once hadiths had satisfied the above criteria, they were classified into accepted categories of 'agreed' (or 'sound'), 'good', 'weak' or 'fabricated'.

COLLECTING HADITH

Scholars who dedicated their lives to locating and codifying hadith became known as *al-Muhaddithun*. Imam Bukhari (d.870) was one of the greatest Sunni hadith scholars and is attributed with collecting some six million hadith before accepting only 7,275 for his nine-volume work. Five other major classical volumes of hadith are still widely used throughout the Muslim world: Muslim, Tirmidhi, Ibn Majah, Abu Dawood and An-Nisai.

Above One of the most famous hadith collections, the nine-volume Sahih al-Bukhari contains more than 7,000 narrations.

STORIES FROM THE PROPHET'S LIFE

MUHAMMAD'S INTERACTIONS WITH PEOPLE, ANIMALS AND THE ENVIRONMENT ARE SEEN BY MUSLIMS AS A TESTIMONY TO HIS COMPASSION AND EVIDENCE OF HIS EXEMPLARY BEHAVIOUR.

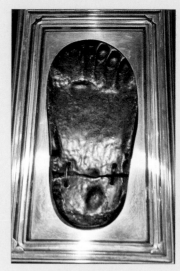

Hadiths and biographies of the Prophet Muhammad contain a wealth of detail about his life – not only about how he worshipped, but also how he dressed, what he preferred to eat, and so forth. There are also many interesting stories and anecdotes that provide an insight into his society. Muslims throughout the world see a humanity and compassion in these stories of the Prophet that they try to emulate in their own lives.

According to Islamic tradition, Muhammad was not only a consummate leader and statesman, but also someone full of kindness, empathy and warmth. Indeed, the stories tell that on occasions he would laugh so much that his molars were visible. It is said that he was approached constantly by people in his community asking him to explain the new religion to them, and that on many occasions he did so with great humour.

TWO OLD WOMEN

One story tells that an old woman once asked Muhammad if she would enter paradise. He teased her by replying no, there would be no old women in paradise. The poor old woman cried, only to be comforted by

Right Muhammad, seen here in green surrounded by a halo of light, hears the complaint of a doe. His treatment of animals is the subject of many anecdotes from hadiths.

Muhammad's smile as he explained that she would enter paradise, but in a young form – no one would remain old there.

On a different occasion, Umm Ayman, another old woman, is said to have come to Muhammad and asked for a camel. He told her that he would give her only the offspring of a she-camel. She was rather disappointed, and worried that a small camel would not carry her weight, until she realized he was teasing her, for of course all camels are the offspring of a she-camel.

Above The Prophet Muhammad's footprint has been preserved. Images of the Prophet are frowned upon; however, sacred relics from his life are revered.

THE COMPANIONS AND THE BIRDS

Both the Quran and hadith are very clear on the need to treat animals with kindness and love, and stories about the Prophet's life tell that he always acted toward animals with care and sensitivity.

It is told that one day, while Muhammad was travelling with his companions, they stopped to rest. While he went away from them for a short time, his friends spotted a sparrow flying with her two fledglings above their heads. The tiny birds were not steady flyers, and as they flew lower, his companions thought it would be fun to try to catch them as they were so beautiful.

Although the men were very gentle, the fledglings struggled in fear in their hands, while the mother bird flew around in great distress. When

Muhammad returned, he asked 'Who has terrorized this bird by taking her young ones?' He explained to his companions that, while they meant no harm, they had in fact distressed the mother. He then released the birds, who flew away to their mother.

THE OLD NEIGHBOUR

The rights of neighbours have been so emphasized in Islam that Muhammad even commented on one occasion that Archangel Jibril impressed their rights so much on him that he thought he would have to include them in his will! This statement emphasizes the importance Islam places on keeping good relations with neighbours so that disputes can be minimized and the home can indeed be a haven.

Muhammad's patience is said to have been severly tested on many occasions. A story tells that he had an old neighbour who was hostile to his message of Islam and threw rubbish at him whenever he passed her house. He never retaliated, nor did he enter into an argument with her. This went on for a considerable length of time. One day, however, the woman was not there. Although

Above This casket is said to contain the Prophet's tooth. Such relics allow people to connect with Muhammad, and are a reminder of a messenger who once lived and walked among people.

he was understandably pleased not to have rubbish thrown at him, Muhammad was concerned when on the following day she was still absent. He asked another neighbour about her and was told she was ill.

Muhammad decided to visit her, but she feared that he had come for retaliation when she was weak. In fact, he had gone simply to see if

Above Socializing is an important facet of Muslim life. According to stories of the life of the Prophet, he was renowned for generously spending his time with people.

she was alright and to fulfil his duty to visit the sick. His kindness won the old woman's heart, and she subsequently entered the faith.

APPLYING HADITH

A STUDY OF QURANIC TEXT AND PROPHETIC HADITH ESTABLISHED
THE AUTHORITY OF A CORE OF RELIGIOUS SCHOLARS, WHO
CODIFIED HADITH AND DEVELOPED THE PRINCIPLES OF ISLAMIC LAW.

By the third century after the death of Muhammad, Islamic scholarship had gravitated around a small group of specialist teachers who had devoted themselves to hadith study. These teachers also developed a system of learning, complete with a graduation. Students would study manuscripts with their master scholars, or *ulama*, either by dictation or from the original text.

CONTROVERSY

As devoted scholars of hadith worked methodically to authenticate the millions of hadiths attributed to Muhammad, other less scrupulous Muslims were engaged in their distortion and fabrication.

There were two main sources of erroneous and forged narrations. The first came from the *qussass*, or professional storytellers, who earned a living as public entertainers, relating the ancient oral narratives of the Arabs. Their tales incorporated ancient mythology, biblical legends, Quranic stories and prophetic traditions, which they fused into elaborated, entertaining plots. While the *qussass* were popular cultural communicators, the errors contained in their religious tales were often translated to the masses as fact. The result was a popular but incorrect version of many hadiths.

The second source of faulty hadiths were certain political and sectarian figures, who, for whatever reason, needed to support their claims of religious orthodoxy. In the temporary absence of a widely agreed authentic body of hadith literature, these people were able to fabricate prophetic narrations to provide justification for their various heterodox positions.

CODIFICATION

Once hadiths had been verified as genuine, it became necessary to begin codifying them into specific categories according to their

Above The imam delivers the Friday sermon to his congregation in the Grand Mosque in Almaty, Kazakhstan, praising the virtues of the Quran and hadith.

reliability and subject matter. The thematic arranging of hadith aided religious rulings relating to ritual practices and the application of Islamic law. Scholars then employed the hadith literature to explain principles of jurisprudential law known as *fiqh*.

One of the first works of this type was *al-Muwatta* (literally 'The Beaten Path') by Imam Malik (717–801). This book was followed by a number of equally important works that formed the basis of the major jurisprudential schools. Students from each of these law schools would present their own newly completed manuscripts, copied from the works of their teachers, for correction. Sometimes manuscripts would be reproduced through correspondence; others were simply copied without any supervised oral readings. Most

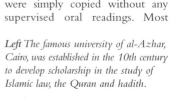

Left The famous university of al-Azhar, Cairo, was established in the 10th century to develop scholarship in the study of Islamic law, the Quran and hadith.

commonly, however, the scholar would provide a certificate (*ijazah*) to his student, granting him permission to transmit what he had learned.

Classical jurists, such as Imam Malik, were careful to stress that their individual opinions and rulings should not be accepted uncritically and that wherever a more appropriate ruling was available it should be preferred. Over time, the rulings of the four leading scholars, Malik, Abu Hanifah, Ash-Shafii and Ibn Hanbal, came to dominate Sunni thought, while the rulings of Imam Jafar al-Sadiq formed the leading legal school among the Shiah.

HADITH AND LAW

Islamic jurisprudence, *fiqh*, is derived from prescribed canonical laws contained in the Quran that relate to criminal and civil rulings (*muamalat*) and personal and religious commands (*ibadat*). The Quran deals with both these types of issues in broad and general terms. For example, it instructs Muslims to make ritual ablution and establish prayers, but it does not give the details of how, where and when.

The Prophet's hadith and sunnah provide precise information on these and all other matters relating to Quranic teachings. The hadith is therefore extremely important in helping Muslim scholars understand the practical application of divine laws and instructions. Had early Islamic scholars neglected to collate, authenticate and codify the hadith, the much-needed minutiae of religious law and practice would have been lost to subsequent generations of Muslims.

Right The minaret of the Uqba Mosque at Kairouan, Tunisia, which dates back to the 9th century. Its university is a bastion of Islamic learning and civilization.

HADITH COLLECTIONS

The five major collected volumes of hadith, and the special science concerned with their transmission, validation and authentication, became a distinguishing feature of Muslim civilization. The hadith collections also facilitated a unique and vast body of religious legal literature that remains available to Islamic scholars and lay Muslims.

As Muslims continue to migrate and settle into new domains, the Prophet's hadith and sunnah continue to be extremely significant

Above Students study hadith literature in the traditional manner – at the feet of their shaykh*, or teacher – in this 13th-century manuscript painting.*

in developing and establishing a functioning community, complete with its traditional values and beliefs. The wide availability of the volumes of codified hadith literature allows contemporary Islamic scholars to address new situations in accordance with the primary religious teachings of Islam.

LAWS AND SCHOLARS

THE BODY OF AUTHENTICATED PROPHETIC HADITH PROVIDES THE
MUSLIM *UMMAH* WITH A UNIQUE SOURCE FOR ISLAMIC SCHOLARSHIP
IN THE FIELDS OF THEOLOGY AND RELIGIOUS LEGAL RULINGS.

Islamic scholarship has developed over 1,500 years through the study of the Quran and sunnah. As Islam spread beyond Arabia, the need to understand and apply its teachings in new geographical and cultural contexts grew. Muslim theologians, philosophers and legal scholars engaged in intense debates, formulating diverse theological and legal stances based on their varied interpretations of text.

ISLAMIC LAW

The laws of the Quran are called the Shariah. The method by which these rules of Shariah are applied to specific or new situations became a

Below Muslim students from Oman study the Quran, the contents and ordinances of which guide Muslims through every aspect of their daily lives.

science known as *fiqh*. Fiqh has four methodological principles, known collectively as *usul*: the Quran, sunnah, reasoning by analogy (*qiyas*) and consensus of opinion (*ijma*).

Fiqh scholars are known as *fuqaha* (singular *faqih*), and issues relating to legal questions are dealt with by a specialist jurist called a *mufti*, whose considered opinion is a *fatwa*. A judge dispensing with criminal and civil disputes is a *qadi* or 'grand judge'.

THE IMPORTANCE OF LEGAL SCHOOLS

Shariah is a dynamic and elaborate system that has evolved from Muhammad's time to the present. It is of major importance to the Muslim *ummah*, for whom its rules and teachings form the guiding principles and values of daily life. Although there is no notion of

Above An ancient Quranic manuscript handwritten in kufic *script. The Quran provides the foundations of Islamic jurisprudential law, or* fiqh, *through Shariah, or canonical, law.*

absolute religious authority in Islam, there is a general consensus of scholars (*ijma*) concerning the fundamental beliefs and practices. The dominant theological position within the *ummah* is referred to as *Sunni* – those who adhere to the major teachings of the Prophet and the majority opinions of the *ulama* or religious scholars.

MAJOR ISLAMIC SCHOLARS AND SCHOOLS

During the periods of the ruling Muslim dynasties of the Umayyads and the Abbasids, *fiqh* scholarship evolved into major recognized legal schools called *madhhabs*, founded on the teachings of individual scholars. Originally there were many schools, but eventually five main ones emerged. In order of their founding, these were Hanafi, Maliki, Shafii, Hanbali and Jaafari.

The founders of these legal schools were all exceptional scholars and they share similar biographies. All spent their early lives mastering hadith literature, which they later taught. Notably, they all also resisted oppressive Umayyad and Abbasid Muslim rulers, for which most of them received public humiliation, imprisonment and even death. For example, the founder of the Hanafi School, Abu Hanifah (702–67), was born in Kufa, Iraq, and became a leading scholar in the Umayyad court, where he was offered, but declined, the position of *qadi*. Despite imprisonment, he refused another royal appointment under the Abbasid caliph al-Mansur (754–75) and thus remained in prison, where he died. Despite the fact that during their lifetimes these scholars were considered by a succession of Muslim rulers to be heterodox or heretical, their scholarship has continued to influence Muslim thought right up to the present day.

Today, the Hanafi School predominates in Turkey, Eastern Europe, Iraq, Central Asia and South Asia; the Shafii School is the main school in Yemen, Egypt, Somalia and East Asia; Muslims in North Africa and Sudan largely

Right Female law students study in a university library in Egypt. Islam has a history of women scholars specializing in religious law and jurisprudence.

follow the Maliki School; while the Hanbali school is predominant in Saudi Arabia. The main Shiah legal school, the Jaafari School, dominates Iran, Lebanon and southern Iraq.

INTERPRETATIONS

Significantly, the written script of the Quran was the first book in the Arabic language and it is the foundational text of all the various original branches of early Islamic sciences. In order to grasp the Quran's context, and thus interpret the text correctly, it is essential to understand the chronology of the Quranic revelations – the when, where, why and to whom they were given. Likewise, it is important to have an awareness of the Quran's specific language and diction, and its particular rhetorical style has been the subject of numerous detailed studies.

Above Ornately decorated copies of the Quran, some of which contain interpretations of the text, are displayed in an Islamic bookshop.

These explanatory works, which are known as *tafsir*, have three major approaches. *Tafsir bil-ra'i* gives an explanation by comprehension and logic based largely on an exegete scholar's considered interpretation of the text. *Tafsir bil-riwayah* expounds what has previously been transmitted through either other correlating verses from the Quran, specific hadiths relating to the text, or the generally agreed consensus of meaning by exegete scholars. *Tafsir bil-isharah* deals with the esoteric interpretations of the text. No individual has absolute authority on the Quran's exact meaning, but these commentaries offer a deeper knowledge of its contents.

CHAPTER 2

THE HISTORY OF ISLAM

In 706–15, Caliph al-Walid I, ruler of the vast and still-growing Umayyad Islamic empire, built the Grand Mosque of Damascus in the historic Syrian city that his forerunner Muawiyah I had chosen as his capital. Al-Walid was the sixth ruler in the Umayyad caliphate (line of successors to the Prophet Muhammad). By the time of his rule, less than 90 years after the death of the Prophet Muhammad (in 632), the faith of Islam had already won wide territories for Allah by military conquest.

Subsequent Umayyad caliphs continued this expansion of territories, creating a powerful Islamic empire. They are revered by Arab nationalists, who see their rule as a 'golden age', but reviled by Shiah Muslims because they came to power through violence and at the expense of the descendants of Ali ibn Abu Talib, cousin and son-in-law of Muhammad. Many Sunni Muslims also see the Umayyad as worldly kings rather than true caliphs (religious leaders and successors to the Prophet).

Opposite At the Great Mosque in Damascus, remains of beautiful mosaics installed by Byzantine craftsmen can be seen on the façade of the transept facing the courtyard

Above Under Sultan Suleyman I (reigned 1520–66), the Topkapi Palace in Istanbul was a great centre for calligraphy and other arts, attracting artists from all over the empire.

SUCCESSORS TO THE PROPHET

THE FIRST FOUR CALIPHS – OR SUCCESSORS TO THE PROPHET MUHAMMAD – ESTABLISHED ISLAM AS A MAJOR RELIGIOUS AND POLITICAL FORCE IN THE MIDDLE EAST AND NORTH AFRICA.

Above Muhammad is pictured with the first three men to serve as caliphate Rasulillah ('Successor to God's Prophet') – Abu Bakr, Umar and Uthman.

Sunnis claim that the Prophet did not name a successor before his death in 632. His followers chose Abu Bakr to be political and religious leader of the faith. Abu Bakr was named caliphate Rasulillah ('Successor to God's Prophet, Messenger of Allah'), and his rule as caliph lasted just over two years (8 June 632 until 23 August 634).

A merchant from Makkah who, like Muhammad himself, was a member of the Quraysh tribe, Abu Bakr had been a long-term companion of the Prophet, whom he had known since boyhood. He was the fourth convert to Islam, and the first outside Muhammad's own family. According to later tradition, he purchased the freedom of eight slaves who converted to the new faith in its early days.

His principal achievement was consolidating the nascent Muslim state by establishing control over the whole of Arabia. In central Arabia, his forces put down several rebel uprisings in the Ridda wars (from Arabic for 'Wars of Apostasy', and so called because a number of rebel leaders declared themselves prophets to rival Muhammad).

The most powerful rebel prophet was Musaylimah, but he and his tribe, the Banu Hanifah, were defeated at the Battle of Yamama on the plain of Aqraba (now in Saudi Arabia) in December 632. Moreover, under Abu Bakr's leadership, Bedouin tribesmen won the first of many astounding victories for the new faith against the Persian Sasanian empire and the Byzantine empire in what is now Iraq and Syria.

THE SECOND CALIPH

In August 634, Abu Bakr fell seriously ill. Before he died, he appointed Umar ibn al-Khattab to succeed him as caliph. Umar was another Makkah-born merchant and a long-term follower of Muhammad,

Left The Prophet's daughter Fatimah and her husband Ali ibn Abu Talib, the fourth caliph, witness Muhammad's death in 632 in Madinah.

and another member of the tribe of Quraysh. He proved a tremendously effective leader: directing operations from Madinah, in his ten-year rule (634–44) he oversaw major Islamic military expansion as his armies continued the assault against the Byzantine and Sasanian empires.

Umar's Arab armies attacked the Byzantines in Syria and captured Damascus in 635. Further south, they took control of Jerusalem from the Byzantines in 638. They also moved against the Byzantines in North Africa and took Alexandria. They seized Ctesiphon, the Persian capital, in 637, forcing the Sasanian king Yazdegerd III to flee, and vanquished the Persian army at the Battle of Nahavand in 642; in 651, Yazdegerd was killed at Merv, and the Sasanian dynasty was at an end.

To consolidate their gains, Umar's followers built garrison towns such as Kufa and Basra in Egypt. Umar was the first caliph to call himself *amir al-mumineen* ('Commander of the Faithful').

Above The Imam Ali mosque in Najaf,
Iraq, contains the tomb of Ali ibn Abu
Talib and is a major pilgrimage site for
Shiah Muslims.

Below Ctesiphon (now in Iraq) had
been a major city for 700 years when
it was captured by Arab troops in 637
in the time of Caliph Umar.

UTHMAN SUCCEEDED BY ALI

In 644, Umar was stabbed in the
mosque in Madinah by a Persian
slave named Pirouz Nahavandi (or
Abu-luluah); he died two days
later. A council of elders chose
Uthman ibn-Affan, – another
former merchant from Makkah and
another of Muhammad's original
converts – as his successor, and third
caliph. Some Muslims were unhappy
at the choice, and dissent burst
into the open after Uthman was
murdered in 656.

Ali ibn Abu Talib, Muhammad's
cousin and son-in-law, assumed the
position of caliph and moved the
capital of the Islamic community
from Medina to Kufa (now in Iraq),
where he had substantial support.
He encountered opposition, causing
the first great schism in the *ummah*.

First, he crushed a faction led
by Ayesha, one of Muhammad's
widows, together with Talhah and
al-Zubayr, two *sahabi* ('companions
of the Prophet', Muslims who were
alive in the Prophet's lifetime). He
defeated them decisively at the
Battle of the Camel at Basra, Iraq.
He also met opposition from a
leading member of the Ummayad
clan named Muawiyah, who
refused to accept his authority.

SHIAH AND SUNNI VIEWS

Shiah Muslims regard Ali ibn Abu
Talib as the first legitimate leader of
the Islamic religious community by
virtue of his blood relationship
with the Prophet and his status as
Muhammad's first convert to Islam.
Entirely rejecting the authority of
the first three caliphs, Shiah
Muslims regard Ali as the first in a
line of infallible religious leaders
called imams.

Sunni Muslims, however, identify
Abu Bakr and his three followers as
the equally rightful successors to
the Prophet in ruling the *ummah*.
The Sunni celebrate Islam's first
four caliphs as the *Rashidun* (the
'rightly guided caliphs'). This term
and idea originated during the
Abbasid caliphate (750–1258).

CIVIL WAR

THE CIVIL WAR SPARKED BY THE CLASH BETWEEN ALI AND MUAWIYAH
CONTINUED INTO THE NEXT GENERATION AND LED TO THE INFAMOUS
MURDER OF ALI'S SON HUSSAIN BY MUAWIYAH'S SON YAZID IN 680.

Not long after assuming power as caliph, Ali ibn Abu Talib dismissed the regional governors appointed by his predecessors. Muawiyah, Governor of Syria, refused to obey, and proved a formidable opponent. A leading member of the Umayyad clan who had been named Governor of Syria in 640 by Umar, Muawiyah had a significant independent power base and had won major military victories, including the conquests of Cyprus in 649 and Rhodes in 654.

In response to this show of defiance, Ali led his army into Syria and fought Muawiyah in the three-day Battle of Siffin in July 657; the battle was inconclusive and the two men agreed to a six-month armistice followed by arbitration of the dispute. However, when the time came, neither man backed down and the standoff continued –

with Ali as caliph and Muawiyah still defying him and acting as Governor of Syria.

Some Muslims hatched a plot to end what they saw as a damaging conflict: on the 19th day of Ramadan in 661, both Ali and Muawiyah were stabbed with poisoned swords while at prayers. Muawiyah recovered, but Ali died from his wounds two days later.

MUAWIYAH GAINS POWER

Ali's supporters named his son Hassan caliph, and Muawiyah marched against them with a vast army. The two armies fought a few inconclusive skirmishes near Sabat and subsequently, after negotiations, Hassan agreed to withdraw his claim to the caliphate. Muawiyah was at last the undisputed caliph. Under the terms of the agreement, Muawiyah was to be caliph for his lifetime. According to Sunni accounts,

Above Ali is shown fighting the forces of Ayesha, a widow of the Prophet, at the Battle of the Camels in this 17th-century Persian wall painting.

Muawiyah agreed that on his death, a leadership consultation (*shura*) should be held to determine the next caliph, but according to Shiah accounts, Muawiyah agreed that the caliphate would pass to Hassan's brother Hussain ibn Ali.

Below Outnumbered perhaps 500 to one, Hussain and his followers took on impossible odds at the Battle of Karbala.

Right The Imam Hussain Shrine at Karbala, close to the battlefield, contains the tombs of both Hussain and his half-brother Abbas.

Muawiyah ruled as caliph with no further challenges until his death in 680. He governed from Damascus, which he developed as a city and where he established a liberal court. His rule was notable for its tolerance towards Christians, who came to occupy many prominent government positions, and for its introduction of Byzantine-style bureaucracies, especially a postal service and chancellery. When he died, however, the terms of his agreement with Ali were ignored in his desire to found a dynasty: the caliphate was passed to his son Yazid.

EVENTS AT KARBALA

Hussain ibn Ali, brother of Hassan and grandson of Muhammad, claimed the caliphate. He marched from Makkah to Kufa in Iraq, the base of his father Ali's support. At Karbala on 10 October 680, he was intercepted by a 40,000-strong army sent by Yazid and commanded by Umar ibn Said. Hussain was vastly outnumbered, with only 72 men in his travelling party. The only survivor was Hussain's son Ali ibn Hussain, who was too sick to fight and was taken prisoner, carried off to Damascus and kept as a prisoner of Caliph Yazid. However, many years later he was freed, and in time he became the fourth Shiah imam.

The Battle of Karbala was a key cause of the centuries-long split between Sunni and Shiah Muslims. Shiahs, descendants of the supporters of Ali (their name comes from that of their party in the 7th century, the *shiat Ali*, 'the party of Ali'), do not admit the legitimacy of any of the other early caliphs nor of the Umayyad descendants of Muawiyah. Sunnis (so called because they claim to follow Muhammad's sunnah, or 'example') celebrate Abu Bakr, Umar, Uthman, Muawiyah and the Umayyads in addition to Ali as the rightful successors of Muhammad.

A SECOND CIVIL WAR

Yazid ruled, as second caliph of the fledgling Umayyad dynasty, for three years, until his sudden death in 683. He had to fight an uprising in the Hijaz region led by Abdullah ibn al-Zubayr, a member of the *sahabi* ('Companions of the Prophet'). This war is known, together with the struggle between Yazid and Hussain, as the Second Fitnah, or Islamic Civil War. Yazid captured Madinah and besieged Makkah. In the course of the fighting, the *Kaabah* was damaged, making Yazid and the Umayyad dynasty more unpopular still. Yazid's death in 683 did not bring an end to the war, which continued through the reign of the next three caliphs.

Right Around 1 million Shiah Muslims travel to Karbala each year to take part in the ceremony of Ashura that commemorates Hussain's death there.

THE POWER OF THE UMAYYADS

THE FIRST GREAT CALIPHATE DYNASTY, THE UMAYYADS, RULED THE ISLAMIC WORLD FOR 90 YEARS, FROM 660 TO 750, AND CREATED A GLITTERING CAPITAL IN THE HISTORIC SYRIAN CITY OF DAMASCUS.

The Umayyad caliphate was founded by Muawiyah I, the provincial governor who had challenged the authority of the fourth caliph, Ali ibn Abu Talib. The Umayyads took their name from Muawiyah's great-grandfather, Umayya ibn Abd Shams, and from the Banu Umayyad clan named after him. The Umayyad clan were members of the same Quaraysh tribes as the Prophet Muhammad and shared an ancestor with him – Abd Manaf ibn Qusai.

THE EARLY YEARS

Muawiyah ruled for 19 years (661–80) and established a powerful court in Damascus, Syria, but the next three caliphs of the line – Yazid, Muawiyah II and Marwan – ruled for just five years between them. The fifth Umayyad caliph, Abd al-Malik, however, imposed his authority and established the dynasty on a firm footing.

Early in his reign, Abd al-Malik defeated a rebellion in Kufa led by al-Mukhtar, who had wanted to establish another of Ali's sons, Muhammad ibn al-Hanafiyyah, as caliph. By 691, he had reimposed Umayyad authority in Iraq, and in 692, he recaptured Makkah, so ending the long-running uprising in the Hijaz; the prominent rebel, Abdullah ibn al-Zubayr, was killed in the attack.

UMAYYAD GOVERNMENT

Abd al-Malik built on the achievements of dynastic founder Muawiyah by improving and centralizing the administration of the caliphate. He introduced a new Muslim coinage with non-figurative decoration and established Arabic as the caliphate's official language.

The Arab armies and the rulers that came in their wake differed from many of their predecessors as conquerors in that they did not

Above The impressive remains near Jericho in the West Bank were once part of the Umayyads' Kirbat al-Mafjar Palace, built there in c. 743–4.

force people to convert to their faith. Christians, Zoroastrians and Jews were free to continue to follow their own religion so long as they paid a head tax to their new rulers. However, many conquered peoples chose to convert to Islam. Conversion was simple: the only requirement was that the new believer acknowledge formally that there is no God other than Allah and that Muhammad is his Prophet. The principal benefits were freedom from slavery – for Islam

Below The peaks of the Eastern Lebanon Mountain range rise behind the ruins of the Umayyad trading city of Anjar, which was probably built in 705–15.

guaranteed that no Muslims could be slaves – and the right to pay the lower tax that was generally levied on believers.

This financial concession, and the willingness of conquered people to convert, in fact posed a problem for the expanding empire, since the spread of conversions necessarily reduced the amount of head tax raised; there were reports of provincial governors discouraging conversions in order to protect revenue. According to traditional accounts, this problem was addressed by the Umayyad caliph Umar ibn Abd al-Aziz (717–20), a ruler revered by later generations for his wisdom, tolerance and the ascetic life he led as a ruler.

UMAYYAD DEGENERACY?

Muawiyah established – and many of his descendants maintained – a cosmopolitan court in Damascus. They appointed Syrian Christians to important administrative positions and they patronized non-Islamic artists, such as the poet al-Akhtal (640–710), who was a Christian. According to some accounts, life at court was degenerate. Not only did senior Umayyads flout Islamic law by permitting the drinking of wine, but it is claimed that one Umayyad prince even enjoyed swimming in wine. However, as tales of this kind

were circulated by the opponents of the Umayyads, there must be some doubt as to their truthfulness.

CITIES AND PALACES

The Umayyads developed the city of Damascus. Under Byzantine rule, it had been a fortress town, but the Umayyads transformed it, albeit briefly, into a great imperial city. They also built cities in the desert to facilitate the by-then flourishing international trade that made Damascus and the empire rich. One was Anjar, around 50km (31 miles) from Beirut in Lebanon, which was built by Abd al-Malik or al-Walid at the intersection of the trade routes to Damascus, Homs and Baalbek (in southern Lebanon).

Umayyad caliphs also built fine desert castles and palaces, many of which appear to date from

Above The plain exterior of the 8th-century Umayyad desert castle of Qasr Amra in Jordan conceals remarkable surviving murals depicting hunting scenes.

the brief reign of Caliph al-Walid II (743–4). Qasr Amra, in eastern Jordan, was used as a hunting lodge; its walls are covered in hunting scenes, images of fruit and naked women. Khirbat al-Mafjar, at Jericho in Palestine (c.725–50), contains a palace and bathhouse, an audience hall and a mosque. Mshatta Palace, around 30km (19 miles) south of the modern city of Amman, Jordan, was also probably built under al-Walid II; its very impressive stone façade can now be seen in the Pergamon Museum in Berlin.

Below The façade of the Umayyad Mshatta Palace, given by Ottoman sultan Abd al-Hamid II to Emperor Wilhelm II of Germany, is now in Berlin.

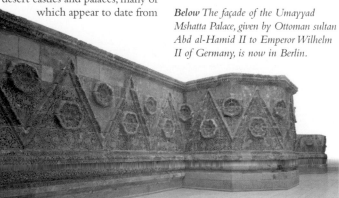

JERUSALEM: HOLY CITY TO THREE FAITHS

THE ANCIENT CITY OF JERUSALEM CONTAINS SITES SACRED TO JEWS, CHRISTIANS AND MUSLIMS, AND ITS POSSESSION HAS BEEN HOTLY CONTESTED BY ADHERENTS OF THE THREE FAITHS FOR CENTURIES.

The Jews revere Jerusalem as the centre of creation, the place where they believe that God made the world and the first man, Adam. For them, it is also the city of the biblical King David, who established the united kingdom of Israel and Judah, and the place where his successor, Solomon, built the first great temple.

To Christians, the city is sacred because it was the place where Jesus Christ, whom they believe to be the son of God, was crucified, buried, then rose from the dead.

Muslims honour the city, which is known in Arabic as al-Quds, principally as the place to which the Prophet Muhammad took his Night Journey and from where he made his ascension to heaven. In addition, Jerusalem is honoured in Islam because of its association in Judaism with earlier prophets, whom Muslims revere as Muhammad's forerunners and fellow prophets. Jerusalem, to Muslims, is the third most sacred city on earth after Makkah and Madinah.

FOUNDATION STONE

In the area of the city in which Solomon's Temple once stood is a large rock, which is known as the

Right Beautiful Iznik tiles were added to the Dome of the Rock's outer walls in a decorative programme under Ottoman sultan Suleyman the Magnificent (reigned 1520–66).

Foundation Stone. According to Jewish tradition, this is the place not only where God created the world, but also where Abraham prepared to sacrifice his son Isaac, where Jacob dreamt of a ladder ascending to heaven, and where the Ark of the Covenant resided within the Holy of Holies in Solomon's Temple.

Muslims honour the stone because of its associations with earlier prophets, although they believe that Abraham's sacrifice was of his other son, Ismail (forefather of the Arabs), and that it took place elsewhere, in the desert of Mina (east of Makkah, in Saudi Arabia). They also believe that the stone was the place from which the Prophet made his ascension to heaven – according to tradition, the rock even tried to rise with him but was held down by Archangel Jibril, and a mark on the stone is the hoof print of his supernatural steed, al-Buraq.

Above The Dome's octagonal plan is clearly shown in this 18th-century Arab manuscript illustration. The upper image is of the al-Aqsa Mosque.

THE DOME OF THE ROCK

In 687–92, fifth Umayyad caliph Abd al-Malik built the Dome of the Rock over the Foundation Stone. According to 10th-century traveller and geographer al-Maqdisi, the caliph wanted a lavish building to match the splendour of the Church of the Holy Sepulchre and to create a unique structure for Muslims that would be 'a wonder to the world'. He built the Dome as a pilgrimage shrine.

The shrine was constructed on a magnificent scale. The octagonal dome is 20m (65ft) tall and the same across, and stands above an arrangement of 12 columns and four piers within an octagonal walkway of 16 columns and eight piers and octagonal outer

Above Within the Dome of the Rock, an inscription celebrates Jesus as prophet and servant of Allah but attacks the Christian doctrine that he is God's son.

walls. Each of the eight outer sections of the wall is approximately 11m (36ft) high and 18m (59ft) wide. It is lavishly decorated within and without with mosaic, marble, tiles, carpets and faience. The dome, originally made of lead, was re-covered using a gold-coloured aluminium and bronze alloy as part of renovations in 1964 and again in 1993. The Dome of the Rock is the world's oldest surviving Islamic sacred monument.

'THE DISTANT MOSQUE'

The faithful do not pray in the Dome of the Rock but in the al-Aqsa mosque at the southern end of the Temple precinct. According to tradition, the original al-Aqsa mosque was raised by the second *Rashidi* caliph, Umar ibn al-Khattab, after the capture of Jerusalem in 638, and incorporated part of the *chanuyot*, or storehouse, of the ancient Jewish Temple of Jerusalem. It was rebuilt then in the time of the fifth Umayyad caliph, Abd al-Malik, and completed by his son al-Walid I (reigned 709–15). It was probably first called the al-Aqsa mosque at this time. The name means 'the distant mosque' and refers to a passage of the Quran that describes the Prophet's Night Journey: 'Glory be to Him Who carried His servant by night from the Sacred Mosque to the Distant Mosque, the environs of which We have blessed, that We might show him some of Our Signs. Surely, He alone is the All-Hearing, the All-Seeing' (17:2).

Above The Holy Sepulchre (reputedly the tomb in which Jesus was buried) is a free-standing structure within the church to which it gives its name.

GREATER THAN ROME

BY 732, A CENTURY AFTER THE DEATH OF MUHAMMAD, THE AREA
UNDER THE RULE OF THE UMAYYAD CALIPHATE WAS GREATER THAN
THAT COVERED BY THE ENTIRE ROMAN EMPIRE AT ITS HEIGHT.

By the beginning of the Umayyad caliphate in 661, the *Rashidun* caliphs had already taken Syria, Armenia, Egypt and most of the lands belonging to the Persian Sasanian empire. Under the Umayyads, the caliphate then expanded further east and north-east towards India and China, and far to the west and north-west across North Africa and into the Iberian Peninsula.

By 750, when the Umayyad caliphs were ousted by the Abbasids, they had created a vast empire that stretched from north-west India in the east to the Pyrenees in the north-west, and incorporated much of Central Asia, the Middle East, North Africa and what is now Portugal and Spain.

Below The army of the Goths flees before the Arab–Berber cavalry at Guadelete, in this detail from a 19th-century painting by Martinez Cubells.

EXPANSION EASTWARDS

The crushing of the Sasanian army in 642 at the Battle of Nahavand near Hamadan in Iran – a triumph celebrated by Muslims as 'the victory of victories' – delivered most of Persia into Arab hands. Afterwards, the Arabs moved on eastwards, taking Herat in 652 and Kabul in 664.

They also pressed north and north-east beyond the Persian plateau into Khorasan (an ancient region comprising parts of modern Afghanistan, Tajikstan, Uzbekistan, Turkmenistan and Iran) and Transoxiana (another ancient region in central Asia). By the early 8th century, most of this area was under Muslim control, and Arab armies pressed on still further, right to the borders of China.

After the capture of Kabul, the Indian subcontinent beckoned. The Arab armies launched attacks into the southern Punjab (in modern

Above The fortified desert palace of Qasr al-Hayr al-Sharqi in Syria was built in 728–9 in the reign of Caliph Hisham (reigned 723–743).

Pakistan) from 664 onwards. A great expedition led by Muhammad ibn-Qasim in 711 established Umayyad rule in Sindh by 712.

In one major military endeavour, however, the Umayyad armies failed. In a series of attacks in 674–8 under Caliph Muawiyah I, and again in 717–18 under Caliph Suleyman ibn Abd al-Malik, the Umayyad military machine tried and failed to capture the Byzantine capital, Constantinople.

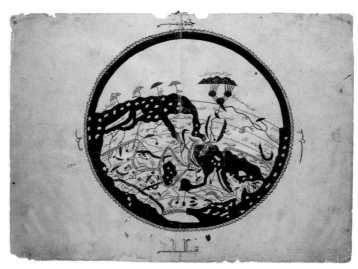

Right A world map drawn in the 12th century by Spanish Arab geographer Abu Abdallah al-Idrisi. As is common in Islamic maps, the south is at the top.

EXPANSION WESTWARDS

Alexandria in Egypt had been taken in 643. The Arabs then pressed westwards across North Africa, taking Tripoli in 647, but met fierce resistance from the Berber peoples of the Atlas Mountains. In 670, they subdued the Berbers in building the fortress city of Kairouan (around 160km (100 miles) south of Tunis in modern Tunisia).

Once conquered, the Berbers mostly converted and joined in the expansion. Arab–Berber armies swept through the Maghreb region of north-northwest Africa, reaching Tangier (now in northern Morocco) by the early 8th century. In northern Africa, they established a Muslim territory, known to historians as Ifriqiya, which encompassed coastal regions of what is now eastern Algeria, Tunisia and western Libya. They then looked further: across the narrow Straits of Gibraltar lay the former Roman province of Hispania, ruled by the internally divided kingdom of the Visigoths.

An Arab–Berber army invaded southern Spain in 711. Berber general Tariq ibn Ziyad inspired the invaders to defeat a much larger force commanded by King Roderick of the Visigoths at the Battle of Guadalete on 19 July 711. Roderick fled, or was killed, and his kingdom was quickly taken. The invaders captured the city of Seville and swept northwards. A second army, commanded by Musa bin Nusair, Governor of Ifriqiya, arrived in 712, and the combined Umayyad forces conquered almost the entire peninsula in five years. Only in the far north did the Visigoths survive.

Umayyad forces made a number of excursions further north into southern France, but these ended in 732 at the Battle of Tours when they were defeated by Christian troops. Thereafter the Umayyads withdrew into the Iberian Peninsula, where they established the territory of al-Andalus, initially as a province of the Umayyad caliphate.

THE BATTLE OF TOURS

On 10 October 732 near Tours in France, an Islamic army of some 80,000, commanded by Abd al-Rahman al-Ghafiqi, Governor General of al-Andalus, was defeated by a Frankish–Burgundian army commanded by Charles Martel in a battle known to Muslim chroniclers as the 'Battle of the Court of Martyrs'.

Traditionally, European historians have seen this battle as a key moment in the history of the continent, when the seemingly unstoppable global progress of Islam was turned back. Certainly, after this crushing defeat, Muslims abandoned attempts at northward expansion and settled in the Iberian Peninsula, where they maintained a presence until 1492.

Right The Battle of Tours is imagined as a single combat between commanders Charles Martel and Abd al-Rahman al-Ghafiqi in this 19th-century bronze sculpture by Théodore Gechter.

TRIUMPH OF THE KILLER

IN 750, THE CALIPHATE WAS SEIZED BY THE ABBASIDS, DESCENDANTS
OF MUHAMMAD'S UNCLE AL-ABBAS. THE RUTHLESS FIRST CALIPH,
ABU AL-ABBAS, WAS NICKNAMED *AS-SAFFAH* ('THE KILLER').

The Umayyads faced recurrent
opposition to their rule from
Shiah Muslims, who would not
allow the murder of Ali ibn Abu
Talib in 661 and the slaughter of
Hussain ibn Ali and family at
Karbala in 680 to be forgotten.

The Abbasids, cousins of and
long-term rivals to the Umayyads,
began to agitate for a change in
leadership. The Shiah Abassids were
members of the Hashim clan,
descended from the Prophet's
great-grandfather Hashim through
Muhammad's uncle al-Abbas. Their
rebellion against the Umayyads is
known as the Hashimiyyah.

THE HASHIMIYYAH

In 747, Abu Muslim became leader
of the Hashimiyyah in eastern Iran.
A native of the region and a convert
to Islam who had become a fervently
committed Shiah Muslim, Abu
Muslim won the support of a group
of fellow converts and non-Muslim
subjects of the Umayyads to name
the prominent Abassid Abu al-
Abbas as a rival ruler to the
Umayyad caliph Marwan II.
The rebels fought under the
sign of a black flag. In 749, a
Hashimiyyah army captured
Kufa and proclaimed Abu al-
Abbas caliph there.

Marwan II attempted to
put the revolt down, but on 25
January 750, an Abbasid army
commanded by Abu Muslim
defeated the Umayyads in the
Battle of the Zab (fought on the
banks of the Great Zab River, now
in Iraq). Marwan escaped with his
life. The Abbasids took Damascus in
April 750, and in August the same
year, Marwan was killed at Busir in

Egypt. The struggle between the
Abbasids and Umayyads is often
referred to as 'the Third Islamic
Civil War'.

Some Shiah clerics promoted
this war as the great final conflict
between good and evil prophesied
for the last days of creation. They
said that Abu al-Abbas was the
Mahdi, or 'Redeemer', whose
appearance will, according to
Islamic tradition, usher in the Day
of Resurrection (*yawm al-qiyamah*).
Belief in the Mahdi is strong among
Shiah Muslims, but generally less
important to Sunni Muslims.

'THE KILLER' TAKES POWER

Abu al-Abbas established himself as
caliph by ruthlessly eliminating all
opposition. He invited all the
leading Umayyads to a dinner at
which they were all clubbed to
death – all save only one. Abd al-

*Above Abu al-Abbas was brutal with
the Umayyads, but otherwise mild in
victory. He allowed Jews, Christians
and Persians in his service.*

Rahman, a grandson of Caliph
Hisham, escaped and fled to al-
Andalus, where he forcibly
removed the provincial governor of
Córdoba and set himself up as
Umayyad caliph, in opposition to
Abu al-Abbas in Baghdad.

In Iraq, every enemy, every
potential threat, was put to the
sword. In their indignation, the
Abbasids even despoiled all the
tombs of the Umayyad caliphs in
Syria, sparing only that of Umar
ibn Abd al-Aziz (717–20), whose
golden reputation as a wise ruler
had won him the enduring
respect of later generations,
both Sunni and Shiah.

After establishing his family
in power, Abu al-Abbas ruled
for just three years, until 754.
His reign is notable for the
setting up of the first paper mills
in the Islamic empire at
Samarkand (an ancient city, now in
Uzbekistan). The Arabs had learned
the secret of paper making from
prisoners taken in the Islamic
victory at the Battle of Talas (751)
against an army of the Chinese
Tang dynasty.

*Above This silver dirham was issued by
the Abbasid caliph al-Mahdi (reigned
775–85), and minted at Bukhara
(now in Uzbekistan).*

On the death of Abu al-Abbas from smallpox in 754, the Islamic world was plunged into civil war once more: Abu al-Abbas had named his brother al-Mansur as his successor, but the latter had to fight to win power. With the support of the great general Abu Muslim, al-Mansur eventually won control of the empire; however, once established in power, he proved himself every bit as ruthless as his brother 'The Killer', ordering the execution of Abu Muslim, the man to whom the Abbasids owed their position.

UMAYYAD DOWNFALL

The Umayyads may have failed because they were so successful in secular terms. The empire expanded so extraordinarily fast, and millions of newly subject peoples converted to Islam. However, these mass conversions caused problems: the Umayyads tended to favour Arab Muslims (and particularly those of the old Arab families) over converts, and in time, the non-Arab Muslims – known as *mawali* ('clients') – grew unhappy at their treatment. This *mawali* unrest was exploited very effectively by the rebel Hashimiyyah movement that swept the Abassids to power.

Above On arriving in Spain, Abd al-Rahman, the sole survivor of Abu al-Abbas' coup, was greeted with great honour as an Umayyad prince.

Below Shiah women perform their devotions at a mosque in Baghdad, the city built by the second Abbasid caliph, al-Mansur.

THE GOLDEN AGE OF THE ABBASIDS

FROM A NEW CAPITAL AT BAGHDAD, THE ABBASIDS PRESIDED OVER A FLOWERING OF ARTISTIC, SCIENTIFIC AND COMMERCIAL LIFE THAT ESTABLISHED THE EARLY YEARS OF THEIR RULE AS A 'GOLDEN AGE'.

In 762, the second Abbasid caliph, al-Mansur, built a new imperial capital called Madinat as-Salam ('City of Peace') at the village of Baghdad, beside the river Tigris in Iraq. The first Abbasid power base was at Harran (now in Turkey), but al-Mansur moved to Iraq partly to be closer to the Persian *mawali* supporters who had helped the new dynasty to power.

THE NEW CAPITAL

Al-Mansur laid out the city in the form of a circle 2.7km (1.75 miles) in diameter, with three concentric walls – and it became known as 'the

Below Al-Mutawakkil (reigned 847–61) greatly expanded the new capital at Samarra and built a splendid palace and parks beside the river Tigris there.

Round City'. At the centre stood a mosque and palace complex: four roads led outwards to the cardinal points of the compass, dividing the area within the city walls into four equal quarters, which consisted of administrative buildings and residential quarters for the caliph's guards and other members of his administration.

The city expanded outside the walls: in the area around the south gate, later known as al-Karkh, merchants built housing and bazaars. At the north-east gate, a bridge of boats led across the Tigris to the river's east bank, where the palace of the heir to the caliphate, al-Mahdi, was built.

The Abbasid capital quickly eclipsed Damascus as the trade capital of the Islamic empire. Its

Above The Mustansiriya madrasa, built from 1227–34 during the reign of the Abbasid caliph al-Mustansir, was a centre for the four schools of Sunni law.

streets were packed with craftsmen and buyers, and merchant ships from India, China and East Africa unloaded and loaded on the city's wharves. Baghdad became a city of international standing, at the height of its prosperity and fame in the late 8th and early 9th century.

Above The minaret of the Great Mosque of Samarra, built by al-Mutawakkil in c.848–52, is 52m (170ft) tall. A spiral ramp leads to the top.

PERSIAN INFLUENCE

Under the Abbasids, the Islamic world took on Persian influence; the round design of Baghdad was based on that of cities such as Ardasher-Khwarrah, or Firuzabad, in the Persian Sasanian empire. The caliphs welcomed non-Arab Muslims to their court, and many Persians rose to powerful positions in the imperial administration.

A new position of vizier, or chief administrator, was introduced, and the caliphs became more isolated from the day-to-day exercise of power, living instead in a palace amid great luxury and elaborate court ceremony, much of it derived from Sasanian models. Nevertheless, the language of the empire, spoken by caliph, courtiers and people alike, remained Arabic.

The 'golden age' of the Abbasids saw a great flowering of learning. Caliph al-Mamun founded the Bayt al-Hikmah ('House of Wisdom') as a library and centre for translation of ancient Greek, Roman, Indian and Persian works of science and philosophy, agriculture, geography, medicine, zoology and chemistry.

Yet for all their wealth and success, the Abbasids were never secure, and they faced persistent opposition. Having come to power with the support of Shiah Muslims, they had embraced Sunni Islam. Shiah Muslims living in Baghdad regularly scrawled slogans against the caliphate on the city walls, and riots in the so-called 'City of Peace' were not uncommon.

MOVE TO SAMARRA

In 836, riots engineered by the Abbasid regime's Armenian and Turkish slave soldiers persuaded Caliph al-Mutasim to move his capital to Samarra, 125km (78 miles) along the river Tigris in central Iraq. He and his successors built a beautiful palace there as well as the Great Mosque of Samarra (852); at its height the city stretched 32km (20 miles) along the banks of the

A THOUSAND AND ONE NIGHTS

The fifth Abbasid caliph, Harun al-Rashid, and his vizier Jafar al-Barmaki feature as characters in several tales of *A Thousand and One Nights* (in Arabic *Alf laylah wa laylah*). Its main source seems to have been a translation into Arabic of a Persian story collection, but all kinds of elements were added, including Islamic religious stories from the time of the Abbasids. The oldest surviving manuscript of the work is a fragment found in Syria and written in Arabic in the 800s.

Above The Thousand and One Nights inspired many later works of art, including the ballet Scheherazade *by Nikolai Rimsky-Korsakov in 1888.*

Tigris. Samarra remained the Abbasid capital until 892, when Caliph al-Mutamid moved the empire's chief city back to Baghdad.

The Abbasid caliphate lasted from 750 until 1258, but for much of this period the caliphs had little real power. Beginning in the mid-900s, they became increasingly marginalized by the explosive rise of Turkish military power. They retained merely nominal authority under the rule of the Buyid and Seljuk Turks.

ARCHITECTURE OF MOSQUES

THE MOSQUE (*MASJID*, 'PLACE OF PROSTRATION', IN ARABIC) IS AT THE HEART OF EVERY ISLAMIC COMMUNITY. IN ITS ARCHITECTURE, MUSLIMS GIVE EXPRESSION TO PROFOUND ELEMENTS OF THEIR FAITH.

Among key features of mosque architecture are the *musallah,* or prayer hall, the *qubbah*, or dome, above it, and the minaret or tower, from which Muslims are traditionally called to prayer.

The earliest developed form of the mosque was a square enclosure with a flat-roofed prayer hall and an open courtyard. The first mosques, founded by Muhammad – the Quba Mosque, outside Madinah, and the Mosque of the Prophet in Madinah itself – were probably originally of this type. Such simple mosques were easy to construct and, in a warm climate, large numbers of believers could worship in the open courtyard. They did not originally have domes or minarets. The *adhan*, or call to prayer, could be made from the flat rooftop – or perhaps by a man running through the streets.

QUBBAH

Domes were adapted from Persian palace architecture and from the basilicas of Orthodox Christianity. They gave a mosque grandeur and an imposing presence, while also providing good acoustics in the prayer hall within. Among the first domed Islamic religious buildings was the pilgrimage shrine of the Dome of the Rock in Jerusalem.

Domes were used widely in the typical Iranian form of the mosque, in which one or more domed halls, or *iwans*, were arranged around a central courtyard used as the prayer area. The *iwans* were open at one end and opened directly on to the yard. The Ottomans built very grand domed mosques, which sometimes had a large central dome over the prayer hall and several subsidiary domes around it.

Above The dome of the Süleymaniye Mosque (1550–7) in Istanbul is typical of mosque interiors: beautifully decorated without using representational images.

MINARETS

The first minarets were built by the Umayyad caliph Muawiyah I in Damascus in 673. In 703, Umar ibn Abdul-Aziz built four minarets on the Prophet's Mosque in Madinah, each 9m (30ft) tall. Minarets served to mark out the mosque, as they could be seen for miles around, and by their size were designed to inspire and impress. They also had a functional role as a raised position from which the *muezzin* could make the call to prayer.

Some of the early minarets were also used as watchtowers. In other places, for example the Qutb Minar in Delhi, they doubled as victory columns, marking military conquest. Another practical use – of great significance, given that these mosques were built in countries with hot climates – was as a cooling

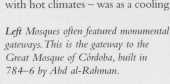

Left Mosques often featured monumental gateways. This is the gateway to the Great Mosque of Córdoba, built in 784–6 by Abd al-Rahman.

tower: air flowing into the *musallah* beneath the dome would be drawn by natural convection up the minaret tower, thereby reducing temperatures in the prayer hall.

These days, the call to prayer is made in the prayer hall with a microphone and speakers, and the minaret has a purely symbolic function. Yet as a statement of the glory of Islam and of the aspirations and faith of believers, modern minarets are often built to extraordinary heights. The world's tallest is at the Hassan II Mosque in Casablanca, Morocco, which stands 210m (689ft) high.

MINARET STYLES

A great variety of minaret styles developed over the centuries, with regional variations. In Samarra, Iraq, the Great Mosque built by

Abbasid caliph al-Mutawakkil in 849–52, had a square-based conical minaret, 52m (170ft) high, with a wide spiral staircase winding around the exterior of the tower. According to tradition, Caliph al-Mutawakkil used to ride up the staircase to the top on a donkey. The conical minaret with a spiral exterior staircase became the typical form in Iraq.

In Turkey, minarets were usually slim and circular, and were often built in larger numbers – up to six, depending on the size of the mosque. A fine example are the six minarets of the Sultan Ahmed Mosque, also known as the Blue Mosque, one of the finest of all the beautiful mosques of Istanbul, which was built by the Ottoman sultan Ahmed I (reigned 1603–17). Another alternative was to build twin minarets flanking an entrance gateway, as in the magnificent Mosque of al-Hakim in Cairo (c.1003).

DECORATION

Mosques often feature beautiful decoration, both interior and exterior. As Islam does not permit

Above This decorated mihrab or prayer niche is in the 16th-century Mosque of Prince Lotfollah, built in Isfahan, Iran, by Shah Abbas I.

representational images, artists developed decorative forms based on floral patterns and various geometrical shapes. The repeating geometric arabesques that are often found on the walls of mosques symbolize the infinite creation of Allah.

Below The Blue Mosque (1609–16), also called the Sultan Ahmed Mosque, in Istanbul has one large, several subsidiary domes and six slim minarets.

MATHEMATICS, MEDICINE AND ASTRONOMY

DURING THE ABBASID CALIPHATE, SCHOLARS TRANSLATED PERSIAN, GREEK AND INDIAN TEXTS TO CREATE A REMARKABLE BODY OF WORK, MOST NOTABLY IN MEDICINE, MATHEMATICS AND ASTROLOGY.

For a period, Abbasid Baghdad was the intellectual capital of the world. The vast Islamic empire brought under one ruler the descendants of several ancient civilizations of the Middle East, Asia and southern Europe for the first time since the age of Macedonian empire-builder Alexander the Great in the 4th century BCE. Frontiers were opened and Abbasids' former enemies were drawn to al-Mansur's 'City of Peace', where Greeks, Persians, Indians, Chinese, Berbers and Egyptians exchanged and compared ideas.

One of the essential features of the Abbasid 'golden age' was its tolerance. The Abbasid caliph and his administration generally promoted according to merit, and allowed Jews, Buddhists, Hindus and Christians to serve them.

THE HOUSE OF WISDOM

In 830, Caliph al-Mamun (reigned 813–33) founded the Bayt al-Hikmah ('House of Wisdom') as a library and translation centre, modelling the institution on the Imperial Library of the Sasanian Persian emperors. Authors whose works were translated include the ancient Greeks Pythagoras (c.580–c.500BCE), Hippocrates (c.460–c.377BCE), Plato (c.427–c.347BCE), Aristotle (384–322BCE) and Galen (129–c.216CE), and the Indians Sushruta (c.6th century BCE), Brahmagupta (598–c.665CE) and Aryabhata (476–c.550CE).

Now Arabic – the language in which Allah is believed by Muslims to have made his divine revelations to the Prophet Muhammad – replaced Greek as the international language of ideas.

Above Muhammad ibn Musa al-Khwarizmi's work in the House of Wisdom makes him one of the greatest figures in the history of mathematics.

MATHEMATICS

In 830, with the Byzantine emperor's permission, Caliph al-Mamun sent a delegation of scholars to Constantinople to seek classical texts for translation. Among these scholars was al-Hajjaj ibn Yusuf ibn Matar, who brought back and translated a copy of the ancient Greek mathematician Euclid's 13-volume masterpiece *Elements* (c.300BCE). Al-Hajjaj's successors translated from Latin a commentary on Euclid's geometry by the ancient Roman mathematician Hero of Alexandria (c.10–70CE) and several works by another ancient Greek mathematician, Archimedes (c.290–c.212BCE).

Perhaps the most important Islamic mathematician of the period was Muhammad ibn Musa al-Khwarizmi (c.780–c.850CE), who

Left These pages of the al-Qanun fil-Tibb (Canon of Medicine) of Ibn Sina, or Avicenna, discuss illnesses that affect the heart, stomach, skull and lungs.

Right Ibn Sina teaches medical colleagues to make remedies for smallpox in this illustration from a 17th-century Ottoman manuscript painting.

worked in the House of Wisdom under al-Mamun. Beginning in the 4th century BCE, ancient Indians had developed the figures 1, 2, 3, 4, 5, 6, 7, 8, 9 and 0 and their use in the place-value system that allows us to write any number using only these ten figures. Al-Khwarizmi learned the system through Arabic translations and explained what he called the 'Indian numbers' in his book *On Adding and Subtracting in Indian Mathematics*; this work was translated into Latin, and from it, the system he had outlined passed into European mathematics as 'Arabic numerals'.

MEDICINE

Scholars in Baghdad also made a significant contribution to later knowledge of medicine. Hunain ibn Ishaq (809–73) was a noted translator of key Greek medical works, including those of Galen and Hippocrates, and also wrote no fewer than 29 medical books of his own, including a series on ophthalmology, which were the first of the Arabic medical books to include anatomical artwork.

Two other important Islamic medical figures were the men known in the West as Rhazes and Avicenna. The first, Abu Bakr Muhammad ibn Zakariyy Razi, wrote more than 50 medical books and practised as a physician in the Iranian town of Rayy. The second, the physician and philosopher Abu Ali al-Husayn ibn Abd Allah ibn Sina (*c.*908–1037) wrote *The Book of Healing* and *The Canon of Medicine*.

ASTRONOMY

Encouraged by the Quran – 'And He it is Who hath set for you the stars that ye may guide your course

by them amid the darkness of the land and the sea' (6:97) – scholars in Baghdad focused on astrology and astronomy. Under Caliph al-Mamun and the direction of Sahl ibn-Harun, the House of Wisdom concentrated, in particular, on astrology and mathematics; under

Caliph al-Mutadid (reigned 892–902), another gifted translator named Thabit ibn Qurra (836–901) was appointed court astrologer. Many astronomical observatories were built throughout the empire and several navigational stars have Islamic names.

ARAB ORIGINS OF SCIENTIFIC TERMS

Several key mathematical and scientific words have their origins in Arab terms, or derive from the names of Muslim authors. The name for the mathematical discipline of algebra, for example, derives from the word *al-jabr* in the title of one of Baghdad mathematician al-Khwarizmi's books, written in *c.*825, *al-Kitab al-mukhtasar fi hisab al-jabr wa-l-muqabala* (*Overview of Calculating by Completion and Simplification*). According to one theory, 'chemistry' also has an Islamic origin, deriving from the Old Persian word *kimia* ('gold').

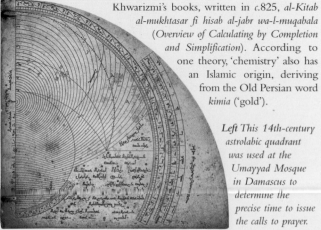

Left This 14th-century astrolabic quadrant was used at the Umayyad Mosque in Damascus to determine the precise time to issue the calls to prayer.

THE SHIAH EMPIRE OF THE FATIMIDS

FROM 909 TO 1171, THE SHIAH FATIMID CALIPHATE WAS A RIVAL POWER TO THE ABBASIDS OF BAGHDAD IN NORTHERN AFRICA AND PARTS OF THE MIDDLE EAST. IT FOUNDED CAIRO AS ITS CAPTIAL.

***Above** Begun by al-Aziz in 990, the al-Hakim Mosque in Cairo was finished in 1003 by al-Hakim and named after him.*

The Fatimids were militant Shiah Muslims who rejected the authority of the Sunni Muslim Abbasid caliphate. They were members of the mystical Ismaili sect of Shiah Islam and their rulers were Shiah imams (religious leaders). The Fatimid imams are recognized by most Muslims as holders of the office of caliph, and as a result, the period of Fatimid rule represents the only period (aside from the caliphate of Ali ibn Abu Talib) in which the caliphate and the Shiah imamate coincided.

THE FOUNDING OF THE FATIMID DYNASTY

The Fatimid dynasty was founded by Ubayd Allah al-Mahdi Billah, who claimed descent from the Prophet through Muhammad's daughter Fatimah and her husband Ali ibn Abu Talib, the first Shiah imam. Starting in Tunis in 909, al-Mahdi extended his power to cover all of the central Maghreb region (Tunisia, Libya, Algeria and Morocco), and ruled from a newly built capital at Mahdia on the Tunisian coast.

Egypt was at this time ruled by the Ikhshidid dynasty, under overall authority of the Abbasid caliph in Baghdad. The Fatimids invaded and conquered the Ikhshidids, took their capital, Fustat, and founded a new royal city in Qahirah (Cairo) in 969. Cairo became a royal enclave for the Fatimid caliph, while the administrative government of his territory was carried out from nearby Fustat.

FORCEFUL EXPANSION

At the height of the Fatmids' power in the late 10th and early 11th century, their empire included the whole of northern Africa, the Hejaz and Yemen, the island of Sicily and the Mediterranean coast as far north as Syria (including Palestine and Lebanon and Syria itself).

The Fatimid imams, by virtue of their descent from the Prophet, declared themselves infallible and incapable of wrongdoing, and they denounced the Abbasid caliphs as usurpers. Their aim was not simply to establish a regional power base independent of Baghdad but to supersede Abbasid power altogether to become leaders of a universal Islamic religious state. They sent missionaries throughout the Islamic world, attempting to make converts, and were a constant ideological as well as a political threat to the Sunni Abbasid caliphate.

FATIMID CAIRO

The Fatimids named their new royal enclave Qahirah after the planet Mars (then called *al-Najim al-Qahir*, 'the destroyer', or *Qahirat*

Left The beautiful al-Azhar Mosque in Cairo dates right back to the city's foundation. It was named after Fatimah az-Zahra, daughter of Muhammad.

al-Adaa, 'Vanquisher of foes'.) The enclave was built in 1069–73 by workers under the command of General Jawhar al-Siqilli during the reign of the Fatimid imam al-Muizz. General Jawhar himself laid the foundation stone for the splendid Mosque of Qahirah (later called al-Azhar Mosque) in 970. In 988, a *madrasa* (religious college) was established in its vicinity; this would become the prestigious al-Azhar University of Cairo.

TRADE AND GOVERNMENT

The Fatimid empire thrived on trade, particularly after an earthquake in the port of Siraf on the Persian Gulf drove traders to divert shipping into the Red Sea, close to Cairo. The empire traded in the Indian Ocean as well as the Mediterranean and established diplomatic and commercial links as far afield as the Chinese Song dynasty.

Although the Fatimids were staunch Shiah Muslims, they generally promoted to the imperial

Below Prominent Fatimids were buried in fine mausoleums in the cemetery at Aswan in southern Egypt from the 10th century onwards.

administration according to ability rather than religious orthodoxy, and Sunni Muslims, Jews and Christians all achieved high office. One major exception to this rule, however, was the eccentric and radically religious Caliph al-Hakim bi-Amrillah, (996–1021), who was violently anti-Christian and responsible for the destruction of the Church of the Holy Sepulchre in Jerusalem.

FATIMID DOWNFALL

During the last decades of the 11th century in Syria, Lebanon and Palestine, the Fatimids suffered a number of losses at the hands of the

Above These thick, sea-washed walls are remains of the 10th-century defensive fortifications at the original Fatimid capital of Mahdia on the Tunisian coast.

Buyid and Seljuk Turks and the European Christian crusaders, including that of Jerusalem to the army of the First Crusade in 1099. Their empire fell away and the Fatimids were reduced to their territory in Egypt.

During the 12th century, Fatimid power continued to wane, and they were finally defeated by Shirkuh, general of the Syrian Zangid leader Nur ad-Din, in 1169.

THE ISMAILIS

The second largest branch of Shiah Islam after the 'Twelvers', the Ismailis take their name from that of Ismail ibn Jafar (*c.*721–55), whom they recognize as the divinely chosen spiritual successor to his father, the sixth Shiah imam, Jafar al-Sadiq (702–65). (The Twelvers regard Musa al-Kazim, Ismail's younger brother, as the seventh imam.) The Ismailis follow a more mystical approach in their religion than do the more conservative Twelvers.

BUYIDS AND SELJUKS

IN THE 10TH CENTURY, THE ABBASID CALIPHS WERE OVERPOWERED BY PREVIOUSLY SUBJECT PEOPLES, AS FIRST THE IRANIAN BUYIDS AND THEN THE SELJUK TURKS TOOK CONTROL IN BAGHDAD.

The collapse of Abbasid power began with a waning of central authority. A key development was the decision of Caliph al-Mutasim (reigned 833–42) to form an imperial bodyguard from non-Muslim Slavs, Turks and Berbers, who had been taken as prisoners of war. These bodyguards, called *ghilman*, were answerable only to the caliph. The soldiers converted to Islam, but they proved a hugely disruptive force as soon as they realized the power that lay in their hands: in the 860s, they revolted a number of times and even killed four caliphs.

The Abbasids' difficulties arose, in part, from the structures of their imperial government. With a vast empire to rule, the caliphs and their viziers, or administrators, allowed regional governors a large degree of independence, and over

time, these men became increasingly autonomous and even created their own dynastic power bases.

A profusion of more or less independent dynasties – they paid only nominal respect to Baghdad – began to establish themselves. They included the Samarids of Khorasan and Transoxiana, the Hamdanids of Syria, and the Taharids, Alids and Saffarids of Iran. In North Africa, the Idrisids in the Maghreb and the Tulunids and Ikhshidids of Egypt were already effectively independent of Abbasid control by the time that the Fatimids arose in open opposition to Baghdad after 909.

BUYIDS TAKE CONTROL

The Buyids – Shiah tribesmen from western Iran – built up their power in western Iran and Iraq in the years after *c.*930 and then effectively took

Above Both Buyids and Seljuks imposed military authority on the lands of the caliphate but left the Abbasid caliphs in religious authority.

power in Baghdad in December 945 under Ali, son of Buya, who declared himself *amir ul-umara* ('Great Commander'). He demanded from the Abbasid caliph al-Mustakfi (reigned 944–6) that the Buyids be allowed to rule their several territories in western Iran and Iraq as independent states. Under the nominal control of the Abbasid caliph, and with the honorific name of Imad ad-Dawlah, Ali shared power with his younger brothers Hasan and Ahmad.

The Buyid state was strongly Shiah Muslim and also had a pronounced Iranian character. Its rulers revived the Sasanian (ancient Persian) royal title of Shahanshah ('King of kings'). They were patrons of the arts, supporting both the pre-eminent Arabic poet of the day, al-Mutanabbi, and the great Persian poet Firdawsi, author of the Iranian national epic *Shahnama* (*Book of Kings*). Their rule is known for its very fine metalwork marked with Sasanian motifs, and its pottery, some of it decorated with scenes from stories found in Firdawsi's superb epic. The Buyids encouraged

Left The Seljuks built the Sultan Han caravanserai, *which stands on the Silk Road traders' route between Konya and Aksaray (both now in Turkey).*

أصح ما شا لدة الزرف والاخرى ميل الى السواد
ولحد الهما انظر الى الفوق والاخرى الى اسفل وكانت
اشنانه دقيقة حادة الرؤوس وكان وجهه كوجه
السد وكان شجاعاجريا على الحروب مناصلاله بزرباله الروحة

Byzantine empire at the Battle of Manzikert in 1071; the third Seljuk sultan, Malik Shah I, built on Alp Arslan's success, winning further victories over the Byzantines and defeating the Fatimids in Syria, where he established client principalities in Damascus, Aleppo and Edessa. Meanwhile, in Anatolia, his cousin, Suleyman bin Kutalmish, captured Nicaea (modern Iznik) and Nicomedia (modern Izmit) from the Byzantines in 1075 and established an independent Seljuk state in the area, called the Sultanate of Rum, with a capital at Nicaea.

The Seljuks are celebrated for restoring unity to the Islamic world under the nominal rule of a Sunni caliph. They left a great legacy to the Islamic world, building a large number of *madrasas*, or religious colleges, throughout the empire. They were also responsible for making major improvements to the Great Mosque at Isfahan, Iran, in 1086–8, adding two great brick domed chambers. Persian influence in literature, pottery and other arts continued through the Seljuks' era.

people to observe Shiah festivals and to make pilgrimages to Shiah holy places, such as Karbala and Najaf.

ERUPTION OF THE SELJUKS

In the 11th century, the Buyids were swept away by the Seljuk Turks. The Seljuks were descendants of originally Oghuz tribes from Turkestan, who had migrated southwards and settled in the Persian province of Khorasan and eventually converted to Sunni Islam. They are named after an early tribal leader, Seljuk, who led these migrations. In 1055, one of Seljuk's grandsons, Toghrul Beg,

took power in Baghdad, where he was given the title 'Sultan of the East and the West' by Caliph al-Qaim (reigned 1031–75), himself no more than a figurehead.

Toghrul took control of the imperial armies in battles against the Byzantine empire and the Fatimids of Egypt. His nephew and successor as sultan, Alp Arslan ('Brave Lion'), inflicted a crushing defeat on the armies of the

Right Alaeddin Kekyubad I (reigned 1220–37) rebuilt many towns and fortresses, including the Red Tower at Alanya on the Mediterranean coast.

WARS OF THE CROSS

IN 1096-9, EUROPEAN ARMIES FIGHTING UNDER THE CROSS OF CHRIST INVADED THE MIDDLE EAST, ESTABLISHING CHRISTIAN STATES THERE. MUSLIM POWERS FOUGHT BACK IN THE 12TH CENTURY.

On 27 November 1095, at Clermont in France, Pope Urban II, leader of the Roman Catholic Church, issued a stirring call to arms to the knights (the landed warrior class) of Europe. Urban spoke out in response to a plea from Alexius Comnenus I, ruler of the Christian Byzantine empire of Constantinople, for help in fighting the Sunni Muslim Seljuk Turks. The Seljuks had established the Sultanate of Rum in central Anatolia and were threatening the Byzantine empire.

In his sermon at Clermont, Urban called on the knights of Europe to travel to the aid of their beleagured Christian brethren in Byzantine lands who were suffering terribly at the hands of 'Turks and Arabs'. According to some accounts of the speech, he also called on the knights to liberate Jerusalem, the scene of Christ's crucifixion, personifying the city and telling his listeners, 'from you, she asks for help!'

THE PEOPLE'S CRUSADE

Alexius Comnenus had envisaged an army of mercenaries; Urban directed his call at the princes, great lords and leading knights of Europe. Both were surprised: a great popular movement arose, known to historians as the People's Crusade. A 25,000-strong army, with a core of experienced soldiers supplemented by vast numbers of ill-equipped hangers-on, set out overland in April 1096 and reached Constantinople by 1 August. They crossed the Bosphorus into Anatolia but were crushed by the Seljuk Turks led by teenage Sultan Kilij Arslan I.

The few bedraggled survivors of the People's Crusade were joined by five great princely armies, led by

Above The crusader knights offered military service to Christ. They each took a vow to reach Jerusalem and pray in the Church of the Holy Sepulchre.

Count Raymond of Toulouse, Duke Robert of Normandy, Godfrey of Bouillon, Bohemond of Taranto and Hugh of Vermandois, younger brother of King Philip I of France. The united force captured Nicaea, the capital of the Sultanate of Rum in May-June 1097.

Kilij Arslan had not expected a serious assault and had departed to fight a local war; now he hurried back. But in the Battle of Dorylaeum, on 1 July 1097, he and his men were shocked by the power of the western knights' mounted charge and impressed by the strength of their chain-mail armour. They called the knights 'Franj' (for Franks, men of France, since a large part of the army was from France) and 'men of iron', in

Left Godfrey of Bouillon, one of the leaders of the First Crusade, leads heavily armed and armoured crusaders in battle against Muslim warriors.

honour of their armour. Ibn al-Qalanisi, chronicler of Damascus, wrote: 'The Franj sliced the Turkish army to pieces. They slaughtered, pillaged and seized many prisoners.'

The Christian army took Antioch in Syria from the Seljuks in June 1098, then defeated a vast relief army under Kerbogha, ruler of Mosul in the Seljuk empire. The following year, they marched on, and captured Jerusalem itself from the Shiah Muslim Fatimids of Egypt on 15–16 July 1099, slaughtering its inhabitants – Muslim and Jew alike. Arab chronicler Ibn al-Athir wrote 'The Franj spent a week slaughtering Muslims...the Jews had come together in their synagogue and the Franj roasted them alive. They also attacked the monuments of saints and the tomb of Abraham himself, may peace be upon him.' The crusaders consolidated the victory when they defeated a 50,000-strong Fatimid relief army led by the vizier (administrator) al-Afdal Shahanshah at the Battle of Ascalon on 12 August 1099.

During the crusade and in its aftermath, the westerners created four Christian territories in the Middle East: the Kingdom of Jerusalem; the County of Edessa, which was based on the ancient city of that name (now Urfa in Turkey); the Principality of Antioch; and the County of Tripoli, which was centred on that coastal city (now in Lebanon). Together these lands were known as Outremer, from the French for 'the Land overseas', so called because they lay on the far shore of the Mediterranean.

Right In this image from an English psalm book of c.1265, Christ is depicted presiding over a map that shows Jerusalem as the centre of the world.

Above Capturing Antioch after a long siege in June 1098, the crusaders ran wild. Citizens fled for their lives, some leaping from the battlements in terror.

CRUSADES AND CRUSADERS

The troops who fought in 1096–9 did not call themselves crusaders: they believed they were making a journey, or *peregrinatio* (pilgrimage). Because their clothing was marked with the sign of the cross (*crux*) they became known as *crucesignati* (meaning people marked with the cross); they were also sometimes called the *milites Christi* (knights of Christ). The word 'crusade' was not used until the 12th–13th century.

The campaign of 1096–9 was later known as the First Crusade, because it turned out to be the first of a long series of Christian wars against Islam. Traditionally, writers numbered nine main crusades, fought in the Middle East and North Africa between 1096 and 1272, but modern historians argue that the crusades continued for many hundreds of years and were still being fought in wars against the mighty Ottoman empire in the 17th century.

MUSLIMS RESURGENT

The Artuqid Turkish ruler Ilghazi led the Muslim fightback early in the 12th century. He won a crushing victory over a Christian army in 1119 in a clash in the Principality of Antioch known to western chroniclers as the Battle of the Field of Blood. Then, in 1144, Imad ed-Din Zangi, ruler of Mosul and Aleppo, captured Edessa from its Christian rulers. A new crusade was called in 1145 and launched in 1147, but this Second Crusade was a disaster that ended in 1149 in a failed siege of Damascus.

Zengi's son Nur ed-Din took control of Damascus in 1154 and reunited Syria. A pious Sunni Muslim, Nur ad-Din was revered for just rule and commitment to his faith; he built many mosques, *caravanserais* (inns for Muslim travellers) and *madrasas*. He made a series of attempts to conquer the Shiah Muslim Fatimid regime in Egypt, which resulted, eventually, in the emergence of Salah al-Din Yusuf ibn Ayyub (later called Saladin), the nephew of Nur ad-Din's foremost general, as the vizier (administrator) of Egypt in 1169.

RIGHTEOUSNESS OF FAITH: SALADIN

SALADIN, FOUNDER OF THE SUNNI MUSLIM AYYUBID EMPIRE, PROVED A FORMIDABLE FOE TO CHRISTIAN SETTLERS IN THE HOLY LAND, FROM WHOM HE RECAPTURED JERUSALEM IN 1187.

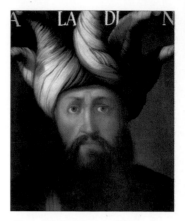

Muslims honour Saladin for his learning, refinement and brilliance as a general – for establishing the great Ayyubid empire, uniting Muslim forces, humbling the crusader armies and recapturing the holy city of Jerusalem. But even those hounded by his armies afforded him a far-from-grudging respect, celebrating him for his military strength, proud bearing and magnanimity in victory. Indeed, in an extraordinary contradiction for 12th-century Christians, who generally believed that being a Christian lord was a key component of chivalry, they praised him as a 'chivalrous infidel'.

LEARNED AND INTELLIGENT

Salah al-Din Yusuf ibn Ayyub, more commonly known as Saladin, meaning 'Righteousness of Faith', was born in Tikrit, Iraq, to a Kurdish family. The Ayubbid dynasty he founded takes its name from that of his father, Najm ad-Din Ayyub.

He was educated in Damascus at the court of Nur ad-Din, where he studied Arabic grammar, rhetoric and Islamic theology. From early in life, Saladin was known as a refined and brilliantly intelligent man, entertaining in conversation, well versed in the traditions of Arab tribes, an expert in the genealogies of the best Arab horses, and a peerless polo player.

He also had a brilliant military upbringing, serving alongside his uncle Shirkuh, Nur ad-Din's leading general, with whom he three times invaded Egypt in the 1160s. On the third campaign in Egypt, Saladin helped his uncle oust the Fatimid vizier Shawar, establishing Shirkuh as vizier and then succeeding him in the position on his death just three months later.

RISE TO POWER

As vizier of Egypt, Saladin was nominally subject to Nur ad-Din, but his scarcely concealed desire was to take power himself and unite Syria and Egypt in a new empire,

Above Saladin's fame in Christendom meant that he was the subject of European works of art, such as this 16th-century Italian portrait.

and he became increasingly estranged from his overlord. Nur ad-Din and Saladin were both Sunni Muslims and one initial point of his conflict was Saladin's refusal to oust the Shiah Fatimid caliph in Cairo, al-Adid. Saladin waited until al-Adid died in September 1171, then ended the Fatimid caliphate and declared the authority of al-Mustadi, the Sunni Abbasid caliph in Baghdad.

Below Saladin and Richard 'Coeur de Lion' were exemplars of chivalry. This (imagined) jousting clash between them is from the English Luttrell Psalter.

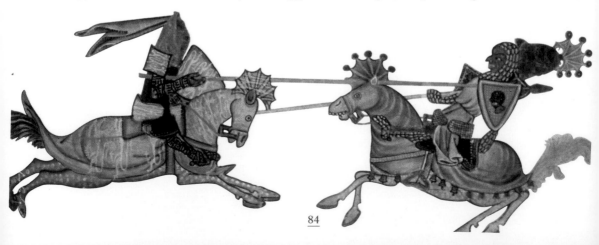

Matters came to a head on Nur ad-Din's death, from fever, in 1174. Saladin marched to Damascus, where he was welcomed by the people. He bolstered his position by marrying Nur ad-Din's widow and publicly setting himself up as leader of a *jihad*, or a 'just war', against the Christian kingdoms of the Middle East. He established his authority in Syria, northern Iraq, the Hejaz and Yemen and led several campaigns against the Christians, culminating in the Battle of the Horns of Hattin in 1187. Here, he captured the most sacred relic of the Christians – reputedly a piece of the cross on which Jesus Christ was crucified – and destroyed the military strength of the kingdom of Jerusalem.

ENCOUNTERS WITH
COEUR DE LION

After capturing Jerusalem in 1187, Saladin encountered the Christian armies of the Third Crusade (1189–92) led by Richard I *Coeur de Lion* ('the Lion-hearted') of England and King Philip II of France. In Richard, Saladin met his match, and the encounter of these two great generals was widely celebrated in European chivalric literature, ensuring Saladin undying fame in the West as well as the East.

Although he twice marched towards Jerusalem, Richard did not attempt to retake it, and the Third Crusade ended in a negotiated settlement at the treaty of Jaffa, under which the Christians were guaranteed access to Jerusalem as pilgrims and could keep certain chiefly coastal territories, including the ports of Acre and Jaffa.

Saladin died at Damascus on 4 March 1193, shortly after the end of the crusade, and was buried in a mauroleum beside the Umayyad Mosque in Damascus. A member of Saladin's entourage, Baha ud-Din ibn Shaddad, wrote a biography, in which he praised his master's character and his unswerving commitment to *jihad*. According to Baha ud-Din, Saladin did not spend a single coin on anything other than *jihad* and pious work and was a fascinating and learned man, who would not hear ill spoken of other Muslims and was always caring for the elderly and for orphans.

Above Saladin lost twice to Richard 'the Lion-hearted' in 1191, at Acre and Arsuf, and at Jaffa in September 1192 agreed a peace treaty.

Below Saladin's tomb in Damascus. Kaiser Wilhelm II of Germany donated a marble sarcophagus, but Saladin's body lies in the wooden one at the rear.

THE BATTLE OF BAGHDAD

THE NOMINAL RULE OF THE ABBASID CALIPHATE IN BAGHDAD ENDED IN 1258, WHEN AN INVADING MONGOL ARMY DESTROYED THE CITY, BUT THE ABBASIDS SURVIVED IN EGYPT UNTIL THE 16TH CENTURY.

The Battle of Baghdad, which took place in January and February 1258 between the city's defenders and a vast besieging Mongol army, was a devastating event for the Muslims of the Middle East. The attack culminated in a week-long orgy of pillaging and looting, from which the beautiful city of Baghdad took centuries to recover. The Mongol army moved on, and with the support of local Christian powers, conquered Aleppo and Damascus in 1260. In just two years, the two great centres of Islamic power in the Middle East, Baghdad and Damascus, were lost. The principal surviving centre of Muslim rule in the East was Mamluk Egypt.

BACKGROUND TO THE CONFLICT

By the mid-13th century, the Abbasid caliphate in Baghdad had regained a measure of power, although the caliphs were still essentially dependent for their position on the Turkish and Mamluk military power. In 1258,

Above When the Mongols took Baghdad, the last Abbasid caliph, al-Mustasim, was captured and forced to watch the destruction of his city.

Below A 14th-century manuscript painting shows the Mongol army making preparations prior to attacking Baghdad.

the caliph was al-Mustasim Billah (reigned 1242–58). His opponent, Hulagu Khan, who was a grandson of Genghis Khan, had been despatched by his brother Mongke, the Great Kahn, to lead the military destruction of Islamic states in Iran, Iraq and Syria.

Commanded by Hulagu and Chinese general Guo Kan, a vast Mongol army, which reputedly contained a tenth of the fighting force of the entire Mongol empire, approached Baghdad in November 1257 and initially offered a peaceful takeover. Although he had made no preparations for the assault, al-Mustasim was defiant. Evidently unable to appreciate the gravity of the situation, or else deliberately deluding himself, he had reputedly accepted the advice of his vizier that the Mongols would be easily driven away by the simple tactic of ordering the women of Baghdad to throw stones at them.

THE FALL OF BAGHDAD
The Mongol army laid siege to the city on 29 January, and on 10 February, al-Mustasim surrendered. The Mongols swept into the city, pillaging, raping and looting, and hundreds of thousands of people were killed as they tried to flee.

Mosques, libraries, hospitals and palaces were burned down. The invaders did not spare even the Grand Library, repository of much of the wisdom of the ancient world: one account reports that the river Tigris was turned black with the ink from the manuscripts hurled into its waters.

The Mongol army moved on from Baghdad to attack and capture Damascus from its last Ayyubid ruler, An-Nasir Yusuf, in alliance with Christian armies from the Principality of Antioch and Cilician Armenia.

THE RISE OF THE MAMLUKS IN EGYPT
Following Saladin's death in 1193, the Ayyubid empire he had created survived for around 50 years, with Ayyubid lords in power in Syria and Egypt. In 1250, however, the Ayyubid sultan of Egypt, Turanshah, was murdered. His Mamluk slave general, Izz al-Din Aybak, took power and founded the Mamluk sultanate, which ruled Egypt (and later Syria) until 1517.

The Mamluk army won a series of astounding victories, defeating the previously invincible Mongols at the Battle of Ain Jalut in 1260 and afterwards driving the Christians from the Holy Land. To

Above Mamluk general Baybar was ruthless in conflict: it is said he beheaded Christian knights who had surrendered in the belief that they would be spared.

legitimate their rule, Mamluk sultans re-established the Abbasid caliphate, now in Cairo rather than Baghdad. The first caliph under this dispensation was al-Mustansir (reigned 1226–42). With strictly nominal authority, Abbasid caliphs succeeded one another in Cairo until 1517, when, after Ottoman sultan Selim I defeated the Mamluks, the final Abbasid caliph al-Mutawakkil III was taken to Constantinople. On al-Mutawakkil's death, by prior agreement, the title of caliph passed to Selim I.

END OF OUTREMER
After the loss of Jerusalem to Saladin in 1187, the capital of the Christian kingdom of Jerusalem was moved to Acre. In the late 13th century, the crusader states lost a series of their territorial possessions – including Arsuf, Caesarea, Antioch and Tripoli – to the armies of the Egyptian Mamluk sultans. The Christians made a last stand in Acre in 1291, but, despite heroic defensive efforts by the military orders of the Knights Templar and Knights Hospitaller, the city was captured by the Mamluk sultan Khalil on 18 May 1291. Within a few weeks, the final remaining crusader towns of Beirut, Haifa, Tyre and Tortosa were surrendered to the Mamluks. The Christian kingdoms of Outremer were at an end.

Left Astride the city's crumbling walls, French knight Guillaume de Clermont leads the final stand of the kingdom of Jerusalem as Acre falls to the Mamluks.

LIGHT IN THE DARKNESS

THE SCHOLARS OF ISLAMIC BAGHDAD AND CAIRO KEPT THE FLAME
OF SCHOLARSHIP ALIGHT AT A TIME KNOWN AS THE 'CHRISTIAN DARK
AGES', WHEN LEARNING WAS NOT GREATLY VALUED IN EUROPE.

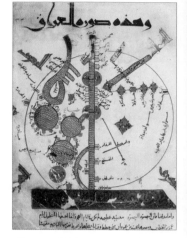

When European cultural life enjoyed a Renaissance, or 'rebirth', in the 14th century, much of its knowledge of classical Greek, Roman and other ancient learning came from translations into Latin of Islamic authors who had written in Arabic at the Abbasid House of Wisdom in Baghdad and at other Islamic establishments of learning.

THE TRANSMISSION OF KNOWLEDGE

The principal works of Islamic mathematician Muhammad ibn Musa al-Khwarizmi (*c.*780–*c.*850) were translated into Latin, and introduced Europe to the concept of what came to be known as the Arabic numerals, the concept of zero and the positional value system. Another highly influential mathematical work was the *Book of Measuring Plane and Spherical Figures*, which was translated into Latin by the Lombardian scholar Gerard of Cremona (*c.*1114–87). Gerard also translated into Latin

Ibn Sina's *Canon of Medicine* and the key writings of Aristotle from Arabic translations made in the 9th century by gifted Mesopotamian linguist Thabit ibn Qurra (known in Latin as Thebit), who worked at the House of Wisdom. The *Canon* of Ibn Sina became a key medical textbook in western universities and was still in use in some places in the mid-17th century.

The translator Hunain ibn Ishaq's work on ophthalmology was likewise translated into Latin and became a key reference book in universities both in Europe and in the East for many hundreds of years. Arab philospher al-Farabi (*c.*878–*c.*950) wrote a book called *The Catalogue of Sciences*, in which he noted the following key areas of study, listed in order of importance: languages, logic, mathematics, physics, metaphysics, politics, law and theology. Later translated into Latin, the work became a major influence on the curricula of study that was followed in many early European universities.

Above Baghdad, great centre of learning, is marked on this page from the 11th-century Book of Routes and Provinces *by Abu Ishaq Ibrahim al-Istakhri.*

AL-ANDALUS

Classical philosophy and learning was also preserved and passed to Western European scholars through the work of Islamic thinkers and authors in al-Andalus, the Muslim territories of the Iberian Peninsula. A key figure was Abu'l-Walid Muhammad ibn Ahmad ibn Rushd (1126–98), known in the West as Averroes. Another great Muslim polymath, he wrote on philosophy, theology, law, medicine, astrology, geography and physics. Among his works were a medical encyclopedia and commentaries on the *Canon* of Ibn Sina and the works of Aristotle and Plato, for which his sources were the Arabic translations made in the 10th century in Iraq.

SCHOLARLY PRACTICES

A number of key scholarly methods were pioneered at the House of Wisdom, many of which are still in

Left East meets West in this painting by Julius Köckert as Harun al-Rashid receives envoys from Charlemagne, King of the Franks, in Baghdad.

Above One of the great Islamic scholars of Spain, Averroes wrote commentaries on the works of Aristotle and Plato for Almohad caliph Abu Yaqub Yusuf.

use today, for example a library catalogue system in which works are categorized by genre or other characteristics. Scholars at the House of Wisdom were also the first to collate various manuscripts of a work in order to make a definitive edition, to add annotations to the margins of works, to write glossaries and to draw up dictionaries of key technical words.

REASON AND REVELATION

The Islamic scholars who saved so much classical learning for future generations had a deep intellectual curiosity and profound commitment to the study of philosophy, mathematics and logic, medicine, mechanics and physics.

At first sight, it might seem curious that adherents of a faith founded on Allah's revelation of truth to the Prophet Muhammad should be interested in the

Right Ancient Greek philosopher Aristotle was honoured by many Islamic thinkers. He wrote on theatre and politics, on logic, ethics and physics.

reasonings of pagan thinkers from the ancient world. But Islam had a strong commitment to learning from the beginning. Muslims are enjoined to seek knowledge by the Prophet himself: according to hadith literature, Muhammad said 'Seeking knowledge is obligatory for every Muslim' and 'go after learning, even to China'.

Muslim chronicles recount how philosopher Aristotle (384–22BCE) appeared to the Abbasid caliph al-Mamun, founder of the House of Wisdom, in a dream. The Aristotle of the dream was a figure of profound beauty, and when al-Mamun asked him the cause of his beauty, Aristotle replied that it derived from 'the beauty of the laws of reason'. Aristotle also assured al-Mamun that there was no clash between the human reason he exercised and praised and the revelation of God's law to the Prophet Muhammad.

AL-ANDALUS

ISLAMIC RULERS GOVERNED PART OF THE IBERIAN PENINSULA FOR ALMOST 800 YEARS. MUSLIM LANDS, WHICH INCLUDED THE CITIES OF CÓRDOBA, SEVILLE AND GRANADA, WERE KNOWN AS AL-ANDALUS.

The Arab–Berber invasion of the Iberian Peninsula, begun in April 711, was one more in a series of stunning military successes for the armies of Islam. Under first Tariq ibn Ziyad and then Musa bin Nusair, the Islamic troops captured almost the entire peninsula in only five years. The land was initially a province of the Umayyad caliphate under overall rule of Caliph al-Walid I (reigned 705–15) in Damascus. From 717, this province made its capital at Córdoba.

In these early years, the Christian Visigoths, previous rulers of much of the Iberian Peninsula, were driven to the far north, but there they maintained a foothold that proved to be the base for a centuries-long fight back, known to Christian historians as the *Reconquista* ('Reconquest').

EMIRATE OF CÓRDOBA

In Iraq, the Hashimiyyah revolt led to the establishment of the Abassid caliphate by Abu al-Abbas in 750, and Abd al-Rahman, sole surviving member of the Umayyad royal family, fled to what is now southern Spain. In 756, he defeated the ruler of Al-Andalus, Yusuf al-Fihri, in battle, and set himself up as Amir of Córdoba, an independent Umayyad ruler in opposition to the Abbasids in Baghdad.

Abd al-Rahman ruled in Córdoba until *c.*788. He put down a number of revolts, including a major uprising backed by Abbasid caliph al-Mansur (reigned 754–75) and led by al-Ala ibn Mugith, who was the governor of the province of Ifriqiya (Africa). Besieged in Carmona, Abd al-Rahman led a daring breakout, defeating the Abbasid troops. He then sent the heads of al-Ala and his generals, pickled in salt, in a bag all the way to Makkah, where al-Mansur was making the *Hajj*.

Above The Arab–Berber army under Tariq ibn Ziyad captures Córdoba in 711. The city would remain in Muslim hands until 1236.

CALIPHATE OF CÓRDOBA

Abd al-Rahman III (reigned 912–61) was the most powerful of the Umayyad rulers in Spain. In 929, he defied the Abbasids and the rising power of the Fatimids in Egypt by declaring himself Caliph of Córdoba, claiming authority over the entire Islamic world. He won several victories against the Christian kings of northern Spain and was hailed as *al-Nasir* ('Defender of the Faith').

During the reign of Abd al-Rahman III and his son al-Hakam II, Al-Andalus was at the height of its glory, but decline set in within 50 years of his death in 961. The caliphate did not recover from civil war among rival claimants to power in 1010, although it limped on until 1031, when it was broken up into smaller *taifa* ('successor') kingdoms.

ALMORAVIDS AND ALMOHADS

These *taifa* states proved vulnerable to the advance of the Christian kingdoms of northern Iberia and

Left The Reconquista was gathering pace by the 9th century. However, the heroic victory of Christian King Ramiro at the Battle of Clavijo (844), shown here, is in fact legendary.

then were swept away by the Almoravids, a Berber power from North Africa. The Almoravid ruler Yusuf ibn Tashfin declared himself as *Amir al-Muslimin* ('Commander of the Muslims') in opposition to the caliph in Baghdad, who was revered as *Amir al-Mumineen* ('Commander of the Faithful').

Power switched hands again in the second half of the 12th century, when Abu Ya'qub Yusuf, leader of another Berber confederation, called the Almohads, took control of Muslim Iberia and established his capital at Seville. Abu Ya'qub Yusuf was known as al-Mansur ('the Victorious') following his great victory over King Alfonso VIII of Castile in the Battle of Alarcos on 19 July 1195. However, his successor, Muhammad III al-Nasir, suffered a devastating defeat in the Battle of Las Navas de Tolosa on 16 July 1212 at the hands of a Christian army. Following this defeat, the power of the Almohads unravelled swiftly, and King Ferdinand III of

Above Islamic rule in Spain ends as Sultan Boabdil surrenders Granada to crusaders led by Ferdinand and Isabella.

Below Ferdinand and Isabella are depicted leading their troops into Granada in 1492 in a wooden panel from an altarpiece of c.1522.

Castile recaptured the great Islamic cities of Córdoba in 1236 and of Seville in 1248.

Thereafter, the sole surviving Islamic territory in Iberia was the Muslim kingdom of Granada in the far south, which was ruled from 1232 by the Nasrid dynasty, or Banu Nazari, as a client state of the local Christian kingdoms.

LAST STAND IN GRANADA

The days of Islamic rule in al-Andalus were numbered, yet remarkably – principally because of infighting among the Christian kingdoms – the end did not come until 1492. Besieged in Granada by a Christian army that was equipped with the latest weaponry and bolstered by crusading troops from many parts of Europe, Nasrid sultan Boabdil surrendered. After making a triumphant entry into Granada, the fervently Catholic King Ferdinand and Queen Isabella set about rebuilding the main mosque as a church.

THE ISLAMIC RENAISSANCE IN SPAIN

THE YEARS OF ISLAMIC RULE IN SPAIN, NOTABLY UNDER THE CALIPHATE OF CÓRDOBA (929–1031), WERE A GLORIOUS AGE OF LEARNING, ARTISTIC ACHIEVEMENT AND RELIGIOUS TOLERATION.

Abd al-Rahman III, the man who proclaimed himself caliph in Córdoba in 929, was a great patron of architecture and reputedly spent one-third of the income from his vast territories on building works. Beginning in 936–40, he built the palace-city of Madinat al-Zahra outside Córdoba. Although little remains of the city today – it was sacked in 1010 during the civil war that brought the caliphate to its knees – it was once vast and magnificent, described in accounts by contemporary travellers as a series of palaces filled with extraordinary treasures.

GLORIES OF CÓRDOBA

Caliph Abd al-Rahman III greatly developed Córdoba itself. Scholars estimate that in the 10th century, the city had a population of up to 500,000 people. He built a new minaret for the superb mosque in Córdoba, begun in 784 by dynastic founder Abd al-Rahman I. This magnificent sacred building, which was originally called the Aljama Mosque in honour of Abd al-Rahman I's wife but is now known as the Mezquita of Córdoba, was built on the site of a 6th-century Christian church. The mosque was further extended by Abd al-Rahman III's son, al-Hakam II, and work on it continued until 987. After Córdoba was captured by King Ferdinand III of Castile in 1236, the building was reconsecrated as a church, and today it is a Christian cathedral, although its celebrated arches, beautiful blue-tiled dome and magnificent *mihrab* can still be seen.

The second caliph in Córdoba, al-Hakam II, made peace with the northern Christian kingdoms

Above Abd al-Rahman III: according to legend, he named his palace city outside Córdoba after his foremost concubine and raised her statue over the main gateway.

and concentrated his efforts and wealth on the improvement of the caliphate's infrastructure and the advancement of learning. Under his rule, irrigation works advanced agriculture, while in cities, the building of markets and widening of streets promoted commerce.

In Córdoba, al-Hakam II created a vast library containing 400,000 books and established a committee of learned men, including both Arab Muslims and Mozarab Christians, to translate works from Latin and Greek into Arabic. (Mozarab Christians were the descendants of Iberian Christians who had lived on under Muslim rule and, while keeping to their own faith, had adopted Arabic customs and language.)

Left The illuminated Mezquita, begun in 784 by Abd al-Rahman I, looks down on the Guadalquivir, the longest river in Andalucía, which connects Córdoba to the Gulf of Cadiz.

Left The beautiful octagonal dome in the Mezquita rises above the mihrab and maqsura enclosure and was built by al-Hakam II.

conquered the city. However, because it was so well established as an international centre of learning under Islam, it remained a meeting place for scholars, where both Arabs and Jews were welcome and Christian scholars, such as Gerard of Cremona (*c*.1114–87), could come to meet them.

RELIGIOUS TOLERATION

This great cultural flowering of Al-Andalus was made possible – as had been the golden age under the Abbasid caliphs in Baghdad – by a remarkable degree of religious toleration. Despite the fact that for almost the entire history of Al-Andalus, the territory's Islamic rulers were engaged in a stop–start war against Christians seeking to win control of the Iberian Peninsula, within Al-Andalus itself, Muslims, Jews and Mozarab Christians were able to live in peace, and together played a major role in the cultural flowering of Islamic Spain.

CENTRES OF LEARNING

The great cities of Al-Andalus, such as Toledo and Córdoba, were the intellectual capitals of Western Europe. Students came from as far away as England and northern France to learn from the Arab, Jewish and Christian scholars who gathered there.

The great Jewish poet, physician, astrologer and scholar, Abraham ben Meir ibn Ezra (1093–1167), was born in Tudela under Muslim rule and lived for many years in Córdoba. Jewish philosopher and physician Moshe ben Maimon better known by his Greek name Moses Maimonides and generally recognized as the greatest Jewish

philosopher of the Middle Ages, was also a product of this culture, and was born in Córdoba in 1135.

Córdoba was celebrated for its copyists, producers of religious manuscripts, and artisans, who made leatherwork, jewellery, brocades and woven silks that were among the best in the world and were traded both in Western Europe and across the markets of the East.

Toledo was a great centre for scholars, home both to a large community of Mozarab Christians and a sizeable Jewish colony. Conquered for Islam by Tariq ibn Ziyad in 711, it was part of Al-Andalus until 1085, when Christian King Alfonso VI of Leon

Right Jewish philosopher Moses Maimonides rose to prominence in Córdoba, then lived in Morocco and in Egypt, where he was doctor to Saladin.

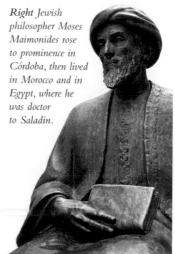

THE GARDENS OF ALHAMBRA

THE MOORISH GARDENS OF ALHAMBRA EPITOMIZE THE BEAUTY AND SPLENDOUR OF MEDIEVAL SPANISH ISLAM AND ARE AN ATTEMPT TO IMITATE THE GARDENS OF PARADISE DESCRIBED IN THE QURAN.

The Muslim Moors of North Africa were ruled by the dynastic Umayyads when, led by their Berber general, Tariq ibn Ziyad, they invaded Spain in 711. Muslim expansion across the Iberian Peninsula was swift, and a sophisticated culture grew up in the region, which produced a very distinctive architectural style known as the Hispano-Mauresque.

THE FORTIFIED PALACE OF ALHAMBRA

Typical of this style, Alhambra is a fortified palace that extends over some 10.5ha (26 acres). Originally constructed separately from its medina, Granada (from the Arabic, *Gharnata*), it is connected by four large wooden gateways. The stunningly ornate palatial dwellings are decorated throughout with the Arabic calligraphic motif, *wa la ghalib-a-illa Allah* ('and there is no victor but God').

Alhambra (the word means 'red palace') was first built in about 860CE, but major reconstruction and development was undertaken by the Nasrid amir Muhammad bin al-Ahmar in the 13th century. Modifications to the palace and gardens were continued until the ruling Moors of the region, led by Boabdil (Abu Abdullah), conceded defeat by handing the keys to the palace and the city to the Catholic monarchs Ferdinand and Isabella on 2 January 1492.

Surrounded by the towering peaks of the Sierra Nevada, Granada is perhaps the most beautiful of Spain's cities. Its unique topography provides a breathtaking backdrop for the green and fertile plain, around 700m (2,300ft) above sea level, called the *vega*, in which the city is set. Even today, water is still carried from the mountain range along the plains and into the city and

Above In the Generalife Gardens, a sophisticated hydraulic system of canals and fountains constantly supplies water to an abundance of vegetation.

the palace gardens by ancient Moorish-built aqueducts through earthen pipes. The sight and sound of moving water is a particular feature that constantly recurs throughout both the palace and gardens of Alhambra. It is said that the Moors' love of water stemmed from their roots in the arid desert lands of North Africa and that all life stems from water. Hence, wherever they settled in Spain, water was their first necessity.

THE GENERALIFE GARDENS

Adjacent to the walled Alhambra are the splendid Generalife gardens (Arabic, *jannat al-rafiah*, meaning, 'garden of lofty paradise'), which were designed to imitate the Quran's description of the celestial gardens, complete with flowing waters and fruit, flowers and vegetation of every kind. The complex is watered by a sophisticated hydraulic system, directed through a central canal,

Left This view of the Moorish palace of Alhambra is taken from Albaicin, and shows the snow-capped Sierra Nevada Mountains in the background.

acequia, resulting in a series of elegant fountains that adorn the many ornate patios.

Alhambra and Generalife were eventually linked by Jardines Nuevos del Generalife ('the new gardens'), which were completed in about 1930 and include an ornate maze garden.

ALHAMBRA HIGHLIGHTS

The Court of the Lions, which dates from the 14th century, was built originally as a series of private residences connected via a rectangular patio bounded by columns and familiar horseshoe arches. At its centre is a fountain powered by an ingenious ancient hydraulic system that ensures the water feed is kept at a constant level. The dodecagonal bowl is perched on the backs of 12 stone lions, from whose mouths flow jets of water that feed four intersecting channels in the courtyard. The flowing water symbolizes life, and each of the lions represents a sign of the zodiac. Together they allude to both the divine symmetry of the universe and eternal life, as reflected in the carved Arabic couplet by Ibn Zamrak (1333–94), vizier and poet of Alhambra, that decorates the fountain's rim.

Overshadowing the Court of the Myrtles is the highest of Alhambra's many towers, the Torre do Comares, which traditionally housed the Moorish throne. Set on the north side of the courtyard, the tower is accessed by the magnificent *muqarnas* arch, a highly and purely decorative carved Arabesque stucco facia. On the southern side of the patio is a splendid two-storey building that houses an arched balcony overlooking the courtyard. Below, myrtle hedges flank a rectangle pool that is fed by a fountain and bordered by a marble pathway.

Above Each stone lion in the impressive Court of the Lions is meant to represent a sign of the zodiac, while the free-flowing water symbolizes eternal life.

Below The Court of the Myrtles is a stunning symmetrical pooled entrance, flanked by myrtle bushes and marble pathways, to the Torre de Comares.

ISLAM IN ASIA

AFTER MUSLIM AFGHANS ESTABLISHED THE DELHI SULTANATE IN THE
LATE 1100S, ISLAM BECAME A MAJOR FORCE BOTH IN THE INDIAN
SUBCONTINENT AND BEYOND IN MALAYA, SUMATRA AND JAVA.

In 711, Arab troops under Syrian general Muhammad ibn-Qasim conquered Sindh (in the south-east of modern Pakistan), and many locals converted to Islam. However, there were no further invasions until Muslim Afghan ruler Mahmud of Ghazni launched a series of raids from eastern Afghanistan in the 11th century. Mahmud achieved control over much of north-west India and what is now Pakistan, but he came principally to loot the wealth of temples, and his rule was only periodically enforced.

The first permanent Muslim presence in India was achieved by the troops of another Afghan ruler, Muhammad of Ghor, when they captured Delhi in 1193. Muhammad's general, Qutb-ud-din Aybak, declared himself Sultan of Delhi (reigned 1206–10) and founded the Mamluk dynasty, first of the Delhi sultanate. By *c.*1235, the Mamluks had taken control of the whole of northern India.

TUGHLUQ POWER

The Delhi sultanate ruled India until 1526. In the 14th century, its sultans achieved power over almost the entire subcontinent under the Tughluq dynasty. Only the native Pandava kings (in the far south) and Rajputs (in the north-west) held them at bay.

However the sultanate's power was smashed in a devastating raid on Delhi unleashed in 1398 by

*Right The tomb of the second ruler
of the Mughal dynasty, Humayan, in
Delhi has Persian-style gardens and
was built in 1562–70.*

Timur (or Tamerlane), Mongol ruler of Samarkand. Thereafter, the sultanate could not recover its former status, although it survived until 1526, when Ibrahim Lodhi was defeated in battle by Afghan ruler Babur at Panipat, north of Delhi. Babur went on to conquer large parts of India and to found the Mughal dynasty, which created a vast Islamic empire in the region.

MUGHAL GLORIES

The Mughal state founded by Babur suffered early setbacks but was doubled in size and established as an empire by Akbar the Great in 1556–1605. By 1600, his empire covered most of north India as far south as the river Narmada. The empire continued to grow under his sons Jahangir and Shah Jahan, and achieved its greatest extent, covering the entire Indian subcontinent save the southern tip, in *c.*1700 under Aurangzeb.

*Above This scene from the superb
Hamzanama, created at the court
of Akbar the Great in c.1562–77,
shows an escape from prison.*

Akbar the Great presided over a magnificent court with a vibrant cultural life. He created a vast library, with books in English, Greek, Persian and Hindi as well as Arabic and including Hindu scriptures and the Bible. He also oversaw the creation of an illustrated manuscript of the *Hamzanama*, an originally Persian romance, telling the adventures of a fictional uncle of

Left *Mughal emperor Shah Jahan wrote that the sight of the beautiful Taj Mahal, which he built in memory of his wife in 1631–54, provoked 'sorrowful sighs'.*

dynasty (618-907). China's first mosque was built in Guangzhou at this time. A modest number of Arab and Persian merchants settled in China and became dominant in the import/export trade. Then, under the Mongol Yuan dynasty (1274–1368), Muslims settled in China in large numbers, where they served as administrators for the Mongol rulers.

Islam was also a major force elsewhere in Asia. The Sultanate of Malacca in southern Malaysia was an important Islamic regional power at its height in the 15th century, while the Sultanate of Demak on the north coast of Java in Indonesia was founded in the late 15th century. The Masjid Agung Demak, or Great Demak Mosque, in Demak, on Java, was built at this time. The Sultanate of Aceh was another important Islamic regional power, with its base in Sumatra, Indonesia, in the 16th and 17th centuries. Its capital was Kutaraja (modern Banda Aceh).

the Prophet Muhammad, Amir Hamza. With 1,400 canvas miniature illustrations, this manuscript is one of the masterpieces of Islamic art.

Akbar rebuilt the celebrated red fort of Agra and constructed nearby the city of Fatehpur Sikri as his capital. His grandson, Shah Jahan, built the most celebrated of all Mughal monuments, the Taj Mahal in Agra (1632–54), to house the tomb of his favoured wife, Mumtaz Mahal. He also built the magnificent Jama Masjid, one of India's most famous mosques, in Delhi in 1656.

Ultimately, the Mughal empire declined in the face of a rival Hindu confederation, the Maratha empire, and the growing power of

the British East India Company in the region. Nevertheless, it survived in various forms until 1857, when the last emperor, Bahadur Shah II (reigned 1838–57), was exiled to Rangoon in Burma by the British.

BEYOND INDIA

Islam was introduced to China in 651, within 20 years of the death of the Prophet Muhammad, when the latter's maternal uncle Saad ibn Abi Waqqas was sent as an envoy to Gaozong, an emperor of the Tang

Right The Kampung Kling Mosque in Malacca, Malaysia, was built in 1748, using the traditional square design of the earliest mosques.

BEYOND THE SAHARA

ISLAM WAS ESTABLISHED IN NORTHERN AFRICA IN THE EARLY DAYS OF
THE FAITH, AND SPREAD SOUTHWARD ALONG TRADE ROUTES. MAJOR
AFRICAN ISLAMIC EMPIRES INCLUDED THE MALI AND SONGHAI.

Arab Muslims had invaded Egypt in 639 during the reign of Caliph Umar (634–44), capturing Alexandria in 643 and establishing Sunni Islam there. The faith had spread along the north of the continent as far as Morocco by 711, when general Tariq ibn Ziyad carried it across the Straits of Gibraltar into the Iberian Peninsula. Right from these early days, Arab trade caravans bore the Islamic faith along with their goods as they made their way across the Sahara into sub-Saharan Africa. At around the same time, Arab merchants sailed down Africa's east coast and established Islamic trading ports there.

GHANA EMPIRE

In western Sudan, between the upper Senegal and Niger rivers, an empire called the Ghana, or Wagadou ('Land of Herding'), grew very rich on trade in gold, ivory and slaves from the 8th century onward. The empire was ruled by a Muslim elite and was at its height in c.1050. It is said to have comprised two linked cities, one inhabited by Muslims, containing at least 12 mosques and the royal palace, and a second around 10km (6 miles) away for the pagan natives.

The capital was sacked by the Muslim Almoravids of Morocco in 1076. Then, in the 13th century, the lands of the Ghana empire were

Above The 14th-century Djinguereber Mosque in Timbuktu, Mali, is made entirely from mud, straw and wood. It has space for 2,000 people to pray.

Below The Great Mosque of Djenné in Mali is the world's largest mud-brick building. The mosque was built in 1907 on foundations dating from the 1200s.

subsumed by a new power, the kingdom of Mali, established by a Muslim ruler named Sundiata Keita in c.1240.

MALI EMPIRE

Beginning from a small state on the upper Niger River, Sundiata Keita conquered many neighbouring kingdoms and created a sizeable state that acquired enormous wealth from controlling trade throughout West Africa and even beyond, to Asia and Europe.

Sundiata Keita's great-nephew Mansu Musa (reigned 1312–37) conquered the cities of Timbuktu and Gao and established Mali as a great empire. A celebrated account survives of the *Hajj* pilgrimage to Makkah that Mansu Musa made in 1324: when passing through Cairo he gave so many gifts of gold that it created inflation across Egypt.

Mansu Musa brought the Arabian architect and poet Abu Es Haq Es Saheli back from Makkah and, under his influence, built religious schools and a university in Timbuktu. In 1327, Es Saheli built the Djinguereber Mosque in Timbuktu. Along with the mosques of Sankoré and Sidi Yahya, it formed part of the university, which itself played a major role in the spread of Islam in Africa.

SONGHAI EMPIRE

The Mali empire thrived until the mid-15th century, when it was eclipsed by another West African Muslim state, the kingdom of the Songhai. Under Ali the Great (reigned 1465–92) and Askia Muhammad I (reigned 1492–1528), the Songhai created a trading empire to rival that of the Mali. Its leaders were just as devout as their predecessors and fostered the growth of learning in Timbuktu. Under Askia Muhammad's rule, scholars made translations of ancient Greek philosophers Plato

Above The Sankoré Mosque in Timbuktu was built in the 15th century. Its courtyard is said to have been built to match the dimensions of the Kaabah.

and Aristotle, Abd al-Rahman al-Sadi compiled the great African history *Tarikh al-Sudan* ('Chronicles of Africa') and the great legal scholar Ahmed Baba was at work.

The Songhai empire survived until 1591, when it was crushed by a Moroccan invasion, and afterward, minor kingdoms attempted without success to fill the gap left by the Mali and Songhai.

In West-central Africa, the Muslim Kanem–Borno empire to the north and west of Lake Chad was at its height in the 16th century. Under Mai Idris Alooma (reigned 1571–1603), the imperial army used firearms purchased from the Ottoman Turks to take control of trade with Egypt and Libya. The empire faded after c.1650, but survived in name until 1846, when it was eclipsed by another regional power, the Adai empire.

EAST AFRICAN CITY-STATES

In East Africa, Muslim Arab traders settled along the coast from c.900 and created city-states such as Mogadishu (today the capital of Somalia), Mombasa and Malindi

(both now in Kenya), and Kilwa Kisiwani (an island port off the coast of modern Tanzania). Islam spread inland from these port cities, and in East Africa became better established among the people than in West Africa, where the faith remained largely the preserve of the governing elite for many years.

Above The atmospheric prayer hall of the Great Mosque on the island of Kilwa Kisiwani is still standing. The mosque was founded in the 900s and rebuilt in the 11th and 12th centuries.

LAND OF THE SHAHS

FROM 1502 UNTIL 1722, THE SHIAH MUSLIM SAFAVIDS RULED A
GREAT ISLAMIC EMPIRE IN PERSIA. WITH ITS MAGNIFICENT CAPITAL AT
ISFAHAN, IT WAS AT ITS HEIGHT UNDER SHAH ABBAS I IN THE 1620S.

The rise of the Safavids was a
major development in the
history of Islam: theirs was the first
large and enduring Shiah Muslim
state since the Fatimids. They
established the Shiah branch of the
faith as the dominant form of Islam
in the Caucasus and much of
western Asia, especially Iran.

The Safavids were descended
from Turkish adherents of the
mystical branch of Sunni Islam
named Sufism who had converted
to Shiah Islam in the 15th century.
They came to believe that they
were called to spread Shiah Islam
through military conquest.

THE 'HIDDEN IMAM'

At the start of the 16th century, a
young Safavid leader, Ismail, claimed
to be a representative of the 'Hidden
Imam', the 12th Shiah imam
Muhammad al-Mahdi. According to
Shiah tradition, after the 11th Shiah
imam, Hassan al-Askari, was killed
in 874, his successor was hidden by
Allah through a process called
ghaybah (occultation) in order to

*Below The beautiful Imam Mosque
in Isfahan, central Iran, was built by
Abbas I in 1611–29. The minarets
flanking the main gateway are
42m (137ft) high.*

*Above The greatest of Safavid rulers,
Abbas I, restored the dynasty's power,
winning a string of military victories.*

save his life. Shiah Muslims claim
that he remains miraculously alive
and will one day return to guide the
faithful. In this guise, Ismail gained a

In central Iran, Abbas I built a new capital alongside the ancient city of the Sasanians. At its peak, Isfahan was one of the wonders of the world: it had no fewer than 163 mosques, more than 250 public baths and around 1,800 shops. The city was also rich in beautiful parks, large squares, libraries and religious schools. The mosques included the stunning Shah Mosque, begun in 1611, with its elegant calligraphic inscriptions and mosaic tiling; it is often described as one of the world's greatest examples of mosque architecture.

devoted following, despite the fact that he was only 12 years old, and led troops to capture the kingdom of Shirvan (now part of Azerbaijan) and the city of Tabriz. He declared himself Shah of Azerbaijan, and proclaimed the Shiah faith to be the official religion in his lands.

Ismail then announced that he was the Hidden Imam himself, returned to rule and to lead the faithful. Within ten years, Ismail had taken control of all of Iran, and captured Baghdad and Mosul in Iraq. In the north-east, he defeated and drove back the Uzbeks.

OTTOMANS HIT BACK
The Safavids now posed a threat to the might of the Ottoman empire: Ismail's Shiah missionaries converted many Turkmen tribes in Ottoman territories in Anatolia and Iraq. Ottoman sultan Selim I marched into Iran and defeated Ismail in the Battle of Chaldiran in 1514. Though wounded and nearly captured, Ismail survived, but his position was seriously weakened, for he lost his aura of invincibility.

The Safavid empire was crucially undermined during the reigns of the next three shahs, Tahmasp I

Above In the elegant Ali Ghapu palace on Nagsh-i Jahan Square, Isfahan, Abbas I received ambassadors and dignitaries from around the world.

(1524–76), Ismail II (1576–77) and Muhammad Khudabanda (1578–88), which saw civil war and internal power struggles as well as repeated attacks by the Ottomans and the Uzbeks, but the dynasty rose to the height of its power and glory under Abbas I (1587–1629).

CONQUESTS OF ABBAS I
The Safavids had lost Baghdad and much of Iraq to the Ottomans, and Abbas recognized that his army needed updating. He negotiated a peace treaty with the Ottomans, and, with the help of two Englishmen, Anthony and Robert Shirley, set about reorganizing the military on the European model of a standing army fully equipped with artillery and muskets.

The new force recaptured Herat and Mashhad from the Uzbeks, and then Baghdad, the eastern part of Iraq and the provinces in the Caucasus from the Ottomans. He regained control of the port of Hormuz on the Persian Gulf from

Above A superb edition of Iran's national epic, the 11th-century Shahnama by Firdawsi, was made for Shah Tahmasp I.

the English and developed lucrative trading links with the Dutch and English East India companies.

Following the death of Abbas I in 1629, the Safavid empire endured for around 100 years, but this was generally a period of slow decline, enlivened only by the reign of Abbas II (1642–66). The Safavid dynasty ended in 1760, when Karim Khan Zand founded the Zand dynasty.

RISE OF THE OTTOMANS

FROM MODEST BEGINNINGS IN THE 14TH CENTURY, TURKISH TRIBES IN ANATOLIA CREATED THE GREATEST ISLAMIC EMPIRE IN HISTORY, THE OTTOMAN EMPIRE, WHICH LASTED FOR MORE THAN 600 YEARS.

The Ottoman dynastic founder, Osman, was a descendant of the nomadic Kayi tribe, originally from Turkestan in central Asia, who settled in Anatolia in the 12th century and established a base in Sögüt, north-western Anatolia (now in Turkey) in the late 13th century. According to one legend, Osman's father, Ertugrul, was leading a force of around 400 horsemen across the region when he chanced upon a battle: he joined in support of the losing side and turned the conflict in their favour, and as a reward the Seljuk sultan he had helped gave him land on which to settle.

Osman (reigned 1258–1324) expanded the territory, and under his son Orhan (reigned 1324–60), the Ottomans became a major regional power. Among other cities, Orhan captured Bursa (in 1326), which he made into a great centre for Islam. He also helped John Kantakouzenos take the Byzantine imperial throne from his rival John V Palaeologus and was rewarded with the hand of the emperor's daughter, Theodora, in marriage and the right to raid with impunity in Thrace (a historical region of south-eastern Europe).

THE FIRST SULTAN

Orhan's son Murad I (reigned 1359–89) expanded Ottoman power in Thrace. He was the first Ottoman ruler to adopt the title sultan, in 1383. He founded a number of enduring Ottoman institutions, including the elite military corps of the Janissaries, and the offices of *beylerbeyi* (military commander-in-chief) and grand vizier (principal government minister).

Within the rapidly expanding empire, the Ottomans allowed local rulers to remain in nominal control so long as they paid annual tribute and provided troops for the imperial army. Many Christian rulers in south-east Europe, and even the Byzantine emperor John V, became client rulers under Ottoman overlordship.

Above Osman's name means 'breaker of bones' and Ottoman writers saw in this a prophecy of the military strength of the empire he founded.

THE THUNDERBOLT

Murad's son Bayezid I (reigned 1389–1402) was known as *Yildirim* ('Thunderbolt') because of the speed of his military campaigns. He imposed Ottoman authority in Anatolia, then occupied Bulgaria, and, though the Europeans launched a crusade against him, he defeated them in the Battle of Nicopolis in 1396. Bayezid maintained a siege of Constantinople for no less than seven years (1391–98), but he met his match in the Mongol leader Timur (or Tamerlane), who invaded Anatolia and defeated the Ottomans at the Battle of Ankara in 1402. Bayezid died in captivity the following year.

Timur did not press home his advantage: his interest lay in conquering India, so he restored power in Anatolia to Turkmen princes and allowed control of the Ottoman empire to pass to Bayezid's sons.

Left The Great Mosque in Bursa was built by Sultan Bayezid I to celebrate victory over European crusaders at Nicopolis in 1396.

Above In preparation for his attack on Constantinople, Mehmed II built a great fortress, Rumeli Hisar, to control shipping in the Bosphorus.

In 1421, Bayezid's grandson, Murad II, re-established Ottoman power over Turkmen principalities of Anatolia, forcing the Byzantine emperor to become his vassal once again. He besieged Constantinople in 1422–3, and withdrew only on payment of vast tribute.

CONQUEST

Murad's son Mehmed II laid siege to Constantinople with a vast army backed up by a fleet of 280 ships. After several weeks, in May 1453, the city fell in a matter of hours.

The conquest of Constantinople was a momentous day in the history of Islam: one of the most famous cities in the world, founded as a Greek trading colony, then re-established by Constantine as a new capital for the Roman empire and a centre of the Christian faith, was now the capital of an Islamic empire. The rapid Ottoman expansion that delivered this prize had been made possible by military might but was also powerfully driven by trade, which accrued wealth as well as necessary goods, and by religion, in particular by the activities of Sufi *tariqahs* (fraternities). The Ottomans renamed the city Istanbul and converted the Hagia Sophia and other churches into mosques.

THE CRESCENT MOON

The crescent moon and single star is an international symbol of the Islamic faith, and appears on the flags of several Muslim countries including Pakistan and Turkey. According to legend, its origin lies in a dream of Ottoman founder Osman I, in which he saw a crescent moon arching from one side of the world to the other. The Ottomans later saw in this a prophecy of their greatness.

In fact, the crescent moon and star was an ancient religious symbol in central Asia, also associated with the Greek goddess Diana. It became the symbol of the Greek colony of Byzantium, which was later transformed into the great city of Constantinople. When the Ottomans conquered Constantinople in 1453, they adopted the symbol as their own.

Left Ottoman triumph in Constantinople is depicted as the slaughter of haloed Christians in this 16th-century fresco from a Romanian monastery.

SULEYMAN THE MAGNIFICENT

THE OTTOMAN EMPIRE WAS AT ITS HEIGHT DURING THE REIGN OF SULTAN SULEYMAN 'THE MAGNIFICENT' (1520–66), WHO RULED OVER VAST TERRITORIES AND 115 MILLION PEOPLE.

The conquest of Constantinople in 1453 by Sultan Mehmed II (reigned 1451–81) was the foundation for a period of continuous Ottoman territorial expansion that brought the empire to the peak of its power and influence. Mehmed's numerous victories won him the byname of 'the Conqueror'. He captured Serbia, Bosnia, Albania and most of the territories around the Black Sea, and re-established Ottoman control in Anatolia.

His successor Bayezid II (1481–1512) consolidated these gains, with victories over Poland, Hungary and Venice. Selim I led campaigns against the Safavids of Iran and the Mamluks of Egypt, and by the end of his reign in 1520 all the territories of the old Islamic

Above Suleyman the Magnificent receives Prince Sigismund of Transylvania at his glittering court in Istanbul in this 16th-century manuscript illustration.

caliphate – aside from Iran and Mesopotamia – were now in Ottoman hands.

Suleyman I (reigned 1520–66) went even further, capturing the territory of modern Hungary from the Hapsburgs and even besieging Vienna in 1529. In the East, he won several victories over the Safavids and captured Baghdad in 1535. He extended Ottoman power all the way through Mesopotamia to the Persian Gulf, while in North Africa, he annexed Tripoli. His navy, which was commanded by the widely feared Barbarossa, dominated the eastern Mediterranean.

'THE MAGNIFICENT'
Suleyman was regarded by his contemporaries – both Christian and Muslim – as the world's

Left At the time it was built, in 1550–57, the Süleymaniye Mosque's dome was, at 53m (174ft) high, the tallest dome in the Ottoman empire.

pre-eminent ruler. Abroad, he was known as 'the Magnificent' because of the vastness of his domain and the splendour of his court. In his era, the Ottoman empire matched the Byzantine or east Roman empire in its pomp, and the extent of its territories almost exactly matched that of the eastern Roman empire under Emperor Justinian I the Great 1,000 years earlier.

Suleyman called himself 'ruler of the lands of Caesar and of Alexander the Great' and 'master of the world'. But although he promoted his own greatness, he remained devout and subject to Allah. His inscriptions also declared him to be a 'slave of Allah' and 'deputy of Allah on earth, obeying the commands of the Quran and enforcing them around the world'.

'THE LAWGIVER'

By his own people, Suleyman was called *Kanuni* ('the Lawgiver'). He revised and developed the *Kanun Nameh*, a code of imperial law first collected and promulgated by Mehmed II 'the Conqueror'. The Kanun code of law was independent of the Shariah law derived from the Quran. By tradition, Shariah law

Above The splendid Topkapi Palace in Istanbul was home to an imperial entourage of 4,000 people at its peak.

was applied in all Islamic states; the Ottoman Kanun law derived from the Turkish tradition, under which the law of the emperor was sacred. The code issued by Suleyman principally covered criminal law, taxation and landholding.

A number of his laws safeguarded the rights of Jews and of the *rayas* ('protected'), Christians living in their own communities within the empire. In the Ottoman empire, religious groups were permitted to set up their own communities called millets, in which they kept their own religious and other customs under their own leaders and the Sultan's protection.

In an inscription in the Süleymaniye Mosque, Suleyman was lauded as *Nashiru Kawanin al-Sultaniyye* ('Spreader of Sultanic laws'). He is traditionally viewed as the successor to the biblical King Solomon, who is praised in the Quran as the embodiment of justice. Muslims revere him as the perfect Islamic ruler.

POET AND PATRON

Suleyman was a highly cultured man. Writing under the pen name Muhibbi, he was an excellent poet, his work celebrated by Muslims as some of the finest in Islamic history. He was also a skilled goldsmith. Above all, he was a discerning and immensely generous patron of the arts. From the Topkapi Palace in Istanbul, he funded and presided over artistic societies named *Ehl-i Hiref* ('Groups of the Talented') that were a magnet for the empire's finest artists, artisans and craftsmen. During his reign, Istanbul became the artistic centre of the Islamic world, where craftsmen developed distinctively Ottoman styles.

Suleyman also embarked upon a vast building programme in Istanbul and the cities of the empire, raising bridges, palaces and mosques in great numbers. He was patron to Mimar Sinan, perhaps the greatest architect in Islam, whom he commissioned to build his first masterpiece, the beautiful Sehzade Mosque (1513 0) to honour his favourite son, Mehmed. Sinan also built the majestic Süleymaniye Mosque in Istanbul (1550– 7).

Above Barbarossa ('Red Beard') was the scourge of western fleets in the Mediterranean for 40-odd years, first as a pirate, then as an Ottoman admiral.

From World Power to 'Sick Man of Europe'

FOLLOWING THE DEATH OF SULEYMAN I IN 1566, THE OTTOMAN EMPIRE BEGAN A LONG, VERY SLOW DECLINE THAT MADE IT, IN THE WORDS OF TSAR NICHOLAS I OF RUSSIA, THE 'SICK MAN OF EUROPE'.

For more than 100 years following Suleyman's death and the accession of Sultan Selim II in 1566, the Ottomans continued to increase their empire. However, the roots of the ultimate Ottoman decline have been traced by historians to this period.

The imperial economy was badly hit when the Dutch and British developed a sea route to Asia to replace the overland one through Ottoman lands. The economy was further damaged by inflation, partly caused by the influx of Spanish silver from 'New World' colonies in South America. A succession of weak sultans allowed decay of the previously strong administrative and military structures. The Ottoman navy was defeated by a Holy League formed by Pope Pius V and lost control of the Mediterranean. Then, during the course of the 17th

Above Under Sultan Mahmud II, the Ottoman empire began to break up as Greece won independence and Algeria was taken by the French.

century, ever more powerful nation states emerged in Europe and made alliances to curb Ottoman power.

STAGNATION AND REORDERING

Matters worsened in the 18th and early 19th centuries. The empire stagnated; many successive sultans were unsuccessful in their attempts to introduce reforms; the Ottomans failed to keep up with European developments in science, technology and military tactics. Central power waned drastically, and many areas of the empire, such as Algeria and Egypt, became effectively independent.

During the Tanzimet period (so-called from the Arabic word for 'reordering') from 1839 until 1876, Sultans Abdulmecid I and Abdulaziz

Left In the revolution of 1908–9, Young Turks fought and defeated soldiers loyal to the sultan in the streets of Istanbul.

made reforms that included the introduction of factories, an education system and a modernized army. In 1856, Abdulmecid issued the *Hatt-i Humayun* ('Imperial Reform Announcement'), which guaranteed equality for all Ottoman subjects, regardless of religious faith. Yet Ottoman power and prestige continued to fade.

LOSS OF TERRITORIES

Throughout the 19th and early 20th centuries, the Ottoman empire shrank. Nationalism was on the rise, and many former imperial territories won independence: Greece in 1829, then Montenegro, Romania and Serbia in 1878. In North Africa, Egypt was occupied by the British in 1882, while Algeria and Tunisia were colonized by the French in 1830 and 1881 respectively. During the Balkan Wars (1912–13), the empire lost all its Balkan territories except Thrace and the city of Edirne.

CONSTITUTIONAL REFORM

In 1876, Western-educated reformers named the Young Ottomans led a military coup to try to establish a constitutional monarchy. This resulted in the empire's first constitution, the *Kanun-I Esasi* ('Basic Law'), issued by Sultan Abdulhamid II in 1876. But just two years later, the sultan suspended the parliament and once again assumed absolute rule. In 1908, the revolution of the Young Turks (a coalition of reformers including secularists and nationalists) forced Abdulhamid II to restore the parliament he had suspended and reinstate the 1876 constitution.

SECULAR REPUBLIC

Following defeat in World War I, the empire was partitioned under the Treaty of Sèvres (signed in August 1920), Istanbul was occupied by

Above *Mehmed Vahideddin VI was the 36th and last of the Ottoman sultans. Deposed in 1922, he died in exile in 1926 in Sanremo, Italy.*

British and French troops, and a Turkish national movement mobilized to fight the Turkish War of Independence (1919–23). Mustafa Kemal led the nationalist army to victory. The Ottoman sultanate was abolished on 1 November 1922 and the last reigning sultan, Mehmed VI (reigned 1918–22) left Istanbul on 17 November. The Republic of Turkey was declared on 29 October 1923, with Mustafa Kemal as its president.

Mustafa Kemal introduced a series of secular reforms. In 1924, he abolished the Islamic caliphate and Shariah law and closed Islamic religious schools. The following year, he outlawed the wearing of

Right *The memory of revolutionary leader Mustafa Kemal, the 'Father' of the Turks', is celebrated in this equestrian statue in Ankara.*

the fez, on the grounds that it was a symbol of the Ottoman regime, and took moves to dissuade women from wearing the veil and to encourage all to wear Western clothing. In 1926, he introduced new legal codes, under which polygamy was abolished, and religious weddings were replaced with a compulsory civil service. In 1928, he introduced a new Turkish alphabet (based on the Latin one) to replace Arabic script, and declared the state to be secular, removing the constitutional clause under which Islam was named as the official state religion. In 1933, a new law required the call to prayer and the reading of the Quran to be in Turkish rather than in Arabic.

In 1934, another law required all Turks to take Western-style surnames and the Turkish Grand National Assembly awarded Mustafa Kemal the surname Ataturk – 'Father of the Turks'.

REPUBLICS AND KINGDOMS

THE PRINCIPAL SELF-DECLARED ISLAMIC STATES ESTABLISHED IN THE 20TH CENTURY – INCLUDING PAKISTAN, SAUDI ARABIA, SUDAN, IRAN AND MOROCCO – CHOSE DIFFERENT MODELS OF GOVERNMENT.

Some Islamic states were founded as monarchies. The kingdom of Saudi Arabia (al-Mamlakah al Arabiyah as Saudiyyah), for example, is an absolute monarchy, established as a unified kingdom in 1932. The kingdom of Morocco (al-Mamlakah al Maghribiyah), which gained independence from France in 1956, is a constitutional monarchy, with a hereditary crown and a two-house parliament under a constitution agreed in 1972 and amended in 1992 and 1996.

Other states declared themselves 'Islamic republics', but this title can mean very different things. The Islamic Republic of Pakistan (*Jamhuryat Islami Pakistan*) was the first country to use the title, in its constitution of 1956. In this case, 'Islamic republic' was primarily a statement of religious and cultural identity: the constitution was a largely secular one, and Pakistan had no state religion until a revised

constitution, naming Islam as the state religion, was adopted in 1973. Iran was a monarchy until the Iranian revolution of 1979, which resulted in it being declared the Islamic Republic of Iran (*Jomhuri-ye Eslami-ye Iran*). The form of government in Iran is termed a 'theocratic republic': its official religion is Shiah Islam and the chief of state or supreme leader is a Shiah imam. Its legal system is based on Shariah law.

A CALIPHATE?

Some Muslims today call for the abolition of Islamic monarchies on the grounds that they are too authoritarian. Some believe that the very notion of a republic – whether secular or Islamic – is necessarily contrary to the proper form of government as established by the Quran and Islamic tradition of the sunnah. Government, according to this theory, should be by a caliph as religious leader and successor of the Prophet, basing governance on Shariah law and Islamic religious tradition. Some call for the re-establishment of an international caliphate uniting disparate Islamic countries under religious rule. Sunni Muslims hold that when a state is ruled according to Shariah law, then this is, in fact, caliphate government in practice, whether or not the leader uses the title 'caliph'.

HISTORICAL PERSPECTIVE

The great Islamic empires were ruled by caliphs: the first four, or *Rashidun*, caliphs, the Umayyads, the Abbasids, and the Ottomans. The

Above The 12th-century Hassan Tower stands amid the ruins of an unfinished mosque in Rabat, the capital of the kingdom of Morocco.

Ottomans initially took the title *bey* (a Turkish tribal name for a ruler), then sultan and only began to use the title caliph from the reign of Selim I (reigned 1512–20) onward. When Selim defeated the Mamluk Sultanate in Egypt in 1517, the final Abbasid caliph, al-Mutawakkil III, was carried off to Istanbul; al-Mutawakkil was permitted to rule

Above Zulfikar Ali Bhutto was President of Pakistan in 1973 when a new constitution declared Islam to be the state religion of the country.

Above The Republic of Sudan, in north-eastern Africa, has been mostly ruled by military Islamic governments since its independence from Britain in 1956.

RELIGION AND SECULARISM IN TURKEY

The country created from the heartland of the great Ottoman empire, the Republic of Turkey (*Turkiye Cumhuriyeti*) has a secular constitution. There is no state religion, although Islam is a dominant force. Ninety-nine per cent of the Turkish population is Muslim, 75 per cent of these being Sunni Muslims, and around 20 per cent Alevi Muslims. (Alevis have links both to Shiah Islam and to Sufism.)

Individuals in Turkey have freedom of religion guaranteed in the constitution. Religious communities are not permitted to establish faith schools or form religious parties and no political party can claim that it represents a particular form of religion.

until his death, whereupon the title of caliph was attached to the Ottoman sultanate. Following the removal of the last Ottoman sultan Mehmed VI Vahideddin (reigned 1918–22) and the declaration of the Republic of Turkey, the first President of the Turkish Republic Mustafa Kemal abolished the caliphate as an institution in 1924.

SELF-PROCLAIMED CALIPHS

In the wake of Ataturk's decree, various individuals tried to proclaim themselves caliph. Hussein bin Ali, Sharif of Makkah and self-appointed King of the Hijaz, declared himself caliph of all Muslims just two days after Ataturk's statement. However, few paid attention to his claim and he was in any case forced to abdicate later the same year by Ibn Saud, subsequently the first King of Saudi Arabia. Mehmed VI Vahideddin, the deposed Ottoman sultan, himself attempted to declare himself caliph in the Hijaz but this also came to nothing.

The kings of Morocco and Mullah Muhammad Omar, leader of the Taliban regime of Afghanistan in the 1990s, later gave themselves the title of *amir al-mumineen* ('Commander of the Faithful') that was associated with caliphs from the 7th century onward. However, none of them claimed international jurisdiction over all Muslims, choosing to limit their power to those within their borders.

Below Built in 1971, the Shahyad Tower ('Memorial of Kings') in Tehran, Iran, was renamed Azadi ('Freedom') Tower in the 1979 Iranian Revolution.

THE MUWAHIDDUN MOVEMENT

THE REFORMIST MOVEMENT IN ISLAM THAT STRESSES *TAWHID* (THE UNITY AND UNIQUENESS OF ALLAH), WAHHABISM HAS BEEN A NOTABLE FORCE IN THE MUSLIM WORLD SINCE THE 18TH CENTURY.

Followers of scholar and religious reformer Muhammad ibn Abd al-Wahhab (1703–92) were given the name Wahhabi (*Wahhabiyyah*) by their opponents. For this reason, they reject it, preferring to be known as 'unitarians' (Muwahiddun) because of their emphasis on the oneness of Allah. This is the predominant form of Islam in Saudi Arabia and Qatar.

MUWAHIDDUN BELIEF

Muwahiddun believe that Islam should be practised as it was in the first three generations after the death of the Prophet Muhammad in 632, as revealed in the Quran and the hadith, and they reject later innovations (bidha). They denounce traditions such as venerating Islamic 'saints' and visiting the tombs of former religious leaders as idolatry, and declaim against the practice of *Tawakkul* ('drawing near to Allah'), which, in the religious practice of some Sufi, other Sunni and Twelver Shiah Muslims, involves praying to Allah through intercession to a prophet, imam or scholar.

Muwahiddun theology is largely based on the teachings of medieval Sunni Islamic scholar Taqi ad-Din Ahmad ibn Taymiyyah (1263–1328), who called for a return in Islam to following its sources in the Quran and sunnah. Its jurisprudence

Above The defenders of the first Saudi state fought bravely but were overcome by an army led by Muhammad Ali Pasha, Viceroy of Egypt, in 1818.

Below At al-Diriya (today on the outskirts of Riyadh), Muhammad ibn Saud and Ibn Abd al-Wahhab became allies. The town was capital of the first Saudi state in 1744–1818.

Left Ibn Saud, first ruler of the Kingdom of Saudi Arabia, spent most of his teenage years in exile in Kuwait after the rival Al-Rashid clan seized his ancestral lands.

is derived from the school of Ahmad ibn Hanbal (780–855), Persian Sunni Muslim scholar and theologian. Muwahiddun hold that a Muslim state should be governed solely according to Shariah Islamic law.

The Muwahiddun movement is identified by some as a form of the Sunni Islamic tradition of Salafiyyism, which draws on the actions and speeches of the Salaf (ancestors in the era of the Prophet Muhammad). The word *salaf* goes back at least until 1166, when Abu Sa'd Abd al-Kareem al-Samani wrote of '*al-Salaf* as exemplars for Muslims in his book *Al-Ansab*. Some trace the phrase to the Prophet himself, who, according to hadith, said 'I am the best *salaf* for you'. For all the possible connections to Salafiyyism, however, Abd al-Wahhab himself condemned over-reliance on scholarly tradition and stressed the capacity of the individual to discern Allah's will.

BIRTH OF THE MOVEMENT

Muhammad ibn Abd al-Wahhab established his movement in his birthplace of al-Uyayna, a village

north-west of Riyadh in Saudi Arabia, in *c.*1740. He led his followers in a number of public actions that expressed their puritan reforming zeal, including ordering the stoning of an adulteress and levelling the grave of Zayd ibn al-Khattab, brother of Caliph Umar (reigned 634–44) and one of the *sahabah* ('Companions of the Prophet'). This provoked the ire of local ruler Sulaiman ibn Muhammad ibn Ghurayr, who ordered Ibn Abd al-Wahhab to leave al-Uyayna.

Exiled in the nearby town of al-Diriya, Ibn Abd al-Wahhab won the support of its ruler, Muhammad ibn Saud, an event that would have enormous consequences over the following centuries. Ibn Abd al-Wahhab agreed to make Ibn Saud and his family the temporal leaders of his movement on condition that the Saud family would implement his teachings when they established themselves in power.

SAUDI CAMPAIGNS

Over the next 150 years or so, Ibn Saud and his heirs mounted a long succession of military campaigns to win power in the Arabian Peninsula. These campaigns brought the Saudi Wahhabis into violent conflict with other Muslims, driven particularly by their strong opposition to the practice of revering the tombs of early Muslim figures. In 1801–2, for instance, Wahhabis commanded by Abd al-Aziz ibn Muhammad ibn Saud attacked the Shiah cities of

Najaf and Karbala in Iraq, where they violated the tombs of Muhammad's son-in-law, Ali ibn Abu Talib, and grandson, Hussain ibn Ali, both of which were (and are) revered by Shiah Muslims.

Their military campaigns created what historians call the first Saudi state. The Ottoman empire, which derived prestige and authority in the Muslim world through its possession of the holy cities of Makkah and Madinah, sent troops under Muhammad Ali Pasha, Viceroy of Egypt, and he regained control of the region in 1818. A second Saudi state was created in 1824, but was brought down in 1891 by rival Arab clans. Finally, the long campaigns of the House of Saud culminated in the establishment of the Kingdom of Saudi Arabia by Abd al-Aziz ibn Saud, a direct descendant of Muhammad ibn Saud, in 1932. King Abd al-Aziz ibn Saud established his territory as a Muwahiddun state.

Above As King of Saudi Arabia, Abdullah ibn Abdul al-Aziz Al Saud is ruler of a Muwahiddun state and head of the House of Saud.

THE LAND OF THE TWO HOLY SANCTUARIES

SAUDI ARABIA, BIRTHPLACE OF ISLAM, WAS ESTABLISHED IN 1932 AS AN ISLAMIC KINGDOM, GOVERNED ACCORDING TO SHARIAH LAW AND IN LINE WITH THE PRINCIPLES OF THE MUWAHIDDUN MOVEMENT.

The kingdom of Saudi Arabia (al-Mamlakah al Arabiyah as Saudiyyah) derives great status in the global Muslim community because it contains the faith's two most sacred cities in Makkah and Madinah. The Holy Mosque in Makkah and the Prophet's Mosque in Madinah are the two holiest mosques for Muslims worldwide, and as a result Saudi Arabia is referred to reverentially as 'the Land of the Two Holy Sanctuaries'.

The Saudi king's official title is 'Custodian of the Two Holy Sanctuaries': this title was first adopted by King Fahd bin Abd al-Aziz Al Saud (reigned 1982–2005), and his successor, King Abdullah ibn Abd al-Aziz Al Saud, also uses it.

The country's motto is the first *kalimah*, or statement of the Islamic faith: 'There is no God but Allah and Muhammad is his messenger'. The motto is written on the Saudi flag, in white Arabic script against a green background and above a horizontal sabre, also in white.

ABSOLUTE POWER

King Abdullah is an absolute monarch, his powers not limited by the constitution. He himself serves as prime minister, and every four years appoints those on his Council of Ministers and the principal legislative body, the Consultative Council (*Majlis al-Shura*). In 2005, however, elections were held for half the members of 179 local assemblies, and further elections are to provide one-third of the members of the Consultative Council.

The Basic Law of Saudi Arabia, also known as the Basic System of Governance, was issued by royal decree by King Fahd in January 1992. It is based on Shariah law: limited secular legal codes have also been introduced, but these do not override Islamic laws.

Above The kalimah – 'There is no God but Allah and Muhammad is his messenger' – is the central feature of the flag of the kingdom of Saudi Arabia.

CREATION OF THE KINGDOM

The kingdom was established by Abdullah's father, Abd al-Aziz ibn Saud in 1902. Ibn Saud first captured the city of Riyadh, ancestral base of the Saud family, from the rival al-Rashid clan in a daring night raid on 15 January 1902. Over the following two years, he took large parts of the Nejd, the interior Arabian highlands that had been the basis of earlier states governed by the Saud dynasty in the 19th century. However, his cause suffered a major setback when, following an appeal from Ibn Rashid, leader of the al-Rashid clan, Ottoman troops marched into the region and defeated the Saudis decisively in June 1904.

Ibn Saud relaunched his campaign of expansion in 1912. During World War I, he gained British financial backing and military supplies to help in an attack on Ibn Rashid, on the grounds that the al-Rashid clan were allies of the Ottomans, and in 1922, he finally conquered all Rashidi territories. Then, in 1925, Ibn Saud captured the Hijaz, the long territorial strip along the eastern bank of the Red Sea that contains Makkah and Madinah. Ibn Saud was declared King of the Hijaz in the Great Mosque at Makkah on 10 January 1926, and the following year, under the Treaty of Jeddah, the

Left Muslim pilgrims making the Hajj reach up to touch the Black Stone and door of the Kaabah within the Holy Mosque in Makkah.

Above The Prophet's Mosque in Madinah contains the tombs of Muhammad and of early caliphs Abu Bakr and Umar.

British recognized the independence of his realm as the kingdom of the Nejd and the Hijaz.

Finally, in 1932, Ibn Saud renamed his unified realm the kingdom of Saudi Arabia. The new country comprised the regions of the Hijaz and the Nejd plus al-Qatif and al-Hasa (two oasis regions in eastern Saudi Arabia).

OIL AND RELIGIOUS FUNDING

In March 1938, vast reserves of oil were discovered in Saudi Arabia, and following World War II – in which the new county remained neutral – development began. By 1949, oil production was under way on a large scale. Saudi Arabia became the world's largest exporter of petroleum and grew very wealthy

on the proceeds. Particularly after the sharp rise in the price of oil in the mid-1970s, the Saudi government reputedly spent lavishly around the world promoting Islam.

After Iraq invaded Kuwait in 1990, Saudi Arabia accepted the exiled Kuwaiti royal family and 400,000 Kuwaiti refugees, and then, in 1991, allowed US and Arab troops to deploy on its soil prior to

attempting the liberation of Kuwait. The fact that US troops remained on Saudi soil following the liberation of Kuwait in 1991 caused rising domestic tension until the final US troops left in 2003.

Below Scores of pilgrims take part in noon prayer (dhuhr) outside the al-Masjid al-Haram Mosque (Holy Mosque) in Makkah during the Hajj.

AN ISLAMIC REPUBLIC

AS THE END OF BRITISH RULE IN INDIA NEARED, THE MUSLIM LEAGUE SUCCESSFULLY CAMPAIGNED TO ESTABLISH MUSLIM-MAJORITY PAKISTAN. IT WAS DECLARED AN ISLAMIC REPUBLIC IN 1956.

The modern state of Pakistan was formed on 15 August 1947. British rule ended and the Indian subcontinent was partitioned into Hindu-majority India and Muslim-majority East and West Pakistan. Both Pakistan and India were initially dominions within the Commonwealth of Nations. India became a republic on 26 January 1950 and Pakistan was declared an Islamic republic on 23 March 1956.

THE CAMPAIGN FOR INDEPENDENCE

Within India, the Muslim League led by Allama Iqbal campaigned for an independent state in north-western India for Indian Muslims from 1930 onward. In 1933, Indian Muslim nationalist Choudhary Rahmat Ali put forward the name 'Pakistan' for the proposed country. In 1940, the Muslim League adopted the Lahore Resolution, which called for the establishment of 'autonomous and sovereign' states in those parts of north-western and north-eastern India where Muslims were numerically in a majority.

In June 1947, Muhammad Ali Jinnah, as representative of the Muslim League, agreed at a meeting with representatives of the Hindu Indian National Congress, the Sikhs and the Untouchables to the creation of Pakistan. The new country of West Pakistan comprised the provinces of Baluchistan, Northwest Frontier Province, Sindh and West Punjab; meanwhile, in the north-eastern corner of the subcontinent, the province of East Bengal formed East Pakistan.

Above In September 1947, Muslims wait to leave India in a protected convoy bound for the new country of Pakistan.

VIOLENT BIRTH

The decision to split the provinces of Punjab and Bengal was highly controversial and led to wide-scale rioting and as many as 500,000 deaths. In the Punjab, millions of Muslims migrated eastward into Pakistan, while millions more Sikhs and Hindus migrated westward into India; a similar cross-border migration took place in Bengal. In total, around 14 million people were forced to relocate.

Disputes arose over the princely states, which theoretically were free to remain independent or to join either India or Pakistan. Of enduring consequence was the disagreement over Kashmir, whose Hindu ruler chose to join India, despite having a Muslim majority population; this led to a long-running dispute between India and Pakistan over the territory. The countries fought two wars – in 1947–8 and 1956 – without resolving the issue.

Left This map shows India with East and West Pakistan at the moment of their creation in 1947 as dominions within the Commonwealth of Nations.

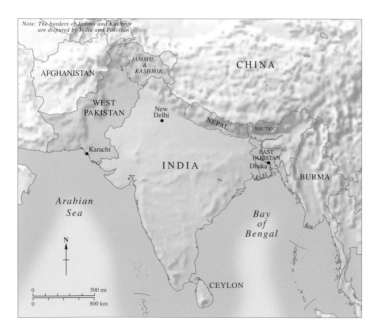

Note: The borders of Jammu and Kashmir are disputed by India and Pakistan

JAMMU & KASHMIR
AFGHANISTAN
CHINA
WEST PAKISTAN
New Delhi
NEPAL
BHUTAN
Karachi
EAST PAKISTAN
INDIA
Dhaka
BURMA
Arabian Sea
Bay of Bengal
N
0   500 mi
0   800 km
CEYLON

Left Benazir Bhutto was twice Prime Minister of Pakistan, in 1988–90 and 1993–6, and was the first woman elected to lead a Muslim state.

CONSTITUTIONS OF PAKISTAN

Pakistan's first constitution was drawn up by the Constituent Assembly, a body established under the terms of independence from British rule in 1947. It declared the country an 'Islamic republic', provided for a parliamentary form of government and decreed that Muslims in Pakistan should be enabled to order their lives in accordance with principles in the Quran and sunnah, and that no laws 'repugnant to the injunctions of Islam' could be passed. Muslims would be required to study the Quran, and only a Muslim could be president of the country, but citizens of Pakistan would have the freedom to practise and propagate any religion they chose. It provided for parliamentary government.

In 1958, the constitution was abrogated and martial law imposed. A new constitution in 1962 renewed the majority of the above provisions; the form of government was to be presidential. Martial law continued until 1972, then a third constitution was agreed in 1973 under the rule of Zulfikar Ali Bhutto. For the first time, Islam was declared to be the state religion of Pakistan. At various times, these constitutions have been suspended and martial law imposed in Pakistan. Shariah law was introduced in the 1980s under General Muhammad Zia-ul-Haq.

THEOCRATIC RULE IN AN ISLAMIC REPUBLIC

Ayatollah Ruhollah Khomeini, Shiah Islamic scholar and an outspoken critic of the regime of the Shah of Iran, returned to Iran after 15 years of exile. Throughout his exile, he had continued to oppose the Shah's regime, and by the late 1960s, was established as a *marja-e taqlid* ('model to be imitated') by Shiah Muslims around the world. The country declared itself an Islamic Republic on 1 April 1979 and in December that year, adopted a theocratic constitution. Khomeini became Supreme Leader.

The system of government was based on the Shiah theory of *wilayat al-faqih* ('Guardianship by the Islamic Jurists'). According to this theory, Shariah laws are sufficient to cover all areas of life, and countries should be governed by a *faqih* (an expert in Shariah law). Such a system is deemed necessary to guard against oppression, injustice and corruption, and representative parliamentary systems of government are considered to be contrary to the teachings of Islam. Under the constitution of Iran, all political decisions have to be approved by the Supreme Leader before they become legal.

On Ayatollah Khomeini's death on 3 June 1989, Ayatollah Ali Khamenei became the Supreme Leader of Iran.

Right Khomeini was an ayatollah *(Shiah religious leader) from the 1950s, and was in his late 70s by the time he became Supreme Leader of Iran in 1979.*

RADICAL ISLAMISM

IN THE 20TH CENTURY, WHILE MANY MUSLIM GROUPS ENCOURAGED MODERNIZATION, SOME ISLAMIC ACTIVISTS URGED RADICAL POLITICAL OR TERRORIST ACTION TO REFORM SOCIETY AND GOVERNMENT.

Several groups over the course of the 20th century called for a revival of Islam through a return to the faith's central tenets and most ancient traditions. Writers and teachers proposed that Islam was more than a religion, and that social and political systems should be remade according to the faith. This theory was generally called *al-Islamiyyah* ('Islamism').

THE MUSLIM BROTHERHOOD
The Muslim Brotherhood, or the Society of the Muslim Brothers (*al-Ikhwan al-Muslimun*) was established in Egypt in 1928 to promote a return to the Quran and sunnah as the basis for modern Islamic societies. The Brotherhood spread quickly to Palestine, the Lebanon, Syria, the Sudan and North Africa.

In the late 1930s and 1940s, the Muslim Brotherhood became politicized, and in Egypt in 1952, it supported the coup led by Gamal Abdel Nasser, whom they expected to found an Islamic religious government. Disappointed by his development of secular nationalism, the Brotherhood attempted to assassinate him in 1954.

One of the leading figures of the movement in the 1950s and 1960s was the Egyptian intellectual Sayyid Qutb. While in prison for his involvement in the planning of the failed assassination (he was later hanged), he wrote a strongly anti-Western and anti-secular book

Below Mujahidun *are those who struggle in jihad – in opposition to* qaid, *a person who does not join* jihad. *These* mujahidun *were fighting in Afghanistan.*

Above Shaykh Ahmad Yassin was co-founder, with Abdel Aziz al-Rantissi, of the militant Islamist organization Hamas in the Palestinian Territories in 1987.

Ma'alim fi-l-Tariq (*Milestones*). In this influential book, Qutb denounced all existing governments, even those of the Muslim countries, as subject to *jahiliyyah* (ignorance). He appealed to Muslims to form a revolutionary vanguard that would

oppose *jahiliyyah* through preaching and by removing governmental systems that supported *jahiliyyah,* through 'physical power and *jihad*'.

HAMAS

In the Palestinian Territories, members of the Gaza wing of the Muslim Brotherhood founded Hamas, the *Harakat-al-muqawamah al-islamiyyah* ('Islamic Resistance Movement') in 1987. The organization is associated with suicide bombings and other attacks on the Israeli military and on civilians; its founding charter called for the state of Israel to be destroyed and replaced with an Islamic state. Hamas is also a political party and won a majority of seats in the elected council of the Palestinian Authority in Gaza in January 2006.

AL-QAEEDA

Qutb's writings were a direct influence on the international Islamic *jihad* movement of al-Qaeeda, which was behind the terrorist attacks on New York City and Washington on 11 September 2001 and subsequently became one of the central targets of the United States' 'war on terror'. Qutb's brother, Muhammad Qutb, became a professor of Islamic studies and

Above A propaganda billboard in the Lebanese capital Beirut promotes the armed struggle of the Shiah militia Hezbollah in the Lebanon.

promoted Qutb's theories. One of his students was Ayman al-Zawahiri, who was reputedly a mentor of al-Qaeeda leader Osama bin Laden and eventually a leading member of al-Qaeeda himself.

There is considerable debate over what al-Qaeeda actually is. Its name perhaps means the 'base' and, according to some accounts, it grew out of the organization set up to train *mujahidun* (Muslims fighting *jihad*) fighting against the Afghan Marxist regime and Soviet troops in Afghanistan in the 1980s.

In 1998, its emerging leader, Osama bin Laden, and Ayman al-Zawahiri issued a *fatwa* calling on Muslims to expel foreign troops and interests from Islamic lands, to 'fight the pagans…until there is no more tumult or oppression…and there prevail justice and faith in Allah'.

Many writers suggest that although training camps in Sudan and Afghanistan were reputedly run under its aegis, al-Qaeeda is not actually a centralized organization, but is, in fact, a loose-knit group of Islamists dedicated to *jihad*.

Above Osama bin Laden, alleged founder of al-Qaeeda, ranked Shiah Muslims alongside heretics, the US and Israel as the four main 'enemies of Islam'.

CHAPTER 3

ISLAMIC BELIEFS

There are a number of fundamental doctrines in Islam that all Muslims are expected to adhere to faithfully. Collectively known as the six articles of belief and the five pillars of faith, all are enshrined in the Quran.

The six articles of belief can be described as the core religious truths of Islam: belief in the oneness of God, his angels, his divinely revealed scriptures, his prophets and messengers, his predestination of all things, both good and bad, and resurrection and divine judgement after death. The five pillars of faith are the physical manifestation of Islamic beliefs: declaring that there is no God but Allah and Muhammad is his messenger, praying five times a day, fasting during the month of Ramadhan, paying the charity tax and making pilgrimage to Makkah.

Muslims believe that they will be held in individual account for their beliefs and practices on the Day of Judgement, when every action and thought will be recalled and judged by God.

Opposite Congregational tarawih, *optional prayers offered by devout Muslims, are observed in mosques throughout the world during the fasting month of Ramadhan.*

Above A 17th-century Mughal manuscript painting captures the beauty of nature and reflects the great diversity of God's creation.

ONE GOD

ALLAH SIMPLY MEANS 'THE ONE GOD', AND PROFESSION OF THIS RELIGIOUS BELIEF SHOULD OCCUPY THE CENTRAL POSITION IN A MUSLIM'S CONSCIOUS THOUGHT AND ACTION AT ALL TIMES.

The *shahadah*, witnessing that 'there is no God but the one God' is the central Islamic creed. It is a doctrine that has transformed numerous civilizations across many continents, from Arabia to Africa, Asia and beyond. But monotheism is not new, and Muhammad was not calling his pre-Islamic Arabian society to a religious concept that was unknown to their civilization.

ISLAMIC MONOTHEISM

The ancient Arabs of Makkah were a Semitic people who traced their ancestry to Ibrahim's son Ismail. The belief in one God was therefore familiar to their history and civilization, while Ibrahim's temple, the *Kaabah*, was a constant reminder of their monotheistic heritage.

Linguistically, the idea of God's uniqueness is crystallized in the Arabic word *Allah*. To proclaim *Allah* in Arabic is to deny the possibility of any co-existing deities, which is why the pagan Arabs avoided using the term. Muhammad's call of *tawhid*, the 'oneness of God', was essentially a revival of the ancient teachings of Ibrahim and the other monotheist Semite patriarchs.

The concept of *tawhid* asserts that divine unity and divine truth are one and the same. This means that for Muslims to declare that the truth is one is to declare not only that 'God is One' but also that there can be 'no other God but God' (*la ilaha ilallah*). This combination of assertion and negation is contained in the *shahadah* (the Muslim declaration of belief).

THE PROPHETS

Connected to the notion of divine unity and truth is the concept of *risalah*, or 'divine communication'. In Islam, *risalah* is the means by which God reveals his nature, purpose and truth to men and women by the election of human prophets and messengers (10:47, 13:7, 35:24).

Muslims believe that God has sent many prophets to humankind, the first being Adam and the last Muhammad. According to a hadith, there have been 124,000 prophets, although the Quran refers to only 25 by name, among them Adam, Noah, Ibrahim, Ismail, Isaac, Moses, David and Jesus.

Islam teaches that all these prophets taught the same message of monotheism to their people.

Above Allah – 'The one God', written in calligraphic Arabic, adorns a high minaret in the former Turkish sultan's palace at Topkapi in Istanbul.

A number of them brought divinely revealed scriptures (2:213, 7:52), but Muslims believe that the Quran is God's final and perfected book of guidance.

THE NATURE OF GOD

Philosophers and theologians have argued about the exact nature of God for centuries. The arguments of Muslim philosophers were based on the cosmological order of things: the created realm is ordered by natural laws in which events happen by cause, and causes, therefore, cannot be without their proper effects, they argued. Like the ancient Egyptian, Greek and Mesopotamian thinkers before them, Muslim philosophers conceived that a world of both chaos and order must necessarily be inconsistent with the idea of a sublime, transcendent being.

Meanwhile, the Muslim theologians feared that an emphasis on the orderliness of the universe could result in the belief that God is detached from the apparent mechanical causality of his own creation. This could lead to the conclusion that either God is

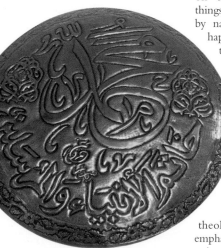

Above A decorative brass plate that hangs in the Tanyal Mosque in Tripoli, Lebanon, declares 'Muhammad is the seal of the Prophets and Messengers'.

Right The Blue Mosque in Istanbul, Turkey. Its huge domes tower high above the congregation in a symbolic portrayal of God's abode in the highest heavens.

divinely unique, wholly 'other' and transcendent, or he is immanent and physical, if not human-like.

OCCASIONALISM

In the view of Muslim theologians, such reasonings regarding the nature of God compromise the doctrine of *tawhid* and seemed to echo not only pagan Arabia's polytheism, but also Judaism's reference to God in the plural as *Elohim* and Christianity's developed trinity – three persons in the deity, each of whom is fully God.

The theologians responded by rejecting the philosophers' views and developing the doctrine of 'occasionalism': at each moment in time, God continues to recreate the universe. In this way, the theologians made the notion of causality dependent on God's 'divine presence'.

Above Ibrahim's belief and faithfulness is tested when God commands him to sacrifice his son, but Ismail is spared by the miraculous substitution of a ram.

QURANIC TRANSCENDENCE AND IMMANENCE

'If there were therein Gods besides God then verily both (the heavens and earth) would be in disorder and chaos. Glorified be God, Lord of the Throne, Transcendent beyond all they ascribe to Him.' (21:22)

'We verily created man and We know what his soul whispers to him and We are nearer to him than his jugular vein.' (50:16)

THE ATTRIBUTES OF ALLAH

THE QURAN ASCRIBES 99 DIFFERENT NAMES TO ALLAH, EACH OF WHICH DESCRIBES A PARTICULAR ASPECT OF HIS NATURE. MUSLIMS LEARN ABOUT GOD AND GAIN MERIT BY MEMORIZING THESE NAMES.

Understanding the nature of God is important in helping Muslims to establish and submit to his will. For example, those who believe that God is *al-Aleem*, 'all-knowing', and *al-Sami*, 'all-hearing', will be convinced that God knows their innermost thoughts, hears all that they say, and sees all that they do. Such an understanding of God's attributes will have a direct effect on the way they live their lives, both publicly and in private.

THE POWER OF GOD

Muslims believe not only that God created the universe but also that he is the all-pervading (*al-Muhit*) controller (*al-Qadir*) and reckoner (*al-Hasib*) of all unfolding events, which have been predetermined by his *qadar*, or 'divine measure'. In other words, Allah knows the present, past and future of all creation because he is the bestower or giver (*al-Wahhab*) of all things.

However, Islam teaches that the fact that God has power and authority over all creation and events does not mean that human beings do not have free will or choice; for example, no one is compelled to obey God or believe in him. Freedom of action does not contradict the foreknowledge of God. An individual does not know his final destiny and is given the freedom of choice to take any course of action he wishes.

Nevertheless, Muslims believe that there will be a final Day of Judgement (*yawm al-hisab*, or 'the day of account'), when God will judge and reward or punish each action in accordance with its intention, with the ultimate reward of eternal heaven or hell.

THE 99 NAMES OF GOD

The Prophet Muhammad stated that there are 99 names of Allah and said that he who commits them to memory will enter paradise. For Muslims, to know or remember the names of God is to understand who he is. All of God's names are found in the Quran.

Left The 99 divine attributes of God are ornately displayed in a beautiful calligraphic style above an entrance to the Blue Mosque in Istanbul, Turkey.

Above Congregational prayer at the Great Mosque in Lyon, France. The prayer begins with Allahu Akbar *('God is Greatest'), an acknowledgement and declaration of God's ultimate authority.*

Islam teaches that not only is each of these attributes of God complete in itself, but they are also perfect in their collective harmony. This means that, for example, while God is *al-Jabbar*, the 'compeller' or 'punisher', he is also *al-Ghafir*, the 'forgiver' or 'clement'. According to Nawawi's *Forty Hadith Qudsi*, Muhammad explained that 'when God decreed His creation, He pledged Himself by writing in His book that is with Him: My Mercy prevails over my Wrath.'

Muslims believe that by recounting and reflecting on the divine attributes of God, their hearts can find both solace and strength of faith (13:28).

REMEMBERING THE DIVINE

Dhikr means 'to remember' and refers to the particular devotional ritual of repeating or reflecting on the attributes of the divine (*dhikr Allah*). The practice of *dhikr* is usually associated with Muslim

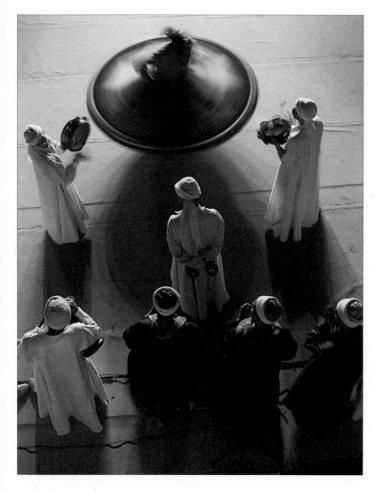

Left An Egyptian Sufi twirls rhythmically in a trancelike state, accompanied by a religious devotional song, nasheed, *as he contemplates God and celebrates the Prophet's birthday.*

mystics or Sufis but is also observed by Muslims from various other Islamic theological expressions.

The Quran explicitly instructs Muslims to engage in remembrance of God as a means of spiritual self-development and attaining inner peace: 'And the remembrance of God is the greatest (of actions)' (29:45), 'O Believers! Remember God with abundant remembrances' (33:41). Muslims are assured that when they remember the Divine and give gratitude to him, he returns the favour with great blessings and rewards (2:152).

The Prophet Muhammad said that everything has a 'polish' and that the 'polish' of the heart is *dhikr*. Muslims engage in *dhikr* in many varied ways, from offering extra ritual prayers to attending special gatherings to recite the Quran, or to exclusively remember God, as with the Sufis. But Muslims also recall God while engaged in their everyday activities, whether they are at work or study, eating or undertaking a journey.

CELEBRATING THE DIVINE

Remembering God is a celebrated encounter that is manifested in various artistic forms across the Muslim world. The most obvious of these is the arabesque, a unique abstract form of interconnected symmetrical designs that have been applied to painting, architecture, calligraphy and horticulture. The arabesque is designed to represent not God himself, but rather his inexpressibility.

Modern calligraphic works by artists such as Ahmed Moustafa, whose work is derived from, and inspired by, the original Quranic text, are products of remembering and celebrating the Divine. Equally, devotional songs of *nasheed* (Arabian), *sama* (Turkomanic) and *qawwali* (South Asian) are the result of a musical contemplation and remembrance of the Divine.

Right Quranic verses in an earthenware mosaic are set around a 16th-century necropolis created by Sultan Ahmed al-Mansour in Marrakech, Morocco.

DIVINE WILL

MUSLIMS BELIEVE THAT THE SACRED TEXT OF THE QURAN REVEALS GOD'S WILL TO HUMANS AND TEACHES THEM HOW TO ACHIEVE PEACE AND HARMONY IN THIS LIFE AND ETERNAL REWARD IN THE NEXT.

Submission to God's will is a central teaching of Islam, and the relationship between God and human beings is presented as that of Lord (*Rabb*) (1:1, 51:56) and slave (*abd*). The term Abdullah means 'servant of God', and the concept of worship (*ibadah*) in Islam is derived from the root word *abd*, which means slave, servant or worshipper. Men and women are seen as completely dependent on their creator for all their needs, both spiritual and physical, yet they have been granted freedom of choice.

DIVINE SOVEREIGNTY

Islam teaches that God is sovereign over all creation, including the human realm, and that everything is subject to God's 'primordial and harmonious condition' (*fitra*), or universal natural laws. Because they have free will, people can choose to act in accordance with *fitra* or against it by rejecting God's will. This conscious rejection is known as *kufr*, meaning 'to cover'. *Kufr* is seen as the antithesis of Islam because it represents the 'covering' or denial of the truth of God's supremacy.

Above In Islam, gardens reflect the beauty of God's creation and represent paradise as an eternal abode for the righteous.

DIVINE PURPOSE

The Quran declares that God's purpose for creating human beings was so that they might worship him: 'And I did not create *jinn* [creatures of the unseen realm] and mankind except to worship me' (51:56). However, while the reason for human existence is explicitly given, the Quran teaches that God, in his infinite wisdom, compels no one to believe in him (2:256).

A prophetic tradition recounts that before God made human beings, he created both heaven and hell and decreed that both should have their fill. Muslims believe that only God knows who will dwell in paradise and who will dwell in hell,

Left A musallah, *an Islamic prayer mat, shows birds of paradise perched upon heavenly flowers, which symbolize God's promise for the faithful.*

but that there is no need for people to be fatalistic or resign themselves to hell; instead, they should endeavour to seek God's grace by submitting to his divine will.

ACHIEVING GOD'S WILL

Islam teaches that divine revelation exists so that men and women might learn and live in accordance with God's will. Muslims believe that in the process of revelation, the divine nature of God is also made known: throughout human history, God has communicated his will through prophets and messengers who translate God's will into practice, leaving a living example for people to follow.

These two means of establishing divine order – God's scriptures and his prophets – both invite and enable people to submit themselves to God and be of service to their fellow human beings. The idea of living in peace and harmony with the creator and the created is, in fact, what is understood by the word Islam, which means 'peaceful submission'.

THE END OF THINGS

According to Islamic theology, the idea that people have that they are self-sufficient is a result of them becoming detached from the divine will for human evolution. The Quran teaches that humankind is on a journey that originated within the presence of God, who then sent us down to earth as a means of testing our faith.

Islam teaches that on this journey through life on earth, men and women will be tempted by Satan, or Shaytan, 'the rejected one', before experiencing a physical death and thereafter an eternal resurrection, either with God in paradise or with

Below Qurans are not only written in beautiful calligraphic styles, but are also handled with great reverence by Muslims.

the devil in the hellfire. To this end, all deeds and thoughts of every person are scribed by two recording angels (*kiraman katibeen*) and will be presented before God on Judgement Day (50:17–18). He will then reward or punish according to the individual's account.

According to the Quran, each human being is the creator of his or her own destiny, which is determined at any given point in life by the exercise of freedom of choice – to do good and obey God or to commit sin in disobedience. 'This Quran guides one to what is more straightforward and reassures believers who act honourably that they shall have great earnings. Yet We have reserved painful torment for those who do not believe in the hereafter' (17:9–10).

Above A Turkish manuscript from the 16th century shows eternal damnation in hellfire for those who reject faith.

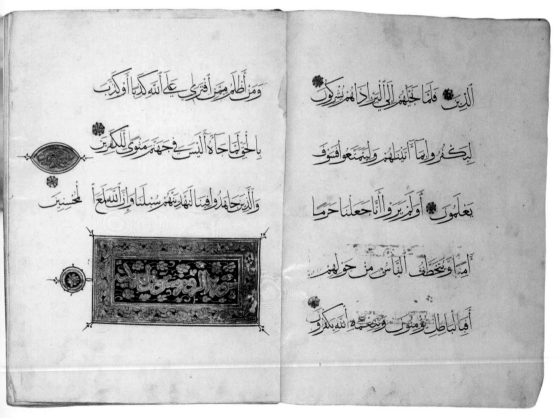

COSMOLOGY

THE QURAN INVITES ITS READERS TO REFLECT UPON THE
CREATION OF THE UNIVERSE AS AN OBSERVABLE REALITY THAT
REFLECTS THE GREATNESS OF GOD AS ITS CREATOR.

Above This micro-organism –
Paramecium caudatum *– is part of
God's beautifully proportioned creation.*

The genesis of humankind and the creation of the heavens and the earth is a recurring theme. The verses relating to creation are invariably linked to the idea that the world is a temporary abode and that believers will ultimately return to their Lord.

GOD, THE CREATOR

The Quranic narrative of the genesis of creation has many similarities to that of the Old Testament, but whereas the Bible alludes to the apparently human-like qualities of God, the Quranic text is devoid of all such descriptions. The Old Testament states that God created the heavens and earth in six days and on the seventh he rested. While the Quran confirms that God created all things in six days, it states that then he 'established Himself on His Throne' (32:4). In the Quran, a 'day' (*yawm*) is not viewed as one complete course of the earth around the sun, but refers to the conditions that existed before the creation. In one passage, it describes God's reckoning of a day to be equivalent to 1,000 of our days; in another to 50,000 (32:5, 120:4). Similarly, the word 'throne' is used symbolically, implying God's absolute authority, direction and control of the cosmos as the ever-living, immanent creator.

The Quran teaches that God is *al-Awwal*, the first, before whom there is nothing, and *al-Akhir*, the last, after whom there is nothing. He is also described as being ever-active within it as *al-Dhahir*, the 'outward', and *al-Batin*, the 'inward', privy to all that exists within the unseen realms of our being and what is around us.

FREE FROM EVIL

The Quran claims that God's creation is in itself good, beautifully proportioned and perfectly adapted for the functions it has to perform (32:6–7). This concept is known as *fitra*, or 'natural pre-disposition', and it includes the notion that all humans are born in a similar state to the rest of creation, that is free from evil (30:30). Dissension and disorder are believed to be the result of men's and women's excessive pride and practice of injustice leading to the harming of God's world (10:23) and their succumbing to Satan's temptation.

The Quranic worldview sees the creation as perfectly balanced and harmonized, on condition that men and women perform their appointed role as God's earthly vicegerents, peacefully submitting themselves to God's divine will. Muslims believe that at an appointed time in the future – the Last Day – God will reclaim his creation and the souls of men and women (15:85–6).

ABUNDANCE ON EARTH

The Quran's defined purpose for the creation of the earth challenges the idea that it is the result of cosmic chance. Instead, the earth is described as a place of abundant sustenance for human beings, with both animal and plant produce of incredible variety as a sign of God's bounty (15:20, 26:7). Ecological sustainability is implicated through the idea of agricultural cultivation

*Left A medieval Islamic manuscript on
astronomy illustrates shooting stars: 'light
missiles to drive away the devils' (67:5).*

and preserving the earth's natural resources. The earth's terrain is presented as a surface that men and women can easily travel across by land or sea. Its volatile landscapes are said to be fixed by lofty mountains, described as 'stakes' (*awtad*), like those of a tent, anchoring the deep foundational geological folds (78:6–7).

The earth is viewed as a temporary abode for humankind, which will eventually be brought to an end by God (99:1–3), and is always mentioned in the context of humankind's final destination and return to God (14:48).

INFINITE UNIVERSE
The Quran contains quite detailed information relating to the creation of the universe, referring to the existence of an initial, unique gaseous mass (*dukhan*), whose elements are fused together (*ratq*)

Right Islam teaches that human life and creation is not a chance occurrence but part of God's predetermined plan.

and subsequently separated (*fatq*) (41:11–12). The separation process resulted in the creation of multiple worlds in orbital solar systems.

The Quran teaches that 'God is the One Who created the night and the day, the sun and the moon, each one is travelling in an orbit with its own motion' (21:33). Specific celestial bodies are mentioned: the

Above The Horsehead Nebula in the Orion constellation is considered to be God's creation in Islam – like all the other stars.

sun, the moon, stars and planets. The universe is constructed of 'seven firmaments' (41:12), and its vastness is a testimony to the creator's power and greatness.

THE BIG BANG

RECENT SCIENTIFIC THEORIES REGARDING THE ORIGINS OF THE UNIVERSE APPEAR TO HAVE MANY SIMILARITIES TO VERSES FROM THE QURAN THAT REFER TO THE GENESIS OF THE HEAVENS AND EARTH.

The modern era is founded on scientific inquiry and the application of reason, which has brought humankind many benefits. But some people argue that the application of scientific analysis to sacred scriptures has increased religious scepticism and disbelief. Muslims conversely claim that the Quran, which was revealed more than 1,500 years ago, contains many verses that appear to agree with modern scientific discoveries.

ISLAM AND THE BIG BANG

The Quran does not provide a continuous narrative or an exact chronology for the origins of the universe, but Muslims claim that there are verses in a number of chapters that, taken together, could

be said to offer a brief synthesis of the events that led to its formation: 'Then He directed the Heaven when it was smoke, saying to it and the Earth, merge you willingly or unwillingly; they said we merge in willing obedience' (41:11), 'Do not the unbelievers see that the Heavens and Earth were one mass, then we split them asunder and that we created every living thing from water; will they then not believe?' (21:30), and 'Then He ordained the seven Heavens in two periods and He assigned to each Heaven its duty and command, And We adorned the lower Heaven with lights and protection, Such is the decree of The Exalted, The Mighty' (41:12).

All of the above, many Muslims would say, appear to agree with scientific theories on the existence of primary nebula and the process of secondary separation of the elements that had formed in the initial unique mass of the 'Big Bang' theory.

INTERMEDIARY CREATION

It is generally accepted by scientists that the separation of the primary gases resulted in the formation of galaxies, which, after dividing, formed stars, from which the planets came into being. The Quranic verses on creation also refer to an intermediary creation existing between the heavens and earth: 'it is He who created the Heavens and Earth and all that is in between them...' (25:59).

Left The Milky Way constellation provides us with an illustration of how cosmic matter from the 'Big Bang' has scattered across the universe.

Above A Turkish Muslim astronomer is shown consulting an armillary sphere and compass as he maps out the universe in this 16th-century manuscript illustration.

Muslims claim that this intermediary creation bears striking similarities to the modern discovery of bridges of matter, present outside organized astronomical systems. The Quran also accords with the modern theory regarding how the celestial organization is balanced by the particular orbits of stars and the interplay of gravitational fields related to their speed of movement and mass, each with its own motion: 'And it is He who has created the night, the day, the sun and the moon; each one is travelling in an orbit with its own motion' (21:33).

EXPANDING UNIVERSE

The first chapter of the Quran, *al-Fatiha* (the Opening), describes God as *Rabb al-aalameen* ('Lord of the worlds'), and the use of the plural term 'worlds' conveys both the spiritual and physical realms. The heavens are referred to as multiple not only because of their plural form, but also as a mystical and symbolic quantity of seven.

Right According to Islamic cosmology, the earth, although a complete and natural ecosystem, is only a temporary abode for humankind.

Other references to celestial bodies in the Quran suggest a fixed place for the sun within the solar system and the on-going evolution of the heavens, both of which are in agreement with modern science.

There is also an allusion to the universe being in a state of continuous expansion, with the idea that at the 'end of time' it will be 'folded in' and 'the Earth flattened' (84:1–3). The Quran also suggests the possibility of the conquest of space – though claims that this will be achievable only by God's grace: 'if you so wish to penetrate regions of the Heavens and the Earth, then penetrate them, you will not penetrate them except by [God's] power' (55:33).

SOLAR SYSTEM

The Quran describes the sun, which we know to be a celestial body in a state of continuous combustion and a source of heat and light, as a *siraj* (torch), and the moon, an inert body that reflects a light source, as *nur* (light). The rotations of the earth around the sun and the moon around the earth are eloquently portrayed in the Quran (39:5) by the use of the verb *kawwara* (meaning 'to coil' or 'to wind'). The word is that used to describe the way in which a turban is wound around the head, which, like the earth's orbit, is elliptical.

The contribution of Muslim astronomers to scientific progress has been widely acknowledged, but the details contained in the Quran are often overlooked.

Right The planets revolve around the sun at the centre of our solar system. The Quran states that 'each floats along according to its own orbit' (36:37–40).

THE QURANIC GENESIS

THE STORY OF ADAM AND EVE IS COMMON TO THE TRADITIONS OF
JUDAISM, CHRISTIANITY AND ISLAM, BUT THE GENESIS ACCOUNT
GIVEN IN THE QURAN CONTAINS SOME SIGNIFICANT DIFFERENCES.

According to the monotheistic religions, Adam and Eve are the parents of the human family, who originally dwelled in the presence of God in his heavenly kingdom. The story of their temporary exile from paradise to earth becomes the primordial narrative of humankind, but the Quran does not refer to the 'Fall'.

IN THE BEGINNING
The Quran account emphasizes the common origin of men and women: 'O mankind! Be conscious of your Sustainer, who has created you out of one living entity, and out of it created its mate, and out of the two spread abroad a multitude of men and women' (4:1).

According to the Quran, the angels panicked when they saw God creating Adam, for they feared that he would make mischief on earth. However, God informed them they did not know his plans (2:30). According to a hadith, he then created Adam from soil taken from different parts of the earth and

eventually breathed into him. Later, when Adam was in need of a mate, God created Hawwa (Eve).

'MAN-MADE' WOMAN
Unlike the Old Testament story, the Quran relates that Eve was not derived from Adam, who, indeed, was not the first creation in male form. According to the Quran, God made a *nafs*, a soul, from which he then made Adam as a gendered male, then brought forth its female counterpart, Eve (4:1). Therefore, Adam and Eve share the same original source, one living entity, out of which both were made.

Eve's purpose in being created was, like Adam, to worship God. Yet, Adam desired her as a mate, 'so that he might dwell in peace with her' (7:189). The roles of men and women are therefore seen as wholly complementary in Islam.

THE 'ENEMY'
The Quran story relates that after God had created Adam, he asked the angels and *jinn* (genies) to bow

Above *The Genesis narrative from a 16th-century Ottoman Bible illustrates Adam and Eve's rejection from paradise to earth to toil on the land and procreate.*

to him, which they all did, except Shaytan (the devil, Iblis) (2:33-34). In his pride, Satan refused, arguing that he was made of a superior matter: smokeless fire. This disobedience led to his rejection from heaven (7:12). However, he vowed to lead men and women astray as revenge against God for this fall from grace. Adam and Eve enjoyed peace in heaven and closeness to God, until Satan seduced them to approach the forbidden tree. As a result of this, they earned God's displeasure and were sent to earth for a life of toil (7:16–21).

Islam differs from the Judaeo-Christian tradition, though, in teaching that Adam and Eve's disobedience did not result in the 'Fall' of humankind, because although they transgressed, Adam and Eve later repented for their sins and were forgiven by God (7:23). Nor do Muslims believe in

Left *This modern representation of Adam and Eve approaching the forbidden tree is by Egyptian artist Karima Ali.*

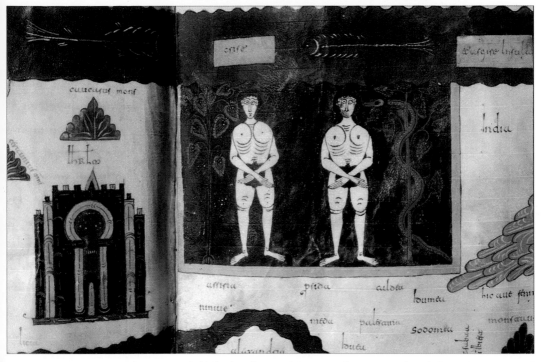

Above This 11th-century Spanish manuscript charts Adam and Eve's settlement on earth in the Middle East after their exclusion from paradise.

original sin, rather that every man and woman is born free of sin. According to the Quran, God did not blame Eve as the temptress, but held both Adam and Eve equally responsible (2:36). (In fact, according to one verse, 20:121, Adam alone was judged to be guilty.) The Quran relates that Adam and Eve both turned to God in repentance and that God accepted their repentance, promising them guidance from him (2:38).

Muslims believe that men and women, as well as Satan, will live on earth for an appointed term, after which they will face a Day of Judgement before God. Thereafter, according to their beliefs and deeds, they will face eternal paradise in heaven or punishment in hellfire (7:24–5, 6:51).

Above Some Muslim scientists have used evidence of fossilized life, especially fish, to argue that humankind did not evolve.

THE THEORY OF EVOLUTION

Among Muslims there is no consensus on the theory of evolution – that all living things are made from simple cell structures, which mutated, evolved and transformed into other life forms by becoming complex cell structures – especially as many perceive that this theory is incompatible with a belief in God. Islamic literature upholds that all living things are made from water (21:30) and claims that creation came about through the will of God. The Quran describes how Adam and Eve were made in perfect human form, and that different tribes and nations were then made to populate the earth (30:22, 49:13).

While many Muslims have rejected the idea that all creation was an accidental occurrence of cause and effect, some Muslim scientists have engaged with the theory.

ANGELS

ACCORDING TO THE QURAN, GOD CREATED ANGELS BEFORE HE MADE ADAM. FORMED FROM DIVINE LIGHT, ANGELS SERVE AS THE MEDIUM BETWEEN GOD'S HEAVENLY DOMAIN AND THE EARTH.

According to Muslim belief, Muhammad's first encounter with the divine was through Archangel Jibril, and believing in the existence of angels is therefore one of the six articles of faith in Islam. Angels are frequently referred to in the Quran in connection with a number of divine activities, from conveying holy scriptures and divine communications from God to his prophets and messengers, to aiding ordinary humans in their pursuit of righteousness.

THE NATURE OF ANGELS
In Islamic theology, angels (*malaaikah*) are celestial beings, who, according to prophetic hadith, are created from divine light (*nur*),

in contrast with humans, who are said to have been formed from dried clay and black mud (15:28). Unlike men and women, angels have not been given free will: they can carry out only the duties and tasks ascribed to them by God and can never disobey him nor act other than in accordance with his command (66:6).

According to a hadith, angels never sleep, nor do they require sustenance or have needs as humans do. They are usually invisible except when they choose to appear to humans, as Archangel Jibril frequently did to Muhammad. In order to implement God's divine will and commands, angels have been given certain qualities and powers in accordance with their particular functions: The Quran describes the angels as generally possessing two, three or four sets of wings (35:1), though it is believed that some individual angels have hundreds of wings.

ANGELIC DUTIES
The Arabic word for angel, *malak*, literally means 'to send on a mission', as does the Hebrew *malach* and the Greek *angelos*.

In addition to conveying God's divine revelations and carrying out his will, Islam teaches, angels

Left Angels and demons surround the enthroned King Solomon, in this scene from a Manuscript of the Khamsa *of Nizami.*

Above A 16th-century Ottoman Turkish text, Ajaibul-mukhluqat, *contains this illustration of angels prostrating in ranks.*

also bring God's blessings to humankind (33:43) and his warnings of impending punishment or catastrophes (16:2). Angels communicate between the *dhahir* (seen) and *batin* (unseen) worlds, and the Quran promises angelic support to believers who commit themselves to righteousness and sincere faith (41:30–2).

Some angels are believed to have been created to assist humans in employing their free will: each person decides what he or she wishes to do and angels help them in that decision or task (82:10–12). Each human being is appointed two 'recording angels', known as *kiraman katibeen*, each of whom records both good and bad deeds. According to a popular hadith, others roam the earth, searching to join gatherings where God is remembered, praised and

worshipped. There are also said to be hordes of angels that will both escort the wrongdoers to hell and greet those who enter paradise, whom they will welcome with the words 'Peace be unto you! Enter the Garden on account of the things you were doing' (16:32).

ARCHANGELS

Islam teaches that there are countless numbers of angels in existence with countless more constantly being created. From among these heavenly hosts, the Quran mentions a few angels by name that have a higher rank: Jibril (Gabriel), the archangel of revelation, who brought the divine message and scriptures to the prophets; Izrail, the angel of death, who is responsible for taking each human soul; Mikail (Michael), the angel of sustenance, who brings provision to the earth for humankind; and Israfil, the angel who is charged with blowing the trumpet at the 'final hour' before the Day of Judgement.

Above In Islam, jinn are unseen beings, created before humans and, like us, endowed with free will.

THE *JINN*

According to Islamic theology, Shaytan, also named Iblis, was not a 'fallen angel', but was one of the unseen spirit creatures known as the *jinn* (genies). In Islamic theology, the *jinn*, like humans, have been given free will and are divided into various categories and groupings: believers and non-believers, ethnic and racial groups, etc.

The Quran teaches that the *jinn* were created by God before humans (15:27), and while they are usually invisible to humans, the *jinn* are able to observe us (7:27).

The Prophet Muhammad taught that the *jinn* take one of three general forms: one type flies through the air, another type takes the physical form of an animal, appearing to humans sometimes as snakes and dogs, and the third is based in one place but travels around. The *jinn* do not normally interfere with the human realm unless they are disturbed or provoked by humans.

DIVINE REVELATIONS AND PROPHETHOOD

MUSLIMS BELIEVE THAT GOD COMMUNICATES TO HUMANKIND BY REVEALING HIS WILL THROUGH REVELATIONS AND HOLY SCRIPTURES BESTOWED ON SELECTED INDIVIDUALS KNOWN AS PROPHETS.

The process of communication between God and humankind is known in Islam as *risalah*, or 'prophethood'. According to Islam, divine communication began with the creation of Adam, the first man and prophet, and thereafter includes a series of divine messengers and holy scriptures to guide humankind from generation to generation in the straight path.

Muslims believe that God, in his infinite wisdom and mercy, has not only created men and women and given them a beautiful world in which to live, but that he has also provided them with guidance to enable them to follow the right course and live in peace and harmony with each other.

DIVINE MESSENGERS

Since the beginning of creation, Islam teaches, God has selected individuals to receive his divine guidance and act as perfect examples for men and women to follow. All of these divine prophets and messengers were human and all of them taught the same basic message as they called men and women to worship the One God. The Quran states that deprived of God's continued guidance, men and women would be lost and without purpose (103:1–3).

SENT TO ALL NATIONS

The Quran asserts that God has sent his divine prophets and messengers to every nation at different times (10:47, 13:7, 35:24). Muslims believe that not only did the prophets receive and transmit divine revelations and guidance to humankind, but also their lives serve as an example for believers on how to live a steadfast and virtuous life, in the face of both adversity and ultimate success.

Above Muhammad is believed to have received Quranic verses from Archangel Jibril. Other prophets, for example, Lot, also had angelic visitations.

According to the Quran, God guides his prophets in a number of different ways, including inspired dreams (Joseph), angelic visitations (Lot) and divine revelations (Moses). Muhammad said that the number of prophets sent to earth is 124,000, but the Quran mentions only 25 by name. Of these, 22 are also referred to in the Bible.

Islam distinguishes between prophets (*anbiya*), those who receive divine guidance, and messengers (*rusul*), who receive both divine guidance and holy scriptures. Thus, while all messengers are prophets, not all prophets are messengers; however, the role of both is to guide men and women to God. Muslims believe in all the prophets and messengers of God, from Adam to Muhammad, and the scriptures they received (2:285).

Left Quranic verses include 2:136, which confirms belief in the revelations and prophets that preceded Muhammad as mentioned in the Bible.

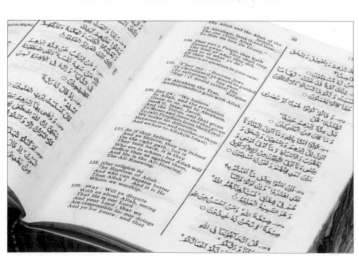

Above Muslim pilgrims offer prayers and blessings at the shrine containing the head of John the Baptist inside the Umayyad Mosque, Damascus, Syria.

SCRIPTURES

The Quran refers to a number of messengers and their scriptures by name, claiming that Moses (Musa) received the Torah (Tawrat), David (Dawud) the Psalms (Zabur), Jesus (Isa) the Evangel (Injil) and Muhammad the Quran. Muslims believe that while the details of how each of these scriptures was revealed differs, their purpose was the same: to carry God's guidance and laws for humankind to follow.

These scriptures have shaped and formed the religious and cultural practices of monotheistic faith communities throughout the ages. While some believers have strived to preserve their texts and religious laws, others have preferred to engage with the spirit of their religious scriptures, allowing for changes to translations, alternative interpretations and new meanings to the text. However, Muslims believe that of all the holy scriptures, only the Quran remains in its original form from the time of revelation (15:9). Nevertheless, the Quran claims that faithful believers from all the monotheistic traditions – Muslims, Christians and Jews, including the Sabians (possibly followers of John the Baptist) – will be rewarded by their Lord, without fear or grief, if they remain faithful to their original teachings (2:62).

Above A 16th-century bible showing Moses parting the Red Sea. Many Biblical narratives are considered divine and are replicated in the Quran.

OTHER HOLY BOOKS

In addition to the holy scriptures of the Torah of Moses, Psalms of David and the Evangel of Jesus, the Quran mentions the 'Scrolls of Abraham' (*Suhuf-i-Ibrahim*) (87:19). Although no record of Abraham's scriptures exists, the Old Testament recognizes Abraham as a prophet (Genesis 20:7). The Quran also refers to the Pentateuch, the first five books of the Old Testament, attributed to the original revelations of Moses.

The Quran does not rule out the possibility of revelations having been given to earlier religious figures in other traditions, such as Hinduism and Buddhism, because, it says, prophets of God were sent to every nation (10:47).

JESUS, PROPHET OF ISLAM

WITHIN ISLAM, JESUS (ISA IN ARABIC) IS CONSIDERED A UNIQUE AND IMPORTANT PROPHET. BOTH HE AND HIS MOTHER, MARY, ARE PORTRAYED IN SOME DETAIL WITHIN THE QURAN.

Mentioned by name many times in the Quran, Jesus is also referred to by other titles, including the *Masih* (Messiah). He is an important figure in the 'End of Time' events related in the Quran and hadith, and his mother, Mary, has a whole chapter of the Quran named after her (*Surah Maryam*, chapter 19).

MIRACULOUS CONCEPTION

The Quran calls Jesus (Isa) 'the word of God' (4:171, 3:45), 'servant of God' (19:30) and 'messenger of God' (61:6). In themselves the titles given to Jesus are not unique – for all of God's prophets are deemed to be his 'word', 'servant' and 'messenger' – but the miraculous birth of Jesus is exceptional.

The Quranic text compares Jesus' conception to that of the first man, Adam: 'Indeed, the likeness of

Above Muhammad prophesied Jesus' return, claiming that he would appear at the Umayyad Mosque, Damascus, Syria, and would then defeat the Antichrist.

Jesus in God's eyes is as Adam's likeness, he originated him from dust, and then said unto him "be" and he was.' (3:59). Many Muslim scholars of the Quran interpret this verse to explain Jesus as 'the word of God', because of the particular way in which he was conceived by God's simple word 'be'.

But the story of Jesus' birth as told in the Quran lacks elements of the Biblical narrative – there are no stable, wise men or stepfather Joseph. Instead, the story relates, Mary retreated to the desert and gave birth under the shade of a palm tree, in some considerable discomfort (19:22–6).

JESUS AND DIVINITY

Although the Quran affirms Jesus' miraculous conception (3:47), it rejects outright the notion of Jesus as divine or as 'the Son of God' (5:18, 19:88–92). To ascribe Jesus' divinity is a major and unforgivable sin in Islam known as *shirk* (associating partners to God).

While the Bible does not directly mention the Trinity (one God existing in three persons and one substance, Father, Son and Holy Spirit), the Quran refers to it in admonishment: 'They do blaspheme who say: "God is one of three, in a trinity: for there is no God except One God" '. (5:73)

Jesus is often referred to in the Quran as 'Jesus, son of Mary' (for example 19:34, 61:6) as a reminder of his humanity, and his genealogy is traced through the Israelites to Isaac, son of Ibrahim (Abraham), through his mother's lineage (the Bible, Luke 3:23–34). The Quran

Above A late 18th-century Ethiopian Christian liturgical parchment written in Geez, an ancient Ethiopian language, portrays Christ teaching his followers.

attributes a number of miracles to Jesus, but it gives details only of the first. The story tells that Jesus, as a newborn child, spoke in his mother's defence after she was accused of being unchaste by her people when she returned after giving birth to him (19:27–33).

THE CRUCIFIXION

As Islam is devoid of the notion of 'original sin' and the subsequent 'fall of man', so, too, the Christian theology of salvation of humankind through the sacrifice of Jesus as the 'Lamb of God' is absent. However, just as the Quran addresses the Christian claims of Jesus' divinity and the Trinity, it also contains verses relating to the event of his crucifixion. The Quran states: 'And they said, "We killed Christ Jesus, the son of Mary, the messenger of God" – but they killed him not, nor crucified him, but so it was made to appear to them'. (4:157)

This passage, although denying outright the crucifixion of Jesus and his death, continues to confirm his ascension to heaven: 'No, God raised him up unto Himself...'

(4:158). The Islamic teaching, then, is that Jesus was not crucified (or killed in any other way) by his enemies, although it was made to appear as such, but rather, God raised him up to paradise, where, the Quran relates, he dwells alive until he will reappear just before the Final Day (4:159).

JESUS AND THE END OF TIME
There are many hadiths relating to Jesus that give descriptions of his appearance and details of his miracles and prophetic mission. In the prophetic narrations relating to the events of the 'End of Time', Jesus is featured as an important character, who, it is claimed in a famous hadith, 'will break crosses, kill swine and abolish the *jizyah* (an exemption tax for religious minorities under Islamic rule) and wealth will pour forth to such an

Right The Quranic narrative of Jesus rejects the crucifixion but accepts the ascension, as illustrated in this 16th-century Ottoman manuscript painting.

extent that no one will accept it and one prostration of prayer will be better than the world and what it contains.'

Jesus is also mentioned in connection with the appearance of the Antichrist and the upheavals of the events connected to him. Another hadith informs that after defeating the Antichrist, Jesus will marry, have children and remain for 45 years before his death, when he will be buried next to the Prophet Muhammad in Madinah.

Below A medieval painting of Jerusalem features the al-Aqsa Mosque – the third holiest shrine in Islam. The city is central to Christianity, Judaism and Islam.

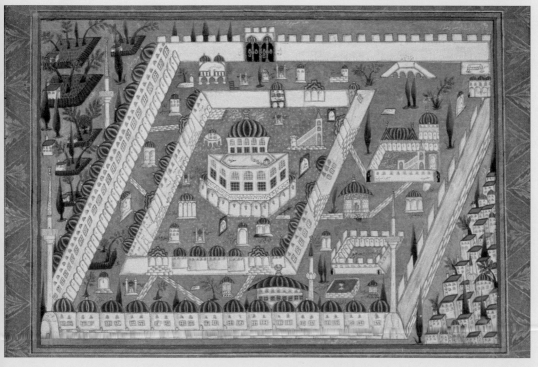

ISLAM AND OTHER FAITHS

RELIGIONS OFTEN EXCLUDE OTHER FAITHS FROM SALVATION AND HEAVEN. HOWEVER, THE QURAN HAS MADE SPACE FOR OTHERS, PARTICULARLY THOSE OF OTHER MONOTHEISTIC RELIGIONS.

The literate activity of polemics, where the world is seen in clearly divided black and white categories, has produced a spate of apologetic works, defending and explaining the faith for believers, that condemn other religions. This thinking has also featured in some Muslim societies through exclusivist interpretations of the Quran, in which only Muslims are considered worthy of heaven. However, there are also inclusive interpretations, which state that people of other faiths, as well as Muslims, are guaranteed a place in heaven.

THE QURANIC VIEW

As Islam presents itself as a continuation of previous divine religions, it is no surprise that it should encompass many people beyond its own religious tradition. The Quran affirms this in no uncertain terms: 'those who have faith, those who are Jews, Christians and Sabians (possibly followers of John the Baptist) – whoever has faith in God and the Last Day, and performs good deeds – will have their reward from their Lord. No fear will come upon them, nor shall they grieve' (2:62).

However, there is an apparent contradiction: while many Quranic verses include Jews and Christians, others chide them for the exclusive rights they claim over paradise: 'if the Last Home with God be for you specially, and not for anyone else, then seek ye death…' (2:94)

It also criticizes Jews and Christians for trying to make Muslims be like them, and instructs Muslims that their response should be 'Nay, (I would rather follow) the religions of Ibrahim, and he joined

Above A painting from 1686 depicts Muslim men in paradise. Debates about who goes to paradise have occupied many pages in Muslim writings.

not partners with Allah' (2:135). The finality of Islam is confirmed by the Quranic revelation 'if anyone desires a religion other than Islam, never will it be accepted of him…' (3:85)

Scholars of the Quran have attempted to explain this apparent contradiction in several ways. Some have suggested, for example, that certain verses were applicable only until the faith of the early believers was strengthened, after which subsequent revelations were given that nullified the previous rule. This would mean that while Jews and Christians were initially accepted into God's heaven, they were eventually excluded, because God accepted only Islam as a faith and way of life.

INCLUDING OTHERS

This exclusive interpretation of the Quran has sat very uncomfortably with some Muslim scholars. Their argument is that whatever God has revealed must surely be applicable for all times and places, until the end of the world. Therefore, they claim, scholars must not take on the 'role of God' and limit the

Left A Christian service at the Chaldean Seminary in Baghdad. Christianity is a continued feature of the religious landscape of Iraq.

Above A collection of Qurans in a bookcase in the Prophet's Mosque in Madinah. The Quran has many verses relating to people from other faiths.

application of those verses that include those of other monotheistic religions into the fold of faith.

Those that support this view claim that 'Islam' does not refer simply to the religion but to anyone submitting in peace to one God – 3:77 defines 'religion of Allah' as being that of everyone who submits to him. Muhammad's acceptance of *hunafa* would seem to corroborate this view – *hunafa* shunned paganism and believed in one God, but did not follow a formal religion.

Some historians of Islam have commented that the exclusivist interpretations of the Quran seem to have been in circulation and

popular at times when Islam was strong as a ruling entity: it has been argued, in other words, a position of superiority has led some Muslims to exclude others.

Many other commentaries of the Quran note that verses that are hard to interpret (*mutashabihah*) should not be interpreted, on the grounds that only God knows their true meanings. Instead, they should be taken at face value.

While other religions may not accept Muslims as a believing people, Muslims have a clear instruction in the Quran to accept others. This viewpoint urges Muslims to treat 'others' as equals, with respect and affection. Islam teaches that the final judgement is

God's, as only he knows who is truly devoted to Him, regardless of religious structures. Ultimately, heaven is his kingdom and he alone decides who enters it.

Right Jewish boys wearing kippas in Torah class in Tehran. The Jewish teacher is observing the Iranian dress code.

FREE WILL

ISLAM TEACHES THAT HUMAN BEINGS ARE UNIQUE AMONG EARTHLY
CREATURES IN HAVING BEEN GIVEN FREE WILL TO ENABLE THEM TO
CHOOSE RIGHT OR WRONG AND TO BELIEVE OR DISBELIEVE IN GOD.

Islamic theology teaches that men and women are to exercise their God-given free will. However, being endowed with choice entails both accountability (*masulliyyah*) and responsibility (*caliph*). Islam asserts that human free will is best employed in the establishment of God's will as revealed to his prophets and their holy scriptures.

DIVINE ORDER

According to Islam, the universe has been beautifully and perfectly created and divinely ordered, with the whole of nature and its innate goodness placed at the disposal of humankind. The purpose of nature is to enable men and women to do good and achieve felicity by divine design and order: 'The earth is full of signs of evidence for those who have certitude' (51:20).

Islam teaches that God is the ultimate cause of every event (*al-Awwal*) and the end of all action and things (*al-Akhir*), and men and women should therefore deem his will to be greater in moral worth than their own. This is not to say that they are removed of individual responsibility or account, but rather that they should reckon all that they do and choose to be in accordance with God's divine initiative.

The Quran claims that to assist humans in pursuit of their purpose, God has continuously provided evidence of his will through divine revelations (30:30, 33:62, 40:85).

Above The Quran teaches that although God knows everything, he has given humans free will over their beliefs and actions to test their obedience and faith.

Below A detail from a 14th-century Persian manuscript by al-Qazwini illustrates the endless possibilities of unlimited free will.

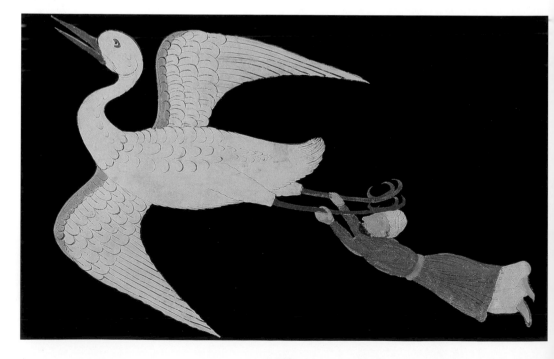

Indeed, Muslims see the universe itself as a living proof of God's sublime existence and predestined command (10:5–6).

PREDETERMINATION

Islam posits that the essential element of choice or free will in humankind results in only two outcomes, which are predetermined by God before each person's worldly existence. In God's schema, however, individual choice manifests itself as an exercise of free will that is devoid of divine predetermination. Because God knows that which angels and human beings do not, he alone has prior knowledge not only of what each man and woman will or will not do, but also of the final abode of every human being.

KNOWING GOD'S WILL

The Quran contains many passages concerning the divine attributes and names of God but offers little in the way of theological doctrine. Hadiths seem to advise against trying to fathom divine will (*qadar*): 'Do not cogitate on God, but on the creation of God' and 'earlier communities perished because they dwelled on discussions regarding *qadar*.'

Traditionally, Muslims have divided into two distinct – if not opposing – groups in their pursuit of knowing God. The first, the legates (*fuqaha*), have historically focused theological discussions on what is manifest (*dhahir*) of God's will through law (Shariah) and jurisprudence (*fiqh*): that is, they explore what God has permitted to be known about himself through the Quran and sunnah.

The second group, the Sufis, or ascetics, have maintained that God is best known through experience. They believe that God unveils his divine nature to those who seek to draw near to him through inner dimensions (*batin*) of worship. The medieval scholar Ibn Tamiyyah

(1263–1328) concluded that 'the truth [regarding Divine will] does not belong to one party exclusively but is divided among all groups'.

Neither the legates' scriptural conformity nor the inner spiritual purification of the ascetics could in themselves solve the problem of tensions that surfaced around the arguments about divine will. However, the classical scholar al-Ghazali (1058–1111) synthesized the rationalism of the legates with Sufi practices of 'living faith' in his *Revival of the Religious Sciences*, which set the Shariah in the context of an experienced religion, in which love of God was the main motivator.

Above This miniature Ottoman astrological zodiac chart dates from 1583. It neatly, if speculatively, illustrates man's divine predestination.

HUMAN WILL

Theological discussions regarding the correct understanding of divine will can detract from the Islamic teaching that every individual is in fact responsible for his or her own actions. Humankind's true vocation, according to Islam, lies in the moral realm, where fulfilment of God's will can take place only in freedom. In other words, to truly prosper, humankind must exercise free will in accordance with God's will.

THE STAGES OF HUMAN EXISTENCE

IN ISLAMIC THEOLOGY, THIS WORLD IS SEEN AS A TEMPORAL AND TRANSIENT ONE, THROUGH WHICH HUMAN BEINGS ARE JOURNEYING ON THEIR WAY TO THE PERMANENT REALMS OF THE AFTERLIFE.

The Quran reminds humankind that 'to God we belong and to Him is the return' (2:156), and the reality that, 'every soul shall taste death' (3:185). But death is not seen by Muslims as the final end, only the termination of worldly life and physical existence.

THE ABODE OF SOULS

Muhammad taught that there are stages of human existence that both precede and succeed this worldly life. The first stage is said to be the 'abode of the souls' (*dar al-arwah*), the place where the spirit (*ruh*) of every human being abides before the creation of its physical body.

Muhammad said that when a person senses familiarity on first meeting someone, it is because their souls have recognized each other from the previous abode, suggesting a continuum and direct connection between the abode of the soul and earthly existence.

Muslim scholars have concluded that the ego-self has three states of being, which are determined by the Quranic terms: *ammarah* (12:53), prone to evil; *lawwamah* (75:2 – *wa la uqsimu bin nafsil lawwamah*, 'And no! I swear by the accusing soul'), aware of evil but resistant through patience, faith and repentance; and *mutmainnah* (89:27), the highest

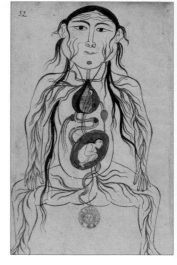

Above This 15th-century drawing by a Muslim artist shows a woman carrying a baby. A hadith explains the soul is blown into the foetus by an angel.

stage of belief, satisfaction and peace. Islamic theology teaches that the soul's earthly struggle is largely believed to be that of the contesting desires between his or her ego (*nafs*), which yearns for worldly materialism, and his or her soul (*ruh*), which seeks the higher spiritual state of being.

EXISTENCE IN THE WOMB

The Quran refers to the creation of human beings in stages (*atwara*) (71:14), drawing attention to several points in the reproductive process (75:37, 23:14, 39:6). A hadith explains the connection between the pre-existing soul and the physical body: 'Verily the creation of each one of you is brought together in his mother's belly for forty days in the form of seed, then he is a clot of blood for a like

Left This 18th-century Ottoman-Armenian dish shows Mikail (Michael), in angelic form, removing the pious soul from the mouth of a deceased person.

period, then a morsel of flesh for a like period, then there is sent to him an angel who blows his soul (*ruh*) into him.'

WORLDLY EXISTENCE

According to the Quran, when God declared that he was about to create humankind, he commanded the angels: 'When I have fashioned him and breathed into him of my spirit, then obediently prostrate before him' (15:29). The verse is taken to imply that only when the spirit was breathed into Adam's body did he become superior to the angels and God's befitting vicegerent (caliph) (6:165).

In Arabic, worldly life is termed *dunya*, which means something lowly, insignificant, without value. The Quran makes a value distinction between this life and the afterlife, or hereafter, which is seen as the first as well as the final resting place of humankind: 'What is the life of this world but play and amusement? But best is the home in the hereafter, for those who are righteous, will you then not understand?' (6:32)

EXISTENCE IN THE GRAVE

Death is the inevitable end of worldly life, but the Quran teaches that 'He [God] created death and life, that He may try which of you is best in deeds' (67:2). According to hadith, Muhammad claimed that the soul is taken from the body at the point of death, but that it is reunited with it after burial.

Some Muslims believe that in the grave, the human soul is visited by angels, who question it about its religious beliefs and its deeds. If the soul has believed and worked righteousness, it is given a view of paradise as a reward to come. However, if the soul has denied God and committed evil, it is tormented and punished in the grave as a taste of the eternal punishment of hell (6:93–4).

THE AFTERLIFE

For Muslims, death is seen not as the end but merely as a transition from one state of being into another in the soul's journey back to the creator, who will reward righteous believers and punish evil wrongdoers (10:4).

The Quran claims that at the 'Final Hour', a trumpet will sound and all souls will be resurrected and recreated in their original physical

Above The city of Najaf, Iraq, has one of the largest cemeteries in the world and is a preferred place of burial for Shiah Muslims globally.

form to stand in rows before their creator (18:99–101, 78:17). Each person will then be questioned by God regarding what he or she believed and did, and will be rewarded accordingly, with either paradise or hellfire.

143

FRIDAY: DAY OF CONGREGATION

THE IDEA OF GOD RESTING ON THE SEVENTH DAY AFTER CREATING THE WORLD IS REJECTED IN ISLAMIC THEOLOGY. RATHER, THIS IS SEEN AS THE DAY ON WHICH HE ESTABLISHED HIS THRONE OF AUTHORITY.

Above In Christianity, Sunday is the traditional day of corporate worship and rest and it is observed from the teachings of the Old Testament creation story.

In Muslim countries, Friday is the day of congregation (*Jumuah*), but it is not a day of rest. While many people may not attend work on the day of *Jumuah*, working or earning a living on this day is not prohibited by Islamic law. This reflects the Muslim belief that, for God, 'no tiredness can seize Him, nor sleep' (2:255).

THE 'SEVENTH DAY'
Although Friday is the day of congregation in Islam and is even *Jumuatul Mubarak* ('Blessed Friday') in some hadiths, it is not equated with the Judaeo-Christian concept of the Sabbath as the 'seventh day' or a 'day of rest' (Genesis 2:1–3).

Islamic theology terms God as *al-Kahliq* (the creator), who is also *al-Hayy* (the ever-living) and *al-Qayyum* (the self-subsisting), and, as such, he is transcendent and wholly other. That is, God as creator is far removed from the qualities of his

creation and the frailties of humankind (2:55). The Biblical concept that God exists as a 'Heavenly Father' (Matthew 23:9, 24:36 and 26:39) suggests that he may possess human-like qualities or traits: anger, jealousy, hunger and tiredness. The notion that God would have human attributes or that he would need to rest after the creation, or even at all, is contrary to the concept of God in Islam.

In the Quranic accounts of the genesis story, after God created the world, he established his Throne of authority over his creation as the final act of his supremacy over it.

THE 'THRONE' OF GOD
A number of verses in the Quran refer to the 'Throne of God' (*al-arsh*), and one verse is known specifically as *ayat al-kursi*, or 'the verse of the seat' (2:255). Here, God's 'Throne' symbolizes his authority, the seat of his power and

knowledge. The Quran asserts that to imagine the realm of the ever-expanding universe and everything contained within it is a totally unfathomable task for any human being, yet so great are God's power, will, wisdom and authority, that they encompass everything within the cosmos and beyond.

According to Islamic theology, the expansive infinity of the universe is a reflection of God's absolute reality (16:12, 22:18). God's activity, eternal nature, perfection and self-sustenance represent his constant and direct involvement with all the realms of his creation.

ADAM AND FRIDAY
The Quran implies that Adam was the last of creation because God informs the angels 'I will create a vicegerent on Earth', to which the

Left Friday is the day of Jumuah or congregation in Islam, but business and social interactions are not prohibited, either before or after prayers.

Left Adam and Eve are depicted playing innocently in paradise. Muslims believe they were created on a Friday and that Judgement Day, too, will occur on a Friday.

hadith relates that Satan, Adam and Eve were sent down to earth from paradise on a Friday.

A DAY OF WORSHIP

The monotheistic traditions of Judaism, Christianity and Islam each have a day of congregational worship: the Jews celebrate Shabbat on Saturday, Christians worship together on Sunday and Muslims participate in *Jum'a* on Friday.

Beyond the theological and canonical justifications for the different days of congregation within these three religious traditions, the overarching principle is that each religious community should meet together to remember, celebrate and praise God on a weekly basis. The instruction in Islam to suspend work and trading in order to attend *Jumuah* is prescribed in the Quran, in a specific chapter entitled *Al-Jumuah*. The passage continues 'and when the prayer is ended, then disperse in the land and seek God's bounty, and remember God much that you may be successful' (62:9–10).

angels ask, 'will you not place therein a thing that will cause much bloodshed while we praise and glorify Your hallowed name?' In his reply, God affirms his all-encompassing knowledge and wisdom: 'Indeed, I know that which you know not' (2:30).

In a hadith, Muhammad said that God had created Adam on a Friday, and that he then taught Adam the names of all things, something the angels could not do, He then commanded all created things to bow before Adam in acknowledgement of his supremacy. All did so except for Satan, a *jinn* (a

genie, or creation of the unseen, who, like humans, has been endowed with freedom of choice), who chose to disobey God because he was jealous of Adam (2:34).

According to the Quran, human beings have been created in the 'best of moulds', but those who follow their temptations and lusts become debased, whereas the righteous shall have unfailing rewards (95:4–6). A prophetic

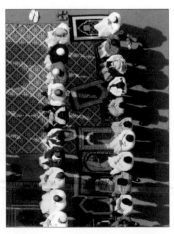

Right Muslim men attend Friday prayers at the Prophet Muhammad's Mosque in the holy city of Madinah, Saudi Arabia.

THE DAY OF JUDGEMENT

THE QURAN SPEAKS OF A 'FINAL HOUR' – THE END OF THE WORLD –
WHEN MEN AND WOMEN WILL BE RESURRECTED FROM THEIR GRAVES
AND GATHERED TOGETHER TO STAND IN JUDGEMENT BEFORE GOD.

Belief in the Day of Judgement (*al-yawm al-akhir*) is a fundamental creed and one of the six articles of faith in Islam. Muslims believe that on this day, every person who has ever lived will be called to give individual account in front of their creator for what they believed and did during their life on earth.

The Day of Judgement is an aspect of Islamic faith that belongs to the unseen realm (*al-ghayb*) – as do God, his angels, resurrection and the hereafter of paradise and hellfire. All the Islamic prophets taught their people to worship God and to believe in the hereafter with certainty of faith.

END-TIME EVENTS

The Prophet Muhammad taught that a number of minor and major events, or signs, will precede the Day of Judgement. According to sayings attributed to him, minor events would include a change in the male–female ratio, with women outnumbering men by 50 to 1, the construction of lofty buildings by the Bedouin Arabs and a decrease in religious knowledge among the general populace.

Major events that are mentioned in the Quran include the appearance of the Gog (*yajuj*) and Magog (*majuj*), wild people who, it is said, will break free from the barrier that restrains them and swarm the world, spreading mayhem (21:96). The Quran also refers to a 'beast' that it says will come out from the earth and address humankind with lies and falsehood, which they will believe because they doubted

the promise of God (27:82). Other hadiths also inform and warn of the Antichrist (*al-Masih al-Dajjal*), who will misguide humankind and create wars and strife.

According to hadith, other major catastrophic events will include the appearance of the promised Muslim Mahdi ('guided one'), who will fight the Antichrist; the eruption of volcanic fires in Yemen; the rising of the sun from the West, and the descent of the prophet Jesus from heaven.

SIGNS IN NATURE

Although the Quran does not make clear the precise chronology of these events, it does tell of signs in the natural world that will precede the 'Final Hour', including 'gales that rage on and on, scattering things around…'. It also promises that it will be a day 'when stars fade away and the sky splits open, when mountains are pulverized…'. (77:2–3, 8–10) According to the Quran, once all of the above events

Above An illustration of the beast of the Apocalypse taken from Zubdat al-Tawarikh *by Sayyid Loqman Ashuri.*

have occurred, the angel Israfil will blow a trumpet. Every person (except martyrs) will then be brought from their graves (78:17–20), where, Islam teaches, they will already have experienced a form of reward or punishment in a transient spiritual state – either *al-araaf* (heights) or *al-barzakh* (purgatory) – that will have been decided by what they believed and how they lived during their worldly existence.

The pre-Islamic Arabs mocked Muhammad's warning of a bodily resurrection, and in the Quran are quoted as saying, 'What! When we are reduced to bones and dust, should we really be raised up as

Left This medieval French painting shows the three-headed Antichrist being aided by the devil and by humans. The Antichrist is central to Islamic – as well as Christian – eschatology.

a new creation?' (17:49) But the Quran gives the reply that he who created humankind in the first instance will do so again (17:50–1).

JUDGEMENT BOOK

The Quran says that on the Day of Judgement, most of humankind will be lined up in ranks and every person will be brought forward to be judged by God, and a 'book' accounting for every deed will be placed before them. The sinful will be terrified, saying, 'Ah! Woe to us! What a book this is! It leaves out nothing small or great, but takes account thereof!' (18:49). The verse continues, 'They will find all that they did, placed before them: and none will thy Lord treat with injustice.' For this reason the Day of Judgement is also known in Islam as 'the Day of Absolute Truth' (*yawm al-haq*) (78:39).

Above Muslim martyrs await the Day of Judgement with Ali – depicted symbolically as the 'Lion of God' – watching over their graves.

HEAVENLY MARTYRS

Islam teaches that anyone who dies in the path of God, pursuing righteousness and defending justice in the service of humanity, should be considered a martyr. It is believed that these martyrs will enter paradise directly, without experiencing death as others do (2:154, 3:169), and without being judged. Muhammad said that they will be allowed to intercede on behalf of their loved ones on Judgement Day and will have lofty mansions with many spouses in paradise near God.

The Quran warns that while successful believers will be rewarded by God with eternal paradise, disbelieving wrongdoers will be punished for ever in hellfire.

Below Medieval representations of the damned commonly depict horrific scenes of eternal blazing torture and punishment, often based on the descriptions of divine texts.

HEAVEN

IN ISLAM, HEAVEN IS SEEN AS THE DOMAIN OF ALLAH, AND THE
ETERNAL RESTING PLACE AND ULTIMATE REWARD FOR ALL HIS
RIGHTEOUS SERVANTS. IT IS THE GOAL OF EVERY MUSLIM.

The Quran and hadith contain many descriptions of heaven, but it is a place that belongs to the unseen aspects (*al-ghayb*) of Islamic beliefs and as such can be imaged only by analogy. Indeed, Muslims believe that its realities are far removed from any descriptions of worldly language and the limits of human imagination.

ORIGINAL ABODE

Muhammad foretold that God has prepared for his servants delights that 'no eye has seen nor any ear has heard and has never occurred to a human heart'. Paradise, or heaven, is the place where God and his Throne are believed to exist, surrounded by countless angels singing his praises and extolling peace (23:86, 39:75).

Islam teaches that the righteous and faithful who attain paradise will find that the desire of their soul will be fulfilled, because they will be returning to their original abode and that of the primordial parents of humankind, Adam and Eve. The Quran teaches that before Satan's jealousy led him to tempt Adam and Eve to take fruit from the forbidden tree, this first man and woman lived in peace and bliss within the Garden of Paradise (2:35). Ever since the momentous event of their expulsion from this garden, their believing and righteous descendants have been striving to return to their original abode in the company of Allah and his angels (6:60, 10:45–6).

DWELLERS OF PARADISE

The reward of returning to the Garden of Paradise is not open to all, however, and the rightful dwellers, according to the Quran and hadith, need to be very worthy souls. Entrance to heaven is not automatic simply on profession of a religious creed or doctrine. Indeed, the Quran warns against such complacency: 'it is not by your wishes, nor by the wishes of the People of the Book [Jews and Christians]: whoever does wrong shall be punished for it, and he will not find other than God as protector or helper' (4:123). Paradise, therefore, is believed by Muslims to be reserved for those who have pure faith and good deeds (2:62).

DESCRIPTIONS OF HEAVEN

The reward promised to the righteous is clearly presented in the Quran, but there is no structure

Above In this 10th-century drawing from a Persian manuscript, Adam and Eve are depicted in the Garden of Paradise – they spent the first part of their lives in heaven.

to paradise suggested in the text. However, it is generally believed to consist of various realms – and some Muslims conclude that people are admitted to each realm depending on their righteousness.

Both the Quran and hadith offer descriptions of heaven's features. It is said to have eight entrances, one of which, the gate of *rayhan*, is as an exclusive entrance for those who were faithful in their religious fasting. The Quran describes its gardens having rivers and fruits of every kind and desire (47:15) and says that it will be neither too hot nor too cold and will provide shade for its inhabitants (76:13–14). There are special fountains of pure water, milk, honey and heavenly wines free from intoxicants and drinks of camphor and *zanjabil*.

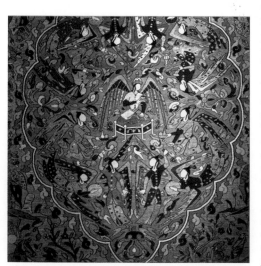

Left This Indian carpet displays the many pleasures of paradise. Faces have been obscured, as some Muslims prohibit figurative art.

Above In Islam, paradise is believed to have various levels of rewards, as shown in this 11th-century Persian painting.

and *talh* (thought to be a fruit similar to plantain or banana) trees in abundance (56:28–9). Other food delights will include inexhaustible selections of meats, particularly the flesh of fowls (56:21).

LIVING IN PARADISE

As a reward for their goodness, proclaims the Quran, the dwellers of paradise will have all that they desire (9:21–2), and describes how they will spend their time. They will wear musk and clothes of the purest silk, with gold and pearl jewellery (22:23) and, reclining on raised thrones, they will be greeted by their Lord (36:56–8) in an atmosphere free of idle or vain talk (19:62). They will be served by youths with plates and goblets of silver and gold (56:17–18) and will live in tents 97km (60 miles) high and made of pearls. The Quran also refers to heavenly companions (2:25), wide-eyed maidens (56:22–4) and beautiful, pure spouses for the righteous (55:70).

Above A beautiful green bird perches on a rock by flowers at a riverside. A hadith states the souls of Muslim martyrs will be housed in the bodies of green birds in paradise.

(a ginger-based beverage), all served from ornate golden goblets (47:15, 76:15–17). It is said that the fruits of the Garden of Paradise are in pairs (55:52), with pomegranates, dates

HELL

ISLAM TEACHES THAT AS GOD CREATED HEAVEN, SO HE ALSO MADE HELL, WHICH THE QURAN DECLARES IS PREPARED FOR ALL THOSE WHO REJECT FAITH AND COMMIT SINS AND GRAVE INJUSTICES.

When God granted humans free will, teaches the Quran, it was conditional to a covenant that they would faithfully worship none but God and live in accordance with divine will (2:38–9). Muslims believe that while the faithful will live forever in paradise, disbelieving evildoers will have their recompense in hell (3:131, 78:21–2).

DESPISED ABODE

Prophetic sayings regarding hell imply that it already exists as a place of punishment waiting to receive wrongdoers. The Quran confirms this: 'truly Hell is lying in wait' (78:21), and says that it will be filled with *jinn* and men (11:19).

Where hell is positioned in relation to heaven is not made clear, but it is described as a bottomless pit of fiercely burning fire (101:8–11), into which evildoers will be thrown, suggesting that it lies some way underneath heaven. Like heaven, it is believed to have different levels, which relate to the quantity and gravity of the sins of its inhabitants (6:123).

The Quran vividly describes hell as a place of unimaginable terror and suffering, in which dwellers receive no respite from their eternal punishment. Hell also appears to be an abode of continuous purgatory, whose inhabitants 'will neither die nor live' (20:74).

Above A 15th-century painting provides a gruesome insight into the punishments of hell.

DWELLERS OF HELL

Compared with other sacred texts, the Quran contains far more descriptions of heaven and hell, particularly in the earlier revealed verses from the Makkan period. This increased focus on the hereafter appears to underline the central theme of inevitable divine judgement. While there are numerous depictions of the abodes of heaven and hell in the Quran and prophetic traditions, it would be wrong to interpret them literally. This is because the real nature and exact descriptions of the hereafter are known only to God. However, Islam teaches that there definitely will be compensation and reward for good deeds and punishment for all evil ones.

On the Day of Judgement, relates the Quran, hell will be asked if its blazing eternal fire has been satiated with the souls of men and women as its fuel, to which it will reply, 'Are there some more (available)?' (50:30)

Left This painting from the 16th century gives a frighteningly graphic and detailed portrayal of the torments and fires of hell.

The response will be that hordes of humans will be dragged in chains into the fire by cursing angels (69:30–2). The Quran names a few dwellers of hell, including: the Pharaoh who drove out Moses and the Israelites (7:103–41, 11:96–9); and Abu Lahab (the disbelieving uncle of Muhammad) and his wife (111:1–5).

DESCRIPTIONS OF HELL

There are various different words used in the Quran to describe hell: *al-hutamah* (human crusher), *al-jaheem* (ferocious fire), *jahannam* (hellfire), *ladha* (fire of hell), *saeer* (burning fire) and *saqar* (flaming inferno). In addition to these six terms, the generic Arabic word for fire (*an-nar*), is also used, and, collectively, the passages create an acutely disturbing and horrifically graphic idea of the place of hell.

According to a hadith, the depth of hell is such that a stone thrown into it would take 70 years to reach the bottom, and so vast that it will be dragged forth on the Day of Judgement by 70,000 angels pulling 70,000 reins. The Quran teaches that hell has seven gates, suggesting seven levels, each assigned to a different class of sinner (15:44), and that 19 angels guard it (74:30). At the centre of hell, its fiercest point, is said to be a tree called *az-zaqqum*, bearing fruit of flaming fire that is served as food to the worst evildoers (37:62–7, 44: 43–6, 56:51–6).

PUNISHMENTS OF HELL

The Quran claims that the fuel of the fire of hell will be humans, *jinn* and stones (2:24, 72:14–15). Hell's punishments will be in relation to the sins committed (15:43–4). Scholars are keen to point out that once in heaven, the fear of being removed does not hang over a dweller, but once in hell, the hope of escaping is always possible – God's mercy is infinite. The allegorical

interpretations which stress God's love also indicate that despite evil actions, a person may escape the torments of hell, if God so wishes. Those who used money belonging to orphans will be made to eat raw fire (4:10), as will those who changed or tampered with the scriptures of God for a small profit (2:174).

Above A vision of hell on earth as a volcano erupts. Prophetic narrations describe hellfire as being 70 times hotter than any earthly fire.

Below A detail from an 18th-century Geez manuscript shows sinners burning in the eternal fire as hell's guardians hold them in chattels and taunt them.

CHAPTER 4

WORSHIP AND RELIGIOUS PRACTICE

An oft-quoted hadith states that Islam is built upon five pillars: the declaration (*shahadah*) that there is no God but the One God, Allah, and that Muhammad is his final messenger; the five daily prayers (*salah*); paying alms to the poor (*zakah*); fasting in the month of Ramadhan (*sawm*); and performing a pilgrimage (*Hajj*) to Makkah, if resources permit.

Festivals capturing the essence of these pillars are celebrated throughout the year. The most frequent is the celebration of *Jumuah*, Friday, the day of congregational prayer. The greatest Muslim festivals of the year are the two *Eids*, marking the end of Ramadhan and *Hajj*. Several others, such as *Mawlid*, the birthday of the Prophet, and *Miraj*, Muhammad's night journey to heaven, are widely celebrated in some parts of the Muslim world.

Because worship and prayer are the central purposes of life, places of prayer are an important part of Muslim civilization. The mosque, as both a building and an institution, is a proud place of gathering.

Opposite The five pillars are the realization of faith in Islam. Prayer is central, and when combined with celebration, as here on Eid ul-adha *in al-Abbas Mosque in Kerbala, Iraq, all the family attend.*

Above Nepali Muslims attend the last Eid ul-fitr *prayer at the Kashmiri Mosque in Kathmandu, which marks the end of the holy fasting month of Ramadhan.*

SHAHADAH: DECLARING BELIEF IN ONE GOD

THE CENTRAL DOCTRINE IN ISLAM IS THE *SHAHADAH*, WITNESSING AND DECLARING THE BELIEF THAT THERE IS NO GOD BUT THE ONE GOD (*ALLAH* IN ARABIC), AND THAT MUHAMMAD IS HIS MESSENGER.

Religious civilizations can often be summed up by one central doctrine or figure: in Islam, the *shahadah* embodies *tawhid*, the doctrine of belief in one God, and *risalah*, that of the prophethood of Muhammad, the central figure of Islam. These two facets of the creed are connected and interdependent; for Muslim belief to be present, both parts of the declaration must be affirmed.

NEGATION IN BELIEF

For Muslims, belief in God cannot exist without first negating the possibility of any other form of deity. Thus, the conviction in one God is first by the negative statement 'there is no god...', followed by the affirmation '...but Allah'. This briefest of affirmations is the richest in meaning in Islamic life, and, according to a hadith, it is also the weightiest in God's eyes. The entire body of Islamic civilization is seen as being encapsulated in the phrase *la ilaha illal-lah, Muhammad rasulul-lah*.

SHAHADAH AS LIFE

As a recitation, or declaration, the *shahadah* constitutes the first words that a Muslim baby hears, and the

Above An Iraqi Muslim holds up his prayer beads after Friday prayer in Baghdad, as he recites the shahadah *as praise of God.*

last words heard by a dying Muslim. In between these points of birth and death, the entire circle of life hinges on these words, which a Muslim will recite countless times in one day – when waking up, when washing, in the five daily prayers, in supplication. In fact, the opening words of Muslim speeches

Below An oil painting by Jean-Léon Gérôme from 1865 depicts Muslim men declaring their faith through prayer.

THE HADITH OF THE PILLARS OF ISLAM

'Islam is built on five pillars: declaring that there is no god but Allah and that Muhammad is the messenger of Allah; establishment of the five daily prayers; payment of the poor due; pilgrimage to the House (Makkah); and fasting (in Ramadhan).'

Bukhari's hadith collection

and documents are usually the *basmalah*. Even in conversation in social settings, Muslims will often intersperse their talk with this declaration, as a reminder of the presence of God, his existence, his oneness and his love.

MUHAMMAD IN THE *SHAHADAH*

For a Muslim, the belief in God is via Muhammad the Messenger. It is therefore incumbent upon Muslims to affirm Muhammad's prophetic mission. In order to follow God's laws, a Muslim must study the life example and teachings of the Prophet, as he is believed to embody the perfect way to live. It is impossible for a Muslim to separate belief in God and his Prophet.

Uttering the simple sentence of *shahadah*, devoid of any other ritual, brings people into the fold of Islam, and, regardless of their actions, they are henceforth considered 'Muslim', meaning 'submitting to God's will'.

CERTAINTY OF KNOWING

However, some scholars believe that the best form of Muslim life is that where the *shahadah* is not just orally uttered, but practised, held in the heart and translated into peaceful actions.

Indeed, a true confession of faith should not be an intellectual activity exclusively – but also an emotional, sensory (hence physical), rational and spiritual one. Muslims believe that experiencing the declaration of faith on all four levels leads one to *yaqin*, the absolute certainty of knowing, seeing and believing the truth (69:51 and 102:5–7).

While the other four pillars of Islam are ritual acts of worship, evolving around this declaration, the *shahadah* is a pillar of belief.

Left A silver vessel bearing the shahadah: la ilaha illal-lah, Muhammad rasulul-lah *(there is no God but God, and Muhammad is his messenger).*

SHAHADAH AS A PRACTICE

The *shahadah* is illustrated in practice through the Treaty of Hudaybiyah, where peace was concluded between Muslims and the Makkan pagan Arabs. Many then came to pledge their allegiance to the Prophet and God, with him placing his hand over theirs (48:10).

Muhammad was instructed later that if pagan women came to him, swearing belief in one God, obeying the Prophet and vowing not to commit major sins, he should accept their oaths (60:12). However, the women would hold the end of a cloth that he held, rather than taking his hand.

In modern times in the West, *shahadah* often takes place by confirming belief in the one God and in the prophethood of Muhammad in both the vernacular and Arabic. The declaration of a convert is often witnessed by two people, although this is not regarded as strictly necessary, as God Himself is believed to be a witness to belief.

Above A South Korean soldier converts to Islam. Conversion is a private matter before God, but many new Muslims choose to recite the shahadah *before witnesses.*

SALAH: THE FIVE DAILY PRAYERS

SALAH IS THE MEANS WHEREBY, FIVE TIMES A DAY, MUSLIMS HOLD COMMUNION WITH GOD. IT MUST BE CARRIED OUT IN A STATE OF RITUAL PURITY, AND WITH THE INTENTION TO WORSHIP HIM ALONE.

Salah, the second pillar of Islam, has both individual significance and communal importance. While often translated as 'prayer', the Arabic word *salah* specifically refers to 'communication'. The worshipper is therefore believed to be in direct communion with God: a hadith claims that *salah* is the ascension to heaven for the believer. The purpose of *salah* is solely to worship and remember God (20:14).

THE FIVE PRAYERS

Salah is compulsory, offered five times a day – at dawn (*fajr*), noon (*dhuhr*), late afternoon (*asr*), sunset (*maghrib*) and night (*isha*) (11:114) – facing the *Kaabah*. It is always recited in Arabic, the language of the Quran: Muslim brotherhood is central to *salah*; thus, Muslims can join *salah* in mosques in any part of the world.

Salah is preceded by the *adhan*, the call to prayer, which pours out of mosque minarets with the melodious voice of the *muadhdhin*, the caller. In many cities, such as Istanbul, one *adhan* is joined by another until the whole city rings with God's call. *Salah* itself is made up of units of prayer, *rakaah*, which vary in the prayers. The opening chapter of the Quran is recited in every unit, followed by other verses. God is praised and his blessings are invoked on Muhammad.

Performed standing, bowing, prostrating and sitting, *salah* can be offered individually or, preferably, in congregation. While it can be recited at home, at work, in the open or when travelling, *salah* carries most spiritual rewards when offered in a mosque.

WUDU

Salah can only be performed in a state of ritual bodily purity. This means that Muslims and their clothes must be clean at the time of prayer. *Wudu*, ritual ablution, therefore precedes *salah*,

Above *Minarets of the al-Azhar Mosque in Cairo, Egypt. The* adhan, *call to prayer, which precedes* salah, *is heard from the minarets ringing across cities throughout the Muslim world.*

and consists of washing the hands, mouth, nose, face, ears, head, arms and feet. Without sacred purity, and without intention, *salah* cannot be offered.

While *wudu* suffices for general purity, such as after waking up or using the toilet, a full bodily wash (*ghusl*) is required after sexual intercourse or menstruation.

PRAYER AS DISCIPLINE

Salah offers Muslims discipline and the chance to empty the mind entirely of its preoccupations. For Muslims, *salah* can be a powerful reorientation both spiritually and physically, as the body is engaged in prayer just as much as the soul. For believers, each movement of prayer carries deep spiritual significance,

Left *Before prayer, ritual ablutions,* wudu, *are performed from a fountain at Qarawiyyin Mosque in Fez, Morocco.*

where every limb is seen as turning its attention to its Creator. Muslims demonstrate their belief in God's greatness and their dependence on him in the act of prostration, of putting the most noble and prized part of the body, the head, before God, in submission to his will.

ORDAINING OF *SALAH*

When Muhammad was chosen as a prophet, he was at first told to purify himself and stand before God in worship. Eventually, he was asked to encourage his followers to do the same. However, it was not until 620, the tenth year of Muhammad's prophethood, that *salah* was institutionalized. This is said to have happened during the Prophet's night ascension to heaven (17:1), when, Muslims believe, he was miraculously transported to Jerusalem and then to the heavens via al-Buraq, a winged horse.

A hadith states Muhammad had conversations with God, during which 50 prayers a day were ordained. However, the story relates that on his way back through heaven, Muhammad met Moses, who told him to return to God and ask for the prayers to be limited in

*Above Sunset prayer (*maghrib*) is offered in the Haram Mosque in Makkah. The* Kaabah *sits in the centre.*

number. God reduced the required prayers to five a day, but promised that those offering them would receive the rewards of at least 50.

Above A group of Muslims bowing in prayer at a mosque in Ibadan, Nigeria. In the Muslim world, all of life is organized around salah.

ORGANIZING THE DAY BY THE PRAYER CYCLE

Salah naturally imposes discipline on believers, for each day is divided and regulated by prayers. Whether Muslims are studying, working or playing, they will stop at intervals to remember God. Everyday life is temporarily suspended by a natural rhythm of 'taking time out' from the world and its pressures. In the Muslim world, people plan events and meetings according to these set prayer times.

ZAKAH: GIVING ALMS TO THE POOR

ISLAM AIMS TO PRODUCE AN EGALITARIAN SOCIETY, WHERE THE SOCIAL AND ECONOMIC GAP BETWEEN THE RICH AND THE POOR IS REDUCED THROUGH THE PAYMENT OF *ZAKAH*, OR ALMS-GIVING.

Islam teaches that wealth is a blessing from God, and those who lawfully amass wealth are entitled to enjoy it. However, to prevent one person living in total luxury while others suffer in abject poverty, *zakah*, alms-giving, is an obligatory requirement for Muslims.

SOCIAL JUSTICE
This third pillar of Islam requires a portion of one's wealth to be distributed among the needy (9:103). It is a reminder to Muslims that all wealth is ultimately God's, and that people are merely trustees of it. *Zakah* is a fiscal policy through which social justice can be secured.

The Arabic word *zakah* means to purify, to bless and to increase. Giving alms is believed to purify wealth from greed: a hadith states that a man came to Muhammad, asking him, 'O Messenger of Allah,

I have plenty of property and wealth, tell me how to conduct my life', whereupon he was told to pay *zakah* to purify it. The Quran warns against amassing wealth and not spending on others (9:34–5) and promises that whoever spends for Allah will find an increase in what Allah bestows on him (2:245).

Alms-giving is fundamental in Islamic life and is mentioned 82 times in the Quran, in conjunction with *salah*. It is also recorded as having been observed by earlier prophets, such as John, Jesus and Ismail (chapter 19).

WHO PAYS *ZAKAH*?
Zakah is to be paid by any Muslim – minor or adult, male or female – who has held money, gold, silver, property or capital (including cattle and crops) above a determined amount, the *nisab*, for a year. The

Above A zakah *collection box from Shiraz, Iran. Zakah requires all Muslims to give 2.5 per cent of their substantial savings in charity per year.*

nisab is a minimum calculation: gold must weigh at least 85 grams for *zakah* to be payable, and cash must be above the minimum value of 595 grams of silver. The rate of *zakah* also varies depending on the property: for gold, silver and cash, it is 2.5 per cent; for agricultural produce, it is 5 per cent.

THE SOCIAL WISDOM BEHIND *ZAKAH*
Although sometimes collected by governments, *zakah* is seen to be the responsibility of the individual. *Zakah* avoids the tension that often exists between the state and the citizen in matters of tax payments

Left A British Muslim couple calculate the amount of zakah *they are due to pay on their savings. Giving* zakah *is self-regulated.*

because it is not a tax levied by the state, but a social and legal obligation fulfilled by the individual, who takes personal control over their wealth and pays the money due themselves. This is important, because for the benefits of *zakah* to be truly felt, there should be no resentment in the heart of the giver.

WHO RECEIVES *ZAKAH*?

The Quran states eight categories of people who may receive *zakah*. They are the poor, the needy, the officials collecting the *zakah*, those recently converted to Islam whose hearts still need reconciling to the faith, those in captivity or bondage, debtors, those working in the cause of Allah (running community or education projects, for example) and the wayfarer.

Non-Muslims and Muhammad's descendants are forbidden from receiving *zakah*, as too are a donor's direct relatives, because the believer already has an obligation to maintain them.

ZAKAH IN HISTORY

During Muhammad's lifetime, the Islamic state collected *zakah*, but after his death, there was resistance to it. The first caliph, Abu Bakr, declared those resisting *zakah* as apostates and fought them until they acknowledged its legal status. *Zakah* continued to be collected under the Umayyad and Abbasid

Above Food, as a form of charity, is distributed at the end of a fasting day in Ramadhan. Here, bread is being given to women in Peshawar, Pakistan.

dynasties, but it was eventually abandoned at state level. Payment of *zakah* is now generally upheld on voluntary moral grounds by individual Muslims.

Above A teenager in Birmingham, England, gives charity through the well-known Islamic Relief clothing bank system.

SADAQAH: CHARITY

Like *zakah*, *sadaqah* is charitable giving, and is mentioned many times in the Quran and in hadith. Muslims are told that *sadaqah* must be practised, but when and how much is up to the individual. *Sadaqah* means to give truthfully, lawfully and with sincerity, and it should therefore be given whenever possible, in addition to *zakah*. It need not be money: even smiling or removing something harmful from the road can be considered as *sadaqah*.

SAWM: FASTING

FASTING DURING THE MONTH OF RAMADHAN IS BOTH AN INDIVIDUAL AND A COMMUNAL ACT OF WORSHIP AND SPIRITUAL EXERTION, WHICH HAS THE AIM OF BRINGING MUSLIMS CLOSER TO GOD.

Sawm, meaning abstaining, is the fourth pillar of Islam, and refers to fasting from sunrise to sunset in Ramadhan, the ninth month of the Muslim calendar. Healthy Muslims abstain from food, drink and conjugal relations during these hours. The end of this testing month is followed by the *Eid* celebrations. As the Islamic lunar calendar is ten days shorter than the solar calendar, Ramadhan falls ten days earlier each year, travelling through the seasons.

Outside Ramadhan, people are free to fast voluntarily, though not on the days of festivities or on Friday. Fasting was prescribed in 623, after migration to Madinah, purely as an act of obedience to Allah. The Quran states, 'O you who believe, fasting is prescribed

Above Palestinian women pray in front of the Dome of the Rock Mosque in the Old City of Jerusalem at the last Friday Prayers during Ramadhan.

for you as it was prescribed for those before you, so that you might remain conscious of God' (2:183). For Muslims, the only reason for *sawm* is to attain piety and God-consciousness (*taqwa*).

THE IMPORTANCE OF RAMADHAN

The month of Ramadhan is known by Muslims as 'Blessed Ramadhan' because it is the time in which they believe that the Quran was revealed, and in which Muhammad stated that the gates of heaven are opened and those of hell closed and the devils chained. According to the Quran, fasting is solely for God's sake; therefore, he will reward it how he sees fit in this world and the next.

Muhammad said that in the first ten days of Ramadhan, Allah's mercy descends on believers; in the next ten days, his forgiveness is showered on them; while, in the final ten days, immunity from hell is promised. It is a time for Muslims to exercise forgiveness and patience and to think of the less fortunate – so empathy with the poor, feeding them and giving daily charity is extolled. Muslims hasten to feed

Left Indonesian women pray the tarawih *prayer in the nights of Ramadhan in Bali. Prayer is segregated in Islam, as this women's section shows.*

fasting neighbours at the time of *Iftar*, breaking the fast, in order to gain God's blessings. The meal is supposed to be simple, nutritious and not too filling.

THE BENEFITS OF FASTING

Muslims believe that fasting is a shield from wrongdoing, because abstention leads to self-control – whether from over-eating or from gossip. Muhammad said that whoever fasted in Ramadhan and abstained from all forbidden things would have all their sins forgiven.

Supplicating is recommended at *Iftar*, as Islam teaches that God answers the fasting believer. (A hadith relates that Muhammad comforted his companions by telling them the odour from a fasting person's mouth was more pleasing to Allah than the smell of musk.)

Abandoning normal life, Muslims engage in far more worship than they can usually manage, reciting the Quran, remembering God and meditating. It is a month of intense spiritual renewal and reflection for Muslims, when they call upon God and re-establish their covenant with him. The nights of Ramadhan are marked by an extra prayer, the *tarawih*, where the whole Quran is recited over the month.

CONDITIONS OF FASTING

Children and the elderly are not expected to fast, though the latter are required to feed the poor instead. For those who are ill, travelling, menstruating, pregnant or breastfeeding, fasting can be postponed until a later date (2:185). Muslims can enjoy ordinary life during the nights of Ramadhan, but must begin fasting at sunrise. Eating the *suhur* meal at dawn was a

Right More than 100,000 people break their fast with the Iftar *meal at sunset in the Prophet's Mosque in Madinah, Saudi Arabia.*

prophetic tradition that carried many blessings, and it is still faithfully emulated the world over.

Deliberate eating or drinking will break a fast, but eating or drinking through forgetfulness does not constitute a break in the fast.

THE LAST TEN DAYS AND *EID*

The Quran is believed to have been revealed on one of the last ten odd nights of Ramadhan, known as the *Laylat al-Qadr*, the Night of Power/Decree. As it is not clear when this night occurs, Muslims spend all ten nights in prayer, and some believers retreat to mosques to excel in their worship.

Above A family taking an Iftar *meal in the privacy of their home. While* Iftar *is a time for sharing, it is also an important family time for Muslims, when children are taught the importance of Ramadhan.*

As the crescent is sighted and Ramadhan ends, the *Eid* festivities follow. The poor are remembered throughout the celebrations, as *zakat ul-fitr*, alms to end Ramadhan, are paid by every Muslim to help the poor enjoy the celebrations. *Eid salah*, a communal prayer, is offered, new clothes are worn, gifts are exchanged and celebration follows. All this, however, is with a tinge of sadness that Ramadhan has ended.

HAJJ: THE PILGRIMAGE

THE FIFTH PILLAR OF ISLAM IS *HAJJ*, THE PILGRIMAGE TO MAKKAH, WHICH TAKES PLACE IN THE LAST ISLAMIC MONTH, *DHUL-HIJJAH*. MUSLIMS AIM TO PERFORM *HAJJ* AT LEAST ONCE IN THEIR LIFETIME.

Prescribed in 631, the year before Muhammad's death, the *Hajj* is elaborated in the Quran (22:26–33), where it is ordered as a symbol of devotion to God in the footsteps of Ibrahim. Whoever fulfils this pillar of Islam, 'for them it is good in the sight of their Lord' (22:30).

PREPARING FOR *HAJJ*

Hajj is perhaps the most complex of Islamic rites as it requires a great deal of preparation. It is considered a calling from God, but Muslims must ensure that they possess the financial means to go, have paid off all debts, distributed *zakah* and left no dependents unprovided for. *Hajj* demands intention and purity of heart, so pilgrims are encouraged to cultivate an attitude of repentance, mercy and God-consciousness.

THE RITES IN *HAJJ*

Muhammad showed how the rites of *Hajj* were to be performed, and clarified that he himself was emulating the practice of Ibrahim. As Islam teaches that all people are equal before God, Muslims are required to shed any symbols of their social status when making *Hajj,* so the same *ihram, Hajj* clothing, is worn by all as far as possible. For men, this consists of two unsewn pieces of cloth, often white, which represent the shroud. For women, it is any simple plain clothing that covers them fully, according to Islamic dress codes.

Right The white tents at Mina where pilgrims camp for four days during Hajj *in Makkah. The three million pilgrims are grouped in tents according to nationality: these are European ones.*

No jewellery or perfume is worn during *Hajj*. On approaching the stations around Makkah (*miqat*), all pilgrims assume a 'state of death', where only necessary physical acts are allowed: even nail-clipping is prohibited. A rigorous state of consciousness follows, where no disagreement or violation of any living thing must take place.

According to the Quran (22:27), God asked Ibrahim to proclaim the pilgrimage to the House of God (*Kaabah*) that he built. Ibrahim responded by climbing on a rock and calling the *talbiyah*, 'I am at your command, O Lord, I am at your command.' Pilgrims continuously repeat the *talbiyah*.

On the eighth day of *Dhul-Hijjah*, the pilgrims camp at Mina, one of the eastern entrances to the Makkan valley, where they offer *salah* from noon to dawn. They then travel to the plain of Arafah, 16 km (10 miles) south-east of Mina. This is the most important day of the

Above A manuscript painting by al-Hariri shows a caravan of Hajj *pilgrims on camel and horseback. In the past, the* Hajj *was arduous and often perilous.*

rites, as Muhammad said that Arafah is the pinnacle of the *Hajj*. This is where, according to Islam, Adam and Eve met after their descent to earth; and beseeched God for guidance. Here, Muslims spend the entire day in prayer close to the Mount of Mercy (*Jabal-al-Rahmah*).

At sunset, the pilgrims retrace their steps 8km (5 miles) north to Muzdalifah, where Muhammad is said to have camped for the night.

Right Pilgrims ritually walk seven times between the two 'hillocks' of Safa and Marwa, which are now enclosed within the Great Mosque in Makkah.

Here, they offer prayers and collect pebbles for the following rituals. The morning of the tenth day of *Dhul-Hijjah* sees pilgrims returning to Mina to ritually stone three stone pillars that represent the devil, who is said to have tempted Ibrahim and his family away from God. A sacrificial animal is slaughtered in recollection of the Ibrahim story, pilgrims clip or shave their hair and the final rites at the *Kaabah* begin.

The pilgrims circle the *Kaabah* seven times, kiss the Black Stone, which they believe came with Adam from heaven, and offer prayers at Ibrahim's Station, the place where he is said to have raised the *Kaabah* and prayed to God. Finally, they run between the two hillocks of Safa and Marwa as, according to tradition, did Hajar in her search of water for Ismail. Water from the Well of Zamzam is drunk, and after the stoning of the devil at Mina, the *Hajj* is complete.

Most pilgrims then make their way north to Madinah, where they offer their salutations to the Prophet and seek to absorb the blessings of his city. Muslims believe that performing the *Hajj* purifies them from sin, and they return home amidst great celebrations of their new sinless status.

SPIRITUAL SYMBOLISM

Hajj is one of the world's largest religious conventions, with more than three million people gathering at Arafah. The experience of brotherhood is breathtaking, as Muslims from every corner of the world flock to worship together.

Hajj is very complex, for while it is outwardly physical, it is laden with spiritual symbolism. To make sense of all the rites, Muslims must search for meaning deep within their hearts. According to Islamic tradition, even Ibrahim was asked by Archangel Jibril whether he understood the meanings of *Hajj*.

The majority of Muslims do not manage to perform the *Hajj*, but they are nevertheless equally valued and included, for on the day of Arafah, they fast, and the day after, they celebrate *Eid*.

Below Pilgrims on the day of Arafah, on the Mount of Mercy, Jabal-al-Rahmah, beseeching God, as, according to hadith, did the prophets Adam, Ibrahim and Muhammad.

Makkah as a Place of Worship

MUSLIM HISTORIANS CONSIDER MAKKAH TO BE THE CENTRE OF THE EARTH. AND FOR MUSLIMS IT ALSO HAS MODERN SIGNIFICANCE: IT IS TO THIS CITY THAT THEY TURN THEIR ATTENTION DAILY IN PRAYER.

Above *Pilgrims are depicted performing the* Hajj *rituals at Makkah in a painting produced for Timurid prince Iskandar Sultan, c.1410–11.*

Makkah is important for Muslims not just because the Prophet Muhammad was born there and spent most of his life in the city, but also because it houses the *Kaabah*, the cubelike edifice that is known as *Bait-Allah*, the first House of God established for his worship. Throughout the *Hajj*, there are rites that take pilgrims back in history to the roots of the city.

ADAM'S MAKKAH

Makkah as a place of worship is thought by early historians to have been first established by Adam, who, Muslims believe, was guided to Makkah after he descended from heaven. It was there that he is believed to have found God's Throne, and honoured it, on the site of the present-day *Kaabah*. It was also in Makkah, on the plain of Arafah, that he is said to have been reunited with Eve and, together with her, sought God's forgiveness and guidance, as do millions of Muslim pilgrims on the *Hajj* today.

Muslims believe that the *Hajar al-Aswad*, the Black Stone in the eastern corner of the *Kaabah*, was brought by Adam out of heaven, and that after Adam's death and burial in Makkah, his son Seth continued to honour God's Throne until it was recalled to heaven.

According to hadith, Noah's Ark later sailed through the area in which the city now stands, and many years afterward, Ibrahim is believed to have taken Hajar and her son Ismail to settle in this land.

Below Al-Masjid al-Haram in Makkah, commonly known as the Grand Mosque, is the largest mosque in the world.

IBRAHIM'S MAKKAH

The rites associated with Ibrahim and his family are immortalized in the *Hajj*, from circling the *Kaabah*, which Muslims believe he rebuilt with his son Ismail, to praying at the Station of Ibrahim, where his footprints are said to be preserved in the stone slab, and drinking from the Well of Zamzam, which is believed to have quenched the thirst of his son Ismail as a babe.

According to Islamic traditions, the rite of running between the two hillocks of Safa and Marwa was begun by Ibrahim to remember his wife Hajar's search for water. The curved arch by the side of the *Kaabah*, the *Hajar Ismail*, is included in its circling, as it is believed to have once been part of the holy house as well as the place where Hajar and Ismail are buried. A story tells that before building the *Kaabah*, Ibrahim visited Ismail when he was a boy, for he had a vision to sacrifice his son to God. On their way outside Mina, Ibrahim, Ismail and Hajar were tempted by the devil, whom Ibrahim stoned. Again, Muslims

remember the great patriarch as they stone the pillars of *jamarat* at Mina. Finally, to pay homage to Ibrahim's willingness to sacrifice Ismail, all pilgrims offer a sacrificial animal and feed the poor.

MUHAMMAD'S MAKKAH

It is in this mystical city that the Prophet Muhammad was born, and his endorsement of the Ibrahimic *Hajj* rites gave it new authenticity. His life also added new sites to visit during pilgrimage: many Muslims visit the places where he lived and walked, in order to retrace his spiritual footsteps. However, this custom is not part of the *Hajj* rites, and the present Saudi authorities' fear of pilgrims practising innovative worship, and thus compromising their attention to God, has almost completely erased any monumental historical sites from Makkah. Although the place of Muhammad's upbringing with his wet nurse, Halimah, is preserved (albeit surrounded by a market), other sites, such as where he lived with his wife Khadijah, her burial place and his wife Ayesha's house, though believed to be known locally, are not officially marked.

Many Muslims visit the Cave of Hira, where Muhammad is believed to have received the first revelation, and the Cave of Thawr, his hiding place on the migration to Madinah. Some scholars claim to know the whereabouts of the pillar in the precincts of the al-Haram, from where Muhammad is believed to have been taken on the night journey to Jerusalem. Leaving Makkah, pilgrims can see the mountain that the Prophet is said to have miraculously split with a gesture from his finger.

Memories of the old Makkah of Adam and Ibrahim mingle with the newer Makkah of Muhammad, who brought new meaning to the city.

Above A view of the Kaabah, *the surrounding mosque, and the city of Makkah in the distance.*

Left Worshippers kiss the Hajar al-Aswad, *the Black Stone set in the eastern corner of the Kaabah. The stone, according to hadith, is from heaven, and was brought to earth by Adam.*

JUMUAH MUBARAK: BLESSED FRIDAY

FRIDAY, *JUMUAH*, IS THE DAY OF CONGREGATIONAL PRAYER, WHEN, AT NOON, THE MUSLIM COMMUNITY GATHERS IN THE LOCAL MOSQUE TO HEAR A SERMON AND TO PRAY TOGETHER.

Chapter 62 of the Quran, named *al-Jumuah*, is said to have been revealed to Muhammad during the first few years after migration to Madinah. In it, God commands Muslims to pray the congregational prayer: 'O you who believe, when the call is proclaimed to prayer on Friday, hasten to the remembrance of Allah, and leave off business...' (62:9). Friday is named *Jumuah* from the Arabic *al-Jam*, meaning 'gathering'. This day of congregational prayer is considered honoured in Allah's sight.

BLESSED FRIDAY

Muhammad said that as the Jews have Saturday and the Christians Sunday, so Muslims have Friday as their special day. However, it is not a day of rest as such, but rather a day of collective worship and particular remembrance of God. It is the day,

Muslims believe, on which God created Adam, the day Adam was sent to earth from heaven, the day he died, the day when the Final Judgement will come and the day on which there is an hour, toward the end, just before sunset, when all prayers are answered. Islam teaches that all prayers are witnessed by the angels, but that on Friday, the angels record all those who go to the mosque and pray. As a reward, they are forgiven all sins committed between that Friday and the next.

Friday is also a day on which Muslims pray for blessings on the Prophet, and recite chapter 18, *al-Kahf* ('The Cave') specifically, for its esoteric message of guidance.

Below Muslims pray in Malaysia during the Friday prayer. Offering collective worship in mosques is an important part of Muslim community life.

Above The Friday prayer at al-Azhar Mosque. Built in the Fatimid city of al-Qahira (Cairo), it claims to be the oldest university in the world.

PREPARING FOR *JUMUAH*

In Muslim countries, preparations for *Jumuah* usually begin after sunset on Thursday, when groups assemble to sing God's praises and blessings on the Prophet. Friday is normally a holiday in the Muslim world, with families preparing for time together in a spirit of worship. Muslims take an obligatory bath on Friday, wear

Left As well as giving Friday sermons, imams give religious instruction on other days – as shown in this painting of the Mosque of the Metwalis, Cairo.

second *adhan*, the imam leads those present into two *rakaah* (units) of prayer, from a niche at the front of the mosque. Afterward, people usually spend some time greeting each other and catching up with their news, for *Jumuah* is just as much an opportunity to come together as a community and socialize as it is to remember God.

AFTER THE PRAYER

The Quran teaches that all business and worldly affairs should be put aside for the remembrance of Allah, but that afterward, people are free to disperse and go about their businesses (62:10). This means that trade in the Muslim world does not stop on a Friday. In fact, it is a day when most Muslim families relax and spend time eating and shopping together, thus boosting trade on a Friday.

Jumuah Mubarak is, in essence, a day of joy, peace and community spirit – a holiday as well as, most importantly, a holy day.

their best attire, perfume themselves, pay attention to oral hygiene and then make their way slowly and peacefully to the mosque.

Jumuah prayer is compulsory for all adults, except women who may find it difficult to go out due to family duties, the infirm, travellers and those under environmental constraints, such as extreme hot or cold temperatures or rain.

THE *JUMUAH* PRAYER

Jumuah replaces the noon *salah* when prayed in congregation. It is preceded by an *adhan* (call to prayer) and a *khutbah* (sermon), given by the imam from the pulpit, facing his congregation. The sermon praises

God and his Prophet and quotes verses from the Quran, encouraging people to do good. The theme varies from week to week and may address contemporary concerns of the congregation. The imam then sits and the congregation offers silent supplications before he gives a second *khutbah*, ending in prayers for believers globally, and for all who are oppressed and poor.

The congregation is asked not to speak at all during the sermon, and to reflect on the words. After a

Right Friday prayers at the mosque of Shaykh Abdul Qadir al-Gailani, Baghdad, Iraq. The women enjoy the prayer as spiritual time, but also as social bonding.

THE TWO *EIDS*

THE END OF RAMADHAN AND THE PERFORMANCE OF *HAJJ* ARE EACH MARKED BY A MAJOR FESTIVAL, *EID*, WHEN MUSLIMS THE WORLD OVER CELEBRATE, EXCHANGE GREETINGS, SING AND SHARE MEALS.

Festivals in Islam are a time for great joy, but at the core of the celebrations is devotion to God, for Muslims believe that all happiness and joy emanate from him. The two great festivals in Islam, the *Eid*, are a testimony to this: both events take place after rigorous devotional training programmes – fasting and pilgrimage – and both are imbued with thanksgiving throughout.

EID UL-FITR:
THE END OF RAMADHAN

After an arduous month of fasting and self-control, Muslims mark the end of Ramadhan with great festivity. They begin the day by bathing, perfuming themselves and putting on their best clothes, usually new ones for children. (It is said that Muhammad himself wore his best clothes on *Eid*, including a special cloak.) Believers then eat something sweet, such as dates or milk pudding, before going to pray.

A congregational *Eid salah* is normally offered early in the morning, in an open space if possible. The whole community – men, women and children – is required to attend, as it is seen as a day of joy for all. Thanks are given to God in a *khutbah*, or sermon, for the blessings of Ramadhan, and supplications are offered for the month's efforts to be accepted and the spirit of the month to be carried throughout the year. People then greet and congratulate each other.

Above *Members of a Palestinian family in the West Bank city of Nablus share a modest Eid meal to celebrate the end of Ramadhan.*

Below *Eid prayers are offered at the Regent's Park Mosque in London, a racially and ethnically mixed community.*

Above Meat is distributed during the Eid ul-adha *in Senegal. Animals are slaughtered and the meat divided between family, friends and those in need.*

As this is usually a holiday of three days, a wonderful array of food is prepared, which is shared with friends and family. Muslims visit each other and give gifts to the children, and play and singing are encouraged. According to hadith, Muhammad and his community enjoyed watching Abyssinians perform in the Prophet's mosque during *Eid* festivities, and, later, girls sang in the Prophet's house.

Remembering those who are less fortunate is incumbent upon Muslims with enough money to be able to celebrate. It is therefore compulsory to pay the *zakat ul-fitr* on the days of *Eid* or just before. This is a nominal amount, paid by the head of the family for each family member, to be distributed to the poor and needy so that they can also enjoy the celebrations of *Eid*.

EID UL ADHA: THE END OF *HAJJ*

Those unable to participate in the *Hajj* can nevertheless join in the great ritual through celebrations.

On the day of Arafah, only those not performing the *Hajj* are encouraged to fast. The day after, *Eid* is declared and festivities begin. Again, Muslims will bathe, beautify themselves and wear their best clothes. It is customary on this occasion to eat after the morning *Eid salah*. Many Muslims offer a sacrifice, in honour of Ibrahim's readiness to sacrifice Ismail, and they will therefore eat part of that, rather than sweet pudding, on returning from the prayer.

PRAISING GOD

As in *Eid ul-fitr*, the prayer is offered in congregation and is followed by a sermon, praising God for the opportunity of pilgrimage for humankind and extolling the benefits of sacrificing an animal and distributing the meat among family, friends and the poor. Finally, God is praised in abundance. Afterward, the congregation spends time greeting and congratulating each other, giving gifts to children and sharing lavish meals.

During the two *Eids*, praising God with *takbir* – singing that he is great – is prescribed as a way of thanking God for his guidance. It is sung intermittently from going to

GIFTS AND THE MEANING OF *EID*

Celebrating on the *Eid* is encouraged, particularly with good food and gifts. However, in this age of materialism, Islam is keen to guide Muslims away from extravagant celebrations, and to remind them that no joy is devoid of the presence of God. Gift-giving is meant to please and satisfy children, but making it the centre of the day is discouraged. The day must begin with the prayer, and should be filled with prayers and thanks, and thoughts and charity given to the poor, so that God is the focus, not material objects.

Above Young British Muslims exchange gifts with their friends on Eid. *While* Eid *is a joyous occasion and gifts are part of the celebrations, the emphasis is on spiritual aspects of the festivals.*

prayer until the sermon begins on *Eid ul-fitr* and on the *Eid* marking the end of *Hajj*, for three days from the day of Arafah. Men and women all join in: '*Allahu akbar, Allahu akbar, la ilaha illal-lah. Allahu akbar, Allahu akbar, wa lillahil-hamd.*' ('God is the greatest, God is the greatest, there is no god but the one God, God is the greatest, God is the greatest, and for Him is all Praise.')

MUHARRAM: THE MARTYRDOM OF HUSSAIN

THE MARTYRDOM OF IMAM HUSSAIN IN THE MONTH OF MUHARRAM IS THE PIVOTAL EVENT OF THE ISLAMIC YEAR FOR SHIAH MUSLIMS, WHO COMMEMORATE AND MOURN HIS DEATH WITH GREAT PASSION.

Muharram is the first month of the Islamic calendar, and one of the four months in which fighting has been prohibited in the Quran. However, it carries another significance for Shiah Muslims, for it is the month in which Hussain, Muhammad's grandson, along with 72 others, was killed in Karbala, Iraq, by the forces of the second Umayyad ruler Yazid I (645–83).

THE 'PRINCE OF MARTYRS'
After Muhammad's death, many followers of Ali believed that he was the rightful successor for being from the Prophet's family, they believe he had been appointed by the prophet himself. The fact that he was not chosen as first caliph is considered a usurpation of his power by Shiah Muslims. This tragedy was replayed in the life of Ali's son Hussain, who stood up against the corruption of the second Umayyad caliph Yazid.

Hussain set off in 680 with his family and small band of followers in Muharram toward Karbala in Iraq, where he was promised support. However, at Karbala, their water supply was cut off and eventually, on the tenth day of Muharram, the day of Ashura, Hussain, along with his family, was killed in battle. His head was

Above Shiah Muslims inside the inner sanctuary of Imam Hussain's shrine in Karbala. Nearly two million pilgrims visit Najaf and Karbala during Muharram.

severed and taken to Damascus, and the children and womenfolk were taken there as captives.

Imam Hussain's head is thought by Sunnis to be buried in Syria, his body being interred in Karbala.

Below The narrative of Imam Hussain's life and death – the focal event in Shiah history – is depicted in this tapestry at the imam's shrine in Karbala, Iraq.

However, most Shiahs believe that his family, on being freed from captivity in Syria, took the head with them and had it interred either in Najaf, at his father Ali's mausoleum, or indeed with his body in Karbala.

Shiah Muslims consider the event to be the most heinous crime ever committed, because the blood of Muhammad's family was spilled by Muslims, and they view Hussain as the 'Prince of Martyrs'.

KARBALA MOURNING

Many Sunni Muslims, too, consider the events at Karbala to be a tragic blot on the history of Islam. However, they prohibit mourning, as the Prophet Muhammad himself forbade people from ritual and passionate displays of bereavement. The Shiahs, however, think it is a duty of believers to commemorate the event, and to mourn Hussain. Indeed, they claim that this will bring redemption to humankind.

From Iraq to Pakistan, Iran and Indonesia, elaborate lamentation ceremonies are held, usually in buildings known as *Hussainiyyas*, or in the open. Recitations, elegies, dirges and public processions are common. Professional reciters sing and recount the life of the martyrs. While the scholars familiarize those gathered with basic Shiah doctrines, this is essentially a time to arouse people's emotions at the injustice of Hussain's death. Rather than being presented as a willing martyr, Hussain is seen as a tragic victim, and his killers and enemies are openly cursed.

Taziyah, passion plays by theatrical re-enactors, were common until the early 20th century, but, since 1940, these have not been seen as much. Instead, models of the scenes of Hussain's martyrdom and of his mausoleum, along with representational banners of his army, are carried in processions. As

Above A procession by Iraqi Shiahs to mark Imam Hussain's martyrdom in Karbala, Iraq. Many more will join in on the day of Ashura itself.

emotional accounts of the events lead gatherers to cry in mourning, they are promised redemption, for Shiah Muslims believe that it is only through mourning Hussain that sinners will be forgiven. Believers also recount miracles attributed to Hussain – his severed head allegedly recited the Quran – as a testimony of his righteousness as opposed to Yazid's wrongdoing.

EXPRESSIONS OF GRIEF

An important feature of the gatherings is *matam* (chest-beating and self-flagellation), with men

Above Shiah Muslims in Peshawar, Pakistan, self-flagellate during a procession on the ninth day of Muharram.

often incorporating knives, chains and swords, whether in India, Iran or Lebanon. Some Shiah scholars allow this controversial part of the mourning rituals, but others have declared it unlawful.

The mourners at the gatherings are provided with meals by donors. Finally, on the tenth day of Muharram, the day of Ashura, mourners will fast. (It is interesting that Muhammad also ordered fasting on this day. However, this was not in prediction of the Karbala tragedy, but because it is believed to be the day on which God delivered Moses and his people from Pharaoh across the Red Sea.)

Muharram is a time of great community bonding and sharing for Shiah Muslims, as well as an opportunity for renewing their faith, when they reflect over the injustices of the world and vow to stand up for what is right.

MAWLID: THE PROPHET'S BIRTHDAY

MAWLID (OR MILAD) COMMEMORATES THE PROPHET MUHAMMAD'S BIRTHDAY. CELEBRATIONS ARE HELD THROUGHOUT THE MUSLIM WORLD, PARTICULARLY IN EGYPT, SYRIA AND PAKISTAN.

The celebration of *Mawlid* is held on the day believed to be the Prophet's birthday – the 12th day of *Rabi al-Awwal*, the third month of the Islamic calendar – with great pomp and ceremony. Passages from the Quran are recited, along with poetry in praise of the Prophet, and meals are distributed as charity.

THE HISTORY OF *MAWLID*

Mawlid is not universally marked in the Muslim world, but generally it is celebrated in Sufi circles. According to historical sources, the Prophet's birthday was first observed in Makkah by the mother of the famous Abbasid caliph Harun al-Rashid, who turned the house in which her son was born into a place of prayer. However, it was not publicly marked until the 11th century, when the ruler of the Shiah Fatimid dynasty in Egypt played a major role in the public procession and celebrations, laying

claims to descent from the Prophet's family, and also thereby securing popularity.

By the 12th century, the Sunnis of Syria and Iraq had also begun to celebrate *Mawlid*. As the practice grew in popularity – as a way of renewing faith and remaining connected with the Prophet – it assimilated local customs and practices, notably in India and Egypt. The Ottomans observed it from the 16th century, and, in 1910, they gave it the status of a national holiday throughout the empire. Today, *Mawlid* remains an official holiday in many Muslim countries.

MAWLID CELEBRATIONS

In India, Pakistan and Egypt, *Mawlid* is often commemorated with public processions. Banners are made; homes, mosques and official buildings are decorated; and poems and songs in praise of the Prophet ring out from

Above A view of a mosque in Pakistan on the eve of the Mawlid *celebrations. In Pakistan, it is the norm for mosques to be decorated and illuminated like this.*

loudspeakers. People are encouraged to reconnect with the Prophet Muhammad and his message, and to celebrate his birth and life on earth with great fervour. Believers wear their finest clothes to attend gatherings, where the Prophet's life story is recounted.

Below The Muslim world celebrates the Prophet's birthday in many ways. This man in Egypt is displaying his strength at a family talent entertainment show.

Right Throngs of Pakistanis take to the streets in celebration on the Mawlid. *This man has dressed his son as an Arab, as a way of claiming a link with the Prophet.*

Children play a significant role in *Mawlid* and spend weeks beforehand rehearsing poetry and songs, which they perform at gatherings. Distributing food and charity is a significant feature of the festivities, particularly in poor countries, where people are fed en masse in the name of the Prophet.

Among the poems recited are those that honour the Prophet's birth and miracles surrounding it – Muhammad's mother, Amina, reportedly suffered no labour pains and was nursed and attended to by heavenly beings. Both Muhammad's mother and his foster mother, Halimah, are praised and revered.

The Sufi circles (spiritual brotherhoods) have traditionally played a major role in *Mawlid*. In Syria, men and women attend single-sex gatherings to sing Sufi poetry, such as the *Qasidah Burda* of Busayri, the 13th-century Sufi mystic. In Turkey, particularly in Konya, the Mevlevi Sufi order of whirling dervishes perform and sing poetry from Jalal-ud-Din Rumi's famous *Mathnawi*. These

cultural expressions have also entered into *Mawlid* celebrations in the West via settled Muslim communities, particularly in Britain and Canada.

Although *Mawlid* started life as an elitist celebration initiated by the Fatimids, it has since spread among the masses, and, in fact, it gives many poor communities a cause to be hopeful as they look toward the Prophet Muhammad for salvation and escape from the difficulties of daily life.

MAWLID CONTROVERSY

Although *Mawlid* is widely observed, there is controversy as to whether it is a genuine Islamic celebration. Muhammad himself never initiated it, nor did the following generations of Muslims. For this reason, scholars from countries such as Saudi Arabia, as well as some from India and Pakistan, forbid the festivities as an innovation that corrupts the purity of the religion.

However, many Muslim scholars support *Mawlid* on the basis that it brings people closer to the roots of their faith, providing an occasion when believers can reflect on the importance of the Prophet and his message of peace and submission to God. Provided that great pomp, free mixing between the sexes and over-indulgence in food, drink and singing be avoided, they claim that the celebrations should be encouraged as spiritually uplifting.

Left In Egypt, Mawlid *is marked with great celebration and the giving of gifts to children. This young boy holds his toy horse while his sister shows off her doll during* Mawlid *festivities in Cairo.*

THE NIGHTS OF POWER AND ASCENSION

TWO OTHER MUSLIM CELEBRATIONS, *LAYLAT AL-QADR* (NIGHT OF POWER) AND *ISRA WAL MIRAJ* (NIGHT JOURNEY AND ASCENSION TO HEAVEN), MARK IMPORTANT POINTS IN THE PROPHETIC MESSAGE.

Muhammad's life is said to have carried many miracles, but Muslims consider two of the greatest to be the revelation of the Quran, which according to the Quran began on the Night of Power, and Muhammad's miraculous Night Journey to Jerusalem and then Ascension to Heaven. Both events are celebrated throughout the Muslim world with special prayers, meditation and contemplation.

THE NIGHT OF POWER

According to chapter 97 of the Quran, it was on *Laylat al-Qadr*, the Night of Power or Decree (*qadr* means both power and decree), that Archangel Jibril visited Muhammad, bringing the first revelation. *Laylat al-Qadr* is seen as a night of great power, when Muslims believe that all the matters for the coming year are decreed by Allah, and that Jibril and other angels descend from heaven, to spread peace on earth. The Quran declares that worship on this one night is equal to that of a thousand months (that is, more than 80 years), and Muhammad said that anyone who spent this night in worship would have all his previously committed sins forgiven.

Below Pakistani Muslims offer prayers at a mosque in Karachi on the night of Laylat al-Qadr, *when they believe the first verses of the Quran were revealed.*

Above Men and women praying (separately) during Laylat al-Qadr *in Kuwait's grand city mosque. Muslims spend the entire night in worship.*

The night falls on one of the last ten days of Ramadhan, on an odd night. Muslims view Ramadhan as a tremendously holy month, but this night adds further spiritual importance to it. As believers intensify their spiritual worship toward the end of the month of fasting, they combine it with their search for the Night of Power.

It is not clear on which of the odd nights *Laylat al-Qadr* falls; therefore, Muslims spend the last ten days of Ramadhan in constant worship. Many retire to mosques to sit in isolation, while others spend the night at home, praying, reciting the Quran and meditating. Some believers claim that they experience a spiritual awakening or 'happening' on a particular night that convinces them that this is the Night of Power.

THE NIGHT JOURNEY AND ASCENSION TO HEAVEN

Laylat al-Isra wal Miraj is Arabic for the night of the journey and ascension to heaven, an event that Muslims believe occurred on the 27th of Rajab, the seventh month of the Islamic calendar, in the tenth year of *hijrah*. It is said that having lost his wife Khadijah, and suffered in the town of Taif in the same year, Muhammad was consoled and strengthened in his mission by this timely miracle.

According to Islamic tradition, Muhammad spent the evening with his family and then went to visit the *Kaabah*, where he fell asleep in the *hijr Ismail*. He was woken by the Archangel Jibril, who led him to where a white winged beast named al-Buraq stood. He mounted the beast and they sped toward Madinah and Jerusalem. There, according to hadith, Muhammad led

all the previous prophets in prayer at the site of the farthest mosque, al-Masjid al-Aqsa. He was offered two cups of drink – wine and milk – but chose to drink the milk. Jibril approved of his choice, confirming that wine was prohibited.

Finally, it is told, al-Buraq flew him up to heaven from the site of a rock, now the Dome of the Rock Mosque. Muhammad met all the prophets again, but they were now in their heavenly forms. He went as far as the 'lote tree of the uttermost end', mentioned in the Quran (53:14), beyond which no one has ventured. God's divine light descended on the tree, and unlike Moses, Muhammad was able to gaze at it. Muslims believe that God

Above A tapestry of al-Buraq, the winged horse that, according to Islamic traditions, took Muhammad from Makkah to Jerusalem and thence to heaven.

instituted the five daily prayers here, first as 50, but finally reducing them to five. Muhammad claimed that he revealed only a part of what he and Allah discussed that night, and even that only over time.

While returning to Makkah, Muhammad saw trading caravans, which he later described to his companions. The caravans arrived just when he predicted, exhibiting all the details that he had described.

Like the Night of Power, this night is marked by Muslims with devotion, prayers and shared meals.

Above This is the rock, in the Dome of the Rock Mosque in Jerusalem, from where Muhammad is said to have begun his ascension to heaven on al-Buraq.

THE NIGHT OF FREEDOM

Laylat-ul-Bara, the Night of Freedom (from hell), occurs on the 15th day of Shaaban, the eighth Islamic month. Some Muslims believe that God's mercy and blessings descend on this night, and in many countries, including Yemen, they mark the event with prayers, remembrance of God and recitations from the Quran.

According to hadith, Muhammad said that Allah forgives all his servants on this night, except those who do not forgive each other and have malice in their hearts. While there is no evidence to support the popular belief that all matters for the forthcoming year are decreed on this night, many renowned scholars have extolled the virtues of observing prayers on this night and fasting on the following day.

MASJID: THE MOSQUE

MUSLIMS CAN PRAY ANYWHERE, SO THE WHOLE EARTH COULD BE
SEEN AS A *MASJID* ('PLACE OF PROSTRATION'). THE TRADITION OF THE
MOSQUE BEGAN WITH THAT ERECTED BY MUHAMMAD AT MADINAH.

The mosque is a focus for congregational worship and community affairs. *Masjid* in Arabic means a place of prostration; therefore, a *masjid* is primarily a place for *salah*, a place where Muslims kneel and prostrate themselves before God. The word 'mosque' is derived from the Spanish *mesquita*, which is the Latinized form of *masjid*.

OWNERSHIP OF MOSQUES

No matter what their size or location, all mosques fulfil the same function, which is to serve the Muslim community as a house of God. No one is allowed to own a mosque, for all mosques are considered to belong to God; those who fund them are viewed as donors, while those who 'own' mosques for legal purposes are simply trustees. The mosque is considered a *waqf*, or endowment, where any Muslim is free to enter, pray and participate. Muhammad encouraged people to fund the building of mosques, declaring that anyone who did so would find a home built for him in paradise.

MOSQUE DESIGN

As Muslims are commanded to pray toward the *Kaabah*, so mosques in Muslim countries are designed facing the *qibla*, the direction of the *Kaabah*, and the imam will lead the prayers from the back wall, the one facing the entrance.

Most mosques are virtually identical in the basic architecture of the back wall, which houses a *mihrab*, an arched, curved niche, usually featuring very subtle decoration. The imam will stand in front of this niche when leading his congregation in prayer.

To the right of the *mihrab* is the *minbar*, or pulpit, which is made from either wood, stone or mud, depending on the materials used in the mosque's construction. It has a flight of steps leading to the top, where the imam will stand to deliver his Friday sermon.

Above The mihrab, *or prayer niche, at the Gurgi Mosque in Tripoli, Libya. The striking tile work of this* mihrab *reflects its central purpose in the building.*

Most large mosques in Muslim countries have a huge entrance that opens on to a central courtyard. The courtyard is not only an important place where individuals and families can sit and reflect, but also houses fountains, taps and basins, where the ritual ablutions are performed.

Mosques invariably have at least one *midhanah*, a tower or minaret, attached to them. The minaret is the place from which the *muadhdhin* calls the faithful to prayer. The *Kaabah* has many minarets, but the Blue Mosque in Istanbul, Turkey, is the only mosque to have six.

As Muslim men and women pray separately, mosques will provide women with either a prayer space at the back of the main hall, as in the Sultan Ahmet Mosque, Istanbul, or separate prayer rooms from which they can hear the imam, as in the Prophet's Mosque in Madinah.

Left The simplicity of the interior of the Red Mosque in Islamabad, Pakistan, means that worshippers are not diverted from the mosque as a place of prostration.

THE PROPHET'S MOSQUE

The first mosque to be constructed by Muhammad was in Madinah, where he is now buried. Although now extremely grand, with an advanced air-conditioning and sunshade system, the mosque started life very humbly.

The simple mud-brick enclosure had a courtyard, open at one end, with two rows of palm-trunk columns and a roof of mud and palm leaves. A small roofed area at the front was reserved for the poor, and rooms were built off the courtyard, with doors opening on to it, to house Muhammad and his family.

The mosque was a vibrant, community place, where both people and animals sought shelter, and where religious instruction was given and guests entertained.

Above A Turkish manuscript painting of the Prophet's Mosque in Madinah. This early layout shows the simplicity of the mosque as a functional prayer and meeting space.

FUNCTIONS OF A MOSQUE

As well as furnishing prayer spaces for men, women and children, mosques also need to fulfil other community functions in order to be officially designated as such. Each mosque must have kitchen facilities, so that guests and wayfarers can be fed, as well as washrooms, because ablutions are a compulsory requirement before prayer. Finally, mosques must

Above A muadhdhin calls Muslims to prayer from an ornate midhanah (tower) of a Chittagong mosque, Bangladesh. Its style and colour are typical of this country.

provide facilities for washing and shrouding the dead. Some mosques also contain an accommodation unit for the imam and his family, where they can live if it is convenient and comfortable for them to do so.

MOSQUE PERSONNEL

THE MOSQUE IS A VIBRANT COMMUNITY CENTRE, OFTEN PHYSICALLY SITUATED IN THE MIDDLE OF A TOWN, AROUND WHICH ALL OF MUSLIM RELIGIOUS AND SOCIAL LIFE IS CONSTRUCTED.

There is no ordination of 'clergy' in Islam as every Muslim is considered 'ordained' by virtue of the covenant, mentioned in the Quran, that God made between himself and all people, when Adam's descendants recognized Allah as their Lord (7:172). The Quran also states that humans are trustees of the earth (27:62), which means that every Muslim is believed to be endowed with a certain amount of authority.

However, learned scholars have jurisdiction over the community as a whole, particularly those who are imams and mosque personnel. They play a significant role in running mosques, and serving and teaching the community.

IMAMS

Every mosque, whether large or small, has an appointed imam. The imam will be a person of letters – that is, qualified and well-versed in Quran and hadith studies and Islamic law – and will need to have good social skills, to equip him to lead the community.

The imam's main functions are to lead the five daily prayers, the Friday sermon and the *Eid* prayers. Other duties include officiating at weddings and funerals, dealing with domestic matters and representing his congregation in the wider community. The imam is always male, as traditional Muslim teaching claims only a man may lead a male or mixed-gender congregation.

Above The muadhdhin *plays an important role in the daily functioning of the mosque. This one calls the* adhan *from the Aqsunqur Mosque in Cairo.*

Below The imam, the most important of the mosque personnel, fulfils a religious as well as a pastoral role.

Above Teaching the Quran in mosque madrasas is a daily activity. These young children are studying the religion in a mosque in Xian, China.

OTHER MOSQUE PERSONNEL

The imam's pastoral and religious work is supported by other mosque personnel, which often include women. In the West, mosque personnel are usually elected on to a mosque committee, which deals with a range of matters, from organizing study circles (halaqah), youth learning and recreational events and children's Quran classes to local public relations and interfaith work. In the Muslim world, mosque personnel are also usually elected. Their responsibilities include facilitating study circles and social and political events, as well as dealing with finances.

In addition, each mosque has an appointed *muadhdhin*, who calls the *adhan* five times a day. The tradition of being a *muadhdhin* is often kept in one family, each generation taking great care to train the next to call the prayer. In Makkah, one family has supplied the *muadhdhin* at the Sacred Mosque for the last three generations.

THE *MADRASA* SYSTEM

A main function of the mosque is to educate the Muslim community in matters of the faith. This is usually through single-sex *halaqah*, or study circles. However, the education of children is one of the most important roles of the mosque. Learned men and women, approved by the mosque, hold classes to teach boys and girls from the ages of five to seven years onward. In these classes, some of which are held privately in homes, the children learn Quranic Arabic, prayer and the basic tenets of the faith.

In the 11th century, *madrasas* – colleges of learning – were set up, independent of mosques, to train scholars. These community colleges were primarily governed by the ruling authorities. Today, many *madrasas* still exist, and while the majority of them provide free education, they tend to be funded by donations rather than by governments. Most are attached to local mosques.

Over recent years, *madrasas* have received negative media attention as being terrorist 'boot camps' with anti-Western rhetoric. Many have been linked with terrorist organizations and extremist views,

Above Young children study the Quran in Arabic at Brick Lane Jami Mosque, London, England.

often with little evidence. This misconception, however, does not do justice to the majority of *madrasas*, whose primary concern is the nurturing of Muslim children in the tenets of religion, to equip them for daily life.

While Muslim countries do not generally deliver free education through the school system, the mosques and *madrasas* do provide free religious instruction. This means that while official figures may indicate low literacy rates in the vernacular, many poor Muslims are literate in Quranic Arabic.

MOSQUE DIVERSITY

THE GLOBAL MUSLIM COMMUNITY IS UNITED BY THE MOSQUES, YET THESE CENTRAL PLACES OF COMMUNITY WORSHIP ALSO DISPLAY THE CULTURAL AND HISTORICAL DIVERSITY IN THE MUSLIM *UMMAH*.

The wide variation in mosques throughout the world can be seen by comparing, for example, the humble converted terraced buildings in England with the grand mosques of Turkey and Indonesia. The differences in size, architecture and cultural expression of these mosques and others provide a rich testimony to Islamic piety and civilization, where houses of worship have often been the epitome of artistic beauty.

VARIED STYLES

The historical evidence of former Muslim power and rule is spectacularly preserved in many buildings, especially mosques. The three most important of these – breathtaking in their architecture, spiritual importance and splendour – are the sacred mosques in Makkah, Madinah and Jerusalem. In addition to these, Islam has a legacy of varied architectural styles

in the mosques of Mali, Iraq, Spain, Pakistan and Egypt, among many other countries.

The different periods of Muslim rule and civilization are reflected in the design of mosques, but while they display distinct historical and cultural styles, all mosques are united in their attempt to reflect something of the beauty of Allah as perceived by Muslims throughout the ages. Because they believe God to be incomparable and, therefore, beyond any form of representation, Muslims avoid any pictorial depictions of Him in either the simple or the ornate houses of worship they have dedicated to Him.

MAGNIFICENT MOSQUES

In most countries, the major congregational mosques, the *jami*, have huge courtyards to house all the worshippers, and these are often very regal. In Turkey, many mosques lack these but do have towering

Above The Dome of the Rock Mosque in Jerusalem has unique bold blue colours and impressive calligraphy. The verses are from chapter 36 of the Quran.

minarets. Elsewhere, domes and columns have played a major role, for example, in the Great Mosque in Córdoba, Spain, which has arcaded columns.

For Muslims, the aesthetic beauty of mosques serves one function: the remembrance and worship of Allah. To reflect his infinite nature, Muslim architects developed Quranic calligraphy and arabesque abstract art, which has no beginning or end. Small composite parts of the designs add to their often-complex sum total. The aim of such designs is to lead the eye – and the soul – into a creative expanse, where there is nothing but God. Floral and geometric arabesque patterns are reinforced by Quranic calligraphy, the divine words of Allah's guidance etched into the stone walls and the domes. Thus, wherever worshippers turn in a mosque, they can find reminders of the presence of God.

Left Muslims pray in Ramadhan at the largest mosque in India, the Jama Mosque in Delhi, an imposing mosque with a huge courtyard.

Above An aerial view of the Ali Saifuddin Mosque in Brunei, which unusually is built over water. Its architecture reflects the local culture.

HUMBLE MOSQUES

The great *jami* mosques are equal in purpose to humble neighbourhood mosques, for the practical function of a mosque is to provide prayer space. Local mosques tend to be very simple buildings, but are heavily used, particularly in districts in Turkey and Pakistan. The simplicity of these structures gives them a beauty of their own.

In England, local mosques are often not purpose built, but rather converted houses or churches. The thoroughly English architecture of such buildings highlights the unique acculturation of Islam. Just as the Seljuk mosques of Turkey and the Mughal ones of India reflect their time and place, so, too, do the newer mosques in England. In addition to converted buildings, there are now also several purpose-built mosques in England, notably the Shah Jahan Mosque in Woking, Surrey.

Right Constructed in 1889, the Shah Jahan Mosque in Woking, Surrey, was the first purpose-built mosque in Britain. Although not large, it is striking.

THE THREE SANCTIFIED MOSQUES

The three sacred, inviolable mosques (*haram*) in Islam, which Muslims are encouraged to visit, are the *Kaabah* in Makkah, the first house of worship; the Prophet's Mosque in Madinah, the first mosque built by him; and the al-Aqsa in Jerusalem. According to Islamic tradition, Muhammad travelled to Jerusalem in his Night Journey, and this was the first *qibla* (direction of prayer), until revelation changed it to Makkah.

All mosques are sanctified, but these three sites convey special religious significance. A prayer offered at the *Kaabah*, for example, carries far more reward than *salah* offered elsewhere. All three mosques are inviolable, which means there must be no blood shed there. It is the collective duty of Muslims worldwide to preserve all three sites – each of which is unique architecturally – as houses of worship.

EXTRA RITUAL PRAYERS

FOR MUSLIMS, A MAJOR PURPOSE OF LIFE IS TO WORSHIP GOD.
MUHAMMAD GAVE MANY FORMULAE FOR PRAYER SO THAT
BELIEVERS COULD HAVE CONSTANT COMMUNICATION WITH ALLAH.

Countless Muslim scholars have reflected on life comprising of many dimensions, in which internal (*batin*) and external (*dhahir*) aspects of life are fused together. To maintain balance, worship must reflect all dimensions, therefore outer forms of worship (*salah*) must have an inner reality.

SUPEROGATORY *SALAH*

In a classical treatise on prayer, Imam al-Ghazali (1058–1111) writes about the different forms that prayer takes, but he begins with the premise that 'prayer is the pillar of religion, the mainstay of conviction, the chief of good works and the best act of obedience.'

The minimum that is required from any Muslim in terms of prayer is the establishment of the five daily *salah*, which should be performed properly and on time. In fact, Islam teaches that if a Muslim fulfils this obligation with God-consciousness and humility, that would be acceptable to God, even if he or she offers no further prayers.

However, believers may also offer optional *salah*. The first kind consists of extra units of prayer (*rakaah*) that are offered along with the five canonical prayers. In this way, the *salah* can be extended, allowing worshippers to spend longer in communion with Allah.

Many devout Muslims pray four further *salah*, offered in the times between the five prayers. The most valuable of these is believed to be the night prayer, *tahajjud*, which is said to be highly rewarded as it involves great commitment to forsake the comfort of sleep and bed for worship. Keeping a night

vigil of prayer, *qiyam-ul-layl*, is especially recommended, because Islam teaches that it will enable believers to draw closer to God. Certain times are believed to be particularly auspicious for the granting of prayers, the middle of the night being one of them. Devout Muslims will therefore spend a part of the night asking for forgiveness and guidance and offering other personal prayers.

At any point during the day or night, Muslims may pray for God's blessings in fulfilling a need (*hajah*), His divine intervention and guidance in making important decisions (*istikharah*), or His mercy in a prayer of penitence (*tawbah*).

Along with these individual prayers, there are several optional *salah* that can be offered in congregation. These include the *tarawih* prayer in Ramadhan, the *kusuf salah* at the time of solar or lunar eclipse, and indeed a prayer for rain, *istisqa*, which was often

Above This 19th-century painting by Carl Haag shows a Muslim raising his hands in supplication, an important aspect of devotional prayer.

performed by Muhammad. During times of fear or war, the *salah* of *khauf* allows half the congregation to pray while the rest keeps watch.

DUA

The formal prayer of *salah* is supplemented by *dua*, supplication, which is prayer in its wider sense, that is calling upon God at any time either to sing his praises or to beseech him. Making *dua* to seek God for his blessings is highly recommended as it is an essentially held belief in Islam that there is great power in prayer. Muslims will make *dua* for those that they love, for their deceased, for the world at large and for themselves. The Quran teaches that Allah will never turn away anyone calling upon him, though it states that when and how he answers *dua* is up to him.

Left Famous philosopher, Sufi and theologian, Abu Hamid al-Ghazali (1058–1111), wrote extensively on the nature of worship and prayer.

DHIKR AND MEDITATION

Remembrance of God, *dhikr*, is a further way of communion. The Quran refers to itself as *dhikr* (15:9), and it urges people to glorify God morning and evening (33:41), for it claims that only 'in the remembrance of God do hearts find satisfaction' (13:28).

The practice of *dhikr*, which involves inner dimensions of love, humility and sincerity with God, is meant to purify hearts and souls. It can be performed individually or in gatherings. Hadiths assert that God remembers those who remember him, and that the angels seek out *dhikr* gatherings in order to join them. Praising God, reciting the Quran, repeating his 99 names and invoking peace and blessings on the Prophet form the core of *dhikr*.

In the Sufi practice of meditation, worshippers shut their minds off from the sensory world and focus on their breath – the divine breath of life – and on God's holiness.

LIFE AS PRAYER

For Muslims, all life can be an act of worship: a deed done to help another person, earning money to support the family, even peeling vegetables can be prayer. Muslims believe that all actions are sacred if they are performed for the sole pleasure of God, so eating and sleeping are also acts of worship.

Above Two men praying in the desert in Afghanistan. Muslims often claim that those who live and call on God in harsh terrains do so with especial devotion.

Below Sufis gather to recite prayers and praise of God as extra ritual worship. At this Friday dhikr session in Omdurman, Sudan, they recite and jump in unison.

CHAPTER 5

MUSLIM LIFE

The home is the heart of Muslim life and the family the bedrock around which the rest of society is moulded. The Prophet's life is taken as the best example of human conduct and is emulated in rites of passage and life in the home. The family as a social institution provides not only a home as haven, but also the first site of learning and experiences. Harmony in marriage leads to peaceful relationships between parents and children, in which the rights and responsibilities of each member are clear.

The life cycles of birth, marriage and death are celebrated by rituals that mark the occasions as worthy of God's praise: newcomers are welcomed into the family and the souls of the deceased are returned to God.

Each aspect of life is regulated by laws of permissibility (*halal*) and prohibitions (*haram*), which are to be applied in spirit, not just literally. Many of these laws relate to dietary requirements and modesty in social relations. Islam regulates social interaction between people, especially between men and women, and, for this reason, rules on dress for men and women are considered an important part of Muslim observance.

Opposite The family is at the heart of Muslim life, and the home is the place where daily life is shared and where children are raised in accordance with the teachings of Islam.

Above Three girls in traditional Islamic dress converse at a Muslim school in central Tehran, Iran. The co-operative school is funded through government subsidies, donations and tuition payments.

THE FAMILY

THE FOUNDATIONAL INSTITUTION AROUND WHICH MUSLIM SOCIETY
IS ORGANIZED IS THE FAMILY, AND ISLAM ESTABLISHES RESPECT AND
HONOUR AS A HALLMARK OF FAMILY LIFE.

Great emphasis is placed on Muslim family life, where all members participate together to form a peaceful and cohesive community. Although family is the nucleus of society, Islam does not limit this to parents and children, but extends the understanding of family to include grandparents, uncles, aunts and cousins.

Above In Islam, the wider family plays an important role and several generations will often share one family home.

MARRIAGE AND SEX

The life of Muhammad elevates marriage as the best way of life; therefore, Islam discourages celibacy. Couples who enter into marriage are blessed by God. As Adam and Eve were created to live together in peace and love, so each couple entering into a marriage contract emulate that practice. Sex outside marriage is not allowed; therefore, Islamic traditions teach that marriage completes half of your faith, and that sex and procreation within marriage are not base physical acts, but natural pleasures like eating and drinking. Indeed, they carry spiritual rewards.

Choosing a pious partner is encouraged, and because the *nikah*, or marriage, is a civil contract (*aqd*), both consenting parties are bound by its terms. The husband carries the responsibility of financial maintenance, and the wife, while she is free to pursue a career, is seen as the source of peace and comfort in the home.

HOME AS HAVEN

At home, the door can be shut on the pressures of the outside world, and peace and love can rule. In this vibrant place, husband and wife

Left This image of the marriage of the three daughters of Serv, King of Yemen, from Shahnama *(The Book of Kings), an epic poem written c.1000, endorses the importance of marriage.*

Right A mother fulfils the duty to raise children according to Islamic values by teaching her daughter the Quran.

find comfort in each other, women are free to celebrate and enjoy their daily lives, grandparents are respected and cherished and children flourish and are nurtured with love. Muslim family life, therefore, centres on the home, the private sphere, rather than public places. Here, taking meals together and socializing are just as important as prayer. The Prophet encouraged his companions to spend time with their families.

THE RIGHTS OF CHILDREN

One of the first responsibilities of parents is to raise their children according to the teachings of Islam. Within the family, children are introduced to an Islamic way of life through love and kindness. Parents are encouraged to set a good example themselves. As one hadith states, there is no better gift from a father to his children than a good education and behaviour. Socializing children with good

manners and training them how to function in a Muslim society is important, and teaching them the Quran, prayer and basic knowledge of God and his prophets is obligatory, but this ought to be done in an environment of love and play.

The obligation to raise children as good Muslims, however, must not be put over and above children's basic rights to food, shelter, love and gentle nurturing. In fact, the spirit of Islam makes love and kindness a condition for nurture, and the beauty of the extended family is that children are naturally socialized and eased into social relations, where everyone has a companion from their generation.

THE RIGHTS OF PARENTS

Parents also have rights due to them, for the Quran states that 'We (God) have made it a duty for humankind to be good to his parents. His mother bears him with strain upon strain...' (31:14) (Mothers are elevated higher than fathers.) Chapter 17 states that God has decreed kindness to parents, and that when they attain old age, they should not be pushed aside.

While parents are expected to give their growing children the right to make decisions regarding their own lives, parents nevertheless hold a position of experience, and seeking their advice is therefore highly recommended.

Above A father in Afghanistan spends time with his son. The parent–child relationship is fundamental in Islam.

HADITHS RELATING TO THE FAMILY

The Prophet said that the most perfect of believers were those who were most considerate to their wives. Kind and moral relations between husband and wife are considered to spread goodness in the family, and in society at large. It is said that a desert Arab came to Muhammad and asked him if he kissed his children, for his people did not. The Prophet replied sadly, 'What can I do for you if God has taken mercy away from your heart?'

RITES OF PASSAGE

EACH TRANSITIONAL STAGE IN THE LIFE OF A MUSLIM – FROM BIRTH, TO MARRIAGE, THROUGH TO DEATH – IS SEEN AS IMPORTANT AND IS ACCOMPANIED BY A SIGNIFICANT RITUAL CELEBRATION.

The special rituals that initiate the Muslim into each new phase of his or her life provide an opportunity for the community to come together, celebrate life and offer thanks to God, as people continuously remember him throughout life. God's laws are upheld in the rites of passage as life is dedicated to him.

BIRTH
A newborn child is welcomed into the Muslim community with much joyful celebration. The parents or elders pronounce the *adhan*, the call to prayer, in the newborn child's ear, testifying that 'there is no God but the one God', and that 'Muhammad is his messenger'. This ritual signifies the child leading a life in accordance with God's laws. Sweetmeats are then distributed in celebration of the birth.

Birth is later followed by a naming ceremony – in which the child is given a good, meaningful name – and an *aqiqah,* or meal, where an animal is sacrificed. Friends and family are invited to partake in thanking God for the child.

Newborn Muslim children often have their heads shaved. The hair is then weighed and charity is given, according to the weight of the hair, in the child's name. The baby thus begins life through good deeds of generosity.

Boys are circumcized, to honour the tradition of the prophet Ibrahim. This is usually done between seven days and a few months after birth. However, in some countries, such as Turkey, boys are circumcized when they are much older – at about seven years – with great ceremony.

PUBERTY
While there is no particular ritual ceremony to mark its onset, puberty is a time of a fundamental change in the life of a Muslim boy or girl, as he or she begins to enter adulthood. At this time, the age of innocence is left behind and life as an accountable and responsible Muslim begins. The five daily prayers become incumbent, as do fasting and other religious obligations. For both sexes, the correct rules of modest dressing now need to be observed.

***Above** An image of a procession in honour of the circumcision of the Turkish prince Mehmed. In Turkey, boys are often circumcized much later than they are elsewhere in the Muslim world.*

MARRIAGE
As sex outside marriage is not allowed, young marriages are generally encouraged in Muslim societies, so that morality can be upheld. To assist in the choice of a good partner, families have traditionally aided the process by introducing prospective couples. Marriage brings together families, not just two individuals; therefore, several people are often consulted. Ultimately, the decision lies with the couple, however, and force can never be justified. The Prophet himself annulled forced marriages.

Marriage is marked by the *nikah* contract, where both parties give consent and the groom pays the bride a dowry, watched by two witnesses. The groom's family then

***Left** Kuwaiti children pray and read the Quran. While prayer is not compulsory for children, it becomes obligatory after puberty.*

Right Marriage is a monumental rite of passage, in which two families are united by a couple taking vows to live in peace together.

invite friends and family to a *walimah*, the marital meal. The marriage is thus made public, and thanks are given to Allah.

While marriage is important, it sometimes fails, and, in such cases, divorce, also, is a rite of passage. Again, the community is involved, as the Quran urges both parties to appoint arbitrators and to part with goodness and justice. The divorce must be witnessed, and any outstanding dowry must be fully paid to the wife.

DEATH

As birth brings a soul into the physical world, so death is seen as a positive experience, where life on earth ends and the soul returns to God. Despite knowing that death is decreed by God, it nevertheless represents a great loss for the family. Burial rites are therefore required not only to prepare the body and soul for return to its Lord, but also

to allow closure for the family. Muslims will gather at the house of the deceased to offer their prayers and condolences, and the whole community will provide food for the grieving family for the first few difficult days.

The body is treated with great respect, and at no point is it exposed in its entirety. Close family and friends ritually wash the body, perfume it and shroud it, with reverence and prayers. A funeral prayer is then offered by the whole

community – men, women and children – as they return the soul of the departed to God.

Muslim burials are eco-friendly as no coffin is used, unless local laws require it, which is usually the case in non-Muslim countries. The Quran and prayers are recited to aid the soul's passage to the next world.

Below Death completes the cycle of life, with the soul returning to its Lord. Here, the community pays its respects and says prayers at a burial in South Africa.

The Lawful and the Prohibited

MUSLIMS BELIEVE THAT GOD HAS GUIDED HUMANKIND BY PROVIDING RULES THAT CLEARLY STATE WHAT IS ALLOWED AND WHAT IS PROHIBITED, IN ORDER TO BALANCE LIFE AND CREATE HARMONY.

The notion of lawful (*halal*) and unlawful (*haram*) has been used as a way of regulating societies since time immemorial. What constitutes these two categories of permissible and prohibited lifestyles has varied throughout time as individuals and societies have carved out their own understanding of good and evil.

Muslims believe that people need laws from God in order to carry out his divinely appointed role as God's vicegerents on earth. These laws therefore exist for the regulation and good of humanity.

SHARIAH

The word 'Shariah' literally means 'road' but is taken to mean Islamic law. Islamic scholars have elaborated that Shariah is a wide road, whose boundaries are quite far apart, allowing a great deal of movement and freedom. The edges of the road represent the limitations and prohibitions that exist in different spheres of life. For the Muslim, all actions are lawful unless expressly prohibited by Shariah.

WORSHIP

While Islam is considered to be a *din*, or way of life, a clear distinction is made in Islamic law between matters of worship and other aspects of life. Daily habits, lifestyle and cultural norms are all considered lawful unless expressly prohibited, but in matters of worship, the only actions and rituals permissible are those that are expressly affirmed by the Shariah.

In worship, there are five categories, which have been developed by jurists. Firstly, there are those acts, such as *salah*, which must be performed (*fard*) and that carry a reward. At the other extreme, those which are prohibited and carry a punishment are *haram*: for example, compromising on God's oneness by giving precedence to

Above A painting (c. 1675–1725) shows legal scholars discussing and formulating juristic opinions. For Muslims, living righteously involves observing the laws.

other things. In between are three graded stages: *mandub* acts are rewarded and recommended but not compulsory: for example, voluntary fasts; *mubah* acts are those on which the law is silent – they are allowed

Below A horse race at the Equestrian Club in Baghdad, Iraq – betting on horse-racing is perfectly acceptable under Islamic law.

but do not carry any merit; and *makruh* acts, which are not *haram* and therefore are not punished, but neither are they encouraged: for example, fasting on a Friday not followed or preceded by a day or more of fasting.

DAILY LIFE

Shariah categories of *haram* are far more limited in scope on matters of lifestyle and habits. This law is not formulated by jurists: the Quran itself explains what is prohibited and no one can add to this category. The Prophet Muhammad stated that what Allah allowed in his book is lawful, what he forbade is prohibited, while what he was silent on is also allowed.

Muslims believe that God prohibits certain actions because they are harmful and impure; in this way, he aids humans in controlling their base appetites and the ego and thus in nurturing the soul. For example, a Muslim man may lawfully marry a Jewish or Christian woman because she is monotheistic,

Right Shariah and the Quran strictly regulate finance, especially interest-free banking. This bank in Indonesia follows Islamic banking laws.

but is prohibited from marrying a polytheistic woman because her ideology would be in contradiction to Islam and it would, therefore, be difficult to establish peace and harmony in the family home.

However, certain matters are not clearly stated as either *halal* or *haram* and are therefore 'doubtful'. Muhammad advised caution in such 'grey areas', saying that it was better to steer clear of them in order to strengthen one's faith. For example, while eating pork is forbidden, using the skin of pigs is considered a grey area: while some

Above Muslims eating at Beurger King Muslim, a halal *fast-food restaurant in Paris. ('Beur' is a French slang word for North African.)*

jurists allow it, maintaining that only the consumption of animal meat is forbidden, others argue that all pig products should be avoided. Smoking is another such area: some Muslims argue that it is close to being *haram* as it is effectively self-violation and can cause illness; others claim that smoking in moderation is allowable as a social habit and a relaxant.

EAT OF THE GOOD THINGS

THE QURAN URGES MUSLIMS TO EAT THOSE FOODS THAT ARE *HALAL*, LAWFUL, AND *TAYYIB*, GOOD (2:168), IN ORDER TO UPHOLD GOD'S COMMANDS AND LIVE A LIFE OF PURITY.

Islam takes a holistic view of human life, believing that the mind, body, emotions and soul are all interconnected and, therefore, interdependent. Food and drink directly affect the body, and spiritual worship very much depends on a healthy body. Islam, therefore, has clear laws on eating and drinking.

TAYYIB, HARAM AND HALAL

The Quran commands, 'O ye who believe, eat of the good things that We have provided for you, and be grateful to Allah: it is Him you worship' (2:172). In Islam, good, or *tayyib*, foods are all those fruits, grains and vegetables that are naturally produced by the earth. Their goodness lies in their nutritional benefits and in the different pleasing colours and tastes that have been created by God. Some Muslims argue that *tayyib* in its purest sense means organic, non-genetically modified foods.

The Quran prohibits the eating of carrion, blood, pig and any animal that has not been slaughtered in God's name (2:173). Further categories of prohibited, or *haram*, foods are carnivorous animals, birds of prey and those partly devoured by wild animals. Islam teaches that the logic behind *haram* foods is simply that God prohibits only those things that are not good for health and wellbeing. All other meats – beef, lamb, fowl and fish – are accepted as lawful, or *halal*, foods.

SLAUGHTERING

Recent controversies over animal welfare have questioned methods of killing animals for food. Islam has always promoted animal welfare, and so prohibits any methods of slaughtering that cause pain or distress to the animals. Slaughtering is sanctioned only by the cutting of the animal's throat in one swift knife action, in which the windpipe and jugular vein are severed.

Above Painting of a meal being prepared from the anthology of Hafiz, a 16th-century poet. Food should be prepared with prayers, peace and love.

Kindness to the animal is paramount – both in life and at the time of its death. It is important that it is reared correctly and freely, is treated kindly at the time of slaughtering, does not see the knife, is not seen by other animals when being slaughtered and has Allah's name invoked over it.

ALCOHOL AND DRINKS

Water, milk and all fruit juices are highly recommended. The only prohibition is fermented drinks: that is, alcohol, or *khamr*. *Khamr* means 'a cover', for alcohol and drugs 'cover' (cloud) the mind through intoxication. As they can impair mental and physical faculties, they are prohibited.

Left Eating tayyib and halal food is a requirement of Muslim life. Animals should be reared organically and treated with kindness in life and at their death.

Above Eating together carries many blessings and is always preferred to eating alone. Here, a traditional meal is shared in a Yemeni home near Taizz.

Because drinking alcohol was such an embedded practice in pre-Islamic Arabia, the Quranic verses prohibiting it were revealed in three phases. Firstly, around the 16th year of Muhammad's prophethood, people were told that there were some benefits in it, but that the harm was greater (2:219). The year after, Muslims were instructed not to approach their prayers when intoxicated (4:43). Finally, in the 17th year of prophethood, the total ban on alcohol was revealed, linking it with the works of the devil (5:90).

NECESSITY NEGATES PROHIBITION

The Quran is emphatic, and the Muslim community is united, in the view that if a person will otherwise die of hunger or thirst, and there is no other food or drink available but the *haram*, or if a person is forced to eat unlawfully under oppression, then such food and drink are to be treated as lawful, without any blame being laid on the consumer. Preserving life is seen as a more sacred duty than obedience to dietary laws.

MANNERS AND ETIQUETTE OF EATING

Not only what but how Muslims eat is important. Muhammad encouraged people to eat with their right hand, and to start with a prayer in God's name. He also recommended that people eat slowly, and from what is nearest to them on their plates first. He emphasized that only a third of the stomach should be filled with food, another third with water and the final third left empty. This is so that overeating, and all the problems associated with it, can be avoided. Finally, praise and thanks to Allah should complete the meal. For attaining further blessings, Muslims believe that it is better to eat in company, rather than alone.

THE QURAN AND HEAVENLY FOODS

The Quran mentions many earthly foods, including lentils, corn, onions, dates, olives, water and milk. But in heaven, the Quran states, there are fountains and flowing springs, and drinks that will be sweet but without any headiness. There are also pomegranates, dates, other fruits, the *talh* tree, bearing perhaps a kind of plantain, and the flesh of fowl.

Above Referred to several times in the Quran, dates are believed to be one of the foods of paradise.

SOCIAL REALITIES FOR WOMEN

THERE ARE A VARIETY OF OPINIONS REGARDING WOMEN'S POSITION IN SOCIETY. WHILE ISLAM APPEARS TO GIVE WOMEN MANY RIGHTS, THE SOCIAL REALITY IS QUITE OFTEN VERY DIFFERENT.

Above In 2003, a Pakistani Muslim female politician outside the Parliament building in Islamabad calls for an end to Pervez Musharraf's dictatorship.

Women in some Muslim societies do not have the safety and freedom of movement enjoyed by others, but appearances can be deceptive: in the early period of Islam, Muslim women had far more rights than were enjoyed by women under English law, even up to the 20th century, as regards property and education. Muslim women in the West are free to choose a public or private life. While many have excelled in education and the workplace, others have chosen a domestic role.

PATRIARCHY AND WOMEN
Muslim societies, like many other societies throughout the world, are traditionally patriarchal: that is, they are organized and run by men. This has meant that Muslim women's movements have often been restricted. For example, in Saudi Arabia, women are banned from driving, and cannot usually leave their home without the company of a male relative. Not only has this curtailed women's movements in the public sphere, but it also contradicts the Prophet's teaching that all Muslims, whether male or female, should be able to ride a horse, which implies the use of any means of transport.

In Afghanistan, the Taliban closed many girls' schools, claiming that if girls were out in society they might freely mix with men, thus corrupting society. (In so doing, they squarely placed the blame for immoral behaviour on women's shoulders.) This again contradicts the prophetic teaching: in this case, that seeking knowledge should be compulsory for men and women. These erosions of women's rights are cultural malpractices that are oppressive to women, not religious injunctions, as Islamic teachings clearly state the opposite.

MOSQUE SPACES
Although the Prophet Muhammad said that women should be allowed to go to mosques to offer prayers, he is also reported as saying that it is better for women to pray at home. Though seemingly contradictory, these two statements can be reconciled from the perspective that it is not compulsory for women to pray in the mosque: that could be an imposition for those

Left In many countries, Muslim women are free to pursue whatever career they want – such as this teacher at a primary school in London, England.

Above Dr Amina Wadud leads mixed-gender Friday prayer in New York. Women imams of mixed congregations are not usually permitted.

who would find it difficult, such as mothers with young children. Unfortunately, the second teaching has been interpreted so literally in some Muslim communities that mosques do not always provide prayer spaces for women.

This extreme position, and the discomfort of some feminist scholars with male-only imams in mosques, led to Dr Amina Wadud, Professor of Islamic Studies at Virginia Commonwealth University, conducting, to much controversy, a mixed prayer congregation in New York in 2005.

DIVERSITY IN MUSLIM SOCIETIES

Such problems for some women, however, must be balanced with the fact that many Muslim societies are surprisingly diverse and egalitarian. Official statistics show that Iran's higher education population is made up of 65 per cent women. In Morocco and Tunisia, women make up 20–25 per cent of judges, compared with 22 per cent in

Britain at district judge level and 8 per cent at appeal level. In Pakistan, 17.5 per cent of politicians in the lower house are women, which compares favourably with 18 per cent in Britain's House of Commons, yet Pakistan is often viewed as a less progressive society than Britain. This illustrates that while some Muslim societies are very traditional and insist on strict

dress codes and segregation, others, such as Malaysia, for example, are not so curtailing of women and allow them free movement.

As Islam puts great emphasis on the home providing a stable life, some women have chosen home-making as a vocation. What might appear as an imposed private life for some Muslim women is, in fact, an expressed choice.

WOMEN IN EARLY ISLAMIC HISTORY

Seeking knowledge is a must for all Muslims, according to a prophetic tradition. This injunction was taken particularly seriously in the early centuries of Islam: after the Prophet's death, his widow Ayesha was often consulted for her wisdom and knowledge of Muhammad's life. Further, women appear in records of Islamic universities from the 8th century.

Many of the early compilers of hadith record female scholars as their source of authority. The same women were renowned teachers, their popularity reflected in records detailing the large numbers of students in their classes. One such distinguished woman was Karima al-Marwaziyya (d.1070), who was considered the best commentator on Bukhari's hadith.

Dr Muhammad Akram Nadwi has written that in the 13th century, Fatima bint Ibrahim, a famous teacher of the Bukhari collection, travelled for *Hajj* to Makkah. On reaching Madinah, she was asked to teach in the Prophet's Mosque. Because she was elderly, she taught while leaning on the Prophet's grave. This is enlightening, considering that some mosques do not allow women to enter. Similarly, Shaykha Shuhda, from the same period, was a renowned lecturer at Baghdad University, the Oxford and Cambridge of its time, yet Britain did not permit women into its universities until the late 1870s.

WOMEN IN THE QURAN

MUSLIM WOMEN CAN ASPIRE TOWARD AND LEARN FROM A WIDE RANGE OF FEMALE CHARACTERS FEATURED IN THE QURAN, FROM THE PRIVATE AND PEACEFUL TO THE POWERFUL AND PASSIONATE.

The many women portrayed in the Quran are admired for various reasons, and show clearly that there is no one ideal woman. Different character traits are depicted so that Muslim women can draw inspiration from the characters that most resemble them.

EVE THE HELPER

The narrative relating to Eve in the Quran presents her as Adam's mate and helper, the one with whom he sought to live in peace. Eve therefore represents domestic harmony and bliss, the other half of Adam, and she is not solely blamed for the couple's subsequent descent from heaven (7:19-25).

MARY THE DEVOUT WORSHIPPER

Mary the mother of Jesus is likewise presented as a peaceful character, but one who is a model of spirituality. Although she is living under the care of her uncle Zakariyya, her life is dedicated to serving God through the temple.

Because of Mary's great piety, her communication with God is very direct. Indeed, whenever her uncle approaches her in the temple with provisions, he finds that she already has food. When he questions her about where this food comes from, Mary simply replies that it has been brought to her from God (3:37).

Above Archangel Jibril appears in human form to Mary, to announce the birth of Jesus, from The Chronology of Ancient Nations, *al-Biruni, 1307.*

Perhaps the most unique event in the narrative of Mary is that angels speak to her directly. (Only men called as prophets are usually addressed by angels.) She is told that she has conceived a child as a virgin and that he will be devoted to God, and is later instructed to withdraw from her people to give birth to the child, then to bring him to her people.

Mary is a figure whom Muslim women aspire toward: she is pious, sincere in her worship of God and innocent – the perfect image of femininity and tenderness. She is so revered in the Quran that chapter 19 is named after her.

BILQIS THE RULER

While both Eve and Mary are very private figures, Bilqis, the Queen of Sheba, is the opposite. In the Quranic account, a hoopoe brings King Solomon the news of a queen from Sheba, a city in Yemen prided for its civilization and produce

Left Adam and Eve and their twins in earthly paradise, from The Fine Flower of Histories, *by Sayyid Loqman Ashuri, 1583.*

Above Verses from chapter 19 of the Quran narrate Mary's story. Mary is highly revered in Islamic thought.

(27:22). The extent of the queen's power and status can be judged from her magnificent throne. However, the kingdom worships the sun, and Solomon therefore invites Bilqis to Islam via a letter.

The narrative shows her to be both a diplomatic and a well-liked ruler – she seeks advice from her ministers regarding Solomon's letter (27:32), but they show allegiance to her by submitting to her decision. She prudently avoids war by sending gifts to Solomon, and eventually accepts the one God.

ASIYA THE OPPRESSED

Most of the women presented in the Quran are married to God's devout prophets, but women who are tyrannized by oppressive men are not to be seen as weak. The wife of Pharaoh, Asiya, is seen as the epitome of women who suffer in such circumstances but who arc still striving toward goodness in their silent struggles. Not only does Asiya raise Moses with love (28:9), but she is also devoted to God, asking him to free her from Pharaoh's crimes and build a house for her in paradise close to him. She is shown in the Quran to be exemplary for both men and women: 'And Allah sets forth as an example to those who believe, the wife of Pharaoh' (66:11).

ZULAIKHA THE PASSIONATE

The wife of the Aziz of Egypt, Zulaikha, is a passionate character. The Aziz has given shelter and work to Joseph, son of Jacob, in Egypt, but as Joseph grows up, Zulaikha falls in love with him and pursues him with passion. On being caught in her pursuit, she pleads innocence, crying (attempted) rape. Joseph's innocence is acknowledged, but Zulaikha still manages to ensure he is imprisoned (12:21-32). She is seen as a woman blinded by anger and passion, bent on making Joseph suffer. Although the story makes it clear that Zulaikha is helpless in being attracted to Joseph, it is also made plain that natural desires can be contained and purified only by a belief in God. Joseph is saved by his God-consciousness (12:24).

While discouraging unlimited passion, the Quran acknowledges that passion is a human trait. In this story, Zulaikha eventually repents and seeks God's forgiveness.

CHAPTER 6

MORALITY, ETHICS AND LAW

I n Islam, morality and ethics are not abstract concepts that are defined simply by individual conscience. Rather, they are concrete values that are enshrined in the Quran and regulated by the Shariah. Muslims believe that because moral and ethical concepts are prescribed by Islamic laws and teachings, Muslim society is able to function with harmony and cohesion.

This does not deny the importance of conscience, however, which Islam teaches has been given to every individual by God. Rather, the norms are determined by the Shariah for certain basic actions, while individuals have the responsibility of applying the moral teachings and ethical dictates of Islam to each human interaction, in accordance with their conscience. For Muslims, such an approach is seen not as the product of mechanical instruction, but as a set of clear directives that appeal to a person's intellect (*aql*) and sense of social justice (*adl*). There is a balance (*mizan*) between man as spiritual being and social actor: God is obeyed and others served.

Opposite An imam studies the Quran before prayers in the Larabanga Mosque, Ghana, West Africa. The Quran contains a blueprint for moral and ethical values.

Above A man and his child attend prayers in Dhaka, Bangladesh. Family values and practices are shaped by the ethical teachings of Islam.

ACCOUNTING FOR THE SOUL

ISLAM TEACHES THAT INDIVIDUALS HAVE MORAL AND ETHICAL DUTIES TO GOD, THEMSELVES, THEIR FAMILIES, THEIR COMMUNITY, THE WIDER SOCIETY, HUMANITY AT LARGE AND EVEN OF THE WHOLE CREATION.

Humankind is seen as the best of God's creation, and as such has a moral responsibility to establish God's will on earth. Muslims believe that God has instructed men and women in their responsibilities by sending a series of divinely guided prophets, some with holy scriptures, to show them the 'straight path'.

Islam teaches that humankind's divinely appointed task is to establish prayer and charity in the service of God and to forsake all evil in thought and deeds, to be morally upright and ethically principled in accordance with God's decrees.

INDIVIDUAL RESPONSIBILITY

The Shariah sets down clear instructions concerning the duties of men and women at every level. Firstly, it maintains, they should worship God as the owner of all creation. The Quran teaches that

***Above** Muslims believe that giving zakah purifies one's possessions and deeds, as well as ensuring that poverty is addressed through wealth distribution.*

God has given humankind unique faculties – reason, intelligence and free will – in return for earthly vicegerency (caliph).

Each individual has responsibility for himself or herself – to nurture his or her body and soul, be morally upright and ethically conscious and accept God's divine decree for his or her life. Each person has a duty to love, respect, protect and provide for the material, emotional and spiritual wellbeing of his/her family, which includes extended family.

Individuals also have duties in respect of their community and neighbours (defined as those living within a radius of 40 houses). Responsibilities toward society include issues of allegiance and loyalty, distribution of charity, community service and civil participation. The Shariah gives both specific rulings and general guidelines in terms of Muslims' wider responsibilities toward humanity, which vary depending on the community's theological and cultural proximity to Islam.

***Left** This early 17th-century Persian painting shows a Safavid princess in the tranquillity of her garden. Islam calls for humans to look after the natural world.*

Above A Muslim family in Britain visit the local mosque. Children are encouraged to attend congregational prayers and other religious events.

Finally, Islam presents itself as an environmentally friendly religion: the Shariah enshrines laws relating to water wastage, destructive tree-felling and the rights of animals, among other ecological issues.

TRUSTEESHIP

A Muslim's thoughts and actions are regulated by a set of moral values and ethical actions bound by the Shariah. Islam teaches that God is unique (the doctrine of *tawhid*) and therefore all creation belongs to him, but that he has given the earth to humankind as a sacred trust. This concept of trusteeship is fundamental in Islam.

The Quran describes trusteeship as 'enjoining what is good': that is, establishing what God has permitted (*halal*) and 'forbidding evil', or stopping transgression and what is harmful (*haram*)(3:104). In doing so, Muslims believe that divine peace (Islam) will be established.

In Islam, men and women are duty bound to co-operate with each other to meet their religious

Right Thai Muslim civilians and soldiers are observed as God's caliphs, or vicegerents, as they plant grass seeds together to protect the soil from erosion.

obligations, and are both considered caliphs on God's earth. As such, they have an equal responsibility in preserving the natural order of God's creation and the ecological balance of their environment.

This sacred trusteeship is bound with accountability, and Islam teaches that abuse or injustices to fellow humans, animals and plants, or the landscape and atmosphere will be judged and punished by God accordingly, both in this world and the hereafter. Human injustices and inequalities cause strife and conflict, and abuses of nature, such as pollution, upset the divinely ordained balance and result in ecological catastrophes.

ESTABLISHING JUSTICE

Another moral responsibility is establishing justice (*adl*). It could be argued that the purpose of all the prophets was to establish divine justice, and, in Islam, the concept begins with the individual. Muslims are taught that they must be mindful of the needs of their own body, mind and soul, avoiding any activity that harms the self. Justice must also be shown to others, particularly to those who are poor and vulnerable.

The Quran and hadith make many references to the status of women. Cultural malpractices can impose a dominant patriarchy on some Muslim societies, but Islam promotes the idea of gender equity. The instructions given relate to the role of women in terms of their religious obligations, their rights and their position in society. While many verses honour and protect women, enshrining their legal rights, others imply a biological gender equity: '...He created for you from yourselves spouses so that you might find solace in them...' (30:21), and 'men and women are protectors of one another' (9:71).

HUMAN AGENCY

ISLAM TEACHES THAT HUMANKIND IS BOUND TO SERVE GOD BY A
PRIMORDIAL COVENANT, ENTERED WHEN ALL SOULS WERE CREATED,
PROMISING TO SUBMIT TO HIM AND BE HIS VICEGERENTS ON EARTH.

Human agency is based entirely on the idea of free will being exercised, for Islam teaches that God himself gave human beings the faculty of choice. However, in exercising their free will, individuals must recognize the responsibility of ensuring peace and goodness on earth, not oppression.

Muslims use the creation story of Adam to understand human agency and the purpose of humankind on earth. According to the Quran, after God created the physical form of Adam, he stroked his back and made all the souls who were to be born between then and the Day of Judgement to come out from between his back and loins. He then made all the souls stand before him, and asked them, 'Am I not your Lord?' (7:172). When they affirmed their choice, Allah took the primordial covenant with them, telling them that he was going to make the heavens and the earth a witness to their promise of recognizing him as Lord. The prophets, who were also among the souls, were then made to take a further covenant with God, with regard to their missions (33:7).

FREE CHOICE

The first thing this covenant clarifies is that humans are different from the animal world, not only because God breathed into them, but also because he allowed them to have choice. This free will to choose is interpreted by scholars as meaning that each person has an innate consciousness (*fitra*), which allows them to discriminate

Above A Saudi Arabian man stands alone in the desert. The Quran says that all souls took a covenant with God, recognizing him as worthy of worship.

between right and wrong. Whether individuals act according to that moral consciousness is another matter, but Islam asserts that at the time of taking the covenant, every man and woman clearly understood truth, falsehood and the importance of following God's laws.

ACCOUNTABILITY

In taking the covenant with God, men and women accepted the responsibility of being his earthly representatives. This involved being accountable for establishing peace and order, not being unjust toward anyone, ensuring through kind and gentle reminders that God was duly worshipped and protecting the existence and rights of all people, animals, plants and the earth at

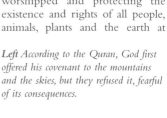

Left According to the Quran, God first offered his covenant to the mountains and the skies, but they refused it, fearful of its consequences.

Left Islamic literature teaches Muslims what their role is on earth and how they are to represent God's plan for peace.

are consequences of disobeying God, but individuals should always have the choice to act or not act.

Taking responsibility is seen as very noble: humankind was brave enough to accept God's vicegerency on earth. But at the same time, this choice has exposed humans to pressures that divert them from their original role. For this reason, the Quran describes humankind as unjust, claiming they took the covenant without reflecting fully on their new responsibility. The covenant is seen not as an ideal that cannot be fulfilled, but rather as one that must be borne with maturity and accountability.

Muslims believe that they have individually promised to worship God and represent him on earth. In practice, this means that they are bound to fulfilling the five pillars, protecting kith and kin, preserving the earth and spreading peace and harmony. In short, it means true, wilful submission: Islam.

Below A 15th-century miniature shows mystics engaged in discourse. Being God's vicegerent requires wisdom and justice.

large. In turn, the whole of creation was made subservient to mankind (31:20). At the same time, in taking this covenant, humankind accepted the reality of free will. This was clearly a huge responsibility for men and women to undertake.

The Quran clarifies that God did not thrust this burden upon humankind: before making the covenant with all souls, he asked the heavens, the earth and, indeed, the mountains if they

wanted this responsibility (33:72). But according to the Quran, they all declined, because they did not want to have the choice of obeying or disobeying God but rather wanted to submit to his will at all times.

CHOOSING VICEGERENCY

In Islam, humanity is considered to be superior to the rest of the natural world, for men and women choose whether or not to obey God. This freedom to act is fundamental: there

---

THE MANTLE OF RESPONSIBILITY

'We did indeed offer the Trust to the heavens and the earth and the mountains, but they refused to undertake it, being afraid thereof: but man undertook it – he was indeed unjust and foolish.'

(33:72)

'When thy Lord drew forth from the children of Adam descendants from their loins, and He made them testify about themselves, "Am I not your Lord?", they said, "Yes! We do testify!" '

(7:172)

COMBATING THE EGO

WHILE ISLAM TEACHES THAT HUMAN NATURE IS BASICALLY GOOD, HUMANKIND MUST NEVERTHELESS ENDURE A STRUGGLE TO MASTER THE EGO–SELF (*NAFS*), WHICH WARS AGAINST THE SPIRITUAL SELF (*RUH*).

Above *A Shiah man prays, holding a rosary, at the Imam Ali shrine. The lives of Muslim saints inspire many Muslims to live a virtuous life, free from the ego.*

Muslim philosophers, and in particular Sufis, have argued consistently that humankind exists in two simultaneous and parallel realms. One is the physical, sensory and known world, referred to as the exoteric (*dhahir*), which is bound by natural laws and experienced realities. The other is the inner world of the unseen or spiritual, called the esoteric (*batin*). Both realms are clearly referred to in the Quran and hadith literature: 'God holds the unseen in the heavens and the earth, And unto him does every matter return, So serve Him and rely on Him, Your Lord is not unmindful of what you are doing' (11:123).

Muslims believe that the external world is ordered by divine instructions, laws and teachings, which are aimed at developing a cohesive and harmonized society. Similarly, the internal realm, which is comprehensively seen and known only by God, is believed to be subject to divine command: God instructs human beings to master or combat the ego and thereby elevate their souls.

BODY AND SOUL

Islamic theology teaches that the ego (*nafs*) and the soul (*ruh*) are essential components of humankind's metaphysical being. While both entities are believed to be contained within the physical being, the *nafs* and *ruh* have different constitutions. The *nafs* is a human being's physical, worldly nature, created from earth and clay and then given the 'breath of life' (literally, *nafas*) by God. Islam teaches that as God created and gave life to every individual, he also placed within each person something of himself. This divine presence that exists within all human beings is the *ruh*, or soul, and Muslims believe that it emanates from God's own essence, or divine light (*nur*).

This implies that man's nature is inherently good, rather than inclined to evil. Muslims believe that it is humankind's base and earthy physical nature that is at the root of his occasional succumbing to his own lower desires. The Quran explains that it is to the *nafs* that Satan whispers his temptations, in order to lead men and women away from their higher spiritual being and natural disposition of obedience to God. Each person therefore faces an internal battle between the earthly, sensory and pleasure-seeking self, or the ego, and the pure, spiritual soul, which desires only to be reunited to the one from whom it came.

SELF-STRUGGLE

Islamic mystics (Sufis) understand the internal struggle of ego and soul in terms of *tazkiyah*, or spiritual self-purification. *Tazkiyah* is the means by which all bad habits and

Left Spiritual emotions run high as a Kashmiri Muslim woman prays in reverence at the shrine of the Sufi saint, Shaykh Hamza Makhdoomi.

traits are tempered through worship of and devotion to God. In their desire to conquer their egos, some Sufis cut themselves off from the world, choosing a life of isolation and spiritual piety.

However, Muhammad advised his followers not to emulate the ascetic practices of the people of previous scriptures, but rather to live among people in order to spread goodness and serve humankind. His own methods of spiritual self-development included a number of specific forms of worship: a night prayer vigil (*tahajjud*), voluntary fasting, regular recitation of the Quran and remembrance of God (*dhikr*) and frequent charity.

The struggle between one's lower desires and the soul's yearning for a higher spiritual plain is a life-long endurance. Muslims view this striving for spiritual perfection as a test of belief, and the Quran offers encouragement in this struggle: 'And whoever desires the Hereafter and strives for it with due effort, and believes, those are the ones whose striving will be appreciated' (17:19).

INNER *JIHAD*

The word *jihad* actually means 'to struggle'. In the Islamic context, *jihad* signifies 'struggling in the way of God' and it covers all activities associated with the establishment of Islam or its defence. This extends from the individual's struggle for spiritual excellence to defending one's country, community or home from oppression and invasion.

At the individual level, the notion of *jihad* is concerned with combating the ego and submitting oneself sincerely to God. On one occasion, while returning from a battle against the pagan Arabs, Muhammad told the Muslims, 'we return from the lesser *jihad* to the greater *jihad*', explaining that 'greater *jihad*' was the constant struggle to combat the ego and lower desires.

Above Contemplation, or dhikr, *is an essential part of Muslim worship, which encourages spiritual self-development through remembrance of God's attributes.*

Below Offering night prayers, or tarawih, *at Ramadhan – here, shown at the al-Aqsa Mosque in Jerusalem – is one way in which Muslims honour the soul's yearning for spiritual perfection.*

JIHAD: A JUST WAR?

THE WORD *JIHAD* IS OFTEN MISINTERPRETED AS A 'HOLY WAR', BUT
OCCASIONALLY FIGHTING TYRANNY AND AGGRESSION IS VIEWED AS A
RELIGIOUS DUTY IN ISLAM. IT IS THEN UNDERSTOOD AS A 'JUST WAR'.

*Above A 14th-century depiction of
Averroes, who engaged with Aristotelian
philosophy and published detailed legal
treaties on the conduct of war.*

Historically, Western scholarship on Islam has tended to present Muhammad as a 'holy warrior', who sanctified violence and intolerance, spreading his religion by the sword to impose his beliefs on others. This misrepresentation has dominated non-Muslims' perception of Islam since the Middle Ages. But association of the term *jihad* with armed conflict has more to do with the hostilities of the medieval European crusades than with any true understanding of the word's multifarious meanings.

LESSER AND GREATER *JIHAD*
Jihad literally means 'struggle', and it implies a physical, moral, spiritual and intellectual effort. As the term *jihad* covers a wide range of activities relating to the struggles of faith, providing a precise definition for the term is difficult.

Islamic scholars identify two types of *jihad: al-jihad al-asghar*, or 'the lesser struggle', and *al-jihad al-akbar*, meaning the 'greater struggle'. *Al-jihad al-asghar* is concerned with the fight against oppression and tyranny, where armed conflict can result in loss of life. *Al-jihad al-akbar* is the internal battle waged by Muslims against their physical desires and baser instincts. It is perhaps because the enemy within, represented by the unfettered ego, is less discernible than one on the battlefield that Islam considers the internal struggle to be a greater *jihad*.

MILITARY *JIHAD*
The Quran states clearly the circumstances in which war is permitted, giving three major ones: Muslims are allowed to fight in defence of their freedom of religion; their country; and their community

(22:39–40). Military *jihad* must also comply with conditions of Islamic law as contained in the Shariah, which details the moral duties and ethical actions of armed conflict.

The Quran refers to the defence of 'cloisters and churches and synagogues' (22:40), implying that religious freedom must be accorded to minority faith communities (*ahl al-dhimmah*) living in Muslim lands or under their protection. *Ahl al-dhimmah* are exempt from military *jihad* by payment of the *jizyah* (exemption tax).

ETHICS OF *JIHAD*
The Shariah contains a wide range of instructions and prohibitions relating to the ethics of *jihad*, and medieval Islamic scholars, such as Ibn Rushd and Ibn Khaldun, wrote detailed treatises on the ethics of military *jihad* and its permissibility.

According to the Quran, 'Permission to fight is given to those against whom war is being

*Left Artist Edwin Lord Weeks imagines
the call to 'holy war' against Christians
in this 19th-century representation of
the Great Mosque of Córdoba, Spain.*

wrongfully waged, And God is indeed able to help them; those who have been unjustly driven out of their homes only because they said our Lord is God' (22:39–40). But the prohibition of aggression is unambiguously stated: 'Fight in the way of God against those who fight against you, but do not yourselves commit aggression; for behold, God does not love aggressors. And fight against them until there is no more persecution and people are free to worship God. But if they desist, then all hostilities shall cease, except against the oppressors…' (2:193)

The Prophet also gave explicit orders to Muslim soldiers in the theatre of war in order to prevent atrocities. He commanded them to seek permission from dependent parents before going to war, and he prohibited the molestation of harmless innocents and the weak and infirm, the demolishing of the dwellings or property of unresisting inhabitants and the destruction of their means of subsistence, such as livestock and agriculture, and of trees or date palms.

POLITICS OF *JIHAD*

Although the Quran interdicts Muslims from waging a war of aggression (2:190), the majority of scholars conclude that when the existence of the Muslim community or the borders of its lands are under attack, military *jihad* should be declared until all oppression has been abated. Conversely, if a Muslim political ruler declares an illegal war, the citizens of that state would be justified in disobeying a call to arms and becoming 'conscientious objectors'. However, if a declaration of hostilities is seen as a just war by the vast majority of religious scholars – and only a just war can be called a *jihad* – and if the state conforms to the principles and instructions of the Shariah, then every eligible Muslim must take up arms.

Above The Muslim ruler Timur, or Tamerlane, is depicted attacking a walled city in this 16th-century illustration. The Quran clearly states when war is justified.

Below Bosnian Muslims in training during the Bosnian War in the 1990s. Many Muslims defended their people and land from Serbian aggression.

MARTYRDOM AND SUICIDE

SHAHADAH IS THE FIRST PILLAR OF ISLAM AND THE ARABIC WORD CARRIES THE SENSE OF BOTH 'TO BEAR WITNESS' AND 'MARTYRDOM', BUT IN ISLAM DYING FOR ONE'S FAITH DOES NOT INCLUDE SUICIDE.

Above A coffin shroud bears the Muslim declaration of faith. Islam teaches that those who die fighting tyranny and oppression enter paradise as martyrs.

Recent decades have witnessed a disturbing rise in the phenomenon generally described as 'Islamic fundamentalism'. The most obscene feature of this particular form of Muslim extremism is the alarming occurrences of terrorist suicide bombings and attacks. It is clear that there are many complex issues surrounding the political motivations for the use of violence, but the question remains: does Islam permit such indiscriminate acts of suicidal murder?

ISLAMIC MARTYRDOM

Islam has permitted war against tyranny and oppression through *al-jihad al-asghar*, or 'the lesser struggle', and recognizes those who die in such a 'just war' as martyrs. The Quran describes those fighting injustices as *mujahidun* (from the word *jihad*) and those who lose their lives in battle as *shuhadaa* (from *shahadah*, meaning 'martyrs').

Like the prophets, *shuhadaa* (sing. *shahid*) will not be brought to account on the Day of Judgement, and the Quran instructs believers to 'Think not of those who are slain in the way of God as dead, Nay, they are living, With their Lord they have provision. Jubilant (are they) because of that which God has bestowed upon them of His bounty, rejoicing for the sake of those who have not yet joined them but are left behind: that there shall no fear come upon them, neither shall they grieve' (3:169–70).

According to the Prophet, it is not only those who die in war

Left The iconography of martyrdom is illustrated in this fresco at the Martyrs Museum in Tehran, Iran. Shiahs revere martyrdom as exampled by Muhammad's grandson (d.680).

who are considered martyrs, but also mothers who die in childbirth, victims of unjust killings through accident or murder and those who die as a result of severe illness, starvation or natural catastrophes.

MUSLIM FUNDAMENTALISM

The term 'fundamentalist' usually denotes someone who believes in the literal meaning of his or her religious scripture. In this sense, all Muslims might be understood as fundamentalist because they believe the Quran is literally God's word, but it would be wrong to assume that the majority of Muslims are literalistic in their interpretation and application of their scripture.

Nevertheless, there exists a minority of Muslims who insist on a single interpretation of the Quran that divides the world simplistically into two categories: believers (Muslims) and non-believers (*kuffar*). Some such literalists use extreme and violent means that are contrary to the teachings of Islam in an attempt to impose their restricted views upon the majority. Often motivated by fanatical political aims, these extremists employ distorted religious interpretations to justify acts of terrorism.

SUICIDE TERRORISTS

Certain of these extremist Muslim fundamentalist groups will even attack and kill innocent people in an attempt to further their political and religious aims. Such acts of terrorism are increasingly carried out in the name of Islam by Muslim 'suicide' attackers or bombers.

Such acts of violence are in opposition to Islam: the Quran stipulates that 'whosoever kills a human being for other than murder or corruption in the earth, it shall be as if he killed all humanity' (5:32), and the Prophet exhorted that there shall be no harming and no reciprocating of harm. The overwhelming majority of Islamic jurists conclude that Islam categorically forbids both the act of suicide and the killing of innocents or 'non-combatants'.

While there can never be a justification for such heinous and reprehensible crimes, a distinction needs to be made between the terrorist acts of individual Muslims,

Above A female suicide bomber poses with her son before blowing herself up and killing four Israelis at a checkpoint on the Gaza Strip in January 2004.

which are perpetrated in the name of their religion, and what Islam teaches and the Muslim community (*ummah*) believes and practises. Suicide bombings and killings are more symptomatic of the political, social and economic inequalities existing in a number of Muslim countries than of any inherent violence or aggression in Islam.

MODERATION IN ISLAM

Islam forbids both zealous fanaticism (*ghuluw*) and lapsed indifference (*dhalal*). To be Muslim is to belong to what the Quran describes as *ummatun wasata*, or 'the community of moderation', and to abide by the consensus (*ijma*) of the wider community, its scholars and leaders.

During times of fission and unity, where Muslim political and spiritual leadership is established, the *ummah* is able to identify both legitimate governance and religious orthodoxy. However, fragmentation and disunity can result in a shared loss of direction and even violence and extremism. Muhammad warned his followers about the decline of Muslim rule, advising them to always take the 'middle path' and remain faithful to the Quranic teachings and his example.

Below The Iran–Iraq war of the 1980s saw Muslims killing Muslims, leaving more than a million dead. Both sides claimed that those killed were martyrs.

ISLAMIC ETHICS

LAW AND ETHICS, THE PRECEPTS OF MORAL CONDUCT, ARE VERY
SIMILAR IN ISLAM: BOTH ARE ROOTED IN THE QURAN, AND MUSLIMS
ARE REQUIRED TO ACCOUNT TO GOD FOR THEIR FULFILMENT.

Islamic ethics are found not only
in the Quran, but also throughout
the entire records of Islamic history.
In their personal moral behaviour
and in relations with family, in
business matters or when making
political treaties, Muslims are
exhorted to be just and merciful.

TEACHINGS OF THE QURAN
The Quran describes itself as the
furqan, the criterion by which
humankind can judge between
right and wrong: 'Blessed is He
who sent down the Criterion to
His servant, that it may be an
admonition to all creatures' (25:1).
Later in this chapter 25, metaphors
of light and darkness illustrate the
Quran's claim that it alone can lead
humankind to God's light, and
thereby his blessings, and that a life
away from this moral code leads
one into darkness. The teachings of
the Quran form the foundation for
all social interaction for Muslims.

Muslim ethics are also based on
the example of the Prophet, known
as sunnah, and his fulfilment of the
command to 'enjoin the good and
forbid the evil' (3:104). The Quran
and the sunnah are put into practice
with the application of human
'reason', the faculty each person has
to discern right from wrong, which
is referred to more than 750 times
in the Quran. Muslims believe that
relying on a combination of all
three sources promotes moral
responsibility, the basis of ethics.

ETHICS AS *AKHLAQ*
The Arabic term for 'ethics' is *akhlaq*.
In its singular form, the word means
character trait, but in its plural, it
carries the sense of morality or
ethics. It is used to refer to good
manners, politeness, justice and
kindness. Islam teaches that only
through personal reform and
morality can a Muslim draw near to
God and grow in his or her faith.

In a well-known hadith, the
Prophet said, 'I was sent to perfect
good character/ethics', thus placing
ethics and morality at the centre
of his prophetic mission. The
Quran says of him '…you are

Above An Iraqi Mullah at Prayer, *by
Konrad Filip, depicts an imam holding
the Quran – the Muslim's criterion for
judging right and wrong, which sets out
a statement of ethics.*

indeed of an exalted character'
(68:4). On many occasions, the
Prophet asserted that the best
Muslim, and the one dearest to
Allah, is the one with the best
moral character. Indeed, another
oft-quoted hadith even claims that
'a person can reach a high status in
the hereafter by his good conduct,
though he may be weak in matters
of worship, and he can also go
down to the lowest part of hell
by his wicked character'.

ETHICS IN PRACTICE
The Quran, sunnah, law and local
customs have together shaped the
whole body of rules known today
as Islamic ethics. The first rule put
into practice by the Prophet was
dispensing with idol worship and
focusing on monotheism. He then
enjoined his followers to replace

*Left These Saudi Arabian men are
engaged in a business meeting. Moral
and ethical conduct must be observed
by Muslims at all times, whether in
personal, social or business relations.*

Right A 16th-century manuscript painting shows the Prophet's Night Journey, which is seen as an allegory for each Muslim's journey toward God, through worship and ethical conduct.

kinship and tribal bonds with the idea of a larger Muslim community, teaching that the hereafter is more important than ancestral legacies, and that humility and justice are of greater consequence than pride and image.

A STATEMENT OF ETHICS

Many scholars claim that the most detailed statement of Islamic ethics contained in the Quran is to be found in chapter 17, verses 22 to 39. The chapter opens with the Prophet's night journey to heaven, which is seen as an allegory for every Muslim's own journey toward God. It then outlines humankind's fall from God's grace before giving the good news of his guidance.

However, in order to receive this guidance, it states that human beings must fulfil a code of ethics. This requires them to worship God alone; to be kind to parents, particularly in their old age; to assist the wayfarer and those in need; to avoid squandering wealth, but without being niggardly; to speak kindly even to those with whom one disagrees; not to kill children out of fear of lack of provision; not to commit adultery; not to take life unlawfully; not to usurp the property of orphans; to measure and conduct business deals fairly; not to be idly curious; not to 'walk on the earth in arrogance'. This comprehensive charter of human ethical conduct has been compared with the Ten Commandments.

Right An Iraqi family is breaking its fast at sunset in Ramadhan, having fasted from dawn until dusk. Sharing meals, sitting and socializing together are all activities that the Shariah rules upon.

THE SANCTITY OF LIFE

ISLAM TEACHES THAT LIFE IS PRECIOUS AND GIVEN BY GOD, AND PROCREATION AND THE BLESSINGS OF CHILDREN ARE SEEN BY MUSLIMS AS A NATURAL CONSEQUENCE OF MARRIED LIFE.

Islam can be said to be generally pro-life, and any action that preserves, prolongs and protects life is encouraged, on condition that it conforms to the moral and ethical teachings of Islam as defined within the Quran and sunnah. Conversely, taking a life by any immoral or unethical means is expressly prohibited in Islam.

MARRIAGE
Islam prohibits fornication and adultery and carefully inhibits all pathways leading to them. Islam is also against celibacy and the suppressing of the sexual urge by castration or any other physical means. Instead, it encourages marriage as a means of living a wholesome and fulfilled life. Sexual relations within the sanctity of marriage are considered both a natural act and a blessing from God.

If a Muslim has the means to marry, then he or she should do so; and refraining from marriage in order to dedicate oneself to the worship and service of God by

monasticism or renunciation of the world is discouraged. The Prophet forbade his companions from shunning marriage and withdrawing from the world, declaring such a lifestyle to be a deviation from Islam and a rejection of his sunnah.

BIRTH AND PATERNITY
Children are a natural consequence of marriage and are seen as a great blessing in Islam, and Muslims believe that God grants their sustenance. Female infanticide was a common practice among the pre-Islamic Arabs, but Islam prohibits the killing of one's children for fear of poverty or shame (17:31).

The right to family lineage and bloodline descent are often taken for granted, but many children do not know who one or other of their parents is. Muslims believe that God has ordained marriage in order that paternity can be established without ambiguity or doubt. Equally, a father is not allowed to deny his paternity of any child born within marriage.

***Above** Marriage is a sacred institution and the cornerstone of Muslim society. It has always been a cause for celebration in Islamic communities across the world.*

Muhammad declared that 'every child is attributed to the one on whose bed it is conceived', by which he meant that every child is a product of a specific sexual relationship, whether or not the man and woman are married.

In exceptional circumstances, where infidelity and subsequent illegitimacy is suspected, an Islamic judge (*qadi*) can decide paternity either via blood tests or by *lian*, a process where both parties swear an oath against each other's accusations before divorcing (24:6–9). In such a case, the child will thereafter take the mother's name.

LEGAL ADOPTION
Just as it is prohibited for a man to deny his paternity of a child born in wedlock, so it is forbidden

***Left** Muslims believe all life to be sacred, and that the illegal taking of a single life is equal to killing the whole of humanity.*

214

for him to legally claim that he is the father of any child he has not biologically conceived. In Muhammad's day, the pagan Arabs had a custom known as *tabanni* ('to make one's son'), whereby a child could be adopted by receiving the name and lineage of his or her adopting father. This practice was allowed even when the biological parents and family lineage of the child were known.

By contrast, the Quran states, 'Nor has He made your adopted sons your [real] sons, that is simply as saying from your mouths...call them by [the names of] their fathers, that is more just in the sight of God. But if you do not know their fathers, they are your brothers in faith and your wards' (33:4–5). Islam posits that the pronouncement

Right Marriage, and sexual relations within the marriage, are strongly encouraged in Islam.

of adopted children as one's own does not alter the biological and genealogical realities. Such a ruling safeguards lineage and protects any rights of inheritance. The Quran teaches that 'blood relatives are nearer to each other in the ordinance of God' (8:75). Legal adoption in expressed terms of claiming children who are not

Above A Qatari Arab Muslim with his daughter. Children are considered a great blessing from God in all Muslim societies.

biologically one's own is therefore forbidden. However, where the child's identity and paternity are presevered and protected, adoption and fostering is considered an extremely virtuous act in Islam.

ISLAMIC LAW

MUSLIMS BELIEVE THAT FULFILLING GOD'S WILL THROUGH UPHOLDING
HIS LAWS LEADS TO A JUST AND SAFE SOCIETY. ISLAMIC LAW IS THE
SYSTEM BY WHICH THE WILL OF ALLAH IS MADE MANIFEST.

*Above A Shariah lecture at Khosrakh,
Daghestan. The importance of the law and
scholars learning from each other has
always been a part of Islamic tradition.*

Islamic law is often erroneously
described as the Shariah, and
presented as being fossilized
and immutable. However, the
Shariah is only that part of Islamic
law which is derived from the two
sacred primary sources: the Quran
and sunnah. The rest of the body of
law, known as *fiqh*, evolves as Islamic
legal scholars arrive at new
understandings of Shariah.

Muslims believe, however, that
while God's laws need to be
established on earth, God himself is
the final judge, who will weigh all
actions in his scale of justice.

SHARIAH

An Arabic word, Shariah means a
'path to a watering course'. Muslims
believe that just as water sustains
life, so, too, does Islam. A clear path
is set before Muslims in the shape
of the Shariah, which ensures that
the principles and values laid out by
God in the Quran are upheld with
justice and compassion between
individuals and the state.

Shariah forms the basic core of
Islamic law, which is seen as eternal,
for it is enshrined in the two
primary sources: the Quran and the
sunnah. Shariah contains core
principles to preserve life, and sets
limits for human behaviour, thus
ensuring that everyone's property
and person remain sacred. It is
worth noting, however, that of more
than 6,000 verses in the Quran,
only around 250 are legalistic, for
while the law is important, it is only
the basis of a godly Muslim life.

Muslims view the Prophet's life
as the best example to follow in
terms of his fulfilment and
explanation of the law. Together
with the divine revelation (the
Quran), his sunnah provides a
blueprint for Islamic law. These two
sources together contain the few
universal and concretized canonical
laws that are at the heart of Shariah.

Eternally written principles are
not problematic for Muslims, for
they contain moral laws that are
important for all times, such as just
economic rules and control on
crimes to make society safe.

PRINCIPLES OF LAW

Fiqh is an Arabic word that loosely
translates as 'jurisprudence', but
more literally means 'understanding
and intelligence', and refers to

*Left An Islamic scholar in Damascus,
Syria, studies Shariah in the Quran.
Muslims believe that God manifests
his will through these core principles.*

principles derived from Shariah by scholars reflecting on the application of the law. It is not eternally binding, but rather interprets and translates the few eternal principles.

There are several branches of *fiqh* that might find their way into the corpus of law. The first is *ijma*, the 'consensus of scholarly opinion': where a law is not clear from the Quran or sunnah, the views of scholars and their interpretations are taken into account. If there still is no clarity, or a new situation arises, then an analogy is drawn between the new case and a similar previous one, so that a new precedent can be created (*qiyas*). In another source of law, known as *ijtihad*, an individual scholar gives his opinion on a new situation in the spirit of the Quran and sunnah. Local norms and customs are also taken into account when applying and extending laws to new situations (*urf*).

Because *fiqh* evolves and changes, depending on the needs of time and place, there are several schools of law, all of which adhere to

Above The Grand Mufti of Egypt is one of the most important Islamic figures in the world and highly respected for his knowledge of law.

the divine laws but have slight differences in their interpretations. A growing number of scholars are of the opinion that it is now time for a further school of law to develop that will meet the needs of Muslims in the West.

Above At a conference in Baghdad in 2007, Shiah and Sunni clerics discuss Muslim unity and the application of Islamic law in Iraq.

GOD, THE INDIVIDUAL AND SOCIETY

The relationship between God, the individual and society can be viewed as a triangle where God is at the apex: his laws bind individuals in relationship with him through personal laws, *ibadat*, such as prayer and fasting, but he also links individuals with wider society through the *muamalat* laws, which protect public interest: for example, as in criminal law.

In Islamic law, actions are not simply viewed as either obligatory or forbidden. In fact, there are three degrees between these two extremes: actions may also be classified as being meritorious, permissible or reprehensible. For example, helping out at a local hospice may not be compulsory, but would be seen as meritorious, because the Prophet practised community care.

ESTABLISHING
GOD'S WILL

MUSLIMS SEEK GUIDANCE AND ATTEMPT TO DETERMINE THE WILL
OF ALLAH BY READING THE QURAN AND FOLLOWING THE SUNNAH,
THE DEEDS AND SAYINGS OF THE PROPHET.

A Muslim's principal religious duty is to submit to and accept the will of Allah. The word Islam, which is usually translated as 'submission', derives from an Arabic root (s-l-m) that also suggests 'acceptance' and 'peace'.

In seeking and then attempting to follow Allah's will, Muslims believe that they can find equilibrium and inner peace and can begin to live in harmony with the laws of the created world as established by God. A Muslim's central source of guidance in

determining Allah's will is the Quran and the sunnah, the traditions concerning the Prophet's words and deeds. By studying these sources, a Muslim is guided to be charitable and compassionate, to be trusting and sincere, to show fortitude and patience and always to be mindful of, and to fulfil, his or her personal commitments.

An oft-quoted verse in the Quran (2:177) offers a definition of 'righteousness' and suggests that a good Muslim life combines faith in God and religious observance with

Above Men read the Quran at the Great Mosque in Damascus, Syria. *By following the word of God, Muslims believe they can be guided to inner peace.*

Below Here, the teachings of the Quran provide guidance for Muslim women in the Jamia Mosque in Srinagar, northern India.

Right In Samarkand, Uzbekistan, a clock reminds the devout of the times for the five daily prayers. Religious observance is part of God's will.

being patient and displaying ethical behaviour, such as caring for travellers and the poor.

THE SUNNAH

Even before Muhammad's lifetime, the Arabic word 'sunnah' was in circulation and meant 'inherited customs and precedents'. Early in the history of Islam, Muslims began to use the term to refer to traditions relating to the Prophet's words and deeds. Hadith (sayings and reported actions of the Prophet) were collected by scholars dedicated to the purpose, and carefully identified by source. *Al-Sirah al-nabawiyyah*, or expanded and rather less strictly reliable narratives of Muhammad's life, also fed into the sunnah.

Muslims believe that the knowledge collected in the sunnah complements the Prophet's divinely inspired teachings, which are recorded in the Quran. Indeed, the Quran itself encourages Muslims to seek guidance in the example of the Prophet's life and actions: 'Verily in the messenger of Allah ye have a good example for him who looketh unto Allah and the Last Day, and remembereth Allah much' (33:21).

SHARIAH

In the early centuries of Islam, study of the sunnah and of the Quran fed into the developing Shariah ('pathway'), guidance on all aspects of how to live as a Muslim in the world. In some Muslim nations, Shariah developed into a legal system with courts and judges, and definitions provided by jurists (*fuqaha*), who were experts in the science of law (*fiqh*).

In the various Muslim traditions, the foundations of and authorities for *fiqh* were different. Shiah Muslims gave special authority to imams and those representing them. For Sunni Muslims, the basic sources for *fiqh* were the Quran and the sunnah, complemented by jurists' reasoning by analogy (*qiyas*) and the agreement of learned scholars and jurists (*ijma*).

For Muslims, Shariah is more than a legal system: it is a framework within which they can make a life in accordance with Allah's will, the basis of an individual's relationship with Allah and with others, and a framework for ethical decisions.

INNER GUIDANCE

Some Muslims believe that they can also find guidance in seeking the will of Allah within their own

hearts, through their own inner leadings. A verse from the Quran quoted in support of this position is 6:125: 'And whomsoever it is Allah's will to guide, He expandeth their bosoms unto Islam', which suggests that Allah develops an individual's ethics and inner understanding so that they are guided through the process of surrender. The Quran praises 'he whose bosom Allah hath expanded for Al-Islam, so that he followeth a light from his Lord' (39:22).

Sufi Muslims consider that the most profound understanding of the will of Allah can be discerned through inner seeking by way of meditation and other spiritual disciplines, such as fasting. Sufis follow an inner path or 'way' *(tariqah)*, led by a spiritual teacher, based around contemplation and meditation, often on verses from the Quran. This spiritual journey is believed by Sufis to culminate in an experience *(fana)* of the individual self being extinguished and united with its divine source in a deep experiential understanding of *tawhid* (the oneness of Allah).

Left A judge in a Shariah court. For Muslims, Shariah law provides guidance on how to live in accordance with God's will.

JUSTICE: APPLYING THE LAW

CIVIL ISLAMIC LAW IS CONCERNED WITH ASPECTS OF PROTECTING AN INDIVIDUAL'S RIGHTS IN A FAMILY LAW DISPUTE, AS WELL AS REGULATING CORPORATE CLIENTS IN BANKING LAWS.

Islamic law touches every aspect of Muslim life, and holds as central principles of freedom, equity and justice – social, political and economic. Promoting equality and the welfare of the community is a major task when enforcing the law. In civil law, this means ensuring justice both in the private sphere, such as family law, and in the public arena, such as business and banking law. The courts are expected to live up to the ideal of the law.

ECONOMICS

The right of the individual to pursue economic gain is recognized in Islamic law, but this must at all times be carried out in a permissible (*halal*) manner. Laws ensure that the world's wealth does not find its way into the hands of a few, and prevent the growth in disparity between the rich and the poor. The rich, therefore, are expected to pay *zakah* as a welfare system.

Economic and business systems are lawful only if they operate on principles of ethical and moral financing. Therefore, trade dealings with 'economic giants' who exploit poor countries through unfair trade practices are forbidden (*haram*).

Below An Islamic bank in Dubai. Ethical Islamic banking forbids the charging of interest, so interest-free loans and mortgages are arranged.

Above The headquarters of the Islamic Development Bank in Jeddah, Saudia Arabia. Under Islamic law, businesses must not exploit the poor.

ISLAMIC BANKING

One example of ethical economics law is banking: usury (*riba*) is not allowed in Islamic banking, because it takes advantage of people in a weak position. Because charging interest is considered unjust and inequitable, all Islamic banks loan money without demanding interest repayments, although they do apply administrative charges.

Islamic banking principles have been in force since the beginnings of the religion in the 6th century, because the taking of interest is forbidden in the Quran itself (2:275–6). But over the last few decades, Islamic banks have emerged as major international economic players.

Malaysia is a Muslim country that is leading the way in interest-free banking. In Britain, the HSBC bank began to offer Islamic mortgages in both Malaysia and Britain around 2003 and was surprised to find that half of its customers were not Muslim. Islamic economics thus benefits the whole of society.

Above Pregnancy outside marriage is seen as proof of adultery. Single Nigerian woman Safiya Hussaini was sentenced to death when pregnant with her daughter, but later acquitted.

FAMILY LAW AND DIVORCE

Fundamental aspects of civil law relating to the private sphere of domestic disputes are enshrined in the Quran. If a woman has been subjected to, or fears, cruel treatment at the hands of her husband, then she can ask for a *khul*, a divorce instigated by the wife (4:128). The parties can come to their own amicable settlement.

Fiqh rules have stipulated that a wife must apply to a court if she wishes to divorce her husband, and that she must return all her dowry in exchange for the divorce. However, if the divorce is requested on grounds of cruelty, the husband is legally obligated not to ill-treat his wife financially by demanding the dowry be repaid to him. He must also maintain her during the three-month separation period.

Above A Muslim man and woman sign a civil contract. Civil law gives women many legal rights, particularly in marriage and divorce laws.

CRIME AND PUNISHMENT

ALLAH FORBIDS INDIVIDUALS FROM TAKING AWAY THE FREEDOM AND
RIGHTS OF ANOTHER. SUCH ACTS ARE SEEN AS CRIMINAL AND WORTHY
OF PUNISHMENT, BUT THIS MUST BE METED OUT VERY CAREFULLY.

The purpose of criminal laws in the Quran is to give believers guidance based on spirituality, ethics and justice, so that life and property can be preserved and protected. The Quran lays down *hudud* (limits of human behaviour), which must not be transgressed, and also prescribes the punishments that are to be applied if these laws and precepts are broken.

CRIMINAL LAW

Because they are considered to be so significant in Islam, criminal laws have been enshrined in the Quran. These laws are of a universal moral nature, and many have been around for centuries in different societies.

Contrary to popular opinion, Islamic criminal law is not an expansive list of rules with stringent punishments for those who break them. In fact, only a few actions are viewed as criminal in the Quran. These include treason, murder, highway robbery, theft, slander and

adultery and sexual offences. Such acts are criminalized in order to protect the individual and uphold the authority of the state with justice, compassion and reason.

In all cases, witness evidence to the act itself must be proved without any doubt. Circumstantial evidence in favour of the accused must also be taken into account. So, for example, the punishment for an accidental killing would be less severe than that for murder.

The criminal laws listed in the Quran have been enshrined there to prevent states from criminalizing or decriminalizing certain acts at whim, depending on their particular moral standpoint. Muslims believe that God alone is fit to decide what people can and cannot be allowed to do against others; to permit men and women to make such decisions is to invite subjectivity.

Islam's criminalizing of adultery provides a good example of Islamic law in practice. While Western

Above Iraqi former president Saddam Hussein, seen here on the first day of his trial, was executed in 2006 under Iraqi law for war crimes against humanity.

societies no longer view adultery as a crime but simply as a misconduct, Islamic law argues that the resulting breakdown of family and society justifies its criminalization. Proving adultery requires four eyewitnesses, however, and as this is so difficult, the law is rarely enforced. Rather, it is intended to act as a deterrent, to retain public morality in society. The fact that such cases rarely come to court can be seen as allowing scope for personal repentance and change.

PENAL POLICY

The few crimes listed in the Quran also carry divinely specified (*hudud*) punishments. The decision to take a criminal's life or liberty is a very grave undertaking, and Muslims believe it is one that cannot be left up to humankind: thus, God has prescribed appropriate punishments. Any Muslim can access this knowledge – it is not the sole domain of lawyers, rulers and law

Left Iranian dissident Hashem Aghajari, left, defends himself during his trial for apostasy. His original death sentence was eventually reduced to imprisonment. A fair trial is fundamental in Islamic law.

books. However, the laws must be administered by recognized Shariah courts with fully trained Islamic judges, because the responsibility of enforcing divine law is great.

Islamic penal policy, which includes the death sentence for murder and amputation of a limb for theft, has been criticized by many people for being too harsh. However, punishments are rooted in *adl*: justice and compassion must prevail at all times. According to a hadith, Allah has made his mercy predominate over his judgment, or wrath. Therefore, judges, although they must be firm, are also required to be clement. The law allows for flexibility in penal policy and judges have licence to pronounce a range of punishments for a given crime.

It is also important that the victim (or the victim's family) feels that justice has been done. While there are prescribed punishments for particular crimes, the victim (or family) can choose to be merciful.

Above A young woman receives a public caning in Aceh Province, Indonesia, after being found having illegal sex with her boyfriend at her house.

For example, in a murder case, the victim's family may choose to dispense with a death sentence, opt for compensation instead, or as the Quran advises, they may forgive (5:45). In practice, a judge may rule that some form of punishment is needed for a serious crime.

In theft cases, amputation of limbs is not mandatory. If the theft was due to poverty, for example, then blame lies with the failure of the state's welfare system rather than with the accused. Judges may also choose to imprison an offender, or try to rehabilitate him. Fear of amputation can be a deterrent to

Right A Muslim prisoner reads the Quran on his bunk. Imprisonment is meant to reform, and spiritual support is provided to facilitate reflection.

crime: in some Muslim countries where amputation for theft is the law, many a shopkeeper will leave his shop unattended to go and pray in the mosque without fear of theft. In this respect, the laws fulfil a fundamental purpose of providing a safe society with a low crime rate.

SHARIAH RULE

IN RECENT TIMES, THE APPLICATION OF SHARIAH AND ISLAMIC LAW
HAS RAISED CONTROVERSIES. IN THEORY, THE RULES TO BE FOLLOWED
BY THE COURTS AND JUDGES ARE VERY CLEAR, BUT PRACTICE VARIES.

Islam is a way of life that is rooted in hope and mercy. Islamic laws reflect this: they are not intended as literal pronouncements, but should convey a spirit of hope and stability in their application. To this end, trained and impartial legal judges are given licence in interpretation and enforcement of Shariah.

The Quran is emphatic that witnesses must stand up for justice, even if they have to give testimony against relatives, and that judges (*qadis*) must be utterly impartial, regardless of whether the accused is rich or poor (4:135). God is seen as the law-maker, while the Muslim community, acting through the judges, is the law enforcer.

Judges are expected to be just, impartial and upright in their personal practice of Islam and to have a deep understanding of the laws. They should not pass judgements in anger and, according to a hadith, should refrain from pronouncing *hudud* (divinely ordained) punishments (for crimes such as theft and adultery) as far as possible, especially where there is the slightest doubt in evidence.

THE FIRST JUDGES

The Prophet enforced the law by judging in disputes brought before him, as instructed in the Quran (4:105). He also set a precedent for appointing judges, by installing Ali (his cousin) as a judge in Madinah and Muadh ibn Jabal in Yemen.

After the Prophet's death, the first four caliphs arbitrated in cases brought before them, but as the Muslim empire began to expand, they also appointed judges in various areas: the second caliph, Umar, is known to have appointed Abu

Above Brass scales represent the scales of justice. Muslims believe that on the Day of Judgement, their actions will be weighed in scales before God.

Darda in Madinah and Shurayh in Basra and placed a female judge in charge of the markets. He also advised his judges to take evidence on oath and retract a judgement if a *qadi* later felt it was wrong. He encouraged the use of the judge's own reason (*ijtihad*) where necessary, and, above all, he advised patience.

DIFFERENT COURTS

Today, Shariah courts are found in many Muslim countries: in some, for example Pakistan, they run in conjunction with a semi-secular legal system. In others, such as Saudi Arabia, they are the only form of judiciary. In non-Muslim countries, such as the UK, Shariah courts deal largely with personal and domestic matters. Often, Shariah courts uphold the law, but on occasions they fall foul of the Islamic ideal.

In Pakistan, the legal system is built on a combination of Islamic laws and the legacy of the Anglo–Muhammadan laws of the British empire. However, Shariah law is invoked in religious

Left A qadi, *Islamic judge, Khartoum, Sudan, late 19th century. Qadis are expected to be just, impartial and upright, with a deep understanding of the laws.*

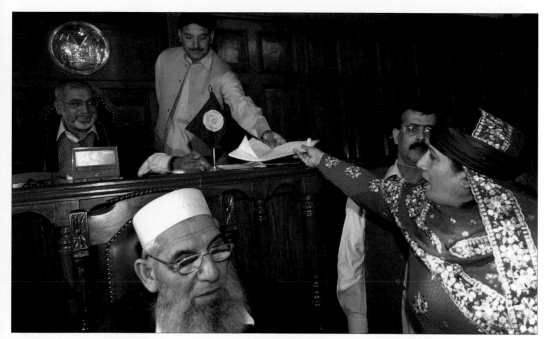

matters, such as blasphemy. Several years ago, an Islamic judgement ruled that two Christians could not be charged with defaming and blaspheming against the Prophet, on the grounds that Islamic law cannot be applied to non-Muslims. The judge upheld a basic Islamic legal principle, much to the dismay of the populace.

In Saudi Arabia, the application of Shariah responds to the times. A traditional ruling that the meat from the sacrificial animals during *Hajj*, must be distributed among family and the poor of Makkah has been sensitively updated, as there is no longer poverty in Makkah: various Saudi scholars have ruled that the meat may be processed, canned and distributed outside Makkah, in countries where there is a dire need for food.

In Britain, the Shariah court in London hears cases of domestic disputes. Although it cannot replace the English court system and

law, the court helps parties to reach legal settlements regarding matrimonial disputes, gives advice relating to reconciliation and issues *talaq* (Islamic divorce), where necessary.

Above A Pakistani legislator in Peshawar in 2006 protests the proposed establishment of an Islamic accountability bureau to suppress vices. Here she is returning a copy of the Accountability Bill to the assembly speaker.

Above Indonesian protestors at a rally in Makassar, South Sulawesi, in 2004 call for implementation of Shariah law.

IS SHARIAH LAW RELEVANT TODAY?

The purpose of the law is to protect the rights of individuals, but, unfortunately, not all Muslim states apply Islamic law fairly and consistently. Some scholars argue that where there is no real Islamic state, then the *hudud* rulings must be suspended, for they should never be applied with force and without justice.

Furthermore, where Muslims live as a minority in a non-Muslim land, they cannot enforce Shariah in public matters and are obliged to follow the law of that land, provided that they are not forced to contravene Islam.

WOMEN'S RIGHTS UNDER SHARIAH

IN ISLAMIC SOCIETY, THE POSITION OF WOMEN IS OFTEN HOTLY DEBATED, BUT, IN FACT, AS MOTHERS AND WIVES, WOMEN APPEAR TO BE GIVEN MANY MORE RIGHTS THAN MEN UNDER SHARIAH LAW.

Above In pledging his daughter Fatimah in marriage to his cousin Ali, Muhammad can be seen to be encouraging marriage as a way of life.

A close examination of the Quran reveals many divinely enshrined rights for women. Although the Quran addresses both men and women as believers, encouraging them to lead a godly life to attain Allah's reward (33:35), there are also verses that specifically relate to women: for example, regarding their rights of inheritance (4:7-12). Women also have political rights to vote and rights to education, as prescribed by hadiths. These are modern rights, given the political struggles of women in Europe during the last century.

MARRIAGE

As the family is central to Islamic life, many laws relating to women pertain to marriage. In Islam, marriage is considered a civil contract between two sane adults with free choice. Certain blood relations prohibit a marriage, and a Muslim woman may only marry a man who is also a Muslim. She receives a dowry, and her husband has full financial responsibility; he is considered the maintainer of the family (4:34). But any income that a Muslim woman has is entirely her own; that is, she is not obliged to contribute financially to the family.

Interestingly, the only legal requirement of a Muslim wife is to fulfil her conjugal role: she is not compelled by divine law to cook, clean or, indeed, rear her children. If she chooses to do so out of a sense of love, compassion or ethical duty, then she will find her reward with God. She is also not required to change her name on marriage: her independent identity is God-given and ought to be preserved.

The marital relationship is described in the Quran in sublime metaphors. One passage states: 'And among His signs is that He created for you mates...so that you may dwell in tranquillity with them, and He has put love and mercy between your hearts' (30:21). These attributes of love and mercy are suggestive of privacy and sacredness. Just as one covers the body with clothes for privacy and beautification, so, too, according to the Quran, '(Your wives) are a garment to you and you are a garment to them' (2:187).

In spiritual matters, husband and wife are equal before God (33:35). In fact, the most noble is believed to be whoever is more God-conscious (49:13). As another verse from the Quran says, 'The best garment is the garment of God-consciousness' (7:26).

Islam recognizes that human relationships can fail. It therefore permits divorce, but reconciliation must first be sought (4:35).

ONE WIFE OR MANY?

Patriarchy was the norm in the Middle East in the 7th century, but it was not created by Islam; rather it was endorsed as the existing system.

Left A qadi examines the case of a young couple wishing to divorce. Divorce forms the bulk of the work of the Shariah courts in Iran.

Right An Iranian female athlete, participating in a cycling competition, is shown having fun and enjoying sports while still observing Shariah dress codes.

Measures were put in place to curtail certain patriarchal practices that had gone unchecked, such as polygyny. The verse in the Quran allowing a man to have four wives put a restriction on the unlimited polygyny of the time: 'and if you fear that you will not deal fairly by the orphans, marry of the women who seem good to you, two, or three or four: and if you fear that you cannot do justice then (only) one' (4:3). As a subsequent verse proposes that a man could *not* treat all four wives equally; however, only one is usually allowed: 'you will not be able to deal equally between your wives, however much you wish' (4:129).

MOTHERHOOD

Although only one facet of most women's lives, motherhood is elevated beyond all relationships: well-known hadiths state that paradise lies under a mother's feet and that a mother has three times more right than a father to be served. The Quran is emphatic that pregnancy and weaning are difficult, and, therefore, people should show gratitude to their parents (31:14).

VEILING

The Quran requires men and women to observe dress codes. For women, this is interpreted in different ways in different countries and sects. Many women cover their hair and entire body, apart from face and hands. The laws state that covering is so women are known as believers and are protected from men's lusts.

Right Young girls at a Quran class in a women's madrasa *in Pakistan. Most* madrasas *provide free religious education for girls from poor families.*

LAWS ON PURITY
Purity laws and cleanliness are central to Muslim life. Quranic references to menstruation are a natural acceptance of, and engagement with, bodily functions: 'They will ask you concerning the monthly course: say it is a hurt, so go apart from women during the monthly period and do not approach them until they are purified' (2:222). Some commentators have translated 'hurt' as a 'pollution' and interpret the exclusion of women from religious rites – prayer and fasting – during menstruation as unfair, but many women believe that such verses show a respectful acknowledgement of the female body and are grateful for the dispensation from prayer and sexual intercourse that allows a woman to 'take it easy'.

CHAPTER 7

UNITY AND DIVISION

There is a surprising unity among the global Muslim community, where fraternity extends beyond nations and cultures. However, although core Islamic beliefs remain the same everywhere, Muslims in various parts of the world interpret and practise their faith in different ways.

Muslims are no longer under the rule of a caliphate but are members of nation states, so they live under different political authorities. How they organize themselves politically remains a contentious issue. Although the majority of Muslims are Sunni, ten per cent of the global community are Shiah, and their concept of political authority differs from that of the Sunnis, as do their schools of law.

Religious practice also varies immensely: some Muslims stress the importance of adhering to laws and ritual, while others, such as the Sufis, lay greater emphasis on the esoteric nature of their faith. Together, these different expressions of Islam make up the body of the Muslim *ummah*.

Opposite An Afghani man prays at the Blue Mosque of Ali ibn Abu Talib at Mazar-e Sharif. The global Muslim community shares fundamental beliefs, but is very diverse in culture and practice.

Above Pilgrims from all over the world pray as they arrive at the Mount of Mercy at the centre of the plain of Arafah, near Makkah. Here on the Hajj, Muslim unity outweighs diversity.

THE *UMMAH*: ISLAMIC UNIVERSALISM

THE MUSLIM *UMMAH* IS A COMMUNITY BOND OF FAITH THAT LINKS MUSLIMS THROUGHOUT THE WORLD TOGETHER, DESPITE THEIR DIFFERENCES IN GEOGRAPHY, CULTURE AND LANGUAGE.

Above *Although this young girl learning in Brunei is reading the Quran in Arabic, her daily language is Malay.*

Muslims are estimated to make up approximately 20 per cent of the world's population, and the religion is represented globally. Although Islam sprang up in what is now called Saudi Arabia, the current population of the country, estimated to be 100 per cent Muslim, is only 28 million, whereas there are more than 120 million Muslims in Bangladesh, 160 million in Pakistan and 200 million in Indonesia. As minorities, Muslims number 1.6 million in Britain, and approximately 150 million in India.

Widespread geographically, the global Muslim community is also very diverse in terms of culture and language. The one uniting factor is its belief system: all Muslims have a strong sense of belonging to a single brotherhood of believers.

MUSLIM UNITY

Umm in Arabic means 'mother', and *ummah*, derived from it, means the 'mother source'. In Islam, *ummah* refers to the primary group to which a Muslim belongs ideologically. The word appears more than 60 times in the Quran, where all prophets are said to have had their own *ummah* (10:47) and Muslims are described as *ummatun wasata*, or moderate community (2:143).

Ummah does not replace other identities of tribe, culture or language, but it certainly takes priority over them. Some scholars have argued that this makes the concept of nations virtually redundant, for while people are divided and defined by state identity, as Muslims, they surpass geographical boundary limitations

by a sense of belonging to a wider ideological community, regardless of language and culture.

The originator of the *ummah*, or universal Muslim community, was the Prophet Muhammad himself: after he migrated to Madinah, a constitution was signed by the indigenous Madinans and the new migrants, stating that Muhammad and his followers constituted one single *ummah*. Belonging to the *ummah*, therefore, means belonging to the *ummah* of the Prophet.

Beyond time and space, then, all Muslims – past, present, and future – are seen as belonging to one community. Islam is a universal religion and its fellowship is open to all people, regardless of their race, ethnicity, culture or economic status. Each member is equal: the only distinction in God's eyes is made on the basis of piety. Indeed, the Prophet Muhammad's last sermon at *Hajj* is a testimony to what *ummah* means in practice as a universal brotherhood.

Left A Muslim woman and her child in Ghana. Only about 16 per cent of Ghanaians are Muslims.

Above A Russian man prepares to kill a sheep for a feast to mark Eid ul-adha. There are 20 million Muslims in Russia.

CULTURAL DIVERSITY

As Muslims spread into new places, indigenous peoples often accepted Islam as a belief system. However, the new converts did not reject their traditional languages and cultures but, rather, Islamized them. Therefore, Muslims in different parts of the world have a great diversity in dress, language and ethnicity. These differences, which often give varied expressions to Islamic practice and interpretation, are celebrated in the Quran (49:13).

Muslims claim that Islam is a missionizing religion, but only to the extent that Muslims follow a mission of *daawah* – 'inviting' people to the peace of Islam. This invitation carries no obligation: those invited have a fundamental right to accept or refuse the offer, as 'there is no compulsion in religion' (2:256). For this reason, Islam insists that people of other faiths living under Islamic rule must be given legal rights and protected as part of the Muslim polity.

Right The 'burqini' worn by this Australian woman was specially designed for female Muslim lifesavers.

THE UNIVERSAL BROTHERHOOD OF ISLAM

'O mankind! We created you from a single pair of a male and a female, and made you into nations and tribes, so that you may know each other. Verily the most honoured of you in the sight of Allah is the most righteous. And Allah has full knowledge of things and is most discerning.'

(The Quran, 49:13)

'All mankind is from Adam and Eve: an Arab has no superiority over a non-Arab nor a non-Arab over an Arab; also a white person has no superiority over a black person nor does a black person have any superiority over a white person, except by piety and good action. Learn that every Muslim is a brother to each other and that Muslims constitute one brotherhood...Do not, therefore, do injustice to yourselves.'

(The Prophet's Last Sermon)

RELIGIOUS AND POLITICAL AUTHORITY

ISLAMIC AUTHORITY IS FORMULATED ON THE VALUES AND CONCEPTS CONTAINED IN THE QURAN, WHICH TEACHES THAT MAN IS GOD'S CALIPH, OR VICEGERENT, ON EARTH.

Islam teaches that the laws prescribed for human conduct and social interaction have been set by God through the Shariah. As God's caliphs, Muslims have a duty to establish divine law and moral order as exampled in the first Muslim community at Madinah.

GOD'S VICEGERENTS

In Islam, men and women are seen as God's earthly representatives and are therefore instructed to rule in accordance with his laws (24:55). A Muslim ruler (caliph) is answerable both to God and to the Muslim community: he must ensure, therefore, that he rules by Shariah and with the community's consent (*ijma*). If he does not, then he can be removed from office and even punished for any misdemeanours. The preconditions of the caliph's rule are that he must be a Muslim, possess qualities of justice, virtue and piety and have knowledge of the Shariah and principles of *fiqh* (jurisprudence). The political and religious caliph is usually a man.

To ensure that the caliph fulfils his divine obligations, the institution of *shura* (consultation) exists as a means of mutually agreeing the correct application of Shariah and assuring the interests of the whole community (42:38). Through the process of *shura*, the head of state is chosen and executive state decisions are agreed. Although the Shariah does not dictate the exact nature of state institutions, the general principles (*maqasid*) encourage the common good (*istislah*) of the community through good council and fair representation.

THE ISLAMIC STATE

While the Prophet Muhammad's city of Madinah is seen as the paradigm for all Muslim societies and modern ideas regarding the 'Islamic State', the Quran and

Above A young Bedouin nomad reads the Quran, written in ink on a wooden slab. Muslims believe that authority lies in God's divine words.

hadith do not, in fact, offer much detail regarding a specific design of government or rule.

After Muhammad's death, the first four caliphs were elected by due process; therefore, a democratic model is endorsed. (Although the caliph was elected for life, he could be removed for misconduct.) There is also an absence of detail relating to definitions of Islamic nation states or sovereign countries. Nevertheless, the increase in religious identity and the mobilization of Islamic political parties mean that debates and theories regarding the precise nature and political shape of the 'Islamic State' are ongoing.

Left For Muslims, Makkah and Madinah are sacred places – and in art they are represented time and again as models of Islamic rule.

Some consensus has been reached on the general principles upon which an Islamic state should be founded; in particular, the religious or devotional aspects of community life and practical social matters (*din wa dunya*), which are concerned with the common good or the collective enforcement of public morals (*istislah*). This general accord has led to greater acceptance of the need for unity of both religious and political authority as a practical application of God's laws administered by humankind.

MODERN ISLAMIC STATES
A number of Muslim countries — Iran, Morocco, Pakistan, Saudi Arabia and Sudan — have declared themselves Islamic states, based on the principles of both Shariah and sunnah. Not surprisingly, these countries differ from each other, but there are some similarities in their prohibition of *riba* (usury) and application of the *hudud* (punishment laws) of the Shariah.

Constitutionally, too, these countries differ greatly — from those with hereditary monarchical systems of rule to those that have a democratically elected president with a limited term of office.

POLITICAL DIVERSITY
These variations indicate that while all Islamic states lean toward the adoption and implementation

Above Muslims in Tehran, Iran, hold aloft posters of Ayatollah Khomeini, who believed political authority was the domain of religious scholars.

of the Shariah in areas relating to moral and social issues, their governmental structures, forms of leadership, specific political features and social and economic orientations are quite disparate.

MODERN ISLAMIC POLITICAL THOUGHT
Some Muslim thinkers argue that there is indeed a distinct model of the Islamic state and Muslim government referred to in the Quran, which, they claim, condemns those who do not judge by what God has revealed (5:44).

Some modern political Islamists see the caliph and *shura* style of government as a 'theodemocracy' — a theory propagated by Abul Ala Maududi (1903–79). Others, notably Sayyid Qutb (1906–66), view Muslim government as a 'social contract'.

Few, however, with the exception of Ayatollah Khomeini (1902–89), have envisaged caliph and *shura* as being the exclusive domains of the *ulama* (religious scholars). Thus, the 'Islamic State' was presented in Iran as the establishment of God's sovereignty, as governed, and even legislated, by man, with religious law guiding society along the 'straight path' (1:5–7).

THE *MADHHABS*: SCHOOLS OF LAW

POLITICAL AND RELIGIOUS AUTHORITY WAS AT FIRST UNITED, BUT AS
DYNASTIC RULE WAS ESTABLISHED, SCHOLARS AND JURISTS — PEOPLE
WHO INTERPRETED ISLAMIC LAW — BECAME MORE IMPORTANT.

*Above A 16th-century illustration shows
a Mongol ruler holding court, listening
to petitioners, while outside Islamic law
is upheld, with thieves being punished.*

As Islam spread rapidly into new
territories, Muslims came into
contact with different cultures and
contexts. In the absence of specific
answers from the Quran and
sunnah to unprecedented problems,
new legal rulings became necessary.
This meant that well-known
scholars passing such judgements
eventually became the main
authoritative voice of Islamic law in
different areas of the Muslim world,
thus giving rise to different
madhhabs, or schools of law.

EXPLAINING ISLAM

The jurists' task was to explain
Islam to ordinary Muslims, so that
they could best apply the rules of
the Quran and sunnah to their own
lives. According to traditions, the
Prophet had already started training
some of his companions during his
lifetime to use reasoned judgement
(*ijtihad*) in reaching just conclusions
in new circumstances.

The first four caliphs set a
precedent for problem-solving by
first referring to the Quran: in the
absence of an answer there, they
would examine the Prophet's
sunnah. If that, too, failed to provide
an explicit solution, they would try
to come to a unanimous agreement
(*ijma*). Where they were unable to
reach such a consensus, they would
form their own opinion through
ijtihad, often by applying analogical
reasoning (*qiyas*). Later jurists
followed this same pattern when
applying and explaining the law in
new circumstances.

Thus, while the politicians took
care of governance, jurists took care
of souls through religious laws. Very
often, they rejected the patronage
of the ruling Umayyad and Abbasid
caliphs, which in many cases
resulted in bouts of imprisonment,
but this independence guaranteed
their impartiality.

THE MAIN LAW SCHOOLS

There were many schools of law in
the early centuries of Islam, as many
able scholars gave *fatwas*: al-Awzai,
al-Layth, al-Thawri, to name but a
few. The great number of early
schools shows that scholars were
responding to the needs of their
community by formulating laws

*Left The ornate calligraphy of this 17th-
century Shiah legal text is a testament
to the importance of Islamic law.*

Right In the mosque of Sultan Hassan in Cairo, the complex courtyard allowed for the study of Islamic law from all four schools: each occupied a separate recess.

through *ijtihad*. Over time, some of these schools disappeared, while others consolidated.

There are four main Sunni law schools, which are followed in and around those parts of the world where they developed. All are named after their founding scholars, who followed the same primary sources but gave different weighting to secondary sources. Each scholar held the others in mutual respect and said that his own opinion should be disregarded if proved wrong by a hadith. There was thus no rigidity of outlook in these schools; their aim was to respond to the needs of their people and places. In their support of this diversity, scholars referred to a prophetic hadith, which claimed that difference among the scholars was a mercy for the *ummah*.

IMAM MALIK (717–801) believed that the consensus of the scholars of Madinah, where he was born, was a most important source of law. However, he refused to have his seminal work, *al-Muwatta*, imposed as unifying state law by the Abbasids on Muslims in other regions, whom he believed were entitled to come to their own reasoned conclusions. Today, the Maliki School is mostly followed in North and West Africa and the Gulf States.

IMAM ABU HANIFAH (730–67) was born in Kufa, Iraq. He valued consensus and local customs (*urf*), which gave rise to a multicultural and diverse practice of Islam. The Hanifi School operates today in and around Iraq, the Indian sub-continent and Turkey.

Right The Al-Azhar University in Cairo, Egypt, is perhaps the most prestigious school of Islamic law.

Right In the mosque of Sultan Hassan in Cairo, the complex courtyard allowed for the study of Islamic law from all four schools: each occupied a separate recess.

IMAM ASH-SHAFII (769–820), who was originally from near Gaza in Palestine, travelled to Madinah to study with Imam Malik. In Iraq, he studied Hanifi law before moving to Egypt, where he remained until his death. His juristic opinions combined the Maliki and Hanifi rulings while he was in Iraq, but in Egypt, faced with new hadiths and legal reasonings, he developed a new school of thought. He is known mostly for his work, *al-Risalah*, on the fundamentals of *fiqh*. Today, the Shafii School is followed in Egypt, Yemen and South-east Asia.

IMAM IBN HANBAL (778–855) was born in Baghdad, Iraq, and studied Hanifi law. He is well known for his *Musnad*, a collection of hadiths. Hanbal taught that only the consensus of the *sahaba* (the companions of the Prophet) was authentic. The Hanbali School is followed today in Palestine and Saudi Arabia.

PROMISED REFORMERS: THE MAHDI AND JESUS

MAJORITY SUNNI DOCTRINE CLAIMS THAT JESUS WILL RESTORE ORDER ON EARTH, BUT SOME SUNNIS AND ALL SHIAHS NAME THE PROPHET'S DESCENDANT, KNOWN AS AL-MAHDI, AS THE REFORMER.

Above Alexander the Great builds a wall between the fighting Gog and Magog. Muslims believe that these warring tribes are eschatological, not just historical, and that Jesus will eventually destroy them.

Belief in the hereafter is a fundamental article of Muslim faith, but, according to hadiths, the afterlife will be preceded by the Day of Judgement, a final reckoning of all souls, who will collectively stand before God. Islam teaches that this last day will follow a series of apocalyptic events that

Below The Al-Askari Mosque in Samarra, Iraq, is dedicated to the 12th imam, whom Shiahs believe to be the promised reformer. The mosque also houses the tombs of the 10th and 11th imams.

will centre around two main figures in hadith literature: the Mahdi and Jesus.

THE END OF TIME

Hadith collections give extremely detailed predictions of events on earth before the end of time. Some scholars believe that these hadiths should be understood literally, whereas others assert that they are metaphorical in nature. They envision, for example, the sun rising from the West, devastating earthquakes occurring with

Above One of the signs of the end of time, according to Islamic eschatology, is a change in the weather systems and an increase in natural disasters – such as the earthquake here.

increasing frequency, time passing more quickly than usual and afflictions appearing from the East.

Hadiths also claim that there will be widespread moral decadence, which will manifest itself in unjust rulers oppressing people's rights, miserliness, sexual immorality and killing. At this point, they foretell,

the Mahdi, and later Jesus, will enter the apocalyptic scene, and through them, Islam and peace will be re-established on earth.

It is said that some time after the Mahdi, the Antichrist, Dajjal, will appear as a young man from between Syria and Iraq. He will be blind in his right eye and will terrorize people, and he will also have miraculous control over fire and water. Setting up camp outside Madinah, he will kill a man, then will bring him back to life. Thus ensuring his might and power, he will call people to a false religion. However, the prophecies claim, Jesus will fight the Dajjal and will vanquish his rule of tyranny.

THE REFORMER MAHDI

The Mahdi, meaning 'the guided one', is believed to be Muhammad Ahmad bin Abdullah, a descendant of the Prophet. According to Shiah belief, he is the 12th imam, currently in occultation, who will come to earth before the end of time to lead a battle of good forces against evil.

This idea is also found to varying degrees in Sunni Islam, for though not clearly formulated in Sunni theology, it has a significant hold on popular beliefs. Some scholars claim

that ascetics and Sufis introduced the messianic figure to Sunni thought, while others still claim that the Mahdi and Jesus figures are eschatological, not just historical.

The Prophet Muhammad is reported to have said that when oppression covers the earth, a member of his tribe, bearing his name, will appear and will be guided to fight injustice. However, his rule will be short, and will be followed by the return of Christ.

JESUS RETURNS

Many hadiths claim that as, according to Islam, Jesus has not yet died, he has yet to return to earth. It is said that this will happen at the end of time, and that he will destroy all false claims to religion. Once the Dajjal appears, Jesus will reportedly descend in Damascus. He will search for and kill the Dajjal, after which he will slay the evil forces of Gog and Magog. After these great trials, hadiths claim, peace will reign, and Jesus will marry, have children, die a natural death and be buried in Madinah beside the Prophet. It is after the second coming of Jesus that life on earth as we know it will end, and God's final judgement will take place.

ORTHODOXY VERSUS HETERODOXY

Various figures have appeared throughout Islamic history and cultures claiming to be promised reformers. However, there also exist some differences in religious belief among Muslims, particularly between Shiahs and Sunnis. Within these two main groups, there are further distinctions in doctrine.

Such 'diversity', however, has its limits: many splinter factions claim to be adherents of Islam, yet the majority of the Muslim community considers them to be outside orthodox Islam. The Ahmadiyyas from India and the Druze, who exist mainly in Lebanon, are two such heterodox groups. The former do not consider that revelation and prophethood are final, while the Druze believe that individuals of unusual spiritual attainment can manifest divine attributes.

Above The Druze, an offshoot of the Ismaili Shiah branch of Islam, are found mostly in Lebanon, Syria and Israel. They are considered to be heretical due to their incorporation of gnostic and neo-platonic philosophies into their faith.

SHIAHS:
THE PARTY OF ALI

THE MUSLIM COMMUNITY IS SPLIT INTO TWO MAIN THEOLOGICAL
CAMPS: THE LARGEST, REPRESENTING 90 PER CENT OF THE WORLD'S
MUSLIMS, IS SUNNI; THE REMAINDER ARE SHIAH.

Muhammad's death around 632 not only deprived the nascent Muslim community of its temporal and spiritual leader, but it also threw his followers into a quandary about who the next leader ought to be. The Quranic revelation dictated democracy, which meant that Muslims were free to debate, differ about and elect a leader (4:59, 42:38). However, nobody could have predicted that this one event – the election of a successor to Muhammad – would lead to such a serious divide in the Muslim community.

ELECTING A SUCCESSOR

Hadith accounts relate that when Muhammad passed away, his family and companions gathered outside his house. Ali ibn Abu Talib, his

Above A Turkish painting depicts Muhammad and his cousin Ali, who is for Shiahs the true successor to the Prophet.

son-in-law and cousin, withdrew to his own house with a few others, but the majority of people began to elect a leader. Umar and Abu Bakr learned of this and joined them.

Abu Bakr persuaded the people that it would be best for a member of the Quraysh tribe to lead the community because of their central position among the Arabs. Umar immediately elected Abu Bakr, on the grounds that he had been appointed by Muhammad to lead prayers at the end of his life, and because he had been mentioned in the Quran (9:40). The whole congregation pledged allegiance to Abu Bakr as their leader – all, that is, except Ali.

THE DISSENSION OF ALI

Ali's position, and that of the *Ahl al-Bayt*, members of the Prophet's family, is unique in Islam because hadiths record Muhammad as having extolled their importance. Indeed, Muslims send peace and blessings on a daily basis on the Prophet and his descendants.

For some members of the early community, this meant that Ali was the natural successor to the Prophet. Not only was he a member of Muhammad's family, he pledged allegiance to the Prophet and his faith at the age of ten, had been trusted by Muhammad with special missions and was renowned for his bravery and justice. As a direct relative, he was entrusted with the responsibility of preparing the body for burial, and lowering it into the grave. Indeed, no one could doubt the importance of Ali.

Above Arabic calligraphy with the names of Muhammad and his family members. Reverence for the Ahl al-Bayt, house of the Prophet, is central to Shiah belief.

However, most members of the *ummah* believed that succession should not be based on blood ties, and that an elected elder would be a better leader. Not until months later, after his wife Fatimah's death, did Ali express his dissatisfaction with the electoral process to Abu Bakr. His objection was that as everybody had rallied around Abu Bakr, without taking absentees into account, no one was given the right to dissent and choose a different leader.

SUPPORT FOR ALI

The matter did not come to an end, however, for there was still a minority of people who were

rallying support for Ali, believing that succession ought to remain with the Prophet's descendants. Indeed, they claimed that at the last pilgrimage, at Ghadir Khumm, Muhammad himself had designated Ali as his successor.

Eventually, the Shiah, 'party' of Ali, was appeased when he became the fourth caliph. But his murder five years later again plunged the community into a dilemma about succession. This time, however, neither those who proposed an elected leader nor those who wanted a direct descendant of the Prophet succeeded: instead, power was vested in a politically and militarily strong might, Muawiyah, the governor of Syria, who then established a dynastic line.

SUNNIS VERUS SHIAHS

While the early differences between the two factions may seem to have been largely political, they were fraught with religious tensions, too, for Islam did not (and does not) make a division between the social, political and religious. The choice

Right A Pakistani Shiah Muslim procession during Ramadhan marks the anniversary of Imam Ali's martyrdom.

of a suitable leader was thus a deeply religious matter. This conflict continued down the centuries.

The emerging Sunni Muslims were those who believed they were following the Prophet's sunnah (hence their name). Their faith was patronized by the rulers, but scholars did not necessarily either trust or support these rulers. The dissenting Shiahs became a minority who stood up against the

Above Shiahs make up well over half the population of Iraq. Here, Shaykh Muhammad al-Gharawi addresses a Shiah conference in Baghdad.

state-patronized religion and continued their loyalty to the Prophet's family. For them, Ali would remain the exemplary ruler: a blood relative loved by the Prophet, who was brave, humble, spiritual and literarily accomplished.

THE SHIAH IMAMS

SHIAH ISLAM DEVELOPED SOPHISTICATED THEOLOGY REGARDING
THE SUCCESSION AND LEADERSHIP OF THE COMMUNITY VIA DIVINELY
APPOINTED 'IMAMS', WHO WERE DESCENDANTS OF THE PROPHET.

*Above Ali Zayn al-Abidin, the 4th
imam and the son of the martyred
Hussain, preaches in a mosque in
defence of his father.*

After Muhammad's death, those who supported Ali believed that succession should be via the Prophet's male descendants: as he had no surviving sons, this would be through his daughter Fatimah's marriage to Ali. The Shiah imams, of whom there are 12 in total, are all descendants from Fatimah and Ali's marriage. Over time, the deeply rooted differences between Sunni and Shiah Islam, originally political, became theological.

HISTORICAL DEVELOPMENT

Shiah Islam is a highly organized branch of the faith, which, unlike Sunni Islam, has a clergy. As the first division in Islam occurred over the issue of leadership of the *ummah*, a central tenet of Shiah thought is that authority must be lawfully and divinely vested in leaders.

For Shiahs, the term 'imam' refers to those of Muhammad's descendants who are believed to have been divinely designated by God as the Prophet's heirs. Each imam appointed his successor before his death and Shiahs believe that he was inspired by God in this choice.

Early divisions increased with the establishment of the Umayyad dynasty, which was seen as corrupt and tyrannical, not upholding the values of Islam. Dissension was therefore viewed as a religious act. After Ali's death, his followers turned their attention to his son Hassan, and recognized him as imam. Hassan was very quietist, whereas his brother Hussain, the third imam, became a pivotal public figure in the development of Shiah Islam with his martyrdom at Karbala in 680. After Karbala, the Sunni–Shiah divide took on further theological shape.

THEOLOGY OF THE SHIAH

Shiah theology developed over time to claim that as God is merciful and just – *rahman* and *adl* – he would not leave his creation without guidance. As prophethood was now closed, Shiahs asserted that God would guide humankind through divinely appointed imams. Imams are therefore viewed by Shiah Muslims as *ayat-Allah*, signs of God's mercy, and as *hujjat-Allah*, proof of God.

Shiahs also believe that these imams were created from the same light as Muhammad and Fatimah, thereby making them *masum*, sinless and hence infallible. The role of

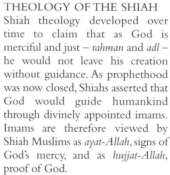

*Left A scene from the Battle of Karbala
showing Hussain's brother being
attacked. The Prophet and Ali are
depicted looking on from heaven.*

these imams was simply to elucidate the inner meanings of the Quran. According to the Shiahs, the ruling imam would be imbued by God with full knowledge, which he would pass on to his chosen successor just before his death.

Eleven imams lived earthly lives. However, since the death of the 11th, the 12th imam is believed by Shiahs to have gone into hiding, or occultation (*ghaybah*), as a child, to reappear at an apocalyptic time near the ending of the world. In the meantime, Shiah governments have been legitimized by claiming to be 'caretaker' governments in the 12th imam's absence; such is the case in Iran, for example.

Shiahs have their own hadith collections of the teachings of the imams, which explain the Quran's esoteric meanings, and the Prophet's life example. *Nahjul Balaghah* is an important collection of Ali's sermons, in which he elucidates the faith in the light of the Quran and prophetic teachings.

Above An Iraqi Shiah woman lights a candle in Karbala as part of festivities to mark the birthday anniversary of the 12th imam, Muhammad al-Mahdi.

Different branches of Shiah Islam developed because of disputes over the persona of the imams. The Twelvers evolved largely in urban Iraq and believe in the 12 imams listed above. The Ismailis lived in rural North Africa, leading to the formation of the Fatimid dynasty in Egypt. They believe Ismail ibn Jafar was the rightful seventh imam.

Twelver Shiahs represent the largest Shiah group, with a majority in Iran and southern Iraq and a significant minority in Lebanon, Kuwait, Pakistan and India. Ismailis form the second largest group and exist mainly in India and East Africa.

Zaydis, the third largest Shiah group, are found mainly in Yemen. Zaydis believe that an imam did not have to be a direct descendant of Ali and Fatimah: it would be sufficient for him to be the son of the ruling imam, albeit from a wife whose genealogy could not be traced to Fatimah. On these grounds, they rejected Muhammad al-Baqir for his brother Zayd.

Below Some 6,000 members of the Nizari Ismaili sect of Shiah Islam pray as they wait for the arrival of their leader, Aga Khan IV.

SHIAH PILGRIMAGES

IRAN AND IRAQ ARE KEY PLACES OF PILGRIMAGE FOR SHIAHS. IRAQ CONTAINS HOLY SHRINES IN KARBALA, NAJAF AND SAMARRA, WHILE IRAN HAS MASHHAD AND THE CENTRES OF SHIAH LEARNING AT QOM.

The world's principal pilgrimage site is the same for Shiah and Sunni Muslims: Makkah in Saudi Arabia, the destination for the *Hajj*, which is compulsory once in a lifetime for all able-bodied Muslims who can afford it. Like their Sunni counterparts, Shiah Muslims travel to the Great Mosque and make seven circuits of the sacred *Kaabah*.

The other main destination for Muslim pilgrims in Saudi Arabia, Madinah, has special significance for Shiahs as the site of shrines to the second and fourth imams, Hassan ibn Ali and Ali Zayn al-Abidin.

KARBALA AND NAJAF

After Makkah and Madinah, the most sacred place for Shiahs is Karbala in Iraq. Karbala is the site of the battle in which Hussain ibn Ali, grandson of the Prophet, was killed on 10 Muharram 680. Around one million Shiahs travel as pilgrims to Karbala to commemorate his death in the month of Muharram.

South-east of Karbala is the holy Shiah city of Najaf, site of the tomb of Ali ibn Abu Talib, the first Shiah imam. Pilgrims visit the Imam Ali Mosque and the Wadi as-Salam, a cemetery nearby that contains the graves of many holy men of the Shiah faith. Najaf is also a great centre of Shiah scholarship.

SAMARRA

Another centre for Shiah pilgrims in Iraq is the city of Samarra, which was the capital of the Sunni Muslim Abbasid caliphate (833–92). It contains the extraordinary Great Mosque of Samarra, built by Caliph al-Mutawakkil (reigned 847–61), but its main significance for Shiah Muslims lies in its being the place where, they believe, the 12th imam, Muhammad al-Mahdi, was miraculously hidden by Allah in a process known as occultation. Pilgrims visit a shrine marking the place at which al-Mahdi was last seen before his occultation.

Above Pilgrims gather at the Jamkaran Mosque near Qom, Iran, where the hidden imam, al-Mahdi, is said once to have made a miraculous appearance.

Samarra is also the site of shrines to the 10th and 11th imams, Ali al-Hadi al-Naqi and Hassan al-Askari. All three are contained within the Al-Askari Mosque, built in 944, which also houses the tombs of Ali Hadi al-Naqi's sister, Hakimah Khatun, and the hidden imam's mother, Narjis Khatun. The mosque once had a dazzling golden dome, 68 metres (223 feet) across, and two golden minarets, each 36 metres (118 feet) tall, but both dome and minarets were destroyed in bomb attacks attributed to Sunni militants in February 2006 and June 2007.

Shiahs also visit the Iraqi capital, to make devotions at the shrines to the seventh and ninth imams, Musa al-Kazim and Muhammad Jawad al-Taqi, in Kazimayn, now a suburb of Baghdad. The shrine to the imams was built by Shah Ismail I (reigned 1502–24) of the Safavid dynasty.

Left Thousands of Shiah pilgrims gather at the Imam Ali shrine in Najaf, Iraq, just before dawn to celebrate the birthday of the hidden imam, al-Mahdi.

Right The tomb of Hussain ibn Ali at the Imam Hussain Shrine in Karbala, Iraq, is topped with a golden dome 27 metres (89 feet) high.

MASHHAD AND QOM

In Iran, the principal pilgrimage destination for Shiah Muslims is the city of Mashhad. It contains the shrine of Ali al-Rida, the eighth Shiah imam, who is said to have been poisoned by Abbasid caliph al-Mamun (reigned 813–33) and is viewed as a martyr. A domed shrine was built over this tomb as early as the 9th century, but this has been rebuilt several times since. The tomb of Abbasid caliph Harun al-Rashid (reigned 786–809) stands opposite the shrine to Ali al-Rida. Mashhad became a major place of pilgrimage under the Safavid dynasty, and Shah Abbas I (reigned 1588–1629) walked there as a pilgrim from Esfahan.

Qom, the principal centre for Shiah scholarship in the world and the place where Ayatollah Khomeini trained, is another Iranian pilgrimage site for Shiahs. Qom is considered a holy city because it contains the shine to Fatema Masume, sister of Ali al-Rida. Pilgrims also make their way to the Jamkaran Mosque on the outskirts of the city. According to tradition, the 12th, and hidden, imam, Muhammad al-Mahdi, miraculously appeared at the mosque and pilgrims there make intercessions to him at a sacred well, from which it is said he will one day emerge. In 2005, the Iranian government reportedly donated US$20 million to develop Jamkaran Mosque into a major Shiah pilgrimage centre.

Left In Mashhad, the faithful draw inspiration from an image of Ayatollah Khomeini, Supreme Leader of Iran, and his successor, Ayatollah Khameini.

MAULANA RUMI AND HIS *MATHNAWI*

JALAL-UD-DIN RUMI (1207–73) IS THE MOST CELEBRATED MYSTICAL POET AND TEACHER IN MUSLIM HISTORY, AND HIS MAGNUM OPUS, *MATHNAWI*, IS ONE OF THE GREAT CLASSICS OF SUFI LITERATURE.

While scholars used Arabic as their literary language, Sufis wrote their poetry and treatises in the vernacular. This use of local languages, especially Persian, became legendary in Rumi's epic *Mathnawi* (meaning 'couplet'), a six-volume poem with more than 25,000 verses of parables, metaphors and tales about prophets and saints.

RUMI'S LIFE

According to his biography, Rumi was born in Persian Khorasan (now in Afghanistan) in 1207. His family moved to Rum in Anatolia around 1222 and to Konya in 1229. Rumi's father was a scholar and Rumi took his place as a teacher at the *madrasa* in Konya, after the latter's death in 1231. Here, his new teacher, Burhanuddin, instructed him in Sufism and sent him to Aleppo and Damascus for further study. Rumi returned to teach in Konya again when he was 30 years old.

Rumi was already accomplished as a jurist and Sufi when, in 1244, he met Shams Tabrizi, an Iranian Sufi mystic, on his way home from teaching. The meeting changed Rumi's life – it is said that he fainted after the spiritual and verbal exchange that took place – and after this time, he neglected his teaching duties to devote himself to Sufi development under the guidance of Shams.

Only 15 months later, however, Shams disappeared. Rumi, despondent and dejected, poured his anguish into verse. Shams did return but disappeared again only a few months later. Legend has it that the teacher was murdered by Rumi's son Ala-uddin. More rational accounts claim that Shams, a highly evolved soul, sought like-minded men to train further in God's way, and that once his task was complete, he would leave so that their great work on earth could begin. Certainly,

Left Rumi holds court and warns his son, Sultan Walad, against sin in this manuscript painting from The Legend of Maulana Jalal ud-Din Rumi *(1599).*

Above A common representation of Rumi: his size denotes his importance. In reality, however, he was known to be a slight man, much given to fasting.

it was after Shams' disappearance that the now mature and refined Rumi wrote his major works.

Rumi died in 1273, after a short illness. It is recorded that people of all races and religions attended his funeral, which took place in Konya. To this day, his burial place is a pilgrimage site for his many devotees. Rumi is fondly known throughout the Muslim world as Maulana, 'our teacher', from which the Mevlevi (whirling dervishes) Sufi order, founded by his son Sultan Walad, takes its name.

THE *MATHNAWI*

Rumi began writing and dictating the *Mathnawi* in 1260 and the work continued until his death. Its many verses teach that although scholars and theologians are important, they lost their way in the depths of books and laws, and that the spirit of God is of paramount importance and knowing him the aim of life.

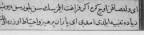

The work opens with 'The Poem of the Reed', a lament by a reed when it is cut off from the reed-bed. The poem is a metaphor of human anguish: pain emanates from the fact that humankind is cut off from God since being rejected from heaven and longs to return to him.

The Mathnawi combines hadiths and Quranic verses with parables, anecdotes, paradoxes and moral teachings. These elements often flow naturally, while at other times a narrative is resumed after interruption by another.

While as an accomplished Sufi, Rumi no longer experienced a separation of the temporal and spiritual realms, he acknowledged that most people did. He is also said to have been very conscious of the limitations of words to describe the divine and the spiritual. Perhaps it is for this reason that he often uses very bawdy, coarse language and imagery to portray spiritual truths.

EXCERPTS FROM THE *MATHNAWI*:

'Listen to the reed how it tells a tale, complaining of separations – saying "ever since I was parted from the reed-bed, my lament has caused man and woman to moan.

I want a bosom torn by severance, that I may unfold the pain of love-desire.

Every one who is left far from his source wishes back the time when he was united with it..."'   *(The Poem of the Reed, vol. 1)*

'When the mirror of your heart becomes clear and pure, you will behold images from beyond this world of water and clay.

You will behold both the image and the image-Maker, both the carpet and the carpet-Spreader.

The image of the beloved is like Abraham – outwardly an idol worshipper, inwardly an idol-breaker.'

(The Prophet Abraham, vol. 2)

Above Whirling dervishes dance in the Maulana hall at Rumi's mausoleum. Murids, or seekers, are not admitted to the dance until they have attained certain stations in their spiritual quest.

SUFISM IN PRACTICE

SUFI PRACTICE IS BASED ON THE IDEA THAT GOD IS LOVE, AND THEREFORE THE ONLY AIM OF THE SUFI IS TO LOVE GOD, OTHERS AND HIMSELF. WELL-KNOWN SUFI MAXIMS ELABORATE THIS BELIEF.

Sufism can be summed up as the fulfilment of the Quran and sunnah so that the exoteric laws are understood through esoteric dimensions. This emphasis on inner spirituality was ardently promoted by some Sufis, who insisted that Sufis should not wear noticeably different clothes, because outward appearance should not be the hallmark of a Sufi.

According to various treatises, Sufis are seekers of gnosis (*marifah*), or knowledge of spiritual mysteries, which cannot be attained until the ego has been fully controlled through prescribed practices.

BODY AND SPIRIT

An interesting tension exists between the body and the spirit in Islam: while humankind is both, the body is understood, in Sufi terms, to be that earthly element (*al-nafs al-ammarah*), which distances man from God. Sufis therefore believe that a rigorous programme of worship, night vigils and fasting is necessary in order to starve the ego and body and purify the soul. Only in this way, they claim, can the 'ever-reproachful soul' (*al-nafs al-lawwamah*) become the 'contented soul' (*al-nafs al-mutmainnah*).

Sufis teach that constant recitation of God's divine names and praises will purify the heart until it is ready to receive divine grace. For Sufis, the legal injunctions of Islam are valid only if performed with God's presence and pleasure in mind.

THE STATIONS AND STATES

For Sufis, knowing God is such a serious business that it cannot be achieved without a teacher. The Prophet, himself the guide (*murshid*) who showed the way to God, is cited as the precedent for this practice. Sufis believe that God bestows this task on pious souls who themselves have travelled the same journey. These teachers are usually affiliated to Sufi orders (*tariqahs*), and trace their chain of authority (*silsilah*), to the Prophet and his companions. They are seen as God's friends, or *awliya* (10:62).

Above Dhikr, *remembrance of God, is a Sufi practice that takes different forms. Members of the Qadriyya sect, like this Sudanese Sufi, whirl rapidly in prayer.*

Each Sufi, then, is required to attach himself to such a teacher, who will give him or her various spiritual and physical exercises to perform. The stages of Sufi development are described as *maqamat*, or stations, and include repentance, patience, gratitude, acceptance, trust and love. The paradigmatic journey to God was the Prophet's ascent to heaven (*Miraj*). While on the path, a Sufi is believed to experience various transcendent states (*ahwal*), such as fear and hope. Imam al-Ghazali asserted that the stations are permanent changes gained through acts of devotion, whereas states are temporary, dependent on the grace and favour of God.

Finally, through the stations of love and gnosis, the Sufi is said to reach the position of *fana*, or

Left Depicted here at his execution, al-Hallaj was thought to have blasphemed by claiming to have attained union with God, a controversial theme in Sufism.

self-annihilation, where he can then exist and dwell (*baqa*) wholly in God. Such ideas, alluding to union with God (*wahdat-ul-wujud*), have been very controversial, often resulting in what appear to be blasphemous statements: Mansur al-Hallaj (d.922) was eventually executed in Baghdad for having uttered, 'I am the Truth'. In an attempt to defend and clarify this union with God, several Sufi writings explain that the Sufi becomes one with the divine will, rather than actually joining with the essence of God.

Above An illustration from a manuscript by the renowned Persian Sufi poet, Farid-ud-Din Attar.

CELEBRATING THE DIVINE

Sufis celebrate the divine in many different ways. While some have very puritan rituals, such as silent meditation, others have produced trancelike dance movements (whirling dervishes), music (Abida Perveen's *qawwalis* in Pakistan), poetry (Bulleh Shah) and literature (al-Ghazali, Jalal-ud-Din Rumi's *Mathnawi*, Farid-ud-Din Attar's *Conference of the Birds*).

Above Sufis pray at the tomb of Shaykh Salim Chishti, at Fatehpur Sikri in Uttar Pradesh, India. The Chishti is a very influential Sufi order in India.

RABIAH AL-ADAWIYYAH

RENOWNED FOR HER WISDOM AND LOVE OF GOD, RABIAH AL-ADAWIYYAH (717–801) IS OFTEN DESCRIBED AS THE FIRST SUFI WOMAN BECAUSE OF HER FAR-REACHING INFLUENCE.

In the 8th and 9th centuries, Basra (in present-day Iraq) was a great centre of asceticism, where women ascetics, in particular, flourished. It is here that Rabiah spent her life, giving advice and moral teachings and introducing pure love in mysticism. Sufism is often more inclusive of women than ritual Islam, and Rabiah is seen as the model of female sainthood.

Rabiah is so important in Sufi thought that she is cited by later seminal historical treatises, such as those by Al-Sulami (d.1021) and Farid-ud-Din Attar (d.1229). Al-Sulami begins his work on women Sufi saints with Rabiah, not because she was the first, but because her influence was so profound and far-reaching. Attar, her main biographer, describes her as a 'man' in appreciation of her status and achievements.

RABIAH'S LIFE
It is thought that Rabiah was born in Basra and sold into slavery as a young girl. The story tells that following her conversion to Islam, Rabiah was observing all-night devotions after having worked all day. Her master saw her and was so amazed that he set her free. She is said to have spent the rest of her life as an ascetic, never marrying, despite receiving numerous proposals.

Various sayings and anecdotes have been attributed to Rabiah, both about her love for God and relating her intellectual debates. She reportedly defeated the old jurist Hassan al-Basra in many intellectual contests, for unlike him, she managed to synthesize theology with the practice of self-discipline in her debates. Her thinking and approach was to pave the way for later Sufism.

Above This 16th-century Persian-style manuscript painting depicts a Sufi preaching in a mosque.

LOVING GOD
Rabiah is well known for having explained the concept of *sidq*, or sincerity with God. Brutally critical of those who claimed to be ascetic, she argued that if they had truly shunned the world, then they ought to be so consumed with affirming God that there would be no scope in their life to shun anything. In other words, detachment from the world was not a verbal confession, but a state of being.

Linked with this was her most famous argument: that believers should be so truthful and devout to God that notions of hell and heaven, despite being present in the Quran, would cease to matter. The goal of worship, she asserted, was not heaven but nearness to God and his pleasure (*rida*). There are famous legendary accounts of her running down a street with fire in one hand and water in the other, because she wanted to burn heaven and douse hell so that people would love God, heedless of reward or punishment.

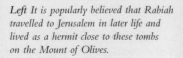

Left It is popularly believed that Rabiah travelled to Jerusalem in later life and lived as a hermit close to these tombs on the Mount of Olives.

Above Women members of a Sufi order at the festival of Sboue in the oasis town of Timimoun in Algeria. The festival is in honour of the Prophet's birthday.

This sincere love (*mahabba*), was so crucial to her that she is said to have exclaimed that she could not hate Satan, for she had no need to think of him, nor could she love the Prophet, with all due respect, for she was too busy loving the One God. This was the epitome of her trust (*tawakkul*), in Allah, for her life consisted of turning exclusively to him.

CATALOGUE OF MIRACLES

Rabiah is said to have annihilated her ego to such an extent that her life became a catalogue of miracles. One story tells that when she went on pilgrimage to Makkah, the *Kaabah* came to greet her rather than her visiting it. It is told that she was thoroughly disappointed by this, for unlike others, she had not travelled to visit the *Kaabah*, but rather its Master.

Below A woman whirling dervish in Istanbul. Women are very visible in Sufi orders, sometimes even leading them.

251

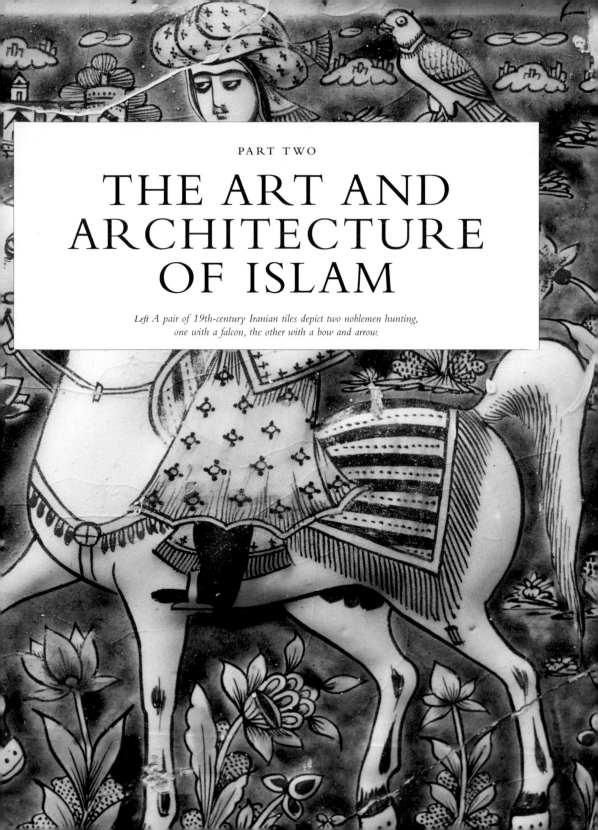

PART TWO

THE ART AND ARCHITECTURE OF ISLAM

*Left A pair of 19th-century Iranian tiles depict two noblemen hunting,
one with a falcon, the other with a bow and arrow.*

THE PROPHET AND THE RISE OF ISLAM

THE RELIGION OF ISLAM WAS FOUNDED BY THE PROPHET MUHAMMAD (DIED 632) IN THE ARABIAN CITIES OF MAKKAH AND MADINAH. THE ARABIC WORD 'ISLAM' LITERALLY MEANS 'SUBMISSION'.

The Prophet Muhammad was born in Makkah, around 570. Orphaned at a young age, he was raised by his extended family, a minor clan of the powerful Quraysh tribe. Makkah was a merchant city with an important pilgrimage sanctuary at its heart. Known as the *Kaabah*, the sanctuary was dedicated to a pantheon of pagan deities. As a young man, Muhammad travelled widely beyond his hometown. He married Khadijah (died 619), a wealthy merchant widow, and they ran her business together. In 610, during a period of solitary reflection on Mount Hira outside

Makkah, Muhammad, now about 40, began to receive divine revelations instructing him to preach a new, monotheistic faith, that would challenge and eventually overturn the pagan beliefs of his own community.

THE EMERGENCE OF ISLAM
Revelations came to the Prophet periodically over the rest of his life, for the next 22 years. They were carefully remembered and retained

Below It is estimated that one million or so pilgrims visit the Kaabah in Makkah every year for the annual Hajj rituals.

***Above** During the annual* Hajj *to Makkah, pilgrims also visit the Mosque of the Prophet in Madinah.*

by the Prophet and his growing community of Muslim converts, and together these revealed passages constitute the Quran, the Holy Book of Islam. As such, Muslims consider the Quran to be of divine authorship, a perfect text. The

essential message of this new religion was monotheism: Muslims believe in only one God, and avoid idolatry. Islam also holds sacred a long lineage of ancient prophets including Adam, Noah, Abraham and Jesus. In these aspects, Islam shares a great deal with both Judaism and Christianity, and these fellow monotheistic faiths are described in the Quran as the 'People of the Book' because Jews and Christians also possess sacred texts (the Torah and the Bible).

THE PROPHET'S MISSION IN ARABIA

Following his first revelation, Muhammad obeyed the divine command to 'Recite!' and started to preach. He began seeking converts, first among his family and friends, and then gradually from the wider Makkah community. This soon met with hostility from the dominant Quraysh tribe, whose power in Makkah rested on their responsibility for the pagan sanctuary of the *Kaabah*. The new religion also undermined the tribal system of family loyalty, as it created a new community bound by religious commitment rather than blood relationships. After many years under threat, the Prophet and his followers were finally forced to leave Makkah in the year 622, and they fled to the security of a small Muslim community recently established in nearby Yathrib. There they built a house for the Prophet and his family, which became the first mosque. This migration, or *hijrah*, was an important moment for the first Muslims, and marks the beginning of Islamic history: 622 is the first year in the Muslim calendar, 1AH ('Anno Hegirae') the year of the *hijrah*. In honour of this reception, Yathrib was renamed Madinat al-Nabi ('The City of the Prophet'), and is now known as Madinah.

Muslims prospered in Madinah and surrounding tribal areas, extending their political and religious influence, but hostility with Makkah remained unresolved. Eventually, in 630, the Muslim forces conquered Makkah, defeating the Quraysh, and reclaimed the *Kaabah* pilgrimage sanctuary for Islam. This had long been the Prophet's intention: he had already designated the holy *Kaabah* as the direction for Muslim prayer; now

Above The text of this 16th-century Quran is beautifully framed within panels of illumination.

he cleared the site of its pagan idols, and it became part of Muslim tradition – and the destination for the annual *Hajj* pilgrimage, one of the five basic requirements of Islam. Following this victory, the Prophet continued to live in his house in Madinah, where he passed away in 632.

THE FIVE PILLARS OF ISLAM
Islam requires that all Muslims perform five basic duties, as follows:

1. *Shahadah*, or profession of faith, reciting the creed statement 'There is no god but God, and Muhammad is his messenger'.
2. *Salat*, or daily prayers, to be performed every day at five determined times between early dawn and evening.
3. *Zakat*, or charitable donation of alms to the poor.
4. *Sawm*, or annual fasting during the daylight hours of the month of Ramadhan every year.
5. *Hajj*, the pilgrimage to the *Kaabah* in Makkah which must be undertaken at least once in every Muslim's lifetime.

PROPHET MUHAMMAD'S SUCCESSOR

FOLLOWING THE DEATH OF THE PROPHET MUHAMMAD IN 632, THE
MUSLIM COMMUNITY, OR *UMMAH*, SOUGHT A MEANS OF AGREEMENT
ON HIS SUCCESSOR, OR CALIPH.

*Above The Kufa Mosque in Iraq was
the headquarters of Ali ibn Abu Talib
(died 661).*

THE RIGHTEOUS CALIPHS

Until the emergence of the
Umayyad dynasty in 661, leadership
of the new Islamic state was
determined by consensus rather
than family inheritance. The initial
principle was based on the
Prophet's own views about his
succession, which were unclear
and hotly debated. When weak and
close to death, the Prophet
Muhammad had asked his
companion and father-in-law, Abu
Bakr, to lead the community's
prayers on his behalf. This was
considered significant, and the
community chose Abu Bakr (died
634) as the first of the four
Righteous Caliphs, or al-Rashidun.
The following three caliphs were
also close friends or family of the
Prophet: Umar (died 644), Uthman
Ibn-Affan (died 656) and Ali (died
661), and all were elected with the
consensus of the community. The
years of the Rashidun Caliphs saw
the Islamic state expand with great
military energy from its Arabian
heartland, conquering first Syria,
then Palestine, North Africa and
Iraq, and then Iran. The Byzantine
emperor was beaten into retreat in
Anatolia, and the
last Sasanian Shah
Yazdagird III (died
651) was completely
defeated. Both great
empires were severely
damaged by Muslim
conquest, but both
also contributed a
considerable cultural
heritage to the new
Islamic state – in
terms of government
infrastructure and
court ceremony, as
well as art and
architecture. This was
particularly felt after
the capital moved
to Damascus in 661,
and eventually to
Baghdad in 750.

*Left A manuscript
illustration that depicts
the first three Shiah
Imams: Ali with his sons
Hasan and Husayn.*

THE EMERGENCE OF SHIAH ISLAM

The fourth caliph was Ali ibn Abu
Talib (d.661), who ruled from Kufa
in Iraq. He was a close companion
of the Prophet Muhammad, as the
first three caliphs had also been.
Ali was the Prophet's younger
cousin. He had been fostered
by him as a child, and later married
the Prophet's daughter Fatima.
Ali and Fatima had two sons,
Hasan and Husayn, who were
therefore part of a bloodline
descending directly from the
Prophet – who had had no
surviving sons. This lineage became
ever more significant with
regard to the Muslim leadership:
while Ali was caliph, he was
challenged by Muawiyah, the
governor of Syria and eventual
founder of the Umayyad dynasty
(661–750). Importantly, Ali was
from the same clan as the Prophet,
while Muawiyah and the third
caliph, Uthman, were from the
Umayyad clan (another branch of
the Quraysh tribe of Makkah).
When Ali was murdered in 661 by
members of the radical Khariji
sect, Muawiyah was quick to seize

Above A painting of the Battle of Karbala, showing Husayn's half-brother, Abbas, heroically defeating an Umayyad soldier.

the Caliphate – establishing his own dynasty, which ruled from Damascus. Ali's son Hasan (died 669) did not pursue the Caliphate, but on Muawiyah's death in 680, his brother Husayn claimed the leadership as a direct descendant of the Prophet. Husayn led his forces to Karbala in Iraq, and was greatly outnumbered by the Umayyad forces of Muawiyah's son, Yazid. Besieged, Husayn and his supporters were eventually massacred by the Umayyads (10 October 680). Ashura, the anniversary of Husayn's martyrdom, is mourned every year by Muslims, but has an especially strong significance for the sect that emerged from orthodox or Sunni Islam. Known as Shiat-Ali, or the partisans of Ali, Shiah Muslims hold that the leadership of the Islamic state should fall only to

those descended directly from the Prophet: Ali is therefore regarded by them as the first such leader, or Imam, with Hasan and Husayn the second and third, and a succession of further Imams thereafter. The first three caliphs are therefore regarded by Shiah Muslims as invalid, while the Umayyad dynasty and its successor, the Abbasid, are considered usurpers. There are different important branches within Shiism, according to views about the succession of later

Imams: these include Twelver Shiism, the state religion of Iran since the 16th century, and Ismaili Shiism – of which the Aga Khan is the current leader. Shiah reverence for the tombs of Imams and their families is very strong, particularly for the shrine of Imam Ali in Najaf, of Imam Husayn at Karbala (both in Iraq), and of Imam Reza in Mashhad in Iran. These and other Shiah shrines remain important pilgrimage destinations to this day.

Right Shiah pilgrims visit the holy shrine of Imam Ali in the Iraqi city of Najaf.

Above A courtyard in the Alhambra, the 14th- and 15th-century residence of Muslim rulers in Granada.

Above Floral patterns feature on this 13th–14th-century Islamic dish, made during the Mongol period in Iran.

Above The Azadi Tower, built in Tehran in 1971, marked the 2,500th anniversary of the Persian Empire.

- 1749 Ottoman governor Asad Pasha al-Azem builds the Azem Palace in Damascus.
- 1836 In Istanbul, Krikor Balyan completes the Nusretiye Mosque for Ottoman Sultan Mahmud II (reigned 1808–39).
- 1848 Muhammad Ali Pasha, Wali of Egypt, completes the grand Muhammad Ali Mosque in Cairo.
- 1855 Architects Garabet Amira Balyan and Nigogayos Balyan complete the Dolmabahçe Palace in Istanbul for Ottoman

Below The Islamic world extended across Africa, Europe and Asia.

Sultan Abdulmecid I (reigned 1839–61).
- 1961 The Dhahran International Airport in Saudi Arabia is completed, designed by American architect Minoru Yamasaki.
- 1971 The Shayad Tower ('Memorial of Kings') is built in Tehran, Iran. After the Islamic Revolution (1979) it is renamed the Azadi (Freedom) Tower.
- 1973 The Great Mosque of Niono in Mali, western Africa, is completed using traditional techniques and materials.
- 1984 The Freedom Mosque in Jakarta, Indonesia, is

completed by Indonesian architect Frederick Silaban.
- 1986 The King Faisal Mosque is completed in Islamabad, Pakistan. The architect, Vedat Delakoy, is Turkish.
- 1989 Architect Abdel-Wahed el-Wakil completes the King Saud Mosque in Jeddah, Saudi Arabia.
- 1990 Architect Rasem Badran completes the King Abdullah Mosque in Amman, Jordan.
- 1993 The King Hassan II Mosque in Casablanca, Morocco, is finished. It is designed by French architect Michel Pinseau. Its minaret, at 210m (689ft), is the world's tallest.
- 1999 The Kingdom Tower office and retail complex in Riyadh, Saudi Arabia, is completed. It is 311m (1,020ft) tall. A rival Riyadh tower, the Al Faisaliyah Centre, is completed in 2000.
- 1999 The Burj al-Arab ('Tower of the Arabs') hotel is completed on a man-made island off Dubai.
- 2007 The Rose Tower built in Dubai. At 333m (1,093ft) tall, it is the world's tallest hotel.

Opposite An illustration of the city of Baghdad, showing the famous bridge of boats across the Tigris, from a 1468 anthology by Nasir Bukhari.

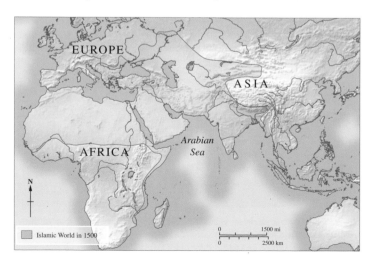

EUROPE

ASIA

AFRICA

Arabian Sea

N

Islamic World in 1500

0   1500 mi
0   2500 km

CHAPTER 8

THE ART OF THE ISLAMIC WORLD

Western art historians have long used the expression Islamic Art to describe the wide range of visual culture that has been created in the extensive regions of the world – from Spain to India, Turkey to North Africa – that have at some time come under Muslim rule. The glorious architecture, from palaces to whole cities, from mosques to bazaars; the arts of the book, such as calligraphy, painting, manuscript illumination and bookbinding; not to mention luxury items made from precious metals and alloys, ivory, rock crystal, gemstones, glass, ceramics and wood, and textiles and carpets, all qualify as Islamic Art. Their splendid refinement signifies a longstanding culture of taste and discernment and an educated, perhaps elite, audience. The common factor in this great output from so many different cultures is the religion of Islam, for although the civilian populations of Western Asia and other parts of the Islamic world were never exclusively Muslim, they have long been ruled by caliphs, sultans, shahs and amirs who were.

Opposite Beautiful mosaics, including prayers and quotations from the Quran, line the interior walls of the Dome of the Rock in Jerusalem. Pilgrims visiting the shrine follow the ambulatory around the sacred Rock at the centre.

Above The Quran is the holy book of Islam, and is always produced with great care and respect for the text.

THE QURAN

THE HOLY QURAN, WHICH CONTAINS THE TRANSCRIBED WORDS OF
ALLAH AS RECEIVED BY THE PROPHET MUHAMMAD IN 610–32, HAS
BEEN A FOCUS FOR ISLAMIC ART AND CULTURE ACROSS THE CENTURIES.

Over 22 years, beginning in 610, the Prophet Muhammad received 114 divine revelations through Jibril (the angel Gabriel). The revelations are collected in the Quran, which Muslims believe to be the complete and faithful record of what Muhammad was told. The teachings he received from Jibril – who is also referred to as the 'Spirit of Holiness' (Surah al-Nahl: 102) – are understood by Muslims to be the actual words of Allah.

Muhammad did not write the Quran (according to tradition he did not read or write). He passed on the words of Allah orally, repeating the revelations he had received to his early followers, who memorized them and passed them on to others.

SINGLE DOCUMENT
Scribes did write down some of the revelations using available materials, such as parchment, palm leaves, stone tablets and even animal bones. In these cases, Muhammad is believed to have had the records read back to him to check that the scribes had accurately written down his words. However, no attempt was made to gather the

revelations into a comprehensive written document until after Muhammad's death in 632. The situation changed when, in the Battle of Yamama (633) between Abu Bakr and followers of self-styled Prophet Musaylimah, at least 700 men who had memorized the Quran were slain. Leading Muslims saw the pressing need to make a written version for future generations before all those who had known the Prophet and his teachings at first hand had died.

A WRITTEN QURAN
One of the principal scribes, Zayd ibn Thabit (c.611–56), gathered the written revelations and wrote down all those existing in only memorized form. The results were approved by the *ashab* (Prophet's Companions) as being an accurate record of Muhammad's teachings. In c.654, during the era of Caliph Uthman ibn-Affan (reigned 644–56), a standardized version was drawn up and sent to the four cities of Kufa, Madinah, Damascus and Basra.

Some secular scholars claim that this traditional Islamic account of the collection of the Prophet's

Above Jibril transmits the words of Allah to the Prophet in this image from the Siyer-i Nebi, an epic biography detailing the Prophet's life.

teachings in the Quran is incorrect and that the book was gathered from various sources over centuries. For Muslims, however, it is a binding obligation of their faith that the Quran contains the words of Allah as received by Muhammad, full, complete and unchanging.

STRUCTURE
The Quran contains 114 suwar (singular surah), or 'chapters', each containing one of the revelations received by the Prophet. They vary greatly in length: some have 3 *ayat* (singular *ayah*), or 'verses', and some as many as 286. A chapter heading will usually indicate the number of verses in the chapter, and also the location of revelation: some were received in Makkah, and others in Madinah after Muhammad and the Muhajirun made the *hijrah* (migration). The revelations received in Makkah are generally shorter and are often mystical in character; those that were received in Madinah are longer and many

---

HISTORICAL QURANS
Fragments of the Quran found during restoration of the Great Mosque of San'a' in Yemen in 1972 have been carbon-dated to 645–90, so do certainly date back to this time. These pages are laid out in horizontal format and written in a slanting script called *Hijazi*. One remarkable page depicts an arcaded building which could be an Umayyad mosque. These fragments may be remains of variant forms of the book that were in existence before the standardized version was sent out by Uthman. This early painting is a unique example of an illustration in a Quran manuscript. Normally the Quran is never illustrated, because of the sacred primacy of the original written text.

Above Muslim students study the Quran word by word. In Mali, Africa, a student copies a passage from the holy book on to a reusable wooden board.

revelations from Madinah appear before the earlier ones from Makkah. According to the Sunni tradition, Jibril dictated the order to Muhammad, and this gives the book an added, esoteric layer of meaning that pleases Allah but is not immediately apparent to readers. In the Shiah tradition, before the Quran was standardized under Uthman, the first Imam, Ali ibn Abi Talib, had a written version of the book made, and this was in a different order; but subsequently Ali accepted the order of the official Uthman version.

ARABIC RECITATION

In the 7th century, many of the Prophet's contemporaries in Arabia were skilled in memorizing and reciting poetry. Muhammad passed on his revelations to his followers, who taught them to others through public recitation. Muslims today are encouraged to memorize the Quran and believe that its words are meant to be spoken aloud and heard by the faithful. The way the words sound is an important part of their effect on believers, which is why Muslims believe they should be recited in the language in which the revelations were given – Arabic.

Above A Bangladeshi girl recites a passage from the Quran in Arabic, the original language in which the revelations were given.

give detailed practical guidance on ethical and spiritual matters. All the chapters, except *surah* 9, begin with the phrase of dedication known as the *basmalah*, 'In the name of Allah, most Beneficent, most Merciful'.

The material in the Quran is arranged in order of length, with the longest revelations first, with the exception of the first surah al-Fatiha. This means that the longer, later

HOLY BOOK

The Quran is revered in book form. Some beautifully produced manuscripts or hand-written copies of the Quran are among the greatest of all Islamic works of art, with elegant calligraphy on the finest quality paper, verse markers and chapter headings in gold and coloured illumination, within skilfully worked leather bindings. Moreover, the very fact that the holy words of Allah can be physically bound within a book gives Muslims a deep reverence for books in general. The Quran is often quite simply referred to as al-Kitab, or 'the book'.

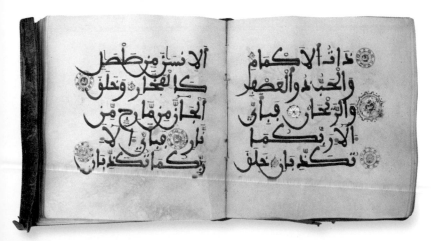

Left This Quran was made in North Africa in 1344.

THE MOSQUE

STARTING AS A SIMPLE HALL AND COURTYARD, THE MOSQUE
DEVELOPED IN INCREASINGLY ELABORATE FORMS UNTIL IT REACHED
THE GRAND, MANY-DOMED STRUCTURE BUILT BY THE OTTOMANS.

The original use for the mosque was as a place for Muslims to gather. They meet there to pray together, and also to perform communal, social and educational activities. The word 'mosque' derives from the Arabic *masjid*, meaning a 'place of prostration', where five times a day Muslims can bow their heads to the ground, thus making the act of submission in prayer to Allah that is required by their faith.

FIRST MOSQUES

The house of the Prophet in Madinah, built in 622, was the prototype for early mosques. Worshippers gathered in large numbers in its enclosed courtyard. The early courtyard mosques were based on this pattern: a flat-roofed prayer hall led to a *sahn*, or an open courtyard, which generally had arcades at the sides. In the centre of the courtyard was often a fountain at which worshippers performed ritual ablutions. A *mihrab*, or niche,

in one wall indicated the direction of the *Kaabah* shrine in Makkah, toward which Muslims must face when praying. Gates or doorways were cut in any of the three walls, other than the *qibla* wall that contained the *mihrab*.

Tall towers called minarets were added to the mosque in the late 7th century. Among the first were the four built at the Great Mosque in Damascus, built in 706–15 under the Umayyad Caliph al-Walid I. The minarets were initially watchtowers in which lighted torches were kept – 'minaret' derives from the Arabic *manara*, meaning 'lighthouse' – but they became elevated positions from which the *muezzin* sent out the five daily calls to prayers.

ARAB-STYLE MOSQUES

The mosque developed in different styles. In Syria, and afterward in Spain and North Africa, mosques were built on a rectangular plan, with an enclosed courtyard and a vast rectangular prayer hall with a flat roof divided internally by rows of columns. Architectural historians call these Arab-plan, or hypostyle, mosques. They were typically built by early Arab Muslims. A hypostyle hall is an architectural term for a large building with a flat roof supported by rows of columns.

This design was followed in 706–15 in the Umayyad Great Mosque of Damascus, which has a prayer hall 160m (525ft) long with a wooden roof supported on

Above This illustration shows the 8th-century Great Mosque of Damascus, with its prayer hall facing a courtyard and an early example of the minaret.

columns and a great courtyard; the same pattern was used in 817–63 for the Great Mosque at Kairouan, Tunisia, where the prayer hall contains 8 bays and upward of 400 columns. At the Mezquita in Córdoba, Spain (begun in 784–86 under the Umayyad ruler Abd al-Rahman I), builders constructed a vast prayer hall containing 850 pillars that divide the hall into 29 aisles running east–west and 19 aisles north–south. Commentators note that the rows of columns in Arab-style mosques create a sense of limitless space.

FOUR-*IWAN* MOSQUES

In Iran, a new form was developed in the 11th century. It included four domed *iwans*, or halls, one in each of the walls surrounding the courtyard. Architectural historians call this the 'four-*iwan*' or cruciform design, because it creates a ground plan in the form of a cross. The form appears to have been introduced by the Seljuk Turks from central Asia, who took power in Baghdad in 1055. The Grand Mosque in Zavareh, Iran, built in

Left The Mosque of the Prophet in Madinah has changed from the simple courtyard and prayer hall that was the original prototype for mosques.

TYPES OF MOSQUE

Of the three types of mosque, the first one is the daily mosque, or *masjid*, a small building used by local people for the five daily prayers. The second is the *jami*, or congregational mosque, also known as the 'Friday Mosque'. This much larger type of mosque is used by crowds of people for Friday service. It contains a *minbar*, or pulpit, used for sermons in Friday prayer. The third type is a large outdoor place for assembly and prayer containing a *qibla* wall with *mihrab* niche to indicate the correct direction for prayer, but without other facilities. These are often built outside towns.

Above This delicate stucco mihrab, *commissioned by Ilkhanid ruler Uljaytu (reigned 1304–16), is in the Friday Mosque in Isfahan, Iran.*

1135–46, followed this design and is the earliest surviving four-*iwan* mosque. Behind the *qibla iwan* (the one aligned toward Makkah) there is another domed chamber containing the *mihrab*.

CENTRAL-DOME MOSQUES

In Turkey and the cities of their empire, the Ottomans developed the vast monumental mosque with a central dome surrounded by semidomes, often called 'central-dome' mosques. They were inspired by the local religious architecture of the Byzantine Empire, and in particular by the magnificent Hagia

Above The central dome in the Sultan Ahmet Mosque (1609–16) in Istanbul is decorated with calligraphy by Seyyid Kasim Gubari, who was the leading calligrapher of the period.*

Sophia (Church of Holy Wisdom) in the Byzantine capital, Constantinople. Within days of Mehmet II 'the Conqueror' (reigned 1444–46, 1451–81) capturing Constantinople, he made the Church of Holy Wisdom into a mosque. Ottoman sultans and architects soon rose to the challenge of competing with the glorious Hagia Sophia.

Foremost among them was Mimar Sinan (1489–1588), chief Ottoman architect under sultans Suleyman I, Selim II and Murad III. Examples of magnificent central-dome mosques he built include the Şehzade Mosque (1543–48) and Süleymaniye Mosque (1550–57) – both in Constantinople – and the Selimiye Mosque (1568–74) in Edirne. The central-dome mosque was built at the heart of a complex of related buildings called a *kulliye*: the Selimiye Mosque, for instance, is surrounded by caravanserais (inns), schools, bathhouses, marketplaces, hospitals, libraries and a cemetery.

The Qibla

MUSLIMS ARE REQUIRED TO FACE TOWARD THE *KAABAH* SHRINE IN MAKKAH WHEN PRAYING DURING THE FIVE DAILY PRAYERS. THIS DIRECTION OF PRAYER IS CALLED THE *QIBLA*.

Within a mosque the *qibla* is indicated by a *mihrab*, a niche in a wall. The wall with the *mihrab* is known as the *qibla* wall. The word *mihrab* originally meant 'a special room'. In the Prophet's lifetime, he began to use the word for the room he used for prayer in his house in Madinah. He entered the mosque established in his house through this room.

Early Muslims prayed toward Jerusalem. It was Jewish custom to pray facing the Temple Mount, where the Jewish Temple stood

(and also, subsequently, the location of the Dome of the Rock and the Al-Aqsa Mosque). One day during prayer in Madinah, the Prophet was inspired to turn toward the *Kaabah* in Makkah, a pagan sanctuary that Muslims claimed for monotheism. The revelation that he received, instructing him to change the direction of prayer, was recorded in the Quran (Surah al-Baqara: 144): 'We have seen the turning of thy face to Heaven (for guidance, O Muhammad). And now verily we shall make thee turn (in prayer)

Above This mihrab *within the Friday Mosque in Kerman, Iran, has a simple arch shape but is elaborately decorated with glazed ceramic tiles.*

toward a *qibla*, which is dear to thee. So turn thy face toward the Inviolable Place of Worship, and ye (O Muslims), wheresoever ye may be, turn your faces (when ye pray) toward it…'

The place in which this event occurred is now called the Masjid al-Qiblatayn ('Mosque of the Two Qiblas'). It is unique in having two *mihrabs* to indicate the two directions of prayer, although at the time of the event Muslims were not yet indicating the direction of the *qibla* with a *mihrab*.

THE FIRST *MIHRAB*

The *mihrab* niche appears to have been introduced in the early 8th century. According to tradition, Caliph Uthman ibn-Affan (reigned 644–56) ordered a sign indicating the direction of the *Kaabah* in Makkah to be posted on the wall of the Mosque of the Prophet, at Madinah. When this mosque was renovated by Caliph al-Walid (reigned 705–15), a niche was made in the *qibla* wall and the sign made by Caliph Uthman

Left *This 17th-century tile bears an illustration of Makkah with the black-draped* Kaabah *at its centre.*

placed within it. It became traditional for the *mihrab* niche to have the shape of a doorway, possibly to indicate that the worshipper can make a journey in spirit through the *qibla* wall to the *Kaabah* at Makkah. The arched *mihrab* shape can also be found on many objects, such as prayer mats, embroideries and tiles.

NOT FACING MAKKAH

A few *qibla* walls and *mihrabs* are not aligned toward Makkah. The most celebrated is that of the Mezquita (Spanish for 'mosque') in Córdoba, Spain, where the *mihrab* faces south rather than south-east (the correct direction for Makkah). Some historians believe that this is because the mosque was built on the remains of a Visigothic cathedral; others say that when building the mosque Abd al-Rahman I aligned the *mihrab* as if he were still at home in Damascus rather than in exile in Spain.

This *mihrab* was reworked under al-Hakam II, Caliph of Córdoba in 961–76, using skilled Byzantine craftsmen. Situated beneath a breathtaking dome, it is regarded as one of the greatest masterpieces of Islamic religious building. An inscription in Arabic begins 'Allah is the knower of all things, both concealed and apparent. He is full of power, and of pity, the living one…'

DETERMINING *QIBLA*

When building a mosque or when praying, Muslims had to determine the precise direction of Makkah. Their need to be able to do this inspired scientists to develop and improve scientific instruments,

such as astrolabes. The astrolabe is an astronomical device that can be aligned with the position of the sun and other celestial bodies, such as the moon and planets, to determine latitude and local time. It was invented in the 1st or 2nd century BCE by the ancient Greeks. The first Islamic astrolabe was developed by the 8th-century CE Iranian mathematician Muhammad al-Fazari. Because they could be used to determine local time, they were also extremely valuable for setting the hours of prayer.

Above The astrolabe is a stereographic map of the night sky which can be set for one's exact date, time and latitude.

THE MOSQUE INTERIOR

MOSQUES VARY GREATLY IN SIZE AND FORM. SOME FEATURES, SUCH AS THE *MIHRAB*, ARE PRESENT IN ALL MOSQUES, BUT OTHERS, INCLUDING THE *MINBAR*, ARE FOUND ONLY IN LARGER MOSQUES.

The essential elements found in a mosque are the *qibla* wall (indicating the direction of the *Kaabah* in Makkah), the *mihrab* in this wall and a fountain at which the faithful perform ablutions before prayer. A congregational mosque will also contain a pulpit called a *minbar*, from which sermons, proclamations and readings are delivered as part of Friday service. The *minbar* has always stood to the right of the *mihrab*.

PURPOSE OF THE *MIHRAB*

The holiest place in the mosque is the *mihrab* archway. It is often highly decorated and is usually made of part of the mosque wall. The imam or other prayer leader leads prayers in front of the *mihrab*. Today, his voice might be broadcast using microphones and speakers, but in pre-electronic times the opening of the *mihrab* amplified the imam's voice so that all present could hear him. The *mihrab* is often decorated with lamps, symbolizing

Above A cantor kneels on the kursi, *or lectern, while reciting the holy words of the Quran in the Mosque of Sultan Barquq in Cairo, Egypt.*

the light of Allah's grace. A small window is sometimes cut in the wall above the *mihrab* to give a sense of the alignment outside the mosque.

MINBAR AND *MAQSURA*

The *minbar* is a free-standing structure, often carved from wood, to the right of the *mihrab*. In some traditions it is decorated, in others it is plain. Steps rise to the *minbar*: the *imam khatib* (preaching imam) who delivers the sermon stands on the lower steps – the top one is reserved in perpetuity for the Prophet Muhammad himself.

The first *minbar*, used by the Prophet, had three steps and was made from tamarisk wood; the Prophet stood on the top step, but the first caliph, or successor, Abu Bakr, would go no higher than the second one as a mark of respect and then the third caliph, Umar, used only the third step. Since that time, however, the preacher has stood on the second step from the top. In the early days of Islam,

political and religious power were one: the Prophet and caliphs led prayers, and the governor first climbed the *minbar* to give a sermon, then descended to lead prayers in front of the *mihrab*.

In some early mosques, the *mihrab* and *minbar* were behind a carved wooden screen known as a *maqsura*. These screens were probably introduced to protect the caliph while at prayers after a rash of attacks on notables in mosques such as that on Caliph Umar, who was stabbed by a Zoroastrian slave as he led prayers in the mosque in Madinah in 644. However, over time the *maqsura*, which was often beautifully and lavishly decorated, functioned also as a statement of the ruler's power and wealth. Although the mosque belonged to the entire community of believers, the area beyond the *maqsura* was set aside for the prince or caliph as a celebration of his glory and the greatness of his rule.

Left A grand minbar *stands to the right of the* mihrab *in the eastern* iwan *of the Sultan Hasan Mosque in Cairo, Egypt.*

Right Some early maqsuras, *as in the Ibn Tulun Mosque, Cairo, were simple raised platforms with protective screens.*

RECITING THE QURAN

Most mosques have a *kursi*, or lectern, at which a cantor recites the Quran. The recitation of the Quran is a highly regarded art. Muslims believe that the Quran has the most profound impact on a believer's mind and heart when it is heard aloud. The *kursi* is a heavy but movable piece of furniture, often with a low platform on which the cantor kneels, facing the *qibla* wall, as he recites from the Quran.

Many larger mosques contained a *dikka*, a platform for the *muezzin* to sing the responses to the prayers chanted by the imam. It was usually aligned with the *mihrab*. Today, the prayers of the imam are heard through loudspeakers, but in large mosques in the days before amplifiers the responses of the *muezzin* on the *dikka* helped those at the rear of the mosque follow the service if they were unable to hear the prayers being chanted in front of the *mihrab*. Their task was also to adopt the positions taken by the imam so that those who could not see him were able to follow this part of the service. In most mosques today, the *dikka* is not used because the *muezzin* no longer stands on the platform during worship.

PRAYER RUGS

Mosques always contain prayer rugs, because worshippers kneel and lower their foreheads to the floor during prayers. They are also usually equipped with bookrests to support copies of the Quran and keep them off the floor, as well as containers to hold the Quran when it is not in use.

Right This 18th-century Turkish prayer rug bears an image of a mihrab *with two columns and a stylized hanging lamp.*

THE *MADRASA*

RELIGIOUS COLLEGES WERE OFTEN ATTACHED TO A MOSQUE, BUT THEY COULD ALSO BE INDEPENDENT INSTITUTIONS FUNDED BY HOSTELS AND MARKETS OR BY AN ENDOWMENT.

The Arabic word *madrasa* means 'a place where teaching and learning takes place', and refers to a religious school, university or college. The *madrasas* specialized in educating religious leaders and legal experts. Where they were funded by a *waqf* (religious endowment), the person who provided the endowment was usually buried in an associated mausoleum.

EARLY *MADRASAS*

In early Muslim communities, mosques were social centres in which a range of activities, such as teaching, took place. Informal teaching sessions were held by educated Muslims, who became known as shaykhs, and the *madrasa* is thought to have developed out of this custom.

The oldest known *madrasa* is in the Qarawiyyin Mosque (also known as the University of al-Qurawiyyin or al-Karaouine) in Fez, Morocco. It was established in 859 by Fatima al-Fihri, daughter of a wealthy merchant. Another early *madrasa* was the one at the al-Azhar Mosque in Cairo, Egypt, in 959; this became al-Azhar University.

SELJUK *MADRASAS*

In the 11th century, the Persian scholar and Seljuk vizier Nizam al-Mulk (1018–92) set up a series of *madrasas* in cities such as Isfahan and Nishapur (both now in Iran) and Balkh and Herat (both now in Afghanistan). These were well-organized places of higher education called *nizamiyyah* after Nizam, and they had a reputation for teaching throughout the Islamic world and even in Europe.

The *nizamiyyah* became the model for later *madrasas*. The first and most celebrated of these was al-Nizamiyya, set up in Baghdad in 1065. The widely admired Iranian Sufi mystic, philosopher and theologian al-Ghazali (1058–1111) was a teacher at al-Nizamiyya. It became common for Seljuk rulers to build and fund a *madrasa* attached to the mausoleum in which they would be buried.

Above Built in Konya (Turkey) in 1256 by Seljuk vizier Fakhr al-Din Ali, the Ince Minareli madrasa is celebrated for its grand gateway.

TYPES OF *MADRASA*

The *madrasa* came in a variety of forms. Some had a single large hall beneath a dome, but a typical configuration was the two-*iwan*, three-*iwan* or four-*iwan* plan, in which a central courtyard adjoins two, three or four large vaulted halls. *Madrasas* typically have grand gateways with imposing portals and towering minarets.

A splendid early example of a three-*iwan* design is the Mustansiriya *madrasa* built in Baghdad by the Abbasid caliph al-Mustansir in 1227–34. Standing beside the river Tigris, the large rectangular brick building is two storeys high and measures 106m by 48m (348ft by 157ft). Students travelled from far-flung parts of the Islamic world to this centre of learning, where they could study the Quran, theology, medicine, jurisprudence, mathematics and literature. It was the first of many *madrasas* to provide facilities for all four principal schools of Sunni Islam – the Hanbali, Shafii, Maliki

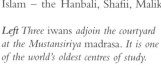

Left Three iwans adjoin the courtyard at the Mustansiriya madrasa. It is one of the world's oldest centres of study.

Right The Chahar Bagh complex in Isfahan, built by Shah Sultan Husayn in 1706–15, incorporated a caravanserai.

and Hanifi. Followers of each of the four schools had one corner of the *madrasa* to themselves.

Under later rulers, notably the Ottomans in Turkey and the Safavids in Iran, *madrasas* were built as part of a large complex centred on a grand mosque. In Iran, complexes often also contained a *caravanserai* (or inn) and a bazaar, and the commercial areas served to fund the educational and spiritual activities in the *madrasa*.

The Ottoman complexes were called *kulliyes*. Sultan Mehmet II built such a complex in Istanbul, the Mehmet Fatih Kulliye, in 1462–70. It had a hospital, kitchens, *caravanserai*, bazaar and several *hammams* (bathhouses), along with a *madrasa* 200m (656ft) in length for up to 1,000 students. Also in Istanbul, the Süleymaniye Mosque complex, built in 1550–57 by the great architect Sinan for Sultan Suleyman, contained, in addition to the superb mosque with its four minarets and dome, a hostel, a medical college, a school for boys, an asylum, a *hammam*, two mausolea and four *madrasas*.

THE SULTAN HASAN COMPLEX

In Cairo, Egypt, the Mamluks built many splendid *madrasas*. Of these, the most celebrated is probably the Sultan Hasan mosque and *madrasa* complex, commissioned in 1356 by Mamluk Sultan Hasan. The sultan intended it to house teachers of all four legal schools in Sunni Islam: it has four *iwans*, one for teachers and students of each school, adjoining a large central courtyard. Its façade is extremely impressive and measures 36m (118ft) high and 76m (249ft) long. Only one of the original two minarets is still standing, but at 84m (275ft) high it is the tallest of all the minarets surviving from medieval Cairo. The other minaret collapsed during construction and killed 300 people.

Left When it was established in 1356–62, the mosque and madrasa of Sultan Hasan was the largest structure ever built in Cairo, Egypt.

MEMORIALS FOR THE DEAD

ORTHODOX ISLAM DISCOURAGES LAVISH FUNERARY MONUMENTS, BUT FROM THE 10TH CENTURY ONWARD MANY MUSLIM RULERS LEFT EVIDENCE OF THEIR WEALTH IN GRAND TOMBS AND MAUSOLEA.

Some of the most spectacular Islamic architecture was created in memory of the dead.

FATIMID TOMBS

In the 10th–12th centuries, Ismaili Fatimid rulers of Egypt, North Africa and Syria (909–1171) created the earliest surviving group of mausolea in Islamic history. At least 14 Fatimid-era mausolea survive in Cairo, Egypt, compared to just 5 Fatimid mosques. Several generations of Fatimid caliphs were buried in a tomb in the Eastern Palace in Cairo, which is now lost.

In Aswan, Egypt, an entire city of mud-brick mausolea was built under the Fatimids. In the early years of Islam, elaborate mausolea were not permitted, because the Quran teaches that tombs should be humble. One way around the religious restriction on building fine tombs was to identify them as celebrations of warriors fallen in *jihad*: the cemetery at Aswan is called 'Tombs of the Martyrs' but historians do not know whether or not it actually contained the bodies of those killed fighting for the faith.

The Aswan cemetery contains about 50 tombs in different forms and sizes. Many are compact, square

Below The Tomb of Humayan in Delhi was a forerunner of the Taj Mahal. The main chamber is beneath its dome.

Above The tombs in the Fatimid cemetery at Aswan are mostly modest square buildings with small domes.

buildings topped with small domes; some have adjoining courtyards. One type is known as the *mashhad* ('site of martyrdom' or pilgrimage shrine), and is a small domed building with a walkway around it. Two notable mausolea in this form, the Mashhad of al-Qasim Abu Tayyib (*c.*1122) and that of

Yahya al-Shabih (*c*.1150), were built under the Fatimids in Cairo.

SELJUK INNOVATIONS

The style of mausolea was changed by Seljuk rulers, who built *turbe* (square domed buildings) or *gunbads* (tomb towers). A fine example of a *turbe* is the Gunbad-i-Surkh of 1147–48 in Maragha, Iran, decorated with mosaic faience tiles. Instead of being square, some *turbe* had 8, 10 or 12 sides, for example the decahedral (10-sided) mausoleum built for Seljuk Sultan Kilij Arslan II (reigned 1156–92) in the courtyard of the Ala al-Din Mosque in Konya (now in Turkey).

Most *gunbads* were tall towers with conical roofs: perhaps the finest of these is the Gunbad-i-Qabus built in 1006–7 in Gurgan, Iran, for Ziyarid ruler Shams al-Maali Qabus.

In the 14th century, the Ilkhanid ruler Uljaytu (reigned 1304–16), is commemorated at Sultaniyya near Qazwin, Iran, with a magnificent mausoleum. With an elegant dome 53m (174ft) tall, it stood in a vast complex of buildings raised by craftsmen from all over the Ilkhanid empire.

The breathtakingly beautiful Taj Mahal at Agra in India – perhaps the most famous Islamic building – was built in 1632–54 by the Muslim Mughal Emperor Shah Jahan (reigned 1628–58) as a shrine for his favourite wife, Mumtaz Mahal. The mausoleum is set in gardens divided into four areas, with waterways, designed to represent the Islamic paradise.

THE *CHAHAR BAGH*

A tomb placed in a walled, four-part garden with flowing waters, as at the Taj Mahal, was called a *chahar bagh*, from the Persian words *chahar* ('four') and *bagh* ('garden'). It was originally a Persian garden scheme, first used by

SIMPLE BURIALS

For all the exuberance exhibited in the impressive tombs and mausolea, both the Quran and Islamic law call for simple burial of the dead and discourage the use of lavish funerary monuments. The preferred mode of burial is to inter the body wrapped in a shroud, rather than placed in a coffin, with the head facing toward Makkah. Graves of this sort were often left unmarked or identified with simple grave markers.

Above A woman prays at a cemetery in Iraq. Most Muslim graves are simple and unadorned.

the emperors of the Achaemenid Empire (550–330BCE) and by Emperor Cyrus the Great (reigned 576–530BCE) in Pasargadae (now an archaeological site in Iran).

In India, the *chahar bagh* design was first used for the Tomb of Humayan in Delhi, built to honour the second Mughal ruler Humayan (reigned 1530–40 and 1555–56) by his widow Hamid Banu Begum. Other lavish Mughal mausolea with

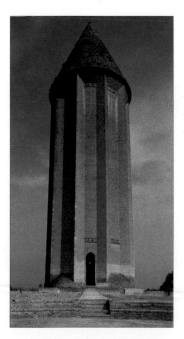

chahar bagh designs include Akbar's tomb at Sikandra near Agra, built in 1612–14 by his son Jahangir (reigned 1605–27), and Jahangir's tomb, built *c*.1637 near Shahdara Bagh, Lahore, Pakistan.

At Sasaram, an ornate mausoleum commemorates Pashtun ruler Sher Shah Suri who briefly overcame the Mughals to rule in Delhi 1540–45. His domed red sandstone memorial stands 37m (121ft) tall and – like the Taj Mahal, which it rivals in beauty – is reflected in a lake.

OTTOMAN SPLENDOUR

The mausolea of the Ottomans were impressive structures in vast complexes centred on mosques. The Süleymaniye Mosque complex (built 1550–57) in Istanbul, for instance, contains two mausolea in the garden behind the mosque; these house the remains of Suleyman I (reigned 1520–66) and his family, and those of Suleyman II (reigned 1687–91) and Ahmet II (reigned 1691–95). Also in Istanbul, the beautiful Blue Mosque (built 1609–16) likewise contains the tomb of its founder, Sultan Ahmet I (reigned 1603–17).

Left Ten triangular flanges show on the sides of the tomb tower Gunbad-i-Qabus, at Gurgan, Iran.

THE CITY

ISLAMIC RULERS MADE A PUBLIC DISPLAY OF THEIR POWER AND
AUTHORITY BY BUILDING GREAT GATEWAYS, PALACES AND CITADELS
– OR EVEN BY LAYING OUT ENTIRELY NEW CITIES.

Many major cities were established by Islamic rulers. In 762, the second Abbasid Caliph, al-Mansur, established Madinat as-Salam (the 'City of Peace'), now known as Baghdad, on the river Tigris in Iraq. The city was round and enclosed by three walls with a great gate at each of the points of the compass, which was named for the province or city that lay in that direction. Commercial and residential areas lay in the outer parts of the city, while at the centre of Baghdad stood the dynasty's imperial palace and mosque.

At Samarra, also on the Tigris in Iraq, al-Mansur's successor al-Mutasim (reigned 833–42) established a new royal capital in the years after 836. The city, which included several beautiful palaces as well as the inspiring Great Mosque, extended no less than 32km (20 miles) along the banks of the river Tigris. The name, according to medieval Islamic historians,

meant 'A delight for he who sees it'. Samarra served as the capital city until Caliph al-Mutamid (reigned 870–92) returned to Baghdad.

Other examples of splendid new cities built to glorify rulers and dynasties include: Cairo in Egypt, founded in 969 by the Fatimid dynasty; Madinat al-Zahra near Córdoba in Islamic Spain, built in 936–40 by Umayyad caliph Abd al-Rahman III; and Sultaniyya in north-western Iran, built by Ilkhanid ruler Uljaytu (reigned 1304–16). Little remains of these early structures, but magnificent monuments and complexes that were built from the 15th century onward, notably in Iran, India and Turkey, have survived.

MUGHAL GLORIES

In India, Mughal Emperor Akbar built Fatehpur Sikri as a new capital in 1569 to celebrate the longed-for birth of a male heir – the future Emperor Jahangir – and raised the

Above The Bab al-Amma in Samarra, Iraq, was once the gateway to the caliph's palace. The gateway stood at the top of steps that led up from the river Tigris.

monumental Gate of Victory in front of the Courtyard of the Great Mosque. He built the city on the site of the camp previously occupied by Sufi mystic and saint, Salim Chishti (1478–1572), who had blessed Akbar and thereby apparently brought about the birth of Jahangir. The courtyard contains the Tomb of Salim Chishti, which

Below The elegantly domed Shaykh Lutfallah Mosque, built 1603–19, stands on the eastern side of the vast Naqsh-e Jahan Square in Isfahan, Iran.

Akbar built in red sandstone but which was refashioned as a marble mausoleum. The city was largely abandoned later.

WONDERS OF ISFAHAN

In Iran, Shah Abbas I (reigned 1587–1629) built new monumental quarters in the city of Isfahan to demonstrate the greatness and prosperity of the Safavid dynasty. He built mosques, bathhouses, bazaars, parks, bridges and palaces. In the centre he laid out the palace, congregational mosque and Grand Bazaar around a vast open space known in Persian as Maidan-e Shah (now Maidan-e Imam). A popular phrase at the time was *Isfahan nesf-e jahan*: 'Isfahan is half the world', referring in part to its splendour and also to the presence of a large international community.

A CITY TRANSFORMED

In Turkey, the Ottoman emperors set about remaking the ancient Christian city of Constantinople as the capital of an Islamic empire, eventually renaming the city Istanbul. Mehmet II began the rebuilding after he conquered the city in 1453, making a bold statement of the greatness of the Ottoman sultan and his religion in the Grand Bazaar, the Topkapi Palace, the Fatih Mosque complex and the Eyyüp Sultan Mosque. A substantial part of the Ottoman rebuilding was carried out through the construction of complexes of buildings centred on mosques and containing hospitals, *madrasas, caravanserais* and other structures.

The Topkapi Palace, begun by Mehmet II in 1459, was not a single imposing building like a typical European palace, but instead consisted of a sequential system of small buildings, some plain and some practical, such as kitchens, but many splendid and lavishly decorated. The Topkapi Palace remained the residence of Ottoman sultans until 1853, when Sultan Abdulmecid I moved to the newly constructed, European-style Dolmabahçe Palace.

CITADELS

Set behind fortified walls the buildings of the Topkapi Palace are an example of an architectural feature unique to Islam – an enclosed city within a city, called a citadel. The Alhambra, built in Granada (southern Spain) by the rulers of the Nasrid dynasty in 1238–1358, is another well-preserved example of this feature.

The citadel in Aleppo, Syria, stands on a partly natural, partly man-made mound that dominates the city. The mound was fortified from ancient times, then the citadel was developed for military uses. Substantially rebuilt in the 12th century by Zangid rulers Imad al-Din Zangi and Nur al-Din, it was remade in the form in which it survives today by Ayyubid ruler al-Malik al-Zahir Ghazi (son of Salah al-Din) in 1186–1216. He strengthened the walls, redug the moat around the citadel, built the bridge across the moat and furnished the citadel with all the necessities of urban life, including granaries and cisterns.

Above At Aleppo, al-Malik rebuilt the entrance block in 1213 as part of his work on the citadel. The arches are those of the bridge across the moat.

TRADE AND TRAVEL

THE MUSLIM TRADERS AND PILGRIMS WHO TRAVELLED VAST DISTANCES ACROSS THE ISLAMIC WORLD RELIED ON A NETWORK OF HOSTELRIES, CISTERNS, MOSQUES AND MARKETS.

From the early days of Islam, travellers made long trade journeys across western Asia. Travel and trade were part of their Islamic heritage: the Prophet Muhammad came from a trading family, and the wider Islamic world is strongly dependent on lively international trade. The Quran recorded Allah's blessing on mercantile transactions: 'It is no sin for you that ye seek the bounty of your Lord by trading' (Surah al-Baqarah: 198).

A WELL-TRAVELLED FAITH

The Islamic faith spread through military conquest, but it was also sustained by merchants and scholars who travelled. Most significant of all, thousands of Muslims set out for Makkah each year, obedient to the demand of their faith that they make a pilgrimage to the *Kaabah* at least once in their lifetime.

Because of all this traffic, trade and pilgrim routes were well trodden and well maintained; the great cities depended on the safe arrival of trade caravans and Islamic rulers invested in the necessary infrastructure. People generally travelled in camel caravans. Getting lost was not usually a danger, because there were some directional markers and watchtowers. However, people needed water and a safe place to rest. *Caravanserais* were secure roadside shelters along the route, where travellers could sleep, rest, wash, water themselves and also pray.

THE *CARAVANSERAI*

Typically, a *caravanserai* consisted of a square enclosure with a single gateway big enough to allow access to heavily laden camels

Above A caravanserai *provides a haven, promising weary travellers a chance to recuperate, in this illustration from a 16th-century Ottoman manuscript.*

and, within, individual rooms and stalls arranged around a large open courtyard; there were separate stables for the animals. There was a well or cistern to provide water for drinking and ritual washing; some *caravanserais* had bathhouses. There was also a mosque, usually a raised building in the centre of the courtyard with a fountain for ablutions beneath. There were shops or a market area for travellers to buy or sell supplies.

In Turkey, the Seljuks built a great network of *caravanserais*: around 100 survive today and there may once have been up to 400 on the trade routes across Anatolia. These were built with a large main gateway leading to an open courtyard, behind which there was a second gateway leading into a

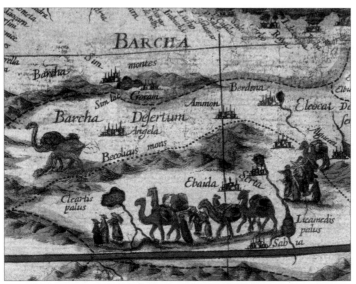

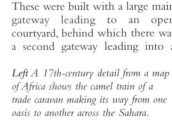

Left A 17th-century detail from a map of Africa shows the camel train of a trade caravan making its way from one oasis to another across the Sahara.

Above The mosque in the caravanserai *built by Seljuk Sultan Ala al-Din Kaykubad I between Konya and Aksaray was raised above the courtyard on arches.*

covered hall whose flat roof was used as sleeping space in summer. The grandest of these *caravanserais* were built near Konya by Seljuk Sultan Ala al-Din Kaykubad I (reigned 1220–37). One on the road between Konya and Aksaray, dated to 1229, has an elaborately decorated stone gateway and covers 4,900sq m (52,743sq ft). It is also the largest *caravanserai* in Turkey. The second, on the road between Kayseri and Sivas, was built in 1236.

In the Ottoman era, a number of *caravanserais* were built on the pilgrim route between Damascus and Makkah. Elsewhere, the Ottomans often built *caravanserais* as part of a *kulliye*, a complex of buildings centred on a mosque. The Tekkiye in Damascus, designed by the great architect Sinan for Sultan Suleyman I in the 1550s, is a fine example in which the *caravanserai* was used by *Hajj* pilgrims before they left for Makkah and after they returned.

KHANS

In urban centres, the equivalent of a *caravanserai* was a *khan*. This was more like a storehouse than a rest stop, and provided greater space for the storage of merchants' goods than for accommodation. Generally, the *khans* were built over several storeys, with the bottom and next floor up used for storage.

Several *khans* were established alongside *madrasas*, or religious colleges, and their profits paid for the religious and legal education of young Muslims. Examples include the splendid *khan* built by Mamluk Sultan Qansuh al-Ghuri in Cairo in 1504–5. It was laid out around a courtyard over five floors, with the lower two set aside for storage and the upper three rented out to merchants as accommodation; profits funded the sultan's adjacent *madrasa*. Similarly, the Khan Mirjan in Baghdad built in 1359 by Amin al-Din Mirjan, wali (or governor) of Baghdad under Shaykh Hasan-i Buzurg (founder of the Jalayirid dynasty of Iraq and central Iran), combined storage space below with extensive accommodation above and paid for the Mirjaniya *madrasa* (1357).

BAZAARS

Goods stored in the *khan* were sold in the market, known as *souk* in Arabic or *bazaar* in Turkish. In an Islamic town or city, the souk or bazaar typically consisted of a network of enclosed shopping streets, with a central secure area that could be locked at night, and one or more *hammams*, or bathhouses. It was located near the congregational mosque, which was at the centre of the community.

Major souks or bazaars survive in almost every great Islamic city, including Istanbul, Cairo, Isfahan, Damascus, Tehran, Delhi and Mumbai. The Grand Bazaar, or Kapali Carsi ('Covered Market'), in Istanbul contains 58 streets and 6,000 shops; the earliest of its two domed *bedesten* (secured areas) was raised in 1455–61 under Sultan Mehmet II 'the Conqueror'. The market was extended under Sultan Suleyman 'the Magnificent' (reigned 1520–66). In Cairo, the Khan al-Khalili souk has its origins in a *khan* built in 1382 by Amir Jaharks al-Khalili in the reign of Mamluk Sultan Barquq (reigned 1382–89 and 1390–99).

Above Merchants lay out their wares in a souk in Cairo in this 19th-century painting by David Roberts.

HAJJ: PILGRIMAGE TO MAKKAH

OVER THE CENTURIES, MILLIONS OF MUSLIMS HAVE MADE THE *HAJJ*, THE PILGRIMAGE TO MAKKAH THAT IS REQUIRED ONCE IN A LIFETIME OF ALL ABLE-BODIED MUSLIMS WHO CAN AFFORD IT.

Before the advent of railways in the 19th century, and of cars and aircraft flights in the 20th century, the *Hajj* often involved travelling in a camel caravan for months at a time, across deserts in punishing heat and under constant threat of attack by bandits.

The routes followed by Hajj pilgrims in earlier centuries can be traced by examining the intricate network of forts, caravanserais, mosques, paved roadways, cisterns, direction markers and milestones built to support them. A sense of the Hajj in medieval times can be gained from the writings of scholars such as the Moroccan traveller Ibn Battuta (1304–77), who made the Hajj four times, and by examining Ottoman travel guides and prayer books.

DESERT ROUTES

Hajj pilgrims came from all over the Islamic world and they made the last part of their journey across Arabia to Makkah following set itineraries. There were six main routes. One went from Damascus in Syria, one from Cairo in Egypt by way of the Sinai Desert and one from Baghdad through Basra in Iraq. For those arriving by boat

Above *The pilgrims' goal is the shrine of the Kaabah in Makkah. This illustration of Muslims at the Kaabah is from the 15th-century Persian classic* Haft Awrang *(Seven Thrones).*

across the Arabian Sea south of the Arabian peninsula, there were three routes: two from Yemen, one along the coast and one inland, and one from Oman.

THE WAY FROM DAMASCUS

The principal routes were those from Iraq, Syria and Egypt, and of these the oldest was the one from Damascus, capital of the Umayyad Caliphate. Major sites on the route through Jordan include the city of Humayma, the square fortress and mosque of Khan al-Zabib, and palaces at Ma'an and Jize, which seem to have been used by leading Umayyads when on pilgrimage and perhaps as *caravanserais* to host passing dignitaries. Both were near large ancient Roman reservoirs.

The route lost importance after the capital moved from Damascus to Baghdad in the 8th century, but

Mediterranean Sea

Damascus

Baghdad

0   500 mi
0   800 km

Ma'an

Tabuk

Persian Gulf

Red Sea

Jeddah
Makkah

ARABIA

N

Atbara

Arabian Sea

Aden

Route from Damascus, the Umayyad capital, was the most important early route

Route from Baghdad, known as Zubayda's Way, became increasingly important after accession of Abbasids in 750

Route for pilgrims from Sudan, Central and West Africa

Left *The main Hajj pilgrimage routes to Makkah. The most used early route was from Damascus.*

it remained in use for many centuries. The Mamluks built forts along it, such as those at Zerka and Jize. In the 14th century, Ibn Battuta followed this route on his first *Hajj* journey, taking the inland route parallel to the western coast of the Arabian peninsula. With the aid of a large camel caravan, he travelled the 1,350km (840-mile) journey from Damascus to the holy cities in about 50 days.

On Ibn Battuta's first *Hajj* pilgrimage, and typically for that era, a desert caravan was like a travelling city, a group bound by a common geographical and religious goal that stayed together for six or seven weeks. There was a *muezzin* to call the travellers to prayer, Imams to lead the prayers and *qadis*, or judges, to provide resolution when disputes arose. Soldiers and guides travelled with the caravan to provide protection from desert bandits.

The position of the leader of the caravan had great political importance and in some cases he could rise to a role in government.

FORTS AND CISTERNS

Under the Ottomans, forts and cisterns were built along the Damascus–Madinah/Makkah route and garrisoned with troops. The forts guarded the cisterns and provided protection for pilgrim camps alongside them against attacks by Bedouin raiders. The Ottomans upgraded these facilities in the 18th century and again in the early 20th century, when a railway was laid along the entire Damascus to Madinah route, with new forts to protect key sites.

Right In a Hajj caravan, people from many backgrounds lived together for weeks at a time. This Ottoman illustration is based on a 13th-century painting.

BAGHDAD TO MAKKAH

From the earliest Islamic period, the road from Baghdad to Makkah was an important trade and pilgrimage route. With the transfer of the capital to Baghdad in the 8th century, it became the major route to the holy cities. Zubayda bint Jafar, wife of Caliph Harun al-Rashid (reigned 786–809), is known to have ordered the construction of a network of wells, reservoirs and buildings along the road to provide pilgrims and travellers with water and shelter; thereafter the road became known as Darb Zubayda ('Zubayda's route'). Several Arab geographers have described how the road was renowned both for its safety and the evenness of its surface, which was tarred and kept free of sand and stones. Archaeologists have identified more than fifty stopping points on the route; these included a cistern for watering camels and

Above This fort at Qatrana in Jordan was built in 1559, one of the network of forts built by the Ottomans along the Hajj route from Damascus to Makkah.

drinking water for pilgrims, a fort or palace, plus a residential area and a mosque. Several caliphs are known to have built palaces to stay in as they made the pilgrimage. Harun al-Rashid is known to have made the Hajj nine times during his reign, more than once on foot.

CALLIGRAPHY

THE MOST HIGHLY ESTEEMED ART FORM IN ISLAMIC CULTURE IS CALLIGRAPHY, PRIMARILY BECAUSE OF ITS SIGNIFICANT ROLE IN TRANSCRIBING THE WORD OF ALLAH, AS WRITTEN IN THE QURAN.

By reproducing the Quran's holy words, the calligrapher was held in the highest respect – far above other crafts and specialist artistic skills. The honour accorded for copying out a text of such spiritual and legal importance reflected the great responsibility of such a task. The writing itself also took on a spiritual quality, as did the *qalam*, or reed pen; in fact, one of the chapters of the Quran is called *Surah al-Qalam*, or 'the Pen'.

A scribe should always pray before commencing the copying of Quranic verses, which should be reproduced without any adulteration whatsoever. Important demands were also made of the Arabic script itself: it had to be legible, respectfully beautiful and unambiguous, worthy to record the word of God. Calligraphic reforms were undertaken in the 10th and 11th centuries on this basis: improvement to the legibility and gravitas of the written Quran was not only spiritually meaningful, but politically expedient.

Above This page of Persian verses copied in nastaliq *script by Mir Ali of Herat was decorated and mounted in a 17th-century Mughal Indian album known as the* Minto Album.

ARABIC SCRIPT

One of the earliest Arabic scripts, used in the first Qurans, is usually referred to as *kufic*. Initially, art historians linked it exclusively with the Iraqi city of Kufa, but this is no longer considered the case. It is a dense rectilinear script, which was often written without the use of diacritics (marks appended to letters) or other conventional orthographic signs, so it could be difficult to read and potentially lead to variant readings of the authoritative sacred text.

In the 10th century, government reforms in Baghdad corrected this issue, and a new *khatt al-mansub*, or proportioned script, was developed under the supervision of the vizier (minister) Ibn Muqla (886–940). Six canonical cursive (joined-up) scripts emerged, known as the *sitta qalam*, or 'Six Pens', and these became the standard repertoire of a professional calligrapher. By the 11th century, cursive script was considered good enough to be used to copy out the

Quran: the earliest extant example was executed in *naskh* by the calligrapher Ibn al-Bawwab.

LEARNING CALLIGRAPHY

Calligraphy was only taught to an apprentice by a master. The student had to learn to reproduce the canonical scripts with perfection, with absolutely no variance from the script of the teacher. The moment of graduation was usually the point when the student could truly replicate his master's hand. Great calligraphers kept proud note of their lineage from renowned masters, down generations of teachers and students. For example, the famous calligrapher Yaqut al-Mustasimi (d.1298) had six pupils, later known

Left This page from a 9th-century Quran was written in kufic *script on vellum; it has an illuminated gold roundel in the margin.*

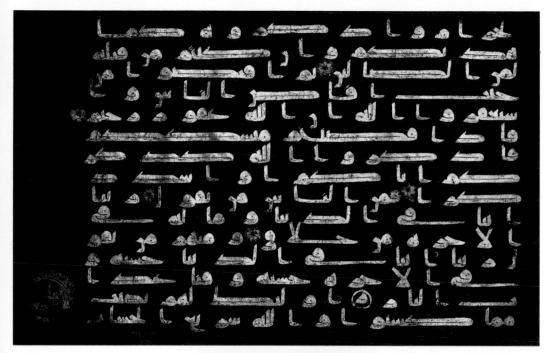

Above A page from a unique 10th-century Quran, known as the Blue Quran, was written in gold kufic script on indigo-dyed vellum.

simply as *sitta*, or 'the Six', from whom calligraphers in Timurid, Safavid and Ottoman times could still trace their descent.

As Islam spread across Western Asia, Arabic script was adopted to write other languages used in the wider Muslim world, such as Persian and Ottoman Turkish. Slight adaptations were necessary to provide new letter forms for Persian and Turkish sounds that did not feature in Arabic, such as 'ch' and 'v'. The fine art of calligraphy continued to be practised in the written literature of these other languages, and indeed a Persian calligrapher, Mir Ali, is credited with inventing a new style of (Arabic) script, entitled *nastaliq*, or hanging *naskh*. This elegant,

Above The thuluth script around the neck of this mid-14th-century enamelled glass mosque lamp aptly quotes the Surah of Light from the Quran.

somewhat italicized script became the characteristic mode for Persian poetry.

A DECORATIVE ART

The art of the pen was not limited to the written page, and calligraphy is found in almost every decorative medium: quotations of Quranic verses on a mosque façade, poetry on a jade drinking cup and informative details about the object's production, such as a patron's name, the artist's signature or the date it was made. Playful script also appeared in the decorative arts, such as 'knotted *kufic*' with plaits or braids adjoining letters, or anthropomorphic text that features human faces peering out from tall letters. The beauty of the script and the prominence of epigraphy demonstrate that text was not just literally informative but also important to the decorative value of the object.

ORNAMENT

ISLAMIC ART AND DESIGN WERE SHAPED BY CERTAIN RESTRICTIONS ON THE DEPICTION OF THE LIVING IMAGE. THIS LED ARTISTS TO DEVELOP STYLIZED FORMS TO GREAT EFFECT.

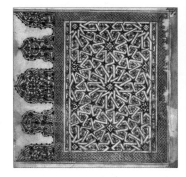

Figurative art, so important in the Christian tradition, has never been as significant to religious art in the Islamic world. Strictly-speaking, image-making has been linked to idolatry, and although there is indeed an historic Islamic tradition of portraying sacred figures, artists decorated religious architecture or objects with different types of design. On a broader level, Islamic art has a very refined design tradition, which extends further than figural subjects.

GEOMETRIC PATTERNS

Often understood as the most typical form of Islamic art, geometric design is used with great precision across the media, in art and architecture. Craftsmen utilized a simple repertoire of shapes – circles, squares, stars, lozenges, polygons – but assembled them in patterns of dazzling complexity.

Above An end-piece from a Quran of 1568, produced for the Sharifi Sultan of Morocco, includes complex patterns constructed around a simple, geometric shape – a radiating star.

Larger compositions could achieve the mesmeric effect of an optical puzzle, using complex radial symmetry. Similarly, in an architectural context, long stretches of geometric patterns could act as a fascinating surface, not necessarily reflecting the physical structure that lay beneath. The walls of the courtyard in the Yusuf madrasa at Marrakesh in Morocco provide a typical example.

Perhaps the most popular of these motifs was the star. Radiating stars were used as basic components in a huge variety of designs: from the colourful decorative panels in manuscripts, to an inlaid wooden panel or a glazed tile façade. Some of the most intricate examples can be found in Egyptian woodwork, especially in the ornate minbars (Islamic pulpits), where they were combined with ivory inlays.

An important three-dimensional form of geometric decoration was muqarnas, or stalactite vaulting, used throughout the Middle East. This was used to create a rich

Left A vaulted arcade from the carpet bazaar in Qom, Iran, displays waves of muqarnas decoration, rippling out from the apertures in the centre of each dome.

honeycomb effect in vaulted ceilings and archways. Celebrated examples can be seen in the halls of the Alhambra, in Granada, Spain.

ABSTRACT DECORATION

The Quran contains grave warnings against the production of idols for worship, and Hadith literature condemns the vanity of equating artistic production with God's life-giving power of creation. At different times and places in history, this has been interpreted as a ban on all reproductions of living things, and it is almost unheard of to find animals or humans depicted within a religious environment or in Quran manuscripts – designs based on geometry or stylized representations of vegetal forms were used instead.

THE ARABESQUE

Stylized foliate scrollwork is a recurrent motif in Islamic art, and has sometimes been named 'the arabesque'. In essence, this is a form of leafy palmette-leaf scrollwork, composed of tightly packed S-shaped tendrils. The inspiration seems to have come from the bands of vine and acanthus decoration popular in the classical world. Early hints of this influence were apparent in the 8th century, in the stonework decoration of the Umayyad palace of Mshatta in Jordan.

Over the centuries designers adjusted the style of this pattern, and created leafy scrolls which were ever more dense and intricate. With ever-increasing stylization, the leafy scrolls became less and less naturalistic. The popularity of this floral ornament was based on its infinite

Above A fine example of 16th-century Iznik tilework, from the Circumcision Chamber in Topkapi Palace, Istanbul, includes birds, peonies and lotus flowers.

Above Flowers were popular motifs, such as the one on an Iznik tile from the Selimiye Mosque, built under Selim II (1566–74) in Edirne (Turkey).

versatility: undulating floral scrolls could be adapted in size and made to fit monumental architectural spaces on tiled or painted surfaces, or reduced to fit the margins of manuscripts, or the decoration of metalwork and ceramic objects.

CHINESE MOTIFS

Islamic craftsmen borrowed a range of Chinese imagery following the Mongol invasions during the 13th century, when large quantities of blue and white porcelain, silk textiles and other goods were imported. The most common motifs were floral: large peonies and lotus blossoms were especially prominent, and were soon adopted into the design repertoire for manuscript illumination, ceramics and glass. Fabulous creatures from Chinese mythology also made an impact, and wiry stylized dragons began to appear in Islamic art, as did the Chinese phoenix.

In Chinese contexts the phoenix and the dragon had imperial connotations and the lotus was associated with the Buddha, but when incorporated into Islamic designs these motifs became purely decorative and lost their original meaning.

The cloud band or cloud scroll was another Chinese import; very stylized ribbon-like clouds were used as space-fillers in the same way as the arabesque. A good example of these is to be found on the monumental tile panels now attached to the exterior walls of the Circumcision Chamber in the Topkapi palace in Istanbul. The contrasting blue and white palette of these tiles was also copied from Chinese porcelain.

THE LIVING IMAGE

FIGURAL REPRESENTATION WAS FREQUENTLY USED IN THE LUXURY ARTS OF THE ISLAMIC WORLD, THOUGH ORTHODOX DISAPPROVAL OF IMAGERY AFFECTED ART PRODUCED FOR SACRED USAGE.

It is often believed that figural images are prohibited in Islamic art, but this is not the case. The Quran forbids the use of idols for religious worship. It does not ban figural representation. However, statements in *hadith* literature do speak out against the depiction of living creatures, and condemn the artist for seeming to create a living form, a power exclusive to God. For both of these reasons, images are never used in the Quran, mosque decoration or any strictly religious context in Islamic art. Instead, sacred books, objects and architecture are decorated with geometric designs, scrolling stylized leaves and flowers, and calligraphy – usually quoting Quranic verses.

FIGURATIVE ART

Outside of the sacred realm, pictures of people, animals and birds have been produced throughout Islamic art history, from Spain to India, in almost every decorative medium. Even three-dimensional sculpture was known: incense-burners, ewers, fountainheads and other figurines in the shape of animals and birds, as well as high-relief stucco wall panels. Particularly popular in the 11th–14th centuries, human and animal figures are the main decorative theme of rock crystal and ivories from Cairo, lustre and *minai* ceramics from Kashan, and inlaid metalwork from Mosul, to name only a few centres of production.

Right The surface of this 12th–13th-century Spanish bronze lion fountainhead is engraved with inscriptions expressing good wishes to the owner.

THEMES AND MOTIFS

Typical subjects dwell on aspects of court life: drinking with musical entertainment and dancers, romantic encounters, hunting on horseback, and formal throne scenes, where visiting dignitaries are received. Motifs of hunting animal pairs, such as a lion or hawk attacking a deer, were also commonly used. They reinforce the theme of power, and the ruler's right to it.

Many figural themes show artistic continuity from pre-Islamic times: Samanid polychrome ceramics made in the 10th century in north-eastern Iran seem to favour royal images recalling the pre-Islamic Sasanian empire of

Above A portrait of the physician and author Dioscorides appears in this 1229 Arabic translation of Dioscorides' De Materia Medica.

Iran. In 10th–12th-century Egypt, Fatimid art shows a vogue for genre scenes, such as wrestlers, which may refer to inherited, classical and coptic traditions.

MANUSCRIPT PAINTING

Across the Islamic world, figures were illustrated in luxury manuscripts. Books have long been treasured in the Middle East, and many bibliophile rulers and the elite collected books with passion. Historic libraries

are recorded having thousands of volumes, and royal and private collectors often made their collections available to visiting scholars.

These were works of science as well as fine literature: the earliest surviving manuscript paintings from the Islamic period are geographical maps, diagrams of the constellations, plants, animals and even mechanical automata. Scientific illustration also extends to scenes of doctors and scholars at work: harvesting medicinal plants, treating a patient or consulting with other sages. The frontispiece portrait usually depicts the author in the company of his patron, whose support is thus acknowledged. This relates to the late classical genre of author portraiture, carried over into the Islamic world. The author's portrait was gradually replaced by that of his patron.

Above This 1330 illustration from *the* Shahnama (Book of Kings) *by Firdawsi shows a king and his court.*

LITERARY PORTRAITS

As long as their patrons could afford the expense, works of literature written in Arabic, Persian and, later, Turkish were also furnished with paintings: history, romantic poetry and heroic epics all provided dramatic subjects for illustration. Luxury copies of the classic Persian works by Firdawsi, Nizami and Saadi were made for rulers and the rich over the centuries, and Persian manuscript painting was produced to an exquisite level. The patron's portrait in the frontispiece remained a standard part of the book, and often provided an insight into the court world, showing princes, guests and entertainers, the architectural setting, furniture and tableware.

Above This 17th-century Isfahan copy *of a 10th-century treatise on the stars discusses the constellation* Bootes.

THE PRINCELY CYCLE

THE MOST FREQUENT FIGURAL SUBJECT IN ISLAMIC ART IS A
THEMATIC RANGE REFERRED TO AS THE 'PRINCELY CYCLE',
DESCRIBING THE PLEASANT PURSUITS OF COURT LIFE.

The theme of the princely cycle can be found across the various media in Islamic art. Works of inlaid metal, painted ceramics and especially manuscript paintings dwell upon the portrayal of the ruler and his world. In order to show appropriate reverence to royal status, the prince is usually depicted slightly larger than his surrounding courtiers, attendants and guests.

BANQUETS

Images of feasting were adopted in the early Islamic period from the Sasanian tradition. The principal figure is the enthroned ruler who is shown seated cross-legged and holding a cup in one hand. He is accompanied by attendants, such as the *saqi* or cup-bearer and courtiers who fulfilled the role of the *nadim* or boon companion.

Male and female musicians formed the entertainment, performing with a range of instruments, such as the lute, tambourine, flute and harp; they sometimes accompany dancers holding trailing scarves, and even

acrobats. Images of such courtly entertainment might be shown taking place in palace interiors or outside within pavilions set within royal gardens.

Such images decorate items of luxury tableware: metal ewers and basins inlaid with copper and silver and ceramic dishes painted with metallic lustre and overglaze colours in the minai technique. The image is most often found in Persian painting, in both historical and poetic manuscripts. Rulers and princes are shown seated on thrones within elaborately decorated and carpeted interiors, surrounded by companions and entertained by musicians and dancers. Often lines of servants bearing dishes of fruits and sweetmeats are also depicted.

HUNTING

The iconography of the ruler out hunting was also adopted from earlier Persian tradition. The ruler is shown on horseback, with a hawk or falcon perched on his wrist ready to be launched in pursuit of prey such as hares or smaller birds.

Above A court assembly is shown in this manuscript painting from a late 15th-century copy of the Shahnama *by Firdawsi.*

Sometimes the hunter is shown with a cheetah riding behind him. This feline could be taught to capture, but not to kill the prey, which conformed to religious requirements; a passage in the Quran proscribes the eating of game killed by animals.

The lion hunt, an image that recurred frequently on silver-gilt bowls of the Sasanian period, demonstrated the ultimate subservience of the lion and symbolized the power of the king

to overcome his opponents. This notion of prey subservient to its predator was also demonstrated in images of lions or hawks attacking deer.

ILLUSTRATING AUTHORITY

The royal audience was another important theme in the princely cycle. The ruler is shown seated on a high-backed throne, usually at the centre of the composition. The throne is often flanked by guards, and in some versions winged spirits hold a canopy over the ruler to signify honour. Ranks of courtiers observe the scene, while visitors kneel or bow at the throne.

Above A pair of 19th-century Iranian tiles depict two noblemen hunting, one with a falcon, the other with a bow and arrow.

Left A 12th-century stucco panel from Iran depicts a ruler being attended by servants, and is framed within a 12-pointed star.

Below This section of a carved ivory panel, made in Egypt or Syria in the 12th century, illustrates scenes from a hunt, one of the many pleasures of court life.

The whole composition is deliberately designed to affirm and idealize authority and power.

A variant of the throne scene was included in some luxury manuscripts as the frontispiece illustration. The ruler is shown sitting in majesty, receiving the book from the author. By crediting him as the all-important sponsor of the work in this way, the artist places the ruler at the forefront of a major intellectual endeavour, thus endowing him with academic glamour.

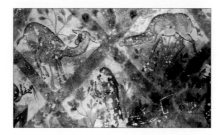

CHAPTER 9

THE UMAYYAD CALIPHATE

The first caliphal dynasty of the Islamic empire was founded by al-Muawiyah of the Umayyad clan in 661 and lasted for 90 years. A former governor of Syria, al-Muawiyah ruled from Damascus, where he set about establishing the governance and profile of the new Islamic empire. The grandeur of Umayyad imperial architecture – seen at its most beautiful and imposing in the Dome of the Rock in Jerusalem and the Great Mosque in Damascus, as well as in several luxurious and richly decorated desert palaces – demonstrates a strong sense of competition with past regimes and religions. When establishing features of the new state, such as coinage and architectural design, however, Umayyad rulers also borrowed from defeated predecessors, such as Sasanian Iran and Byzantium. In the Dome of the Rock and the Great Mosque, there are many typical Byzantine elements, not least the use of wall mosaics, as well as essential Islamic qualities, such as calligraphy and the preponderance of decorative patterns based on plant motifs. Gradually, however, a distinct Islamic aesthetic emerged.

Opposite 20th-century reconstruction of the inner courtyard of the Great Mosque of Damascus, originally built by Umayyad Caliph al-Walid I in 706–15, but severely damaged by fire in 1893.

Above A fresco in the bathhouse area of the Umayyad desert palace of Qusayr Amra in Jordan (c. 712–15) depicts wild animals. The artists were influenced by late classical traditions.

THE UMAYYAD PERIOD

THE UMAYYADS WERE THE FIRST ISLAMIC RULERS TO ESTABLISH A DYNASTY (661–750). THEIR BUILDINGS PROMOTED THE AUTHORITY OF THE REIGNING FAMILY, AS WELL AS THE YOUNG FAITH OF ISLAM.

The first member of the Umayyad family to become caliph was Muawiyah I, a provincial governor who challenged the authority of Ali ibn Abi Talib, the Prophet's cousin and son-in-law, as ruler of the Islamic world.

Muawiyah did not take power until 29 years after the Prophet Muhammad's death, in 632. Abu Bakr, a companion of the Prophet and an early convert to Islam, had been chosen as the caliph, or successor, to be both religious leader of Muslims and political ruler of the Islamic world.

Shortly before his death in 634, Abu Bakr nominated Umar ibn al-Khattab as the next ruler. In 644, Umar's successor as caliph, Uthman ibn-Affan, was elected by a committee of religious elders. On Uthman's murder in 656, Ali ibn Abu Talib, one of the elders who

had elected Uthman, assumed control. However, Ali struggled to impose his authority, and the *ummah*, or Islamic religious community, had its first great schism. Muawiyah was among those who did not accept Ali's authority.

RULERS FROM MAKKAH

Like Muhammad himself, the Umayyad family belonged to the powerful Quraysh tribe of Makkah. They had initially opposed Muhammad but accepted his rule and converted to Islam when the Prophet took control of Makkah in 630. Muawiyah then fought in the Arab Islamic army in Syria against the Byzantine Empire, and in 640 he was appointed Governor of Syria

Below At its peak, c.750, the Umayyad Empire stretched from Spain in the west to Persia in the east.

Above Husayn ibn Ali is attacked during the Battle of Karbala as he tries to obtain water from the Euphrates.

by the second caliph, Umar ibn al-Khattab. Throughout the reign of Ali ibn Abu Talib, Muawiyah maintained his independence and expanded the Umayyad power base by taking military control of Egypt. When Ali was murdered in 661, Muawiyah seized power and forced

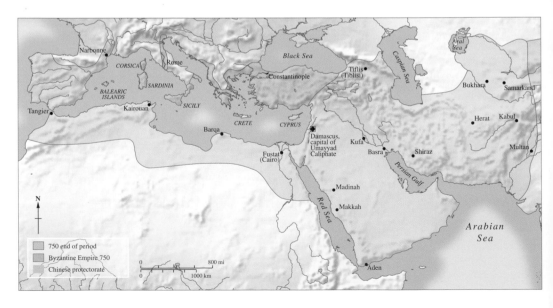

Ali's son Hasan to abandon his own claim to be caliph. Muawiyah declared himself *amir al-mumineen* ('Commander of the Faithful').

Ali's principal power base had been the city of Kufa in Iraq, built as a garrison town following the Arab victory over the Byzantines at the Battle of Yarmouk in 636, but Muawiyah established Umayyad rule in the ancient city of Damascus in Syria. Such had been the military expansion under the first four caliphs that by 661, when Muawiyah took power, the Islamic Empire already stretched from Iran in the east to Egypt in the west.

Muawiyah held these disparate landholdings together through ties of personal loyalty. Government was strong under his rule: he developed bureaucracies on a Byzantine model; in Syria, he appointed Christians – many with experience of government under the Byzantines – to key positions.

SHIAH OPPOSITION

Muawiyah established the first dynasty in Islamic history when he passed the Caliphate to his son Yazid I in 680. This created further conflict: Husayn ibn Ali, son of Ali and, through his mother Fatima, a grandson of the Prophet, claimed the right to rule, but he was killed by Yazid's troops at the Battle of Karbala on 10 October 680.

The Prophet's descendants continued to oppose the authority of the Umayyad rulers: in particular, they never forgave the Umayyads for Ali's death at Karbala. Gradually the group of followers, or Shiah, of Ali grew. In 750, when members of the Hashim clan, who were descended from Muhammad's uncle al-Abbas, led a revolt against

Right The courtyard of the Great Mosque of Damascus, built on the site of the Christian Church of St John the Baptist in 706–15.

the Umayyads, they were supported by several Shiah groups. The Hashim were successful and their leader, Abu al-Abbas, became the first of the Abbasid caliphs.

ARCHITECTURAL GLORIES

The Umayyad rulers, especially Abd al-Malik (reigned 685–705), al-Walid I (reigned 705–15), Sulayman (reigned 715–17), Hisham (reigned 724–43) and al-Walid II (reigned 743–44), financed an imperial building programme, primarily in Syria. They established a splendid court in Damascus and built a series of grand palaces on country estates nearby. In Damascus, they lived in a palace south of the Great Mosque: from contemporary descriptions it is known that the building had a green dome, and included a pool. They also invested heavily in an infrastructure to promote agriculture across Syria, building vast numbers of dams, wells, canals and gardens. Syria became a prestigious place to live.

In these years, Damascus was the capital and Syria the centre of an empire in which a variety of pre-Islamic architectural and artistic traditions still existed. To the east were Iraq and Iran, where the Assyrians, Babylonians, Achaemenids and Sasanians had ruled; to the west,

Above Caliph Hisham built Qasr al-Hayr al-Gharbi in the Syrian desert in 728. It was a palace complex with a bathhouse and caravanserai.

south-west and north were lands that had once been part of the Byzantine Empire, where Graeco-Roman traditions were strong. To the south, in the deserts of Arabia, was the birthplace of Islam. The Umayyads summoned craftsmen from every part of this diverse empire to work on their building projects. Documents found in Upper Egypt provide evidence that a local governor was required to send workers to labour on the Great Mosque of Damascus, built under al-Walid I. These workmen applied their local styles and skills to Umayyad mosques and palaces, such as Coptic carving from Egypt and Persian stucco work.

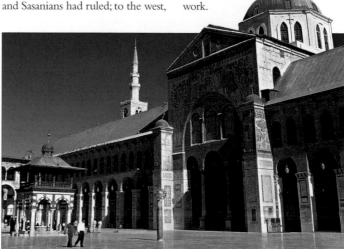

UMAYYAD COINS

AFTER INITIALLY MAKING ONLY MINOR AMENDMENTS TO THE COINAGE OF THEIR PREDECESSORS, THE UMAYYAD CALIPHS GRADUALLY DEVELOPED NEW DESIGNS THAT WERE DISTINCTIVELY ISLAMIC.

Coins known as the dinar and dirham are mentioned in the Quran, but scholars believe that the Arabs had very little of their own money in circulation in Arabia. However, when they took over the government of the former Sasanian and Byzantine empires, the Umayyads understood the importance of continuity in economic matters. To maintain healthy levels of trade, it was essential that merchants had confidence in the coinage, and a sudden change to unfamiliar designs might have endangered this.

ECONOMIC CONTINUITY

The earliest surviving Arab coins in fact just predate the Umayyad era (661–750). These early coins are marked 653, which is 21 years after the Prophet's death in 632 and 8 years before the establishment of

Above This silver drachm bears the head of Sasanian monarch Khosrow II. The Arab conquerors of Iran kept coins of this type in circulation.

the Umayyad Caliphate by Muawiyah I in 661.

When they first came to power, the Umayyads kept familiar coins in circulation. Umayyad coins minted in former Sasanian territory (Iran and Iraq) were adaptations of Sasanian silver coinage; they continued to feature the head of the Sasanian Shah Khosrow II (reigned 590–628) on the front and – because the Sasanian kings followed the Zoroastrian religion – a Zoroastrian fire altar appeared on the reverse.

The Umayyads seem to have continued using Iranian die-makers to mint their coins. The coins bore the mint marks and sometimes the name of the Arab governor in the *pahlavi* script that had been used by the Sasanians.

The date of issue was given both in the Sasanian reckoning and in the Hijra calendar (counted from the Prophet Muhammad's migration from Makkah to Madinah in 622). However, Umayyad rulers also clearly felt the need to promote the Islamic faith that was driving their imperial expansion and coins began to appear incorporating pious Muslim doctrinal slogans in *kufic* script, such as 'All praise be to Allah' and 'In Allah's name'.

Left A coin from the reign of the second Sasanian king, Shapur I (reigned 241–72), features the Zoroastrian fire altar.

BYZANTINE INHERITANCE

In Syria, which had previously been part of the Byzantine Empire, the Arab conquerors also initially issued coins identical in appearance to those of their forerunner. The coins bore images of Byzantine imperial figures, including Emperor Heraclius (reigned 610–41) with his sons. As in Iraq and Iran, the Umayyad rulers had decided to keep the coins looking as similar as possible in the interests of continuity, but they gradually began to make minor changes in order to nullify the Christian symbols used on the coins. For example, they removed the horizontal arm of the crucifix found on the back of some coins, or they cut out the 'I' from the monogram 'ICXC' used to represent Christ's name in orthodox Christianity.

In time, the figure of the Byzantine ruler was replaced with a turbaned and clearly Arab male, standing and holding a sword. This figure has been interpreted by some scholars as an image of the caliph giving the *khutbah* sermon at Friday prayers, and the coins have become known as 'standing caliph' coins.

On the reverse they bore an image of the lance associated with the Prophet, set within a niche – clearly a modification of the Christian image of the cross standing at the top of a flight of steps that appeared on Byzantine coins. According to Islamic tradition, the lance was given to one of the Prophet's companions by an Ethiopian ruler and it was then passed on to Muhammad himself; the image was used in the first mosques to indicate the direction of Makkah. The niche on the coin, although it may appear to suggest the *mihrab* prayer niche found in mosques, is most likely a reference to niches in Byzantine architecture as *mihrabs* were probably not yet in use in mosques.

AN ISLAMIC COINAGE

In around 696–98, Islamic coinage was reformed under Umayyad Caliph Abd al-Malik, builder of the Dome of the Rock in Jerusalem. A new weight standard was set for coins, and all figurative images were replaced with Islamic messages written in Arabic *kufic* script. The

AFTER THE UMAYYADS

The style of coins introduced in the late 7th century under the Umayyad caliphs was the standard one used to produce Muslim coinage for several hundred years, and was used also by the Umayyads' Abbasid successors. The name of the ruling caliph was generally not included on the coins until the Abbasid era, beginning with those issued by al-Mahdi (reigned 775–85). Thereafter, it became standard practice to include the name of the reigning caliph on coins.

purpose of the epigraphs was to remind all subjects of the empire of the success and supremacy of the conquerors' Islamic faith.

Just as the interior of the Dome of the Rock was emblazoned with mosaic messages that set Islamic beliefs apart from Christian and Jewish doctrines, so the new gold dinars issued by Abd al-Malik declared the key beliefs that differentiated Islam from rival faiths. The coins bore doctrinal statements, such as the *kalimah* ('words') *La ilahu illa Allah, wa Muhammad rasul Allah* ('There is no god but Allah, and Muhammad is Allah's Messenger'), and directly dismissed the concept that Christ is

(in the words of the biblical Gospel of John) 'the only begotten Son of God', declaring 'Allah has no associate' and 'Allah does not beget, and was never begotten'. There were two denominations of coins: the copper fals and the silver dirham. Although there was a great variety in the issues of the lesser copper coins, there was remarkable uniformity among the silver dirhams, all of which bore calligraphy of the same type. All the coins bore a date and the name of the mint at which they were struck.

Below These 10th-century coins show that epigraphy became the dominant theme of Islamic coinage.

DESERT PALACES

THE FINEST SURVIVING EXAMPLES OF SECULAR BUILDINGS FROM THE
UMAYYAD ERA ARE THE *QUSUR*, OR DESERT PALACES, SUCH AS QUSAYR
AMRA IN JORDAN AND QASR AL-HAYR AL-GHARBI IN SYRIA.

Although called 'desert palaces', the qusur, were built alongside agricultural land or oases. While some stood on trade routes and incorporated *caravanserais* (travellers' lodgings), and others were perhaps used as hunting lodges, they were principally country houses at the centre of farming estates.

FRESCOES AT QUSAYR AMRA

The small palace of Qusayr Amra was probably built under Caliph al-Walid I in 712–15, and stands beside an oasis in semi-arid land around 80km (50 miles) east of Amman in Jordan. The remains of a castle, tower, waterwheel and well have been uncovered, but the principal surviving buildings are a rectangular throne room and audience chamber and a bathhouse. The internal walls of both are decorated with remarkable frescoes.

One fresco in the audience chamber shows a ruler, probably Caliph al-Walid I, grandly enthroned in the Byzantine fashion beneath a canopy. He faces a fresco in which six kings stand in line as if paying homage. Other subjects include the pleasures of life at the Umayyad court, such as a royal hunt and scenes of relaxation in the bathhouse, together with some of the many crafts activities carried out under the Caliph's patronage. The vaulted ceiling is divided into rectangular sections and also shows craftsmen working.

The walls of the three rooms in the bathhouse are decorated with musicians and dancing girls, and scenes of animals, including gazelles, camels, donkeys, and even a

Below The abandoned complex of Qusayr Amra was rediscovered in 1898 by Czech orientalist Alois Musil.

Above Hunters and maidens cavort in a detail from the wall frescoes at Qusayr Amra. These are the largest surviving group of early medieval frescoes.

bear playing a musical instrument. The domed ceiling in one room is painted with the main constellations of the northern hemisphere – the oldest surviving representation of the stars of the night sky on a domed surface.

The wonderful images at Qusayr Amra are confidently drawn and delicately coloured, using methods and iconography from the classical worlds of Greece and Rome. They are part of a princely propaganda attempt to establish the Umayyad rulers and their court on an equal footing with other imperial rulers and establishments past and present.

FINE STUCCO WORK

Qasr al–Hayr al–Gharbi was built by Caliph al–Hisham about 60km (37 miles) west of Palmyra, a caravan trade city on the road from Damascus. The complex includes a palace, bathhouse and *khan* (travellers' lodge), together with agricultural land, all surrounded by a protecting wall set with semicircular towers. An irrigation system is fed by underground canals that connect to an ancient Roman dam at Harbaqa, 16km (10 miles) to the south.

Within the enclosing wall, the *khan* is laid out around a courtyard. The palace is square in shape with sides measuring 70m (230ft). It originally had two storeys, although only the lower one survives, and a monumental gateway with carved stucco decoration – the oldest Islamic example of this type of decoration, which was derived from the work of Sasanian craftsmen. The stucco work is now in the National Museum, Damascus.

The palace complex at Khirbat al–Mafjar in the Jordan Valley near Jericho in Palestine was built in the years before 743 by Caliph al–Hisham. Set within a protective wall, the grouped buildings include a two–storey palace, a mosque, and a great domed bathhouse with audience room, together with a large courtyard with central fountain and circular colonnade. The very grand bathhouse and audience room contain a bathing pool and a second plunge pool that reputedly once held wine, as well as a latrine with space for 33 guests at once. The bathhouse floor consists of no fewer than 39 adjoining mosaic panels decorated with geometric designs; together these form the world's largest floor mosaic still surviving from antiquity. Another striking mosaic panel, located in the audience hall, depicts a lion attacking a gazelle.

The palace at Mshatta, built in 743–44 by Caliph al–Walid II around 32km (20 miles) south of Amman in Jordan, was seemingly intended to be the grandest of all the Umayyads' royal buildings, but work was abandoned when the Caliph was killed in a battle against rebels in 744. The unfinished square

Above A detail from the stone façade of the palace at Mshatta in Jordan (743–44) shows Sasanian-style rosettes.

complex, built in limestone and brick, includes a mosque, entrance hall, audience hall and residential quarters covering a vast 144sq m (1,550sq ft). Its splendid stone façade reveals many influences: it is decorated with Sasanian–style solar rosettes divided by a zigzag band moulding of a kind often seen in Christian Syrian buildings and backed by a detailed classical–style relief of animals and vines.

Above This beautifully decorated doorway is part of the Umayyad desert palace of Qasr al-Hayr al-Gharbi, built under Caliph al-Hisham in Syria.

CHAPTER 10

THE ABBASID CALIPHATE

In 750, the Umayyad dynasty was ousted in a revolt led by the Abbasids, cousins of the Umayyads and descendants of the Prophet's uncle al-Abbas. The Abbasids established a new caliphate that lasted for 500 years and moved the capital of the empire to Baghdad in Iraq. The city quickly grew to become a vibrant centre for trade, culture and intellectual life. In 836, the Abbasids moved their capital to Samarra. Although the move proved temporary, the Abbasids built luxurious palace compounds there, complete with parks, artificial water basins, barracks and racecourses. The 8th to 10th centuries are renowned as a golden age for Islamic culture. Luxury arts thrived: metalworkers, weavers and potters produced beautiful, highly crafted objects, while scribes created the first Qurans to be produced on paper. This was also the era of the Translation Movement, when scientific texts from the classical world were translated into Arabic. The Caliphate came to an end in 1258, when invading Mongol tribesmen entered Baghdad and executed the last Abbasid caliph, to the dismay of the wider Islamic world.

Opposite The striking 52-m (170-ft) tall minaret of the Great Mosque of Samarra was built in the new imperial capital in 848–52 by the Abbasid Caliph, al-Mutawakkil.

Above A 13th-century work on paper depicts the classical scholar Solon (638–559BCE). Scholars of all faiths and ethnicities were welcomed and given employment at the highly cultured Abbasid court in Baghdad.

BAGHDAD

ONE OF THE WORLD'S MOST POPULOUS AND WEALTHY CITIES,
ABBASID BAGHDAD WAS A GREAT CENTRE OF LONG–DISTANCE TRADE
AND AN INTELLECTUAL AND ARTISTIC CAPITAL.

In 762, the Abbasid Caliph al-Mansur founded a great city called Madinat as-Salam ('The City of Peace'), or Baghdad as it soon became known, beside the river Tigris in Iraq. This was a vast project: according to the 9th-century Arab historian al-Yaqubi, an army of labourers 100,000 strong was drafted in to build the city.

The city was laid out in a vast fortified circle centred on the caliph's palace and a great *jami*, or Friday Mosque. In choosing the circular layout, al-Mansur was following ancient local tradition going back at least to the foundation of the Assyrian city of Dur Sharrukin in the 8th century BCE, and evident in the city of Ghur (modern Firuzabad) established by the Sasanian Shah Ardashir I (reigned 226–41CE).

FORTIFIED CITY

Little remains of the early structures of Baghdad, but contemporary written accounts enable experts to build up a picture of its design. The Round City was 2.7km (1.68 miles) in diameter and stood within a double set of mud-brick walls and a moat flooded from the Tigris. Four gates led to and were named after Basra (at the south-east), Kufa (south-west), Khurasan (north-east) and Damascus (north-west). Each gate had a zigzag entranceway to make it easier to defend against charging attackers, and each stood beneath a chamber accessed by a ramp or stairs. These chambers had a domed roof topped with a weathervane shaped like a horseman.

From the gates, long vaulted and arcaded avenues ran into the centre of the city. Along the inside of the defensive walls was an outer circuit of buildings used as residences for the caliph's family and members of the court. Key government buildings, including the treasury and the weapon store, were part of an inner ring of buildings. In the centre of the city were a building for guards as well as the mosque and palace.

MOSQUE AND PALACE

The central mosque was a square hypostyle design, its sides 100m (330ft) long and enclosing an open courtyard. Next to it, the palace covered four times the area of the mosque. A vaulted reception hall, with sides measuring 15m by 10m (50ft by 33ft), led into an audience chamber with sides 10m (33ft) long.

A second audience hall had a dome called Qubbat al-Khadra ('Green Dome'), which was 40m (130ft) tall and topped with a

Above The Tomb of Zumurrud Khatun was built c.1193. It is celebrated for its tall cone-shaped muqarnas *dome.*

weathervane shaped like a warrior on horseback holding a spear. This figure was celebrated as a symbol of Abbasid power: wherever he faced he looked out over lands ruled by the caliph. According to tradition, the caliph learned of rebellions, as well as of meteorological storms, from the movements of this figure. The dome and the horseman collapsed in 941. This was an ill omen, as just four years later the Buyids established themselves as de facto rulers of the empire, leaving the caliphs in only nominal control.

PALACE OF UKHAYDIR

The buildings of Baghdad owed much to local tradition, marking a shift from Umayyad style. No traces of the original city survive in Baghdad itself, but the nearly contemporary fortified desert palace of Ukhaydir, built in c.775 near Kufa, about 200km (125 miles) south of Baghdad, gives experts an idea of the likely appearance of the Round City. This vast

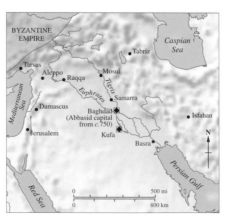

Above Baghdad became the Abbasid capital in 762. Kufa was the original capital.

Above The original buildings of
Baghdad resembled Ukhaydir Palace,
near Kufa, built c.775.

complex stands within walls 19m
(62ft) tall and in a slightly elongated
square measuring 175m by 169m
(574ft by 554ft). It contained
courtyards, halls, a mosque and a
bathhouse. It is characteristic of the
Abbasids' preference for surrounding
audience chambers and palatial
buildings with fortifications – they
combined a commitment to grand
ceremonial with security.

ARTS AND LEARNING

Baghdad was a centre for luxury
arts, attracting artisans from all over
the Islamic Empire while exporting
its metropolitan style far and wide.
This was an important phase in
Islamic art and architecture.
Baghdad, and later Samarra, drew in
eastern influences from Iran and
passed these westward as part of
an identifiable Abbasid style: in
al-Andalus (Islamic Spain), artisans
copied the textiles of Baghdad, and
in Egypt architects used decorative
stucco as found in Samarra. Under

these influences, Islamic artisans and
architects moved away from Graeco-
Roman and Byzantine styles.

Baghdad was also an intellectual
capital, where scholars contributed
to the highly influential 'Translation
Movement', translating into Arabic
ancient Greek works of philosophy,
medicine, mathematics and astrology
by classic authors, such as Aristotle
(384–322BCE), Galen (129–216CE)
and Ptolemy (*c.*100–161CE), and
Indian texts by the mathematicians
Sushruta (6th century BCE) and
Aryabhata (476–550CE).

HARUN AL-RASHID

Harun al-Rashid (reigned 786–809), the fifth Abbasid caliph, ruled Baghdad
at the height of the city's prosperity and prominence as a centre of art and
learning. He was a poet and scholar and a great patron who invited
intellectuals to his court from far and wide. His own fame reached as far as
Western Europe: he exchanged a series of ambassadors and gifts with
Charlemagne, King of the Franks (reigned 747–814). In return for gifts of
hunting dogs and Spanish horses, Harun sent Charlemagne an elephant called
Abdul-Abbas, chessmen made of ivory and a mechanical clock that astonished
all who saw it at the court of the Franks in Aachen (now western Germany).
He even features as a character in the world's most celebrated piece of
literature in Arabic, *Alf laylah wa laylah* ('The Thousand and One Nights'),
which began as an oral tradition.

Left A detail from a 15th-century manuscript from Nizami's Khamsa *(five poems*
or 'Quintet'), showing Harun al-Rashid in a bathhouse.

SAMARRA

THE CITY OF SAMARRA IN IRAQ WAS THE ABBASID IMPERIAL CAPITAL
FOR JUST OVER 50 YEARS, 836–92. ITS NAME REPUTEDLY DERIVED
FROM THE PHRASE *SURRA MAN RA'A* ('A JOY FOR HE WHO SEES IT').

In Baghdad, Abbasid caliphs lived in their vast palace complex isolated from their people. As their authority began to wane in the 9th century, they became increasingly dependent on their Turkish slave troops from Central Asia. In 836, violent clashes in Baghdad between the slave troops and local citizens persuaded Caliph al-Mutasim to move the imperial capital to Samarra 125km (78 miles) north of Baghdad.

In Samarra, al-Mutasim and his successors raised a huge city, which extended for 50km (30 miles) along the banks of the river Tigris and covered 150sq km (60sq miles); it included several sprawling palaces, grand boulevards, extensive barracks and lush gardens, as well as the Great Mosque of Samarra, at the time the world's biggest mosque. Outside the city limits were large hunting parks and three tracks for horseracing. Samarra remained capital of the Abbasid Empire until 892, when Caliph al-Mutamid moved the administration back to Baghdad.

HOUSE OF THE CALIPH

The main palace at Samarra was the Dar al-Khilafa ('House of the Caliph'), a huge assembly of court-yards, chambers, apartments and pools that covered 70ha (173 acres). The structure dwarfed the relatively small palaces of the Umayyad era.

A bank of steps rose from the Tigris to the main public entrance, the Bab al-Amma, which had three large brick archways. The principal audience chamber was a domed hall at the centre of four vaulted *iwans*, or halls, and opening on to a garden overlooking the river Tigris. In the audience hall, the caliph held public audiences on a Monday and Thursday. Nearby and within the palace complex was a field used for polo matches and parades.

THE GREAT MOSQUE

In 848–52, al-Mutasim's son and successor al-Mutawakkil built the Great Mosque, which measured 239m by 156m (784ft by 512ft) and was protected by tall walls supported

Above The outer walls of the Great Mosque in Samarra, restored by Saddam Hussein.

by 44 semicircular towers. The whole was set within an enclosure of 444m by 376m (1,457ft by 1,234ft).

The mosque originally had colonnaded arcades halls around a courtyard: the flat roof of the sanctuary on the south wall was supported by 24 rows of 9 brick-and-stone columns. The *mihrab*, or prayer niche, was decorated with gold glass mosaics with two rose-coloured columns of marble on

Below Qasr al-Ashiq in Samarra, on the right bank of the river Tigris, was built by al-Mutamid (reigned 870–92).

each side. Little remains of the mosque's interiors, except for its distinctive spiral minaret known as al-Malwiya. It stands on a square base, from which a round tower rises 55m (180ft) above ground. A spiral ramp runs counter-clockwise around the outside of the tower to a pavilion at the top. This particular form of minaret appears to have been inspired by ancient Mesopotamian ziggurats, or temple towers.

OTHER PALACES

In addition to the Great Mosque, al-Mutawakkil built as many as 20 palaces, leaving the Abbasid treasury badly depleted by the end of his reign. In the 850s, he laid out a new area north of Samarra, called Jafariya, that contained a vast palace called the Jafari, as well as a second grand congregational mosque (now called the Mosque of Abu Dulaf), built in imitation of the Great Mosque and with a similar spiral minaret, but on a smaller scale.

The building of large palaces set behind high walls probably reflected the development of a more hierarchical society in the Abbasid era, when the caliphs adapted Persian ideas of kingship. At the same time, religious and political authority, once united in the person of the caliph, began to diverge, and the mosque became more the preserve of the *ulama*, or religious legal scholars.

Although most of the buildings, even the palaces, were built of only mud brick, they were lavishly

decorated, with glass mosaics and elaborate wood or marble panelling. The setting was one of high luxury: glass objects, gold and silver dishes and lustreware have been excavated.

STUCCO DECORATION

A distinctive type of carved and moulded multicoloured painted stucco decoration was developed and made popular in Samarra, and from there spread throughout the Islamic Empire. The decoration appears in three distinct styles.

The first was derived from the vegetal carving of the Umayyad period: a surface was divided into compartments by roundels and filled with curling vine tendrils. In the second style, the compartments contained carved plant decoration so stylized that it could no longer be associated with plants; in some, the contemporary Chinese symbols for the properties of yin and yang appeared. In the third, the compartments contained abstract

Above The first style of Samarran stucco wall decoration uses curling plants; this example is from Qasr al-Ashiq.

decorative motifs, such as palmettes, bottle shapes and spirals. Known as the 'bevelled style', this was made with a shallow cut using moulds in symmetrical patterns that could be repeated as far as required, so it could be applied quickly across wide areas of wall. The third style had an important influence on later Islamic art as it led to the development of arabesque decoration.

The walls were also decorated with paintings, including naturalistic images of human figures. These included hunting scenes with wild animals and naked women. A wall painting from the Dar al-Khilafa shows two serving girls dancing while pouring wine into goblets.

Below This is an example of the third Samarran style, made with a shallow cut and using symmetrical designs.

MAJOR ABBASID CALIPHS
Abu al-Abbas al-Saffah (750–54) Dynastic founder
al-Mansur (754–75) Founded Baghdad
Harun al-Rashid (786–809) Great patron
al-Mutasim (833–42) Moved to Samarra
al-Mutawakkil (047–61) Great builder in Samarra
al-Mutamid (892–902) Moved capital back to Baghdad
al-Mustasim Billah (1242–58) Final Baghdad caliph

POTTERY AND LUSTREWARE

IN AN ATTEMPT TO IMITATE IMPORTED CHINESE WARES, ISLAMIC POTTERS DEVELOPED A WHITE TIN GLAZE BUT SOON ADDED THEIR OWN DESIGNS WITH COBALT AND LUSTRE.

The earliest pottery production in the Islamic world was a continuation of local traditions. Functional green- and turquoise-glazed earthenwares were made for the storage and transportation of goods, such as oil, dates and honey. However, in the late 8th to early 9th centuries, the pottery industry in Iraq was transformed, and the first distinctively Islamic ceramics were produced here. This was a development that coincided with the luxurious taste and demands of the Abbasid court, and it was triggered by the importation of porcelain and stoneware items from China. These wares provided inspiration to the Iraqi potters, who sought to imitate them.

FOREIGN INFLUENCES
Basra was the main centre of pottery production: several contemporary writers describe the fine quality of the white clay found in deposits near the city and it was also the port of entry for imported Chinese wares that came by sea. Persian and Arab sailors had recently opened a direct sea route between the Persian Gulf and the South China Sea. They took ivory, incense, spices and pearls to China and returned with silk, paper and ceramics. The goods also travelled by land over the Silk Route. A contemporary account of one diplomatic gift to Harun al-Rashid, the caliph in Baghdad, included: '200 pieces of imperial porcelain, including basins and bowls and other things the like of which had never been seen before at a royal court, and 2,000 other

Chinese ceramic vessels, including covered dishes, large bowls and large and small pottery jars.'

BLUE-AND-WHITE POTTERY
The Iraqi potters could not reproduce the shiny white surface and hard compact body of the Chinese wares exactly because they did not have access to the same type of clay – white kaolin – or the kiln technology that was needed to achieve high firing temperatures. Instead, they closely imitated the Chinese vessel shapes and copied the whiteness of the surface by covering the yellow body of the pots with an opaque white glaze made by mixing tin oxide with a lead glaze.

Initially, the potters left the surfaces of these wares unadorned, like the Chinese prototypes, but it was not long before they began to add decoration in cobalt blue pigment. The colour had a tendency to sink into the glaze, an effect that has been described as 'ink on snow'. The designs were generally limited to floral and geometric motifs or calligraphic inscriptions. The use of writing, in the form of signatures and phrases, such as 'blessing to its owner', was an entirely new and Islamic decorative device. In a second phase, splashes of green were added to the cobalt designs, probably influenced by imported Chinese splashware vessels.

Above Iraqi potters imitated Chinese white wares by coating the earthenware body with an opaque white glaze, as seen in this 9th-century bowl.

LUSTRE GLAZING
Following the commercial success of the blue-and-white pottery, the Basra potters developed a new technique known as lustre glazing, a complex process that required expensive materials. Borrowed from

Above This 9th-century dish has been pressed into a mould to form the relief decoration. The raised dots and lustre glaze were used to imitate metal.

glass technology, the technique used powdered metallic oxides of silver and copper, which when applied to the ceramic body produced a lustrous metallic sheen. The pots were painted with a plain white glaze and fired in an ordinary kiln. When they were cool, the potter painted on the design in a mix of metallic compounds that were finely ground together, mixed with clay and diluted in grape juice or vinegar. The vessel was then put into a reduction kiln and fired a second time; carbon monoxide in the reducing atmosphere extracted the oxygen from the silver and copper oxides and bonded them as a thin layer of metal on to the surface of the glaze.

STYLISTIC CHANGES

The earliest lustre-glazed vessels were decorated with a range of tones known as polychrome lustre and were characterized by busy geometric and floral patterns that entirely covered the surface. Over time the process was simplified and a single golden colour, described as monochrome lustre, was adopted. This simplification may have been intended to reduce the costs of the process, or it could have been that after much experimentation the potters had achieved a real understanding and control of the technique.

With the change in palette, a new iconography was developed and the abstract patterning was replaced with figural imagery. Large-scale figures of men bearing arms, or seated and holding a glass, or animals, such as deer, camels and birds, became popular. These monochrome lustreware pieces are particularly distinctive; the contours of the image are outlined, leaving a narrow white space to separate

Above *This late 9th–early 10th-century bowl is painted with a stylized figure in a cross-legged position. It resembles a bodhisattva, which is a Buddhist religious figure.*

and distinguish it from the background, which is filled with roughly shaped dots or dashes like the punching found on metalwork. In this period, the Abbasid rulers recruited their armies from the tribes of Central Asia and it was probably through these Turkish immigrants that this type of imagery was introduced.

By the late 10th century, pottery production in Basra declined. Many of the potters seem to have moved to Egypt, where the Fatimid court was beginning to flourish.

Above *By the late 9th–early 10th century, potters in Iraq were expertly using lustre and had limited the palette to one colour.*

GLASSMAKING

IN THE 9TH AND 10TH CENTURIES, ISLAMIC GLASSMAKERS DEVELOPED IMPRESSIVE NEW DECORATIVE TECHNIQUES FOR CUTTING AND COLOURING THE GLASS SURFACE.

Above This cup was found in a palace of the Abbasid Caliph al-Mutasim (reigned 833–42). Vertical lines of inscription read 'drink and be filled with delight' and 'made in Damascus'.

Long before the Arab conquest, glassmaking had flourished across the Middle East for more than two millennia. Glassmaking was a conservative craft in which technical methods continued unchanged over long periods. The political upheavals of the Islamic conquest had little impact on the glass workers, except that they increased the production of their wares in response to demand from their new patrons.

AN EXPORTED WARE

Islamic glass was traded widely across the Islamic world and also in Europe, China and South-east Asia. It was exported in the form of luxury vessels but also as broken glass, known as cullet, which was suitable for remelting and making new glass inexpensively. This wide distribution makes it difficult to identify with any certainty where much of Islamic glass was produced. One broad distinction is that glass workers in Iran and Iraq favoured cutting and moulding techniques, whereas those in Egypt and Syria preferred to experiment with colour.

LUSTRE GLASS

A technique known as lustre decoration was invented in the 7th century. This was a complex process where powdered metallic oxides containing silver or copper mixed with vinegar were painted on to a blown glass vessel, which was then reheated in a reducing kiln at a temperature lower than the original firing so that the vessel did not collapse. The oxides left a brownish or yellow stain, sometimes with a metallic sheen, on the pale glass. Several lustre-painted glasses have inscriptions, a few of them naming their patrons, making the value placed on such objects evident. Two lustre glasses have been found with inscriptions stating that they were made in Damascus.

PRODUCING CUT GLASS

The art of cutting glass became highly developed in Iran and Iraq in the 9th and 10th centuries. Glass vessels were blown into the desired shape and then allowed to cool to

Above This 16th-century manuscript painting shows the stages of glass-blowing and the tools required. On the right, a craftsman is blowing a glass bubble.

THE GLASSMAKING PROCESS

Glass is essentially made from silica, or sand, which melts at very high temperatures. To lower the melting point, a flux obtained from the ashes of the glasswort plant or from natron, a mineral widely available in Egypt and also used in the mummification process, was added to the silica and heated in an iron pot in the hottest part of the furnace. When the mixture had melted, the craftsman gathered up a mass, known as a 'gather', on the end of his blowpipe to create a bubble of glass, which he then shaped and decorated with various tools.

let the glass worker grind, cut and polish the surface on a rotating wheel – as he might do if working with gemstones. Facet cutting, a method that was popular in Iran in the Sasanian period (226–651 CE), was achieved by blowing vessels with relatively thick walls and then cutting away parts of the surface to create a honeycomb pattern of shallow facets. Fine geometric and floral patterns could be incised into the surface with a tool set with a diamond point, and this technique is referred to as scratch engraving. Several blue glass dishes of this type were found in the crypt of a temple in China that was sealed in 874.

The technique of relief-cut glass required extraordinary skill and precision. The pattern was created by cutting and grinding the surface to remove the background and most of the inner areas of the main design, leaving the outlines and some details in relief. A version

Left This 10th-century Iranian pitcher was made in several stages: first the body was blown into a mould, which impressed whorls, then the cobalt neck was added and finally the clear glass handle was attached.

of this technique is known as cameo glass: the colourless glass vessel was dipped in molten coloured glass to form a coating, and after cooling, sections of the coloured layer were cut away to form an overlaid decorative design.

TRAILED GLASS

In Syria and Egypt, a number of techniques were used where the glass was manipulated and decorated while it was hot and malleable. Applied trails of glass, in a contrasting colour to the vessel, could be wound around the vessel and then manipulated with a pointed tool or a fine pincer to create patterns in thin strands of glass. A group of small animal figures, shaped as camels or donkeys, have flasks (probably for storing perfume or scented oils) attached to their backs that are enclosed by a network of trailed threads like a basket. If the vessel with its applied trails was rolled on to a flat slab, known as a marver, the trails became integrated into the vessel wall and made striking wavy or festooned patterns; this is called 'marvered' glass.

Left To make this 10th–11th-century glass vessel, the clear glass matrix was dipped in a layer of molten turquoise glass; after it cooled, it was ground on a wheel using gem-cutting techniques.

THE ART OF THE QURAN

ISLAMIC CALLIGRAPHERS DEVELOPED A REPERTOIRE OF FUNCTIONAL YET DECORATIVE DEVICES AS THEY COPIED THE SACRED TEXT, TO HELP NAVIGATE AROUND THE QURAN AND ALSO BEAUTIFY IT.

With the spread of Islam, the text of the Quran inspired some of the world's greatest artworks. Together, calligraphers and illuminators created some of the finest manuscripts ever produced. From the first, the main emphasis was on the beauty and clarity of the written word. As a result, calligraphers enjoyed a higher status than other artists.

EARLY SIGNS AND SYMBOLS

From the outset, the text of the Quran was adorned with a number of markings. Many of these were orthographic signs, added above and below the letters to indicate short vowels, doubled letters and other features of spelling.

In early Qurans, these signs could also indicate variant readings of the text, and they were written in up to four different colours: red, yellow, green and blue. In addition, there were a variety of symbols positioned at the end of verses and chapters, which were designed to help readers navigate their way around the text. In the earliest manuscripts, these symbols could be simple – the end of a verse, for example, might be marked by a cluster of gold dots. However, over the years these adornments grew more elaborate.

CHAPTERS AND VERSES

The text of the Quran is divided into 114 suwar (literally 'degrees', sing: surah), or chapters. From around the 9th century, the headings of these suwar became an important focus for decoration. In most cases, this took the form of an inscription in a decorative, rectangular frame, or *unwan*, specifying the title of the surah, the number of its verses and the site of its revelation (such as Makkah or Madinah). The inscription often featured a different script or colour than the one used for the main body of the text, usually *kufic* or *thuluth*.

Above The title of each surah was written in a different style to the main text and contained within a rectangular frame, as in this 12th-century example.

In the margin adjoining the frame, the illuminator sometimes added a palmette, a hasp ornament to emphasize a break in the text.

Some suwar received more attention than others. The pages relating to the first two, known as al-Fatihah and al-Baqarah, were always especially ornate. Surah al-Fatihah is short, filling just a page, and often recited as a prayer. The two suwar therefore begin on the same page opening. In later Qurans, the entire text of this initial section was enclosed in decorative borders, and the calligraphy itself was superimposed on a background of swirling patterns.

Illuminators also focused on the breaks between the *ayat* (sing: *ayah*), or verses, which made up these suwar. This provided a useful guide for those reciting the text, because the verses were of varying lengths. Different symbols were used, but rosettes or *shamsahs* (sunbursts)

Left In the most expensive Qurans, the decorations were highlighted in gold, silver and lapis lazuli. This 13th-century manuscript from Egypt is a particularly fine example.

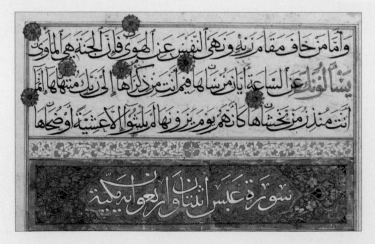

were common. In addition, artists added more elaborate symbols in the margins, to denote every fifth and tenth *ayah*. These symbols mainly took the form of circular rosettes or tear-shaped medallions, with a brief inscription in the inner roundel.

OTHER DECORATION

Many Quran manuscripts also contained marginal designs, which were used in the passages to indicate where ritual prostration was required. Here, the word *sajdah* was inscribed in an ornamental setting. There was no

Below In later Qurans, the margins were often filled with lavish borders. This 18th-century manuscript was commissioned by the Sultan of Morocco.

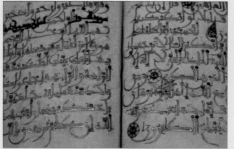

Above A double-page section from a 14th-century Quran produced in North Africa. The ayah divisions are marked by rosettes and the script is Maghribi.

fixed format for this marking, although medallions and stars were popular choices. A more unusual variation can be found in a Mamluk Quran commissioned by Sultan Barquq. Here, the *sajdah*

inscriptions were contained in a tiny image of a mosque.

LATER ERAS

The space given over to illumination in Quran manuscripts continued to expand and from the 14th century, extraordinary double pages of pattern were created. Some of these pages were designed to list the number of verses contained in the individual volume (the text of the Quran was frequently divided into 30 separate volumes).

Qurans were still copied out by hand in the 19th century, many years after the advent of printing, and calligraphers continued to use classic archaic scripts, such as *kufic* and *thuluth*, after they were no longer in general use.

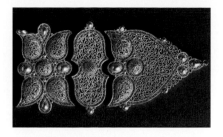

CHAPTER 11

THE FATIMIDS

In the 10th century, the Fatimids, a dynasty based in North Africa and claiming descent from the Prophet's daughter Fatima, challenged the rule of the Abbasids in Baghdad and established a rival caliphate. The Fatimids belonged to the Shiah Muslim sect known as the Ismailis, and did not recognize the authority of the Abbasids who, in turn, regarded the Fatimids as heretics. The Fatimids governed first from Tunisia, and then created a new capital at Cairo, in Egypt, which became the pre-eminent city in the Islamic world. At the height of their power, the Fatimids ruled a prosperous empire that reached north to Syria, west along the North African coast, and south to the Hijaz and Yemen on the Arabian peninsula. With a wide geographical spread through much of the Mediterranean world, Fatimid art was influenced by the late-antique figurative traditions of the classical world. Written accounts from the Fatimid era describe incredible levels of luxury and sophistication at their court, while luxury objects made from intricately carved wood, ivory and rock crystal and lustreware ceramics were also produced for the cosmopolitan merchant elite.

Opposite The Fatimid al-Azhar Mosque dates right back to the foundation of al-Qahira (Cairo) in 969. It was a great centre of Shiah Islam and became one of the Islamic world's premier universities.

Above Fatimid gold work was exported far and wide: this piece was found in Ashkelon (now in Israel). The Fatimid caliph reputedly sat behind a golden filigree screen during court ceremonies.

THE FATIMID CALIPHATE

THE FATIMID CAPITAL OF AL-QAHIRA (THE VICTORIOUS), NOW
KNOWN AS CAIRO, WAS A WALLED PALACE CITY CENTRED ON THE
CALIPH'S RESIDENCE AND A CONGREGATIONAL MOSQUE.

The Fatimids emerged as an Ismaili sectarian movement in Tunisia. There, in 909, Ubayd Allah declared himself the Mahdi, or Holy One, and founded a Fatimid Caliphate in their temporary capital, Raqqada. The dynasty claimed sacred descent from Ali, the Prophet's son-in-law, and his wife Fatima, the Prophet's daughter – from whom the name Fatimids derives.

Supported by missionary activity around the Islamic world, the Caliphate quickly grew, and in 921 Ubayd Allah built the splendid palace city of Mahdia on the Tunisian coast. He was succeeded as ruler by al-Qaim (934–46), al-Mansur (946–53) and al-Muizz (953–75). During al-Muizz's reign, the Fatimids moved eastward to conquer the Ikhshidid governors of Egypt, and in 969 al-Muizz ordered General Jawhar al-Siqilli to found a new dynastic capital on the Nile, to be called al-Qahira 'the Victorious' and now known as Cairo.

This walled settlement was a proud statement of the power and ambition of a youthful dynasty. The walls, which had eight gates set into them, enclosed a large area measuring 1,100m by 1,150m (3,610ft by 3,773ft).

TWIN PALACES

A broad street called Bayn al-Qasrayn ('between the two palaces') ran through the middle of the city. Across this street, two royal palaces faced each other; the Eastern Palace larger than the more

Above An 11th-century wall painting from a bathhouse near Cairo depicts a young man drinking wine. In secular settings, figurative art was common.

secluded Western Palace. The Bayn al-Qasrayn was a parade ground where elaborate processions and public ceremonies were held to celebrate religious holidays and other significant dates, such as the start of the agricultural year.

According to contemporary accounts, these palaces were beautifully planned and furnished, with cloisters of marble and rooms bedecked with the finest textiles. The gardens, which were set within high walls, had artificial trees carved from precious metal with

Below At its greatest extent, the Fatimid Caliphate stretched across North Africa and into the Arabian peninsula. Sicily was also part of the Caliphate.

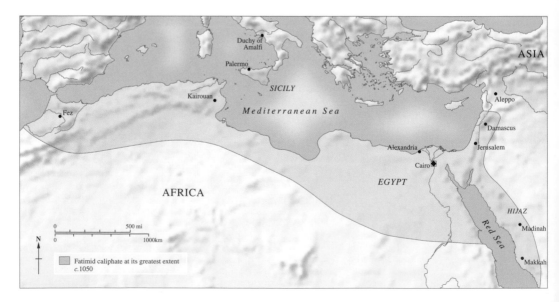

clockwork singing birds. The 11th-century Persian traveller Nasir-i Khusrau visited the Western Palace in 1049, and reported seeing a raised dais carved with hunting scenes and fine calligraphy, a golden balustrade and silver steps.

During a financial crisis in 1068, the unpaid Fatimid army rose up and looted the Fatimid treasury, where they found huge numbers of precious luxury items – and promptly sold them on the open market to the great astonishment of the Cairo public.

MOSQUES

The magnificent Mosque of al-Hakim was begun in 990, under the rule of Caliph al-Aziz, and finished in 1012, by Caliph al-Hakim (reigned 996–1021). Four arcades enclose a courtyard. Within the prayer hall there are five bays: the bay before the *mihrab*, or prayer niche, and, unusually, the two corner bays at each end of the *qibla* wall that indicates the direction of prayer are domed. The outer walls are surmounted by battlements, and there is a three-part façade with a monumental entrance gateway, plus a spectacular minaret at each end – one circular and one square. The design of the façade was derived from that of the Great Mosque (916) in Mahdia.

UNDER THE VIZIERS

In the late 11th and 12th centuries, the power of the Fatimid caliphs weakened. Cairo was governed by its viziers, or ministers. One of these was Badr al-Jamali, vizier to Caliph al-Mustansir (reigned 1036–96), who rebuilt and extended the city walls. The splendid fortified gates of Bab al-Nasr and Bab al-Futuh are from this period. Bab al-Futuh has twin towers 8m (26ft) high, rising to a battlement with a parapet. It was built with the latest defensive features, such as machicolation (small

Above Bab al-Futuh (the Gate of Victories) was built in 1096 for vizier Badr al-Jamali by Armenian builders.

openings through which to drop missiles to enemy forces).

Mamun al-Bataihi, another vizier of al-Mustansir, founded the remarkable Aqmar Mosque in Cairo in 1125. This mosque has a decorated façade with a central porch bearing a medallion inscribed with the names of Muhammad and Ali – who is revered by Shiahs as the first Imam – at its centre.

A distinctive aspect of Fatimid architecture in Egypt is the building of lavish mausolea. The Fatimids and their fellow Shiah contemporaries in Iran, the Buyids, were the first rulers in Islamic history to build funerary monuments. Shiah Islam encourages religious devotions at the tombs of saints and Imams, while orthodox Sunni Muslims are discouraged from venerating any human forebears. For this reason, the building of mausolea was initially found

FATIMIDS IN JERUSALEM

In 969, the Fatimids captured Jerusalem. They rebuilt the citadel, and in 1035 Caliph al-Zahir rebuilt the al-Aqsa Mosque, which had been destroyed by an earthquake two years earlier, in the form in which it survives today. Deciding to promote Jerusalem as a pilgrimage site to rival the holy cities of Makkah and Madinah, Fatimid rulers encouraged writers to create works about the beauties of Jerusalem, and a new genre came into being: *Fada'il al-Quds* (Songs in Praise of Jerusalem).

more in the Shiah tradition than in Sunni Islam. The Fatimid caliphs were buried in a splendid dynastic tomb in the Eastern Palace, but their wealthier subjects built many tombs, principally to celebrate Shiah martyrs and saints in large cemeteries at Aswan and Cairo.

ROCK CRYSTAL

THE FATIMIDS VALUED ROCK CRYSTAL BOTH FOR ITS BEAUTY AND ITS 'MAGICAL' POWERS. ASTOUNDING QUANTITIES OF THIS PRIZED MATERIAL WERE FOUND IN THE FATIMID TREASURY.

Above A crescent carved from rock crystal is mounted in a 14th-century European silver and enamel monstrance. A kufic inscription carved into the crystal gives the name of the Fatimid Caliph al-Zahir.

Several deposits of rock crystal, a transparent quartz, can be found across the Middle East and Asia. Writing in the early 11th century, the Persian scholar and scientist al-Biruni stated that the finest pieces of rock crystal were produced at Basra in Iraq and that the raw material was imported from the Laccadive and Maldive islands and from the islands of Zanj in East Africa. The Iranian traveller Nasir-i Khusrau, who visited Cairo in 1046 and saw rock crystal being carved in the lamp market, mentions that Yemen was the source of the purest rock crystal but that lesser quality crystal was also imported from North Africa and India.

THE CRAFTSMEN

Rock crystal is a hard mineral that requires great expertise to carve. Skilled lapidaries from Basra probably migrated to Cairo to seek the patronage of the Fatimid court, just as the potters are known to have done. The craftsmen cut blocks of crystal roughly the shape of the vessel they intended to make and then laboriously drilled out the interior, leaving walls of remarkable thinness before carving the decoration and polishing the exterior.

Right Carvings of a large bird of prey attacking a horned deer appear on this 10th–11th-century ewer from Cairo. The carvings symbolize the power of the ruler over his enemies.

THE FATIMID TREASURY

When the Fatimid palace was looted in 1068–69, many of the valuable artefacts that had been concealed in the storerooms were dispersed. The *Kitab al-Hadaya wa al-Tuhaf* (Book of Gifts and Rarities), compiled in the 11th century, refers to the gifts exchanged between Muslim and non-Muslim rulers and officials. It contains an eyewitness account of some of the items that were removed. The author refers to 36,000 objects of glass and rock crystal that were found in the treasury, but also lists a number of specific rock-crystal objects, including a spouted ewer of smooth rock crystal with a handle carved from the same block, a large storage jar with images carved in high relief, and a box with a lid cut from a single block of rock crystal, made to store small rock crystal dishes.

The same source that listed the precious items dispersed from the Fatimid treasury also described how these objects were sold in the local markets and bazaars and also sold to the courts of neighbouring countries, such as Spain and Sicily, as well as the Byzantine court in Constantinople. Many of these rock-crystal pieces ended up in church treasuries across Europe, often as containers for storing saintly relics.

SURVIVING TREASURES

Several of the surviving pieces contain inscriptions naming their patrons, who include two caliphs and a general. Eight complete ewers have survived, each one of similar pear-shaped form, carved with pairs of animals beside scrolling foliage and with an intricately pierced handle topped with an animal as a thumb rest. One of these ewers, now in the treasury of San Marco in Venice, Italy, bears a dedicatory inscription to Caliph al-Aziz (reigned 975–96). It is carved with face-to-face lions, the quintessential symbol of royalty. Another ewer, decorated with a pair of birds with elegant curving necks and long beaks, was commissioned for Husayn ibn Jawhar, a general of Caliph al-Hakim. The final inscribed piece is a curious crescent-shaped object that may have been mounted on a horse's bridle as a royal emblem; it contains the titles of Caliph al-Zahir (reigned 1021–36). Other types of objects made from rock crystal include lamps, small bottles that probably contained precious oils, chess pieces and small animal figures.

Right This rock crystal ewer from Fatimid Cairo, carved with a pair of birds below a kufic inscription, is now in the Musée du Louvre, Paris.

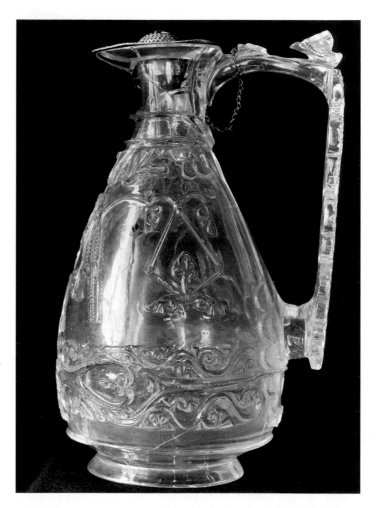

MAGICAL LINKS

Although rock crystal was valued for its aesthetic qualities, it was also held in great esteem by the Fatimids, along with other cultures, because they believed it had magical properties linked with its similarity to water and air. In fact, the Arabic name for 'rock crystal', *maha*, is a synthesis of the two components of which it was believed to be made: *ma,* or 'water' and *hawa,* or 'air'. The Persian-born author and judge al-Qazwini (1203–83) explained that kings preferred to drink out of rock-crystal vessels because they had the power to prevent them from ever becoming thirsty. In the Quran, there are two passages that describe how cups of rock crystal filled with pure water will be offered to the believers in paradise.

Left This rock crystal ewer, now broken, was inscribed with the titles of Husayn ibn Jawhar, a general of Caliph al-Hakim who held the title from 1000 until 1008.

WOOD AND IVORY CARVING

THE SKILLED ARTISANS OF FATIMID EGYPT CREATED SUPERB CARVED WOOD AND IVORY PIECES, PRODUCING INTRICATE ABSTRACT GEOMETRIC DESIGNS AND LIVELY FIGURAL DEPICTIONS.

Several beautiful carved wooden friezes once graced the lavish Western Palace of the Fatimid caliphs in Cairo. The palace was abandoned after the fall of the Fatimid dynasty in 1171, and later made part of the Hospital of the Mamluk Sultan Qalawun (completed 1284). The friezes were discovered by chance during restoration work on the hospital, and, remarkably, are all that survives of the once magnificent setting of the Fatimid court as described in medieval accounts.

SECULAR WOODCARVING

The surviving fragments are typical of Fatimid secular woodcarving in representing the pleasures of court life, such as hunting, musical entertainment, dancing and drinking wine. Human and animal figures are framed by winding plant tendrils or interlaced geometric patterns, and sometimes also by bands of calligraphic inscriptions.

One splendid frieze depicts a hunter spearing a lion and a courtier pouring wine while another plays a pipe. It has a recurring image of long-eared hares and a perched bird, a characteristic element in Fatimid figurative decorations. Fragments of paint found on the frieze suggest that it was once coloured blue with the figures highlighted in red.

Another frieze shows two gazelles, with beautifully fluid heads, horns and haunches. The figurative representations of animals and people

Left This portable mihrab *(1133) from the Mausoleum of Sayyida Ruqayya has wooden panels carved with six-pointed stars, a design known as the star-shaped medallion.*

Above Fluid horses' necks and heads emerge from a delicate geometric pattern on this teak door panel carved by Fatimid artisans in the 11th century.

produced by Fatimid artists in wood-carving are generally more fluid and vital than the stiff images created by earlier Islamic craftsmen.

CARVED *MIHRABS*

One of the best surviving examples of sacred woodcarving is the *mihrab* from the Mausoleum of Sayyida Ruqayya in the Southern Cemetery in Cairo, built in 1154–60. Sayyida Ruqayya was a daughter of Ali, husband of the Prophet's daughter Fatima, though another of Ali's wives was her mother. She went to Cairo with her stepsister Zaynab and the two women are seen as being among the city's patron saints.

Sayyida Ruqayya's tomb is a *mashhad*, or pilgrimage shrine, much visited by Shiah Muslims. The *mihrab* has been removed from the shrine and is housed in the Islamic Museum in Cairo, but a fine wooden screen remains in the shrine.

Another beautiful wooden *mihrab* now in the museum was taken from the Fatimid shrine to Sayyida Nafisa (great-granddaughter of the Prophet's grandson Hasan), who died in Fustat in 824. While alive, she gained a reputation for piety and for performing miracles, and during the Fatimid era her shrine was a great attraction for Shiah pilgrims, who sought to benefit from her *baraka* (divine blessing).

Fatimid wooden panels and fragments of friezes carved with animals also survive. Two rectangular panels, probably originally set within a door, are deeply carved with the sinuous necks and heads of a pair of horses, each wearing a decorated bridle. The panels were carved to different depths, a skilled technique mastered by Fatimid craftsmen and used to work both wood and ivory. One panel is in the Metropolitan Museum, New York, and the other in the Islamic Museum in Cairo.

LUXURY WORK

Whereas in some parts of the Islamic world, such as Turkey and northern Iran, wood was common and was used as a basic building material, in Egypt it was scarce; the woods used for the fine Fatimid carvings that have survived, which include acacia, box, cedar, cypress, ebony, pine and teak, would all have been imported.

As well as palace friezes and internal mosque features, such as wall-mounted wooden *mihrabs*, the woodcarvers of the Fatimid court also produced ceiling rafters, door panels, mosque furniture, caskets and portable *mihrabs*. Large pieces were inlaid with

ivory. Wooden furniture and fittings from mosques were often reused not only because the wood was scarce but also because it had acquired a degree of sanctity from its sacred setting.

IVORY CARVINGS

Fatimid Egypt was a great centre for ivory carving in the Islamic world because of its proximity to the main source of the material in East Africa. Craftsmen in Egypt were concentrated in Fustat in particular, but Fatimid ivory carvers were also at work in what are now Tunisia and Sicily.

Carvers produced inlay panels to decorate objects made from wood, together with small ivory items, such as caskets, combs and chess pieces. They also carved delicate decorations on to pieces of elephant tusk. Initially, only the broad end of the tusk was decorated, but later examples are carved along the whole length. These items – which are often called 'oliphants' from the archaic English word for 'elephant' – were exported to many countries of Christian Europe.

Larger ivory carvings – intended to be inset in wooden furniture or used as room decoration – were similar in style to

Left This carved ivory figure was made at Fustat, Egypt, the principal centre of ivory carving in Fatimid times.

Above This detail from a Fatimid ivory plaque in the Museum of Islamic Art in Berlin shows a figure drinking at a banquet.

those found on woodcarving. They represented scenes of court life featuring huntsmen and animals, dancers and musicians, all so delicately rendered that the details of an animal's fur or the fall of a dancer's costume can be clearly seen.

Four ivory panels in Berlin are carved with a range of different figures enjoying the pleasures of a banquet with wine and musical entertainment all set against a sinuous vine scroll dripping with bunches of grapes. Whether working in wood or ivory, the Fatimid artisans demonstrated a supreme mastery of their materials.

SICILY

ARTISTS FROM THE FATIMID EMPIRE WORKED FOR THE NORMAN
LORDS OF SICILY IN THE 11TH AND 12TH CENTURIES, MOST
PROMINENTLY IN THE CAPPELLA PALATINA (PALATINE CHAPEL).

At the start of the Fatimid era in 909, the island of Sicily was largely under the control of the Aghlabid amirs of Tunisia. They had first attacked Byzantine-held Sicily in 827, but the conquest of the island took almost 140 years, until 965. Under their rule the island thrived: Palermo replaced Syracuse as capital and became one of the great cities of the Islamic Mediterranean world. Architects converted Palermo's basilica into a great mosque and made the former citadel into a splendid royal palace.

Infighting made the amirate vulnerable, and Norman warlord Robert de Hauteville (also known as Guiscard), with his brother Roger, conquered Sicily in 1072. Roger reigned as Count of Sicily in 1072–1101 and was succeeded by his sons Simon (count in 1101–05) and Roger II, who was count from 1105 and then, with papal backing, was crowned King of Sicily in Palermo on Christmas Day 1130.

His glorious coronation mantle made of red silk interwoven with pearls and gold thread must have been made after his coronation, because it bears an inscription with the Hijra date 528, which corresponds to 1133–34. This unique textile depicts two mirror-images of a lion attacking a camel. At this time, the products of the textile workshop in Roger's palace became famous far beyond Palermo.

THE PALATINE CHAPEL

Muslim craftsmen served at the Christian court of Roger II. In 1132–40, Roger had a magnificent chapel built at the royal palace. Dedicated to St Peter, the Palatine Chapel has splendid floors, elegant Byzantine wall mosaics and a grand wooden ceiling painted in tempera in a style similar to frescoes in the 9th-century palaces of Abbasid Samarra and contemporary paintings in royal buildings in Fatimid Cairo. There are almost

Above Water flowed down the shadirwan at the summer palace of La Zisa in the Jannat al-Ardh hunting grounds.

1,000 paintings covering a profusion of *muqarnas* (small vaults arranged in tiers). They mainly depict the pleasures of life at an Islamic court, with images of kings served by attendants, noblemen playing backgammon or chess, dancers, wrestlers, courtiers drinking wine, elephants, beasts of prey and exotic birds, processions, and scenes of racing and hunting. The architectural backgrounds to the images are mostly the arcades and domed roofs of an Islamic palace city.

There are also scenes associated with the zodiac and mythology, such as sirens, griffins and sphinxes. The pictures have beaded edgings and the bands between the images contain *kufic* inscriptions that wish fame, great power and charity on the chapel patron. Other rooms in the palace are as magnificent. The Roger Hall has mosaics depicting

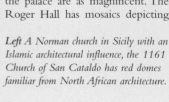

Left A Norman church in Sicily with an Islamic architectural influence, the 1161 Church of San Cataldo has red domes familiar from North African architecture.

and drew a celebrated world map in 1154, probably the most accurate made in the medieval period. Known as the 'Tabula Rogeriana', the map shows all of Eurasia and northern Africa. Al-Idrisi also wrote a geographical work named the *Nuzhat al-Mushtaq*, which appears to contain an account of Muslim sailors crossing the Atlantic and landing in the Americas, where they encountered natives 'with red skin'. He also made a silver planisphere, a circular device for demonstrating the shift of the constellations and the signs of the zodiac.

SUMMER PALACES

The Norman lords hunted in the Jannat al-Ardh ('Paradise of the Earth'), the Kalbid estates outside Palermo's city walls. They laid out summer palaces which, like the Umayyad desert palaces, were set within agricultural fields, in this case, of date palms, citrus and olive trees. The summer palace of La Zisa was built in the last years of the Fatimid era, in 1166.

As was typical of country palaces in the Islamic world, water played a major role at La Zisa: the building had pools around it, and an elegant *shadirwan*, or fountain room.

Above In the Palatine Chapel, fine Byzantine mosaics adorn the end and side walls, while Fatimid-style paintings decorate the ceiling above the nave.

stylized landscapes that feature lions, peacocks, palm trees and leopards.

The co-existence of Christian and Muslim iconography is striking in the Palatine Chapel. The scenes of Fatimid court life in the *muqarnas* suggest that Fatimid culture and the magnificent city of Cairo were the primary reference point in the Mediterranean for those who aspired to courtly splendour. Furthermore, it is

noteworthy that Roger II, who was seeking to enhance the dignity of his position by building an impressive sacred space, turned to Fatimid artists and architects.

MEDIEVAL WORLD MAP

Roger was also a patron of great Islamic scholars and writers, such as the geographer Muhammad al-Idrisi (1100–66), who worked at the court in Palermo for 18 years

Right Muhammad al-Idrisi's world map, known as the 'Tabula Rogeriana', was the most accurate map of its day. North is at the bottom.

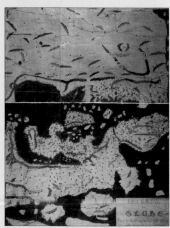

CHAPTER 12

FROM THE SAMANIDS TO THE SELJUKS

From the 9th century onward, the Abbasid Caliphate's provinces in Greater Iran were controlled by local governors, such as the Samanids and Ghaznavids, who became increasingly independent from Baghdad. In the great Iranian cities of the period – Isfahan, Samarkand, Merv, Balkh, Nishapur, Herat and Rayy – Persian cultural traditions became dominant in art and architecture, and a taste for sophisticated objects developed, perhaps owing to an increasingly wealthy and discerning merchant bourgeoisie. The 11th century saw the arrival in the region of the Seljuk Turks, tribesmen from the Central Asian steppes who initially served in the armies of Samanid and Ghaznavid sultans. The Seljuks carved out a vast territory stretching from north-eastern Iran to Anatolia and then, following steppe traditions of power-sharing, they divided their empire between the Great Seljuks, who controlled Iran (1040–1194), Iraq and Syria, and the Anatolian Seljuks, who built an empire in the former Byzantine territory (1081–1307) of Anatolia. Rulers of both Seljuk empires were energetic builders of monumental architecture.

Opposite The south iwan (hall) of the four-iwan Friday Mosque at Isfahan is in the direction of Makkah and leads into the domed sanctuary, behind, built by Nizam al-Mulk in 1086–87.

Above An elegant Quranic inscription in turquoise-glazed tiles on the side of the towering Minaret of Jam, built in the late 12th century in Afghanistan by Muhammad Ghur.

THE SAMANID DYNASTY

THE SAMANID RULERS FOSTERED AN IMPORTANT REVIVAL OF
PERSIAN CULTURE – IN POTTERY, CALLIGRAPHY, METALWORK AND
TEXTILES, FOR EXAMPLE – DURING THE 9TH AND 10TH CENTURIES.

The Samanids first rose to prominence as local governors in Transoxiana (a province spanning modern-day Tajikistan, Uzbekistan and Turkmenistan) under the Tahirids, who served the Abbasid caliphs in Baghdad. The dynasty took its name from Saman Khuda, an 8th-century feudal aristocrat from the province of Balkh in Afghanistan who had served the Abbasid governor of Khurasan. According to many accounts, Saman was a Zoroastrian who converted to Sunni Islam.

In the early 9th century, Saman's grandsons Ahmad, Nuh, Yahya and Elyas helped to defeat an uprising against Abbasid Caliph al-Mamun (reigned 786–833) and in return were given the provinces of Ferghana, Samarkand, Shash and Herat. The Samanids reached the peak of their power under Ahmad's son Ismail Samani (reigned 892–907). Ismail defeated Amr, the Saffarid ruler of Khurasan, in 900, and the following year defeated Muhammad b. Zaid, ruler of

Tabaristan, thus conquering new territory across northern Iran to add to the provinces of Khurasan and Transoxiana. Ismail made his capital at Bukhara (now in Uzbekistan).

The Samanids were staunch Sunni Muslims and were opposed to, and tried to repress, the Ismaili strand of Shiah Islam promoted by their Fatimid contemporaries. Under Samanid rule thousands of Turkish tribesmen converted to Islam. The dynasty claimed descent from the pre-Islamic Sasanian shahs, and were keen sponsors of Persian culture, overseeing a renaissance in art, architecture and literature and the emergence of New Persian as a literary language.

SAMANID ARCHITECTURE

The finest monument of the Samanid era is the mausoleum in Bukhara. It is traditionally associated with Ismail Samani, but may also have been used as a tomb for later Samanid princes. It takes the form of a tapering cube built from bricks topped with an

Above The mausoleum of Ismail Samani and the Samanid rulers in Bukhara now stands alone but was once at the centre of a substantial complex.

elegant hemispherical dome rising from a flat roof with a small cupola at each corner. Both within and without, the mausoleum is notable for its intricate brickwork and the symmetry of its design.

PERSIAN CULTURE

The wealth and sophistication of this period survives in the luxury objects that are known today. Samanid potters produced fine work in the cities of Samarkand and Nishapur, reviving ancient Persian imperial iconography, such as bulls' heads, mounted horse riders, birds and lions, but also courting Islamic culture through the use of pithy Arabic calligraphy. Metalwork of the period also made self-conscious reference to Sasanian artistic traditions, as did textiles. A remarkable pictorial silk fragment, depicting elephants, camels and peacocks, generally known as the St Josse silk, was made for an amir of Khurasan, Abu Mansur Bukhtegin, in c.955.

Left Nuh-Gunbadh Mosque, now in ruins, was one of 40 mosques built in Balkh in the 9th century. This fine example of Samanid architecture was influenced by earlier styles.

Ghaznavid patronage. Another great poet of the era was Rudaki (859–*c*.941), who served at the court of Samanid ruler Nasr II (reigned 914–43). He is celebrated as one of the founders of modern Persian literature and reputedly wrote more than 1.3 million verses.

FALL FROM POWER

From *c*.950 onward, the rulers of the vast Samanid empire began to lose their power, challenged by palace rebellions and external threats from the Qarakhanid Turks to the east. The Samanids were finally defeated by the Ghaznavids, who ruled from Ghazni (modern-day Ghazna in Afghanistan, south of Kabul) and had previously served them as governors.

First, Mahmud of Ghazni (998–1030) led a revolt, deposed Samanid ruler Mansur II (reigned 997–99), and took Khurasan to found the Ghaznavid Empire, which eventually extended as far east as the border with India. The final Samanid ruler was Ismail II, who failed to counter Mahmud and was killed in 1005.

THE FAME OF BUKHARA

Bukhara was a major city and centre of learning under the Samanids. With a population of more than 300,000, it was the largest city of central Asia and, for a period, rivalled Córdoba, Baghdad and Cairo as one of the foremost cities of the world. It was a principal centre of Sufi Islam, particularly of the Naqshbandi Order.

Bukhara is known for its scholars. It is the birthplace of Muhammad al-Bukhari (810–70), revered by Sunni Muslims as the author of *Sahih Bukhari*, a collection of *hadith*,

or sayings, of Muhammad that is considered the most authentic of all extant books of *hadith*. The great polymath ibn Sina (980–1037) was born near Bukhara in the Samanid era. Known in the West as Avicenna, he was a major philosopher as well as the author of the *Canon of Medicine*, used as a textbook for medical students in European universities until the 17th century.

The national poet of Iran, Firdawsi (*c*.935–*c*.1020), was born and worked under the Samanid rulers, although he completed his masterwork, the *Shahnama*, under

Above This detail of the St Josse silk shroud shows a pair of elephants and part of an inscription praising an amir of Khurasan who died in 961.

SAMANID POTTERY

NISHAPUR AND SAMARKAND WERE MAJOR POTTERY CENTRES IN THE
10TH CENTURY, PRODUCING WHITE SLIPWARES WITH CALLIGRAPHIC
DESIGNS AND POLYCHROME WARES WITH FIGURAL DECORATION.

Excavations made in the cities of
Nishapur and Samarkand have
uncovered kilns along with other
evidence of pottery production.
Samanid pottery was made using
slip technology, where a fine clay
diluted with water, known as 'slip',
was poured over the earthenware
body of the vessel to form a
smooth, even layer. When dry, the
surface was decorated with more
slip that had been coloured by
adding different oxides to the
mixture. Finally, a transparent lead
glaze was applied over the ware,
which was used to seal in the slip
colours and intensify their hue.

EPIGRAPHIC STYLE
Some of the most impressive
examples of Islamic ceramics were
made during this period in both
Samarkand and Nishapur. Using a
variety of different styles of *kufic*
calligraphy, the potters inscribed
various aphorisms, or proverbs,
around the walls of large flat dishes
or deep bowls. Wares decorated in
this fashion are known as
epigraphic pottery. Sometimes
the letters were stretched and
elaborately decorated with
knots and foliated terminals
in order to fit the
proportions of the vessel.
The background colour
was generally white and
the calligraphy was usually
applied in a dark brownish
black, sometimes with

*Right The kufic inscription
on this large 10th–11th century
earthenware dish reads: 'The taste of
science is bitter at first but sweeter than
honey in the end.'*

accents appearing in tomato
red. However, in a few examples
this palette is reversed, so that
white calligraphy stands out from
a dark background. Occasional
birds, drawn with spare, bold lines
and sometimes enclosing the word
baraka, meaning 'blessing', are the
only variants found in these wares.

POLYCHROMATIC WARES
In complete contrast to the
monochromatic palette that was
used for producing epigraphic ware,
a colourful and highly patterned
polychromatic ware seems to have
been the speciality of Nishapur. On
these bowls, a vivid yellow colour
serves as a background to a riot of
human figures, animals, birds and
floral motifs arranged in hectic
rotating patterns, which were
coloured in green, dark brown and
with touches of brick red. The wide
range of decorative themes was

*Above Over time the epigraphic style
used in Nishapur and Samarkand
evolved and red was added to enhance
the monochromatic palette. This late
10th–11th-century bowl is decorated
with dark brown and red slips.*

probably drawn from local myths
and folklore: many of the figures
wear Persian costume and hold
objects that have been associated
with Zoroastrian ritual. Other
pieces have explicitly Christian
motifs, such as Nestorian crosses.

ESTABLISHING DATES
Unfortunately, the archaeologists at
Nishapur could not establish a clear
chronology for these two
contrasting types of pottery.
However, Richard Bulliet
(b. 1940), an American
historian who specializes in
medieval Islamic history,
looked at the dated coins
and types of ceramic
excavated with them at
three sites and deduced
that more epigraphic
pottery was found in the
earlier sites and more
figural ware in the later
sites. He extrapolated from
this distribution that the
epigraphic ware appealed to the
earliest settlers and converts who
read Arabic and wanted to uphold

wares; Nishapuri potters do not seem to have had access to cobalt so substituted manganese, which produced a dark purplish colour, but combined with green splashes it produced a fair imitation.

Another popular type of ware excavated in Nishapur, but with a wide distribution across the Middle East and probably made in many centres, was splashed ware. It was made with either a plain surface or with an incised design that is sometimes described as 'sgraffiato' (Italian for 'scratched'). Such pieces were covered with white slip, and then metallic oxides were used to produce various colours: copper for vivid green, iron for yellow-brown and manganese for purple were splashed on to the surface in stripes or spots. One of the few datable vessels is a jar from Susa, which contained a hoard of coins, the latest one dated 955–56.

the traditions of the Abbasid court, whereas the colourful, figurative ware appealed to the indigenous population who were trying to maintain their Persian traditions. Bulliet even suggested that the different shapes of each type of ware represented the different dietary traditions of these two groups: the large flat dishes and bowls with calligraphic decoration were perfect for serving typically Arab dishes of rice and grilled meat, while the rounded bowls of the figurative ware were better suited to the more liquid Persian dishes.

FOREIGN INFLUENCES
The excavations at Nishapur also uncovered large numbers of imported Iraqi wares, such as lustreware pieces and blue-and-white ware with green splashes. The potters of Nishapur had tried to imitate both types, but it is clear they did not have access to the necessary ingredients or the specialized knowledge and were forced to approximate the techniques with locally available materials. They used a yellow-green slip and a glossy transparent glaze to imitate the colour and sheen of lustreware and copied the distinctive style of decoration closely. The same was the case with the blue-and-white

Above The swirling leaf scroll on this 10th–11th-century shallow bowl replaces the more usual band of calligraphy. It was painted in manganese slip.

Below This Nishapuri 10th–11th-century bowl shows a figure on a horse with a cheetah on its rump. Birds, rosettes and calligraphic elements are scattered around the background.

THE GHAZNAVID AND GHURID DYNASTIES

DURING THE 10TH CENTURY, THE GHAZNAVIDS QUICKLY ESTABLISHED A BROAD EMPIRE AND MADE INROADS INTO NORTHERN INDIA. IN THE 12TH CENTURY, THEY WERE SUPPLANTED BY THE GHURIDS.

By the 10th century, the political cohesion of the Islamic world was beginning to disintegrate. In the east, the Ghaznavids eventually became the dominant power, ruling from 962 until 1186. This Turkic dynasty originated from a corps of slave-guards who had served the Samanids and eventually supplanted them. From their capital at Ghazni in Afghanistan, they built up a considerable empire, which, at its height, included most of Iran, Afghanistan, Khurasan and parts of northern India.

GHAZNAVID BUILDINGS
The royal strongholds built by the Ghaznavids seem to have been modelled on those in Abbasid Samarra, in Iraq. This is certainly obvious in Lashkari Bazaar (Qalah-i

Bust), a meandering complex of 11th-century palatial buildings that stretched for several miles along the banks of the river Helmand in south-western Afghanistan. These are now largely in ruins, although the remains of the winter palace, with its four *iwans* (vaulted halls) and its painted frieze of bodyguards, are still impressive.

The most tangible surviving reminders of Ghaznavid power can be seen in a number of remarkable towers. In Ghazni itself are the lower sections of two imposing, early 12th-century minarets. One was built by Masud III (reigned 1099–1114) and the other by his son, Bahram Shah (reigned 1118–52). Constructed in a similar style on a star-shaped plan, the minarets are decorated with inscriptions and geometric patterns

Above Dating from 1007, the tower of Gunbad-i Qabus was a potent symbol of power. Its stark, brick surface was adorned with just two bands of kufic *script.*

created in brickwork. More impressive still is the Gunbad-i-Qabus, the best preserved of all the Islamic tomb towers. Located in north-eastern Iran, the tower was commissioned by a local Ziyarid ruler, Qabus ibn Wushngir. Cylindrical in shape, the tower has ten triangular flanges around the exterior and a very striking and austere appearance.

Nominally at least, the tower was meant to be Qabus's tomb, but at over 60m (197ft) high the sheer size of the structure ensured that it was also an affirmation of his political strength. It is not clear if Qabus was ever buried there, but a medieval account claims that his body was placed in a glass coffin suspended from the roof.

THE GHURIDS
In 1186, the Ghaznavids were displaced by the Ghurids, who took their name from their native

Above A story from the Shahnama *is depicted on this 13th-century Kashan stonepaste cup.*

FIRDAWSI
The poet Firdawsi (*c*.935–*c*.1020) is one of the most celebrated figures in Iranian culture. His masterpiece is the 60,000 couplet epic *Shahnama* (Book of Kings), a monumental account of Persia's early history. Firdawsi is said to have laboured on the project for more than 30 years, beginning it under the Samanids in 977, but only completing it in the Ghaznavid era in 1010. Drawn from earlier accounts and oral sources, the *Shahnama* describes the kings, queens and heroes of pre-Islamic Iran. This beguiling mixture of history and legend provided Islamic artists with a fertile source for illustration in manuscript copies of the stories and in other media.

province (Ghur) in Afghanistan. Like their predecessors, they extended their control over large swathes of Afghanistan, Iran and northern India. They owed much of their influence to the military success of Muhammad of Ghur (1162–1206), who conquered Lahore in 1186.

The Ghurids are associated with two famous minarets, both of which are registered as World Heritage Sites by Unesco. The oldest of these is the Minaret of Jam, which dates back to the 12th century. It is hidden away in a remote Afghan valley – in fact, it is so remote that the tower was forgotten by the authorities until a boundary commission rediscovered it in 1886. Jam stands close to the river Hari Rud. The leaning shaft of the minaret is liberally adorned with decorative panels of calligraphy that cite all of Surah 19 of the Quran.

The purpose of this isolated minaret has been the source of considerable speculation. It is possible that it stands on the site of Firuz Kuh, the ancient summer capital of the Ghurids, and was once associated with a mosque there. Alternatively, it may have been built as a symbol of Islam's victory and never used for calling the faithful to prayer.

The huge minaret of Qutb Minar in Delhi was constructed on an even grander scale. Built on the site of an old Jain temple, it was attached to the Quwwat al-Islam ('Might of Islam') Mosque, the first great Muslim foundation on the Indian subcontinent. The 73m (240ft) high minaret dates from 1202, with many subsequent additions, and is made of red sandstone. The fluted columns of the tapering shaft owe much to local architectural traditions, but the decoration is truly Islamic, consisting of carved ornamental bands of floral, geometric and calligraphic designs.

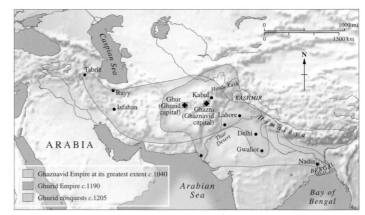

Above The Ghaznavid Empire reached its peak in c.1040 and stretched into most of Iran. The Ghurids displaced the Ghaznavids and by c.1205 had conquered most of northern India.

Below The Minaret of Jam is the finest surviving example of Ghurid architecture. Built for Ghiyath al-Din (1153–1203), it is over 60m (197ft) high and decorated with glazed-brick inscriptions.

CARAVANSERAIS

THE SELJUKS BUILT A NETWORK OF *CARAVANSERAIS* ALONG TRADE ROUTES. THESE SHELTERS PROVIDED SECURE ACCOMMODATION, FOOD AND WATER FOR TRADERS, TRAVELLERS AND THEIR ANIMALS.

A complex of buildings could typically be found inside a *caravanserai*, often with an imposing, decorated gateway as an entrance leading to a courtyard surrounded by lodging and stables, with a fountain and mosque and normally a bazaar or trading area. These *caravanserais* became important trade centres and were often fortified. The usual layout of Seljuk *caravanserais* was of four *iwans*, or halls, surrounding the courtyard.

A traveller was typically allowed to stay for three days without paying because the *caravanserais* were built as an expression of the Muslim duty of charity toward travellers. Local rulers built the entrances in a very grand style to signal their wealth and generosity. Some *caravanserais* were built as part of a complex attached to a mausoleum and paid for by a legacy from the deceased.

The Seljuks built *caravanserais* in Iran, across Afghanistan and Central Asia toward India and Russia, and in Anatolia, where they were usually known as *hans*. (*Han* is simply the Turkish word for *caravanserai*.) They were also known as *ribats*. The *caravanserais* were positioned approximately every 30km (19 miles) along the road.

GRAND PORTAL

One typical *caravanserai* of the early Seljuk period is the Ribat-i Malik in Uzbekistan, built on the road between Bukhara and Samarkand in 1078–79 by the Qarakhanid Sultan Nasr (reigned 1068–80). The sultan was a son-in-law to Seljuk sultan Alp Arslan (reigned 1063–72) and a client ruler under Seljuk overlordship. The splendid portal gateway of the *caravanserai* still stands, bearing an inscription in Persian declaring that it had been

Below The Rabat Sharaf caravanserai near Mashhad in Iran was built in 1128. Behind its tall and elegant entrance portal, it has two courtyards.

Above This portal, all that remains of a caravanserai in Uzbekistan, on the road from Samarkand to Bukhara, would have been a welcome sight for any traveller seeking respite.

raised by the 'sultan of the entire world' and that within, by God's grace, the setting would be like that of paradise. Archaeological excavations have determined that the *caravanserai*'s layout was square and that it was surrounded by sturdy walls that were set with semicircular towers.

Some later *caravanserais* were built with two courtyards, leading into each other. The 11th-century Akcha Qala near Merv (now in

Right The courtyard of the Aksaray Sultan Han covers approximately 2,250sq m (24,220sq ft).

Turkmenistan) and the Rabat Sharaf *caravanserai* built on the road between Nishapur and Merv in 1114–15 are examples. In these, the first enclosure was reserved for stables for camels and areas for storing goods, while the second was used for lodging. This double-enclosure layout was used in the Seljuk-era *caravanserais*, or *hans*, in Anatolia, except that in these complexes the second courtyard was usually covered by a roof.

CARAVANSERAIS IN ANATOLIA

Two particularly grand *caravanserai* were built near Konya by the Anatolian Seljuk Sultan Ala al-Din Kayqubad I (reigned 1220–37). The larger of the two, the Aksaray *caravanserai* on the road from Konya to Aksaray, was built in 1229. With great walls, a large projecting portal almost 50m (164ft) wide and 13m (43ft) tall, 6 corner towers and 18 side towers, it has the look of a castle. However, it is also beautifully finished with elegantly carved marble side panels on the portal,

Above The Incir caravanserai was built near Bucaq, between Isparta and Antalya (now in Turkey), in 1238 by Sultan Keyhusrev II (reigned 1238–46).

featuring polygonal geometric patterns along with naturalistic representations of flowers.

The portal faces south-west. It leads into an entrance room beneath a star-shaped vault, flanked by office rooms. The courtyard has a colonnade along its western side, which was used for stabling and storage; rooms used for kitchens, dining rooms and bath facilities are ranged along its eastern side. Beyond the courtyard a large, nine-aisled, barrel-vaulted hall provided living and sleeping areas for the winter months; in summer, residents slept outside on the roof. The hall covers about 1430sq m (15,400sq ft).

The *caravanserai* found on the road between Kayseri and Sivas (on the route from Konya eastward to Iran and Iraq) was built slightly later, in 1232–36. Like the one at Aksaray, it has an entrance way

flanked by guard or office rooms. This leads into a courtyard with stables and storage areas along one side and accommodation, kitchens and bathhouse facilities along the other. Beyond, as at Aksaray, is a covered hall.

KIOSK MOSQUE

In the centre of the courtyards at both the Aksaray and Kayseri Sultan Hans is a free-standing mosque. The mosque at Aksaray is lifted above the ground on four arches, accessed by steps on the south side, beautifully decorated with stone carving without, and with a fine *mihrab* niche within. Known as a 'kiosk mosque', this kind of structure was typical of Seljuk *caravanserais* in Anatolia. There are similar kiosk mosques in the caravanserais in Agzikara (built 1231–37, near Konya) and Sahipata (1249–50), between Afyon and Aksehir.

THE ANATOLIAN SELJUKS

THE RULERS OF THE INDEPENDENT ANATOLIAN SELJUK EMPIRE
BUILT MOSQUES WITH THREE OR MORE DOMES AND GRAND
MADRASAS AND *HANS* (*CARAVANSERAIS*) WITH CARVED GATEWAYS.

The Seljuks became established in Anatolia in the wake of Sultan Alp Arslan's devastating defeat of the Byzantine Empire at the Battle of Manzikert in 1071. Anatolia is the region formerly known as Asia Minor, bound by the Mediterranean Sea to the south, the Aegean Sea to the west and the Black Sea to the north; it was part of the Byzantine Empire and fell to Seljuk troops that came in the wake of Alp Arslan's army.

Under Suleyman bin Kutalmish, the Seljuks took the Byzantine cities of Nicaea (modern Iznik) and Nicomedia (modern Izmit) in 1075. In 1077, Suleyman declared himself ruler of the independent Seljuk sultanate of Rum (so-called from the medieval Islamic word for Rome, because the territories had been part of the Byzantine or eastern Roman Empire).

The Seljuk state in Anatolia survived in various forms until the early 14th century, when the region became a province of the Ilkhanid empire established by the successors of Mongol invaders who had captured Baghdad in 1258. The Seljuk capital, initially at Nicaea, was at Konya for most of this time, after being moved there by Sultan Kilij Arslan II (reigned 1156–92) in 1181. The greatest of the Anatolian Seljuk rulers was Ala al-Din Kaykubad I (reigned 1220–37), who presided over a glittering court, expanded the boundaries of the empire and oversaw a great age of building in his territories.

Right The Anatolian Seljuk Empire at its greatest extent c.1240 occupied most of modern-day Turkey.

Many more Seljuk-era buildings survive in Anatolia than in Central Asia. The Anatolian Seljuks built congregational mosques, *madrasas* (religious colleges), *caravanserais* (resting places on travellers' routes), palaces, monasteries, tombs and mausolea, bathhouses and hospitals. In addition, they pioneered the construction of building complexes typical of the Ottomans; known as *kulliye*, these incorporated mosque, *madrasa, caravanserai* and mausoleum in one setting. A Seljuk example is the Huand Hatun complex of 1238 in Kayseri, which includes a mosque, *madrasa*, mausoleum and *hammam* (bathhouse). It was built by Mahperi Hatun, the wife of Sultan Ala al-Din Kaykubad.

MOSQUES

The congregational mosque was called the *ulu çami* by the Anatolian Seljuks. They did not follow the four-*iwan* plan used by the Great Seljuks, but instead used variations, for example the 'basilican' design – so called due to its similarity to

Above The *Gök* madrasa *in Sivas, built in 1271, has a dramatic entrance portal. The entrance is behind a niche within a stone frame, flanked by minarets.*

church architecture – used three domes. In some mosques, such as the Ala al-Din Çami of 1223 in Nigde, the three domes were aligned above three bays in front of the *qibla* wall that indicates the direction of prayer; in others, such as the Burmali Minare Çami of 1237–46 in Amasya, the three domes were arranged above the length of the hall at right angles to the *qibla* wall. In another design, used at the Gök Çami *madrasa* of c.1275–1300 at Amasya, the two

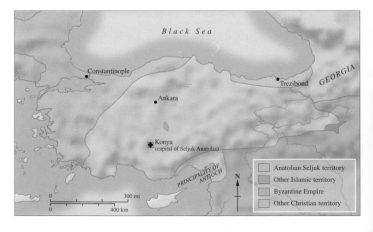

options were combined, so that three domes ran parallel to the *qibla* wall and three also ran at right angles. These mosques were a direct influence on Ottoman mosque architecture.

The Anatolian Seljuks also built mosques based on the hypostyle mosque of Syria and Arabia, in which the prayer hall's flat roof was supported by rows of pillars. In many of the Anatolian examples, architects used wooden rather than stone pillars. The Sivrihisar Ulu Çami of 1232, the Afyon Karahisar Ulu Çami of 1272 and the Arslan Hane Çami of *c.*1290 in Ankara are all examples of this type.

MADRASAS

The Anatolian Seljuks built some *madrasas* on the model of those built by the Great Seljuks, with four *iwans* arranged around a courtyard, but more typically in Anatolian *madrasas* the courtyard was covered with a great dome, while a single *iwan* was built in the centre of the rear wall with one domed room to each side of it, and lines of smaller rooms arranged along the sides of the courtyard.

The two most celebrated surviving Seljuk *madrasas*, the

Above The dramatic façade of the Karatay madrasa *in Konya (1252) features patterns created by alternating light and dark stone, a sign of Syrian influence.*

Karatay *madrasa* of 1251 and the Ince Minareli *madrasa* of 1258, both in Konya, follow this plan. In the Karatay *madrasa*, which was built by Jelaleddin Karatay, vizier to Sultan Izzeddin Kaykavus, the dome, decorated with turquoise, white and black mosaic tiles and calligraphic inscriptions, rises to

an open top that admits daylight, and a pool beneath catches rainwater.

MAUSOLEA AND CARAVANSERAIS

Like their counterparts in Iran and Central Asia, the Anatolian Seljuks built tomb towers and square-domed mausolea. The Anatolian tombs are different, in that they generally have two levels – a vault used for burial and a prayer room above – while the tombs of the Great Seljuks were single-storey, without a vault. Moreover, despite the fact that prayer was not permitted at mausolea and tombs in orthodox Islam, many of the Anatolian mausolea have *mihrabs* – niches that indicate the direction of prayer.

The Anatolian Seljuks built a network of *caravanserais*, along the trade routes that ran east–west and north–south across their territories. Most were built under Ala al-Din Kaykubad I and Ghiyath al-Din Kay Khusrau II (reigned 1237–47).

The typical design, seen in the surviving *caravanserais* of Aksaray and Kayseri, had an imposing portal, a large courtyard and a vast covered hall.

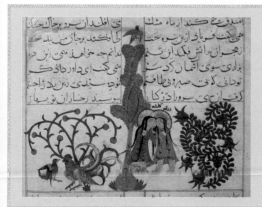

VARQA AND GULSHAH

The 10th-century Persian poet Ayyuqi wrote the *Romance of Varqa and Gulshah*, his masterpiece, in 997, in the era of Sultan Mahmud of Ghazni, founder of the Ghaznavid Empire. In *c.*1250, Abd al-Mumin al-Khuyyi created a magnificent illustrated manuscript of this tragic story. The artist, who signed the manuscript, was probably working in Konya, the capital of the Anatolian Seljuks. The manuscript paintings run across the middle of the page, with the poem continuing above and below. This unique manuscript is now in the Topkapi Palace Museum in Istanbul.

Left Here, the couple embrace in a garden before fate separates them. Their union is echoed by the presence of a cockerel and hen.

SELJUK STONEWORK

ONE OF THE MOST OUTSTANDING FEATURES OF SELJUK BUILDINGS IS
THE CARVED STONE DECORATION, ESPECIALLY ON THE PORTALS, OR
ENTRANCES, WHERE MASONS CREATED AMAZINGLY DETAILED WORK.

The Anatolian Seljuks earned a reputation as great builders. Their architecture has much in common with that of their Iranian counterparts, but they created a distinctive style of their own. In part, this was due to their location. They drew some of their ideas from neighbouring Byzantium and Armenia, and they enjoyed a better supply of building material, much of it salvaged from the buildings of their vanquished enemies.

The Seljuks produced their finest work in stone. They had several grades of mason, ranging from semi-skilled artisans, who prepared roughly shaped blocks from the quarries, to gifted carvers, who produced exquisitely detailed decoration. At their best, these men produced work of outstanding quality. They mimicked the delicate stucco designs of the Great Seljuks, achieving the same lightness and grace in a harder material.

Above The calligraphy on the portal of the Ince Minareli madrasa is intricately designed along two vertical friezes.

CONTRASTING SURFACES

Anatolian craftsmen were fond of the contrast between large expanses of plain, smooth ashlar (square-cut stone used for facing a building) and smaller areas of compressed ornamentation. The latter was often focused around the portals of a building. This architectural approach can be found on every major structure, from mosques and *madrasas* (religious colleges) to *caravanserais* (travellers' lodges) and tombs. In many cases, the carved decoration is made in the form of a triangular, recessed arch, which has been likened to the shape of early Islamic tents.

One of the most spectacular examples can be found at the remains of the *caravanserai* between Konya and Aksaray. There, the

Left Seljuk stonemasons emphasized windows, doors and arches by framing them in receding bands of decoration. This example is from the Gök madrasa in Sivas, Turkey (1271).

portal contains *muqarnas* (stalactites) vaulting above carved calligraphy. Surrounding the recess, there is a shallow, rounded arch composed of interlocking geometric motifs. This, in turn, is flanked by several vertical panels of tightly packed, carved decoration. There is evidence of similar portals at the Gök *madrasa* at Sivas (1271) and the Cifte Minareli *madrasa* at Erzerum (1253).

CALLIGRAPHY IN STONE

The decoration on the Ince Minareli *madrasa* at Konya (1258) – now a museum dedicated to Seljuk stonework – is more elaborate. The entrance is framed by two bands of intertwining calligraphy and imposing sculptures.

The Ince Minareli features a mix of *naskhi* and *kufic* calligraphy, but during the Seljuk period, plaited (braided) *kufic* was the most common form. In this style of calligraphy, the lettering

was interlaced in a rhythmic, ornamental fashion. The trend for plaited *kufic* script began farther east and spread west to Anatolia before the 13th century. Examples can be found on the Ince Minareli and Karatay *madrasas* in Konya, and the minaret of the Ulu Çami at Malatya.

SYMBOLIC WORK

Some of the stonework decoration may carry spiritual symbolism. A number of Seljuk buildings were adorned with panels of flowering or fruit-laden trees. In most cases, the foliage is in the form of palm leaves and the fruit, pomegranates. An eagle is often portrayed on top of the tree.

Traditionally, these emblems were interpreted as invocations of blessings, with the main image representing the Tree of Life and the bird seen as a human soul, ascending to paradise. Variants of

Above A stylized palm tree, with leaves sprouting from a crescent, adorns a panel on the Doner Kumbet, near Kayseri.

this emblem can be found on the Ince Minareli *madrasa*, the Cifte Minare *madrasa* at Erzerum and the Doner Kumbet near Kayseri.

THE TÜRBE

One fine example of a distinctive form of Seljuk architecture is the Doner Kumbet. It is a *türbe* (tomb tower), a mausoleum with a burial vault at the base and a prayer chamber above it. The shape is usually cylindrical, with a conical roof, but square or polygonal versions can be found. The exterior walls are often decorated with blind arcading (rows of arches attached to the walls), with further decoration around the base of the roof. The example at Kayseri features carvings of lions, eagles and human heads.

There is debate about the inspiration for the *türbe*. According to one long-held theory, the design of the conical roof was based on the tents used by early nomads. Other authorities see a closer parallel with the domed churches of Armenia.

SELJUK SCULPTURE

Islamic sculpture is rare, but potters in the 12th–13th century produced fine, glazed ceramic figures of animals, birds and people. The masons also created beautiful carved, high-relief stone sculpture: fine examples can be found in the northern portal of the Ince Minareli *madrasa* (1258) in Konya, where medallions and large leaves, ribbons and calligraphy bands were combined effectively. Also from Konya are pieces of high-relief figurative carving of the highest quality that once decorated the citadel built in *c.*1220 by Sultan Ala al-Din Kaykubad I. These include a two-headed eagle, elephants and crowned and winged spirits or angels.

Above Calligraphy, arabesques and geometric shapes decorate the Great Mosque and Hospital at Divrigi (1229).

KASHAN POTTERY

CERAMIC PRODUCTION FLOURISHED DURING THE LATE 12TH CENTURY IN KASHAN, WHERE NEW MATERIALS AND TECHNIQUES WERE USED TO MAKE WARES WITH ELABORATE DESIGNS.

In the 12th century, an important new ceramic production centre was established at Kashan in central Iran. There are no records of the city's industrial history before this time, but it was located close to the sources of raw ingredients and fuel needed to produce luxury pottery. The Persian words for tiles and pottery are *kashi* or *kashani*; it seems their manufacture became so closely identified with the town that the product came to be named after it.

Below This early 13th-century stool or low table is made from stonepaste with a white glaze and lustre decoration; the six sides are identically decorated.

A NEW BODY MATERIAL

Much is known about the technical aspects of pottery production in this period. A treatise written by Abu'l Qasim al-Tahir in 1301 included a section on the art of glazed ceramics. He was well-qualified to write this manual since four generations of his family worked as potters in Kashan.

One of the triggers for this new production was the development of a new body material known as stonepaste (or fritware), which was white and could be made to appear translucent – both highly regarded qualities of Chinese porcelain. The technology for this new body was

Above The composition of this 1210 Kashan stonepaste dish, with a sleeping boy beside a pond with a naked figure, along with a horse and attendants, has been interpreted as a mystical allegory regarding the quest for the Divine.

probably introduced to Kashan by potters from Egypt, who had moved east in search of new patronage after the collapse of the Fatimid regime. The recipe for the stonepaste body is given by Abu'l Qasim. He lists its ingredients as ten parts of sugar stone (or quartz), crushed and then strained through coarse silk, one part crushed glass and one part fine white clay.

Initially, the potters exploited the whiteness of this new body and made finely potted, thin-walled vessels that were simply covered in a transparent alkaline glaze. The walls were moulded in relief, and holes pierced through the pattern would become filled with glaze, producing a translucent effect. The stonepaste body was an excellent surface for decoration and it was not long before coloured glazes, particularly brilliant shades of cobalt and turquoise, were added.

THE KASHAN STYLE

A technical manual written in 1196 by Muhammad al-Jawhar al-Nishapuri devotes a chapter to the ingredients and processes involved

the vessel and then carved parts away, leaving the design behind in silhouette. Later experimentation revealed that the black pigment could be painted directly on to the surface of the vessel; this discovery allowed the potters greater freedom and fluency in their designs and the earlier clumsily carved decoration was abandoned in favour of quite delicately scrolled floral designs and bands of elegant cursive inscription. Details in cobalt were sometimes added, but this was much less stable and often ran under the glaze.

END OF AN ERA

Kashan was attacked by the Mongols in the 1220s, and although ceramic production suffered, it was not destroyed; lustre production was curtailed and for a time pieces were not signed or dated until production was revived in the Ilkhanid period.

Above This Kashan stonepaste bowl with minai *decoration is from c.1300. It shows a scene from the* Shahnama, *in which the hero Faridun rides the cow Barmaya and leads the captive Zahhak.*

in overglaze *minai* (from the Arabic for 'enamel') decoration, and lustre decoration, in which metallic oxides were painted over the glaze and fixed in a second reduction firing to create a lustre, or metallic, sheen. The Kashan potters became renowned for these two techniques.

Minai ware used a new polychrome technique developed so that the figurative imagery could be rendered with greater clarity. Like lustre decoration, this was an expensive process that required several firings in the kiln. Areas of the design were painted with colours such as turquoise, cobalt, grey and purple on to the white glaze and the piece was fired.

Further details were then applied in black, red and gold before a second firing. The figurative decoration probably reflects designs found on contemporary illustrated manuscripts and wall paintings, although none of these survive.

By 1200, what is known as the 'Kashan' style was fully developed and the majority of dated objects and tiles are decorated in this way.

UNDERGLAZE PAINTING

Another Kashan innovation was the development of underglaze painting. In the first stages of this technique, the potters applied a layer of black slip (a liquid clay) to

Right This early 13th-century stonepaste jug with black painted decoration under a turquoise glaze has a cockerel-shaped head. The outer body is pierced using a technique borrowed from metalwork; a hidden inner body contained the liquid.

KHURASAN INLAID METALWORK

IN 12TH-CENTURY KHURASAN, LUXURY COPPER-ALLOY OBJECTS WERE DECORATED FIRST WITH ENGRAVED CHASED PATTERNS, AND THEN WITH INLAID PRECIOUS METALS.

The period from the 12th to 14th centuries saw great innovations in the technique and style of inlaid metalwork. Production centres appeared first in the Khurasan province of north-east Iran, and from the 13th century in Mosul (Iraq) and elsewhere, where the technique of inlaying brass or bronze objects with silver, copper and eventually gold details was developed to a high level, rivalling the detailed surface decoration found on contemporary ceramics, glass and even manuscripts.

On an ostentatious level, the precious metal inlays added value to an object, with the base metal acquiring the glittering surface of a more precious metal. Emulation of more expensive materials also seems to have occurred in contemporary ceramics, which used lustre glazes to echo the gleam of metal and imitated metal shapes.

INLAYING METAL

Metal inlay is a technique in which a softer and more precious metal is applied to the surface of a cheaper, stronger metal or alloy. The receiving surface is usually lightly punched to make a pockmarked area, and the softer metal is then hammered on, thus easing it into the punched grooves for a more secure grip. The technique could be used to enhance a pattern or inscription engraved on to a metal object, highlighting the lines of script, clarifying a design or framed area, or bringing up the main characters in a figural scene. Dense pictorial detail, elaborate

calligraphic inscriptions, along with sophisticated floral and geometric patterns, were all applied to metal vessels, transforming the style of previous generations of metalwork.

FORM AND FUNCTION

Khurasan metalwork was made in a wide range of forms and functions, but most of these objects were made for hospitality uses in wealthy homes, such as ewers, cups and incense-burners, or for official use, such as pen boxes and caskets. Many pieces of Khurasan metalwork, such as the Bobrinsky bucket (see opposite page), were produced by casting them in a mould. Casting allows for more sculptural variety and flexibility in the final shape, and spectacular pieces, such as a cow, calf and lion group, demonstrate great

Above The c. 1200 *Vaso Vescovali is a cast brass bowl made in Khurasan. The silver inlaid lid is contemporary to the bowl but from a separate object.*

technical skill. According to its own inscription, all three animals were cast simultaneously. Although it is sometimes said that Islamic art features no three-dimensional sculpture, there are many functional objects that contradict this claim, such as a feline incense-burner (see opposite page).

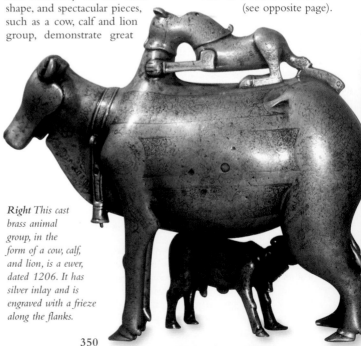

Right This cast brass animal group, in the form of a cow, calf, and lion, is a ewer, dated 1206. It has silver inlay and is engraved with a frieze along the flanks.

Below The body of this 11th-century cast brass incense-burner, in the shape of a lion, has a pierced openwork pattern as well as holes for the eyes and mouth, through which smoke could pass.

DECORATIVE THEMES

The theme of courtly pleasures is ubiquitous in Islamic art of the 12th to 13th centuries, but a second recurring theme, that of astrology, echoed the benevolent wishes so frequently inscribed on luxury goods. Figures symbolizing the planets were often depicted in combination with zodiac signs, showing each planet at its most powerful and useful position, thus invoking good associations for the owners of the metal object. The Vaso Vescovali cast brass bowl features astrology as its main theme, and also includes a minor frieze depicting a party with musical entertainment and drinking guests.

These metal objects usually bore a formal inscription that delivered a consistent formula of good wishes directed at an unnamed owner, such as 'Glory and Prosperity', 'Power', 'Safety', 'Happiness',

'Success' or 'Blessings'. Because inscriptions rarely mention the owner by name, it is thought that these luxury objects were produced for the open market, not for a court context.

While silver or copper could be used to brighten some parts of a design, black substances, such as niello, bitumen or mastic, were sometimes used simultaneously to darken engraved lines. This allowed the metalworker to create a more graphic range of colour contrast.

The stylistic developments that occurred throughout this period meant that engraved designs were becoming increasingly sophisticated on Islamic metalwork. In unskilled hands, these developments could have led to an eventual incoherence of the overall design; however, small areas or lines accented with metal inlay were used as a new way to clarify the design.

THE BOBRINKSY BUCKET

A key piece of Khurasan inlaid metalwork is known as the Bobrinsky bucket, made in Herat in 1163. This remarkable bucket, for use in a bathhouse, is decorated with several layers of inlaid silver and copper, depicting the lively pleasures of drinking, enjoying music, dancing and hunting on horseback. It bears many inscriptions, mainly with the standard long formula of good wishes (such as 'Glory and Prosperity'), but also with the date, names of the patron and commissioning agent, and those of the metalworker and the inlayer. The owner is described as the 'pride of the merchants, trusted by the Muslims, ornament of the pilgrimage and the two sanctuaries', and was evidently a well-travelled merchant and *Hajj* pilgrim.

Above The densely inscribed Bobrinsky bucket is a cast brass bucket with silver and copper inlay decoration and a handle.

CHAPTER 13

ZANGIDS, AYYUBIDS AND MAMLUKS

As the Seljuk Empire declined in power during the 12th century, a number of small, derivative and often short-lived successor states were established in Syria, Iraq and eastern Anatolia (modern Turkey). The Turkish Zangid dynasty ruled northern Iraq and Syria in 1127–1251. Its most celebrated rulers, Imad al-Din Zangi and Nur al-Din, were promoters of Sunni orthodoxy and fierce proponents of *jihad* (holy war) against Christian crusaders. Salah al-Din Yusuf ibn Ayyub (Saladin), a Kurdish officer in the Zangid army, then created an empire based in Cairo that extended to Syria and beyond, and established the Ayyubid dynasty in 1171. In 1249, the Ayyubids were overturned by their own slave army, which took control of Egypt and Syria and founded the powerful Mamluk Sultanate (1250–1517). These rulers of the states that succeeded the Seljuks were Turks and Kurds with a heritage of nomadic tribal life. They may not naturally have been drawn to Sunni orthodoxy, but many were enthusiastic patrons of Islamic religious architecture.

Opposite The Tomb of Qayt Bay in Cairo, built in 1472–74, displays the finest Mamluk stone carving. Some of the grandest stonework can be seen in the reticulation on the dome.

Above A detail of the exquisite silver inlay on the celebrated Mamluk-era brass basin, known as the Baptistère de St Louis (14th century), shows a procession of court dignitaries.

THE ZANGIDS OF MOSUL

THE TURKISH ZANGID RULERS OF NORTHERN IRAQ AND SYRIA IN
1127–1222 WERE CHAMPIONS OF SUNNI ISLAM. THEY WERE ALSO
PATRONS OF THE ARTS, ESPECIALLY IN MOSUL.

Imad al-Din Zangi, the son of the governor of Aleppo under the Seljuk sultan Malik Shah, was the founder of the Zangid dynasty. Zangi's father, Aq Sunqur al-Hajib, was executed for alleged treason against his Seljuk masters in 1094, and thereafter Zangi was raised in Mosul by the city's governor Karbuqa. Zangi established himself as governor of Basra in 1126, Mosul in 1127 and Aleppo in 1128.

In seeking to extend his authority farther, he fought against both Muslim enemies and the Christian crusaders who had established the 'crusader states' (the County of Edessa, the Kingdom of Jerusalem, the Principality of Antioch and the County of Tripoli) during and after the First Crusade of 1095–99.

FIGHTING THE ENEMY
Zangi won a major victory over the crusaders when he captured the capital of the County of Edessa on 24 December 1144. This shocked the Christian world and led directly to the Second Crusade, which was

called for by Pope Eugenius III on 1 December 1145 and mounted in 1147–49.

After Zangi's untimely death in 1146 (he was murdered by a slave), his territories were split between two sons: Nur al-Din Mahmud (reigned 1146–74) ruled Syria from Aleppo, while Sayf al-Din Ghazi I (reigned 1146–49) ruled northern Iraq from Mosul. Nur al-Din, like his father, proved a scourge of the crusaders and personally led the army that broke the Second Crusade by relieving the Siege of Damascus in 1149. Thereafter, Nur al-Din took control of Damascus in 1154, and in doing so he created a united Muslim Syria.

Subsequently, the Zangids came into conflict with the nascent Ayyubid Empire that was established in Cairo by Salah al-Din, who was the nephew of Nur al-Din's general Asad al-Din Shirkuh. The Zangid rulers of Mosul twice survived attacks by Salah al-Din (in 1182 and 1185), but they were forced to accept his overlordship. The Zangid dynasty came to an end in Mosul with the rule of Nasir al-Din Mahmud (reigned 1219–22). He was ousted by his former slave Badr al-Din Lulu, who governed the city until 1259, when it was captured by the Mongols under Hulagu Khan.

Above Nur al-Din commissioned this richly carved minbar *for the Al-Aqsa Mosque in 1169. It stood beside the prayer niche from 1187 until it was destroyed in an arson attack in 1969.*

PROMOTING THE FAITH
Nur al-Din was a zealous promoter of the idea of *jihad*, or holy war, against the Christians in Syria and Palestine. He had tracts read out in mosques praising the beauties of al-Quds (Jerusalem) and the Muslim sanctuaries in the Haram al-Sharif (Noble Sanctuary), the area known as Temple Mount by the Jews. Reports circulated that the crusaders, who had captured Jerusalem in 1099 at the peak of the First Crusade, were desecrating the Dome of the Rock and the Al-Aqsa Mosque in the Noble Sanctuary. Recapturing Jerusalem for Islam became a focus of *jihad*.

As a statement of his confidence that Islamic armies would regain the city, Nur al-Din had a fine new *minbar* (pulpit) made for the Al-Aqsa Mosque by five craftsmen from Aleppo in 1169. The cedarwood pulpit had exquisite intarsia (coloured wood inlay) and panelling in its side walls and was inscribed with a declaration of Islam's superiority and victory over rival faiths. As it turned out, the richly decorated *minbar* could not

Left Remains of the castle built by Nur al-Din at Mosul (northern Iraq) stand against sheer rock. Here, the Zangids were twice besieged by Salah al-Din.

be installed in Nur al-Din's lifetime, but it was fitted in the Al-Aqsa Mosque after Ayyubid ruler Salah al-Din took Jerusalem from the Christians in 1187.

BUILDING IN ALEPPO

Nur al-Din was a great builder, responsible for refortifying Aleppo's city walls and citadel, as well as for repairing the aqueduct. Within the city, Nur al-Din ordered work on the markets and the Great Mosque. Perhaps to establish his credentials as a proponent of *jihad* or possibly through religious fervour, he promoted orthodox Sunni Islam by building a network of *madrasas* (religious colleges), which were designed to combat the influence of Shiah Muslims in Syria. He also built a string of *khanqas* (institutions like monasteries) for Sufis.

PATRONS OF MOSUL

From the late 12th and early 13th centuries, there survive a number of illustrated manuscripts linked with court production at Mosul. One of these is an 1199 copy of a

Above The Nur al-Din Mosque, built in Hama, Syria, in 1172, is celebrated for its fine square minaret.

late classical work on toxicology, *Kitab al-Diryaq* (Book of Antidotes). The manuscript's frontispiece depicts a central, seated figure holding up a large lunar crescent. A pair of entwined dragons coil around this central figure. Four attendant angels, or genies, hover at the corners. In Mosul, this seated figure is the characteristic heraldic image for the Zangid dynasty and is also used on their coinage and other metalwork.

A mid-13th-century copy of the same text was also made in Mosul, but the frontispiece shows a ruler at his court enjoying a reception. Although the exact patron is not known, the style is a close match to depictions of Badr al-Din Lulu made for frontispieces in a multi-volume set of the great poetic anthology, *Kitab al-Aghani* (Book of Songs), produced in Mosul *c.*1216–20. The frontispieces show the typical Seljuk costume – most notably, the *sharbush*, or fur-lined bonnet.

Left An illustration from Kitab al-Aghani (Book of Songs), c.1216–20, by Abu al-Faraj al-Isfahani, showing a ruler listening to musicians.

INLAID METALWORK OF MOSUL

IN THE EARLY 13TH CENTURY, ACCOMPLISHED INLAID METALWORK BEGAN TO BE PRODUCED IN MOSUL IN NORTHERN IRAQ, POSSIBLY AS A RESULT OF SKILLED CRAFTSMEN EMIGRATING FROM IRAN.

The production of precious metal inlay, in which expensive metal is used to decorate the surface of a cheaper metal alloy object, was highly developed in the Khurasan province of eastern Iran. This production seems to have shifted to the city of Mosul, northern Iraq, around the same time that Mongol invasions led by Genghis Khan were creating an impact on cities in north-eastern Iran. Samarkand, Merv, Nishapur and Herat were devastated in the early 1220s, and their citizens massacred. A contemporary historian, Ibn al-Athir, described these dramatic events:

'In just one year [the Mongols] seized the most populous, most beautiful and the best cultivated part of the earth whose characters excelled in civilization and urbanity. In the countries which have not yet been overrun by them, everyone spends the night afraid they may appear there too.'

The sudden shift of metal inlay production has been interpreted as the result of the emigration of Khurasanis fleeing the Mongols. Certainly, the ruination of the region would mean that the local market for luxury wares was damaged, and it

Above This inlaid brass basin, made for Ayyubid Sultan al-Adil II Abu Bakr in 1238–40, is decorated with vivid scenes of hunters and animals.

would make economic sense for producers to move to richer and less turbulent areas in western Iran and Iraq. Most Mosul metalwork is dated later than the invasion of Khurasan, and some signatures show direct connections with the Khurasani producers. One 1229 ewer confirms this connection: it is signed 'Iyas assistant of Abu'l-Karim b. al-Turabi al-Mawsili'. 'Turabi' refers to the city of Merv in north-eastern Iran, and 'Mawsili' refers to the master's new home in Mosul.

AL-MAWSILI, OR 'OF MOSUL'

The metal inlay craftsmen of Mosul often signed their wares using the *nisba*, or toponym, *al-Mawsili*, meaning 'of Mosul'. However, throughout the 13th century and into the early 14th, this *nisba* features on many inlaid metal objects that were made in other places, such as Egypt and Syria. It appears that *al-Mawsili* refers to the craftsman's place of training and its specific reputation, not necessarily where the object was produced.

Mosul inlaid metal objects usually feature lively figural scenes of people or animals, either in long narrow friezes or more often in vignettes within cartouches (a type

Left Dinner guests, musicians and dancers are the main decorative subjects on this 13th-century candlestick, made from brass with silver inlay.

Above The Blacas Ewer, made in Mosul in 1232, is a masterpiece of inlaid metalwork. The vignettes show scenes of court life, hunting and war.

of decorative frame) against densely patterned backdrops. Because the metalworker can chase lines into the inlaid silver areas, even finer detail was possible. Some of these even feature Gospel scenes, implying that not all clients in this cultural environment were Muslim.

Mosul designs are different in style to Khurasan inlaid metal pieces: the visual repertoire is wider and the metal forms they decorate are local to Mosul and the surrounding region. Craftsmen in Mosul, as in Khurasan, exploited the metal inlay technique to make their decoration more pictorial, a practice which was also fashionable in other contemporary media, such as enamelled glass and ceramics. Illustrated manuscripts that have survived from 13th-century Iraq show many parallels of composition and pictorial motifs between these paintings and the exquisite scenes composed on inlaid metal objects.

MOSUL DIASPORA

Only one dated Mosul object is inscribed with the statement that it was produced in Mosul itself: this is the Blacas Ewer, dated 1232, now in the British Museum. It is signed by one Shuja b. Mana al-Mawsili 'in Mosul', and the ewer may have been made for the city's ruler Badr al-Din Lulu (d.1259). It is an object of outstanding quality, decorated with a series of framed scenes, laid in horizontal bands that draw from the 'princely cycle' repertoire of hunting and feasting, as well as astrological figures, calligraphy, and decorative scrollwork and patterns.

There are just six other known objects that most likely come from Mosul itself, as they belonged to Badr al-Din Lulu or members of his court. The *nisba* signature of *al-Mawsili*, however, is on at least 28 known inlaid metal objects, as a diaspora of metalworkers trained in Mosul was active in the rest of Jazira province and further south in the courts of Ayyubid Syria and Egypt. It reflects how craftsmen seek opportunities of rich patronage, and also shows why it is difficult to separate these regions into distinct stylistic categories of metalwork. Meanwhile, the discontinuation of red copper and the introduction of gold inlay show how this technique achieved ever greater luxury and affluence as it moved into the Mamluk period.

Above Dramatically designed with a dragon's head handle, this inlaid brass incense-burner was made in Damascus, c.1230–40, by a Mosuli craftsman.

THE AYYUBID DYNASTY

OF KURDISH DESCENT, THE SUNNI MUSLIM AYYUBID DYNASTY RULED EGYPT, SYRIA, YEMEN AND PARTS OF IRAQ IN THE 12TH–13TH CENTURIES.

Salah al-Din (known in the West as Saladin), the most celebrated of Muslim generals, established Ayyubid rule in Cairo in 1169. He was hailed for both his strategic brilliance and chivalrous bearing by the European crusaders he fought, and was acclaimed throughout the Muslim world for his triumph in recapturing the holy city of al-Quds (Jerusalem) from the Christians on 2 October 1187. The dynasty Salah al-Din founded was named after his father Najm al-Din Ayyub ibn Shadhi, a Kurdish soldier in the service of the Seljuk Turks who became governor of Damascus.

A NEW EMPIRE

Salah al-Din came to Egypt with his uncle Shirkuh, the principal general of the Zangid ruler of Syria, Nur al-Din. He campaigned in Egypt alongside Shirkuh three times – in 1164, 1167 and 1168–69 – and on the final occasion took power after killing the Fatimid Egyptian vizier Shawar (Shirkuh

died of natural causes). Salah al-Din abolished the Ismaili Fatimid Caliphate on the death of Caliph al-Adid in 1171 and declared Cairo to be under the authority of the Sunni Muslim Abbasid Caliph in Baghdad, al-Mustadi. He created an empire, taking power in Syria after the death of Nur al-Din in 1174, then winning control in northern Iraq, as well as the Hijaz and Yemen.

Salah al-Din was a champion of Sunni orthodoxy. As a proponent of the *jihad*, or holy war, he was named 'Protector of the holy sites of Makkah and Madinah' by the Abbasid caliph in Baghdad, and he waged an intermittent war against the crusader kingdoms, which culminated in his victory at the Battle of the Horns of Hattin in July 1187 and the capture of Jerusalem three months later.

On Salah al-Din's death in 1193, the empire was divided among his brothers and other relatives and thereafter was weakened by internal feuding. Nevertheless, the Ayyubids

Above The great Ayyubid ruler Salah al-Din built his citadel on Muqattam Hill in Cairo in 1176–83.

had survived more than 50 years, until the establishment in 1250 of the Mamluk Sultanate by the Ayyubids' former slave soldiers.

CAIRO WALLS AND CITADEL

On taking power in Cairo in 1171, Salah al-Din began work to extend the city walls, uniting the Fatimid royal capital of Cairo (founded in 969) to the older garrison town of Fustat (founded in 641). This task was not completed, but as part of the project Salah al-Din built a citadel and made it the centre of government. Known as the Citadel, it was raised on the Muqattam Hill in 1176–83.

Muqattam Hill had been the site of a pavilion known as the 'Dome of the Wind', built by Hatim ibn Hartama, the city's governor, in 810; Fatimid rulers and nobility had used it to enjoy the breezes and the views of the city. Salah al-Din, however, saw its military significance as a site for a fortified base from which to defend the city at a time when crusader armies were frequent and unwelcome visitors to Egypt. The

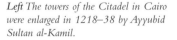

Left The towers of the Citadel in Cairo were enlarged in 1218–38 by Ayyubid Sultan al-Kamil.

citadel raised by Salah al-Din had walls 10m (33ft) high and 3m (10ft) thick with rounded towers from which defenders could fight off an attacking force. Within, Salah al-Din's engineers dug a great well 87m (285ft) deep through solid rock and with a long ramp so that animals could be led down into the depths to drive machinery needed to lift water such a great height.

After Salah al-Din's death, Sultan al-Kamil (reigned 1218–38) greatly enlarged a number of the citadel's towers – notably those known as the Blacksmith's Tower and the Sand Tower, which overlooked the narrow pass between the citadel and hills alongside. He added square towers on the wall perimeter; three of these, 30m (98ft) wide and 25m (82ft) tall, are still standing, overlooking the area today used for parking cars outside the walls. Sultan al-Kamil also built a palace within what is now the citadel's southern enclosure in 1218; this building is no longer standing.

MADRASAS IN EGYPT

As part of a programme to counter the influence of Shiah Islam and establish Sunni orthodoxy, the Ayyubids built the first *madrasas* (religious colleges) in Egypt, principally in Cairo. Their design was based on *madrasas* built by the Seljuks of Anatolia: they had long courtyards lined with accommodation and two *iwans* (halls) at each end. In Cairo, Salah al-Din built five *madrasas* and a mosque, and imported Sunni professors from Syrian legal schools to teach there.

The best surviving Ayyubid *madrasa* in Egypt, however, is the Madrasa of Sultan al-Salih Najm al-Din Ayyub, built by the sultan of that name toward the end of the Ayyubid era in 1242–44, on part of the site once occupied by the Fatimid Eastern Palace in the centre

of Cairo. Like the Mustansiriya *madrasa*, built in Baghdad in 1234 by Abbasid Caliph al-Mustansir, this was designed to house all four Sunni Muslim schools of legal thought – the Maliki, Shafii, Hanifi and Hanbali – with one *iwan* each.

The last of the Ayyubid sultans, al-Salih Najm al-Din Ayyub, died in 1249 and his mausoleum was added to the complex by his powerful widow, Shajar al-Durr, in 1250.

Above A seated ruler represented on this silver coin, made in south-eastern Anatolia in 1190–91.

Below Parts of the Madrasa of Sultan al-Salih Najm al-Din Ayyub, built in Cairo in 1242–44, still survive.

ALEPPO AND DAMASCUS

THE SYRIAN CITIES OF ALEPPO AND DAMASCUS WERE KEY
STRONGHOLDS FOR THE AYYUBIDS. IN BOTH LOCATIONS, AYYUBID
RULERS UNDERTOOK MAJOR BUILDING PROJECTS.

Above A half-dome of muqarnas *rises above a grand entranceway to the palace in the Aleppo citadel.*

Both Aleppo and Damascus had been important bases for Zangid ruler Nur al-Din in his war against the Christian crusaders. Later Ayyubid work complemented building begun by the Zangids: the Ayyubids refortified the citadel, built or rebuilt mosques and founded numerous *madrasas*.

THE ALEPPO CITADEL
Salah al-Din conquered Aleppo in 1183, and his son al-Malik al-Zahir Ghazi was soon made governor (1186–1216). Ghazi set to work refortifying the citadel: his men regraded the sides of the mound on which the citadel stood, re-excavated the moat, built a bridge, strengthened the ramparts and raised a gateway flanked by towers. Within the citadel they built a weapon store, dug a deep well and reservoir, erected palaces and bathhouses and added gardens.

Ghazi also renovated the Mosque of Abraham built by Nur al-Din. According to tradition, the patriarch (and Islamic prophet) Abraham stopped on the mound that became the citadel on his voyage from Ur to the Promised Land and milked his cows there; Nur al-Din's mosque was raised on the spot where Abraham was said to have milked the creatures.

Archaeologists have excavated what they believe to be the remains of Ghazi's principal palace within the citadel, the Dar al-Izz ('Palace of Glories'), which had a grand central courtyard paved in marble with an octagonal fountain at its centre and was surrounded by four *iwans* (halls). The northern *iwan* contained an indoor *shadirwan*, or fountain, running into a pool.

MADRASA AL-FIRDAUS
Daifa Khatun, who was Ghazi's wife, founded two notable buildings in Aleppo: one a *madrasa* (religious college), the other a *khanqa* (Sufi monastery). The Madrasa al-Firdaus (College of Paradise) was laid out around a courtyard paved with marble and centred on an octagonal fountain and pool decorated with a cloverleaf pattern; on the northern side was an *iwan*, with student quarters behind it, while on the southern side was a three-domed mosque between mausolea, and to east and west were halls probably

Left The Mosque of Abraham in the Aleppo Citadel once contained a fine wooden mihrab *donated by Nur al-Din.*

Above Ayyubid Sultan Al-Malik al-Zahir Ghazi added the bridge and fortified gateway to the Aleppo citadel.

used for teaching. The 1237 Khanqah al-Farafra also has an *iwan*, mosque and accommodation built around a fountain in a courtyard.

This arrangement of buildings around a courtyard with octagonal fountain was typical of Ayyubid buildings in Aleppo. In palaces, the courtyard was usually surrounded by four *iwans*, and religious buildings always had the mosque on the southern side. The mosques had a dome raised above the bay in front of the *mihrab* (niche). Their *mihrabs* were often adorned with a stonework pattern of interlinking knots, which inspired Mamluk and Ottoman architectural decoration.

Ayyubid buildings were usually made of dressed stone and left undecorated on the outside, except for entrance portals ornamented with *muqarnas* (stalactite-styled vaulting) or niches. Different types of stone were combined in some buildings, for example, by laying alternating horizontal bands of light and dark stones to create a design. Known as *ablaq*, this technique was an established one in Syria, having been used in the Great Mosque of Damascus, but it may have been inspired by the Byzantine tradition of using alternate bands of white ashlar and reddish baked brick.

IN DAMASCUS

Following the death of Nur al-Din in 1174, Salah al-Din became ruler of Damascus. Under Ayyubid rule, the citadel was strengthened, notably under al-Malik al-Adil in 1208–9. A number of mausolea and *madrasas* were built there, including the Madrasa al-Adiliya, which had been begun by Nur al-Din.

The Salihiyya quarter was established outside the city walls, where the al-Muzaffari Mosque was raised in *c.*1202–13. This historic treasure is the second oldest mosque surviving in Damascus. It contains a fine *mihrab* beneath a semidome adorned with *muqarnas* vaulting and on its right a *minbar* (pulpit) carved with geometric and floral designs, the oldest surviving *minbar* in Syria. Its design was based on the Umayyad Great Mosque of Damascus, with a plain façade, arcaded courtyard and rectangular prayer hall with three aisles on the south side of the courtyard.

Above The mihrab *in the Madrasa al-Firdaus, Aleppo, is made from marble set in a beautiful interlacing pattern.*

TRADE WITH EUROPE

EUROPEANS WERE IMPRESSED BY THE HIGH QUALITY OF MATERIAL GOODS FROM THE ISLAMIC WORLD. LUXURY ITEMS WERE BROUGHT TO EUROPE, WHERE THEY INFLUENCED LOCAL CRAFTSMEN.

Across the Islamic world, a dedicated export market developed. Craftsmen in Egypt, Syria and al-Andalus worked to meet the demand from Europe. The luxury goods purchased by pilgrims and merchants included carpets, glass, ivories and textiles, as well as inlaid metalwork and ceramics.

VENICE AND THE MAMLUKS

The main European trading partners of Mamluk Egypt were Venice and Genoa. The great trade routes through Damascus and across the Red Sea to South and South-east Asia passed through Mamluk lands, and in many cities there was a permanent diplomatic staff from Venice, safeguarding the interests of Venetian merchants. Indeed, Francesco Foscari, Venice's longest-reigning doge (in power 1423–57), was born in Egypt. Venice was particularly important in the trade in glass and ceramics, but also played a key part in the import of metalwork. It is known from trade documents that Venetian merchants exported brass and copper in significant quantities to craftsmen in the Middle East and at the other end of the process imported the finished inlaid products.

At one time historians proposed that Muslim craftsmen actually lived and worked in Venice, producing what was once termed 'Veneto-Saracenic metalwork' for the local luxury market. Modern historians reject this theory, arguing that the crafts guilds in Venice were so tightly managed that no foreign workers would have been able to establish themselves in the city.

STATUS SYMBOLS

Items of inlaid metalwork imported from the Islamic world into Europe included ewers, incense-burners and candlesticks as well as basins. These acquisitions were then proudly and prominently displayed in the homes of the wealthy.

Above This fine engraved 16th-century brass dish with a raised centre may have been made in Italy in an Islamic style.

On many of these items, a space was left blank for a European coat of arms to be added by the customers.

Some of the artefacts, such as the Baptistère de St Louis (see opposite page), found their way into royal collections and from there into modern museums, where we can admire them today, and their provenance and history are carefully detailed. Another key area of evidence for the trade between the Islamic world and Europe can be found in Italian paintings of the Renaissance period. Islamic art objects were often depicted in portraits of patrons and their families, shown standing in a domestic context: many of the objects were beautiful, exotic and expensive – and so, naturally enough, they were symbols of status, wealth and international connections.

Above Danzig merchant George Gisze made a prominent display of his carpet, imported from what is now Turkey, when he was painted by Hans Holbein in 1532.

CERAMICS AND GLASSWARE

Imported wares were copied by local European craftsmen, and in some cases the trade in Islamic products inspired the development of European production centres. For example, craftsmen in the Middle East developed gilding and enamelling techniques for decorating glass. Afterward, in the 13th century, Venice became the European centre for decorated glass objects, in part because of its maritime trade with the Islamic world but also because exiled Byzantine craftsmen settled in Venice. The craftsmen in Venice used forms and decorative styles developed in the Islamic Middle East but also turned for inspiration to narratives and motifs from Italy's classical past.

Glazed lustre pottery from al-Andalus was also imported to Europe. In Italy, tin-glazed wares were named 'maiolica' after the contemporary Italian name for the island of Mallorca, which was a key staging post on the maritime route for pottery from al-Andalus. In Venice, Florence and elsewhere in Italy, craftsmen made their own maiolica wares from the late 1200s onward. From Middle Eastern potters, Italian craftsmen learned how to scrape through the glaze to uncover the darker surface beneath – a technique called 'sgraffiato'.

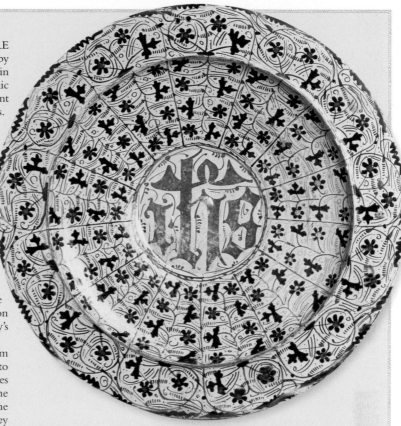

Above A Hispano-Moresque dish of tin-glazed maiolica, with the Christian monogram IHS in the centre. Stylized floral designs surround the central inscription.

THE BAPTISTÈRE DE ST LOUIS

A notable example of Mamluk export wares is the Baptistère de St Louis, an exquisite brass basin covered with figural engraved decoration and inlaid with silver and gold. The basin was signed by Muhammad ibn al-Zayn, probably in the mid-14th century – a time when this figural, decorative style had gone out of fashion among the Mamluk sultans and amirs, suggesting that the item was made for European customers.

The basin passed into the collection of the French royal family and was used as a vessel to hold holy water for the baptism of princes and princesses; it was part of the royal collection of the Sainte-Chapelle ('Holy Chapel') in the Château de Vincennes (built in the 14th century by King Charles V and now in the suburbs of Paris). The Baptistère de St Louis was given its name, which means the 'baptismal vessel of St Louis', because of an anachronistic association with St Louis (the French King Louis IX, died 1270). The basin is now in the Musée du Louvre in Paris.

Above The design on the Baptistère de St Louis shows dignitaries carrying weapons and symbols of their status at court.

CHAPTER 14

ISLAM IN SPAIN AND NORTH AFRICA

The Muslims conquered North Africa ('al-Maghreb') within the first decades of the Umayyad Caliphate, and reached Spain ('al-Andalus') in 711. After the overthrow of the Umayyad Caliphate by the Abbasids in 750, one survivor fled Syria and established an independent Umayyad power in Spain, ruling from prosperous Córdoba and the nearby palace city of Madinat al-Zahra. Political power fragmented following Umayyad decline, and al-Andalus was invaded from al-Maghreb by two consecutive Berber dynasties: the Almoravids (1062–1147) based in Marrakech, and then the Almohads (1130–1269), who made Seville their capital. Increasingly, the Christian kingdoms of northern Spain were pressing southward, and the Almohads were defeated by a Christian confederation at Las Navas de Tolosa in 1212. The last Muslim rulers in Spain were the Nasrids (1232–1492), who retreated to Granada in the south and built the Alhambra, a spectacular palace citadel that survives to this day. In 1492, the last Nasrid sultan was expelled from Spain by the Catholic monarchs Ferdinand and Isabella.

Opposite An exquisitely decorated stucco arcade runs around the Palace of the Lions in the Alhambra Palace, Granada. Originally, the stucco was painted in bright colours. The columns are marble.

Above The mihrab in the 10th-century Mosque of Córdoba is decorated in glass mosaic with kufic script and stylized foliate designs.

THE UMAYYADS OF SPAIN

THE MUSLIM CONQUEST OF IBERIA IN 711 WAS CONSOLIDATED BY THE LONE SURVIVOR OF THE UMAYYAD CALIPHATE OF DAMASCUS, WHO FOUNDED A DYNASTY THAT RULED THE PENINSULA UNTIL 1031.

In 711, an army of Arabs and Berbers, unified under the Umayyad Caliphate of Damascus, invaded the Christian Visigothic Kingdom of the Iberian Peninsula. During the eight-year campaign, the entire peninsula, except for Galicia and Asturias in the north, was brought under Muslim control. The conquered territory, under the Arabic name al-Andalus, became part of the Umayyad Empire.

ESTABLISHING A DYNASTY

When the Umayyad Caliphate of Damascus was overthrown by the Abbasid revolution in 750, the only member of the Caliphate to survive the subsequent massacre of the royal family, Abd al-Rahman I, escaped from Syria and fled to North Africa, reaching southern Spain in 755. Welcomed by Syrian immigrants loyal to his family, he re-established the Syrian Umayyad dynasty in Spain, which was to last for two and a half centuries. Nonetheless, nostalgia for Syria was a key theme in Spanish Umayyad

culture. At his capital of Córdoba, he began the construction of the Great Mosque, which was later enlarged by his successors.

During his 32-year reign, Abd al-Rahman I had to contend with numerous uprisings, some of which were supported by the Abbasids and one by Charlemagne. His successor, Abd al-Rahman II, was a poet and patron of the arts whose rule was marked by peace and prosperity. He brought scholars, musicians and poets from all over the Islamic world to Córdoba. The brief reign of his son Muhammad I was a period of crisis, but his successor, Abd al-Rahman III (912–61), was to reign for half a century. Abd al-Rahman III was the first Spanish Umayyad to declare himself caliph in 929, openly challenging the Abbasids in Baghdad and countering Fatimid claims from Cairo. Under his rule, and that of his son al-Hakam II (961–76) – a great patron of the arts and bibliophile – Umayyad Córdoba was a worthy and aspiring competitor

Above With its double tier of horseshoe arches, the Great Mosque at Córdoba, begun by Abd al-Rahman I in 784, is one of the great medieval buildings.

to the great courts of Byzantine Constantinople, Abbasid Baghdad and Fatimid Cairo. Art, poetry, philosophy and science flourished. Works in the 'courtly love' tradition were carried by troubadours (from an Arabic word meaning 'to be transported with joy and delight') into southern France. Al-Andalus became a centre for the translation of Arabic works (via Spanish) into Latin and Greek, and for innovations in music. Court culture followed sophisticated codes of manners for gastronomy, cosmetics, perfumes, dress codes and polite behaviour. Luxury objects, such as carved ivory boxes, bronze statues of animals and richly patterned silks, adorned the palaces, which were decorated with ornate capitals and marble fountains.

TECHNICAL INNOVATIONS

The introduction of new farming methods and the improvement of the Roman irrigation system turned the Guadalquivir Valley, the wetlands of the Genil and the fluvial areas of the Mediterranean

Left This gilt silver casket, dating from 976, bears the name of the Umayyad Caliph al-Hisham II. Luxurious silver caskets like this one were commissioned by caliphs to demonstrate their wealth and royal authority.

Above The diminutive mosque, Bab
al-Mardum, in Toledo has an inscription
on the façade saying it was built in
999 by Musa ibn Ali.

coast into fertile orchards and
fields. Among the crops that were
introduced into the region are
pomegranates, apricots, peaches,
oranges, rice, sugar cane, cotton and
saffron. Andalusian products were

sold in Baghdad, Damascus and
Makkah and as far away as India
and Central Asia.

Al-Hakam II's son, al-Hisham
II, was usurped by al-Hisham's
opportunistic chamberlain,
Muhammad ibn Abi Amir, who
adopted the title of al-Mansur,
or 'the Victorious One'.
Al-Mansur carried out more than
50 punitive expeditions against the
Christians of northern Spain. It
was during one such expedition
that the Basilica of Santiago
de Compostela, the most famous
Christian sanctuary in Spain,
was sacked. However, these
victories only served to unite the
Christian rulers of the peninsula
against al-Mansur. In 1002, he
was succeeded by his son Abd
al-Malik, known as al-Muzaffar,
who ruled until 1008.

CIVIL WAR

After Abd al-Malik, Sanchuelo,
his ambitious half brother, took
over. However, his attempt to take
the Caliphate for himself plunged
the country into a
devastating civil war
leading to the end
of the Umayyad
Caliphate in Spain.
The region then
fragmented into a
few weaker, rival *taifa*
kingdoms who were
unable to resist
Christian powers that
were encroaching
from the north.

Left This impressive
water wheel was
built on the site of
a Roman mill, during
Abd al-Rahman II's
reign (822–52), to
raise water from the
Guadalquivir river
to the Caliphal
Palace, Córdoba.

CÓRDOBA

UNDER THE UMAYYAD CALIPHATE, CÓRDOBA BECAME ONE OF THE MOST WONDERFUL CITIES OF THE WORLD, ITS OPULENCE AND CULTURE UNRIVALLED THROUGHOUT WESTERN EUROPE.

Situated along the Guadalquivir river, Córdoba had half a million people living in 113,000 houses scattered among 21 suburbs at the height of its prosperity. There were 1,600 mosques, 900 public baths and more than 80,000 shops. The Spanish Umayyad caliphs followed the pleasure-loving ways of their Syrian ancestors, and the elegance of life at court depicted on the ivory caskets was one of the specialities of Córdoba's skilled craftsmen.

During the caliphate of al-Hakam II, one of the most scholarly caliphs, Córdoba became the most cultured city in Europe. The library of al-Hakam is believed to have held 400,000 manuscripts. A great state institution, al-Hakam's library was a hub for a range of intellectual activities on an international level.

THE GREAT MOSQUE

With its complexity of design, decorative richness and delicacy of its superimposed arches, the Great Mosque at Córdoba is the finest surviving monument of Umayyad Spain. Its construction was begun by Abd al-Rahman I in 784, reportedly on the site of a Roman temple and a Visigothic church. Subsequent

Above This ornate doorway, with its horseshoe arch, is part of the additions made by al-Hakam II to the exterior of the Great Mosque at Córdoba.

Umayyad rulers extended and embellished the Great Mosque, creating a truly remarkable building.

The mosque interior is a deep hypostyle hall, featuring a dense forest of arched columns. Set on salvaged classical stone columns, the double arches are striped in red brick and white stone voussoirs, and mounted in pairs. This gives a dazzling visual result, heightening the hall and emphasizing the effect of receding perspective.

In 962, al-Hakam II added a new *mihrab* (niche) area, a small domed room exquisitely decorated in gold glass mosaic and carved stucco panels. Many aspects of the Great Mosque of Córdoba may be deliberate evocative references to the architecture of Umayyad Damascus.

Left The dome in front of the mihrab in Córdoba's Great Mosque is decorated with Quranic inscriptions and flowing designs of plant life.

MADINAT AL-ZAHRA

The splendid palace-city of Madinat al-Zahra, about 5km (3 miles) east of Córdoba, was modelled after the old Umayyad palace in Damascus, and it served as a symbolic tie between Caliph Abd-al-Rahman III and his Syrian roots. Only ten per cent of this remarkable city has so far been excavated, but a palatial complex of great luxury has come to light. Its construction began in 936 and continued for 25 years. Built in three large terraces on the hillside at the base of the Sierra Morena, with the caliph's palace at its highest point, the city was visible for miles around. In 941, the city's mosque was consecrated, and by 947 the government had transferred there from Córdoba.

At its zenith, Madinat al-Zahra was said to have a population of 12,000 people. The city was a vast and luxurious complex of buildings and irrigated gardens, including the caliph's residence, court reception halls, mosques, *hammams,* state mint,

pharmacy, barracks, court textile factory, plus a large urban quarter on the lowest terrace. This magnificent city was to last for only 50 years. It was sacked and looted during the Civil War (1010–13) that led to the end of the Caliphate of Córdoba and marked the beginning of the *taifa* period.

Above With its series of hillside palaces, Madinat al-Zahra commands an impressive prospect over the surrounding landscape.

Below These horseshoe arches in The Audience Hall in the Great Mosque are richly decorated with panels of carved stone applied to the walls.

SPANISH IVORIES

THE INTRICATELY CARVED IVORIES OF ISLAMIC SPAIN ARE EVIDENCE
OF THE ARTISTIC AND TECHNICAL EXPERTISE REACHED BY
CRAFTSMEN DURING THE 10TH AND 11TH CENTURIES.

Craftsmen turned pieces of
elephant ivory into small
containers, and carved them with
beautiful calligraphic inscriptions
and lively depictions of birds,
animals, gardens and human figures.
The earliest Spanish carved ivories
were made at Madinat al-Zahra, the
Umayyad royal city near Córdoba, in
the mid-10th century, at the height
of the Caliphate. Ivory was carved
into two shapes: either into a casket,
a small box with a flat or pitched lid,
or into a cylindrical container with a
domed lid known as a pyxis.

ROYAL COMMISSIONS

The tradition of ivory carving spread
from ancient Syria and Egypt to
Spain in the Islamic period. The
royal court at Madinat al-Zahra
commanded vast wealth and
monopolized the ivory industry of
Islamic Spain. They imported tusks
of ivory from its source in East
Africa and received ivory as gifts
from foreign royalty. It was reported
that 3,630kg (8,000lb) of the most
pure ivory was sent as part of a
present to Caliph al-Hisham II by
a Berber prince in 991.

The craftsmen worked in royal
workshops with the finest ivory
to create their unique objects, often
working in teams. The pyxides were
carved on a lathe, while the caskets
were constructed from 1cm (½in)
thick plaques sawn from the tusk
and fitted to a wooden frame. They
were carved in relief with sharp
chisel-like tools.

INSCRIPTIONS

An Arabic inscription was often
carved around the lid of the
completed ivories in foliate script.

These often tell us the place, for
whom and when they were made
and sometimes even the name of
the craftsmen. Most of the ivories
were specially commissioned for
members of the caliph's family
or courtly entourage. However,
one pyxis at London's Victoria and
Albert Museum was made for the
prefect of police, while two
pyxides and two flat boxes were
made in 964 and 966 for a lady
called Subh. She was a Basque
from Gascony, the consort of
Caliph al-Hakam II and mother of
his son and successor al-Hisham II.
The poetic inscription on another
pyxis in the Hispanic Society of
America hints that these luxury
objects were used as containers
to store precious jewels, spices
and unguents:

*Above A detail of an ivory casket, with
peacock designs, made for the concubine
of Caliph al-Hakam II, Subh.*

*Above This intricately carved lid from
999 bears the name of Sanchuelo,
second son of Caliph al-Mansur.*

'Beauty has invested me with
splendid raiment,
Which makes a display of jewels.
I am a receptacle for musk,
camphor and ambergris.'

AL-MUGHIRA PYXIS

The 'al-Mughira' pyxis was made in
968 and is a masterpiece of intricate
design and skill. It was made for
Prince al-Mughira, second son of
Abd al-Rahman III and considered
a hopeful for the throne of his
brother al-Hakam.

The carvings on the pyxis are
not fully understood. They might
show scenes from the life of the
prince, or perhaps they celebrate
seasonal festivals or pursuits. Four
cartouches, read from right to
left, start under the beginning of
the inscription, with the image
of a youth reaching up to steal
eggs from three eagles' nests. The
second image shows a lute player
flanked by two barefoot youths,
while the third and fourth scenes
show lions attacking bulls and a
pair of youths on horseback
picking dates from a tree. These
images are surrounded by smaller
vignettes of wrestlers, wolves,
fighting animals and pairs of
birds, filled in with delicately
intertwining leaves, resulting
in an intricate mix of agricultural
and hunting images.

Above This ivory casket was made in 1049–50 in the Cuenca workshops, and signed by a member of the Ibn Zayyan family. The enamel mounts are later European additions.

PAMPLONA CASKET

With the decline of the caliph's power in the late 10th century, production of luxury carved ivory moved to Córdoba, where the ambitious chamberlain al-Mansur commissioned a superb casket, which is now in Pamplona.

Al-Mansur had virtually taken over the rule of al-Andalus from the weakened caliph, and the depiction of the chamberlain in royal guise seated on a throne and flanked by attendants is an obvious display of this new authority. The signatures of a whole team of craftsmen are

Right The Pamplona casket, dated 1004, has elaborately carved panels showing the seated ruler and figures playing musical instruments.

hidden throughout this casket. One of them, Misbah, even carved his name on the throne platform under the chamberlain's feet.

THE CUENCA IVORIES

In the 11th century, when al-Andalus was fragmented into *taifas* (small kingdoms), the carved ivory workshops moved from Córdoba

to Cuenca, where craftsmen worked under the ruling family known as the Dhu'l-Nunids. The ivories the family commissioned were made by single craftsmen, such as Ibn Zayyan, who signed the 'Silos' casket of 1026–27. The Cuenca ivories are less richly carved than the earlier ivories, with simple repetitive decorations.

EARLY ISLAMIC RULE IN NORTH AFRICA

THE AGHLABIDS (800–909) RULED THE PROVINCE OF IFRIQIYA IN NORTH AFRICA AND LED INVASIONS OF SICILY, SARDINIA, MALTA AND PARTS OF MAINLAND ITALY.

In 800, the Abbasid Caliph, Harun al-Rashid (reigned 786–809), appointed his army general, Ibrahim ibn al-Aghlab from Khurasan, to pacify and rule the unstable province of Ifriqiya (the area of Tunisia and Eastern Algeria), making him semi-autonomous. The Aghlabids ruled from Kairouan until 909.

THE GREAT MOSQUE
The heart of Aghlabid culture is found in the holy city of Kairouan and, in architectural terms, the jewel in its crown is its magnificent Great Mosque. This was the first building of outstanding quality in the region, and today it is classified as a Unesco World Heritage Site. The mosque was originally founded in 670 by Umayyad general Sidi Uqba b. Nafi, but was

Below The Aghlabid Empire was centred on present-day Tunisia – but extended into Algeria and Libya.

entirely renovated in 836 by the Aghlabid ruler Ziyadat Allah (reigned 817–38). It has a large, rectangular courtyard with ablution pool, and a deep hypostyle hall of arcaded columns, with semicircular, horseshoe arches. Many of the 414 marble and porphyry columns are classical spolia, recycled from earlier Roman buildings on the site. The square, three-storey minaret is said to be one of the oldest in the Islamic world.

The most remarkable feature of the interior is the impressive array of early lustre tiles set around the *mihrab* (niche). These were imported from Baghdad in the mid-9th century, and are considered to be the oldest known example of Abbasid tiles still in situ. The surviving 139 examples display a wide variety of designs, including winged palmettes, crowns and peacock-eye motifs. The

Above Kairouan's Great Mosque, rebuilt in 836, was the most influential Aghlabid building – a prototype for early North African architecture.

mosque's *minbar* (pulpit) dates from the 9th century and was made from 300 pieces of imported teak.

OTHER MOSQUES
The design of the Great Mosque at Kairouan was extremely influential, shaping the development of other Aghlabid mosques in Sfax (849), Sousse (850) and Tunis (864). It also had an impact on the Mosque of the Three Doors in Kairouan. Built

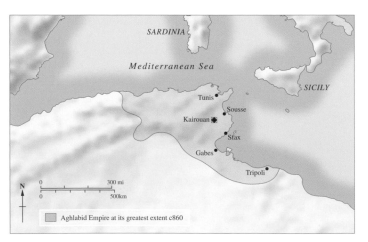

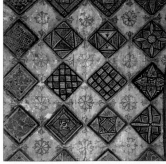

Above These 9th-century lustre tiles from the Great Mosque of Kairouan, Tunisia, feature a variety of vegetal and geometric designs.

in 866 by Muhammad ibn Khayrun, it takes its name from the triple horseshoe arch on the façade, which is surmounted by three bands of decoration, featuring *kufic* inscriptions and floral patterns.

THE BASINS

In a different vein, the Aghlabids created an important civic amenity in Kairouan, a hydraulic system known as the Basins. These two interlinked pools acted as reservoirs, settlement tanks and filters, and provided the city with clean water. They were commissioned by Abu Ibrahim Ahmad ibn al-Aghlab and took four years to complete (859–63).

ISLAMIC *RIBATS*

In the year that Kairouan was granted World Heritage status (1988), Unesco bestowed the same honour on another Aghlabid city: Sousse. This was a major port that held a key strategic and commercial significance, because it was only separated from Sicily by a narrow stretch of water. For this reason, Sousse was well fortified, with powerful ramparts and a *ribat*.

Ribats, which have been described as monastic fortresses, were a distinctive form of Islamic architecture, combining military and spiritual needs. Essentially, they were designed to house the Murabitun (holy warriors), but they also had facilities for prayer and study in times of peace. The minaret at Sousse, for instance, served as a watchtower and a landmark for shipping, as well as its traditional military and religious purpose.

The borders of the Aghlabid territories were protected by a line of *ribats*, with major outposts at Tripoli, Sfax, Monastir, Bizerte and Sousse. The latter is by far the most impressive, but the one at Monastir

is also a fine, early example (796). Built by Ziyadat Allah in 821, the Sousse Ribat is notable for its lofty battlements, pierced with arrow slits, its galleries of arcades enclosing the inner courtyard, its rib-vaulting, and the first-floor cells, which were accommodation for the troops.

Above A stairway leads from the courtyard of the Great Mosque of Sousse (850) to the vaulted sanctuary. A long kufic inscription extends above this arcade.

Below Enlarged in the 10th century, the ribat at Monastir has large fortified walls and a tower which served as watchtower and minaret.

THE ALMORAVIDS AND ALMOHADS

THE BERBER DYNASTIES OF THE ALMORAVIDS (1060–1147) AND THE ALMOHADS (1133–1269) RULED THE MAGHREB AND AL-ANDALUS. THEY BUILT MOSQUES AND PALACES AND OVERSAW A SILK-WEAVING INDUSTRY.

The Almoravids were from the western Sahara and established themselves in the Maghreb under religious leader Abdallah ibn Yasin in c.1030–59. Their name derives from al-Murabitun (meaning 'men of the *ribat*'), as the ascetic and highly disciplined followers of ibn Yasin were known; the word *ribat* refers perhaps to a religious institution, a fortified monastery in which the men trained, or simply to a bond of religious brotherhood, a shared commitment to *jihad* (holy war). At the end of the 11th century, the Almoravids extended their power north into al-Andalus and also south of the Sahara in West Africa, eventually creating an empire that covered 3,000km (1,865 miles) from north to south. Their capital was Marrakech.

Almoravid leader Yusuf ibn Tashfin (reigned 1060–1106) first arrived in al-Andalus in 1085, at the invitation of the small Islamic *taifa* kingdoms, requesting support against the Christians. He defeated King Alfonso VI of León and Castile (reigned 1065/72–1109) at the Battle of Zallaka in 1086 and, in 1090, took control of Andalus and defeated the *taifa* kings as well.

ALMORAVID MOSQUES

The Great Mosque of Tlemcen (in Algeria, near the Moroccan border) is a key surviving Almoravid construction, built in 1082 after Yusuf ibn Tashfin led the conquest of the central Maghreb and captured Tlemcen. The mosque is celebrated for its highly decorated minaret and for the splendid horseshoe *mihrab* (niche) and great dome in the prayer hall, both closely based on the Great Mosque of Córdoba. Built by Yusuf ibn Tashfin, the Great Mosque underwent many alterations under the rule of his son Ali ibn Yusuf (reigned 1106–43). The Qarawiyyin Mosque in Fez was expanded and improved with beautiful domed vaults under Ali ibn Yusuf. The mosque had been founded in c.850 by immigrants from Kairouan in Tunisia, and named after them; Ali ibn Yusuf expanded the already large 18-aisle prayer hall to contain 21 aisles – measuring 83m by

Above Nine aisles run across the prayer hall in Tinmal's Great Mosque, an example of the Almohad T-plan design.

44m (272ft by 144ft). It was one of the largest mosques in the Maghreb. Ibn Yusuf's craftsmen also increased the height of the central aisle that leads to the *mihrab* and added five domed vaults decorated with *muqarnas* (tiers of small niches). Under the Almoravids, this mosque was also developed into a major university.

Other contemporary Almoravid religious foundations include the Great Mosque of Nédroma (near Tlemcen in Algeria), built in 1086, and the Great Mosque of Algiers, built in 1096.

RISE OF ALMOHADS

Known as al-Muwahiddun ('those who believe in the oneness of God'), the Almohads swept the Almoravids from power in 1145–47. They were followers of the preacher Imam Muhammad al-Madhi ibn Tumart, a Berber from southern Morocco who declared himself the infallible imam Mahdi. After ibn Tumart's death in 1130, Abd al-Mumin became

Left The beautifully tiled courtyard at the Qarawiyyin Mosque in Fez.

leader of the movement, defeated the Almoravids at Orhan in north-western Algeria in 1145 and captured Marrakech in 1147.

The Almohads also took control of al-Andalus and made their capital in the city of Seville. However, after 1212, when their leader Muhammad III al-Nasir was defeated at the Battle of Las Navas de Tolosa by a Christian coalition of Aragon and Castile, Almohad power in al-Andalus swiftly failed, and they lost Córdoba (1236), Murcia (1243) and Seville (1248) to Ferdinand III of Castile. Back in the Maghreb, the Almohads survived in Marrakech until 1269, when the city was taken by the rival Berber power of the Merinids.

ALMOHAD T-PLAN MOSQUES
In the Maghreb, the Almohads built a series of mosques to a standard plan, with a many-aisled prayer hall and forecourt in the shape of a rectangle. These are known as T-plan mosques because the prayer hall's central aisle aligned on the *mihrab* met the transept to form a T-shape. Perhaps the principal prototype was the Mosque of Taza in Algeria, founded in 1142 by Abd al-Mumin; another was the Great Mosque of Tinmal (1153),

built in the Atlas Mountains around 100km (62 miles) south-east of Marrakech, in memory of Almohad founder Muhammad ibn Tumart.

THE ALMOHADS IN SPAIN
The remains of Almohad buildings can still be found in Seville. The Almohad Great Mosque, constructed in 1172–98, was later the site of the city's Christian cathedral. The minaret and the mosque's main courtyard survive. Today, the minaret serves as the cathedral's bell-tower. It features significant later additions, including a 17th-century Baroque belfry at its top, together with a rotating weathervane, and is called 'La Giralda'. The courtyard is planted with orange trees.

Among the more significant Almohad remains in Seville are parts of the city walls and a 12-sided tower on the banks of the Guadalquivir river near the city gates. The tower was once covered with glazed golden tiles and is known as the Torre del Oro ('Golden Tower'). Originally, it was matched by a similar tower on the opposite riverbank, which was covered with glazed silver tiles and called the Torre de la Plata ('Silver Tower'); the two towers were connected by a chain, which was

Above Seville's 12-sided Torre del Oro ('Golden Tower') was originally part of the 12th-century city walls.

lifted to allow ships access to the city harbour. Two Almohad palace buildings, the Patio de Yeso and the Patio de Contratacion, survive within the city.

Above This Almoravid silk cloth (c 1100) survived in a tomb in the Burgo de Osma Cathedral, Spain.

SILK PRODUCTION IN AL-ANDALUS
The history of silk weaving in Spain goes back to the Muslim conquest in the 8th century. Under Almoravid rule the city of Almería became the centre for textile production. According to the geographer Muhammad al-Idrisi (1100–66), in the mid-12th century Almería alone had 800 weaving mills, while the geographer Yaqut notes: 'In the land of Andalus there is not to be found a people who make more excellent brocade than those of Almería.' Generally, under the Almohad rulers figurative decoration on silks disappeared, to be replaced by abstract patterns of geometry and calligraphy.

As with many other Islamic art media, luxurious woven silk textiles were often adopted for use in sacred Christian contexts, such as royal burial, because of their remarkable quality. This (illustrated) silk and gold thread Almoravid fragment was re-used as a shroud for Christian relics of San Pedro de Osma: the design features lions, harpies, griffins, hares and people.

RABAT AND MARRAKECH

THE ROYAL CITIES OF MARRAKECH AND RABAT IN MOROCCO
WERE FOUNDED IN THE ALMORAVID AND ALMOHAD ERAS, AND ARE
RICH IN ARCHITECTURAL REMAINS OF THE PERIOD.

Marrakech gives its name to the country of Morocco: from Arabic *Marakush*, it came to English by way of Spanish *Marruecos*. The city was founded by Almoravid leader Yusuf ibn Tashfin (reigned 1060–1106) in 1062. He erected a grand palace named Dar al-Hajar ('House of Stone').

ALMORAVID BUILDINGS

A great mosque was built by the Almoravids in Marrakech, but it was destroyed when the city was captured by the Almohads in 1147. However, a small cube-shaped and domed building built over a well survives from the reign of Ali ibn Yusuf (1106–43). Named after its founder, the Qubbat al-Barudiyin is just 8m (26ft) tall. The walls are decorated with polylobed arches derived from those in the Great Mosque of Córdoba and with composite arches (alternately convex and concave curved outlines) based on the arches in the Palace of Aljaferia in Saragossa (1050–83), a product of the *taifa* (small kingdoms) of al-Andalus. The domed interior has magnificent stucco decoration. Historians believe that the building was a place for ritual washing used by those visiting the mosque.

The Almoravid rulers typically installed large, fine wooden *minbars* (pulpits) in their mosques. The beautifully carved *minbar* that once stood in the Great Mosque of Marrakech was ordered by Ali ibn Yusuf in *c.*1120 from renowned craftsmen in Córdoba. It stands 4m (13ft) high and has 1,000 carved panels featuring a complex design of geometric shapes. When the Almohads sacked Marrakech and destroyed the mosque in 1147, they saved the *minbar* and transferred it to the Kutubiyya Mosque that they built in the city.

ALMOHAD MOSQUES

In fact, the Almohads built two Kutubiyya mosques in Marrakech. The first, constructed in 1147, had

Above Built of red clay, the Bab er Reha gate is part of the 11th-century city wall of Marrakech.

17 aisles and was built to a T-plan design with the principal aisle aligned on the *mihrab* (niche) and a pronounced transept cutting across it at right angles to form a T.

However, this building was demolished almost as soon it was finished, perhaps due to a slight mistake made in its alignment with Makkah. The second mosque, built to the south of the first, beginning in 1158 was on a different alignment.

The second Kutubiyya Mosque has five cupolas above the *qibla* aisle (facing the direction of prayer) and six above the transept; there is also a splendid 67.6m (222ft) high minaret with a square tower surmounted by a lantern-shaped section. It contains six floors and a ramp to give the *muezzin* (who makes the call to prayer) access to the platform at the top. Four copper globes adorn the tower: according to local legend, there were originally three gold globes, until a wife of the Almohad ruler Yaqub al-Mansur (reigned 1184–99) donated the fourth globe after giving up all her gold jewellery to compensate for her failure to fast for a single day during Ramadhan. The minaret was the model for the minaret of the Mosque of Hasan in Rabat.

Left Measuring 67.6m (222ft) in height, the elegant minaret of the second Almohad Kutubiyya Mosque in Marrakech was built from 1158.

At Marrakech, the Almohads also laid out fortified city walls that incorporated monumental gates, such as the Bab Agnaou. Yaqub al-Mansur also built a *kasbah*, or fortified palace (citadel), in the city, as well as an associated mosque, the El Mansouria, completed in 1190.

RABAT

The city of Rabat, the modern capital of Morocco, grew from a *ribat*, a fortified camp or monastery, established by the first Almohad ruler Abd al-Mumin (reigned 1130–63) in 1146 as a base from which to launch the military attacks he was planning against al-Andalus.

Above The 12th-century Bab Agnaou gate at Marrakech bears an inscription from the Quran in Maghribi script. It leads into the royal citadel.

Below The unfinished Mosque of Hasan (1195–99) in Rabat contains 200 columns and a half-built, but beautifully decorated, red limestone minaret.

Yaqub al-Mansur gave it the name Ribat al-Fath ('Victory Camp'), from which its modern name derives, and built the fortifications that still survive.

At Rabat, this proud ruler, who took the name al-Mansur Billah ('Granted Victory by God') after he defeated King Alfonso VIII of Castile at the Battle of Alarcos on 18 July 1195, began building the Mosque of Hasan. This mosque was left unfinished, but survives today as a splendid square minaret and long lines of pillars, originally intended to support the roof of the prayer hall. The mosque was a vastly ambitious project: the surviving minaret is on a base 16m (52ft) square and may have been intended to rise to 80m (262ft), while the planned mosque was to cover 178m by 138m (584ft by 453ft) – bigger even than the Great Mosque of Córdoba, which measured 173m by 127m (568ft by 417ft), after it had been extended many times. The Mosque of Hasan may have been left unfinished because Yaqub al-Mansur overreached himself and could not complete such a vast building. After his death in 1199, building work ground to a halt.

THE NASRIDS

THE LAST MUSLIM SULTANS ON THE IBERIAN PENINSULA, THE NASRIDS (1232–1492) WERE RULERS OF THE SMALL KINGDOM OF GRANADA IN SPAIN, WHERE THEY BUILT THE MAGNIFICENT ALHAMBRA CITADEL.

Almohad power in Spain never recovered from the defeat of Sultan al-Nasir by an army led by King Alfonso VIII of Castile in 1212. The Christians captured Córdoba in 1236, the cities of Murcia and Jaén in 1243 and 1245, and Seville in 1248. During this period, several small Muslim kingdoms were established, and one of these was created in Jaén by Muhammad ibn Yusaf ibn Nasr (reigned 1232–73), self-styled Sultan Muhammad I of Arjona, who made his capital in Granada in 1237. Ibn Nasr was a client-ruler under King Ferdinand III, but he managed to pass on his kingdom to his son Muhammad II (reigned 1273–1302), who consolidated Nasrid power in Granada.

The Nasrid kingdom was at its height under Sultan Yusuf I (reigned 1333–54) and Sultan Muhammad V (reigned 1354–9 and 1362–91), both of whom devoted themselves to rebuilding the fortified palace-city of the Alhambra that was the Nasrids' most enduring legacy.

After the reign of Muhammad VII (1392–1408), the power of the Nasrids entered a slow decline as rival family members fought over the sultanate. The final sultan, Muhammad XII, also known as Boabdil, seized the throne from his father Abu'l Hasan Ali in 1482, but the following year he was captured by Christians. Boabdil's uncle took the throne as Muhammad XIII, then King Ferdinand released Boabdil as a vassal-ruler, and the two rivals fought while Ferdinand's army advanced toward Granada. There, Boabdil was forced to hand the city to the Christians in 1492. The 'Reconquista' (reconquest) was complete.

GLORIES OF GRANADA

The Alhambra's name derives from the Arabic words for 'the red one': it is so-called from the reddish colour

Above A steam bath was part of the harem area of the Comares Palace at the Alhambra. The tiles are original.

of the sun-dried, clay-and-gravel bricks of which its outer walls are constructed. A fort is known from contemporary accounts to have stood on the site as early as 860, but there are no remains dating to earlier than the 11th century, when builders of the Zirid dynasty erected an earlier version of the Alcazaba. The complex began to be established in its current form under the early Nasrid sultans, and the most celebrated features, including the Comares Palace and the Palace of the Lions, date to the reigns of Yusuf I and Muhammad V in the 14th century.

In its final form, the fortified palace-city of the Alhambra stands behind walls 1,730m (5,675ft) long with 30 towers and 4 main gates, on a plateau overlooking the city of Granada. The Alhambra has three main areas: the Alcazaba, or citadel, a barracks area for the guard; the palaces used by the sultan and family; and the madinah, a residential area for officials and artisans.

Left By 1260, Muslim rule in Spain was limited to a small, mountainous area in the south-east of the country.

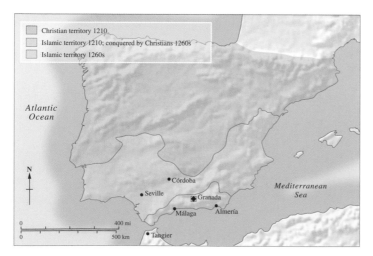

Christian territory 1210
Islamic territory 1210; conquered by Christians 1260s
Islamic territory 1260s

Atlantic
Ocean

N

Córdoba
Seville
Granada
Málaga   Almería
Tangier

Mediterranean
Sea

0   400 mi
0   500 km

Above The fortified palace-city of the Alhambra sits on a plateau in front of the Sierra Nevada mountains.

TWO PALACES

Within the palace complex the two outstanding Nasrid buildings are the Comares Palace and the Palace of the Lions. The former was built by Yusuf I around a series of courtyards that led on to reception rooms. Beyond a highly decorated façade, added by Muhammad V in 1370, the main rooms are arranged around the Court of the Myrtles. The main residential areas are off the long sides of the court, while at one end is an administrative complex and at the other a public room with the large Throne Room (or 'Hall of the Ambassadors') occupying the Comares Tower. With its exquisite ceiling of inlaid wood rising to a *muqarnas* dome, it is one of the most beautiful parts of the entire complex.

The Palace of the Lions was added to the Comares Palace by Muhammad V. At the centre of its main courtyard is a marble fountain, its dodecagonal bowl supported by 12 lions. Verses inscribed into the

Right In the Alhambra's Hall of Justice, a ceiling painting on leather depicts a Christian knight slain by a Muslim warrior.

fountain's edge praise the hydraulic system that supplies its water. A colonnade with horseshoe arches runs around the patio and gives access to royal apartments and reception rooms, including the Sala de los Reyes ('Hall of the Kings'), with a dome featuring paintings of people thought to be the principal Nasrid kings. The Sala de los Mocarabes ('Muqarnas Chamber') once had a *muqarnas* dome.

When the city passed into Christian hands, King Charles V of Spain built a large Renaissance-style palace within the walls of the Alhambra in 1526. The Comares Palace and Palace of the Lions were

thereafter together called the Casa Real Vieja ('Old Royal Palace'), while the Renaissance building was called the Casa Real Nueva ('New Royal Palace').

MADINAH

In Alhambra, the madinah held stores, a mosque, public baths and the sultans' mausoleum. Many of these were built by Muhammad III (reigned 1302–9). There was also a *madrasa* (college). Outside the Alhambra walls were the Generalife Gardens, incorporating vegetable gardens, ornamental plantings, pavilions, fountains and the summer palace of the Generalife.

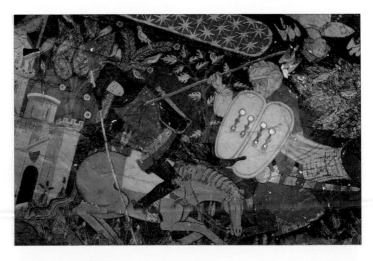

THE GARDEN IN ISLAMIC ARCHITECTURE

THE IMPORTANCE OF ENCLOSED AND IRRIGATED GARDENS HAS A LONG HISTORY IN THE MIDDLE EAST. GARDENS ARE OFTEN DESCRIBED AS AN EARTHLY VERSION OF THE PARADISE PROMISED IN THE QURAN.

The descriptions of the eternal garden of paradise in the Quran refer to springs, brooks and four rivers containing water, milk, honey and a non-intoxicating type of wine. In a landscape 'as large as heaven and earth', thornless trees provide restful shade and fruits.

Chapter 55, the Surah al-Rahman ('The Merciful'), describes four gardens in paradise, all with flowing waters, trees and fruits. There are references to gates, so the gardens are enclosed by walls. Throughout these gardens are shelters and buildings, including tents, castles, houses and rooms that have running water. The buildings are isolated among green spaces and stretches of water rather than gathered in a settlement, because in contrast to Judaism and Christianity – which both look forward to a 'heavenly Jerusalem' – Islam has no city in visions of the afterlife.

THE GENERALIFE

The Generalife gardens are separated from the Alhambra palace by a gorge, and overlook the palace-city. The name may be derived from the Arabic *jinan al-arif*, meaning 'gardens of the overseer'.

The gardens were laid out during the reign of Muhammad III (reigned 1302–9) and used as a summer retreat; the Nasrid rulers and their courtiers would have strolled through the terraces filled with lush, green planting and cooling fountains.

The lowest terrace – the Patio de la Acequía – was formed as a rectangle and divided into four separate quadrants by two intersecting water channels, with a water basin at the centre.

Below The beautiful Shalimar Gardens in Srinagar, India, were laid out by Mughal Emperor Jahangir in 1619.

Above Fountains and flowing water are central to the design of the Patio de la Acequia *in the Generalife Gardens.*

USES OF WATER

In its description of paradise, the Quran tells of 'gardens beneath which rivers flow'. With many Islamic cultures rooted in dry regions, irrigation plans were central to the design of gardens. One scheme, developed in pre-Islamic Iran and exported throughout the Islamic world, was to dig canals underground that carried water around the garden down gentle gradients from a raised water source.

As in the Quranic example, the waterway was beneath the garden; it was covered so the water did not evaporate in sunlight. In other places, where the heat was less intense, open canals were used.

In Islamic culture, water is a symbol of life. Control and provision of water were also the gift of the ruler – symbolic of his gracious generosity and responsibility as a fellow Muslim. Fountains, pools and waterways were given prominence so that visitors could enjoy the air-cooling qualities, movement and music of running water. In princely gardens integrated within palace complexes, water flowed in covered canals into the interior of the palace, where it emerged from fountains, ran down tiled walls and fell in waterfalls down stairs.

FOUR-PART GARDEN

The description of the four gardens and four rivers of paradise in the Quran gave resonance to the four-part Persian *chahar bagh* garden design. The *chahar bagh* was named from the Persian words *chahar* (four) and *bagh* (garden). The design was derived from a pre-Islamic source: the gardens in Pasargadae laid out by Cyrus the Great (reigned 576–530BCE), ruler of the Persian Achaemenid Empire.

The *chahar bagh* layout was used for palace gardens and, particularly in Mughal India, for formal gardens surrounding mausolea. In Delhi, Mughal Emperor Akbar (reigned 1566–1605) placed a mausoleum in honour of his father Humayan (reigned 1530–40 and 1555–56) at the centre of a *chahar bagh* garden. Near Agra, the design was used again for the Taj Mahal, the memorial shrine built in 1632–54 by Mughal Emperor Shah Jahan (reigned 1628–58)

to honour the memory of his wife Mumtaz Mahal. Here, the tradition was slightly altered: in a normal *chahar bagh* layout, the tomb stands at the centre of the quadrilateral garden, but at the Taj Mahal it is at the northern end overlooking the river Yamuna.

A GREEN SHADE

Many of the early Muslims hailed from arid lands, such as the deserts of Arabia and north Africa, and historians draw on this heritage to explain the love in Islamic culture for well-watered shady places. As well as the Quranic

Above The quadrilateral layout of the chahar bagh *gardens at the Taj Mahal is clear in this 18th-century lithograph.*

imagery of paradise as a garden, there was a well-established literary tradition in which gardens were revered as blissful places of refuge. Poets conjured the image of shady retreats from the heat of day, where moving water made soothing music. In the Abbasid Empire from the 8th century and in al-Andalus, particularly in the 11th century, the *rawdiya* ('garden poem') was a popular genre. Many Islamic gardens survive attached to palaces and mausolea, but many more have been described in contemporary literary sources. According to these sources, for example, there were 110,000 gardens of fruit trees in Damascus, magnificent parks outside the city walls in Samarra, and miles of canals and gardens in Basra. In al-Andalus, Valencia, Seville and Córdoba were famous for their beautiful gardens.

Left In Islamic gardens, water in pools, streams and fountains is symbolic both of earthly life and the abundance promised in paradise.

SPANISH LUSTREWARE

THE SKILLED POTTERS OF ISLAMIC SPAIN CREATED MASTERPIECES IN CERAMICS, USING THE ISLAMIC TECHNIQUE OF LUSTRE PAINTING THAT ARRIVED IN SPAIN IN THE 11TH CENTURY.

It is thought that the technique of lustre decoration was invented in Iraq at the end of the 8th century by potters who borrowed techniques from glass technology. Powdered metallic compounds of copper and silver were painted on to the fired ceramic body, which was fired again at a low temperature in a kiln with a reduced oxygen supply. After cooling, the object was polished to reveal the lustrous metallic sheen.

Lustre-decorated ceramics were popular in Egypt during the Fatimid period from the late 10th century. The technique probably spread from Egypt to Spain in the early 11th century, where fragments of imported Fatimid lustreware pottery have been found. Fatimid potters may have moved west to the wealthy patrons of Islamic Spain, bringing the secrets of this complicated technique with them. The earliest lustreware made in Spain is a bowl that can be dated to the early 11th century. There is evidence for the dating of early Spanish lustreware in the so-called *bacini*, the imported glazed bowls that were used to decorate the façades of 12th-century churches in northern Italy, particularly Pisa. These show that the Spanish potters had mastered lustre production by the early 12th century.

EARLY SPANISH LUSTRE

By the 13th century, a lustreware industry was established in the port town of Málaga. The Arabic word *mālaqah* has been found written on a number of lustre fragments, indicating they were made in the town, which had grown in size and wealth under the patronage of the Nasrid rulers from 1238.

Early documentary evidence of Spanish lustreware is found in a document from Britain dated 1289, which mentions that pottery of 'a strange colour' was bought from a Spanish ship in Portsmouth for Queen Eleanor of Castile, who was the wife of King Edward I. In 1303, another document lists the customs duty that was paid on pottery from Málaga, which was described as '*terra de Malyk*', when it was imported into the town of Sandwich in Kent. The fact

Above This dish, made in the pottery-making centre of Manises, near Valencia, in 1496, bears the arms of Ferdinand of Aragon and Isabella of Castile.

that these ceramics were exported as far as Britain shows that lustreware was prized as a luxury object. The Moroccan traveller Ibn Battuta wrote in about 1350 that 'at Málaga is made the wonderful gilded pottery that is exported to the remotest countries.'

ALHAMBRA VASES

The magnificent 'Alhambra vases' have been described as the closest that pottery has ever come to architecture. Standing almost as tall as a human being, they are the largest Islamic ceramics ever made. Ten unique vases survive mostly intact, but excavated fragments suggest a greater production. The vases have been found in Spain, Sicily and Egypt, indicating that they were exported throughout the Mediterranean. Analysis of fragments of a vase found in Fustat, Egypt, confirmed that they were made in Málaga under the Nasrid Empire during the 14th century.

The name 'Alhambra vases' comes from the theory that they may have been made to grace the wall niches in the halls of the

Left This large Hispano-Moresque lustre dish, made from earthenware, dates from the 15th century.

Nasrid Alhambra Palace in Granada. Their distinctive, elegant shape resembles that of traditional unglazed storage jars known as *tinajas*, used to store and transport oil, wine and water. However, the vast size and winged handles of the Alhambra vases mean they could not have been easily lifted, while the rich decoration suggests a purely ornamental function.

The golden lustre and cobalt blue decorative scheme is usually arranged in horizontal bands that are decorated with arabesques, inscriptions and symbolic motifs, such as the *khamsa*, or 'hand of Fatima'. The monumental inscription on the vase in Palermo repeats continuously the word

Left One of the so-called 'Alhambra vases', this vessel stands over 1.2m (4ft) high and has golden lustre and cobalt blue decoration.

Above This earthenware bowl with lustre and cobalt blue decoration was made by Nasrid potters in Malaga, and probably commissioned by a Portuguese merchant.

'al-mulk', or 'kingship', while the vase in St Petersburg is inscribed in Arabic with the words 'pleasure', 'health' and 'benediction'.

MÁLAGA SHIP BOWL

One of the most splendid examples of early 15th-century Nasrid lustreware is a truly magnificent bowl at the Victoria and Albert Museum in London. Measuring 50cm (20in) in diameter, the lustre decoration on the interior depicts a caravel, a type of ship that was developed in the early 15th century by the Spanish and Portuguese for their voyages of exploration. The ship is shown in full sail and bearing the arms of

ancient Portugal. Perhaps the Nasrid potter was commissioned to make it by a maritime merchant from Portugal to commemorate a successful voyage. Analysis of this bowl conducted in 1983 identified the clay as Málagan and therefore of Nasrid production – before then it had been thought it came from Valencia.

After the fall of the Nasrid Empire in 1492, lustre ceramics stopped being made in Málaga. The technique was not lost though, as the lustre tradition was developed by mudéjar artists of Manises and Paterna in eastern Spain, with their famous Hispano-Moresque ceramics that flourished in the 15th and 16th centuries.

MUDÉJAR STYLE

THE DISTINCTIVE ARTISTIC STYLE OF THE MUDÉJARS FLOURISHED
IN THE ARCHITECTURE AND DECORATIVE ARTS OF SPAIN FROM
THE 14TH TO THE 16TH CENTURIES.

Those Muslims who stayed in Spain after the end of Islamic rule and the Christian 'Reconquista' in 1492 were known as the mudéjars. The word 'mudéjar' is probably a medieval Spanish corruption of the Arabic word *al-mudajjanun*, meaning 'those permitted to remain'. During this period, the new Christian rulers were under pressure to repopulate the lands they had conquered, to irrigate and farm the lands and to create vital tax revenue. The mudéjars were allowed to continue practising their religion, customs and language under Christian rule.

The Christian aristocracy, who wanted to emulate the sophisticated art and architecture of the previous Muslim rulers, became patrons of the mudéjar artisans. Even the Catholic monarchs of the Reconquista, Ferdinand and Isabella, commissioned works of mudéjar craftsmanship, including lustreware and carpets. The craftsmen, who sometimes formed guilds, worked in masonry, carpentry, textiles, ceramics and metalwork, areas in which they had amazing technical proficiency. Mudéjar style is characterized by its integration of Islamic decorative style with elements from the Christian arts.

ARCHITECTURE

The new Christian kings and noblemen were fascinated with the luxury and refinement associated with the Islamic style. New palaces were built and old ones renovated by mudéjar craftsmen, who created royal residences in brick, wood and plaster. The 11th-century Islamic fortified palace of Aljaferia in Saragossa was substantially renovated in the 14th century by mudéjar artists working for King Pedro IV. The Alcazar of Seville was

Above These tiles from the Santa Cruz district of Seville are in the mudéjar *style. Tin-glazed and decorated ceramic tiles like these are known as* azulejos.

rebuilt in 1364 for the Christian ruler Pedro I, emulating the style of the Islamic palaces of al-Andalus, with patios and ornamented façades, carved wooden doors, fountains, elaborately carved stucco and even Arabic inscriptions referring to Pedro I as 'sultan'.

The mudéjars were responsible for religious as well as aristocratic and secular art, as Islamic motifs invoked notions of power and wealth in the church as well as the palace to a population that had until recently lived under Islamic rule. In synagogues and cathedrals, they used brick and wood instead of stone as a primary material. The magnificent painted wooden ceiling of Teruel Cathedral in Aragon is a masterpiece of the mudéjar style from the late 13th century. A look up to the ceiling

Left In 1364, the Alcazar of Seville was rebuilt in Islamic style for the Christian ruler, Pedro I.

above the nave reveals a lively and colourful mix of scenes from everyday life, with musicians, knights on horseback, animals and even a group of carpenters.

Mudéjar craftsmen also worked for Jewish patrons, in buildings such as the 'el Transito' synagogue in Toledo. This prayer hall was built in the mid-14th century by mudéjars working for Samuel Halevi Abulafia, tax collector for King Pedro I. Beautifully detailed inscriptions in Arabic and Hebrew are finely carved in stucco on the walls.

CERAMICS

Mudéjar ceramics reached a high point both aesthetically and commercially in the lustreware made in the villages of Manises and Paterna just outside Valencia. Their distinctive ceramics, known as 'Hispano-Moresque' ware, combined motifs from Islamic culture, such as pseudo-Arabic inscriptions and arabesques, with Christian elements

Above This elaborate mudéjar ceiling, built after 1504, is in the monastery of San Juan de los Reyes, in Toledo.

of heraldry and cartouches with Christian inscriptions, to create a distinctive mudéjar aesthetic.

The early pieces were greatly influenced by Nasrid ceramics. It is thought that potters from Nasrid Granada may have emigrated to Manises in the early 14th century at the request of Pedro Buyl, Lord of Manises. Demand outstripped supply as potters began to work on a level approaching mass production. They worked for a wealthy Christian clientele and made plates, bowls, basins, pharmacy jars and pots meant for everyday use. Italian nobility soon became the largest market for Manises lustreware. In fact, many surviving

Right A Hispano-Moresque dish with lustre and cobalt blue decoration, made in Manises in the 15th century.

objects are datable by the Italian coats of arms that decorate them. Images of Manises ceramics are even found in Renaissance paintings from as early as the 15th century.

Mudéjar art declined in Spain during the 16th century, and finally disappeared at the time of the forced conversions, and finally expulsions of Muslims in 1609–10.

وده شب بر بابل بسید | کشتن بر زمین بر نهاده پدید | زمانه شاد درد او باخروب | روکتی که هامون زاده بحوب | کنو برنشید و ندید کس | همه مویه مورد و صحبرد نمای

بیرون رخمه ساخته | پی کوپش را بر زین درتخت | بر نهاد بر زرین دوتخت | زآن خواننده کنی بکنجت | هر نکره که بود ازرستندار | ازاد وازباک دل بیدکان

بکس کخ و دیاره زبر | همو کسی کفت کای نامدار | همو خواستی مشک و عبر نثار | نخواهی همی بادشامی و برم | سوتونی همی سبر حفنان زنم

همی برسری سرای بنج | کنون شاد باشی بحوم | که زیانت از داد و مزربی | بر نخمه بنشنند و کشتند بار | شدان نامور سبر کردن فرار

چون سوات ربم بد | زبری نخاک بر همه زاهنی | کز این بوشتی و ظاهرمی | توبازنده سوی تکوی کزای | مکام یانی میکبرسرای

از مانکار بر کشید | شبه زاهی بیلس باز کرد | تحره خروش آمد نکی نای | جواکه شد شاه کابلستان | همانکوش روبس وهندیستان

زمین را کرد کرد | بخون شید کشا جهان تار بدبر | زکنج نخاست شبه بدن و ناکرد | بدین فرامش شد سباه | ازان نامدازان زابلستان

مرزی بیش سباه | زبر آهین شده هوا لاجورد | آمد کی باد وکردی کبود | پیشه درون شیر کردن راه | بشدد و شبایی زخور شیباد

زان هوا تان شد | جهان شد بر آواز برخاشوی | بیازرم شد بزم جوکبی | قرامرزن باخوان مایه سباه | زبین زآسمان همی بید سود

شبهار سکار کفا تش شد | حو نخاست آواز کبان درود | دیلزان زابلی شیر دار زرک | زهبر سو زیشان کین ساختند | بردحویشتن زان زان قلبک

زین و کودک وما لبکد شند | دل ازمرز وان خانه مرد داشت | بزاکه شد هند وسند برت | که کل شد همه خا آورده | همراز برمنش نامدا زان بسند | خبندان نکردان هند

CHAPTER 15

IRAN AFTER THE MONGOL INVASIONS

Duration the 13th century, the Mongols invaded the Islamic world not once but twice. This seemingly invincible cavalry first emerged from the steppes of Mongolia under the leadership of Genghis Khan (d.1227). The second Mongol invasion was led by Genghis Khan's grandson Hulagu, who established the Ilkhanid dynasty, ruling from Maragha, Takht-i Sulayman and then Tabriz. The Ilkhanids were important patrons of Islamic and Persian culture, particularly architecture and the arts of the book. The dynasty remained subordinate to the Great Khan in China and the visual arts were strongly influenced by Chinese contact. Following the decline of Ilkhanid power in the 1330s, different interests took control across Iran and Iraq, including the culturally rich Jalayirid dynasty of Tabriz. These were swept away by another brutal steppe invasion in the 1370s, led by the renowned conqueror Timur (d.1405). Like the Ilkhanids, the Timurids knew that cultural patronage would guarantee a place in history and sponsored great works of art and architecture at their courts in Samarkand, Herat and Shiraz.

Opposite The Ilkhanids transformed the arts of the book in Iran, with grand projects such as this c.1330s copy of the Shahnama *(Book of Kings) by Firdawsi.*

Above Dramatic turquoise, yellow and blue tiles cover the dome of the Gur-e Amir ('Tomb of the King') in Samarkand. Many Timurid mausolea and mosques have slender ribbed domes with bright blue tiles.

THE ILKHANIDS AND THEIR ARCHITECTURE

AS THEY SET OUT TO DEMONSTRATE THEIR GREATNESS BY BUILDING ON A GRAND SCALE, THE ILKHANID SULTANS FOLLOWED IRANIAN ARCHITECTURAL TRADITIONS ESTABLISHED IN THE SELJUK ERA.

Former nomads, the Ilkhanid rulers spent winters in the region of Baghdad and summers in grassy pasturelands of north-western Iran. There, the second Ilkhanid Sultan, Abaqa Khan (reigned 1265–82), built the vast, lavishly decorated summer palace of Takht-i Sulayman and the fourth sultan, Arghun Khan (reigned 1284–91), established Tabriz as the capital of the Ilkhanate.

When he came to power, Ghazan Khan (reigned 1295–1304) converted to Sunni Islam, and with his Iranian vizier Rashid al-Din he embarked upon an enormous building programme, constructing *caravanserais* (travellers' inns) along major trade routes and building a congregational mosque and bathhouse in each city. Ghazan Khan also rebuilt the walls of Tabriz, which he developed into a major city of international standing. He

then built a grand funerary complex to house his own remains in western Tabriz, with two *madrasas* (religious colleges), an astronomical observatory, library, hospice and other buildings around his tomb. Rashid al-Din constructed a complex in his own name in the eastern part of the city.

ILKHANID MOSQUES

One of the best-preserved mosques of the Ilkhanid period is the Friday, or congregational, Mosque built in 1322–26 under Abu Said, the ninth ruler of the Ilkhanate at Varamin, 42km (26 miles) south of Tehran. The Varamin Mosque was built following the traditional Iranian pattern established under the Seljuks: four *iwans* (halls) built around a central courtyard, with a domed prayer hall with the *mihrab* (niche) behind the *qibla iwan* (the hall in the direction of Makkah).

Above The magnificent dome, spanning an impressive 25m (82 ft), at Uljaytu's tomb at Sultaniyya, in Iran is one of the masterpieces of world architecture.

In Tabriz, however, the mosque of the vizier Ali Shah built in 1315 under the rule of Uljaytu (reigned 1304–16) had a different layout: there was a single *iwan* leading on to the courtyard, which contained a pool and was enclosed by walls 30m (98ft) in length, 10m (33ft) thick and 25m (82ft) high; the *mihrab* was set in a vast semicircular bastion extending behind the *qibla* wall. Originally, there was a grand entrance portal at the far end of the courtyard, and a *madrasa* and hospice for Sufis stood on either side of the *iwan*.

ULJAYTU'S MAUSOLEUM

The eighth Ilkhanid ruler Uljaytu constructed a new capital called Sultaniyya ('Royal Ground') about 120km (75 miles) north-west of Qazvin in north-western Iran, where Arghun Khan had built a

Left Under Hulagu, Genghis Khan's grandson, the Mongol invasions of the 1250s gave the Ilkhanids control over a huge empire.

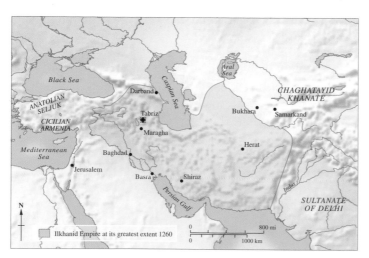

Black Sea

ANATOLIAN SELJUK

CICILIAN ARMENIA

Mediterranean Sea

Jerusalem

Darband

Caspian Sea

Tabriz

Maragha

Baghdad

Basra

Shiraz

Aral Sea

Bukhara

Samarkand

CHAGHATAYID KHANATE

Herat

Indus

Persian Gulf

SULTANATE OF DELHI

N

Ilkhanid Empire at its greatest extent 1260

0   800 mi
0   1000 km

Above The octagonal tomb of Sufi saint
Abd al-Samad is part of a fine early
14th-century complex at Natanz in Iran
that includes a four-iwan Friday Mosque.

summer residence. All that remains
today of the city is the Uljaytu's vast
octagonal mausoleum, 38m (125ft)
in diameter, with eight minarets.
It has a beautiful, pointed dome,
standing 50m (164ft) high, that was
once covered in turquoise
tiles. Beneath the dome is an
arcaded gallery with a ceiling
decorated in coloured stucco and
terracotta carving. There are views
for miles across the plain from a
circuit of vaulted galleries, in
which the ceilings are decorated
with carved plaster designs painted
in patterns markedly similar to
those found in the contemporary
illuminated manuscripts.

This mausoleum's extraordinary
dome is recognized by architects
as one of the greatest architectural
achievements in the world.
According to tradition, it was built
on such a grand scale because

Right Calligrapher Haydar picked out
floral decoration and sacred phrases on
this stucco mihrab of 1310 in the winter
iwan at the Friday Mosque, Isfahan.

Uljaytu, who was a Shiah Muslim,
was originally planning to move
the body of Imam Ali from his
tomb at Najaf in Iraq and re-inter it
beneath the dome at Sultaniyya.
Uljaytu was later dissuaded from
this plan and instead made the
building his own tomb.

CARVED DECORATION

During Uljaytu's reign, in 1310, a
magnificent stucco *mihrab* was
added to the winter *iwan* of the
Friday Mosque in Isfahan. It was
designed and carved by Haydar, the
pre-eminent calligrapher of the day,
and featured arabesque decoration,
floral designs and calligraphic

inscriptions. The building of the
mihrab was ordered to mark the
conversion of Uljaytu to Shiah
Islam in 1309, an event that
had provoked opposition among
the mostly Sunni inhabitants
of Isfahan.

Haidar's work can also be seen in
an inscription band on the north
iwan at the Friday Mosque in
Natanz, central Iran. The mosque
was part of a complex built in
1300–10 by vizier Zayn al-Din
Mastari around the grave of revered
Sufi saint Abd al-Samad, who had
died in 1299. The complex
included a hospice for Sufis, as well
as the tomb and mosque.

TAKHT-I SULAYMAN

THE SUMMER PALACE OF TAKHT-I SULAYMAN IN NORTH-WESTERN
IRAN (C.1275) IS A RARE EXAMPLE OF SURVIVING ILKHANID SECULAR
ARCHITECTURE. A NOTED OBSERVATORY WAS BUILT NEARBY.

When Abaqa Khan, the second ruler of the Ilkhanid Empire, built Takht-i Sulayman, he set out to demonstrate his legitimacy as head of an Iranian empire. The complex stands in a breathtaking natural setting. He chose the site on which it was built because it held a ruined sanctuary used for the coronations of the pre-Islamic Sasanian emperors of Iran (226–651). Dragons and phoenixes featured in the lavish tiled decoration of the palace, because these mythical creatures were established Chinese motifs that symbolized imperial authority. Quotations from the *Shahnama* (Book of Kings), the national epic poem of Iran written by Firdawsi in the 11th century, were also incorporated into the decoration.

Below The lake was central to the design of the once-magnificent royal summer palace of Takht-i Sulayman, built by Ilkhanid ruler Abaqa Khan.

The site was located south-east of Lake Urmia in the Azerbaijan province of north-western Iran. It had been called Shiz by the Sasanians and was the location of an important Zoroastrian fire temple at which Sasanian kings performed rituals before they ascended the throne; in the Ilkhanid era it was called Saturiq. The later name Takht-i Sulayman means 'the Throne of Solomon'. The palace stands on an extinct volcano, where a spring flowing into the central crater had created a lake. According to local folk legend, King Solomon bound monsters in the nearby volcano and created the lake that dominates the site.

COURTYARD AND LAKE
The remains at Takht-i Sulayman were excavated from 1959–78. The palace was built around a vast courtyard running north to south, measuring 150m by 125m (492ft by

Above Astronomers at work in Hulagu Khan's observatory at Maragha, from a 16th-century edition of the Nusratnama.

410ft) and incorporating the lake. The courtyard was surrounded – as was traditional in an Iranian palace (or mosque) – by four *iwans* (halls) situated behind great porticoes.

The south *iwan* was 17m (56ft) wide and featured a grand staircase at the centre rising to a domed hall.

At the other end of the complex, the north *iwan* stood before a domed chamber, probably used as an audience room. The courtyard had to be large because the lake's dimensions could not be altered: as a result it is one of the largest four-*iwan* layouts in the Persian tradition.

TWIN PAVILIONS

Beyond the west *iwan* was a flat-roofed hall between two domed octagonal pavilions; this was the sovereign's living quarters. The remains of what must have been a beautiful set of *muqarnas* (vaulting) were found in the southerly pavilion. The northern pavilion – built on the site that the Ilkhanids believed was once the coronation

Above This celestial brass globe (1275), at Maragha, was signed by 'Muhammad ibn Hilal, astronomer from Mosul'.

area of the Sasanians – was lavishly decorated. The lower walls of the pavilion were covered in tiles in star and cross shapes; above was a frieze of tiles depicting scenes and quotations from the *Shahnama* (Book of Kings) and Chinese symbols of kingship.

Archaeologists also discovered a square stucco plaque with sides measuring 50cm (20in), covered in drawings of part of a *muqarnas* vault at Takht-i Sulayman. Historians believe the drawings were used as a guide by workmen to help them put cast units together to form the dome. From contemporary accounts we learn that designs for buildings of this kind were often drawn up in the capital before being sent to the site in question; this plaque is one of the few pieces of evidence that this occurred.

MARAGHA OBSERVATORY

At the Ilkhanids' summer capital Maragha, 30km (19 miles) west of Takht-i Sulayman, Hulagu Khan (*c*.1216–65) built an astronomical observatory atop a hill around 500m (1,640ft) north of the town, beginning in 1259. The director was Nasir al-Din al-Tusi (1201–74), the notable scientist and astronomer, working with a large team of eminent scientists. There was a central tower of four storeys with a quadrant measuring no less than 45m (148ft) in diameter, a foundry used for making astronomical instruments and a library that reputedly held 400,000 volumes. Observations made at the observatory in 1260–72 were recorded in Persian in the *Zij-i Ilkhani* (Ilkhanid Tables), which included data tables for working out the positions of the planets. By tradition, Hulagu Khan attributed his military successes to the advice he received from

Above Hunting scenes were a favourite subject for palace decoration. This tile shows riders bringing down an antelope.

astrologers, so to ensure future success he built the observatory and funded the collection of information for the *Zij-i Ilkhani*. The Maragha scientists sought to resolve inconsistencies with the geocentric model of the universe and their work influenced the Polish astronomer Nicolaus Copernicus.

ILKHANID POTTERY

BY THE MID–13TH CENTURY, CHINESE MOTIFS WERE APPEARING ON ILKHANID CERAMICS, REFLECTING A CHANGE OF DECORATIVE STYLE THAT WAS INFLUENCED BY THE MONGOL INVASIONS.

During the Mongol invasions in the first half of the 13th century, the production of luxury ceramics at Kashan was severely disrupted. Large-scale production was not resumed until the 1260s, by which time the Mongols had installed themselves as the Ilkhanid rulers of Iran and had established their capital in Tabriz.

There seems little doubt that ceramic workshops would have been active in the capital, and Abu'l Qasim, a contemporary historian and member of the famous Kashani family of potters, refers in his treatise to the type of wood burnt to fire the kilns in Tabriz. So far it has not proved possible to identify what type of wares were made there. However, it is known that the Abu Tahir family of potters remained closely involved in the running of the pottery workshops in Kashan in Iran, because tiles signed by them have survived.

MONGOL INFLUENCES

Ilkhanid pottery shows a distinct change of style in its decoration, which must have reflected the tastes of the new patrons. The so-called Pax Mongolica, or 'Mongol Peace', created an environment of free

Above The Ilkhanids were passionate about hunting. Birds and animals of the chase, such as these startled hares, were popular decorative themes.

cultural exchange across the Islamic world and beyond, and many Chinese motifs were introduced into the Islamic artistic vocabulary. New ornamental motifs included lotuses and peonies, cloud bands, dragons and phoenixes. The new styles also show the influence of Chinese design in vessel shape. Celadon forms, such as the rounded bowl with relief petals on the exterior, known as the lotus bowl, were widely imitated.

Lustreware was still being produced with a different emphasis. Floral and geometric designs replaced the earlier figurative schemes, and turquoise as well as cobalt formed a counterpoint to the lustre. The principle of the overglaze *minai*, or enamelled, technique was not abandoned, but the palette was transformed by 1301, when Abu'l Qasim says that the old style was replaced by *lajvardina*. The word *lajvard* is Persian for 'lapis lazuli', which describes the colour of the cobalt background

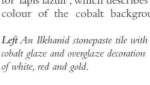

Left An Ilkhanid stonepaste tile with cobalt glaze and overglaze decoration of white, red and gold.

over which was painted a showy combination of white and gold, with gold leaf applied in intricate, often geometric designs.

SULTANABAD WARE

A new style of wares became known as Sultanabad ware, not because they were produced in the city, but many pieces were found near it. With a new monochromatic palette, probably inspired by Cizhou wares imported from China, the body of the vessels was covered with a thin slip (liquid clay) of a purplish grey or pale brown colour on which designs were painted in a thick white slip, outlined in black and set against a black hatched ground. A loose overall pattern of leaves painted in the thick white slip forms the background to the main motif, which often has a Mongol flavour: pheasants, ducks in flight, deer and gazelles, and scenes of figures in Mongol dress.

ARCHITECTURAL TILES

The use of tiles to decorate architectural surfaces was an old tradition in Iran, but it had a new resurgence in the Ilkhanid period. The potters concentrated on fulfilling commissions for producing tiles for shrines, mosques and palaces. A number of tombs commemorating Shiah and Sufi saints were built in the late 13th and 14th centuries with whole walls decorated with eight-pointed and cross-shaped lustre tiles.

Takht-i Sulayman, the summer palace built by the Mongol ruler Abaqa Khan c.1275, consisted of several buildings that were lavishly decorated with tiles. Many fragments were discovered on the site and tiles are thought to have been used to line both internal and external walls. The tiles were of all different shapes and sizes, from large rectangular figural scenes to smaller geometric shapes that would have formed part of interlocking patterns. The production techniques also showed a wide range: lustre, *lajvardina*, monochrome glazed, underglazed and unglazed tiles were found together. A kiln and workshop were also discovered, indicating that the workload was so extensive that craftsmen were transferred to work on the site. Some of the tiles were painted with episodes from the *Shahnama* (Book of Kings), while others were inscribed with quotations from this same epic history, and further tiles show the dragon and phoenix, mythical animals that were Chinese royal symbols. By invoking both Persian and Chinese symbols of authority, the Ilkhanid rulers were clearly underlining their own legitimacy.

Right Walls were often tiled with geometric patterns of eight-pointed star tiles with cross-shaped tiles filling the interstices.

ILKHANID MANUSCRIPTS

IN THE LATE 13TH CENTURY, THE ILKHANID RULERS SPONSORED MANUSCRIPTS THAT HIGHLIGHTED MONGOL LEGITIMACY ALONGSIDE THE HISTORICAL AND LEGENDARY KINGS OF THE WORLD.

After the rulers of the Ilkhanid dynasty converted to Islam in the late 13th century, they set about establishing their cultural legacy as legitimate rulers of the Islamic world. They did this by writing their own history and appending it to older accounts of world history. Many notable illustrated works were produced, including the Compendium of Chronicles and 'The Great Mongol *Shahnama*'.

A WORLD HISTORY

The grandest of these projects was ordered by Ghazan Khan (reigned 1295–1304), who commissioned a multivolume universal history from his minister Rashid al-Din (d.1318).

Below Rashid al-Din's universal history included an account of the Islamic world: this section illustrates the Samanid dynasty of Iran, showing Mansur b. Nuh coming to the throne in 961.

The location of this endeavour was the Rab-i Rashidi precinct, which was founded by Rashid al-Din himself, north-east of the Ilkhanid capital Tabriz. This vast personal suburb included a mosque, the patron's tomb, a Sufi hospice, a hospital (Rashid al-Din was also a royal physician), library and teaching facilities, with over 300 employees. The scale of this foundation is relevant to the magnitude of the universal history project, which was ambitious.

Entitled *Jami al-tawarikh*, or Compendium of Chronicles, the work comprised the history of Ghazan Khan and the Mongols, a world history describing the Arabs, Jews, Turks, Persians, Indians, Franks and Chinese, and a geography volume. Earlier works of history had to be assembled from across the known world, translated and collated together, and, in order to

Above Produced in c.1330 Ilkhanid Tabriz, this Shahnama *painting shows Shah Bahram Gur, a legendary marksman, out hunting onager.*

do this, an international team of scholars was formed, as well as copyists and painters.

According to the foundation documents, two large copies of this compendium were to be produced every year, one in Arabic and one in Persian, and dispatched to different cities of the Ilkhanid realm,

either Arabic- or Persian-speaking. The completed work was officially presented to Ghazan's successor Uljaytu in 1310, but it was an ongoing project of systematic and centralized production.

Densely illustrated, the earliest extant copy is dated 1314, and is now divided between Edinburgh University Library in Scotland and the Khalili Collection, which is privately owned. The painting style is strongly influenced by Chinese illustrated narratives, and reflects the international resources available to artists at the Rab-i Rashidi, but also the quick pace imposed upon them. The project did not last more than a few years. In 1318, Rashid al-Din was accused of poisoning Uljaytu. Following his execution, his foundation and estates were plundered and the project ceased.

MAKING A STATEMENT

The Compendium of Chronicles presented an account of world history with the Mongol Empire positioned in a global context, ennobling their current supremacy in cultural terms. The dynasty also sponsored illustrated manuscripts of Iranian cultural heritage, thereby deliberately reasserting Iranian identity within the Ilkhanid court. The same tactic was applied by Qubilai Khan in Yuan China, where the Mongols also seized power in the 13th century. Dynastic histories were commissioned in order to enlist the support of the Chinese administrative elite.

'THE MONGOL SHAHNAMA'

To this day the *Shahnama* (Book of Kings) by the 11th-century poet Firdawsi remains the national epic of Iran, and the earliest illustrated copies were apparently produced in Ilkhanid centres. This classic poem is extremely long, and describes generations of kings and heroes of pre-Islamic Iran, in their ancient feud with neighbouring Turan. The political meaning of commissioning this text is evident: by promoting ancient Iranian kings, the Mongols were aligning themselves as worthy royal successors in a long and noble line. Several illustrated copies date from the early 14th century. From this point onward, it becomes a characteristic mode of kingship for Persian rulers to commission personal illustrated manuscripts of Firdawsi's work.

Above In 'The Great Mongol Shahnama', Alexander the Great orders the construction of massive iron walls to keep out the savage people of Gog and Magog (shown top left).

The manuscript known as 'The Great Mongol *Shahnama*' is a masterpiece of Ilkhanid painting, and was probably ordered for Abu Said in the 1330s. The paintings reflect some of Rashid al-Din's style, but have a deeper range of colour, more exciting compositions and a more dynamic range of figures recounting the adventures, tragedies and romances of Iran's ancient heroes. The manuscript contained at least 60 paintings. Today, these are dispersed in worldwide collections – due to the fateful decision made by a 20th-century art dealer to dismantle the book and sell the folios.

ILKHANID QURANS

WHEN THE ILKHANIDS CONVERTED TO ISLAM IN THE LATE 13TH
CENTURY, THEY BEGAN PRODUCING QURANS OF THE HIGHEST
QUALITY. THEY WERE THE FIRST TO PRODUCE MULTIVOLUME SETS.

The Mongol invasions of the 13th century marked an important development in Islamic culture. The death of the last Abbasid caliph in 1258 must have felt like the end of an era. At the same time, the change in regime opened up new possibilities, bringing direct contact with Chinese civilization, and introducing stability and wealth.

MULTIVOLUME QURANS

The new Qurans were created on a grander scale than anything seen before. The Ilkhanids pioneered a deluxe format, spreading the text over several volumes. Traditionally, the Quran has 30 sections, each of which is known as a *juz*. Ilkhanid

manuscripts often devoted a separate volume to each of these sections, boxing them together in a container known as a *rabah*. Other divisions of the text can be found, ranging from 2 to 60 volumes.

By enlarging the format, the Ilkhanids offered new opportunities for both calligraphers and illuminators. Most volumes opened with an ornamental, double-page frontispiece and, in some cases, there was an additional decorative endpiece. The calligraphy, too, was far more impressive, as various types of monumental cursive script, using flowing joined-up letters, were

Below A 14th-century Quran copied in muhaqqaq *script – this particular type was often used for Ilkhanid Qurans.*

Above A 14th-century Quran illuminated by one of the great Ilkhanid masters, Muhammad ibn Aybak. The complex geometric design is typical of his work.

adopted. These included different combinations of *muhaqqaq, thuluth, rayhani* and *muhaqqaq-jali*.

The new regime did not, however, sever all connections with the past. The greatest calligrapher of the age was Yaqut al-Mustasimi (d.1298), a Turkish eunuch who had worked

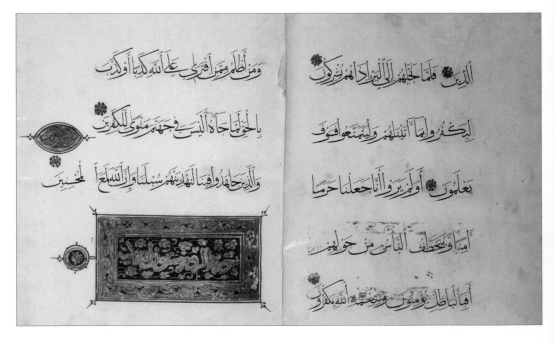

for the last caliph of Baghdad. He is said to have trained six gifted pupils, collectively known as the *sitta*, who preserved and transmitted his style during the Ilkhanid period. Although there is disagreement over the precise identity of some of these calligraphers, they are usually listed as Arghun ibn Abdallah al-Kamili, Nasrallah al-Tabib, Zarin-Qalam ('Golden Pen'), Yusuf al-Khurasani, Gandah-Navis and Shaykh-Zadah.

ULJAYTU AND THE QURAN

The most important Ilkhanid Qurans were produced in Iraq and western Iran, in the early 14th century. The chief patron was Sultan Uljaytu (reigned 1304–16). He founded a new capital at Sultaniyya, which he chose as the site of his elaborate mausoleum, now in ruins. Uljaytu commissioned a magnificent, 30-volume Quran for the memorial. Dating from *c.*1307–13, the manuscript is unusually large at 71cm by 51cm (28in by 20in) and features outstanding calligraphy. The script is mainly *muhaqqaq* or *muhaqqaq-thuluth*, and the lettering alternates between black outlined in gold, and gold outlined in black. The illuminator was Muhammad ibn Aybak, who displayed a preference for complex geometric compositions, with overlapping diamonds, circles and stars.

Uljaytu commissioned a number of other influential Qurans. These include another 30–part manuscript, which was produced in Mosul but was probably destined for the mausoleum in Sultaniyya. In this instance, both the calligraphy and the artwork appear to have been carried out by the same man, Ali ibn Muhammad al-Husayni. At the same time, Uljaytu also ordered a Quran from the Iranian city

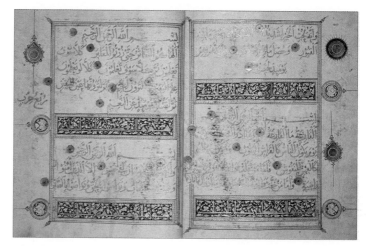

of Hamadan. This appears to have been commissioned as a gift, because the manuscript was sent to Cairo, where it caused a stir in Mamluk circles. The style is different from Uljaytu's Iraqi Qurans. The script is *rayhani*, and the decoration, in predominantly blue and gold, is simple but elegant.

PATRONAGE FROM A VIZIER

The other major patron of the period was Uljaytu's vizier, Rashid al-Din. He commissioned or

Above Calligraphers increasingly opted for more monumental styles of script and made the marginal symbols more ornate.

collected hundreds of Qurans, but, unfortunately, only a few fragments of these have survived. The most significant one was produced in Tabriz and is now housed in the Topkapi Palace.

Below This early 14th-century Ilkhanid Quran is copied in stately muhaqqaq script, written in gold ink, with illuminated panels.

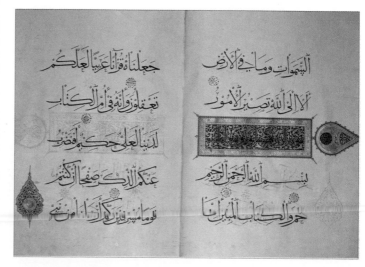

THE TIMURID DYNASTY

TURKIC CONQUEROR TIMUR IS KNOWN CHIEFLY FOR HIS
RUTHLESSNESS. YET, HE AND THE SUCCESSORS OF HIS DYNASTY
CREATED AN IMPRESSIVE ARCHITECTURAL AND CULTURAL LEGACY.

Probably the greatest conqueror in Islamic history, Timur (reigned 1370–1405) rose from being a minor chief near Samarkand, to rule an empire stretching from Anatolia to the borders of China. He achieved this despite a birth handicap that won him the nickname of Timur Lenk ('the Lame') – his upper thigh, right knee and right shoulder were malformed and he could get about only by using crutches or on horseback. The variations of his name, such as Tamerlane or Tamburlaine, are European corruptions of Timur the Lame. In 1941, Soviet scientists examined his skeleton and found evidence of these disabilities.

A MONGOL DESCENDANT

Timur was descended from the Barlas tribe, a Mongol tribal group that settled in Transoxiana (roughly in modern Uzbekistan). With his brother-in-law Amir Husayn, he won control of Transoxiana by 1366; then he turned against Husayn and in

the ancient city of Samarkand declared himself sole ruler in 1370. His culture was Turkic: he used the Turkic title *amir* rather than the Mongol *khan*. But he set out to restore the Mongol Empire created by his ancestors, and kept marriage ties with Genghis Khan's bloodline.

Despite having defeated many Muslim rulers, Timur presented himself as a religious warrior, or *ghazi*. His conquests were brutal. According to estimates, 17 million people were killed in the course of his campaigns; he sacked and burnt many ancient cities, creating gruesome pyramids of his victims' heads, and laid waste to vast areas. He died at the age of 69 in 1405 while leading an invasion of China. Yet, the Timurid dynasty he founded survived until 1526, despite dynastic in-fighting, and in India more than 300 years longer still, as the Mughal Empire that ended only in 1857, which was founded by an Asian Timurid prince, Babur (1483–1530), a direct descendant of Timur.

Above *The battered remains of the vast 50-m (164-ft) tall entrance portal is all that survives of Timur's Aq Saray Palace in Shahr-i Sabz (or Kesh).*

TIMURID PATRONAGE

On campaign, Timur spared artisans and craftsmen when he could, and dispatched hordes of conscripted masons, stucco workers, painters, tilers, potters, weavers and glass-makers to Samarkand. There, they reputedly worked on splendid palaces, fitted with carpets and decorated with mosaics and murals depicting his conquests, but these structures are now lost.

In Timur's lifetime, and in the Timurid era that followed, when princes of the dynasty competed

TIMUR'S REPUTATION

Timur was celebrated in Renaissance Europe as the embodiment of ruthless conquest, particularly for his defeat and capture of Ottoman Sultan Bayezid I at the Battle of Ankara in July 1402, followed by his humiliation of Bayezid in captivity. According to traditional (but probably invented) tales of these events, Timur kept Bayezid in a cage and used his kneeling body as a footstool when mounting his horse. Timur was the subject of the play *Tamburlaine the Great* (1590) by English dramatist Christopher Marlowe, and of the opera *Tamerlano* (1724) by Handel. Today, he is celebrated as a national hero in the former Soviet republic of Uzbekistan, independent since 1991; an equestrian statue of the conqueror stands in the capital, Tashkent.

Left *An equestrian statue of Timur has been erected in Tashkent, where the conqueror is celebrated as a hero of Uzbekistan.*

as patrons of architecture and the arts, magnificent mosques, *madrasas* (religious colleges) and palatial tomb complexes were built in the major cities of the empire, such as Samarkand and Herat. These buildings were characterized by their vast size and beautiful facing of multicoloured tile mosaic.

In his hometown of Shahr-i Sabz (or Kesh), 80km (50 miles) south of Samarkand, Timur built the grand Aq Saray Palace ('White Palace'), with a decorated entrance portal 50m (164ft) high bearing the inscription: 'If you have doubts as to our power, just look at the buildings we raise.' He also built a grand memorial complex named Dar al-Sadat ('House of Power'), which appears to have contained a domed chamber and mausoleum. The Dar al-Sadat was seemingly intended to house Timur's own remains. Both these grand buildings survive only in fragments.

BIBI KHANUM MOSQUE

In Samarkand in 1399–1404, Timur oversaw the construction of the Bibi Khanum Friday (congregational) Mosque, which contained a prayer hall with a dome 44m (144ft) tall that measured 140m by 99m (460ft by 325ft), making it one of the largest mosques in the world. The entrance portal stood between polygonal towers covered in mosaic decoration, and behind it the courtyard was surrounded by galleries beneath domes that were supported by marble columns. There were two smaller domed rooms at the courtyard's cross-axis and a tall, thin minaret at each corner. Soon after construction

Above Small domed side chambers at the Bibi Khanum Friday Mosque in Samarkand are exquisitely tiled in geometric patterns and bands of Quranic inscriptions.

parts of this enormous building began to fall apart under the weight of its own bricks, which was not helped by the region's frequent small earthquakes. In the 1970s it was rebuilt by the Soviet Union at third of its original size.

In Bukhara in 1400–50, the Kalan Friday Mosque was built on the same model, but with a polygonal niche at the entrance portal; the galleries around the courtyard have 288 domes held on pillars, and the prayer hall has a grand *maqsura* (private prayer area) with a beautifully tiled *mihrab*.

MADRASAS OF ULUGH BEG

Timur's grandson Ulugh Beg is remembered as a man of learning, a mathematician and astronomer, and the builder of three great *madrasas*: at Bukhara in 1418, at Samarkand in 1420 and at Gishduwan in 1437. The *madrasa* at Bukhara has a tall entrance portal with pointed arch and two-storey arcade sections on

each side leading to corner towers; behind the entrance a square hall gives access to two domed side chambers (one a mosque for winter use, and one a classroom) and the courtyard, which has two *iwans* (halls).

The *madrasa* in Samarkand had a *pishtaq* (projecting portal) 45m (148ft) tall in the entrance façade, which faces the city's main square. The *madrasa* covers 81m by 56m (266ft by 184ft): its interior courtyard, measuring 30sq m (98sq ft), has a minaret at each corner and four *iwans*, as well as 50 student rooms arranged around the yard over two storeys. In the rear wall there is a rectangular mosque set between domed chambers. This was a highly prestigious *madrasa* and it hosted many great religious and secular scholars of the Timurid period. The *madrasa* at Gishduwan has a grand entrance portal, but is more modest, with just four sets of student rooms on each side of the courtyard. Ulugh Beg also built an important astronomical observatory in Samarkand in 1428–29.

Above The magnificent entrance portal to Ulugh Beg's madrasa at Bukhara was built in 1418.

SAMARKAND TOMBS

TIMUR'S CAPITAL SAMARKAND, NOW IN UZBEKISTAN, IS CELEBRATED
FOR DOMED MAUSOLEA DECORATED WITH EXQUISITE TILE WORK
AND MOSAICS, BUILT IN THE LATE 14TH TO 15TH CENTURIES.

One of the grandest of the Samarkand tombs is the Gur-e Amir (Lord's Tomb) mausoleum, initially built in 1403 to house the remains of Timur's favourite grandson, Muhammad Sultan. The Gur-e Amir was built as part of a complex containing a *madrasa* (religious college) and a *khanqa* (hospice), around a walled courtyard with a minaret at each corner. Today, only the entrance portal, part of one minaret and the foundations of the *madrasa* and *khanqa* remain in addition to the mausoleum, which has been substantially restored.

A DYNASTIC MAUSOLEUM

Timur had built a mausoleum for himself in his hometown of Shahr-i Sabz. However, on his death in 1405, his body could not be carried to Shahr-i Sabz because the route was blocked by snow, so instead he was buried in the Gur-e Amir Mausoleum. Ulugh Beg oversaw the completion of the mausoleum,

and added a grand entrance portal to the complex in 1434: the beautifully tiled portal bears the name of its builder Muhammad ibn Mahmud al-Banna al-Isfahani. During Ulugh Beg's reign, the Gur-e Amir tomb became established as the dynastic mausoleum. Along with Timur and Muhammad Sultan, it was the burial place of Timur's sons Shah Rukh and Miran Shah, and of Ulugh Beg himself.

The mausoleum is octagonal on the outside but has a square chamber within, 10m (33ft) long on each side, and supporting a high drum with decorative facing beneath a ribbed, pointed, azure blue dome 34m (112ft) high. The outside of the drum bears a *kufic* inscription, set in tiles, declaring that 'Allah is eternal', and there are geometric patterns of glazed and plain bricks. This particular use of glazed bricks arranged in geometric patterns within groups of unglazed bricks has become known as the *banna'i* technique.

Above The interiors of the mausolea in the Shah-i Zinda complex in Samarkand are tiled in intricate patterns. No two decorative schemes are the same.

The inside of the building is lavishly fitted and decorated. The internal dome rises to a height of 26m (85ft), its inner surface once coloured with relief work of gilded papier-mâché; hexagons of onyx and painted decoration cover the lower walls rising to a cornice of *muqarnas* (stalactite-like decorative vaulting), and above, an inscription band. Each wall has a rectangular bay beneath *muqarnas* domes. In the south-east corner of the square chamber, steps lead down to the cross-shaped, domed burial crypt beneath. Some historians identify this breathtaking domed building as the model for the mausolea built by the Mughal descendants of the Timurids in India, notably the Tomb of Humayan in Delhi and the Taj Mahal in Agra.

SHAH-I ZINDA COMPLEX

Another beautiful collection of tombs in Samarkand is the Shah-i Zinda ('Living King') complex. This was built up over the years

Left The tomb chamber beneath the Gur-e Amir mausoleum in Samarkand contains the bodies of Timur and several of his descendants.

Right Remains of the Gur-e Amir complex include the grand entrance portal and the distinctive mausoleum, with its ribbed dome set upon a cylindrical drum.

1360–1434 in the vicinity of the reputed Tomb of Qutham ibn Abbas, the cousin of the Prophet, which had been restored in 1334–60. According to tradition, after Qutham ibn Abbas came to the region in the 7th century to preach the new faith founded by Muhammad, he was beheaded but escaped down a well or crevice, where he is said to be living still.

Arranged along a stepped pathway that runs 70m (230ft) to the north from the old city walls, the tombs in this complex were mostly single-room structures. A monumental entrance marks the start of the complex and was added by Ulugh Beg after 1434.

Many of the entrance portals are beautifully decorated with tile mosaics, some with gold leaf added; there are also glazed bricks, glazed terracotta, wall paintings, wood carvings, *muqarnas*, stucco, coloured glass and painted ceramic pieces; and there are beautiful calligraphic inscriptions in both Arabic and Persian that quote from the Quran and from poetic elegies.

There are fine examples of work produced with the minai or *cuerda seca* techniques that were also used by Safavid craftsmen in the holy buildings of Isfahan. *Cuerda seca* means 'dry cord' and refers to lines of a black substance used to mark out areas of glaze: the artists applied the glaze within these lines, which burnt away in the kiln.

OTHER COMPLEXES

Elsewhere in Samarkand, the Ishrat Khane ('Place of Joy') mausoleum complex was built by Ishrat Khane,

Below The necropolis of Shah-i Zinda stands in an elevated position, just beyond the ancient city limits of Samarkand.

wife of Timurid ruler Abu Said in 1464. The structure has survived mostly in its original state without renovation. It has a large, beautifully decorated entrance portal and sizeable central chamber beneath a dome raised on overlapping arches, beneath which is the octagonal domed burial chamber.

The palatial mausoleum Aq Saray (*c.*1450) stands close to the Gur-e Amir complex, but all that remains is the central chamber, with corner rooms, and a hall attached on the north side. The surviving interior decoration is beautiful, with the finest tile mosaics and relief work painted in blue and gold below elegant vaults.

ISLAMIC ASTRONOMY AND ASTROLOGY

EVEN BEFORE THE INTRODUCTION OF ISLAM, ASTRONOMY HAD DEVELOPED THROUGHOUT THE MIDDLE EAST. CELESTIAL IMAGES, THOUGHT TO BE PROTECTIVE, WERE OFTEN USED IN DECORATION.

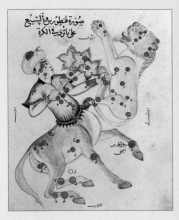

Above A Timurid copy of an illustration from The Book of Constellations, *by Abd al-Rahman al-Sufi, showing the constellations Centaurus and Lupus.*

Thanks to the great efforts of the translation movement in Abbasid Baghdad (8th–10th centuries), a wealth of international scientific literature had been made available for study and research in Arabic. Classical instruments, such as the celestial globe and the astrolabe, were developed further, and ancient texts in Greek, Pahlavi, Sanskrit and Syriac were drawn from and closely analysed. This intellectual culture also influenced the material world: the early 8th-century domed ceiling at the Umayyad palace of Qusayr Amra is decorated with a fresco map of the constellations.

ASTRONOMY AND ISLAM

For Muslims, astronomy held an important role in the service of Islam. The determination of daily prayer times and of the *qibla* (direction for prayer) were essential functions that scientists could address, as was calculating the lunar calendar. The appearance of a new moon, for example, signals the beginning and end of the fasting month of Ramadhan. In the 13th century, the role of the mosque astronomer (*al-muwaqqit*) was established to provide these services.

Astronomy was not restricted to only these religious purposes. Its uses in navigation and timekeeping are singled out for special praise in the Quran: 'He has ordained the night for rest and the sun and moon for reckoning. Such is the ordinance of the Mighty One, the all-knowing. It is He that has created for you

Left Suleyman 'the Magnificent' founded this Istanbul observatory in 1557, and appointed the renowned scientist Taqi al-Din al-Misri as director.

the stars, so that they may guide you in the darkness of land and sea' (6:95–96). This quotation shows that practical astronomy was the norm in 7th-century Arabia, but it also emphasizes that astronomy is gifted by God – and that the stars and planets should not be venerated (as pagan deities) in themselves.

ASTRONOMY V. ASTROLOGY

In Islamic courts, there was a big demand for astronomers, who were employed not only for astronomical work (at times even teaching their patron astronomy), but also to cast horoscopes and advise the ruler of planetary events that were unusual. Because it was thought that the movements of the celestial bodies have an influence on people and objects, major events, such as laying foundations for a new palace, were planned to begin at a certain time, calculated by astronomers. For example, to guarantee a good horoscope for the Abbasids' new capital of Baghdad, two scientists were consulted before building began on 31 July 762, following their precise instructions.

CELESTIAL IMAGERY

The importance of the stars and planets in astrology guaranteed that their imagery circulated far beyond the instruments and texts of specialists in the field. The evidence found on many centuries of decorative objects, furnishings and architectural detail confirms that certain celestial bodies were widely known and respected. These are the zodiac signs, and the seven 'planets' – sun, moon, Mercury, Venus, Mars, Jupiter and Saturn – along with a 'pseudo-planet' associated with eclipses. Furthermore, astrological imagery was typically applied in an organized way, which shows that the manufacturers and indeed consumers of these luxury objects understood a set of core rules about an astrological system, which they deliberately used for their benefit.

According to astrology, each planet has zodiac constellations, where its influence will be at its most powerful. For example, the planet Mars is strongest when combined with the constellation Scorpio, and the sun when with Leo. These powerful pairings are used as decorative motifs on many luxury items of inlaid metal or overglaze-painted ceramics, as they provide the best protection and good luck to the owner.

Above Dedicated to Sultan Murad III, this 1583 map of the universe shows the signs of the zodiac, from Zubdet ut-Tevarih (The Fine Flower of Histories).

This association of astronomy (the study of celestial bodies) with astrology (the study of how these bodies influence us) was both useful and troublesome. On the one hand, rulers were most likely to sponsor major observatories and to hire astronomers in order to benefit from astrology. Also, the technical requirements of measuring the exact planetary positions in order to cast an accurate horoscope encouraged greater observational accuracy and the development of more precise instruments. On the other hand, astrology could also draw religious censure on to astronomical projects, and was used in retrospect to explain why some dynasties had fallen.

A PRINCELY ASTRONOMER

The Timurid Prince Ulugh Beg (d.1449) was more than a patron of astronomical activity: he was also a scholar, mathematician and astronomer. He built an observatory at Samarkandwhere he worked with a staff of scientists and produced new records from their observations. Ulugh Beg has been credited with designing new astronomical instruments, and a contemporary colleague described him as a proficient scientist: 'the Emperor of Islam is (himself) a learned man and the meaning of this is not said and written by way of polite custom...I venture to state that in this art he has complete mastery, and he produces elegant astronomical proofs and operations'.

Right Ulugh Beg's mural sextant at his observatory at Samarkand was used to measure the angle of celestial bodies.

TIMURID HERAT

THE TIMURID DYNASTY MOVED ITS CAPITAL TO HERAT IN THE EARLY 15TH CENTURY. THIS ANCIENT CITY ENJOYED A RENAISSANCE, DURING WHICH SEVERAL IMPRESSIVE MONUMENTS WERE BUILT.

The conquests of Timur had established a powerful empire in the East, but this threatened to disintegrate after his death in 1405, as bitter rivalries surfaced. Shah Rukh – Timur's only surviving son – decided against moving to his father's base in Samarkand. Instead, he chose Herat as the new capital and appointed his son, Ulugh Beg, as governor of Samarkand.

AN ESTABLISHED CITY

Herat, in present-day Afghanistan, was an old city with an illustrious past. Pre-Islamic Persian rulers as well as early Muslim dynasties recognized the city for its military and commercial importance. It also had an impressive cultural reputation and was known in the Islamic world for its high-quality metalwork. Yet, before Shah Rukh's time, the Mongols had demolished the city and, in 1381, Timur had sacked it again.

The accession of Shah Rukh opened a new chapter for Herat. He set about rebuilding the city, transforming his court into a major artistic centre. He is probably best remembered as the patron of a number of outstanding illuminated manuscripts, while the surviving architectural monuments are more closely associated with his wife, Gawhar Shad.

MOSQUE OF GAWHAR SHAD

In nearby Mashhad, Gawhar Shad commissioned a new mosque (1416–18) as part of the renovations around the shrine of Imam Reza, a popular destination for pilgrims. The building is especially famous for its outstanding tile work. Though Islamic architects had for a long time adorned the domes and façades of their buildings

Above The shrine of Abdullah Ansari at Gazargah lies within a hazira – an enclosed burial ground – located within a four-iwan courtyard.

with colourful glazed tiles, this art form reached its peak during the Timurid period. The mosque at Mashhad is a fine example, featuring extensive sections of cut-tile mosaic.

MUSALLAH COMPLEX

The mosque was designed by Qavam al-Din Shirazi (d.1438), one of the most successful of the Timurid architects. When finished, the queen commissioned him to undertake an even more ambitious project – a complex of buildings in Herat. These included Gawhar Shad's mausoleum, a *madrasa* (religious college) and a congregational mosque.

The complex must have been spectacular, but only two minarets and the tomb have survived. Much of it was destroyed during military campaigns in the 19th century, and by an earthquake in 1932. The best-preserved section is the domed

Left Gawhar Shad's mausoleum in Herat has a distinctive ribbed cupola.

mausoleum, which rests on a 16-sided drum base. Eight Timurid princes were buried here, along with Gawhar Shad herself. Only two minarets remain from the *madrasa* and the mosque, but their glazed tiles embellished with floral motifs and *kufic* inscriptions are a hint of their former splendour.

OTHER MAJOR PROJECTS

Progress on the complex of Gawhar Shad was slow, taking almost 20 years to complete. This was because, in 1425, Shah Rukh diverted the architect to build the Abdullah Ansari funerary shrine at Gazargah, just outside Herat.

Ansari was a 12th-century Sufi mystic, revered as the *pir* (wise man and guardian) of Herat. His tomb had long been a place of pilgrimage for Sunnis, and Qavam al-Din's new shrine added to its prestige. The most impressive feature there is a massive *pishtaq* (monumental portal), 30m (98ft) high, which

Above The intricate carvings in Ansari's tomb complex at Gazargah are centred on a 16-point star, flanked by two stylized trees.

Below At Abu Nasr Parsa's shrine at Balkh, the cut-tile mosaics combine floral and geometric designs.

soars over the tomb. The decorations include *banna'i* designs, another form of tile work favoured by the Timurids. Here, the technique was to lay the glazed bricks on their ends, to form zigzag patterns or angular inscriptions.

Qavam al-Din's last commission was a *madrasa* at Khargird, which was completed after his death. The structure is now in ruins, but there are enough remains to clearly demonstrate its similarity to the Ansari shrine. This is evident from the panels of glazed-brick decoration and the arrangement of the entrance bays.

Another important Timurid monument in the region is the Funerary Mosque of Abu Nasr Parsa at Balkh, a spiritual leader in Herat who died in 1460. The mosque was begun shortly after his death, but its completion date is unclear. The entrance has a huge *pishtaq*, and the mosaic decoration displays Chinese influences.

JADE CARVING

IN THE ISLAMIC PERIOD, JADE CARVING WAS WIDESPREAD IN TIMURID IRAN AND IN MUGHAL INDIA. THE RAW MATERIAL WAS ACQUIRED FROM KHOTAN IN CENTRAL ASIA.

Jade has always been noted for its medicinal qualities, a tradition that in China dates back into prehistory. Medieval Arabic and Persian texts describe a wide range of apotropaic and medicinal properties, ranging from victory in battle, protection from lightning and earthquakes, the prevention and cure of illness, and repelling the effects of poison.

WORKING WITH JADE

The jade of objects crafted in Iran and India was nephrite. It is found in a wide range of colours; most commonly in shades of green, but also brown, yellow and red, and a translucent white, the rarest and most sought-after type of all.

To create a vessel, the raw jade is sawed into blocks of a workable size and shaped into the desired form using a hand-operated lathe. Then, the surface is polished using various stone, leather and wooden surfaces, together with abrasive substances to create the desired smoothness. Lastly, the object is often, but not always, decorated with inlays of different precious metals and gemstones.

TIMURID JADE

The main source of jade was in the Kunlun mountains near Khotan in Central Asia, which, in the 15th century, was within the Timurid Empire. It is from this period (1370–1506) that the production of Islamic jades became established.

A number of jade objects are associated with Timur and his descendants. The cenotaph of Timur in the Gur-e Amir is carved from a massive single block of dark green jade brought from Mongolia by his grandson Ulugh Beg.

Two notable jade vessels are inscribed with the name of this ruler: a shallow cup kept in the British Museum, London, is made of green jade with a handle in the form of a Chinese hornless dragon,

Above A dagger handle made from nephrite jade, set with gold and rubies. It dates from the reign of the Mughal Emperor, Alamgir (reigned 1658–1707).

and a pot-bellied jug has a sinuous handle in the form of this same mythical creature.

MUGHAL JADE

The true heirs of the Timurid tradition can be found in India, at the Mughal court, where the work was often carried out by expatriate Persian artists. Jade carving flourished during the rule of Jahangir (reigned 1605–27) and his son Shah Jahan (reigned 1628–57), and continued throughout the 18th century.

The Mughal court chronicler Abu'l Fazl records that a merchant named Khwaja Muin, was received

Left This white jade Mughal wine cup is carved so thinly that it appears translucent.

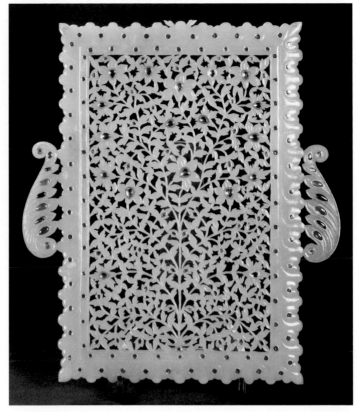

at the court of Akbar (reigned 1556–1605). He controlled the jade monopoly at Kashgar and is said to have stopped at the court with a selection of his wares, while en route to Makkah to perform the pilgrimage. Some sources pinpoint the start of the trend more specifically, linking it with the visit of Khwaja Mucin, who was the grandfather of one of Akbar's (reigned 1556–1605) generals. He controlled the jade monopoly at Kashgar and is said to have stopped at the Mughal court during a pilgrimage to Makkah, with a selection of his wares.

Mughal patrons commissioned a number of jade vessels that carry echoes of the work produced in central Asia. In the British Museum in London, for example, there is a fine cup in the shape of a gourd, which was made for Shah Jahan (reigned 1628–58) in 1647. Dating from the same period, there is also a jade box formed into the shape of a mango.

Increasingly, jade was used as a component of fine jewellery and ceremonial armour. There are many great 17th- and 18th-century examples of daggers produced with elaborate jade handles encrusted with jewels.

The Mughal emperor honoured his princes and high-ranking officials with the gift of such daggers; these were

worn tucked into the waist sash, as highly visible symbols of the owner's status and wealth. Mughal artists produced an extraordinary range of lavish jade plaques. These were used to adorn a variety of objects, from bow cases to belts, and Quran bindings to mirror-backs. Typifying

this trend is a sumptuous jade mirror, now housed in the Victoria and Albert Museum in London. The octagonal object, fashioned out of green jade, is decorated with flower-shaped inlays made out of white jade, and is encrusted with gold mounts and rubies.

TIMURID MANUSCRIPT PAINTING

DURING THE 15TH CENTURY, THE TIMURID PRINCES OF IRAN SPONSORED THE PRODUCTION OF LUXURY MANUSCRIPTS. CLASSIC WORKS OF PERSIAN LITERATURE WERE MADE BY TEAMS OF ARTISTS.

In the late 14th century, the Turkic conqueror Timur sacked many of the great cities of the Middle East, and as he did so, he conscripted the skilled citizens of his conquests into his service at his capital of Samarkand. Centralizing cultural skills was beneficial to Timur's court, because the finest artists, calligraphers, poets, scholars and craftsmen of the day were assembled in one place. Timur's sons and grandsons were educated by an elite selection of masters, and grew up to be connoisseurs of the arts.

After Timur's death in 1405, the empire was subdivided among his male descendants. Timurid princes were posted as regional governors in several Iranian cities, where each

Above Humay arrives on horseback at the palace gates of his beloved Humayan, in an anthology produced in 1396.

had his own atelier, or workshop, of artists and calligraphers to produce illustrated manuscript copies of Persian literary classics. Different schools of Timurid painting style developed in Shiraz, Herat and Samarkand, under these various patrons, whose ambitious military rivalry was also played out in the cultural sphere. At the same time, a commercial industry of manuscript production developed for other wealthy members of society.

PRODUCTION IN HERAT

Baysunghur Mirza (1399–1433), one of Timur's grandsons, was a renowned patron, 'alike in talent and the encouragement of talent', as described by a court biographer. His court welcomed poets and artists. He died young, however, allegedly by falling from his horse while drunk. During his time, the

Left Humay recognizes Humayan in this woodland scene, produced by Junaid Sultani for this Jalayirid manuscript.

Right Muslim pilgrims perform the Hajj *at Makkah, in this Shiraz manuscript from c.1410–11. It was produced for the Timurid Prince Iskandar Sultan.*

exact workings of an atelier in Herat were recorded in a contemporary document, datable to the late 1420s. Entitled *Arzadasht*, this is a progress report apparently written by the atelier director Jafar al-Tabrizi for his patron, Baysunghur Mirza.

Jafar provided a list of more than 20 craftsmen, describing which project each was engaged with: these are calligraphers, painters, illuminators, gilders, bookbinders and leather workers. As well as the ongoing progress of manuscript production, Jafar described repair work and restoration of damaged manuscripts, preparation of designs to be given to craftsmen to decorate tent poles, saddles and ceramic tiles, and problems with staff illness.

Jafar's account shows how designs were produced centrally in Timurid art, and how they were applied to a range of different media. This systematic process of distribution explains the stylistic unity in Timurid art, in which designs and motifs recur with regularity.

It is also possible to see the high level of specialization practised among artists, and to get a glimpse at how a manuscript painting was created. One note specifies that the painter Amir Khalil had finished applying silver to a seascape in a *Gulistan* manuscript (silver was typically painted to represent water), and would now proceed to paint in the colours. Remarkably, this exact manuscript survives in the Chester Beatty Library in Dublin and, indeed, contains two seascapes.

INFLUENCE FROM BAGHDAD

The style of Timurid court painting was strongly influenced by the late 14th-century art of the Jalayirid dynasty from Baghdad and Tabriz,

and manuscripts that were illustrated at Baysunghur Mirza's court atelier are very similar to the exquisite crystalline style of Jalayirid works. Timurid princes not only admired Jalayirid manuscripts, but in the early 15th century, they employed the same artists: the painter Amir Khalil recorded in Baysunghur Mirza's *Arzadasht* had previously worked for Jalayirid rulers in Baghdad, and presumably, had been conscripted by Timur after he took the city in 1401.

In turn, some Late Timurid artists actually went on to work under the subsequent Safavid dynasty in the early 16th century, and so on. The continuity of the Persian painting style from the 14th century onward was clearly noted by the 16th-century commentator Dust Muhammad: in an album preface dated from 1544, he observed of an early 14th-century painter: '[the style of] depiction which is now current was invented by him'.

LATE TIMURID PAINTING: BIHZAD IN HERAT

THE PAINTER BIHZAD WORKED FOR THE TIMURID COURT IN LATE 15TH-CENTURY HERAT, AND IS CREDITED WITH CREATING A NEW AND INFLUENTIAL STYLE OF PAINTING.

In the second half of the 15th century, Timurid military power began to decline, and the dynasty lost western and southern territory to Turkman tribal confederations. The former empire was eventually reduced to the region of north-eastern Iran, where Sultan Husayn Bayqara (reigned 1469–1506) ruled over the last Timurid court in Herat. He was a legendary patron of cultural activity, and hosted an extraordinary coterie of scholars, poets and artists at his court. This included the calligrapher Sultan Ali Mashhadi, the poet Jami and the painter Bihzad, whose masterpieces were all admired and emulated for centuries. Husayn Bayqara's chief minister, Mir Ali Shir Navai, was also a poet, and the prince himself wrote literary debates.

Above Bihzad's illustration of Laila and Majnun meeting at school, from the Khamsa of Nizami *(1494–95).*

EVOLVING PAINTING STYLE

In this milieu, there came about a radical development in manuscript painting, which determined the character of Persian painting in both Iran and Mughal India for the following centuries. The style of depicting figures and landscape changed greatly, as did some of the typical subject matter. This has been characterized as a cool, rational and even humanistic approach, rendering figures in more natural poses and expressions, and using a more modulated palette of colour.

Credit for this change has been given to one artist, Kamal al-Din Bihzad (d.1535), but it is unlikely that he was the only artist to work in this new style. He was probably a leading proponent rather than a lone pioneer. His work bridges the end of the Timurid period and beginning of the Safavids, and his transfer from one court to the next ensured the continuity of Persian painting traditions, from Timurid to Safavid patronage.

Left Bihzad's illustration of Harun al-Rashid at the bathhouse, from the Khamsa of Nizami *(1494–95).*

Above Bihzad's depiction of Iskandar, or Alexander the Great, as he consults the seven sages, from the Khamsa of Nizami *(1494–95).*

As with all respected painters, Bihzad's style was imitated and his compositions were re-drafted by generations of Persian artists as a matter of course. Owing to this renown, 'signatures' of Bihzad may be found widely, inscribed on to paintings, perhaps by later owners making a hopeful attribution, or by painters feeling their work worthy of the great artist's name.

THE *BUSTAN*
The exact corpus of Bihzad's work is not fully agreed, but one of his least disputed works is the *Bustan* (or 'Garden') of the poet Saadi (d.1291), a luxury manuscript dated June 1488, which features five masterpiece paintings: one double frontispiece and four subsequent illustrations. Each illustration is discreetly signed by Bihzad, on a horseman's arrow quiver

Right The royal herdsman reproaches Shah Dara, signed by Bihzad (1488).

on a hand-held book or placed in the calligraphic frieze around an architectural setting. The double frontispiece is a remarkable scene of feasting, no doubt revealing the world of Husayn Bayqara's famous court. The revellers are drinking heavily from wine cups, while servants are kept busy pouring from vessels of porcelain, glass and precious metal. A still is seen in operation on a hill beyond the courtyard.

By contrast, the dignified ruler kneels beneath an illuminated canopy, conversing with a younger courtier and listening to music. An upstairs window opens to reveal the prince's porcelain collection, giving further evidence of his refinement.

KHAMSA OF NIZAMI
A second manuscript generally agreed to be partly illustrated by Bihzad is a copy of the *Khamsa of Nizami*, dated 1494–95, now in the British Library in London. Typically of late Herati Timurid painting, the new subject matter of the 22 illustrations is a little more realistic than the typical jewel-like canon of earlier 15th-century works. They have added genre scenes of an old beggar woman and a busy building site, as well as a working bathhouse, with active figures engaged in their affairs, however humble they may be. These realistic vignettes contrast with the royal scenes of court society, and challenge their complacent, comfortable privilege.

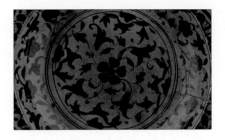

CHAPTER 16

IRAN: THE SAFAVIDS TO THE QAJARS

In 1501, the young Ismail Safawi established Safavid power across Iran, swiftly uniting a vast region. For the first time, Iran became a Shiah state, and the Safavid shahs ruled until 1722. Safavid court art of the early 16th century is regarded as a pinnacle of technical finesse and taste, particularly for the arts of the book. In 1598, Shah Abbas I (reigned 1587–1629) moved the capital to Isfahan, and transformed the profile of Safavid Iran in the eyes of the world's travellers, diplomats and merchants. He added spectacular public and private architecture, much of which remains to this day. Safavid art of this period, particularly the portraits of painter Reza Abbasi, reflects a prosperous society. The Safavid dynasty collapsed in 1722 and the country was beset by political unrest for much of the 18th century. Stability returned with the Qajar dynasty (1794–1925) and Fath Ali Shah brought in a new era of ostentatious imperial imagery. The art of 19th-century Iran combined the archaism in Qajar visual culture with an interest in Western traditions and modern trends.

Opposite One of the most beautiful achievements in Safavid Isfahan is the Masjid-e Imam. It was designed to impress, with a breathtaking pishtaq or entrance portal that features a cascade of muqarnas vaulting decorated with cut-tile mosaic.

Above A 16th-century 'Kubachi' plate produced in Iran, decorated in black under a green glaze. European travellers named the pottery after the village in Daghestan where this type of ceramic ware was discovered.

SAFAVID ISFAHAN

BUILDING STATELY MOSQUES, PALACES AND A BAZAAR AROUND A NEW
CENTRAL *MAIDAN*, OR SQUARE, SAFAVID SHAH ABBAS I TRANSFORMED
ISFAHAN INTO A FITTING CAPITAL FOR HIS DYNASTY'S PERSIAN EMPIRE.

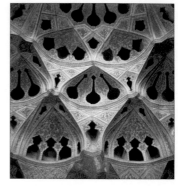

*Above The ceiling in the music room
at the Ali Qapu Palace on Maidan-e
Imam. The Ali Qapu was originally
just a gateway into the royal gardens.*

The sublime architecture built
by Shah Abbas I (reigned
1587–1629), fifth and greatest ruler
of the Safavid dynasty, is regarded as
the supreme achievement of the
Safavid era. Situated on the river
Zayandeh Rud in central Iran
about 340km (211 miles) south of
Tehran, Isfahan had been a town of
note as far back as the Parthian
Empire (238BCE–226CE), and a
capital under the Seljuk Turks
(11th–14th centuries). It reached a
golden age when Shah Abbas made
Isfahan the new Safavid capital and
began a grand building programme
in 1598.

A NEW CITY CENTRE

Abbas I made a new centre by laying
out a vast rectangular *maidan*, or
square, known as Maidan-e Shah
(King's Square), and now renamed
Maidan-e Imam, or Imam Square.
Covering 8ha (20 acres), the *maidan*
was built in 1590–95, initially as a
public space for state ceremonial,
military and sporting events. In a

second building stage, completed by
1602, a double-storey arcade of shops
was laid out around the perimeter.

On the north side of the *maidan*
the shah oversaw the building of a
covered two-storey bazaar entered
by a grand portal decorated with a
tile mosaic of Sagittarius the archer,
because the city was founded under
this astrological sign, and frescoes
showing Abbas I's military victories
over the Uzbek Shaybanid dynasty.
The bazaar contained a 140-room
royal *caravanserai*, baths, a hospital
and the royal mint.

TWO MAJOR MOSQUES

On the east side of the square, the
Lutfallah Mosque, named after the
scholar Shaykh Lutfallah Maisi
al-Amili, was erected in 1603–19. A
grand entrance portal on the square
gives access to the mosque's prayer
hall, a single square-domed room
measuring 19m (62ft) on each side,
and set at a 45-degree angle to the
portal, so that the *mihrab* (niche)
and *qibla* wall (indicating the

direction of prayer) could be aligned
to Makkah. The inner dome is
finely decorated with glazed tiles in
a sunburst design at the apex and
medallions filled with floral designs
running down the dome's sides.
This was the shah's private oratory.

On the south side of the *maidan*
another great entrance portal, finely
decorated with tiers of *muqarnas*
(stalactite-like decoration) domes
and tile mosaic, gives access to the
Masjid-e Imam, or Imam's Mosque.
Originally known as the Masjid-e
Shah (King's Mosque), this large
congregational mosque was built in
1611–30 to replace the older Friday
Mosque in the Seljuk part of Isfahan.

Its traditional layout consists of a
courtyard measuring 70m (230ft)
on each side, surrounded by arcades
and with an *iwan* (hall) in the centre
of each side, with a domed prayer
hall behind the *qibla iwan*. As with
the Lutfallah Mosque, the entrance
iwan fronts the square, but the main
part of the complex behind is
shifted 45 degrees so that the *qibla*
wall is aligned to Makkah. The side
iwans on the courtyard lead into

*Left The Safavid Empire reached its peak
under Shah Abbas I (reigned 1587–
1629). He made Isfahan the capital city.*

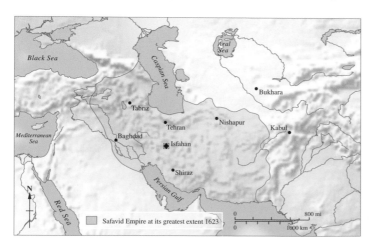

Black Sea

Caspian Sea

Aral Sea

Bukhara

Tabriz

Tehran

Nishapur

Kabul

Mediterranean
Sea

Baghdad

Isfahan

Shiraz

Persian Gulf

Red Sea

N

Safavid Empire at its greatest extent 1623

0   800 mi

0   1000 km

Right The interior of the Lutfallah Mosque in Isfahan is decorated with ceramic tiles on every surface.

domed chambers, while behind the arcading on each side of the main courtyard is another arcaded yard that was used as a *madrasa* (religious college). There are four minarets, but the call to prayer was given from a small building, called *guldasta* in Persian, situated above the west *iwan*. The grand dome above the prayer hall is 52m (170ft) tall; like the Gur-e Amir in Samarkand, it has a double shell, with a bulbous outer dome rising above its inner dome.

GARDENS AND PALACES

On the west side of the *maidan*, Abbas I built the Ali Qapu ('Highest Gate'). Originally an entrance to the royal gardens, this was reworked as a palace with a raised veranda, or *talar*, that was used as a royal viewing platform when displays, parades or sporting events, such as polo matches, were held on the *maidan*.

The Ali Qapu was the entrance to 7ha (17 acres) of royal parkland containing pavilions, garden palaces

Below The view across the square looks south to the Masjid e-Imam which is angled toward Makkah.

and walled gardens. In the park, the Chihil Sutun ('Forty Columns') Palace built by Shah Abbas II (reigned 1642–66) stands beside a rectangular pool. The palace has a flat-roofed *talar* supported by tall pillars of the kind built in pre-Islamic Persia. Despite its name, the palace has only 20 pillars: it appears to have 40 because they are reflected in the pool. The palace contains a large hall and many murals of court life. Also in the gardens is the Hasht Behesht ('Eight Heavens') Palace, built by Shah Sulaiman I (reigned 1666–94).

RIVERSIDE IMPROVEMENTS

Shah Abbas I's redevelopment of Isfahan also included the laying out of the Chahar Bagh esplanade from the *maidan* to the river Zayandeh. This splendid avenue was lined with the palaces of leading nobles. Great bridges were built across the river. The Si-o Se Pol ('Thirty-three Arch Bridge'), constructed in 1602 by Allahvardi Khan, general to Shah Abbas I, is 300m (984ft) long and has pavilions from which pedestrians can take in the view. New Julfa, a quarter for Armenian merchants, was built on the opposite bank.

CERAMICS OF SAFAVID IRAN

IMPORTED CHINESE POTTERY INFLUENCED THE PRODUCTION OF TIMURID POTTERY IN THE 15TH CENTURY. THE SAFAVIDS FOLLOWED THE TIMURID TRADITIONS IN THE 16TH AND 17TH CENTURIES.

From the 9th century onward, Chinese porcelain was highly valued in the Middle East and was almost continuously imported by land and sea. Blue-and-white wares were made specifically for export at the Jianxi kilns of Jingdezhen in China, and were imported into Syria and Egypt from the late 14th century.

Although imported Chinese porcelain was used as tableware, it was also displayed in specially designed pavilions, known as *chini khaneh*. The Mughal Emperor Babur, who visited the collection of Ulugh Beg (d.1449), one of the amirs during the Timurid dynasty, described a hall lined with porcelain tiles ordered from China. The interior was probably lined with wooden panelling cut into niches of various shapes to house vessels of different forms. This type of display has been found illustrated in manuscript paintings of the Timurid and Safavid periods.

When the Turkic Amir Timur (reigned 1370–1405) conquered Damascus in 1400, he brought its craftsmen back to his capital Samarkand, where the conscripts began producing blue-and-white pottery using the manufacturing techniques they were familiar with. The stonepaste body was made using sand, which was at variance with the traditional Iranian practice of using river pebbles.

After Timur's death in 1405, the Timurid capital moved to Herat, and in 1411 conscripted workmen were allowed to travel home. This resulted in craftsmen settling in a number of areas. Three main pottery centres developed from the late Timurid era into the Safavid period at Nishapur, Mashhad and Tabriz.

Above This elegant vessel, with Chinese-inspired scenes, was used for smoking tobacco.

ARCHITECTURAL TILES

Timurid buildings were lavishly decorated with tiles. Tile-makers used a range of techniques: glazed bricks, carved and glazed terracotta, tile mosaic and *cuerda seca*, overglaze enamelled, underglaze painted, relief and occasionally lustre tiles.

Tile mosaic was made from slabs of glazed tile that were cut after firing into interlocking shapes. The individual pieces were put together face down on a drawing of the design and plaster was poured over the back and strengthened by canes; when dry, the panel was attached to the wall. This was a labour-intensive process, but a faster alternative, named the *cuerda seca* ('dry rope') technique, developed in Spain. This overcame the technical difficulties of firing several colours together by outlining each area with an oily substance, which burnt off during firing to leave an outline in relief.

When Shah Abbas I (reigned 1587–1629) moved his Safavid

Left In 1607–8, Shah Abbas I gave the palace collection of Chinese porcelain to his family shrine at Ardabil. Individual niches were built in the shrine to house the pieces.

428

capital to Isfahan in 1598, a great period of construction began. Palaces and other secular structures were decorated with square tiles individually painted in polychrome glazes. These tiles were then combined to form large pictorial scenes with elegant, languid figures arranged in garden settings in the new style developed by Reza Abbasi, chief painter of the court atelier.

SAFAVID BLUE AND WHITE

In 1607–8, Shah Abbas I donated the imperial collection of Chinese porcelain, some 1,162 mostly blue-and-white pieces, to his ancestral shrine at Ardabil in north-western Iran, where they were displayed in a specially renovated building. Inspired by this and the newly popular Wanli porcelain being imported from China, production of blue-and-white increased to satisfy the local demand.

The East India Company had built up a trading network in Iranian ports and when the fall of the Ming dynasty in 1644 disrupted Chinese exports, the Persian workshops became one of the biggest suppliers of blue-and-white to

Europe. Persian and European sources single out Kirman as the centre that was producing the finest blue-and-white wares. Mashhad was also an important centre and potters there revived the use of the lustre technique, producing vessels decorated with delicate landscape and floral designs.

KUBACHI WARE

The term 'Kubachi' ware has been used to describe pottery of both the Timurid and Safavid periods. The name refers to a village in the Caucasus, where 19th-century travellers discovered large quantities of ceramic dishes hanging on the walls of the houses. The dishes were in many different styles – blue-and-white, turquoise-and-black, and polychrome – but were identifiable by the holes drilled in the foot ring for hanging

Above A 17th-century stonepaste dish with coppery lustre, probably from Mashhad, Iran. The design was inspired by marginal decoration on manuscripts.

and a crackling in the glaze. However, it became clear they were never made there and it has only recently been established that they were made in Nishapur, Mashhad, Tabriz and Isfahan.

Below Individually painted square tiles were often combined, as here, to form large pictorial scenes.

PERSIAN CARPETS

UNDER THE SAFAVID DYNASTY, CARPET WEAVING WAS TRANSFORMED
INTO A STATE-SPONSORED INDUSTRY, PRODUCING SPLENDID CARPETS
FOR BOTH RELIGIOUS AND PALATIAL CONTEXTS.

The weaving of carpets was an ancient art form in the Islamic world, and fragments of rugs and carpets survive from Seljuk Anatolia and Mamluk Egypt. The oldest complete, dated Islamic carpets, however, are from Safavid Iran.

Many carpet designs echoed the composition of contemporary book covers, with an elongated rectangular layout in which the central area was set within borders. Figurative designs were often similar to those in book illustrations, and indeed could have been designed by the same artists, while others consisted of repeating abstract patterns.

THE ARDABIL CARPETS

One common carpet design, which gave rise to the term 'medallion carpets', featured a large central medallion, sometimes with quartered medallions placed at the four corners. Two especially large medallion carpets were made on

the order of Shah Tahmasp for the Safavid family shrine in Ardabil in 1539–40. These are known as the Ardabil carpets, and they are probably the most celebrated of all Persian carpets.

Designed as a matching pair, the carpets consist of a densely knotted wool pile on a white silk warp and weft foundation, and feature an intricate design rendered in ten deep colours. A central yellow medallion is surrounded by a circle of smaller oval shapes, and two lamps are represented as if hanging from the medallion. All are set on a dark blue ground filled with curling scrolls of lotus flowers. A quarter section of the medallion is repeated in each corner, giving the sense of a continuing pattern. The whole design is framed by a border of patterned parallel bands.

In the late 19th century, pieces from one carpet were used to repair the other, altering their sizes. The larger carpet, now in the Victoria

Above This detail of this 16th-century *hunting carpet shows a horseman turning in the saddle to fight off a lion.*

and Albert Museum in London, measures an immense 10.5m by 5.3m (34ft 6in by 17ft 6in), and contains 33 million woollen knots. The smaller, now in the Los Angeles County Museum of Art, California, measures 7.2m by 4m (23ft 7in by 13ft 1in).

SAFAVID SILKS

French traveller Jean Baptiste Tavernier (1605–89) claimed that more people worked at silk weaving than in any other trade in Safavid Iran. Shah Abbas I (reigned 1587–1629) revived the textile industry in Iran, establishing factories across the empire in Isfahan, Kashan, Kirman, Mashhad, Yazd and elsewhere. Many silks bore figurative images, derived from contemporary manuscript painting, of courtly picnics, lovers, huntsmen, warriors leading prisoners and scenes from the works of the poets Firdawsi (c.935–c.1020) and Nizami Ganjavi (1141–1209). In England, in 1599, the Earl of Leicester gave a set of Safavid silk hangings to Queen Elizabeth I to be hung in an apartment in Hampton Court Palace.

Left This elegant 17th-century Persian silk panel shows a pair of courtiers, in perfect symmetry, at a country picnic.

Each carpet also features a text-panel of poetry at one end:

'Except for thy threshold, there is no refuge for me in all the world. Except for this door there is no resting-place for my head. The work of the slave of the portal, Maqsud Kashani. 946.'

The number refers to the year 946 in the Hijra calendar, corresponding to 1539–40CE. Maqsud Kashani may have been the designer of the carpets or the court official who organized their production on behalf of Shah Tahmasp.

FIGURATIVE SCENES

The Ardabil carpets do not feature animals or people in their design because they were made for a religious environment. Safavid carpets designed for more secular courtly locations were frequently decorated with figural motifs.

Pairs of animals were artfully depicted in combat poses, and represented natural enemies: lion against bull, snow leopard against mountain goat, and even falcons against waterbirds. Supernatural animals were also very popular:

Above The two hanging lamps on this Ardabil carpet vary in size – perhaps to correct the perspective effect when this gigantic carpet is viewed from one end.

fighting dragons, phoenixes and chilins, all borrowed from Chinese art – without their associated symbolic meanings.

Another category of Safavid carpet depicted hunting scenes. These carpets were decorated with hunters mounted on horseback pursuing their prey, often set within borders containing kings, courtiers and musicians and, sometimes, angels. A celebrated example is the carpet created by master weaver Ghiyath al-Din Jami in 1542–43, and today held in the Museo Poldi Pezzoli in Milan, Italy. The carpet is made of wool, silk and cotton, and is precisely twice as long as it is wide, measuring 3.4m by 6.8m (11ft by 22ft).

The category known as garden carpets represented cultivated flowerbeds and trees; fish and ducks in waterways and ponds; garden pavilions, terracing and fountains; and animals such as deer, peacocks,

hares and even lions and leopards. Other carpet designs showed vases and flowers.

Some of the garden and hunting carpets also featured medallions in their design. On the Ghiyath al-Din Jami hunting carpet in Milan, for example, the hunting scenes were arranged around a medallion, while in the corners of the design were cranes set amid bands of cloud.

EXPORTS

Fine carpets made excellent diplomatic gifts and were also widely exported. Under Shah Abbas I (reigned 1587–1629), a number of carpets were made in the royal workshops in Isfahan and Kashan to be given as gifts to foreign rulers, or were commissioned by patrons in Europe. Examples include a group bought by King Sigismund III Vasa of Poland in 1602, complete with the royal coat of arms, while silk carpets were given to the doges of Venice in 1603 and 1622. Exported Safavid carpets, sometimes known as 'Polonaise' carpets, were discovered in Poland in the 19th century.

SAFAVID MANUSCRIPT PAINTING

IN THE FIRST HALF OF THE 16TH CENTURY, A COORDINATED TEAM OF ARTISTS AND CRAFTSMEN AT THE SAFAVID COURT PRODUCED LUXURY MANUSCRIPTS OF EXCEPTIONAL QUALITY.

When the Safavid young crown prince Tahmasp was sent to Herat to be regional governor, his court there included the company of Herati artists from the last Timurid *kitab-khana*, or atelier (workshop), that of Sultan Husayn Bayqara. The renowned master painter Bihzad was head of the *kitab-khana*, and it was the young Tahmasp's privilege to be tutored by him.

When Tahmasp finally returned to the Safavid capital Tabriz in 1522, his taste for metropolitan Timurid painting would have been at odds with the current idiom of the Tabriz court atelier, which was directed by the painter Sultan-Muhammad in the Turkman style. However, Prince

Tahmasp then studied under Sultan-Muhammad, while the elderly Bihzad was brought to Tabriz and appointed director. From this amalgamation, the placement of a Herati master at the head of the Tabriz painters, the character of 16th-century Safavid court painting was set, as a stylistic synthesis of taste, under a royal patron who was an able connoisseur of both modes, and a competent artist and calligrapher too. The results were spectacular.

TAHMASP'S *SHAHNAMA*

In 1524, Tahmasp became shah and soon after, from *c*.1524 to 1540, his court painters produced the grandest *Shahnama* (Book of Kings) manuscript ever seen. The manuscript has 258 paintings in its current state, most of which appear toward the beginning. It provides an extraordinary showcase of 16th-century Safavid court art, with recognizably Timurid or Turkman aspects, and a successful fusion of the two styles, where fluid figures are painted in finely detailed compositions, using brilliant rich colours.

Although there are few signatures or dates on the paintings, one – the remarkable *Court of*

Left A Shahnama *scene attributed to Sultan Muhammad shows the hero Faridun striking the tyrant Zahhak with an ox-head mace.*

Above *This illustration of Adam and Eve (c.1550) is from the* Falnama, *a work of bibliomancy attributed to the sixth Shiah Imam, Jafar al-Sadiq.*

Gayumars – has been identified as the work of Sultan-Muhammad from a description in a biography of the Tabriz master. The painting shows a crowded court scene set in a rocky landscape, but look closely and it is possible to see an astonishing array of minuscule faces and figures, barely discernible to the naked eye, concealed in the rocks and clouds. The biographer's description is effusive: '[he] has developed depiction to such a degree that, although it has a thousand eyes, the celestial sphere has not seen his like…With the pen of his fingertips, on the tablet of vision, he has drawn a different version at each and every instant.'

A POLITICAL STATEMENT

Firdawsi's epic poem tells the history of generations of pre-Islamic Iranian kings, from the dawn of time up to the last Sasanian shah. It consists of some 60,000 couplets and is packed with eventful narratives of suspense and derring-do, making it an ideal text for illustration. Being a royal commission, a king's personal copy of the *Shahnama* has political significance too, as it bestows the glamour of historical Persian kingship upon its owner – perfect for a Safavid shah, or any Iranian ruler.

It has been suggested that Tahmasp may have had additional motives for commissioning such an ostentatious version. In 1514, his father Ismail had been soundly defeated by the Ottomans at the Battle of Chaldiran. The Ottomans went on to sack the Safavid capital, Tabriz, including the royal treasury. As a key theme of the *Shahnama* is the Iranian triumph over their longstanding enemies, the Central Asian Turkic Turanians, this new version may have brought some solace to the Safavids in a post-Chaldiran world by enabling them to relive earlier victories over the Turks. Tahmasp may also have wanted to replace the *kitab-khana's* losses after the Ottoman sack of the capital by commissioning a major new project.

THE SHAH'S DISAFFECTION

Tahmasp, his brother Bahram Mirza (d.1549) and Bahram's son Ibrahim Mirza (d.1577) were all bibliophile princes, with a connoisseur's eye and personal training in painting, calligraphy and poetry. They commissioned manuscript paintings, collected art and exchanged gifts, such as the precious 1544 album of paintings and drawings given to Bahram Mirza by his brother the Shah. The album is prefaced with an illuminating account of Persian art history as told by a 16th-century compiler named Dust Muhammad.

The history of Safavid painting took an abrupt turn around this time, due entirely to a change of heart on Tahmasp's part. He turned increasingly to religion throughout the 1530s and 1540s, renouncing non-Islamic habits, and gradually abandoned the company of his youth, dismissing from the Safavid court his artists, musicians and poets. They sought employment at

provincial courts and beyond in Mughal India, or simply retired.

In 1567, Tahmasp's monumental copy of the *Shahnama* was one of many spectacular accession presents sent to the new Ottoman ruler, Selim II, in the hope of retaining an important peace treaty agreed with Selim's predecessor Suleyman. In view of this decision, Tahmasp's apparent disaffection shows political

Above This scene from a 1536 Shahnama depicts Khusrau ascending the throne.

maturity. The biographer Qadi Ahmad notes: 'having wearied of the field of calligraphy and painting, [Tahmasp] occupied himself with important affairs of state, with the wellbeing of the country and tranquillity of his subjects.'

THE *KHAMSA* OF NIZAMI

REVERED AS ONE OF THE GREAT MASTERPIECES OF PERSIAN LITERATURE, THE *KHAMSA* (QUINTET) WAS WRITTEN BY THE 12TH-CENTURY POET NIZAMI.

Nizami was the pen name of Ilyas Yusuf Nizami Ganjavi (1141–1209), who was born and spent the great part of his life in the south Caucasian city of Ganja, then part of the Seljuk Empire and now known as Gyandzha, in Azerbaijan. He was orphaned early in life and raised by his uncle, Khwaja Umar.

Nizami lived a simple, quiet life, largely keeping away from court – although he had a number of royal patrons. He was a passionate admirer of the early 11th-century poet Firdawsi's *Shahnama* (Book of Kings) and used it as his source for material in his own epic. In addition to the *Khamsa*, Nizami also wrote many odes and lyrics, but few of these have survived.

Above An illustration of the Ascension of the Prophet Muhammad, as retold in the Khamsa, *dated 1505*

THE FIVE PARTS

The *Khamsa* is an anthology of five epic poems written between 1171 and 1202 in the *masnavi* style of rhyming couplets (*masnavi* means 'the doubled one'). The poems were dedicated by Nizami to local dynastic lords and Seljuk rulers. Comprising 30,000 couplets in total, the work is known as the *Khamsa* (the Arabic word for 'five').

The first of the five poems, *Makhzan al-Asrar* (Treasury of Mysteries), differs from the rest in that it is not a romantic epic but a collection of 20 parables on religious and ethical themes, such as the benefits of just royal rule and the necessity for all to ready themselves for life after death. Written in 1171, the *Makhzan al-Asrar* acknowledges its debt to an earlier work, the *Hadiqat al-Haqiqa* (Garden of Truths) of the 11th- to 12th-century Persian Sufi poet Sanai.

TWO ROMANTIC POEMS

Khusrau o-Shirin (Khusrau and Shirin), the second of the five poems, was written in 1177–80. This is an epic treatment of the celebrated story, also told in the *Shahnama* and in other sources, of the proud and protracted courtship between the Sasanian King Khusrau II and Princess Shirin of Armenia. The pair fall in love before they have even met: Shirin by seeing Khusrau's portrait, Khusrau by hearing Shirin described by poets. The course of the relationship is not smooth, however, and the two endure quarrels, separation and jealousy before they finally agree to marry.

Above A scene from the Khamsa *(c. 1550), showing a game of polo between a team of men and a team of women.*

Layli o-Majnun (Layla and Majnun), completed in 1192, is the third of the five poems, and recounts a legend of tragic love from Arab sources. A poet named Qays falls passionately in love with his cousin Layla at school, but cannot wed her because of a family quarrel and, as a result, is driven into madness. His strange behaviour wins him the name Majnun (from the Arabic for 'mad'). He cuts himself off from normal life, isolating himself in the desert with only wild animals for company and writing love poems about Layla. The star-crossed couple never find union in life, but after death are laid to rest in a single grave.

According to legend, the story was based on real events that took place in 7th-century Umayyad Arabia: a Bedouin poet fell in love with a young woman of his tribe, the Bani Amir, but was refused her hand in marriage by her father and afterward isolated himself in the Najd desert; his family left food in places where they knew he would find it. This story passed into the Persian tradition, and was recounted by the 9th–10th-century Persian poet, Rudaki.

EXPLOITS OF GREAT RULERS

The *Haft Paykar* (Seven Portraits, or Beauties), the fourth poem in the *Khamsa*, was completed in 1196 and recounts episodes from the life of the Sasanian King Bahram V (reigned 421–38), often known as Bahram Gur. While a prince, Bahram is sent to the court of an Arabian king. There, he discovers a secret room containing paintings of beautiful princesses from China, India, Africa, Russia, Turkistan, Byzantium and Iran, representing the seven regions of the world. Bahram learns that when king he will marry all seven princesses.

Once on the throne, Bahram sends out a messenger to find and bring back the seven princesses. Upon their return he has a palace built for each one where they are visited by the king. The central section of the poem is subdivided into seven tales, delivered as the seven stories told to Bahram Gur over seven consecutive nights by each of his seven brides.

Nizami acknowledged his debt to Firdawsi's *Shahnama*, where Bahram's exploits had already been described, but he also presented several adventures from the king's life that were not described by Firdawsi. Literary scholars hail this poem as Nizami's masterpiece.

The final epic in the *Khamsa* is the *Iskandar-nama* (Book of Alexander), written in 1196–1202, celebrating the many legendary and mysterious events from the life of Macedonian general, Alexander the Great (356–323BCE). The poem contains 10,500 couplets arranged in two books: the *Sharaf-Nama* and the *Iqbal-Nama*. The second book

Above A duel between two court doctors, a scene from Nizami's Khamsa, *copied in Tabriz c.1539–43.*

focuses on Alexander's personal qualities, and his emergence as the ideal worldly ruler.

CLARITY AND LEARNING

The *Khamsa* is celebrated for its originality of expression and clear, colloquial use of language. It also shows Nizami to be a man of great learning, capable of drawing on both Persian and Arabic literary traditions, and of making references to astronomy, astrology, medicine,

Islamic law, music, philosophy, botany, alchemy and mathematics. His work was very influential, and the *Khamsa*, a set of five epics, became a literary form in its own right. The Indian Sufi Amir Khosrow (1253–1325), and the Timurid statesman Mir Ali Shir Navai (d.1501) also wrote *khamsas*.

REZA ABBASI

REGARDED AS THE MOST IMPORTANT AND INFLUENTIAL PERSIAN
ARTIST OF THE 17TH CENTURY, REZA ABBASI (D.1635) SPECIALIZED
IN PLAYFUL PORTRAITS OF ISFAHAN'S PEOPLE.

Reza's father was the court artist Ali Asghar, who had served successive Safavid shahs and princes in the late 16th century, at the courts in Qazwin and Mashhad. Following custom, he trained his son as a painter too, so Reza grew up in the company of the elite artists who had served at the royal ateliers (workshops) of Shah Tahmasp, Prince Ibrahim Mirza, Shah Ismail II and Shah Abbas I.

He showed talent at an early stage, and was strongly admired by his contemporaries, as was recorded in a contemporary biographical note: 'it is fitting that the present age should be proud of his existence, for in the flower of his youth, he brought the elegance of his brushwork, portraiture and likeness to such a degree that [the great artists of the past] would praise his hand and brush a hundred times a day. In this age he has no rival; master painters, skilful artists who live in our times regard him as perfect.' Shah Abbas was also appreciative of Reza's talent, awarding him the honorific title 'Abbasi' as a measure of his esteem.

PORTRAIT ARTIST

Reza specialized in the single-page paintings or tinted drawings that were in vogue in Iran in the late 16th century. This romantic genre features slightly windswept lone figures in an idealized natural setting. Reza contributed to at least one manuscript painting project at this period, but then he began his single-page portraiture, with great success. He focused on young courtiers relaxing, but also created powerful images of people in the wider community. His 1598 drawing of a portly official taking his turban off to scratch his head is a masterpiece of observation.

Above A fluid depiction of hunters in the landscape, painted by Reza Abbasi five years after he rejoined the royal workshop in 1610.

CHANGE IN CHARACTERS

In 1598, the Safavid court moved from Qazwin to Isfahan, which was transformed into a vibrant imperial capital thanks to major architectural and commercial projects initiated by Shah Abbas I. New palaces and mosques were built in this old city, as well as monumental public spaces, major avenues, garden quarters and bridges. A great part of Reza Abbasi's surviving works reflect the moneyed society of this new capital, with portraits of foppish youths and dallying girls dressed in high fashion and posed in relaxed mood, enjoying romantic picnics of wine and fruit.

However, in the period from about 1603 to 1610, it would seem that Reza tired of this company, for he withdrew from court circles and entered a different sphere of Isfahan life. This is recorded with

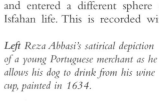

Left Reza Abbasi's satirical depiction of a young Portuguese merchant as he allows his dog to drink from his wine cup, painted in 1634.

Above Sitting alone, this young woman adjusts her make-up. A young man woven into the design of her cushion cover seems to spy on her.

disapproval by biographers of the day. One biographer notes: 'He avoided the society of men of talent and gave himself up to association with low persons', while another comments: 'vicissitudes [of fate] have totally altered Aqa Reza's nature. The company of hapless people and libertines is spoiling his disposition. He is addicted to watching wrestling and to acquiring competence and instruction in this profession.' Sure enough, Reza's portraits from this period typically depict wrestlers, dervishes and other humble characters that belonged to an Isfahan subculture not usually represented in court art.

This period of disaffection may have been triggered by Shah Abbas's departure on a military campaign against the Ottomans in 1603, when Reza was left behind in Isfahan and then wearied of the other remaining courtiers. After about 1610, the artist returned to Abbas's court and resumed his paintings of courtiers, although he also continued to portray older dervishes until his

Above This alcove painting of a young woman, from the Ali Qapu Palace in Isfahan, is in the style of Reza Abbasi.

death in 1635. The double portrait of a younger court dandy paired with an older, wiser dervish was a recurring theme in Reza's work, emphasizing the contrast in lifestyle and outlook of these two different sections of society.

A LASTING INFLUENCE

Reza's influence on contemporary artists was considerable; it lasted throughout the 17th century and can be seen in paintings, murals, ceramics and textiles. This is evident from the work of Reza's students, such as his son Shafi Abbasi and Muin Musavvir, and many other painters, including Muhammad Qasim and Muhammad Yusuf al-Husayni. In addition, there are a large number of 17th-century paintings that appear to be 'signed' by Reza, but which are in fact tributes made by later painters.

AFSHAR, ZAND AND QAJAR PAINTING

IN THE 17TH CENTURY, FOREIGN STYLES AND TECHNIQUES BEGAN TO
INFLUENCE ART IN IRAN. EXPERIMENTS WITH WESTERN TECHNIQUES
INCREASED DURING THE 19TH CENTURY UNDER THE QAJAR DYNASTY.

Later 17th-century Safavid art increasingly began to toy with international styles, such as Mughal themes, and European conventions, such as tonal modelling, perspective and the technique of oil painting.

The late 17th-century artist Muhammad Zaman produced unsettling illustrations of familiar subjects from the *Shahnama* and *Khamsa* featuring (European) classical architecture rendered in steep perspective. Full-length oil portraits were also produced at this time depicting single figures – not unlike the genre established by Reza Abbasi earlier in the century.

In 1722, an Afghan invasion overturned the Safavid dynasty, and the rest of the century was a dismal period of tribal violence and civil war. In 1736, Nadir Shah Afshar founded the shortlived Afsharid dynasty, which was followed in 1751 by that of the Zands. Karim

Khan Zand established his capital in Shiraz. Several full-length portraits have survived from his reign, along with some of the early works of Mirza Baba, who is better known as a Qajar artist.

QAJAR IMPERIAL STYLE

Long-term stability returned when the Qajar dynasty came to power in 1794, led, with some brutality, by Aga Muhammad (d.1797). The Qajar capital was established at Tehran, which remains the capital of modern Iran today.

The distinctive Qajar style emerged during the long reign of Fath Ali Shah (1797–1834), Aga Muhammad's nephew, who commissioned a number of oil portraits of himself and his many sons. He used the portraits, which emphasize his full beard, large eyes and wasp waist and show him wearing heavily jewelled crown and regalia, to cultivate an imposing

Above The Qajar ruler, Nasir al-Din Shah, is shown wearing Western-style military uniform and sitting on a Western chair in this 1857 portrait.

Above This c.1805 portrait of Fath Ali Shah shows him wearing the jewelled crown of the Qajar dynasty.

Left The Qajar Empire reached its peak early in the reign of Fath Ali Shah (1797–1834), but later lost considerable territory to foreign powers.

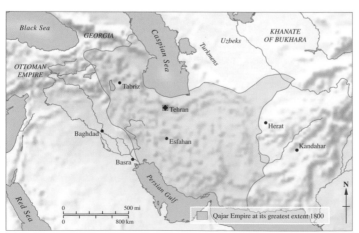

Qajar Empire at its greatest extent 1800

Above This Qajar oil painting of a dancing musician illustrates contemporary female fashions.

As Iran moved into the modern era under Muhammad Shah (reigned 1834–48), Western-style reforms and fashions continued. Military uniform became formal dress at court, as can be seen in contemporary imperial portraiture.

The taste for Western art and culture remained strong during the long reign of Nasir al-Din Shah (reigned 1848–96), who made three official tours of the courts of Europe and was keen to present Iran abroad as a similar imperial nation. He was particularly taken with the new invention of photography and took it up as a hobby – building his own studio and taking up to 20,000 photographs of the court, including his mother, wives and children. His albums remain in the collection of the Gulestan Palace.

In 1851, Nasir al-Din Shah set up a European-style technical college in Tehran called Dar al-Funun (House of the Arts) to train military cadets, engineers, musicians, doctors and interpreters. Photography and lithography were also taught, which encouraged their wider use. Painting was added to the curriculum in 1861. In the later Qajar period, the Ghaffari family from Kashan produced generations of important court painters: Abu'l-Hasan Khan Ghaffari (d.c.1866), who had the title Sani al-Mulk (Craftsman of the Kingdom), was sent to Italy by Muhammad Shah to study academic painting and lithography. His nephew Muhammad Ghaffari (d.1940) was a major court portraitist who studied at Dar al-Funun and also spent five years in Paris.

public image, and he had them distributed around Iran as well as sent abroad to a number of foreign rulers. Fath Ali Shah also commissioned an enormous mural for his Negarestan Palace in Tehran. Depicting an imaginary court reception to celebrate *No Ruz* (Persian New Year), it showed the shah surrounded by 12 of his sons, together with retainers and foreign ambassadors from Britain, France, the Ottoman Empire, Sind and Arabia.

THEMES IN QAJAR PAINTING

Qajar artists also produced paintings of beautiful women, including a series made for the Nigarestan Palace in Tehran. These ranged from royal women to dancers, musicians and serving girls. The most unusual subjects were the acrobats and tumblers who entertained the royal household, and are depicted upside down, balancing precariously on their hands, elbows and even on the tips of knives.

Right A ceramic tile showing musicians and dancers at the court of Qajar ruler, Nasir al-Din Shah.

LACQUER PAINTING

ISLAMIC LACQUER-PAINTED OBJECTS ARE RARE BEFORE THE 17TH
CENTURY BUT BECAME VERY POPULAR IN THE LATE SAFAVID,
QAJAR AND ZAND PERIODS.

In the Islamic world two different techniques were used to produce a lacquered surface. In the first technique, a resinous substance called 'lac' – which is produced by certain insects – was painted directly on to wooden objects. In the second, much more common technique, an object was first painted with an image in watercolour paint, then coated with a thin layer of protective varnish made from resin.

LACQUER BOOKBINDINGS

In Iran, lacquer painting developed during the late 15th century, when it was first adapted for use in Timurid bookbinding in Herat. The technique soon spread to Safavid Tabriz and other cities. Artists painted designs in watercolour on to a prepared surface of papier mâché, or pasteboard, then applied a coat of varnish, thus replacing traditional leather bindings. The varnish could be given an added sheen by carefully mixing it with powdered gold or mother-of-pearl.

The immediate stimulus for this activity came from new polychrome lacquers that had recently been imported from the East. The most influential of these was *qiangjin* – incised black lacquer infilled with gold. Islamic artists hurried to copy this gold-and-black palette. The popularity of lacquer bindings increased under the Safavids and reached a peak in the Qajar era.

Over the years, lacquer artists developed a varied repertoire of themes and design styles. There were simple, ornamental designs, composed of arabesques and scrollwork; elegant scenes of courtly entertainments in idyllic gardens; studies of birds and flowers; and, in the 19th century, rolling landscapes, influenced by European painting.

Royal portraits were also in demand, and a well-known Qajar lacquer binding depicts Fath Ali Shah taking part in a lively hunting scene.

Left A Qajar box from 1867, which depicts Shaykh Saadi in conversation with Nizami and his attendants.

Above This beautiful blue iris, painted by Muhammad Zaman in 1663–64, appears in a manual on bookbinding and lacquerwork.

AN EXPANDING ART FORM

From the 17th century, Iranian artists began applying lacquer decoration to a wider range of objects. Among the most popular uses were on pen cases. These elongated boxes carried all the accoutrements of the calligrapher's art – reed pens, an inkwell, a small, sharp knife for cutting fresh nibs and scissors to trim the sheets of paper. In the finest examples, painting was added to both the interior and exterior of the lid.

Later, in the Qajar period, the range of lacquered objects also included fans, mirror-cases, backgammon boards, musical instruments and playing cards.

Most lacquered objects were adorned with lyrical arrangements of butterflies, birds, and flowers, but some pieces were also decorated with narrative and popular historical scenes. One of the most spectacular items is an ornate chest dated 1840, now kept in the British

Museum in London. The box contains a collection of instruments for weighing jewellery, and its lid is painted with a colourful scene of King Solomon enthroned and surrounded by an array of *jinns* (genies), *peris* (angels) and *divs* (demons).

Another casket, by the leading court painter Muhammad Ismail, shows in minute detail the siege of Herat by Muhammad Shah on the top of the lid and other scenes from the same military campaign are painted around the sides.

19TH CENTURY
In terms of quantity, the 19th century was the high point of Iranian lacquer production. British

orientalist, Sir William Ouseley, who spent two years working and studying in Iran from 1810–12, described in his writings seeing lacquered pen boxes, as well as mirror-cases and an array of caskets piled high in the bazaar. Many of these pieces were signed and dated by their artists. The leading family of lacquer painters during this time

Above This Qajar lacquered papier-mâché pen case, from c.1880, shows Safavid ruler Shah Ismail defeating the Uzbeks in 1510.

was Muhammad Ismail, his brother Najaf Ali and his three sons. Many of their works were inspired by European subjects, but they also dealt with local political leaders, such as Manuchihr Khan, who is featured holding court on a lacquered pen box dating from 1840–50, which is held in London's Victoria and Albert Museum.

Below These lacquer bookbindings, painted in 16th-century Iran, show a hunting scene (left) and a prince, under the awning, enjoying courtly life (right).

CHAPTER 17

ISLAMIC ART IN MUGHAL INDIA

Babur, the first Mughal ruler, invaded India from his Central Asian homeland in 1526 and eventually established a great empire that lasted into the 19th century. Descended from both Genghis Khan and Timur, the Mughals were one of four superpower states in Western Asia at the time, all with Turco-Mongol roots, the others being the Safavids, Uzbeks and Ottomans. Babur's son Humayun was a less effective ruler, and sought political asylum with the Safavid Shah Tahmasp for a time – which proved very formative for Mughal court art as Humayun was much taken by the sophistication of Safavid painting. By the time he returned to India, Humayun had persuaded Persian artists to join his court, and their contributions in the royal atelier combined with Indian art traditions to great effect. The three greatest Mughal emperors were Akbar (reigned 1556–1605), Jahangir (reigned 1605–27) and Shah Jahan (reigned 1628–58), who presided over a period of enormous wealth and power with great creativity and exuberance in art and architecture.

Opposite The construction of Fatehpur Sikri, the new imperial city built by Akbar. Its pavilions and palaces were made of red sandstone and carved with intricate motifs.

Above The decorative art of pietra dura, an intricate technique for inlaying semi-precious stone, was a major design element of Mughal architectural decoration.

MUGHAL TOMBS

ARCHITECTURE UNDER THE MUGHALS ACHIEVED A WONDERFUL BLEND OF HINDU AND PERSIAN STYLES. THE MOST SPECTACULAR EXAMPLES ARE MONUMENTAL TOMBS, OFTEN IN A GARDEN SETTING.

Though the glorification of the dead is alien to the spirit of Islam, there are many outstanding tombs built in Islamic lands. 'The most beautiful tomb,' according to the Prophet Muhammad, 'is one that vanishes from the face of the earth.' Yet magnificent tombs were built by rulers to perpetuate and glorify their names or at the desire of a community of believers to honour their saints. The tombs of

Below The red sandstone exterior of Humayun's imposing tomb in Delhi is picked out in relief with white marble.

rulers were often built by the rulers themselves, whereas those of saints were the gift of their disciples.

Sher Shah (reigned 1540–45), the Afghan ruler who seized the throne and forced Humayun into exile, built his own monumental mausoleum at Sasaram. At the time it was completed, in 1545, it was the largest tomb ever built in India. Its setting in the middle of an artificial lake and its octagonal shape are both allusions to the Islamic notion of paradise. The tomb rises in three tiers of diminishing size and is crowned by a Hindu-style dome.

Above The shadowed interior of the Tomb of Salim Chishti at Fatehpur Sikri is lit by intricately carved marble latticework windows, or jalis.

TOMB OF HUMAYUN

Humayun's mausoleum in Delhi was, and remains, a fine example of Indo-Islamic architecture and was one of the first of many garden tombs built during the Mughal period. It was probably built my Humayun's son Akbar. Construction began in 1562 and continued for nine years. Set on a wide, high platform, the mausoleum has four double-storey pavilions set in a square, creating a central space between them. The space is crowned by a white marble dome mounted on a high drum. The red sandstone exterior is picked out in relief with white Makrana marble. Inside the tomb, a system of corridors allows for the circumambulation of the central cenotaph (a monument for a person whose remains are elsewhere). High walls surrounding the garden are intersected by four gates.

Humayun's son, Akbar (reigned 1556–1605), ordered the construction of a tomb at Fatehpur Sikri to honour Shaykh Salim Chishti, the saint who had

Left The growth of the Mughal Empire across the subcontinent and the sites of the major Mughal tombs.

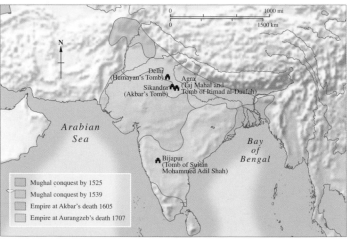

Above With three tiers of diminishing size, the Tomb of Sher Shah at Sasaram is crowned by a Hindu-style dome.

predicted the birth of his son, Jahangir. Built of luminous white marble, the tiny tomb lies at the feet of the red sandstone walls of the city's great mosque. The tomb's canopy is inlaid with ebony and mother-of-pearl. Jahangir (reigned 1605–27) added exquisite marble screens, mosaic flooring and a walkway paved in marble.

GARDEN TOMBS IN AGRA
The garden setting of Akbar's own tomb at Sikandra, near Agra, follows the same basic design as Humayun's tomb. Set in a *chahar bagh*, or four-part garden of Persian origin, the tomb consists of five storeys, surmounted by red domed kiosks supported on pillars. The tomb's upper storey is open to the sky, and in the centre is Akbar's white marble cenotaph. His actual grave lies in a domed hall at ground level, reached

through a portico. The tomb complex is entered by an imposing gateway. At its four corners rise white marble minarets.

OTHER IMPORTANT TOMBS
The tomb of Itimad al-Daulah in Agra was built in 1622–28 by Nur Jahan, the wife of Jahangir, for her parents. The mausoleum, set in a garden, is entirely clad in white marble with subtle inlays in yellow and green stone, differing from earlier use of red sandstone. A small pavilion on the roof is surmounted by a square dome. Here lie the two cenotaphs, surrounded by marble screens. Every inch of the whole mausoleum, inside and out, is decorated with geometrical patterns, floral designs in marble mosaic and *pietra dura* inlay, using semi-precious stones, such as topaz, onyx and lapis lazuli.

Right This corner of the Tomb of Itimad al-Daulah at Agra shows the *pietra dura* inlay on the exterior of the building.

At Bijapur in the Deccan lies another noteworthy mausoleum, the Tomb of Muhammad Adil Shah (reigned 1627–57). Known as Gol Gumbaz, this mausoleum boasts one of the largest domed spaces in the world – 4.9m (16ft) larger than the dome of St Paul's in London. At each corner of the building is an impressive domed octagonal tower.

The Taj Mahal

ONE OF THE MOST FAMOUS MAUSOLEA IN THE WORLD, THE
TAJ MAHAL AT AGRA MARKS THE MOMENT WHEN INDO-ISLAMIC
ARCHITECTURE REACHED A PEAK OF PERFECTION.

The future Shah Jahan (reigned 1628–58), Prince Khurram, was the favourite of his grandfather Akbar and of his own father, Jahangir. A fine soldier, it was Prince Khurram who was responsible for the military successes of Jahangir's reign. To honour his son's victories, his father bestowed on him the title Shah Jahan, or 'King of the World'. While still a prince, he had already demonstrated a passion for architecture and gardens and had carried out a number of building projects, including the Shahi Bagh (Princely Garden) at Ahmadabad and the wonderful Shalimar Gardens in Lahore.

On Shah Jahan's accession to the throne, the prodigious wealth at his command enabled him to carry out

Below Often considered the finest example of Mughal architecture, the Taj Mahal sits at the end of a 300m (980ft) square chahar bagh *garden.*

not only an extravagant building programme but to maintain a court whose magnificence was the envy of all. The sums he expended on his tombs, hunting pavilions, palaces and gardens, even entire planned cities, such as Shahjahanabad in Delhi, would seem astonishing even today. The emperor took a close personal interest in all these undertakings. His pride in his magnificent buildings is reflected in the famous couplet inscribed on the Diwan-i-Khas in the Red Fort at Delhi: 'If there be a paradise on earth, it is this, it is this, it is this!'

THE EMPEROR'S WIFE

The peak of the ruler's architectural achievements is the Taj Mahal, built as a tomb for his favourite wife, Mumtaz Mahal, who was a niece of Jahangir's formidable queen Nur Jahan. Mumtaz Mahal played a discreet but important role in Shah Jahan's government. She was, wrote

Above The decoration on the Taj Mahal includes Hindu-influenced design elements, such as this lotus flower, beautifully carved in white marble.

a Mughal chronicler, the emperor's 'intimate companion, colleague, close confidante in distress and comfort, joy and grief'. He was utterly devoted to her and although he had other wives, he had children only by her. When she died in 1631 while giving birth to his 14th child, he was devastated. It is said that he shut himself up in his private

quarters and refused to eat. When he emerged eight days later, his hair and beard had turned white.

OUTSIDE THE TOMB

The grief-stricken emperor chose a site for his wife's tomb on a bend in the river Jumna at Agra. Instead of following the usual practice of positioning the tomb at the centre of a garden, he placed it at the end overlooking the river, so it is visible at the horizon. The tomb, built by some 20,000 workers over 20 years, is set on a marble terrace, which in turn stands on a wide platform, flanked by two red sandstone buildings. At each corner, at a distance from the tomb, are four marble minarets, 42m (138ft) high.

All four sides of the tomb are identical, but it can only be entered from the garden side. The garden is bisected by a broad, straight canal that stretches from the tomb to the main gateway, an elegant two-storey building of red sandstone. In the centre of the canal lies a square pool in which the inverted reflection of the Taj seems to hang suspended. The huge dome, shaped like a lotus bud – a typically Hindu motif – culminates in a gilded bronze finial. The entire building is faced with pure white Makrana marble decorated with *parchin kari*, a type of inlay stonework that characterizes many of Shah Jahan's buildings.

INSIDE THE TAJ MAHAL

The interior of the tomb consists of a central octagonal chamber, which contains the cenotaphs of Shah Jahan and his wife. Linked to each other, and to the central chamber, are four side chambers. A white marble trelliswork screen surrounds the cenotaph, filtering the light entering the tomb chamber. For the Mughals, light served as a metaphor for divine light, symbolizing the true presence of God.

Shah Jahan's severe illness in 1657 led to a rivalry between his four sons, in which the third son, Aurangzeb, killed his brothers, declared his father unfit to rule and seized the throne. Shah Jahan lived for another seven years, imprisoned inside the Agra fort in one of his own palaces, overlooking his most sublime creation.

Above The cenotaphs of Shah Jahan and his wife Mumtaz Mahal lie at the heart of the Taj Mahal. An exquisite octagonal marble screen, or jali, surrounds the cenotaphs.

Below Extensive stone inlay decoration on the exterior of the Taj Mahal includes calligraphy, abstract forms and designs based on plant forms.

RED FORT

AT THE HEART OF SHAH JAHAN'S NEW CITY STOOD THE RED FORT, A VAST WALLED COMPLEX OF PALACES AND ASSEMBLY HALLS FROM WHICH HE RULED WITH UNRIVALLED POMP AND CEREMONY.

In 1639, Shah Jahan founded a new city at Delhi. He named it Shahjahanabad, meaning 'the abode of Shah Jahan'. The city of 2,590ha (6,400 acres) supported a population of 400,000. The Friday Mosque, the largest mosque in India at that time, was built on a hillock. Shahjahanabad became the new capital of the Mughal Empire.

According to the emperor's librarian: 'It first occurred to the omniscient mind that he should select on the banks of the [Jumna] river some pleasant site, distinguished by its genial climate, where he might found a splendid fort and

delightful edifices...through which streams of water should be made to flow, and the terraces of which should overlook the river.'

A NEW PALACE-FORTRESS

As the emperor had desired, a structure was sited on the banks of the Jumna. Known today as the Red Fort, the complex was situated on Shahjahanabad's eastern edge, dominating the new imperial city but separated from it by walls of red sandstone over 1.8km (1 mile) in circumference. With its palaces, audience halls, bazaars, gardens, mansions for the nobility and an estimated population of 57,000, the Red Fort was a city within a city.

In 1648, nine years after work on the complex began, the Red Fort was dedicated in a magnificent

Above Red sandstone, pillars with intricate low-relief carving and marble flooring are used to decorate this building in the Red Fort.

ceremony. The buildings were decorated with impressive textiles embroidered with gold, silver and pearls, and costly gifts, such as jewelled swords and elephants, were distributed to members of the imperial family and nobility.

Below One of the two imposing entrances to the Red Fort. The fort was a city within a city, housing a bazaar, many workshops and 50,000 people.

CANAL OF PARADISE

The great palace-fortress could be entered by two gates, the massive red sandstone Lahore Gate and the Delhi Gate. The Lahore Gate led to a long covered bazaar street, the Chatta Chowk, whose walls were lined with shops. The principal buildings and the emperor's private quarters were sited along the river side of the fort on a terrace some 600m (2,000ft) long.

A shallow marble watercourse, known as the Canal of Paradise, ran through the centre of all these exquisite marble pavilions. Water for the Mughals was just as vital an element in their architecture as it was in their gardens. 'There is almost no chamber,' reported a 17th-century visitor, 'but it hath at its door a storehouse of running water; that 'tis full of parterres, pleasant walks, shady places, rivulets, fountains, jets of water, grottoes, great caves against the heat of the day, and great terraces raised high, and very airy, to sleep upon in the cool: in a word, you know not there what 'tis to be hot.' This Mughal love of water is particularly evident in the Shah Burj ('King's Tower') pavilion, where the water ripples down a marble *chador*, or water chute, into a lotus-shaped pool, and from there flows into the Canal of Paradise.

COURTLY QUARTERS

In a commanding position at the centre of the fortress-palace was the Diwan-i-Am ('Hall of Public Audience'), which contained the marble throne from which Shah Jahan presented himself to his court. The Diwan-i-Khas ('Hall of Private Audience'), the most richly decorated of all the fort's buildings, was where Shah Jahan, seated on a gem-encrusted peacock throne, held the equivalent of cabinet meetings. Built of white marble, the pavilion's interior was richly

embellished with floral *parchin kari* stone inlays, precious stones and a ceiling made of silver and gold.

Next to the Diwan-i-Khas lay the Khwabagh, or emperor's private quarters (now called the Khass Mahal). Every day at dawn the emperor presented himself to his people from the balcony of an octagonal tower, which overlooked the river bank. Here too were staged fabulous spectacles, such as elephant fights and military reviews. Also along the riverside were the *zenanas*, or women's quarters, and the *hammam*, or bathhouse. Cool in summer and heated in winter, the *hammam* was ideal for discussing affairs of state in private.

Above Beautiful cusped arches enliven the Sawan Pavilion, named after a month in the rainy season. It is one of two pavilions in the Red Fort's garden.

There were two major gardens, the Moonlight Garden and the Lifegiving Garden, where the hyacinths 'made the earth the envy of the sky' and 281 fountains played. The fort's other areas held numerous specialist workshops that supplied the vast court with everything it needed.

Below The Diwan-i-Khas was used to hold meetings. It held Shah Jahan's peacock throne, before it was plundered by Iranian invader Nadir Shah in 1739.

LAHORE

THE CITY OF LAHORE IN NORTHERN INDIA REACHED A PEAK OF ARCHITECTURAL GLORY DURING THE RULE OF THE MUGHALS. FROM 1584 TO 1598, IT SERVED AS THE IMPERIAL CITY.

During most of the Mughal dynasty, the imperial capital was moved to different cities. When the emperor and his army set off on campaign, his entire establishment went with him, from the ladies of the harem to the treasury and from the court artists to the menagerie. However, several cities did become – and remained for a while – the official Mughal capital.

Akbar (reigned 1556–1605) used Agra as his capital until 1571, when he moved it to his newly built city, Fatehpur Sikri. Within 15 years, he had transferred his capital to Lahore in the Punjab. Lahore remained the capital until 1598, when Akbar moved it back to Agra. However, Lahore, which was strategically situated along the routes to Afghanistan, Multan and Kashmir, continued to be one of the most important Mughal cities after Agra until 1648, when Shah Jahan built his new capital at Delhi.

MUGHAL FORT

During his residence at Lahore, Akbar constructed a fortified palace on the edge of the city overlooking the river Ravi, on the site of an earlier fort. The walls of Akbar's fort were brick, a traditional building material of the region. Under Jahangir (reigned 1605–27), Lahore gained increasing prominence – the city was described by Europeans as one of the greatest in the East. The fort was substantially remodelled, and several audience halls and residential pavilions, with private courtyards and gardens, were added.

The fort's exterior walls were decorated with hundreds of brilliantly coloured tiles, a material common in Lahore, arranged in complex geometric patterns. Other tiled mosaics depicted elephant fights, camels, the Virgin Mary and Jesus, while the emperor's bed chamber had friezes of angels around the ceilings.

Above In the Shish Mahal, tiny pieces of mirror on the walls and ceilings create shimmering, reflective surfaces.

AFTER JAHANGIR

In 1627, Jahangir died on the way to Kashmir. His queen, Nur Jahan, constructed his mausoleum at Shadera near Lahore. Set in a large square garden, the tomb's exterior is decorated with marble inlay and the cenotaph inlaid with semi-precious stones representing tulips and cyclamen. Nur Jahan's own tomb in Lahore bears a moving epitaph: 'On the grave of this poor stranger, let there be neither lamp nor rose. Let neither butterfly's wing burn nor nightingale sing.'

Jahangir's succeeding son, Shah Jahan (reigned 1628–58), was born in Lahore. Like his father, he extended the fort and built several other structures in the city. Here, as elsewhere, he was closely involved in the design of his buildings. His love for white marble is evident in the Shah Burj, built inside the fort for his exclusive use. Within the Shah Burj he built the Shish Mahal

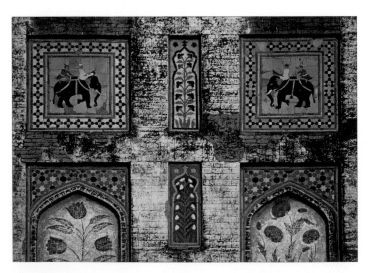

Left The exterior walls of Lahore's fort are made of brick; they are profusely decorated with panels of pictorial tiles and cut-tile mosaic.

('Glass Palace'), so-called because its walls and ceilings were inlaid with a mosaic of mirrors, which created a shimmering effect, that was especially noticeable at night when the interior was lit by lamps.

One of the most beautiful tiled buildings in Lahore is the Wazir Khan Mosque, built in 1634 by Wazir Khan, Shah Jahan's governor of the Punjab. Four towering minarets dominate the building, which is set on a plinth and entered through a high portal. Every inch of the walls is faced with coloured tile mosaics depicting floral sprays, arabesques and calligraphy.

SHALIMAR GARDENS

Shah Jahan's most spectacular addition to Lahore was the Shalimar Gardens, the greatest of the Mughal water gardens. Constructed in 1641–42, the garden is rectangular in shape and has numerous marble pavilions of intricate design and exquisite workmanship. The garden has three terraces, with two changes of level. At the centre of the middle terrace lies a square pool, said to have contained 152 fountains. Looking out across the pool is the emperor's marble throne.

BADSHAHI MOSQUE

Set in a vast courtyard, the Badshahi Mosque was built in 1674 by Aurangzeb (reigned 1658–1707). With its trio of white domes, octagonal minarets and imposing arched portal, the mosque is the largest place of prayer constructed during the Mughal era. Some walls are covered with intricate geometric patterns, others with a mass of tiny flowers and floral sprays springing from vases. Moulded plaster lattices adorn the vaults and domes, taking on an almost textile

Above Lahore's Shalimar Gardens, the greatest of all Mughal water designs, were laid out by Shah Jahan.

quality. Although responsible for the construction of this great mosque, Aurangzeb seldom visited Lahore. Probably because the city lacked an imperial presence, by the second half of the 17th century it was in a state of rapid decay.

Below The courtyard of Aurangzeb's Badshahi Mosque in Lahore can hold tens of thousands of believers for prayers.

DECORATIVE OBJECTS

UNDER THE PATRONAGE OF THE MUGHALS, THE DECORATIVE ARTS
REACHED UNPRECEDENTED HEIGHTS. ARTICLES OF EVERYDAY USE,
SUCH AS INKWELLS, WERE OBJECTS OF OPULENCE AND BEAUTY.

Influenced by the arts of the
wider Islamic world, yet firmly
rooted in Indian traditions,
Mughal style permeated every
element of the Mughal courts. In
the vast network of *karkhanas*, or
imperial workshops, expert artists,
artisans and craftsmen produced
luxurious furnishings and objects
for the Mughal palaces. Even
practical objects, such as *huqqas*
(water pipes), ewers and back
scratchers, were fashioned from
costly materials, such as jade and
rock crystal.

The decorative themes echoed
those found in architecture. Under
Jahangir (reigned 1605–27), images
of plants, animals and people
appeared in a naturalistic style, and
in Shah Jahan's reign (1628–58),
floral plant motifs were popular.

JADE
The Mughal emperors of India
were passionate admirers of jade.
This passion is evident in the
artistic innovation and outstanding
technical virtuosity of jade objects
produced in the court ateliers. Jade
was the favourite hardstone for
decorative objects including eating
and drinking vessels, fittings for a
variety of weapons and also
personal artefacts such as pendants,
mirror backs and inkpots.

For the Mughal emperors, jade
formed a powerful link with their
Timurid ancestors, whose jade
carving traditions and objects
formed the foundation for a
distinctive Indo-Persian style.

One of the most exquisite
pieces to survive is Shah Jahan's
wine cup, dated to 1657. Made of
pearly white jade, the cup is of a
lobed half-gourd shape, tapering
into a curving handle in the shape
of the head of an ibex. The base is
shaped like open lotus petals with
radiating leaves. Other more
utilitarian objects were also carved
from jade. *Huqqa* bases that were
filled with water to cool and purify

Above The interlocking panels of this
vaulted ceiling in the tomb of Itimad-
al-Daulah contain different painted
floral motifs.

the smoke before it passed through
the pipe are known, and also
dagger handles, often in the form
of horse's heads. These were
presented as gifts by the ruler and
worn on ceremonial occasions.

STONE INLAY
Mughal craftsmen were masters of
the art of stone inlay, using a
technique known as *parchin kari* in
India, but also as *pietra dura* from the
Italian tradition. Colourful semi-
precious stones, such as lapis lazuli,
carnelian and agate were inlaid into
white marble, creating elaborate
floral and geometric designs.

The tomb of Itimad al-Dawla in
Agra was the first Mughal building
to use this technique for its
decoration which was also used to
great effect in the Taj Mahal and the
Red Fort in Delhi.

Left A magnificent wine cup made of
milky white jade and belonging to the
Mughal ruler, Shah Jahan, dated 1657.

Right The ancient art of bidri has survived for some 4,000 years. These huqqa *bowls were made in Hyderabad, a centre for bidri manufacture today.*

BIDRIWARE

Bidri is a technique known only in the Indian subcontinent, and takes its name from the city of Bidar, in the present-day state of Karnataka. Its origins are obscure, but the earliest surviving pieces date from the late 16th and early 17th centuries.

Bidri objects are cast from an alloy in which zinc predominates, though small amounts of lead, copper and tin may also be found. The decoration is inlaid with silver, or a combination of silver and brass. The final stage of the bidri process is to apply a saline mud paste over the entire surface which changes the dull grey of the alloy to a dense black colour. The shiny silver and brass inlays contrast very effectively with the matt black background.

ROCK CRYSTAL AND GLASS

The clear, ice-like appearance of rock crystal had a great appeal for the Mughals. Examples of rock crystal inlaid with precious gems survive from the mid-17th century, although the techniques of the inlay process were already known during Akbar's reign. Vessels, such as cups and bowls, were deeply engraved with floral patterns, others were inlaid with gold and set with precious stones.

Glass decanters with long necks had been produced in India for some time, but there is no hard evidence of glass production on a large scale until the Mughal period. Manuscript paintings show bottles of every shape and size arranged in wall niches or placed on the floor beside the emperor.

Right This Mughal wine cup, made of emerald, gold and enamel, *was recently sold at auction for £1.8 million, the highest price ever realized for a wine cup.*

MUGHAL PAINTING

UNDER AKBAR'S LIBERAL PATRONAGE OF PERSIAN AND INDIAN
PAINTERS, THE ART OF THE MUGHAL MINIATURE EVOLVED,
REACHING PERFECTION AT THE COURT OF JAHANGIR.

From the 16th to 19th centuries, artists found almost continuous employment at the Mughal court. They even accompanied the rulers on their hunting expeditions and military campaigns. Akbar (reigned 1556–1605), although reportedly illiterate, had a passion for books, particularly illustrated ones. He had also been taught to paint as a child. Early in his reign, he established a large studio of talented indigenous artists, who worked under the direction of the two great Persian masters, Mir Sayyid 'Ali and Abd as-Samad, who had been brought back from Iran by Akbar's father, Humayun.

Artists learned their trade as apprentices, often from their fathers or uncles as the craft was frequently a family occupation. They were taught how to make paintbrushes from bird quills set with fine hairs, how to grind their pigments and how to prepare the aqueous binding medium of gum arabic or glue. Seated on the ground, with one knee bent to support the drawing board, they painted with opaque watercolour on paper or occasionally on cotton cloth.

NATURALISM

Under Akbar's close supervision, a style of manuscript illustration evolved that combined native Indian traditions – he particularly admired Hindu painters – with Persian technical refinement. These manuscripts were full of vivid representations of plants, flowers, animals and people, despite orthodox religious objections to figurative painting. As Akbar's official historian, Abu'l-Fazl, had commented: 'Bigoted followers of the letter of the law are hostile to the art of painting, but their eyes now see the truth.' This naturalism was also influenced by European prints and pictures brought to the Mughal court by merchants and Jesuit missionaries.

Above Beautiful mounts were a feature of Mughal painting. This example contains a portrait of Emperor Aurangzeb.

AKBAR'S MANUSCRIPTS

In about 1567, Akbar ordered his artists to prepare an illustrated copy of the *Hamzanama*, the story of the mythical adventures of the uncle of the Prophet Muhammad. A team of 100 painters, gilders and binders were assembled for the task. The multivolume work contained no less than 1,400 paintings and took 15 years to complete.

One of the most outstanding examples of the Akbari style was the *Akbarnama*, the official history of Akbar's reign written by Abu'l-Fazl. The vivid, naturalistic paintings illustrate scenes from the emperor's daily life and events from his military campaigns. At his death, Akbar's library contained some 24,000 volumes, including works in Persian, Arabic and Greek, many of which had been copied during his reign to the highest standards of book production.

Left A study of a zebra painted by the artist Mansur in 1621 for the famous 'Minto Album' begun by Jahangir. Exotic animals were commonly presented as diplomatic gifts.

JAHANGIR'S ARTISTS

Akbar's achievement as a patron of artists was refined under Jahangir (reigned 1605–27), who was a great connoisseur of the arts and claimed that he could distinguish the work of each of his painters at a glance. Preferring quality to quantity, and lacking his father's fondness for grand projects, he greatly reduced the staff of the royal studio, concentrating instead on a few favourite masters. As a result, fewer illustrated manuscripts were produced and more individual pictures, usually portraits or animal and flower studies, were created.

During this time, artists were encouraged to paint with increased realism and subtlety, softer colours and more harmonious designs. Much of this work shows the influence of European

painting, such as the use of perspective and shading. The individual paintings were often mounted in exquisitely decorated borders and bound together in albums. Many of Jahangir's artists continued to paint under his son Shah Jahan (reigned 1628–58), but the style changed. One of the last great Mughal historical manuscripts was the *Padshahnama*, a chronicle of the first ten years of Shah Jahan's reign that recorded military victories and court ceremonials. The paintings, although richly detailed, are more formal and lack the dynamism of those produced under Akbar and Jahangir.

Left Emperor Babur and his architect are shown planning the Bagh-i-Wafa near Jalalabad (1589–90).

ROYAL PORTRAITS

A large number of portraits were produced under Akbar. 'His Majesty himself sat for his likeness,' reported his chronicler Abu'l-Fazl, 'and also ordered to have the likenesses taken of all the grandees of the realm.' Jahangir's preference for individual pictures, rather than the historical manuscripts of Akbar's reign, also encouraged portraiture. His admiration for European art saw the beginning of a more naturalistic style of portrait. Toward the end of his reign, his portraits contained Islamic, Hindu and European imagery. Under Shah Jahan and his successors, portraiture became more stiffly official in character, as can be seen from the massed ranks of courtiers in the Padshahnama.

Above A likeness of Emperor Akbar (1542–1605), painted shortly after his death. He encouraged the artist to paint 'individual' works.

Above A portrait of Emperor Jahangir (1569–1627) holding a portrait of his father, Emperor Akbar (reigned 1556–1605).

INDIAN CARPETS AND TEXTILES

THE SPLENDOUR OF MUGHAL INDIAN CARPETS AND TEXTILES MAY BE SEEN IN CONTEMPORARY COURT PAINTINGS, WHICH SHOW THE LUXURY OF COURT DRESS AND FURNISHINGS.

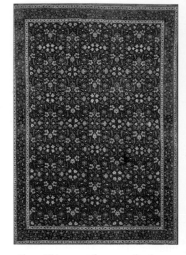

Above This carpet features a floral design organized in a tight lattice.

The luxury textiles of the Mughal court included silk embroidered cottons, velvets and woven silks, as well as carpets with sophisticated designs. The earliest written evidence that knotted pile carpets were being manufactured in Mughal India appears in the *Ain-i Akbari*, the chronicles of the emperor Akbar (reined 1556–1605). The court biographer Abu'l-Fazl relates that in the 1560s, the emperor '…has caused carpets to be made of wonderful varieties and charming textures; he has appointed experienced workmen, who have produced many masterpieces… All kinds of carpet weavers have settled here, and drive a flourishing trade.'

The most valuable carpets and textiles were stored in the *farrashkhana* (private storehouse) at Fatehpur Sikri. In fact, the evidence of Mughal manuscript paintings shows that knotted pile carpets had been used in India before this time, since the early 16th century, at least. Indian carpets were also produced in other courts beyond the Mughal empire, such as the Deccani Sultanate further south.

EARLY MUGHAL CARPETS

The influence of Iranian design is an important aspect of early Mughal art across all media. Classic subjects depicted on Mughal carpets are therefore also found abundantly in the carpets of contemporary Iran: these include hunting scenes, with horsemen racing through an stylized natural environment and spearing game, as well as wild animal hunts, with lions seizing deer, and other animal combats. In spite of this similarity in design motifs, Indian carpets typically follow a different weave structure to carpets woven in Iran.

Left This red silk carpet is decorated with silver thread to create a complex floral design.

From the outset, European visitors to the Mughal court were greatly impressed, and took sophisticated textiles and carpets back home. Some even ordered personalized new carpets which included their family coats-of-arms in the woven pattern, such as the famous Fremlin Carpet now housed in the Victoria and Albert Museum in London. Woven in Lahore around 1640, the carpet was commissioned by William Fremlin, who served in the East India Company from 1626–44, and features his Suffolk family's crest throughout the design. Similarly, Sir Thomas Roe, the English ambassador to the court of emperor Jahangir (reigned 1605–27), recorded that he returned from India with 'a great carpet with my arms thereon'.

FLORAL DESIGNS

Many Mughal carpets with exquisite floral designs survive from the mid-17th century, often focusing on single-stem flowers with attentive detail. These reflect the wider trend for a precise

Right These woven fragments from a large court carpet feature leafy spiral scrolls which are sprouting animal heads as well as flowers.

botanical style in Mughal art during the reign of Shah Jahan (1628–58), which is found in the *pietra dura* stone inlay panels of the Taj Mahal, and in album-paintings of the same period. Plant stems and blossoms were also organized in more stylized patterns, forming spiralling scrolls or trellis grids to create delicate and complex surface designs.

Colourful printed cotton panels with all-over floral designs or bunches of flowers set within niches were hung up on palace walls and inside tents set up for the ruler's comfort and pleasure while he was out on hunting expeditions or campaigning.

CARPETS AND TEXTILES IN PAINTINGS

Manuscript illustrations reveal the important role of carpets and textiles in Mughal visual culture. Carpets were laid down not only on palace floors, but also outside in gardens, tombs and imperial tents. When Shah Jahan received important visitors in his Hall of Private Audience, every surface of the room was covered in exquisite silk carpets.

Mughal paintings show how the court was 'dressed' in this way for major diplomatic events to project the power and sophistication of the empire. Luxury textiles were distributed to courtiers in reward for loyal service, and the wearing of fine costume at court demonstrated a courtier's favourable position, as well as his wealth. Foreign textiles were also offered as diplomatic gifts to visiting ambassadors, and were received with interest.

Left Emperor Akbar Shah II sitting on a dais with his sons.

JEWELLERY

WORN BY BOTH MEN AND WOMEN, MUGHAL JEWELLERY WAS THE
MOST OPULENT IN THE ISLAMIC WORLD. PRECIOUS STONES WERE
ALSO USED IN THE ORNAMENTATION OF OTHER OBJECTS.

An Italian visitor to India in the second half of the 17th century was astonished by the conspicuous consumption and display at the Mughal court. 'In the Mughal kingdom,' he wrote, 'the nobles, and above all the king, live with such ostentation that the most sumptuous European courts cannot compare in richness and magnificence with the lustre beheld in the Indian court.'

The splendour of the court was enhanced by the custom of giving and receiving presents. When the emperor received honoured guests, he presented them with gifts, such as robes of honour, gold, silver and richly decorated swords and daggers. Sir Thomas Roe, the English ambassador at Jahangir's

Above *Emperor Shah Jahan was the most extravagant of all the Mughal emperors. He regularly wore diamonds weighing over 50 carats.*

court, received a gold cup from the emperor, which was 'set all over with small turquoises and rubies, the cover the same set with great turquoises, rubies and emeralds…'

However, the custom also worked in reverse: to gain an audience with the emperor, it was obligatory for the visitor to present him with some precious object. 'For no man,' wrote a visiting French jeweller, 'must come into his presence empty-handed, though it be an honour dearly purchased.' Courtiers, too, were required to give expensive gifts to the emperor and to important members of the imperial household.

SUPPLYING THE DEMAND

This constant demand for jewelled objects was met by the imperial workshops, or *karkhanas*, which employed thousands of skilled craftsmen, many of them foreigners who had been attracted to India by the enormous wealth of the Mughal court. According to an account by one of Akbar's courtiers, gems could be purchased in the town markets. After a visit to Bijapur, he wrote: 'In the jewellers' shops were jewels of all sorts, wrought into a variety of articles, such as daggers, knives, mirrors, necklaces, and also in the form of birds…all studded with valuable jewels, and arranged upon shelves, rising one above the other.'

*Left A naturalistic floral
design is carved into this dark
green, hexagonal Mughal emerald –
a decoration reflecting their love of nature.*

MALE JEWELLERY

All the Mughal emperors, especially Jahangir (reigned 1605–27) and Shah Jahan (reigned 1628–58), were festooned with jewels. 'For the Mughals, though his clothing be not so rich and costly, yet I believe that there is never a monarch in the whole world that is daily adorned with so many jewels as he himself,' reported an English clergyman at Jahangir's court. Akbar's jewels were all given names, while Jahangir had his arranged in such a way that he could wear a different set each day.

Pearls played an especially important role. By the time of Akbar (reigned 1556–1605), double and triple strands of pearls were symbols of nobility. Portraits of the emperors also show them wearing enamelled gold armlets, jewelled turban ornaments, pearl earrings, gold bracelets inset with diamonds and rubies, archer's rings on their thumbs and pendants with rubies and emeralds.

FEMALE JEWELLERY

The imperial ladies wore earrings, armlets, forehead ornaments, rings, bracelets, gem-studded necklaces and several ropes of pearls, which hung down to below their waists. In the harem, the concubines were similarly bedecked: according to one French visitor, they wore the sleeves of their thin dresses short so that 'they may have liberty to adorn the rest of their arm with carcanets (chains) and bracelets of gold, silver and ivory, or set with precious stones…'

OTHER BEJEWELLED ITEMS

The goldsmith's art was even applied to weapons: dagger and sword hilts, which were often made of hard stones, such as jade and rock crystal, were carved and encrusted with gold and precious stones.

However, the object that came to symbolize the splendour of the Mughal court was Shah Jahan's Peacock Throne. This celebrated throne, which took seven years to construct, was commissioned by the emperor at his coronation as a means of displaying the incredible wealth of jewels in the royal treasury. Contemporary accounts give conflicting descriptions, but paintings show Shah Jahan seated cross-

Left Known as 'The Carew Spinel', this gemstone is inscribed with the names of three Mughal emperors – Jahangir, Shah Jahan and Aurangzeb.

Above This early 18th-century Mughal miniature painting depicts a noblewoman wearing earrings and a necklace made with pearls, emeralds and red spinels.

legged on a four-legged dais, with four columns supporting a domed canopy. Above the canopy was a peacock, its raised tail studded with sapphires and other precious stones. In the centre of its breast lay a great ruby, given by Shah Abbas, the Safavid emperor, to Jahangir. Every surface of the throne was encrusted with diamonds, pearls, emeralds and rubies. In 1739, it was looted by Nadir Shah and carried off to Iran, and a decade later it was destroyed.

COMPANY PAINTINGS

AS THE MUGHAL EMPIRE BEGAN TO DECLINE, THE EMPEROR'S PATRONAGE OF ARTISTS WAS TAKEN UP BY OFFICERS OF THE EAST INDIA COMPANY. THESE WORKS ARE KNOWN AS COMPANY PAINTINGS.

The Mughal emperors were receptive to Western artistic ideas and both Akbar (reigned 1556–1605) and his successor Jahangir (reigned 1605–27) had collected European prints and other works of art. Mughal artists copied these imported pictures and began to paint nature with greater realism, adding shading and perspective to their own work.

EARLY COMMISSIONS
Both the Mughal love of nature and their penchant for portraits were shared by many Britons and Europeans based in India. The British were also familiar with the technique of Indian artists – opaque watercolour or gouache on paper – because it was identical to that used by artists in Britain. Having seen and admired the work of Mughal artists, in the mid-18th century officers of the East India Company began to commission their own paintings from them.

The initial commissions were for miniature paintings, executed in the traditional Indian manner but showing scenes with European figures. These portraits often depict a portly European gentleman, sometimes wearing Indian dress, seated awkwardly on a cushion and drawing on a *huqqa*, a type of smoking pipe. With their propensity for documenting everything, the British commissioned pictures of native crafts, castes, festivals and pastimes – indeed, exactly the kind of subjects that are photographed today. The depiction of natural history subjects and topographical views of famous Mughal monuments followed.

One of the earliest and most important collections of natural history subjects was commissioned in Calcutta between 1777 and 1783 by Lady Mary Impey, wife of the Chief Justice of Bengal. While the drawings show a mastery of the subject, they have a power and

Above *Only a few Indian artists were known by name, but Dip Chand signed this charming picture of Dr William Fullarton on his terrace, puffing a* huqqa.

character all their own. Their distinctive quality perhaps indicates that the artists were given complete freedom to express their talents as they wished.

THE FRASER ALBUMS
A remarkable collection of more than 90 watercolours by Indian artists was commissioned between 1815 and 1819 by two brothers, James and William Baillie Fraser. Known as the Fraser Albums, this collection is now generally accepted as one of the finest groups of Company pictures ever painted by Indian artists. They record a broad range of Indian life in Delhi and its surroundings and depict some of the colourful Indian characters encountered by William Fraser in the course of his civil and military employment. One of the most arresting drawings is of a young Indian trooper who had saved his life when he was attacked by a would-be assassin.

Left *These two women and a buffalo were painted by the Indian artist who accompanied William Fraser on his travels for the East India Company.*

Because the Indian artists were regarded by their patrons as no more than employees, few of their names were recorded. Most Indian painters were artists because they had been born into a family whose men followed the caste profession. Although the identity of the artists who worked on the Fraser Albums is uncertain, they are thought to be the work of a single family, that of Ghulam Ali Khan. He is probably also the artist responsible for the illustrations in the Skinner Album, commissioned by Colonel James Skinner, the Anglo-Indian Colonel of the famous Irregular Cavalry Corps, Skinner's Horse.

TOPOGRAPHICAL PAINTINGS

The first purely topographical artist known from late Mughal Delhi was Mazhar Ali Khan. It seems likely that he was commissioned by Thomas Metcalfe, the Agent representing British power at Delhi, to produce 125 paintings of Mughal monuments in the city and surrounding area. One of the most impressive of his pictures, painted in 1846, is a large-scale panorama of Delhi, nearly 5m (16ft) wide. It is a valuable record of the Red Fort and the outlying city before much of it was destroyed in 1858.

One well-known name among Indian artists working for the British in Calcutta was Shaykh Muhammad Amir of Karraya. His paintings depict the British way of life in and around the city: their large, palatial mansions, favourite dogs, horses and carriages. One picture, painted in 1845, shows a little girl on a pony attended by no less than three servants. Her face is entirely hidden by a blue bonnet and her isolation from reality seems to symbolize the colonial position of the British in India before the Mutiny that occurred in 1857.

Above The British often employed local Indian artists to paint their houses or favourite animals. This racehorse, jockey and groom are shown on the racecourse.

Above This bird of prey was one of 44 paintings, bound together in a volume, which were executed by an Indian artist for an East India Company botanist.

CHAPTER 18

THE OTTOMAN EMPIRE

Of Central Asian tribal descent, the Ottoman Turks first formed a small *beylik* (principality) close to the Byzantine frontier in Anatolia in the 13th century. In 1453, the Ottoman Sultan Mehmet II ('the Conqueror') captured Constantinople (Istanbul) from the failing Byzantine Empire, and the imperial city became the heart of Ottoman power, ruling a massive land empire that lasted until 1924. At its greatest extent, Ottoman territory extended from North Africa to Iraq and from Arabia into the Balkans, pressing to the walls of Hapsburg Vienna on two separate occasions. The golden age for imperial Ottoman culture was the 16th century, particularly the long and glorious reign of Sultan Suleyman 'the Magnificent' (1520–66). The architect Sinan transformed the urban landscape of Istanbul and other Ottoman cities with formidable mosque complexes, while the luxury arts promoted an elegant floral style. The Ottoman sultans were great patrons of the arts and attracted the most talented artists and craftsmen, from calligraphers and metalworkers to the renowned potters of Iznik.

Opposite The Topkapi palace courtyards are filled with soldiers and courtiers in this 1558 painting

Above Domes are clustered together at the Bayezid I Mosque complex (1390–95) in Bursa. The foundation includes a dervish lodge, hospital, hammam, madrasa and mausoleum for the sultan.

CONSTANTINOPLE (ISTANBUL)

THE OTTOMANS GAINED A NEW PRESTIGIOUS CAPITAL WHEN THEY
TOOK CONSTANTINOPLE IN 1453. THE CITY ALSO PROVIDED THEIR
BUILDERS WITH THE PROTOTYPE FOR THEIR GREAT MOSQUES.

Istanbul, the Turkish version of the Greek words *eis ten polin*, or 'to the City', became the official name of the city on the Bosphorus only as late as 1930. Until that date, it was still called Constantinople, 'the city of Constantine', a name reflecting its Roman and Byzantine imperial past. The grandeur of this capital of three successive empires inspired several sieges by Muslim rulers, but the prize of conquest was reserved for Sultan Mehmet II (reigned 1444–46, 1451–81), who consequently assumed the epithet of Fatih, 'the Conqueror.'

THE FATIH MOSQUE

The first mosque to be built in the soon-to-be-regenerated capital still bears the same name, Fatih Mosque (1462–70), and despite collapsing and being reconstructed in 1771, it retains its original plan. Like the pre-1453 mosques of Bursa, Edirne and Didymoteicho, it has a large central domed roof and some lateral bays, but it also presents the first occurrence of a feature that later would develop into the main characteristic of classical Ottoman mosques: a large semidome that supports the main dome on the *qibla* side (toward the direction of prayer) over a long and narrow bay, unlike the square side bays to the left and right. Significantly, this bay is separated from the domed central bay by an arch supported by pillars that recede to the sides, creating the illusion of a unified roof consisting of the central dome and the semidome.

THE HAGIA SOPHIA PLAN

This effect was undoubtedly inspired by the patriarchal church of Byzantine Constantinople and eventually mosque of the Ottomans, Hagia Sophia (Ayasofya),

Above *The interior decoration of the reconstructed Fatih Mosque follows the Baroque style of 18th-century Ottoman architecture.*

a building laden with imperial connotations. Built between 532 and 537, it was an inventive and short-lived answer to the problem of a large floor area sheltered by a domed roof. The 'Hagia Sophia plan' was popular with Ottoman builders and characterized 16th-century mosque architecture.

The original 'Hagia Sophia plan,' as in the 6th-century cathedral, was finished with a second semidome opposite, creating an elongated oval shell. The complete version first appeared in the Sultan Bayezid Mosque in Istanbul, built for Bayezid II (reigned 1481–1512) around the turn of the century, in which the central core (semidome-dome-semidome) was flanked to the right and left by eight domes arranged over eight bays.

The most faithful Ottoman version of the plan was erected between 1550 and 1557 by Sinan

Left This aerial view of the Sultan Bayezid Mosque (1501–6) gives some idea of its of its innovative roofing system.

(1489–1588), the principal architect of the Ottoman Empire, for Sultan Suleyman 'the Magnificent' (reigned 1520–66). The Süleymaniye Mosque, the high point of classical Ottoman architecture, bears a striking resemblance to the Byzantine cathedral in both proportions and ground plan, although the lofty arches opening to the right and left toward the side bays represent a step forward by alleviating the restricting effect of the church's side walls.

BEYOND THE PROTOTYPE

While little innovation can be seen in the floor plans of sultanic mosques because they adhere to a venerated prototype, the architectural designs of smaller buildings are often more original. The graceful Şehzade Mosque, built by Sinan in 1543 to commemorate the son of Suleyman I, was a symmetrical departure from the Hagia Sophia plan. Two lateral semidomes balancing the ones on and opposite the *qibla* side create a strong central focus complementing the single large dome. The pillars carrying the main arches are pushed toward the outside walls to allow the play of curved surfaces on the top half of the building's interior to counterbalance the strong vertical lines of the supports. By this stage, walls are simple screens bridging the gaps between load-bearing elements and they are profusely pierced with stained-glass windows in symmetrical arrangements.

Buildings other than mosques, erected around the Ottoman Empire in great numbers, were built within the traditions of earlier Islamic architecture. Surrounding mosques and supporting them financially were complexes of shops and *hammams* (bathhouses), creating income to cover the running costs of mosques and charitable institutions complementing their social role, such as *imarets* (public kitchens) and *madrasas* (religious colleges).

Above A drawing of the Süleymaniye Mosque shows the system of domes and semi-domes based on the Hagia Sophia plan.

Below The Hagia Sophia's domed structure interior decoration and fenestration inspired Ottoman architects.

THE CLASSICAL ERA

CLAD WITH IZNIK TILES AND DRESSED STONE, AND EMBELLISHED WITH STAINED GLASS AND FURNITURE, 16TH-CENTURY OTTOMAN MOSQUES ARE AMONG THE GLORIES OF ISLAMIC ARCHITECTURE.

The grandeur of the classical Ottoman mosques is not only due to their vast size, ground plan and height but also to their interior decoration. The balance between light and dark, straight and curved lines, empty space and decorative excess reaches its pinnacle in the works of the master builder Sinan.

INTERIOR DECORATION
The striking colours of the tiles that adorn the buildings, commissioned from workshops in Istanbul and the town of Iznik not far from the capital, have preserved the splendour of decorative schemes from the 16th century. This is often not true of other decorative materials: few stained-glass windows have survived and the wall paintings have often been renewed several times since first executed. Contrary to current practice, it is possible that the polished marble floors were

uncovered in hot summer months, to reflect light streaming in from the windows. However, cold Istanbul winters called for warmer coverings, and the few period carpets still extant testify to the opulent, colourful woven fields of flowers and elaborate geometry added to the mosque interiors.

Sinan's Rüstem Pasha Mosque (1561–63) in Istanbul – commissioned by the Grand Wazir and son-in-law of Suleyman 'the Magnificent' – is an architecturally unassuming edifice with an ornate interior featuring a profusion of tiles arranged in panels on the walls both inside and under the front porch. The splendour and expense of the decorations enhanced the visual impact of the building.

Even more impressive is the tile cladding of the Sokollu Mehmet Pasha Mosque (1571–72), again by Sinan, for the successor of Rustem

Above The floral pattern on the tiles in the Rustem Pasha Mosque includes an innovative red colour.

Pasha. In this simple domed space with four semidomes over the side bays, the stone surfaces of the walls and bearing elements are only selectively embellished with tiles, custom-made to fit specific spaces. The beautiful effect achieved, despite the unremarkable architecture, must have been worthy compensation for the time and effort needed. The survival in more-or-less original form of the stained-glass windows completes the image of a restrained yet elegant interior.

BUILDING DONORS
The relation between the donors who funded the building of these mosques and the sultan emphasizes the social and political dimension of such religious foundations. The ruler's family and high officials erected extravagant public structures as status symbols advertising their donors' munificence and power to the capital's citizens. Women of the imperial family were also great builders. Mihrimah Sultana,

Left Calligraphy and floral patterns are among the design elements in the blue, green, red and white tiles that adorn the Sokollu Mehmet Pasha Mosque.

daughter of Suleyman 'the Magnificent' and wife of Rüstem Pasha, erected a mosque near the Edirne Gate of Istanbul's walls between 1562 and 1565. The choice of architect was unsurprising: Sinan's dense fenestration of the elevated cube under the dome dematerializes the Mihrimah Sultana Mosque's structure; he would fully deploy this decorative device a decade later in Edirne's Selimiye Mosque. The comparatively modest scale of non-sultanic buildings was a testing ground for ideas that were blended into an elegantly varied yet homogeneous body of work.

THE ARCHITECT SINAN

Sinan was the most important *mimar* (architect) in Istanbul and his long career spanning the reigns of three sultans, from the early 16th century to his death in 1588, marks the classical period of Ottoman architecture. A cross between a civil engineer, an architect and a minister of public works with a portfolio of hundreds of monuments across the Ottoman dominion, Sinan was revered even in his own lifetime.

His masterpiece is the light-filled, delicately detailed Selimiye Mosque, built in Edirne (1569–75) for Selim II (reigned 1566–74). With this mosque he claimed to have surpassed Hagia Sophia in building a larger dome. However, his real achievement is the distribution of interior space under the vast dome, which rests on eight arches supported alternately by semidomes and window-pierced walls. The arches spring from capital-free pillars that recede toward the outside of the building, creating a huge unified space unobstructed by structural elements. The multitude of glazed windows admits abundant daylight, forming an open-air, ethereal illusion. In the Selimiye Mosque, Ottoman architecture had truly surpassed its prototype, pushing the capacity of building materials and geometry to their limits.

The architecture of the late 16th and 17th centuries added few variations to the themes already introduced by Sinan and his predecessors, and there was a decline in the standards of both construction and decoration.

Above *The Mihrimah Sultana Mosque in Üsküdar is another major endowment by a female member of Suleyman's family.*

Above *The impressive dome of the Selimiye Mosque stands 42m (138ft) tall. The slender towering minarets reach a tapered point at about 71m (233ft).*

Left *Pillars arranged in an octagon shape support the massive dome of the Selimiye Mosque, creating a huge area illuminated by natural daylight.*

TOPKAPI PALACE

THE WORLD-FAMOUS TOPKAPI PALACE PRESERVES MOST OF ITS
ORIGINAL ARCHITECTURAL LAYOUT, ALONG WITH AN REMARKABLE
MUSEUM COLLECTION FROM THE IMPERIAL TREASURY.

*Above This reception room is in the
sultan's private quarters of the palace.*

Founded by Mehmet II in the
1450s, the Topkapi is one of the
best-known palace complexes in
the Islamic world. Built on the
acropolis of ancient Constantinople,
it overlooks the Golden Horn, the
Sea of Marmara and the Bosphorus,
and was an ideal location for the
new centre of Ottoman power.
The Topkapi (or Cannon Gate)
Palace was built shortly after
the Ottoman conquest of
Constantinople in 1453. Initially
known as the New Palace, this
was the seat of administration only
– the royal family was housed in
another palace, known later as the
Eski Saray or Old Palace. They
moved to the Topkapi after
the harem was built in the late
16th century.

AN ORDERED UNIVERSE
The palace is organized around a
sequence of courtyards, with
increasingly restricted privilege of
access and high security. This
sequential layout articulated the
state hierarchies with great clarity.

Much more than the sultan's
residence, the Topkapi Palace was the
seat of government for the entire
Ottoman Empire. It was home to
hundreds of courtiers, soldiers and
slaves. The imperial complex included
the Divan, where government
ministers met, as well as military
barracks, workshops, the royal mint,
state treasury and enormous kitchens
situated around beautifully planted
and well-maintained garden
courtyards. The harem was restricted
to the royal family and their servants,
and within these quarters were
facilities to serve the residents' needs.

Being an imperial residence for
some four consecutive centuries, the
interiors of the palace were
regularly updated and rearranged, to
follow new changes in interior
fashions, or to renovate after
occasional house fires. The splendid
palace rooms therefore show the
tastes of different periods – from
16th-century Iznik tiled pavilions to
18th-century Baroque *trompe l'oeil*.

There was an exacting order that
permeated everyday life within the

enclosure. Specific groups were
admitted at particular areas during
determined times to perform
prescribed duties. Some quarters
were altogether out-of-bounds,
except to a few. Famously, the only
non-eunuch adult male allowed in
the harem was the sultan himself.

HIERARCHICAL LAYOUT
The Gate of Majesty leads into the
first court, where the Imperial Mint
and the 8th-century church of
Hagia Irene, used in Ottoman times
as a warehouse and armoury, still
stand. Upon arriving at the Gate
of Salutation or Middle Gate,
everyone but the sultan had to
dismount in order to proceed
into the second court. The second
court was the main gathering place
for courtiers, the location of the
grandest audiences with the sultan
and the point of access to various
areas of the palace – the chimneyed
kitchens, rebuilt by Sinan after a fire
in 1574; the Outer Treasury; the
Divan, seat of the government
council; the Tower of Justice and
the inner harem.

From here, through the Gate of
Felicity, or Gate of White Eunuchs,

*Left A dense array of buildings form the
Topkapi Palace, originally called the Yeni
Saray, or 'New Palace'. The Tower of
Justice can be seen here (right).*

470

the few that were granted access by the sultan could enter the third court, surrounded by the Chamber of Petitions, or Throne Room, the Library of Ahmet III (reigned 1703–30), the Mosque of the Aghas, the Kiosk of the Conqueror (housing the Inner Treasury), the Dormitory of the 39 Senior Pages (the sultan himself being the 40th 'page') and the sultan's apartments.

ROUTE TO THE HAREM
The sultan accessed the harem from the third court – a complex of palatial proportions. The individual apartments featured mosques, ancillary service rooms, *hammams* (bathhouses) and warehouses.

Finally, in the innermost fourth court, visitors can nowadays enjoy the views and lofty quarters once reserved for the sultan, among them the superbly decorated Baghdad Kiosk and Circumcision Chamber,

standing between decorative pools. The slopes leading to the sea are still planted with gardens, and give a flavour of the tranquil atmosphere surrounding the palace. In 1853, the imperial household moved out of the Topkapi Palace, to the more modern Dolmabahçe Palace on the shores of the Bosphorus.

Above The Circumcision Chamber was clad with the finest tiles manufactured during the peak of Iznik production.

Below The love of flowers is apparent in the 18th-century Fruit Room, where painted wooden panels of fruit and flowers decorate the walls and ceiling.

DAMASCUS, ALEPPO AND IZNIK

AS THEY EXTENDED THEIR TERRITORIES, THE OTTOMANS BUILT NOTABLE STRUCTURES IN OTHER CITIES, SUCH AS THE ANCIENT SYRIAN CENTRES OF DAMASCUS AND ALEPPO AND IN IZNIK.

The highly attractive Dervish Pasha Mosque in Damascus was built in 1574 by the Ottoman governor of the city, Dervish Pasha. The use of the traditional Syrian architectural feature of *ablaq* (bands of alternating black-and-white stone) gives the main façade a distinctive look. The entrance consists of an arched doorway with an Arabic inscription naming patron and date and a polygonal minaret with conical roof above. Within, there is a rectangular open-air courtyard with polychrome paving and at its centre a 16-sided fountain; on the yard's south side stands the prayer hall's five-bay portico with five small domes supported by white stone columns. From the courtyard a spiral staircase climbs to the minaret.

The prayer hall is a typically Ottoman square-domed space, with side aisles, each with three smaller domes. The main dome has 16 arched windows. To the south, the *qibla* wall (facing the direction of prayer) is covered with geometric patterns in multicoloured marble; its *mihrab* (niche) arch has a rectangular frame with diamond-and-star decoration made of coloured stones, and is flanked by marble columns. The niche has vertical stripes of white and black marble, and the semidome above it contains white, red and black marble laid in a zigzag decoration. The *minbar* (pulpit) is also marble.

The other walls of the prayer hall are covered with panels of Persian-style tiles and also contain coloured-glass windows. The mosque also has a *madrasa* (religious college) and the shrine of the governor, who died in 1579.

Another fine 16th-century Ottoman mosque in Damascus is the al-Sinanieh Mosque, built on

Above The Azem Palace baths, built in imitation of the main city baths, are now dilapidated, but visitors can see that they were once beautifully decorated.

the Bab al-Jabieh Square just outside the city wall by Governor Sinan Pasha in 1590–91. Like the Dervish Pasha Mosque, the al-Sinanieh also has a striking *ablaq* façade, a rectangular open-air court and a seven-dome prayer hall. It is particularly celebrated for its beautiful cylindrical minaret covered with green and blue tiles.

AZEM PALACE

Near the citadel and south of the Umayyad Mosque in the Old City of Damascus, the splendid Azem Palace was built in 1749 as the residence of Asad Pasha al-Azem, Ottoman governor of Damascus. It comprises several buildings arranged in three wings. The first, the *haremlik*, is a private residential area for the governor and his family, containing baths and kitchens as well as lavish accommodation. An interesting touch is that the baths are an exact replica, scaled down in

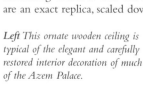

Left This ornate wooden ceiling is typical of the elegant and carefully restored interior decoration of much of the Azem Palace.

Above The minaret of the Ottoman-era al-Sinanieh Mosque in Damascus rises above the façade decorated in black-and-white ablaq *stonework.*

the architects used the *ablaq* technique, creating a pleasing decorative effect in their combination of marble, basalt, limestone and sandstone in the walls; within, the bedroom ceilings were fitted wooden panels bearing paintings of natural scenes, and there were marble mosaics and *muqarnas* (stalactite-like decoration) corners. The palace was damaged in 1925 during the Syrian revolt against French control in the region, but has since been carefully restored and today is a Museum of Arts and Popular Traditions.

ASAD PASHA KHAN

In 1751–52, Governor Asad Pasha al-Azem also built a magnificent *khan* (lodging place) on Suq al-Buzuriyyah in Damascus' Old City. Covering 2,500sq m (27,000sq ft), the *khan* is laid out in traditional style over two floors around a central courtyard: the ground floor contains shops, while on the upper level 80 rooms are arranged as accommodation for merchants.

The courtyard is divided into 9 equal areas, each covered with a dome standing on a drum containing 20 windows; an octagonal fountain stands beneath

its own dome in the centre of the courtyard. It has a magnificent monumental entrance portal with carved stone decoration as well as a beautiful *muqarnas* semidome.

IN ALEPPO AND IZNIK

The Ottomans left a proud architectural legacy in other cities of the empire, notably Aleppo in Syria and Iznik (now in Turkey). Of particular note in Aleppo is the Khan al-Wazir, probably the city's most beautiful *khan*, constructed in 1678–82 on the traditional pattern with buildings arranged around a courtyard, with shops and storage on the ground floor and merchants' accommodation on the upper floor. It has splendid ornamented window frames and a black-and-white marble *ablaq* façade with an arched entrance door.

Among the many Ottoman buildings in Iznik is the Nilufer Hatun Imareti, a charitable hospital built by Sultan Murad I (reigned 1362–89) in 1388 and named after his mother Nilufer Hatun. A five-bay entrance portico leads into a domed central court, and beyond it a raised vaulted building that contains a *mihrab* indicates that it may have been used as a prayer hall.

size, of the main baths in Damascus. The second, the *khadamlik*, or servants' quarters, is attached to the family quarters. The third, the *salamlik*, is a guest wing, and contains grand reception areas, including a hall with a beautiful internal fountain, and superb courtyards with water features; the grounds were kept lush by waters diverted from the river Barada. The palace combines opulent interiors with serene exteriors: once again,

Right In Iznik, the Nilufer Hatun Imareti of 1388, once a charitable hospital, was restored in 1955 and is now the city's principal museum.

IZNIK POTTERY

THE SKILLED CRAFTSMEN OF IZNIK WERE RENOWNED FOR THEIR CERAMIC POTTERY AND TILES, AND THEIR PRODUCTION REACHED ITS PEAK DURING THE 16TH CENTURY.

The production of glazed earthenware at Iznik, formerly Nicaea, went back to the 13th century. In the 15th century, potters from Iran introduced the technology for making the hard white ceramic body known as stonepaste. The tile work of the mosque of Sultan Mehmet in Bursa, dated 1419–24, is signed by 'the masters of Tabriz' (a city in north-western Iran). The typical Iznik pottery body is hard and white, coated in a white slip (liquid clay) made of the same raw materials as the body but ground more finely. The transparent glaze is particularly brilliant and glossy.

EARLY PRODUCTION

The late 15th century was the beginning of large-scale production. The imperial workshops in Istanbul were responsible for many of the designs that were applied to the pottery vessels using stencils. Entire compositions or individual motifs were drawn on wax paper, the outlines were pricked and the design was laid over a tile or vessel and charcoal dust sprinkled though the holes. The first phase of design, inspired by both Chinese porcelain and the radial designs of Ottoman metalwork, consisted of tightly drawn arabesques reserved in white on dense, often

Above The walls of Rüstem Pasha Mosque are covered in tiles. Designs include a repetition of serrated saz leaves, Chinese-style cloud bands, plus tulips and carnations.

blackish cobalt ground. By the beginning of the 16th century, the blue had become paler, there was a greater use of white and the decoration had become looser.

TABRIZ INFLUENCE

In 1514, Sultan Selim I captured Tabriz and brought back 38 master craftsmen, including 2 tile cutters and at least 16 painters; one of these was Shahquli, who became head of the workshop in 1526 and initiated a new, more Persian style typified by the 'saz leaf and rosette' style, a harmonious combination of serrated leaves and large, many-petalled flowers.

One of the most impressive commissions of this period is a series of five massive tiles (each one

Left The floral spray on this late 16th-century dish includes tulip, rose and saz leaf – a classic combination. Red was applied thickly to survive the firing.

Right The distinctive pattern of tight foliated spirals on this mid-16th-century tondino – a small bowl with broad rim – was derived from manuscript illumination, particularly the tughra, *or imperial monogram.*

125cm/50in high), made for the walls of the Sunnet Odasi, or Circumcision Chamber, in the Topkapi Palace. These tiles were decorated with imaginary beasts grazing in a landscape of swirling leaves and flowers in various shades of blue and turquoise.

A new style was developed during the reign of Suleyman 'the Magnificent' (1520–66), in which the motifs were outlined in dark green or black for better definition, and new colours, such as purple and olive green, were introduced. A mosque lamp in this style is signed by its maker Musli.

ARCHITECTURAL TILES

Suleyman was a great patron of architecture, particularly religious buildings, and from 1550 tile making became the pre-eminent concern of the pottery workshops. The palette of soft colours used in vessel decoration needed to be altered, because when viewed from a distance these tones were muddy and indistinct. The colour red was introduced for better impact and visibility but had to be applied thickly to survive the firing. The red colouring was made from Armenian bole, a powerful astringent that the Ottomans used to heal circumcision wounds.

Sinan was made chief architect in 1539 and put in charge of all ceramics and architectural industries. He needed to have a close

relationship with the Iznik potteries to ensure that the tiles were made to the correct dimensions to fit his building plans.

The new palette was so successful on tiles, it was eventually applied also to vessel production. The potters were inventive and developed many new shapes, some of which were based on metal and leather items, and many new designs. The floral style was still the most popular, particularly a spray of carnations, tulips and hyacinths springing from a central tuft, but there were also figural designs with animals and ships.

DECLINING INDUSTRY

In the 17th century, the industry started to decline. This was closely linked with

the decline of Ottoman rule but also with the construction of the Sultan Ahmet Mosque, which while employing many tile makers during the peak of its ten-year construction period, eventually put them out of business. Sultan Ahmet was obsessed with tiles and ordered over 20,000 from Iznik. Extra clay had to be imported from Kutahya, and the tile makers were forbidden to do other work in the meantime. When work was completed, many potters must have gone bankrupt because they had been forced to neglect other production.

Right This 1549 mosque lamp is signed on the base by its maker, 'the poor and humble Musli', and the inscription around the base is dedicated to Esrefzade, a local saint of Iznik.

OTTOMAN CARPETS

FROM THE 15TH CENTURY ONWARD, MANY FINE CARPETS WERE PRODUCED FOR THE IMPERIAL COURT IN ISTANBUL OR FOR EXPORT TO EUROPE. PRAYER RUGS WERE ALSO MADE FOR THE FAITHFUL.

The finest Ottoman carpets were produced in Ushak, in western Anatolia. Carpets from this region, now known as Ushak carpets, were commissioned by the Ottoman court under sultans Mehmet II (reigned 1444–46, 1451–81) and Bayezid II (reigned 1481–1512). The Ottomans held a strong, central control over the artistic production of the carpets, and the designs reflected their tastes.

REDS DOMINATE
The carpets have fine designs, usually organized in a repeated series of motifs and following a strict symmetry. The colour palette was dominated by red, with design elements in green, white, yellow and blue. Some of the Ushak carpets were manufactured in a large format, up to 10m (33ft) in length.

Below This 17th-century Star Ushak rug is the only surviving complete example of a design that uses quatrefoil (four-leaved) medallions with smaller diamonds.

Ushak carpets have been divided into several groups based on design. One major group is known as the 'Star Ushaks' because these carpets bear an endlessly repeating design of an eight-pointed star alternating with a smaller lozenge. Another group is known as the 'Medallion Ushaks' because they were decorated with a medallion design. Designs such as these remained in use for long periods under the Ottomans.

EXPORTS FOR EUROPE
Many fine Ottoman carpets were exported to Europe, especially via Italy, from the 15th century onward. Members of the nobility and church authorities were frequent buyers; the rugs were prestigious possessions, and were represented by leading artists in portraits and in sacred paintings intended for churches (*see* Holbeins and Lottos, opposite). Henry VIII had extensive collections of Turkish and Egyptian carpets: by his death in 1547, there were 500 such carpets in Tudor palaces.

Above The Ottomans added floral designs to the prayer rugs they commissioned. This rug was woven from wool and cotton in c.1600.

PRAYER RUGS
Another category of carpet was the prayer rug or *saf*. These were intended for use by the Muslim faithful in mosques. They carried an image of the *mihrab* (niche) and were laid on the floor pointing toward Makkah when, during prayers, worshippers prostrated themselves in the direction of the holy city.

There were both single prayer rugs for individual use, and longer ones with several woven niches aligned either horizontally or vertically on the rug, designed to be shared by a number of worshippers at prayer. Few of these carpets have survived because they were in daily use during worship, but there are some surviving fragments of communal prayer rugs: some now held in the Museum of Islamic and Turkish Art in Istanbul are badly damaged but are still 8m (26ft) long, giving an idea of how long they once must have been. Ushak prayer rugs often used a cloud-bank border adopted from Persian designs; some represented a pendant to indicate a mosque lamp.

An Ottoman prayer rug in the collection of the Textile Museum in Washington, DC, is a good example of another common design featuring three prayer arches. It dates to the 1600s, and is very similar to rugs represented in 17th-century Dutch paintings, such as *Still Life* by Nicolaes van Gelder (1664), now in the Rijksmuseum, Amsterdam.

Above A prayer rug of c.1500, woven from wool in Cairo, provides ample evidence of the Mamluk artisans' skill that was so admired by the Ottomans.

MAMLUK INFLUENCE

After the Ottomans conquered Egypt in 1517 under Sultan Selim I (reigned 1512–20), they had access to the highly skilled carpet makers of Mamluk Cairo. The Mamluks used finer wool than their Turkish contemporaries, and made tighter knots to create even more elegant flowing designs; they sometimes also used cotton for the white areas of a design and silk for the main weave. Before the Ottoman conquest, they had typically woven carpets with kaleidoscopic designs and patterns of octagons with stars, in blues, green and wine-red colours. The Ottomans dispatched detailed designs for floral patterns featuring hyacinths, carnations and tulips from Istanbul to be followed by the Mamluk weavers.

In 1585, Sultan Murad III (reigned 1574–95) called 11 master carpet makers from Cairo to Istanbul, with a large consignment of Egyptian wool; at this point there were 16 master carpet makers in the Ottoman capital, but the demand for carpets was so high that they could not meet it. As a result of Egyptian influence, some carpets and rugs made in Turkey began to show Egyptian elements: for example, a rug from the mausoleum of Sultan Selim II (d.1574) used typically Egyptian green and cherry-red colours.

HOLBEINS AND LOTTOS

Certain designs of Ottoman carpets exported from Ushak became known as 'Holbeins' and 'Lottos', after the European artists Hans Holbein the Younger (1497/8–1543) and Lorenzo Lotto (c.1480–1556), in whose paintings the carpets were represented as luxury objects. The artists carefully copied the delicate patterns and rich colours of the carpets. Both designs appeared also in the works of other artists. The Holbein design, which featured octagons interlaced with cross-shaped elements, appeared in European art from 1451 onward; the first appearance of the similar Lotto design was in a 1516 portrait by Sebastiano del Piombo (c.1485–1547).

Right An Ottoman carpet takes pride of place in this portrait, Husband and Wife *(c.1523), by Italian artist Lorenzo Lotto.*

OTTOMAN MANUSCRIPT PAINTING

THE OTTOMANS AMASSED AN EXTRAORDINARY LIBRARY AT THE TOPKAPI PALACE. THE COURT ATELIER PRODUCED MULTI-VOLUME ILLUSTRATED MANUSCRIPTS OF OTTOMAN HISTORY AND GENEALOGY.

To this day, the library of the Topkapi Palace houses a remarkable collection of manuscripts, acquired over four centuries by Ottoman sultans and their courts. Some sultans were known bibliophiles, such as Mehmet Fatih and Ahmet III, who built personal collections.

Exceptional books also came to the palace library as diplomatic gifts, and from the sacked treasuries of defeated powers. The Ottoman

Below This portrait of Sultan Selim II (reigned 1566–74) firing an arrow was painted by Nigari, one of the artists working at the Topkapi Palace, Istanbul.

military successes over the Mamluks of Egypt and Syria, as well as the Safavids of Iran, brought substantial riches, including manuscripts.

Books were given as important acts of international diplomacy, which indicates their status as major cultural assets. In 1567, the Safavid Shah Tahmasp of Iran sent a great consignment of gifts to Istanbul to congratulate the Sultan Selim II on his accession. The first two items on the list were books: the first was a copy of the Quran said to be handwritten by Ali, the Prophet's son-in-law, and therefore a sacred relic. The second was a two-volume copy of the *Shahnama* which was arguably the finest illustrated Persian manuscript ever produced. At the time, Ottoman taste favoured the styles of early 16th century Safavid Iran, which is evidenced by a lively export trade of manuscripts from commercial centres in Shiraz to the Ottoman empire. The Safavid court manuscript of *c.*1520–40 was an exceptional example, and constituted an appropriate gift to the Ottoman court, although it may also have implied a message about Iran's supposedly greater artistic heritage.

Above A painting (c.1475) of Mehmet the Conqueror at the height of his power, possibly by Sinan Bey.

COURT PAINTERS

Working at the palace, the court painters may have benefited from the imperial library's holdings of illustrated books from east and west. The stylistic influence of Safavid Iran was important, but the court artists came from lands throughout the empire, as well as former Safavid territories.

Imperial patronage determined the types of manuscripts and paintings the atelier produced, and Ottoman illustrated manuscripts certainly reveal independent ideas which were not indebted to Safavid painting traditions. Court archives record how the artists' workshop was organized, and give details of names, salaries and ethnicity, as well as noting personal presentations of masterpieces, offered directly by the artist to the sultan on a festive occasion or bayram. The sultan would usually reward presentations with a gift of cash or robes.

IMPERIAL HISTORIES

The Ottoman sultans were keen to claim an important place in history, and establish their position as the

Left The 1541 reception of Hungarian Queen Isabella and infant King Stephen is depicted in this commercial manuscript.

of the Sultan's death on his military campaign, the funeral procession and final burial in Istanbul. On a municipal level, illustrated *Surname* manuscripts also described the public festivities accompanying court celebrations as well as guild processions through the city streets.

As Ottoman territory included the two holy cities of Makkah and Madinah, the Sultans promoted and protected the pilgrimage routes, and the facilities at the holy places. This pious undertaking may be related to the production of multi-volume illustrated accounts of the lives of the prophets in the late 16th century, such as the illustrated 1594 six-volume manuscript of *Siyer-i Nebi* (The Life of the Prophet).

Other biographies outline the history of Islam from Adam to the Prophet Muhammad and the Caliphs and, by extension, to the Sultans themselves. Prayerbooks praising the two holy places were produced, with topographical illustrations of the pilgrim sites.

rightful successors to past Islamic rulers and key religious figures. To this end, they commissioned official dynastic histories, genealogies and portrait series.

Historical accounts of the Ottomans were densely illustrated and the paintings provide exciting views of 16th-century court life. For example, most of the reign of Sultan Suleyman 'the Magnificent' (reigned 1520–66) is described in the *Suleymanname* (dated 1558),

written by the court panegyrist Arifi. The biography is the final volume in a series of five, dedicated to the dynastic history of the Ottoman sultans. A subsequent book (dated 1579–80) provided an addendum volume, covering the remaining ten years of Suleyman's reign: this includes dramatic scenes

Right The Procession of the Trade Corporations was illustrated in Vehbi's Surname, *1720.*

481

OTTOMAN CALLIGRAPHY

DURING THE OTTOMAN PERIOD, SHAYKH HAMDULLAH AND OTHER
OUTSTANDING CALLIGRAPHERS REFINED SEVERAL CALLIGRAPHIC
SCRIPTS, EVEN CREATING A NEW OFFICIAL SCRIPT CALLED *DIWANI*.

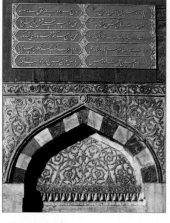

Over the centuries, calligraphy became the foremost Islamic art form, a way of giving physical and visible form to the words of Allah as revealed to the Prophet Muhammad and recorded in the Quran. Calligraphers were highly honoured at the Ottoman court: the foremost Ottoman calligrapher, Shaykh Hamdullah (1436–1520), was befriended by the future Sultan Bayezid II when Bayezid was a prince in Amasya, and on Bayezid becoming sultan in 1512, he was summoned to Istanbul. According to tradition, Bayezid was happy to see himself as a pupil of Hamdullah, and willingly held the *hokka* (ink pot) while his master wrote.

SHAYKH HAMDULLAH
While at Bayezid's court, Shaykh Hamdullah created a new character and style for the *thuluth*, *naskhi* and *muhaqqaq* styles of calligraphy, in particular succeeding in making *naskhi* script unambiguous to read.

According to a tradition originating with Ibn Muqla, 10th-century vizier in Abbasid Baghdad, there were six 'hands', or canonical scripts: *naskhi, muhaqqaq, rayhani, tawqi, riqa* and *thuluth*. Shaykh Hamdullah's work in Istanbul was based on a close study of the writings and calligraphy of a 13th-century follower of Ibn Muqla named Yaqut al-Mustasimi (d.1295), who was revered in the Ottoman era as a master of calligraphy. Shaykh Hamdullah was hailed as Kibletul Kuttab ('Highest of scribes') and founded his own school of calligraphic artists in Istanbul. His followers greatly developed the *naskhi* script for use in copying books.

In the late 17th century, Hafiz Osman (d.1698) worked in the same traditions. He made further improvements to the *naskhi* script by drawing together the works of Yaqut al-Mustasimi and Shaykh Hamdullah. Such was

Above Some fine Ottoman calligraphy is displayed on the water fountain just outside the Topkapi Palace.

the stature of this calligrapher that he was hailed as Sayhi Sani ('the second Shaykh', a reference to Shaykh Hamdullah). His work had a great influence on later calligraphers.

A SCRIPT FOR DOCUMENTS
Ottoman calligraphers developed a new calligraphic style known as *diwani*, which was used for decrees, resolutions, endowments and other official documents. It was named *diwani* because it was used for the official documents of the sultan's *diwan*, or council of ministers. Only a few official calligraphers were instructed in this difficult script. The style was developed in the 16th century and was known to Shaykh Hamdullah – an album of his calligraphy preserved in the Topkapi

Left This elegant calligraphic line above a doorway at the Topkapi Palace reads: 'There is no god but God, and Muhammad is his Prophet.'

Above Verses from the Quran, inscribed in magnificent calligraphy, sanctify the walls and dome of the Süleymaniye Mosque in Istanbul.

Palace contains writing in the *diwani* script as well as in *naskhi, thuluth, muhaqqaq,* Riqa and Tawqi.

Ahmet Karahisari (1468–1556) was another leading calligrapher of the 16th century, a contemporary of Shaykh Hamdullah and a favoured artist at the court of Suleyman I 'the Magnificent' (reigned 1520–66). Karahisari was celebrated for his calligraphic representation of the *basmalah* formula in praise of Allah, which could be inscribed without lifting the pen from the paper.

Two splendid illuminated copies of the Quran largely composed by his hand are kept in the Topkapi Palace. One of these is very large, measuring approximately 61cm by 43cm (24in by 17in), bound in black leather with gilded ornament, and has 300 pages. It is written in the *naskhi, thuluth, muhaqqaq* and *rayhani* styles. The calligraphy, illumination and binding of this Quran are all of the highest quality, and it is viewed as an absolute masterpiece. However, this Quran was not signed by Karahisari, which is unusual. For this reason, textual historians believe that when Karahisari died in 1556 the work was unfinished, and that it was

probably completed by his adoptive son Hasan Celebi, who was another fine calligrapher.

DECORATIVE CALLIGRAPHY
Leading calligraphers also played an important role in other arts, providing designs for textiles, metalwork and ceramics, and notably sacred architecture. Ahmet Karahisari designed the grand calligraphic inscription in the dome of the Süleymaniye Mosque in Istanbul, built in 1550–57. In the same building, Hasan Celebi made a calligraphic piece above the harem door; the same artists produced fine work in the Selimiye Mosque in Edirne, built by Sinan in 1568–74 for Selim II.

THE SULTAN'S SEAL
Each Ottoman sultan had his own *tughra*, a calligraphic form of his name and title, with the words *al-muzaffar daiman* ('ever victorious') used as a signature and seal on official documents and on all coins issued in a sultan's reign. The calligraphy was increasingly embellished with infilled illumination, such as the spiralling foliate style, known as *tughrakesh*.

Above The tughra of Sultan Murad III (reigned 1574–95) also appears over the Imperial Gate of the Topkapi Palace.

OTTOMAN METALWORK

THE OTTOMAN METALWORKERS WERE HIGHLY SKILLED CRAFTSMEN, PARTICULARLY WHEN WORKING WITH GOLD AND SILVER SET WITH PREVIOUS STONES, SUCH AS RUBIES AND GARNETS.

The collection of precious metal objects in the Topkapi Palace museum in Istanbul, although spectacular, represents only a small proportion of what the Ottoman court treasury once contained. Written sources and miniature paintings give documentary and visual evidence of all types of objects made of precious metal.

However, regular military campaigns resulted in the need to melt down silver and gold when the national coffers were empty, and re-use the metal as currency.

COURT PRODUCTION

The wave of Ottoman military conquests in the 15th century brought new lands and new peoples into the expanding empire. As a result, a wide range of metalworking traditions and techniques were introduced into the imperial workshops in Istanbul. The conquest of the Balkans, with their rich deposits of gold and silver, and craftsmen expert in the local traditions of working with precious metals, was particularly important.

Craftsmen from all over the Ottoman Empire came to Istanbul and joined the *ehl-i hiref* – an expression meaning 'communities of the talented', a title given to those working in the court ateliers. By the end of the 16th century, over 100 hundred gold and silver-smiths were listed on the palace payrolls. Other related craftsmen listed include *hakkakan* (jewellers), *kuftgeran* (gold inlayers), *kazganciyan* (coppersmiths) and *zernisani* (gold repoussé workers).

It was the custom of the Ottoman court for the princes to learn a practical skill; both Selim I

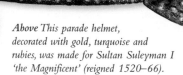

Above This parade helmet, decorated with gold, turquoise and rubies, was made for Sultan Suleyman I 'the Magnificent' (reigned 1520–66).

and Suleyman 'the Magnificent' were trained as goldsmiths and, as a result, this type of work had great social prestige. Although few signed pieces of metalwork survive from the period, one celebrated jeweller, Mehmet Usta, is known from several signed pieces.

According to an Italian merchant resident at the court of Sultan Mehmet II (reigned 1444–46, 1451–81), the sultan ate from gold plate, the viziers from silver and members of the army from base metal.

Court records list great numbers gold and silver vessels, particularly bottles and drinking cups, which were given as gifts, particularly on the important occasion of the circumcision of the young princes. Very few examples of such pieces survive today.

OTTOMAN STYLES

A number of different styles and techniques were used to produce the finest metalwork. Some of the most striking pieces are in a bejewelled style. This seems to have developed during the reign of

Left A patron of metalworkers, Suleyman I commissioned this fine pendant made of gold with pearls and emeralds for the Topkapi Palace.

Suleyman 'the Magnificent' (reigned 1520–66). Precious stones, such as rubies, emeralds or garnets were set into the surface of gold, silver and zinc objects, as well as rock crystal and jade. This most ostentatious of techniques was reserved for the most precious objects, which included Suleyman's parade helmet, decorated with rubies and turquoises, as well as his personal water flask and ceremonial sword which, in one painting, can be seen being carried by pages standing behind the Sultan.

Artisans also continued to use repoussé and other established techniques, including chasing (creating an incised design by hammering lines into the metal surface), filigree (decoration using twisted threads of gold or silver), niello (applying black inlay around engraved designs) and embossing. Unadorned pieces – such as bottles and candlesticks with bold shapes but no additional decoration – were also made. Gilded copper, or tombak, was a popular material for this plainer style of design.

FLORAL DECORATION

Floral designs transformed not only the surface of Ottoman metalwork, but also the basic form: one popular type of brass candlestick was made with the candleholder section cast in the shape of a tulip with pointed petals.

The *saz* style developed by the artist Shahquli, with its combination of serrated *saz* leaves and blossoms, was adopted by goldsmiths; a certain Mehmed the Bosnian excelled at this style and at least three signed examples of his work survive in the Topkapi Palace museum. During the 18th century a Rococo style was adopted from Europe with the

Above These daggers with decorated sheaths date from c.1600, in the reign of Mehmet III.

emphasis on floral bouquets, garlands and fluttering ribbons.

ARMOUR

Craftsmen made all types of ceremonial armour, including helmets, swords, daggers, armour and firearms for use by sultans, princes and military leaders. The blades were inlaid with gold arabesques or calligraphy, while the hilts were often adorned with jade or precious stones. Metalworkers also made practical weapons for active warfare, including swords and

battle-axes, often decorated with jewelled scabbards, sheaths and hilts.

A superb engraved helmet made for Sultan Bayezid II has survived and is kept in the Army Museum in the Hôtel National des Invalides in Paris. Measuring about 33cm (13in) in height, the helmet is made of steel and decorated with gold wire using the technique of *kuft-gari*, in which the steel surface is roughened with a chisel and a design in gold wire is hammered into it. The inscription reads: 'Allah, I am the helmet for the head of the brave imam, the fearless Sultan, the world-Emperor, the bringer of victory to Islam, the leader blessed with Allah's support and aid, al-Malik al-Nasir Sultan Bayezid, on of Sultan Muhammad Khan, may his followers and supporters be granted greatness by Allah.'

An example of a 15th–16th-century Ottoman ceremonial dagger with a steel blade, about 20cm (8in) in length, has survived and is held in the Royal Scottish Museum, Edinburgh. It bears decoration of arabesque foliage and a calligraphic inscription inlaid in gold, from a poem by the poet Necati (d.1509). The hilt is made from grey-green jade.

Left The handle of this 16th-century golden jug, commissioned by Suleyman I, represents a dragon. The jug is encrusted with rubies and emeralds.

OTTOMAN COSTUME

MEMBERS OF THE OTTOMAN COURT – FROM RULER TO SLAVE – WORE OSTENTATIOUS AND THEATRICAL CEREMONIAL CLOTHING MADE FROM LUXURY WOVEN FABRICS.

Expensive and elaborate clothing formed a significant part of court life under the Ottomans, and conveyed important messages about the wearer. The Topkapi Palace in Istanbul houses more than 2,500 textiles, including no fewer than 1,000 kaftans.

On Friday, the Ottoman sultan went in public procession to attend noon prayers at a mosque outside the palace. On formal occasions such as this, he typically wore decorated gold and silver cloth, called *seraser* in Turkish, and a brooch with precious stones in his turban. Foreign dignitaries visiting the Ottoman court were invited to watch the procession, and were impressed by the wealth on display.

A decorative motif of 'tiger stripes' and three spots was often used in Ottoman art. The design was already centuries old by the time of the Ottoman era, and its constituent elements were reputedly based on the stripes and

spots on tiger and leopard skins. It appears on a fragment of a kaftan that belonged to Sultan Mehmet 'the Conqueror' (reigned 1444–46, 1451–81) held in the Topkapi Palace Museum in Istanbul.

On some occasions, however, sultans wore plain materials. At funerals, for example, the sultans dressed in plain purple, dark blue or black kaftans of pure silk or mohair; for accession ceremonies, the new sultan wore white. Beneath the luxury of silk kaftans, they would wear more humble material – to avoid directly contravening the Quranic ban on wearing silk.

The sultan generally changed his silk robes after wearing them once, and afterward they were cared for by the wardrobe master in the treasury. After the death of a sultan his clothes were labelled and placed in the treasury; one of his kaftans, a turban, a belt and a dagger were laid on his tomb for the funeral.

Above Floral designs decorate the robes worn by Sultan Suleyman 'the Magnificent' in this portrait. He wears a jewelled brooch in his turban.

ROBES OF HONOUR

Many fine textiles and kaftans were given as 'robes of honour' by the sultan to leading officials or to visiting dignitaries. Called *khila*, these robes were of varying quality according to the degree of honour bestowed. This ancient Middle-Eastern system therefore expressed a strict and subtle social code. The robes given to the Grand vizier were usually made of gold or silver cloth and given in pairs: one lined with sable fur, one without. Religious scholars would only wear fine wool or mohair, but never silk.

A group of court tailors called *hayyatin-i hassa* were detailed to produce the *khila* robes. A fine silk kaftan with elongated ornamental

Left Courtiers gather for a reception at the court of Selim III (reigned 1789–1807). Splendid costumes added to the Ottoman court's projected image of power.

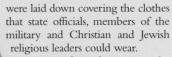

sleeves and a large pattern of leaves embroidered in gold on a silver ground, dated to *c.*1760, was given to and worn by an envoy of Frederick the Great of Prussia (reigned 1740–86) to the court of Ottoman Sultan Mustafa III (reigned 1757–74). It survives in good condition and is held in the Staatliche Museen zu Berlin in Germany.

STATUS AND CLOTHES

Clothes played an important role in Ottoman society, displaying the social status and allegiances of the wearer. Only courtiers and the wealthy elite wore kaftans and fine embroidered clothing, while poorer people wore more practical clothes.

In the era of Suleyman 'the Magnificent' (reigned 1520–66), clothing regulations were issued. Poorer men and women often wore *salvar* (trousers) or *potur* (breeches) with *mintan* (jackets) and *cizme* (boots). Strict rules

Right This silk robe, which belonged to Sultan Bayezid II (reigned 1481–1512), is in the collection at the Treasury of Topkapi Palace, Istanbul.

were laid down covering the clothes that state officials, members of the military and Christian and Jewish religious leaders could wear.

In a reform known as the *Tanzimet* (Reordering) Period in the mid-19th century, Western-style clothing, such as the waistcoat, necktie and high-heeled shoes, became fashionable among the wealthy; poorer people still wore traditional clothing.

FROM TURBAN TO FEZ

Headgear was highly significant in Ottoman visual culture: in the 16th–18th centuries people wore either the *sarik* (turban) or a cone-shaped headdress called *bashlyk*. The *sarik* was made out of particularly fine material. In 1826, under Sultan Mahmud II, the short cone-shaped felt hat called the fez replaced the *sarik*. Then, in 1925, after the foundation of the Republic of Turkey, Mustafa Kemal Ataturk outlawed the fez as part of a series of modernizing and secularizing reforms. As a result, more people began to wear Western-style hats, which were manufactured to meet the increased demand.

OTTOMAN SILK AND VELVET WORK

The Ottomans ran a thriving industry in silks and velvet, with production based at Bursa. Weavers used patterns based on crescents, leopard spots and tiger stripes, and a lattice enclosing flowers, such as tulips. Patterns were often in gold on a crimson ground. Weavers used silk for court kaftans and covers to be laid on the tombs of sultans and great officials; the tomb covers were embroidered with Quranic verses and invocations to Allah. A beautiful 18th-century red silk tomb cover of this kind is held in the Victoria and Albert Museum, London. Velvet was used for divan cushion covers, large hangings and saddle covers. A fine velvet saddle cloth embroidered in silver and gilt wire with flowers and foliage was given to King Gustavus Adolphus of Sweden in 1626 and is kept in the Royal Armoury, Stockholm.

Right A warrior horseman is shown wearing a wonderful silk robe in this battle scene from the Suleymanname.

CHAPTER 19

MODERN ISLAMIC ART AND ARCHITECTURE

From the late 18th century, European interests in Western Asia became increasingly dominant, and many Muslim countries began programmes of modernization and reform. This discrepancy of power and influence was reflected in the art and architecture of the times, by the adoption of certain European media and models, including oil painting, printing, photography, costume, academic training and even urban planning. There was also a new interest in reviving the grand styles of the past, with deliberate archaism. Meanwhile, European Orientalist artists were engaging with the Islamic world with an altogether different agenda, portraying a mysterious and even seductive 'East' for the curiosity of Western audiences.

Come the 20th and 21st centuries, both traditional revivalism and global assimilation have continued to characterize modern art and architecture in Western Asia as a whole. To this day, world-famous icons of modern architecture continue to be built in Muslim countries, particularly the Arabian peninsula.

Opposite The Azadi Tower sits at the centre of one of Tehran's main avenues. The architect Hossein Amanat (b. 1942) won the state-sponsored competition to build the tower in 1971.

Above The blue-domed King Abdullah Mosque in Amman, by Jordanian architect Rasem Badran (b.1945), is typical of much of Islamic architecture in the 20th–21st century.

REVIVALIST TRENDS

MANY ARTISTS OF THE MODERN AGE – BOTH EUROPEANS VISUALIZING MUSLIM CULTURE AND THOSE FROM WITHIN THE MUSLIM WORLD – HAVE BEEN INSPIRED BY THE HERITAGE OF THE ISLAMIC MIDDLE EAST.

In the 19th century, a number of important Western European artists admired the achievements of the Islamic artistic past and revived these traditional methods in their own work.

Prominent among these artists was English tile designer and potter William de Morgan (1839–1917), a friend and collaborator of the artist, writer and designer William Morris (1834–96). Both men were notable figures in the Arts and Crafts aesthetic movement, which turned away from mass production in the wake of the Industrial Revolution, instead celebrating individual craftsmanship.

William de Morgan began to work in ceramics in 1863. He was a great experimenter, and in *c*.1873 rediscovered the techniques of tin-glazing and lustre that had been invented in 9th-century Iraq. He also began to use a colour palette (including turquoise, dark blue and green) and imagery (including fabulous creatures and repeating geometric motifs) derived from wares made by Iznik craftsmen in the Ottoman Empire during the 16th century.

LEIGHTON'S 'ARAB HALL'
In the 1870s, English artist and sculptor Frederic Lord Leighton (1830–96) built a magnificent 'Arab Hall' as part of an extension to his house in Holland Park in London. The hall was intended to house and display Lord Leighton's large collection of Damascus and Middle-Eastern tiles, and the interior was based on the banqueting hall of the summer palace of La Zisa, which was built in Palermo, Sicily, by Fatimid craftsmen working in Norman Sicily in 1166.

The hall's grand decoration includes an epigraphic frieze of tiles with an inscription quoting from Surah 54, verses 1–6, beginning 'In the name of the long-suffering Allah, ever merciful, who has taught

Above English craftsman William de Morgan's Persian-style dish draws inspiration from the designs of 16th-century Iznik ceramics.

me the Quran…'. Richard Burton may have acquired this for Lord Leighton in Sind, Pakistan: he certainly sourced tiles for Leighton in Jerusalem.

Upstairs is a 17th-century wooden *zenana*, a box-like construction designed for segregating women from men during worship, which Lord Leighton transported to London from a mosque in Cairo, along with a 17th-century stained-glass window from a Damascus mosque.

IRANIAN PAINTERS
The revival of miniature painting in early 20th-century Iran is an example of how artists tried to resurrect historic traditions and techniques. A key figure in the renewal was Mirza Hadi-Khan Tajvidi, who in 1929 established the Madraseh-i Sanaye'-i Qadimeh ('School of Traditional Arts') in Tehran. He taught many artists there who formed the School of Tehran.

Other notable painters in this revival included Mohammad Ali Zavieh, Shayesteh Shirazi and Hossein Behzad. Born in Tehran, Behzad produced paintings in an

Left Leighton House's Arab Hall contains an indoor fountain as well as beautiful tiling, slender columns and muqarnas vaulting.

archaizing style imitating traditional Timurid and Safavid manuscript paintings. He won international renown as a miniaturist, beginning with his illustrations to works by the Persian poet Nizami (1141–1209), completed in 1915, and continuing with illustrations to the *Rubáiyát of Omar Khayyám* (1048–1123), finished in 1936. He received several international awards, and many of his works were collected and housed in the Behzad Museum in the Saad Abad Palace in Tehran.

In the wake of these artists came a generation of Iranian painters who were both inspired by the great Persian miniature tradition and introduced modern techniques from other areas of the arts. Among these is Mahmoud Farshchian. Born in Isfahan and educated in the fine arts both in Iran and in Europe, Farshchian won wide acclaim with works inspired by the Iranian epic the *Shahnama* (Book of Kings) and the works of the Sufi mystical poet Rumi (1207–73).

Other artists in this generation include Mohammad Bagher Aghamiri, Majid Mehregan and Ardshir Mojarrad-Takestani.

TRADITIONAL BUILDINGS

Particularly in Africa, some modern architects have maintained traditional forms when constructing mosques. For example, the Great Mosque of Niono in Mali, completed by master mason Lassina Minta with local workmen in 1973, was built in line with centuries-old local Islamic building traditions with wooden beams and walls of clay bricks and roofs made from matting and earth. A number of the historic mosques of the region,

Above The Grand Mosque of Djénné, Mali (1906), is one of several 20th-century West African mosques built from clay and wood in the traditional style.

such as the Great Mosque of Djénné, were rebuilt in the 20th century using similar materials and craftsmanship. The Great Mosque of Niono has a vast prayer hall covering approximately 726sq m (7,815sq ft). The Niono Mosque won an Aga Khan Award for Architecture in 1981–83.

Above John Frederick Lewis drew on memories of life in Cairo for his Orientalist work, An Intercepted Correspondence *(1869).*

IMAGINING THE EAST: 'ORIENTALIST PAINTERS'

From the late 18th century and throughout the 19th century in Britain, many Western artists were drawn to scenes of life in the Orient – which often meant the Mediterranean coastline of Egypt, Syria, Turkey and Palestine. These artists represented harem, bazaar or city scenes, especially in the cities of Istanbul, Damascus, Cairo and Jerusalem, at this time all part of the declining Ottoman Empire. One of the leading Orientalist painters was John Frederick Lewis, who had lived for ten years in Cairo, and later made his name in England with images such as *Harem Life, Constantinople* (1857), *Edfu, Upper Egypt* (1860) and *The Seraff: A Doubtful Coin* (1869). The exotic appeal of Orientalist art lay in authentic reportage of foreign landscape and architecture, as well as in the sexual mores of the harem. Artists made close study of Islamic domestic architecture and painstakingly reproduced latticework screens, as in *An Arab Interior* (1881) by Arthur Melville, but their actual knowledge of local genre situations was extremely restricted.

THE MODERN AGE

AFTER THE 18TH CENTURY, ART AND ARCHITECTURE WERE
INFLUENCED BY EUROPEAN STYLES, AND IN CAIRO AND ELSEWHERE
URBAN DESIGNERS ADOPTED STRAIGHT–BOULEVARD CITY PLANNING.

By the 1800s, the Ottoman
Empire was in decline, and the
balance of political and financial
power swung westward. Former
Ottoman territories, such as Greece
and Serbia, won independence;
North Africa came under varying
degrees of Western colonial control.

In many Islamic countries,
political and social reforms brought
government and administration
closer to Western models: in the
Tanzimet Period (from the Arabic
word for 'Reordering') in 1839–76,
Ottoman sultans Abdulmecid I
(reigned 1839–61) and Abdulaziz
(reigned 1861–76) introduced
reforms of the army, administration,
judiciary and education systems; in
1861, Tunisia was the first Islamic
country to adopt a constitution and
established itself as a Western-style
constitutional monarchy. In line
with this, architecture and the arts
turned to Western models.

THE BALYAN ARCHITECTS
In Istanbul from the 1820s onward,
the architects of the Armenian
Balyan family produced mosques in
a style influenced by Western
Baroque and Empire styles. Krikor
Balyan designed the Nusretiye
Mosque, built in 1823–36 for Sultan
Mahmud II (reigned 1808–39). The
mosque was called the Victory
Mosque to celebrate the abolition
by Mahmud II of the janissary
troops who had been behind many
revolts, and their replacement with a
Western-style military.

Garabet Amira Balyan and
Nigogayos Balyan, Krikor's son
and grandson, were responsible for
several mosques: the Dolmabahçe
Mosque (1853–55), the Ortakoy
Mosque (1854–56) and the Buyuk
Mecidiye Mosque, finished in 1855.
These have a Western European
look, using marble and grand paint-
ings in place of tiles as decoration.

Above Three Western styles of architecture
– Baroque, Rococo and Neoclassical –
combine in the Dolmabahçe Palace. Its
ceilings are covered with 14 tonnes of gold.

These two men also designed
the Dolmabahçe Palace, built in
1844–55, for Sultan Abdulmecid I.
The palace stands in what was once
a harbour on the Bosphorus, indeed
where Mehmet II had once
anchored 70 ships. The harbour was
later reclaimed for use as royal
gardens and the name of the palace
means 'filled garden'. Its white
marble façade, 284m (932ft) long,
faces on to a quay 600m (1,968ft)
in length. The Dolmabahçe was
the first European-style palace in
Istanbul: its interior was beautifully
designed by the French decorator
Charles Séchan (designer of the
Paris Opera) and was lavishly
appointed, with the world's largest
chandelier, weighing 4.5 tonnes
and containing 750 lights, in the
Exhibition Hall and a celebrated
staircase with banisters made from
Baccarat crystal.

Left The Dolmabahçe Mosque stands
on a site measuring 25sq m (269sq ft)
close to the Dolmabahçe Palace beside
the waters of the Bosphorus.

MUHAMMAD ALI MOSQUE

In this period, Egypt was ruled by the Khedives, descendants of Muhammad Ali Pasha (1769–1849). He was an Albanian officer, sent to the country as part of an Ottoman force following the invasion of Egypt by French general Napoleon Bonaparte. Muhammad Ali had taken power and established himself as Wali (Ottoman governor) in 1805, and founded a dynasty that ruled until 1952. In the Cairo Citadel, he built a Grand Mosque in the Ottoman style in 1824–48.

The Muhammad Ali Mosque was at first planned in the local Mamluk style by a French architect named Pascal Coste, but the designs of Greek architect Yusuf Bushnaq were preferred. The mosque has a large main dome and four half-domes with Ottoman spindle minarets, modelled on the 1599 Yeni Valide Mosque in Istanbul.

The Muhammad Ali Mosque was the largest mosque built in the first half of the 19th century, and superseded the nearby Mamluk Mosque of al-Nasir Muhammad as the state mosque of Egypt. It was built on the grounds once occupied by Mamluk palaces, which were destroyed on Muhammad Ali's order. In choosing the Ottoman instead of the Mamluk mosque style, Muhammad Ali made it clear that Egypt was aligned with the Ottomans. At the same time, the decorative style used displayed a strong European influence and harmonized with that used in the contemporary Empire and neo-Baroque mosques of Istanbul, designed by the Balyans.

Muhammad Ali's grandson, Ismail Pasha (reigned 1863–79), was pro-Western. He added a new area on Cairo's western edge in the style of Paris, as remodelled by Baron Georges-Eugène Haussmann, and built a rail network in Egypt. He declared in 1879, 'My country is no

Above The main dome of the grand Muhammad Ali Mosque (1824–48) in Cairo is 21m (69ft) in diameter, and is flanked by Ottoman-style minarets.

longer part of Africa; now we are in Europe. It is natural, therefore, for us to set aside our former ways and to take on a new organization suitable to our social conditions.'

EFFECTS ON OTHER ARTS

These changes had varied effects in other arts. In metalwork, for example, Western influence was felt from the 18th century onward by the elite craftsmen of Istanbul, who produced Baroque and Rococo decorative designs. The craftsmen made mirrors, trays, ewers and coffee sets with intaglio (stone-carved) decoration. Floral decoration became more expansive, with engravings of bouquets and baskets of flowers, bows and ribbons.

In the 19th century, the severe Ottoman decline had dispiriting effects on metalwork and the arts.

Right This clock from the Dolmabahçe Palace clearly shows how Western styles – particularly Baroque – influenced late Ottoman metalwork.

Except for those that were donated to mosques or mausolea, many gold and silver pieces held in the imperial palace were melted down. However, Western influence had little effect on calligraphy, the Islamic art form par excellence.

MODERN ARCHITECTURE

SOME OF THE MOST DYNAMIC ARCHITECTURE OF THE LATE 20TH
AND EARLY 21ST CENTURIES WAS CREATED IN THE ISLAMIC WORLD,
USING MODERN DESIGNS THAT HONOUR THE ISLAMIC TRADITION.

The vast King Faisal Mosque in Islamabad is a symbol of modern Pakistan. Built in 1976–86 under the supervision of Turkish architect Vedat Delakoy, it combines the modern and the traditional: it is based on the design of a central dome with spindle minarets used over centuries by the Ottomans, but here the main dome is opened out into a great folded roof resembling a tent. It is made of concrete without external decoration. The scale is vast: the mosque is part of a complex covering 5,000sq m (53,820sq ft) that can hold 300,000 members of the faithful.

The prayer hall contains a large chandelier, calligraphy by Pakistani artist Sadeqain Naqqash and tiles by Turkish artist Menga Ertel. On the west wall the *kalimah* (the affirmation of faith) is written in *kufic* script set in mosaic.

The King Faisal Mosque is the state mosque of Pakistan, and one of the world's largest mosques; it was named after King Faisal of Saudi Arabia, who suggested its construction in 1966 and afterward funded the building.

OTHER MOSQUES

There are several other modern mosques of note, including the Freedom Mosque (or Istiqlal Mosque) in Jakarta, Indonesia, built in 1955–84 by architect Frederick Silaban, using concrete and steel. The large prayer hall covers an area of 36,980sq m (398,050sq ft) and the mosque can hold 250,000 people. It is the state mosque of Indonesia.

Abdel-Wahed el-Wakil built the King Saud Mosque in Jeddah, Saudi Arabia, completed in 1989. It covers 9,700sq m (104,410sq ft) and has a minaret 60m (197ft) tall. It pays tribute to both Iranian and Mamluk architecture, celebrating the four-*iwan* (hall) design of Iranian tradition in that it contains a rectangular courtyard and four *iwan*-like openings in the surround-

Above The King Faisal Mosque (1966–86) stands at the northern edge of Islamabad, where the city gives way to the foothills of the Himalayas.

ing wall, and honouring Mamluk architecture in Cairo in the pointed dome shape and the minaret style. The main dome is 42m (138ft) tall and 20m (66ft) across.

COMMERCIAL BUILDINGS

In this same period, the vast scale of secular architecture built in Islamic countries is a good representation of their wealth and status. Hotels, apartment blocks and offices have been built in a dynamic, glamorous style.

In Tehran, Iran, the distinctive Azadi Tower was designed in 1971 by architect Hossein Amanat. Initially called the Shayad Tower ('Memorial of Kings'), it was renamed the Azadi (Freedom) Tower after the 1979 Iranian Revolution. The tower contains 8,000 blocks of white marble stone from the region of Isfahan, and was built by the pre-eminent Iranian stonemason Ghaffar Davarpanah Varnosfaderani. It stands at the centre of a great square that was the setting for many of the demonstrations

Left In the rectangular prayer hall of the Freedom Mosque in Jakarta, Indonesia, 12 great columns support a spherical dome 45m (148ft) in diameter.

offices, a hotel, private apartments, restaurants, fitness clubs and shopping floors; there are also three mosques, including the world's highest, the King Abdullah Mosque, on the 77th floor and a public viewing platform at the top at a height of 270m (886ft). The Kingdom Centre was designed by Ellerbe Becket/Omrania. The Al Faisaliyah Centre, completed in 2000 and 267m (876ft) tall with 30 floors, contains offices and shopping areas. The four main corner beams of the centre bend in to join at the tip and beneath them is a great golden ball containing a restaurant. It was designed by UK architects Foster and Partners.

Dramatic skyscraper hotels were built in Dubai, United Arab Emirates, in the late 20th and early 21st centuries. The highly distinctive Burj al-Arab ('Tower of the Arabs') was built in 1994–99 to designs by architect Tom Wright in the shape of a boat's sail on a man-made island 280m (919ft)

offshore from Jumeirah Beach. It has 60 floors and stands 321m (1,053ft) tall, making it the second tallest hotel in the world, outdone only by the Rose Tower, 333m (1,093ft) tall, on Shaykh Zayed Road, also in Dubai. The Rose Tower has 72 floors and was built in 2004–7.

INSPIRATIONAL AIRPORT

A notable building complex in Saudi Arabia is the Dhahran International Airport, built in 1961 and designed by American architect Minoru Yamasaki (1912–86). The airport's blend of traditional Islamic architectural forms with modern elements was highly influential. Its flight control tower has the appearance of a minaret, and the distinctive terminal featured for some time on Saudi banknotes. In 1999, after the building of the King Fahd International Aiport, the Dhahran International Airport was made into a air base of the Royal Saudi Air Force.

Above A luxury restaurant within the golden sphere atop the Al Faisaliyah building revolves so that diners have a changing view of Riyadh, Saudi Arabia.

and rallies of the Iranian Revolution, and it continues to be a focal point for protest.

Many modern buildings that set new standards for size have been built in Saudi Arabia and the countries of the United Arab Emirates. In Riyadh, the twin towers of the Al Faisaliyah Centre and the Kingdom Centre are the two tallest buildings in Saudi Arabia. The Kingdom Tower, 311m (1,020ft) tall with 43 floors, was completed in 1999. It contains

Right The iconic Burj al-Arab hotel in Dubai, United Arab Emirates, mimics the shape of the sail used in the traditional Arab sailing vessel, the dhow.

WHERE TO SEE ISLAMIC ART

THE ISLAMIC WORLD

Museum of Islamic Art, Doha, Qatar

This museum opened its doors in 2008. The building, inspired by Islamic architecture, was designed by the architect I.M. Pei. It houses Islamic artworks from the 7th to 19th centuries, including textiles, ceramics, manuscripts, metal, glass, ivory and precious stones. www.mia.org.qa/english

Iran Bastan Museum, Tehran

This national museum now incorporates two original museums that together cover ancient archaeology and many pre-Islamic artefacts and post-Islamic period artefacts. www.nationalmuseumofiran.ir

Islamic Arts Museum, Kuala Lumpur

This collection of more than 7,000 artefacts aims to be representative of the arts of the Islamic world. An emphasis is placed on works from India, China and South-east Asia. www.iamm.org.my

Museum of Islamic Art, Cairo

The renovated Museum of Islamic Art holds a collection of more than 100,000 objects of mainly Egyptian origin produced from the 7th to 19th centuries. www.islamicmuseum.gov.eg

L.A. Mayer Museum of Islamic Art, Jerusalem

Dedicated to the memory of Leo Arie Mayer, a professor of Islamic Art and Archaeology at the Hebrew University of Jerusalem, this museum aims to cultivate a mutual understanding between Jewish and Arab cultures. www.islamicart.co.il/default-eng.asp

Turkish and Islamic Arts Museum, Istanbul

The Ibrahim Pasha Palace is now home to a 40,000-strong collection of Islamic arts, and is particularly famed for its world-class selection of carpets. www.greatistanbul.com/ibrahim_pasa_palace.htm

Below Museum of Islamic Art, Doha.

Above Entry gate to the Topkapi Palace Museum, Istanbul.

Topkapi Palace Museum, Istanbul

Built in the 15th century and once the imperial residence of the Ottoman sultans, Topkapi Palace is now the setting for one of the foremost museums of Islamic art in the world. It holds first-rate collections of manuscript painting, ceramics, clothing and jewellery. www.topkapisarayi.gov.tr/eng

Tareq Rajab Museum, Hawelli, Kuwait

The private collection of the Rajab family, the museum has around 10,000 objects on permanent display. The collection managed to survive the Iraqi invasion of 1990, and the attached Museum of Islamic Calligraphy was opened in 2007. www.trmkt.com

EUROPE

British Museum, London

Concentrated in the John Addis Gallery, the Islamic collection includes artworks from the full range of Islamic history. The museum is actively collecting contemporary Islamic art. www.britishmuseum.org

Right London's Victoria and Albert Museum.

Victoria and Albert Museum, London

The Jameel Gallery at the V&A contains more than 400 objects out of a collection of 10,000 from across the Islamic world. The star piece of this magnificent collection is the Ardabil carpet, the oldest dated carpet in existence. www.vam.ac.uk

Chester Beatty Library, Dublin

Established by the American collector and magnate, this collection was gifted to the Irish Republic on Chester Beatty's death in 1968. The Islamic section is particularly strong in Mamluk Qurans, as well as Ottoman, Persian and Indian paintings. www.cbl.ie

Musée du Louvre, Paris

As of 2010, the objects from the Islamic Department of the Louvre can be found in an exhibition space in the Cour Visconti. The new building can display 3,000 objects. www.louvre.fr

Museum für Islamische Kunst (Museum of Islamic Art), Berlin

Islamic architectural decoration features strongly in this collection, housed in the south wing of the Pergamonmuseum. Its highlights include the façade of the Mshatta Palace, 13th-century *mihrabs* (niches to indicate the direction of prayer) from Konya and Kashan, and the Aleppo Room. www.smb.spk-berlin.de

The David Collection, Copenhagen

Founded by Danish lawyer Ludvig David in his ancestral home, since his death in 1960 the David Collection has concentrated on acquiring Islamic artworks of outstanding quality, resulting in a superb collection of 2,500 objects. www.davidmus.dk

RUSSIA

State Hermitage Museum, St Petersburg

The Islamic art collection holds pieces from Iran, Egypt, Syria and Turkey. The collection includes more than 700 Iranian bronzes as well as Islamic textiles, ceramics, manuscript paintings, glassware and weaponry. www.hermitagemuseum.org

USA

Freer and Sackler Galleries at the Smithsonian, Washington, DC

The Freer and Sackler Galleries are one of the best places to see Islamic art in the United States. The collection of more than 2,200 objects is strong in the areas of ceramics and illustrated manuscripts. www.asia.si.edu/collections/islamicHome.htm

Metropolitan Museum of Art, New York

The Met's Islamic galleries display pieces from its prized collection of 12,000 objects, including ceramics, calligraphy and metalwork. www.metmuseum.org/Works_of_Art/islamic_art

Los Angeles County Museum of Art

There are more than 1,700 Islamic objects in the museum, making it a significant collection of Islamic art in the country. Areas of note include Iranian pottery and tiles, and the Turkish arts of the book. www.lacma.org/islamic_art/islamic.htm

ONLINE

Museum With No Frontiers (MWNF)

The largest transnational museum on the web, the MWNF's flagship project, Discover Islamic Art, contains Islamic art and monuments from around the Mediterranean, organized by country. www.discoverislamicart.org

The Khalili Collection

With more than 20,000 Islamic artworks, the Khalili Collection is one of the most comprehensive private collections ever assembled. More than 30 museums worldwide have exhibited pieces from the collection and slideshows are available on the website. www.khalili.org

GLOSSARY

ABLAQ Typically Syrian use of alternating dark and light masonry, often marble.

ADHAN The call to prayer signalling the congregational times of the five daily prayers. *See also muadhdhin.*

ADL Justice, equity or equality.

AHL AL-BAYT 'The people of the house', the immediate family of the Prophet, namely Muhammad, Fatimah, Ali, Hasan and Hussain. Significant in Shiah theology.

AHL AL-DHIMMAH Religious minorities living under Muslim rule.

AHWAL (singular *hal*) The different temporary states of spirituality experienced through Sufi practice.

AKHLAQ Morality and ethics. In its singular form, the word means character, manners and etiquette.

AL-BURAQ The winged, horselike beast that Muslims believe carried Muhammad to Jerusalem and then to heaven on the *Isra* and *Miraj*.

AL-DAJJAL The Antichrist who, it is said, will appear before the end of times, wreak havoc on earth and be killed by Jesus after his second coming.

AL-GHAYB The unseen world; a created reality but not seen with the human eye (e.g. *jinn*, or heaven).

AL-MAHDI Literally 'the guided one', a descendant of the Prophet Muhammad, who Muslims believe will appear at the end of time and establish peace on earth. In Shiah theology, he is the 12th awaited imam, the 'hidden imam'.

AL-MASIH Literally 'the anointed one', referring to Jesus.

AL-MUHADDITHUN Scholars of hadith and Islamic jurists.

AL-SIRAH AL-NABAWIYYAH Biographical accounts of the Prophet's life.

AL-YAWM AL-AKHIR The Last Day or Day of Judgement.

AMIR The leader of a Muslim community.

AQD A legal contract or agreement.

ARABESQUE Decorative geometric ornament based on stylized vegetal forms, such as tendrils and creepers.

ARAFAH The valley plain near Makkah where *Hajj* pilgrims spend the day in repentance and prayer.

ARCH A curved area in a building used to spread the weight of the structure above it to the walls, pillars or columns below; important in Islamic architecture, especially for supporting large domes.

ASHLAR Dressed stone blocks.

ASR The third prayer of the day, offered in late afternoon.

AYAH A verse from the Quran.

AZULEJO Tin-glazed ceramic tiles produced in Islamic Spain.

BAB Gate.

BATIN The hidden or esoteric.

BAZAAR Turkish term for covered marketplace and business centre in Islamic towns and cities; also known as *souk* in Arabic.

BURQA A long overgarment, usually black, covering the entire body of a Muslim woman. Also usually covers face with a veil. *See also niqab.*

CALIPH The appointed leader of the Muslim community in early Islamic history until the Ottoman times.

CALLIGRAPHY The art of beautiful writing; in Islam stylized written Arabic is revered as the highest art because it gives visible form to the words of the holy Quran.

ÇAMI Congregational mosque used for Friday prayers (Turkish; called *jami* in Arabic).

CARAVANSERAI Secure and often fortified lodging for merchants and travellers, their animals and goods, usually on a trade route. Known as *han* in Turkish, and *khan* in Arabic.

CASBAH See citadel.

CHAHAR BAGH Persian-style, four-part garden layout.

CITADEL Enclosed, fortified section of a city or town, known as *casbah* (from Arabic *qasaba*) in North Africa.

CLOUD BAND Decorative motif of curling clouds in Chinese art, used throughout Islamic art from the 14th century onward.

CUERDA SECA ('dry cord') Use of lines of a greasy black substance to mark out and contain areas of glaze applied to tiles, enabling artists to contain the colours.

DHAHIR The manifest and known, or the physical and tangible world.

DHIKR Remembrance of God through spiritual practices of repeating his name and praises.

DHUHR The second prayer of the day, offered early in the afternoon.

DIN Religion, a way of life.

DUNYA Earthly existence.

EID The celebration at the end of Ramadhan (*Eid ul-fitr*) and Hajj (*Eid ul-adha*).

ESCHATOLOGY Branch of theology concerning the final events in the history of the world or humankind.

FAJR The first prayer of the day, offered just before sunrise.

FAQIH (plural *fuqaha*) A Muslim scholar of Islamic religious law.

FARD An obligatory action that must be performed by every sane, healthy adult.

FATWA A religious edict; a legal opinion, issued by a *mufti* (legal expert), although it is not binding in nature.

FIQH Body of jurisprudential principles derived from Shariah by legal scholars exercising their understanding of the law.

FITRA The state of natural or primordial disposition.

FURQAN 'The criterion', referring to the Quran as the measure of what is right and wrong.

GHULUW Excessiveness, extremism.

GHUSL Ritual bath to attain purification, a state that is compulsory before offering prayers.

GUNBAD Tomb tower.

HADITH The sayings and narrations of the Prophet.

HAJJ Pilgrimage to the *Kaabah* in Makkah: the fifth pillar of Islam.

HAMMAM Bathhouse.

HAN See *caravanserai*.

HANIF (plural *hunafa*) A believer in one God but without any professed or formal religion.

HARAM Actions that are forbidden/unlawful under Islamic law.

HIJAB A headscarf worn by women to cover all the hair.

HIJRAH The Prophet Muhammad's migration from Makkah to Madinah in 622.

HYPOSTYLE Hall with flat roof supported by columns; type of mosque in which the flat roof of the prayer hall is supported by rows of columns.

IBADAH (plural *ibadat*) An act of worship. This forms the 'personal' part of Islamic law.

IFTAR The meal taken at sunset to break the fast during Ramadhan.

IHRAM The simple two-piece (usually) white cloth worn by pilgrims on *Hajj*.

IJMA The majority consensus of Muslim scholars.

IJTIHAD Exerted effort by the use of analogy to arrive at an Islamic legal opinion.

IMAM In Shiah theology, the leader of the Muslim community from the descendants of the Prophet. In Sunni practice, the religious leader of the mosque community.

INLAYING The technique of inserting one material into another to create a decorative effect, often used in metalwork to add a precious metal, such as gold or silver, to decorate a less expensive metal body, such as bronze or brass.

ISHA The fifth prayer of the day, offered at nightfall.

ISLAM As a verb, wilful submission to God; peace. As a noun, the faith of Islam as taught by the Prophet Muhammad.

ISNAD The chain of hadith transmitters connecting directly to the Prophet Muhammad.

ISRA The Prophet's night journey with Archangel Jibril to Jersualem from Makkah on al-Buraq.

IWAN Vaulted hall with one side left open, giving on to the courtyard of a mosque or *madrasa*.

JAHANNAM Hellfire.

JAHILIYYAH Ignorance; a term used to described the state of polytheist pre-Islamic Arabia.

JAMI Or *masjid-i-jami*; congregational mosque used for Friday prayers (Arabic; *çami* in Turkish).

JIHAD (verb) To struggle. Usually refers to the 'greater' self-struggle of purifying the soul from earthly desires, but also means physical/military struggle (which is known as the 'lesser' *jihad*).

JINN Creatures of the unseen who, like humans, have been endowed with free will.

JIZYAH The exemption tax paid by religious minorities under Muslim rule.

JUMUAH Friday, the day of congregational prayer.

JUZ (plural *ajza*) One portion of the Quran divided into 30 parts.

KAABAH The cubelike edifice in the Haram Mosque, Makkah, which is considered to be the first house of worship.

KAFIR (plural *kuffar*) A theological definition of a non-believer.

KALAM The rhetorical expositions of philosophers.

Right A battle scene from the Suleymanname, *an illustrated history of the life of Suleyman the Magnificent, dating from the 16th century.*

KHAMSA Five in Arabic; in Persian a *khamsa* is a group of five books; in Islamic Africa a *hamsa* (sometimes *khamsa*) is a hand-shaped, good-luck symbol used in jewellery.

KHAN See *caravanserai*.

KHANQA A monastery for Sufis.

KITAB Book; al-Kitab or kitab Allah (Book of God) are sometimes used as terms for the Quran.

KUFIC Early Arabic script, named after city of Kufa in Iraq.

KUFR Disbelief.

KULLIYE Complex of religious buildings centred on a mosque with other establishments, such as *madrasa*, *caravanserai*, *hammam*, kitchens and sometimes hospitals, typically built by wealthy subjects of Ottoman sultans.

LIAN A particular oath relating to alleged infidelity and taken in a divorce petition.

LUSTREWARE Ceramics finished with metallic glazes that produce a shining effect. Developed in Abbasid Iraq in the 9th century.

MADHHAB Islamic jurisprudential school or developed method of legal interpretation.

MADINAH The city of Yathrib, which became known as 'the city of the Prophet'.

MADRASA Islamic educational establishment, often associated with a mosque, where students studied the Quran, law and sciences.

MAGHRIB The fourth compulsory prayer of the day at sunset.

MAGHRIBI Cursive form of Arabic script; developed in western Islamic lands.

MAIDAN Open square, usually in the centre of a town or city.

MAKKAH Muhammad's birth city and the place of Ibrahim's ancient temple, the *Kaabah*.

MALAK (plural *malaaikah*) An angel.

MAQAM (plural *maqamat*) Different stations on the Sufi path that are experienced on the journey toward God (e.g. repentance and gratitude).

MAQASID Established principles or reasons for Islamic rulings and interpretations.

MAQSURA Private area in a congregational mosque used by a ruler or governor, often lavishly decorated.

MASHHAD Shrine; tomb of martyr or Sufi saint.

MASHRABIYA Turned-wood openwork screen.

MASJID See mosque.

MATN Used in relation to hadith interpretation, meaning the hadith's content or principle.

MAWLID The Prophet's birthday celebration; also known as *Milad*.

MIHRAB Wall niche in form of arch indicating the correct direction of prayer (toward Makkah).

MINAI An overglaze technique for decorating pottery used in Kashan Iran in the 12th–13th centuries.

MINARET Tower attached to a mosque, once used as a watchtower but now the place from which the Muslim faithful are called to prayer.

MINBAR Pulpit in mosque from which the *khutbah* prayer or sermon is pronounced.

MIRAJ The Prophet's Night Journey to heaven, on al-Buraq. See also Isra.

MIZAN Scales or balance.

MOSQUE Muslim place of gathering and prayer. In Arabic, *masjid* ('place of prostration').

MUADHDHIN The caller who recites the *adhan*, to call believers to the ritual prayers.

MUAMALAT Those aspects of Islamic law dealing with social relations and interactions.

MUEZZIN Anglicized form of the Arabic *muadhdhin*, the individual who calls faithful to prayer, traditionally from the minaret of a mosque.

MUFTI An Islamic jurist qualified to give a legal ruling.

MUHAQQAQ Cursive script used in calligraphy; one of the 'six hands' of calligraphy identified in the 10th century by Ibn Muqla (d.940).

MUHARRAM The first month of the Islamic calendar, also the month in which Hussain, the Prophet's grandson, was martyred at Karbala.

MUJAHID (plural *mujahidun*) A Muslim engaged in physical *jihad*.

MUQARNAS Small, concave stalactite vaults, often painted or tiled, used widely in Islamic architecture.

MURSHID A Sufi master, attached to a *tariqah* (Sufi order), who guides his/her disciples. Also known as *shaykh*.

MUSALLAH 'A place of prayer'. Refers both to the physical place of prayer and a prayer mat.

Left Now a Christian church, the Mezquita of Córdoba was originally built by Abd al-Rahman I in 784 and remained a mosque until 1236.

MUSLIM One who submits his or her will to worshipping one God: a follower of the religion of Islam.

MUWAHHIDUN Unitarian belief stressing the oneness of God, and used as a self-label by those more usually called 'Wahhabis' by critics. *See also* Wahhabism.

NABI A prophet of Allah.

NAFS The ego encompassing human virtues and desires.

NASKH Style of Arabic script.

NASTALIQ Calligraphic script, used mainly for Persian rather than Arabic.

NIKAH The marriage contract, detailing an offer by the groom, acceptance by the bride, witnessed by two people.

NIQAB Face veil.

PISHTAQ Arched portal leading to an *iwan* at the entrance of a mosque, *madrasa* or *caravanserai* in Iran.

QADI An Islamic judge, who presides over legal matters and proceedings.

QADAR God's divine measure, decree or predestination.

QASR Palace or castle.

QIBLA The direction of prayer facing toward the *Kaabah* in Makkah.

QIYAM-UL-LAYL Night of devotional prayer to achieve nearness to God, through either formal prayer or recitation of the Quran and *dhikr*.

QIYAS Analogous reasoning used in applying Islamic jurisprudence.

QUBBAH Dome or domed tomb.

QURAN The word of Allah (God), as revealed to the Prophet Muhammad via Archangel Jibril in 610–32; the main source of guidance and authority for Muslims.

QURAYSH The ruling Arab tribe of Makkah during the pre-Islamic period of Muhammad's era.

RAMADHAN The ninth month of the Islamic calendar, during which Muslims fast. *See also* sawm.

RASUL God's messenger.

RIBA Usury. The taking or giving of interest in economic transactions is forbidden by Islam because it is considered to be unjust.

RIBAT Fortified monastery, a base for *jihad*, or religious war.

RISALAH Divine messengership. Denotes the messenger bringing a divine text, such as the Quran and Torah, to humankind.

RIWAQ Arcades running around the four sides of the courtyard in an Arabic-style courtyard mosque.

RUH The spirit or the soul.

SAHN Courtyard of a mosque.

SALAH (plural *salawat*) Formal ritual prayer, offered in Arabic, reciting verses from the Quran and other prayers, toward the direction of the *Kaabah*. Apart from the five compulsory prayers, *salah* can also be extra optional units of prayer. *Salah* is the second pillar of Islam.

SAWM Fasting in the month of Ramadhan, the fourth pillar of Islam. Usually begins with *suhur* (a meal taken before sunrise).

SHADIRWAN Fountain inside a palace room or the courtyard of a mosque.

SHAHADAH The first pillar of Islam; the declaration of faith that there is no god but the one God, and that Muhammad is his prophet.

SHAHNAMA Book of Kings. Epic Persian history written by Firdawsi between 977–1010. The text has been illustrated in various media.

SHAYKH An elder, leader or teacher. *See also murshid.*

SHAYTAN Satan, the devil. Also known as Iblis.

SHEREFE Balcony on minaret used when issuing a call to prayer.

SHIAH A Muslim who follows the minority political and theological system that recognizes Ali and his descendants as the rightful heirs and leaders of the Muslim community.

SHIRK Polytheism, or the sin of associating partners with God.

SHURA Consultation, or the act of seeking council by the caliph from learned advisors.

SILSILAH Sufi chain or order of spiritual authority.

SIRAH The biography or historical account of the Prophet Muhammad.

SUFISM/ TASAWWUF Mysticism, spiritual inner journey where remembrance and love of God, together with purification of the heart, is emphasized more than outer dimensions of faith.

SUNNAH The 'way' or life example of the Prophet Muhammad.

SUNNI A term used to describe the overwhelming majority of Muslims, who adhere to the teachings and life example of the Prophet.

SURAH (plural *suwar*) A chapter in the Quran.

TAFSIR Exegesis or explanation and interpretation of the Quran.

TAJWEED Art of reciting the Quran.

TALAR Columned hall (Persian).

TALBIYAH 'I am at your command O Allah, I am at your command', the prayer recited by pilgrims throughout the Hajj.

TAQLID Adherence to established Islamic legal rulings.

TAQWA An all-encompassing awareness of God.

TARAWIH The extra optional night prayer offered in congregation during Ramadhan.

TARIQAH Sufi order of brotherhood, organized with a spiritual guide (*murshid*) helping disciples (*murids*) on their inner journey to God.

TAWBAH Repentance. The process of asking God for forgiveness to attain purity of faith.

TAWHID God's oneness or unicity.

TAZIYAH Passion plays and models of Hussain's mosque, carried in processions to commemorate his martyrdom in Muharram.

TAZKIYAH Purification of the soul. A deeply spiritual exercise.

THULUTH Large and elegant cursive calligraphic script.

TIRAZ Robes given as mark of honour, embroidered with Quranic verses and the name of the donor.

TUGHRA Stylized monogram-signature incorporating the name of an Ottoman sultan.

TURBE Mausoleum.

ULAMA Islamic legal and religious scholars (Arabic; singular *alim*).

UMMAH The universal Muslim community.

UMMATUN WASATA The Muslim nation as a community of moderation.

VICEGERENT A deputy or steward to God on earth.

VIZIER Administrator; chief minister (Anglicized form of the Arabic *wazir*).

WAHHABISM The name often given to the puritanical reform movement founded by Muhammad ibn Abd al-Wahhab in the 18th century, adopted by the ruling family in Saudi Arabia.

WAQF Pious endowment supporting a *masjid*, *madrasa* or secular institution, such as a *bimaristan* (hospital).

WIKALA Hostel for merchants and travellers within a city.

WUDU Ritual ablutions to prepare for prayer.

YAWM AL-QIYAMAH The Day of Resurrection.

YURT Round tent used by Central Asian nomads.

ZAKAH The required Islamic principle of giving alms to the poor. The third pillar of Islam.

ZAMZAM, WELL OF The well in Makkah that, according to Islam, sprang up when Ismail's mother, Hajar, searched for water in the barren valley to quench his thirst.

ZIYADA The enclosure or courtyard between mosque precincts and outer walls.

ACKNOWLEDGEMENTS

This edition is published by
Hermes House, an imprint of
Anness Publishing Ltd
Blaby Road, Wigston
Leicestershire LE18 4SE
info@anness.com

www.hermeshouse.com
www.annesspublishing.com

Anness Publishing has a
new picture agency outlet
for images for publishing,
promotions or advertising.
Please visit our website
www.practicalpictures.com
for more information.

Publisher: Joanna Lorenz
Editorial Director: Helen Sudell
Cover Design: Nigel Partridge
Production Controller: Helen Wang

Produced for Anness Publishing
    by Toucan Books
Managing Editor: Ellen Dupont
Editors: Anne McDowall and
    Theresa Bebbington
Project Manager: Hannah Bowen
Designer: Ralph Pitchford
Picture Researchers: Tam Church,
    Mia Stewart-Wilson and
    Marian Pullen
Cartography: Cosmographics, UK
Proofreader: Marion Dent
Indexers: Jackie Brind and
    Michael Dent

© Anness Publishing Ltd 2012

ETHICAL TRADING POLICY
At Anness Publishing we believe
that business should be conducted
in an ethical and ecologically
sustainable way, with respect for
the environment and a proper
regard to the replacement of the
natural resources we employ.
    As a publisher, we use a lot of
wood pulp in high-quality paper
for printing, and that wood
commonly comes from spruce
trees. We are therefore currently
growing more than 750,000 trees
in three Scottish forest plantations:
Berrymoss (130 hectares/320 acres),
West Touxhill (125 hectares/
305 acres) and Deveron Forest
(75 hectares/185 acres). The
forests we manage contain more
than 3.5 times the number of
trees employed each year in
making paper for the books
we manufacture.
    Because of this ongoing
ecological investment programme,
you, as our customer, can have
the pleasure and reassurance of
knowing that a tree is being
cultivated on your behalf to
naturally replace the materials
used to make the book you
are holding.
    Our forestry programme is
run in accordance with the UK
Woodland Assurance Scheme
(UKWAS) and will be certified
by the internationally recognized
Forest Stewardship Council (FSC).
The FSC is a non-government
organization dedicated to
promoting responsible
management of the world's forests.
Certification ensures forests are
managed in an environmentally
sustainable and socially responsible
way. For further information
about this scheme, go to
www.annesspublishing.com/trees.

A CIP catalogue record for
this book is available from the
British Library.

Previously published in two
separate volumes, *The Complete
Illustrated Guide to Islam* and *The
Complete Illustrated Encyclopedia
of Islamic Art and Architecture*

PUBLISHER'S NOTE
Although the information in this
book is believed to be accurate
and true at the time of going to
press, neither the authors nor the
publisher can accept any legal
responsibility or liability for any
errors or omissions that may
have been made.

PICTURE CREDITS
The publishers have made every
effort to trace the photograph
copyright owners. Anyone we
have failed to reach is invited
to contact Toucan Books,
89 Charterhouse Street,
London EC1M 6HR, UK.

akg-images 24t, 25t, 29t, 33, 37t,
38t, 60b, 69b, 86b, 87t, 88b, 90b,
121b, 134t, 146b, 147b, 150t, 151b,
177b, 238b, 240, 264, 266t, 273b,
286t, 287b, 294t, 309t, 310b, 312t,
313t, 316t, 325b, 350t, 352, 359t,
362b, 363tr, 363b, 369t, 370b,
382b, 401t, 403bl, 420t, 420b,
423b, 430t, 433, 438t, 447t, 464tr,
473b, 475b, 478t, 479t, 483t.
Alamy 4br, 6bml, 6mr, 12t, 30t,
52t, 73t, 79t, 86t, 102b, 110, 161t,
179t, 200, 205t, 215t, 235, 245t,
258tm, 259bm, 260tm, 272b, 277b,
286b, 292, 303t, 303b, 321, 324b,
328t, 328b, 329t, 332t, 340b, 342b,
355t, 358bl, 360, 361br, 364t, 364b,
365t, 365b, 366t, 366b, 381b, 401t,
430t, 434b, 437tr, 444t, 449b, 452t,
465t, 466t, 468b, 469t, 469bl,

471br, 472b, 473t, 482t, 482b, 485tr, 490b, 492t, 492b, 496t, 509.
Ancient Art & Architecture 4bml, 5br, 7bml, 15r, 60t, 68t, 70, 75b, 79b, 81b, 91t, 92t, 96b, 100t, 102t, 105b, 175b, 208t, 295t, 296t, 296b, 326t, 335t, 341t, 350b, 485b, 487b, 507.
The Art Archive 4bl, 5bml, 14, 15l, 19b, 20t, 21, 22t, 24b, 27t, 30b, 31b, 32t, 34b, 40t, 46b, 49b, 50t, 52b, 54b, 55t, 56t, 69t, 70, 73mr, 74b, 75t, 76b, 77t, 78t, 80, 81t, 82t, 83b, 84, 85t, 88t, 91b, 93b, 103b, 104t, 105t, 106, 107b, 108t, 119, 123b, 125, 128t, 130t, 132, 133, 127b, 136, 137t, 141, 142b, 146t, 148t, 149l, 150b, 164t, 186b, 192t, 195t, 198bl, 199, 202b, 205b, 209t, 213t, 214t, 226t, 236t, 246, 249t, 250t, 255, 261br, 262tm, 268t, 269r, 271b, 272t, 274t, 275b, 280t, 280b, 282tr, 283br, 287t, 290t, 299b, 300t, 301b, 306t, 314t, 323b, 324t, 326b, 327b, 333b, 344t, 346b, 349b, 351t, 353, 355b, 356b, 362t, 367b, 368t, 368b, 369b, 371t, 373b, 395b, 402t, 408b, 415t, 418b, 421, 422t, 423t, 431, 438br, 441b, 457b, 467t, 474b, 480t, 481t, 481b, 483b, 484t, 484b, 486b, 487t, 505, 506.
Art Directors/ArkReligion.com 4bmr, 6bl, 6br, 7bl, 16, 18, 20b, 23t, 25b, 50b, 51t, 55b, 61t, 63t, 64t, 65t, 76t, 85b, 97b, 104b, 111, 112t, 113b, 116b, 120, 121t, 122b, 124, 126t, 129, 134b, 139t, 144t, 156t, 158t, 159b, 162b, 181, 182b, 186t, 188b, 189t, 193t, 198br, 204, 212b, 220b, 224t, 228, 232b, 233, 236b, 243t, 243b, 244t, 268b, 269tl, 274b, 278t, 279t, 307t, 316t, 338t, 343t, 375, 410b, 450t.
The Bridgeman Art Library 7bmr, 15m, 26b, 29b, 34t, 42, 46t, 62t, 65b, 66t, 68b, 71t, 87b, 89b, 90t, 137b, 140b, 142t, 147t, 149r, 154b, 198t, 208b, 216t, 238t, 244b, 248b, 252–3, 256b, 270b, 284t, 285b, 288t, 288b, 289t, 289b, 291tr, 291cl, 297b, 305, 307b, 309b, 310t, 311t, 311b, 314b, 315t, 315b, 319, 322t, 322b, 323t, 329b, 334t, 334b,

335b, 349t, 356t, 372t, 372b, 373t, 376b, 380t, 391t, 392t, 392b, 398, 403r, 404b, 405, 406t, 406b, 408t, 409t, 409b, 414t, 414b, 418t, 419t, 419b, 422b, 425, 428t, 429t, 429b, 430b, 434t, 435, 436t, 436b, 437tl, 439t, 439b, 440t, 440b, 441t, 442, 443, 454t, 454b, 455t, 455bl, 455br, 456t, 457t, 458t, 458b, 459b, 460t, 460b, 461t, 461b, 462, 469br, 474t, 475t, 476t, 477t, 477b, 478b, 480b, 486t, 490t, 491b.
Corbis 1, 2, 3, 5bl, 10–11, 13b, 31t, 35b, 39, 40b, 41, 43b, 47b, 48b, 51b, 53t, 57t, 59, 62b, 66b, 71b, 74t, 82t, 83t, 89t, 94t, 95, 96t, 107t, 108bl, 116t, 117b, 122t, 123t, 131b, 139b, 144b, 147, 155br, 157b, 159t, 160t, 161b, 162t, 163, 165b, 166b, 167t, 170, 172t, 173t, 178, 179mr, 180, 183b, 185, 189b, 190t, 191t, 192b, 196b, 197, 206, 207t, 209b, 211t, 212t, 213b, 215b, 218b, 221, 222t, 223, 225b, 226b, 227, 229, 241b, 242b, 245b, 247, 248t, 254t, 254b, 256t, 257t, 257b, 259bl, 259br, 265, 267tl, 267tr, 270t, 276t, 277t, 281t, 281b, 298t, 298b, 299t, 300b, 316b, 317b, 336b, 339t, 343b, 345t, 348t, 348b, 354t, 359b, 367t, 370t, 371b, 384t, 389b, 391b, 394b, 395t, 400t, 404t, 407, 417b, 428b, 432t, 432b, 445t, 453t, 459t, 465b, 466b, 476b, 479b, 494b, 508, 511, 512.
Getty Images 9, 13t, 17, 19t, 22b, 27b, 28b, 44t, 48t, 54t, 94b, 98t, 112b, 114t, 115t, 119, 127b, 138b, 140t, 143, 153, 154t, 157t, 160b, 168t, 171t, 172b, 173b, 174, 176b, 177t, 190b, 191b, 196t, 201, 203b, 207b, 210b, 211b, 214b, 217t, 219b, 222b, 225t, 230, 231, 232t, 234b, 237t, 239b, 241t, 250b, 283tr, 377b, 504.
Heritage-Images 263, 452b.
Imagestate 44b, 45t, 139t, 156b, 167b, 182t.
iStockphoto.com 463t, 503.
NASA 127t.
Paul Harris Photography 449tr.
Peter Sanders 26t, 36t, 37b, 43t, 53b, 108br, 155bl, 159b, 165t, 169, 202t, 203t, 210t, 267b, 377tl, 378tr.

Photolibrary 7br, 8b, 23b, 35t, 49t, 56b, 57b, 58, 61b, 63b, 64b, 67, 72b, 78b, 92b, 93t, 97t, 98b, 99t, 100b, 101, 103t, 109, 113t, 115b, 117t, 128b, 135t, 151t, 164b, 175t, 176t, 216b, 224b, 237b, 260tl, 262tl, 262tr, 271t, 273t, 278b, 279b, 295b, 308t, 312b, 318, 330, 333t, 339b, 346t, 358t, 361t, 374, 376t, 378b, 379, 382t, 383t, 385t, 386t, 387, 389t, 390t, 390b, 396t, 410t, 411b, 412t, 412b, 413t, 413b, 426t, 427t, 427b, 444cl, 446t, 446b, 447b, 450b, 451t, 451b, 467b, 468t, 470b, 471t, 471bc, 472t, 488, 491t, 493t, 494t, 495t, 495b, 496b, 500, 510.
Photoshot 28t, 171b, 183t, 184, 194, 195b, 342t, 347t, 357t, 497.
Reuters 251t.
Rex Features Ltd 152, 166t, 168b, 217b, 218t, 220t, 239t, 242t, 332b, 351b, 357b, 453b.
Robert Harding 72t, 99b, 126b, 188t, 249b, 258tr, 260tr, 261bl, 261bm, 275tr, 293t, 301t, 302t, 304, 331, 336tr, 337b, 341b, 347t, 354b, 386b, 394t, 396b, 399, 402b, 411t, 415b, 416t, 416bl, 417t, 424, 445b, 448b, 470t, 489, 493b.
Shutterstock 47t, 187, 193b, 276b.
Sonia Halliday Photographs 302br, 499.
TopFoto 5bmr, 45b, 77b, 219t.
Werner Forman Archive 8t, 32b, 38b, 130b, 131t, 148b, 234t, 284b, 285t, 290–291b, 313b, 320t, 325t, 327tr, 340t, 345b, 380b, 381t, 383b, 384b, 385b, 388t, 393t, 393b, 397b, 448t, 456b.
Zeynep Mufti/ photographersdirect.com 251b.

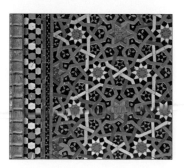

Above Procession of a sacred camel on a pilgrimage to Makkah and Madinah.

*Below Calligraphy from the Topkapi
Palace in Istanbul, Turkey.*

Below Detail of the floral tile work in the Savar Garden, Shiraz, Iran.

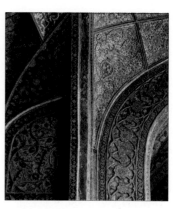

Above Detail of ornate inlay work at Emperor Akbar the Great's tomb at Sikandra, Agra, India.

Below Deep blue mosaic tiling at Samarkand's Shah-i Zinda.